THE WORLD ENCYCLOPEDIA OF
CHRISTMAS

THE WORLD ENCYCLOPEDIA OF
CHRISTMAS

GERRY BOWLER

M&S

Canadian Cataloguing in Publication Data

Bowler, Gerald, 1948-
The world encyclopedia of Christmas

ISBN 0-7710-1531-3

1. Christmas – Encyclopedias. I. Title.

GT4985.B68 2000   394.2663'03   C00-931247-1

We acknowledge the financial support of the Government of Canada through the Book Publishing Industry Development Program for our publishing activities. We further acknowledge the support of the Canada Council for the Arts and the Ontario Arts Council for our publishing program.

Every effort has been made to secure permission to reproduce copyrighted material in this book. Should any error or omission have been made, please notify the publisher and the information will be corrected with the next printing. Page 259 constitutes a continuation of the copyright page.

Design by Sari Ginsberg
Typeset in Minion by M&S, Toronto
Printed and bound in Canada

McClelland & Stewart Ltd.
The Canadian Publishers
481 University Avenue
Toronto, Ontario
M5G 2E9
www.mcclelland.com

1 2 3 4 5   03 02 01 00

This book is dedicated to my parents, Gerald and Elva Bowler,
who first showed me the wonders of Christmas.

Acknowledgements

he arts and sciences," says Montaigne, "are not cast in a mould, but are formed and perfected by degrees, by often handling and polishing, as bears leisurely lick their cubs into form." This book has been licked into shape with the aid of many whose assistance it is now a pleasure to acknowledge.

This work began as a little offering for a Christmas party at the home of John and Kari Stackhouse. John was the first to suggest that a book was waiting to be written on all things Christmassy and has been a supporter of the project from the beginning; without his encouragement at key moments it might not have continued. My family has been no less supportive: Karen, Amy, Kate, and Maria have all contributed and sacrificed in numerous ways in order that this encyclopedia be completed.

The embassies and tourist bureaus of the following countries were helpful in providing information on national Christmas customs: Argentina, Armenia, Belgium, Chile, Croatia, Denmark, the Czech Republic, Germany, Jamaica, Luxembourg, Malta, Philippines, Russia, Sweden, Switzerland, and Venezuela.

Many kind people from around the world took time to answer my questions. Thanks are due to Mama Andromeda for information on the Christmas music of Puerto Rico; Javier de Baraka for Christmas in the Basque country; Brother Carl D. Bartholomew and Father Murray Watson for Roman Catholic practices; Reverend Wil Bloy for Hebridean customs; Marcelo Bruno for Christmas in Brazil; Debbie Haughland Chan and the indefatigable internet newsgroup norwaylist for Christmas in Norway; Dr. Terry Galloway for Christmas beetles; Hilda Gharamani and Waleed and Wendy Yousif for Christmas in the Middle East; David Goss for Maritime Christmas customs; Hardy Kleinsasser and Mark Waldner for Christmas among the Hutterites; Derek Liebenberg and Pat and Len McBeath for Christmas in South Africa; David Meadows for Roman history; Flori Mihailescu for Christmas in Romania; Serge Moes for Christmas in Luxembourg; Dale Hoyt Palfrey for the *posadas* ceremony; Christine Pavacic and WPIX-TV for the televised Yule log; Don Smith, Linda Richards, and the members of the internet newsgroup rec.collecting.postal-history for help with Christmas postage stamps; Dr. Eduard Schludermann for Christmas in Austria and Germany; Alvin Suderman for Christmas in Scotland; and Michael D. Toth, Linda Dalglesh, and Kate Bowler were the most resourceful of research assistants.

Special thanks are owed to Canadian Nazarene University College of Calgary and its librarian Carolyn Alho for ordering Christmas material to support my research.

Finally, I must extend my sincere gratitude to Guy Vanderhaeghe and Doug Gibson for getting McClelland & Stewart interested in this project and Alex Schultz, deftest of editors.

Introduction

n the Czech Republic a child gazes at a carp swimming in her bath tub; in Portugal a man is trying to make a turkey drunk. In Ethiopia men are shouting and waving hockey sticks; in New Zealand a family is barbecuing on the beach. In Denmark they are lighting a candle, while in Mexico they are strolling behind a young couple searching for a place to stay. In Austria costumed figures are driving demons away with brooms, while in Canada warmly dressed singers are trudging door to door through the snow. In Japan someone is reserving a table at an expensive restaurant, while in China someone is reserving a seat in a cathedral. Children everywhere are yearning for the annual visit of Santa Claus, Father Christmas, Mother Goody, Grandfather Frost, Père Noël, Befana, Baboushka, Saint Nicholas, or the Old Lady of Bethlehem. A myriad of different activities indicates that it is Christmas time on planet Earth.

There can be no doubt that Christmas is the world's most popular holiday. It is celebrated on every continent, by Christians for whom it is the second most sacred date on the calendar, and by increasing numbers of people of other faiths and folk with no religious faith at all. Stores specializing in Christmas items now do business all year round; Christmas buying fuels much of the industrialized economy; and every year the festival penetrates new cultures, accruing new meanings and importance.

All over the world, the month of December is scarcely long enough to prepare for all that must be done: baking, cooking, shopping, brewing, wrapping, rehearsing, travelling, decorating, writing, meditating, fasting, and hoping. All around the world people will mark the occasion with celebration: eating, drinking, spending, parading, praying, playing, singing, dancing, gathering, and giving. And what a host of symbols has accumulated about this holy and merry time: bells, stars, snowmen, elves, robins, lights, logs, holly, ivy, gingerbread men, prune people, candy canes, evergreen trees, goats, oxen, asses, camels, reindeer, fat men in red suits, angels, shepherds, weary astrologer-kings, a Virgin, and a baby in a makeshift cradle.

Christmas could not have gained or maintained this astonishing hold on people's lives if it had not developed a number of important, and differing, meanings and claims over time. Its original meaning – and still its deepest – was the celebration of the birth of the baby Jesus in Bethlehem and the solemnities surrounding the profound mysteries by which God took on human form. Marking this event would require of believers two distinct attitudes of the heart: the disciplined preparation that would grow into the season of Advent, and the festive joy that would become the Twelve Days of Christmas.

From its earliest days, Christmas took on different aspects and was a holiday whose meaning could shift with time and place. Centuries of complaints by church councils and reformers attest to the tension between the demands of a sacred season and those of a midwinter festival. At times celebrations have been centred on the whole community, with Christmas coming to stand for neighbourliness and hospitality; at other times the emphasis was on the individual family. In various countries the focus will be on outdoor worship and merriment; in others Christmas is kept indoors. The holiday has stood for international good will, and on the other hand, as in Soviet Eastern Europe, for national identity and resistance. It has been child-centred and adult-centred; alcohol-centred and toy-centred; raucous and domestic; holy and profane. Everywhere, however, and at all times, it has been the season of miracle and surprise, the time closest to the hearts of the people who keep it.

This book tries to gather all of the various meanings, symbols, and expressions of Christmas in one volume. The author hopes that in its more than one thousand articles you will find much that will delight, astound, and amuse you, and that, whatever the time of year, Christmas will take on a richer meaning.

Gerry Bowler
St. Benedict's Day,
2000 A.D.

THE WORLD ENCYCLOPEDIA OF

CHRISTMAS

Abbot of Unreason A version of the LORD OF MISRULE in clerical garb, a popular name for the leader of Christmas revels in late medieval Scotland (where he was also known as the Master of Unreason). In 1489 Henry VII of England had an Abbot of Misrule to direct his holiday events. The office was officially banned in England in 1555, but continued into the 17th century and only vanished during the reign of the Puritan faction in the 1640s and 1650s. In France the Abbot of Misrule was called L'Abbé de Liesse (jollity). In the French town of Cambrai in the late-medieval period, the festivities during the Twelve Nights were run by "Fools' Abbots" and "Simpletons' Bishops," but this practice of riotous good fun and social inversion was ended by the Catholic Reformation.

Adam and Eve, Saints Adam and Eve, the ancestors of the human race, were first honoured as saints in the churches of Eastern Christianity, and during the Middle Ages their cult spread into the West. Though the Catholic Church never officially recognized them with a feast day, popular veneration of Adam and Eve was widespread, particularly on December 24, when it was thought fitting that those responsible for the fall of mankind be linked with the birth of the Saviour who came to redeem humanity.

Medieval dramas telling the story of Adam and Eve had as a stage prop a tree representing the Garden of Eden and the Tree of the Fruit of the Knowledge of Good and Evil. This tree was decorated with apples or round wafers representing the host of the Mass, and it is this "Paradise Tree" that historians see as a precursor to the modern Christmas tree. This link is evident when we note that as late as the 19th century some American and German Christmas trees had images of Adam and Eve and the Serpent underneath them. *Godey's* magazine claimed "an orthodox Christmas-Tree will have the figures of our first parents at its foot, and the serpent twining itself around its stem."

In parts of Lithuania, apples were placed on the table on Christmas Eve to recall those through whose sin mankind first fell, as well as the Virgin Mary, the new Eve.

"Adam Lay Ybounden" The 15th-century text to this carol links the fall of man to the coming of Jesus. Benjamin Britten included it in his CEREMONY OF CAROLS. The most successful musical setting is by Boris Ord (1897-1961), music director at King's College, Cambridge.

> Adam lay ybounden,
> Bounden in a bond;

> Four thousand winter
> Thought he not too long.

> All for an apple,
> An apple that he took,
> As clerkes finden
> Written in their book.

> Ne had the apple taken been,
> The apple taken been,
> Ne had never our Lady
> A-been heavene queen.

> Blessed be the time
> That apple taken was;
> Therefore we moun singen:
> *Deo gracias! Deo gracias! Deo gracias!*

Addresses, Watchmen's or Carriers' It was customary in the 18th and 19th centuries for occupations such as night watchmen and newsboys to present printed addresses, usually in verse form, to customers in hope of soliciting a tip at Christmastime. An example from Suffolk in 1823, replete with puns, reads:

> Your pardon, Gentles, while we thus implore,
> In strains not less awakening than of yore,
> Those smiles we deem our best reward to catch,
> And for the which we've long been on the *Watch*;
> Well pleas'd if we that recompence obtain,
> Which we have fa'en so many *steps* to gain.
> Think of the perils in our *calling past*,
> The chilling coldness of the midnight blast,
> The beating rain, the swiftly driving snow,
> The various ills that we must undergo,
> Who roam, the glow-worms of the human race,
> The living Jack-a-lanthorns of the place.

> 'Tis said by some, perchance, to mock our toil,
> That we are prone to "*waste the midnight oil!*"
> And that, a task thus idle to pursue,
> Would be an idle *waste of money* too!

Addresses A 19th-century watchman with his staff and address.

How hard, that we the *dark* designs should rue
Of those who'd fain make *light* of all we do!
But such the fate which oft doth merit greet,
And which now drives us fairly off our beat!
Thus it appears from this our dismal plight,
That *some* love *darkness*, rather than the *light*.

Henceforth let riot and disorder reign,
With all the ills that follow in their train;
Let TOMS and JERRYS unmolested brawl,
(No *Charlies* have they now to *floor* withal,)
And "rogues and vagabonds" infest the Town,
For cheaper 'tis to *save* than *crack a crown!*

To brighter scenes we now direct our view –
And first, fair Ladies, let us turn to you.
May each New Year new joys, new pleasures bring,
And Life for you be one delightful spring!
No summer's sun annoy with fev'rish rays,
No winter chill the evening of your days!

To you, kind Sirs, we next our tribute pay:
May smiles and sunshine greet you on your way!
If married, calm and peaceful be your lives;
If single, may you forthwith get you wives,
Thus, whether Male or Female, Old or Young,
Or Wed or Single, be this burden sung:
Long may you live to hear, and we to call,
A Happy Christmas and New Year to all!

"Adeste Fideles"   A popular Christmas hymn written by John Francis Wade, an Englishman at the Catholic College at Douai, in northern France, probably around 1740-43. This Latin hymn was long assumed to have only been copied by Wade and to be much older (St. Bonaventure, the 13th-century Franciscan monk, was sometimes credited with it), but Wade is now deemed by most musicologists to have been responsible for both words and music. The most popular English translation, the 1852 "O COME ALL YE FAITHFUL," is by Frederick Oakeley.

Adoration of the Child   The artistic depiction of the infant Jesus being adored by his parents and the animals in the stable. These scenes were not derived from scriptural sources but seem to have emanated from medieval mystical and devotional writings, such as the visions of ST. BRIDGET OF SWEDEN. Botticelli and Filippino Lippi's portrayals both illustrate the alienation of JOSEPH, setting him apart from the scene to emphasize that he was not the true father of Jesus. Corregio's *Adoration* eliminates Joseph altogether. (See colour fig. 1.)

Adoration of the Magi   The Gospel of Matthew tells of how Magi, Persian astrologers and scholars, journeyed from the east in search of a new-born king. "And when they were come into the house, they saw the young child with Mary his mother, and fell down and worshipped him: and when they had opened their treasures, they presented unto him gifts; gold, and frankincense and myrrh." (Matthew 2:11.)

Among the earliest examples of Christmas art are depictions of the Adoration of the Magi, which appear in Roman catacombs and on sarcophagi of the pre-Constantinian period. It is interesting to note that at a time when the number of Magi was still unfixed, these appear as a trio, almost identical (unlike later representations in which they differed in age and race), dressed as Persians with Phrygian bonnets and pantaloons. In these early depictions, all pre-dating the establishment of Christmas celebrations in Rome, Mary and the baby

Jesus are portrayed unsentimentally, seated on a chair or throne as if receiving a diplomatic mission. The Magi process toward them bearing gifts, often on plates, with gold always the first to be offered. The presence of these representations on funereal art has been attributed to the notion of the dead, who are sometimes featured in their togas in the Magian procession, having joined the Magi in hope of achieving salvation in return for the gifts brought to the baby Jesus.

In the fifth-century Roman Church of Santa Maria Maggiore, where the pope celebrates a mass every Christmas Day, the Magi are depicted both standing before Herod and offering gifts to the baby, who is seated on a throne. In the sixth-century mosaics of the church of Sant'Apollinare in Ravenna, we begin to see the three Magi as distinct in dress and age.

In Renaissance art the Adoration of the Magi and the Adoration of the Shepherds are often merged into one scene. (See colour figs. 14, 18.)

Adoration of the Shepherds   "And it came to pass as the angels were gone away from them into heaven, the shepherds said one to another, Let us now go even unto Bethlehem, and see this thing which has come to pass, which the Lord hath made known unto us. And they came with haste, and found Mary, and Joseph and the babe lying in a manger." (Luke 2:15-16.)

The visit of the shepherds to the baby Jesus was at first portrayed in art as a visitation by two or three shepherds with simple gifts such as a lamb. The number of shepherds increased in later medieval art, and the scene was often conflated with the ANNUNCIATION TO THE SHEPHERDS or the ADORATION OF THE MAGI. In Le Brun's 1690 *Adoration of the Shepherds* the host of angels filling the air above the Virgin contrasts with the earth-bound shepherds, who crawl toward the centre of the canvas. The piety and simplicity of the shepherds made the scene a favourite subject for centuries; other artists who have painted the scene include Rembrandt, Bassano, and El Greco, whose *Adoration* was his last work, meant to hang over his tomb.

Advent   The season of preparation for the celebration of the birth of Jesus. In the churches of the West, it is the beginning of the ecclesiastical year and commences on the Sunday closest to St. Andrew's Day, November 30. In the Eastern churches a longer Advent season begins on November 15.

Its name derives from *adventus* (Latin for "coming"), and its origins appear to lie in the mid-fourth century. In fifth-century Gaul it was a penitential period, involving a fast of three days a week, from St. Martin's Day, November 11, to Christmas, but in Rome it seems to have been a shorter, more festive time of anticipation. By the 13th century, Advent had become a four-week fast with activities such as marriage, games, feasting, and sex forbidden, but these restrictions were abolished in the 20th century, and the season is now one of reflection and spiritual preparation.

Church services include the singing of Advent hymns, such as "O Come, O Come Emmanuel" or the great "O" antiphons, and the lighting of Advent candles. In homes Advent wreaths are set out and Advent calendars mark the days before Christmas. Pre-Christmas cleaning is often an important part of the preparation, as is a hectic round of baking breads, cakes, cookies, and treats. Christmas markets present their wares and children write to the gift-bringer to alert him (or her) to the presents they would like to receive.

Around the world Advent is a time for remarkable ceremonies. In Twente in the Netherlands special horns, made of young saplings, are blown to chase away evil spirits and welcome the coming of Christmas. House visits are customary, and include the *asalto* in Puerto Rico, the *posadas* in Mexico, and the *Klopfelnächte* in Germany. Christians in many lands perform dramas during the season, such as the Brazilian *pastorhinas*, the German *Herbergsuchen*, and the Filipino *pastores*. (See DRAMA AND CHRISTMAS.)

Advent also includes a number of saints' days tied into the celebration of Christmas. (See ST. BARBARA'S DAY, ST. LUCIA, ST. NICHOLAS, ST. THOMAS'S DAY, ST. THORLAK'S DAY.)

Advent Calendar Advent calendars note the days in December remaining until Christmas. The most common form of these has little doors that are opened each day to reveal a candy, picture, toy, or verse.

The notion of graphically depicting the time until the arrival of Christmas seems to have begun in 19th-century German homes. Some families marked chalk or paint lines on the floor as Christmas approached, others hung a different devotional picture on the wall or lit a new candle every day beginning December 1. Homemade Advent calendars appeared about 1850, with each day from December 1 to 24 marked by a Bible verse, a sweet, or a drawing. The first printed calendar was the *Münchener Weihnachtskalender* (Munich Christmas calendar), produced in 1903 by Gerhard Lang, but other publishers were quick to follow. By 1914 Germany was exporting ornate Advent calendars in numerous designs involving winter landscapes, Christmas trees, town scenes, or castles; many of these are now valuable collectors' items. As with German Christmas toys and ornaments, this trade was disrupted by world wars I and II, but the country continues to print calendars for a world market.

Though most Advent calendars are now produced commercially, the traditional homemade variety has not been abandoned by craftspeople, who continue to find ingenious ways to mark the count-down to Christmas. Variations include the Advent stocking containing 24 treats, one of which is removed every day, and the Danish calendar-candle marked off into 24 sections.

Advent calendars are particularly popular in Scandinavia, where various tie-ins with television programs both entertain and raise money for charitable causes.

Advent Wreath A wreath, usually of greenery, to which are attached candles, invented by the reforming Lutheran pastor Johann Hinrich Wichern. In Hamburg in 1833 Wichern opened the *Rauhe Haus*, the "Rough House," which sheltered orphaned or neglected children. To make the Christmas story more real to the children, every night of Advent he told them stories, prayed, and lit a candle. To accommodate the candles a wheel-shaped chandelier was built, around which evergreens were twined. Visitors and supporters were impressed by this display and the custom spread, but those who imitated it reduced it in size to four candles, one for each week of Advent.

Many churches and homes mark the progress of Advent by lighting one additional candle a week until, on the final Sunday (Gaudete Sunday), all four are alight. Three of these candles are purple or violet (penitential colours) while the fourth is the pink of rejoicing. After Christmas these candles are often replaced with white ones.

The candles represent the coming of Jesus, the Light of the World, and it was once customary for someone named John or Joan to be the first to light them, because John the Baptist was the first to see the fire of divinity in Jesus and John the Evangelist began his gospel by referring to Jesus as the Light.

The wreath is an ancient symbol of victory, and the greenery represents the everlasting life.

A German variation on the Advent wreath is a seven-branched candle-holder. In the southwestern United States the wreath is occasionally made from bunches of red chili peppers. Acadians in the Canadian Maritime provinces fashion their Advent wreaths in the form of a cross and place them at the foot of the church altar.

The world's largest Advent wreath takes up a whole city block in Münster.

"Adventure of the Blue Carbuncle" *Sherlock Holmes and Doctor Watson question a visitor about a Christmas goose.*

"Adventure of the Blue Carbuncle" Though Arthur Conan Doyle sold his first Sherlock Holmes story in 1887 to *Beeton's Christmas Annual*, "Adventure of the Blue Carbuncle" is the only account of the great detective that deals with Christmas. We learn, in this short piece written for the January 1892 edition of the *Strand Magazine*, how a battered hat and a Christmas goose lead Holmes to the solution of a mystery, the freeing of an innocent man, and the recovery of a giant blue jewel.

Advertising and Christmas Advertising and Christmas have been synonymous for centuries. Probably the earliest form of mass medium designed to bring in money at Christmas was the printed address handed out to clients by newsboys, lamp-lighters, and watchmen in the 18th century. This one from Boston sums up the approach:

> Christmas and New Year, Days of Joy,
> The Harvest of your Carrier Boy,
> He hopes you'll not his Hopes destroy . . .
> [That] His generous patrons may inspire,
> By filling up his Pockets higher!

Merchants were not far behind in drumming up business at Christmas. In 1728 an advertisement in England's *The Country Journal* offered necklaces for sale with the claim that the queen always gave them to her children. Though most Christmas advertising of the time was directed at those buying for young people, servants, or other dependents, a 1770 ad from the *New York Journal* targeted the upper classes: jewellery, teapots, dress swords, and pocket pistols were deemed to be "proper

Presents to and from Ladies and Gentlemen at this Season, when the Heart is more peculiarly enlarged."

The second decade of the 19th century saw an acceleration in seasonal advertising as Christmas giving became more customary and manufactured gifts became socially acceptable. A Broadway emporium bought space in the *New-York Advertiser* to offer the following in 1824:

> a large assortment of Juvenile Pastimes, all of which are calculated to improve as well as amuse the youthful mind, viz: Geographical Games. The Traveller's tour through the United States, performed with a tetotum [a top] and travellers. They are put up in three different modes – on pasteboard and double folded on cloth, with a case, and dissected [i.e., jigsawed]. Dissected Maps. Vernacular Cards, Geographical Cards, The Cabinet Of Knowledge Opened, PHILOSOPHICAL cards, Astronomical Cards, Scriptural Cards, Botanical Cards, Dissected Pictures. . . . In addition, a good assortment of Juvenile Books, in plain and elegant bindings. Also, Pocket Books, Chess Men, Backgammon Boards, Pen-Knives, and Ladies' Work Boxes.

In the 1830s Santa Claus became a popular figure in print advertising. Since he came ready-made as a gift-bringer with a pack full of goods – Clement Moore's influential poem "A Visit From Saint Nicholas" described him carrying "a bundle of toys just over his back / And he looked like a peddler just opening his sack" – merchants could hardly ask for a more propitious icon of Christmas consumerism. J.W. Parkinson of Philadelphia advertised his store in 1846 as "Kriss Kringle's Headquarters," and by the end of the century it was customary for department stores to hire Santa Claus impersonators and ensconce them in special grottoes or on stages where children could flock and tell them what they hoped they would be brought on Christmas Eve. (This appropriation of Santa Claus continued all through the 20th century, and one industry figure in 1940 estimated that the jolly saint generated $500,000,000 in sales annually.)

Department stores also began to use their windows as a means of attracting buyers. Macy's in New York has had special Christmas windows since they opened in 1858, and by the mid-1880s hundreds of thousands of people were jamming the sidewalks as they toured the Christmas store displays. These displays could be enormous and elaborate. In 1894 Macy's staged 13 *tableaux* ranging from Sinbad the Sailor to Gulliver's Travels to King Solomon and the Queen of Sheba. The most impressive of the American department store displays were those staged by Wannamaker's of Philadelphia, which every year turned its Grand Court into a veritable cathedral including wooden statues of the 12 apostles, a recreation of the rose window from Westminster Abbey, and what was then the world's largest pipe organ. The store also offered customers their own annual Christmas hymnal for joining in the carol singing. This pseudo-religious display gave customers the notion that the store was above mere commercialism.

Christmas cards from businesses to their customers became a popular form of advertising in the late 19th century. The first Christmas cards printed in the United States were of this ilk, offered by Pease's Great Variety Store in Albany in the 1850s. Such cards were usually beautifully produced, particularly after the introduction of chromolithographic printing, and often ended up as decorations on the Christmas tree.

Churches, too, used the holiday season to their advantage in raising money for projects; Christmas bazaars or fairs run by North American places of worship were widespread around the turn of the century. A New Brunswick Anglican church in the 1890s ran the following advertisement in excruciating rhyme:

> Christmas gifts you'll find for one and all, for Santa has left them at St. George's Hall. November twenty-seven at seven o'clock, our Shoppes will open just on the dot. We'll continue next day beginning at four, and we'll keep it open to ten or more. Our Shoppes are many, our Goods are new, if you cannot buy them at least come to view.

By 1900 Christmas was the biggest marketing season of the year. The 1899 *Advertising World* told its readers "Do not stint the advertising appropriation." In 1908 *The Merchants Record and Show Window* announced that "Christmas is the merchant's harvest time and it is up to him to garner in as big a crop of dollars as he can." With such high stakes the advertising campaigns were begun earlier and earlier. In 1887 the first Christmas advertisement in the London *Times* appeared on December 12; in 1898 it was November 30. The 1902 *Dry Goods Economist* noted that November 15 or even November 1 was not too early to start the "Holiday Campaign."

Those businesses selling goods or services that might not have been considered suitable for seasonal gifts nonetheless expended much energy in finding ways to advertise their products as Christmas-related. Consider this ad from an insurance company in 1921:

> We all join with Tiny Tim in his beautiful prayer – "God bless us, everyone," and then we are reminded of the old saying that "God helps (or blesses) those who help themselves." There is no better means of self help to those we love than the great institution of Life Insurance, which enables us, by regular payments, to create a fund which will be paid to those we love at a time when, perhaps, they most need it.

In the 20th century the blare of Christmas advertising became omnipresent from late October on. Merchants competing for attention have occasionally devised ways to attract customers that proved so effective they have become woven into the celebration of the holiday. For example, a 1910 advertisement for Ivory Soap showed a child sitting in front of a fireplace with a bowl of water, a towel, and a bar of Ivory so that Santa could wash up after coming down the sooty chimney. After the advertisement had run, parents took to setting out soiled washcloths and dirty water after the children had gone to bed as a way to convince them that St. Nick had paid his visit. Santa Claus or Christmas parades, originating in Canada in 1905, have become popular ways to kick off the buying season; many draw vast crowds and are televised. For much of the century in North America the arrival of the Christmas catalogue was part of the ritual of toy selection and an important means by which parents discovered the material yearnings of their offspring. But the two most significant blendings of advertising and celebration were American innovations of the 1930s.

The Coca-Cola company had adopted the figure of Santa Claus in the 1920s to promote the idea that soft drinks were a winter as well as a summer beverage. In 1931 Haddon Sundblom painted the first of his Santa Claus illustrations for Coke, a job that he continued to perform until 1964. These illustrations of a red-clad Santa, trimmed in white fur with high black boots and a stocking cap, helped to standardize the image of the gift-bringer in the eyes of North Americans.

Sundblom had taken an already-established figure and made

it part of advertising history. In 1939 Robert May created one of the few Christmas figures of enduring appeal to emerge in the 20th century when he invented RUDOLPH THE RED-NOSED REINDEER as a Christmas promotion for the Montgomery Ward department store in Chicago. From the humble beginnings of this illustrated 32-page booklet were to come the song, storybook, movies, toys, and miscellaneous collectibles of an entire industry built around the illuminated reindeer.

Not all advertising at Christmas is commercial. The Christian Advertising Network, a coalition of British denominations, sponsors an annual Christmas ad campaign meant to attract people to churches. The 1996 advertisement depicted the arrival of the Three Kings with a caption reading: "Bad hair day? You're a virgin, you've just given birth, and now three kings have shown up – find out the happy ending at a church near you."

Aguinaldo   A Spanish word, meaning "gift," with a number of Christmas associations: in Cuba it is a vine with blue flowers that blooms in the winter; in the Philippines and Puerto Rico it is an early-morning mass in Advent; in much of Spanish America it is a name for Christmas presents; in Honduras, Costa Rica, and Ecuador the term refers to the annual Christmas bonus given by employers; and in Spain and the Spanish Caribbean it is a song sung by visiting carollers.

Albert, Prince   (1819-61) Prince consort to Queen Victoria and exemplar of a German-style Christmas in Britain.

Prince Albert *Probably the most influential of Christmas illustrations. This 1848 picture from the* Illustrated London News *helped to spread Prince Albert's vision of a domestic Christmas.*

Francis Albert Augustus Charles Emmanuel, prince of the Protestant German state Saxe-Coburg-Gotha, was the chosen husband of the young Victoria, newly crowned queen of England. After their marriage in 1840, Albert was Victoria's chief adviser and firm supporter. Though never popular with the English people while he was alive, his importing of German attitudes to Christmas did much to lend royal sanction to the holiday in Victorian England. The middle class was quick to adopt novelties introduced by Prince Albert, such as the Christmas tree, and to celebrate the season as they imagined the royal family did. The *London News* in 1848 ran an illustration of the royal tree with the following description:

> The tree employed for this festive purpose is a young fir about eight feet high, and has six tiers of branches. On each tier, or branch, are arranged a dozen wax tapers. Pendent from the branches are elegant trays, baskets, *bonbonières*, and other receptacles for sweetmeats, of the most varied and expensive kind; and of all forms, colours, and degrees of beauty. Fancy cakes, gilt gingerbread and eggs filled with sweetmeats, are also suspended by variously coloured ribbons from the branches. The tree, which stands upon a table covered with white damask, is supported at the root by piles of sweets of a larger kind, and by toys and dolls of all descriptions, suited to the youthful fancy, and to the several ages of the interesting scions of Royalty for whose gratification they are displayed. The name of each recipient is affixed to the doll, bonbon, or other present intended for it, so that no difference of opinion in the choice of dainties may arise to disturb the equanimity of the illustrious juveniles. On the summit of the tree stands the small figure of an angel, with outstretched wings, holding in each hand a wreath.

The magazine noted that Prince Albert and Victoria each had a personal tree decorated and hung with presents from the other spouse. In a letter he sent to his father, Prince Albert described the effect of the tree on his own family: "This is the dear Christmas Eve, on which I have so often listened with impatience for your step, which was to usher us into the present-room. Today I have two children of my own to give presents to, who, they know not why, are full of happy wonder at the German Christmas-tree and its radiant candles."

All I Want for Christmas   (1991)   One of the strongest themes in late 20th-century Christmas movies is the notion of reunion and reconciliation. In *All I Want for Christmas* Hallie O'Fallon (Thora Birch) tells a department store Santa (Leslie Nielsen) that her only Christmas wish is to see her divorced parents reunited. Hallie and her brother then set out to thwart their mother's relationship with her new fiancé and bring Mom and Dad back together for Christmas. This Robert Lieberman film won few friends, and only the charm of young Miss Birch, Leslie Nielsen, and Lauren Bacall as the kids' grandmother provide momentary flashes of interest.

"All I Want for Christmas Is My Two Front Teeth"   A novelty tune written by Don Gardner in 1946, it was a hit in 1948 for Spike Jones and the City Slickers. The words were sung in a child's voice by George Rock, one of the Slickers. Danny Kaye, the Andrews Sisters, and Nat King Cole all recorded it, and it was a Top Ten hit again in 1955 when it was sung by seven-year-old Barry Gordon.

All Mine to Give (1955) Glynis Johns and Cameron Mackintosh play a 19th-century immigrant couple on the American frontier, trying to raise six children. When his parents die it falls to the oldest boy, only 12 years old, to find homes on Christmas Day for his siblings. Also known as *The Day They Gave Babies Away*, this tear-jerker was directed by Allen Reisner.

"All My Heart This Night Rejoices" Written as "Fröhlich soll mein Herze springen" in 1653, this carol is one of many by Germany's most popular hymn writer, Paul Gerhardt (1607-76). Two tunes are in common use: the first by Johann Georg Ebeling (1637-76), who was cantor of the St. Nicholas church in Berlin, where Gerhardt was pastor, and another composed in 1893 by American music professor William Henry Parker. The 1858 English translation is by CATHERINE WINKWORTH. Gerhardt's original 15 stanzas were reduced to 10 in Winkworth's version, and most hymnals now use only these three.

> All my heart this night rejoices,
> As I hear, far and near,
> Sweetest angel voices;
> "Christ is born," their choirs are singing,
> Till the air, ev'rywhere,
> Now with joy is ringing.
>
> Hark! a voice from yonder manger,
> Soft and sweet, doth entreat,
> "Flee from woe and danger.
> Brethren, come; from all that grieves you,
> You are freed, all you need
> I will surely give you."
>
> Come, then, let us hasten yonder;
> Here let all, great and small,
> Kneel in awe and wonder.
> Love Him who with love is yearning,
> Hail the star that from far
> Bright with hope is burning!

Amahl and the Night Visitors A Christmas opera by Gian Carlo Menotti inspired by Hieronymous Bosch's painting *Adoration of the Kings* in New York's Metropolitan Museum of Art. Broadcast December 24, 1951, by NBC as the first opera designed for television, it tells the story of a crippled shepherd boy who encounters the Magi on their way to visit the baby Jesus. Young Amahl is moved to offer his crutch as a gift and is instantly cured of his lameness. (Menotti had been lame himself as a child and seems to have been cured miraculously by a visit to a shrine of the Madonna.)

The opera has become an immensely popular Christmas-time presentation and has since been adapted as a ballet. On Christmas Day, 1963, NBC aired a new version with Kurt Jaghijian and Martha King.

An American Christmas Carol (TV) (1979) A remake of Dickens's classic, set in Depression-era New England with Henry "The Fonz" Winkler as a grim Benedict Slade, the Scrooge-like figure whose life is changed by ghosts from his past. Directed by Eric Till. Despite the title the film was made in Canada.

Anastasia, Saint A Christian saint, legendarily a noblewoman noted for her kindness to the poor, martyred on December 25 in Diocletian's persecutions of the late third century. By the fifth century her cult was well-established in Rome, with devotions centred on the Church of St. Anastasia (which may

Hans Christian Andersen *The celebrated Danish writer of fairy tales penned a number of Christmas stories.*

have been named after the Greek word for resurrection). Though her popularity diminished in the Middle Ages, she is commemorated in the second of the three masses celebrated by the pope every Christmas morning in the Church of St. Anastasia.

Andersen, Hans Christian (1805-75) Danish author of fairy tales, many of which are set at Christmas. After building a reputation as a novelist, Andersen turned in 1835 to the genre that would make him internationally famous, the fairy tale. His Christmas stories, such as "The Fir Tree," "The Little Match Girl," and "The Tin Soldier," are usually marked by heavy sentiment and more than a touch of tragedy.

Andrewes, Lancelot (1555-1626) English bishop (Chichester, Ely, and Winchester) and preacher of a notable series of Nativity sermons to King James I. The most famous of these was preached at Whitehall on Christmas Day, 1622, when Andrewes took as his text Matthew 2, the coming of the Magi. His description of their travels – "A cold coming they had of it at this time of the year, just the worst time of the year to take a journey, and specially a long journey. The ways deep, the weather sharp, the days short, the sun farthest off, *in solstio brumali*, 'the very dead of winter'" – influenced T.S. Eliot's "Journey of the Magi," which begins with a paraphrase of Andrewes.

Andrew's Day, St. November 30 is the feast day of Saint Andrew, brother of Saint Peter and one of the original 12 disciples of Jesus. As described in John 1:40, Andrew was the first to follow the Messiah and the first to bring others to him, so the Church has placed his day at the beginning of the church calendar: Advent Sunday is the Sunday nearest to St. Andrew's Day. In parts of Germany it was once the custom for children to put out their stockings on St. Andrew's Eve and to find them the next morning filled with nuts and apples.

Lancelot Andrewes *The bishop who preached Christmas sermons for King James I.*

In much of Europe it was a day for prognostications, especially for girls seeking husbands. In Romania, vampires rise from the grave. In Germany, if a woman throws a shoe over her shoulder toward the door at midnight, and the shoe lands pointing to the door, the woman will receive a marriage proposal within the year.

Angels Literally "messengers," these emissaries of God play an important role in the Nativity and subsequent Christmas celebrations through the ages.

It is an angel, Gabriel, who begins the Nativity story by his appearance in ancient Palestine to announce a remarkable pair of births. To an elderly couple, beyond the normal years of parenthood, he announces that they will have a son who is to be called John (later known as the Baptist). To a young virgin, Mary, kin to the first couple, Gabriel announces that she has found favour with God and will bear a child engendered by the Holy Spirit. In order that Joseph, Mary's betrothed, does not repudiate her, the angel fills him in on the divine secret. When, at length, the child is born in Bethlehem, a great host of angels announces the news to shepherds in nearby fields. When the local ruler, Herod, appears bent on murdering the child, an angel warns the family to flee to Egypt and advises them later that it is safe to return. (See LUKE, GOSPEL OF and MATTHEW, GOSPEL OF.)

Non-canonical accounts of the Nativity of Jesus also find parts for angels to play. In the *Protoevangelium of James* and *Gospel of Pseudo-Matthew*, Mary and her parents are frequented by angels long before her miraculous pregnancy; in the *Arabic Infancy Gospel*, angels stand round the infant Jesus at his presentation in the Temple, and an angel in the form of a star warns the Magi to flee from Herod. ST. EPHRAEM SYRUS in the fourth century and *The Book of Seth* both claim that the star followed by the Magi was really an angel.

Since the Nativity and its narratives, angels have been prominent in the art and music of Christmas. (For the role of angels in the fine arts, see ANNUNCIATION TO MARY,

ANNUNCIATION TO THE SHEPHERDS, and ADORATION OF THE MAGI.) Graphically, angels have also served in the popular and domestic arts. They have long been symbols of Christmas in the form of ornaments, especially as tree-toppers. Christmas cookies are baked in angel shapes; in Lithuania the traditional wafer is termed "bread of the angels." They have always been a popular theme on Christmas cards and are indispensable in manger scenes, where they hover over the stable.

The medieval mystic Henry Suso in his sorrows dreamt that angels came to comfort him, took him by the hand, and led him in a dance while one sang "In Dolci Jubilo." When he woke, he wrote the music down in the form of a carol, which became "Good Christian Men Rejoice." More usually angels have been the subject of Christmas music in many lands, particularly in their role as annunciators of the birth of Jesus to the shepherds. From France came "Les Anges Dans Nos Campagnes," which has been translated into English as "Angels From the Realms of Glory," and from Moravia we have "Angels and Shepherds." From England came "Angels We Have Heard on High," "Hark the Herald Angels Sing," and "While Shepherds Watched Their Flocks by Night." American angel carols include "It Came Upon the Midnight Clear."

Medieval dramas centring on the Nativity made good use of angels. The 12th-century *Play of Herod* begins: "When Herod and the other persons are ready, an Angel shall appear with a multitude of the heavenly host. He shall announce salvation unto them while the rest keep silent." They also abound in Christmas movies, less as heralds than as interveners in the lives of the spiritually needy. In *The Bishop's Wife* an angel rescues a troubled marriage, while in *It's a Wonderful Life* an angel (albeit an apprentice) saves a good but desperate man from suicide.

Christmas pageantry would not be nearly so colourful without the presence of angels. Countless girls and boys have been clothed in white robes for their part in the seasonal dramas staged by churches and schools. Angels accompany street processions re-enacting the journey to Bethlehem in Latin America and the Philippines; in Europe they are part of the Star Boy groups, which go from door to door.

According to Irish legend the Virgin Mary sends angels each Christmas Eve to awaken children and take them to heaven to sing a carol to the Christ Child. Such children are then returned to their beds and are accounted lucky for the rest of their lives. In Europe angels often accompany the gift-bringer and advise which children have been naughty or nice.

"Angels and Shepherds" A carol based on the 19th-century Bohemian folk song "Nesem vám noviny," translated by Mari Ruef Hofer, 1912.

> Come, all ye shepherds, ye children of earth,
> Come ye, bring greetings to yon heavenly birth.
> For Christ the Lord to all men is given,
> To be our Savior sent down from heaven:
> Come, welcome Him!
>
> Hasten then, hasten to Bethlehem's stall,
> There to see heaven descend to us all.
> With holy feeling, there humbly kneeling,
> We will adore Him, bow down before Him,
> Worship the King.
>
> Angels and shepherds together we go
> Seeking the Savior from all earthly woe;
> While angels, winging, His praise are singing,
> Heaven's echoes ringing, peace on earth bringing,
> Good will to men.

"Angels From the Realms of Glory" Carol writer James Montgomery.

"Angels From the Realms of Glory" This well-loved carol appeared first on Christmas Eve 1816, written by radical journalist and hymn writer James Montgomery, author of more than 400 songs. The first tune associated with it was that connected to the 18th-century French carol "Les Anges Dans Nos Campagnes" of which Montgomery's song was a paraphrase. The music with which most are more familiar today was written in 1867 after Montgomery's death by blind composer Henry Smart (1813-67). Smart's tune had first been used for Horatio Bonar's hymn "Glory Be to God the Father" and was then attached by someone to Montgomery's words. The first melody is still used in England.

Angels from the realms of glory
Wing your flight o'er all the earth.
Ye who sang creation's story
Now proclaim Messiah's birth.

Come and worship, come and worship;
Worship Christ, the newborn King.

Shepherds in the fields abiding,
Watching o'er your flocks by night.
God with man is now residing;
Yonder shines the infant Light.

Chorus

Sages, leave your contemplations;
Brighter visions beam afar.
Seek the great desire of nations;
Ye have seen His natal star.

Chorus

Saints before the altar bending,
Watching long in hope and fear,
Suddenly the Lord descending
In His temple shall appear.

"Angels We Have Heard on High" This carol is a blend of an anonymous 18th-century French *noël* and words by Bishop James Chadwick that became popular in England in the 1840s. The last verse is sometimes reworded by Protestants to avoid seeming to invoke Mary and Joseph.

Angels we have heard on high,
Sweetly singing o'er the plains,
And the mountains in reply
Echoing their joyous strains.

Gloria, in excelsis Deo!
Gloria, in excelsis Deo!

Shepherds, why this jubilee?
Why your joyous strains prolong?
What the gladsome tidings be,
Which inspire your heavenly song?

Chorus

Come to Bethlehem and see,
Him whose birth the angels sing;
Come adore on bended knee,
Christ the Lord the newborn king.

Chorus

See him in a manger laid,
Whom the choirs of angels praise;
Mary, Joseph, lend your aid,
While our hearts in love we raise.

Chorus

Animal Crackers The National Biscuit Company introduced "Barnum's Animal Crackers" in 1902 as a seasonal promotion. The box's carrying string was designed for hanging on a Christmas tree at a time when candy and treats were still a typical decoration. Shirley Temple later celebrated the snack with the song "Animal Crackers in My Soup."

Animals and Christmas
Animals in Nativity Legends
The first animal to be connected with the Nativity story is the humble donkey that legendarily carried Mary to Bethlehem and that shared the manger with the infant Jesus. It was believed that, in accordance with messianic prophecies from Isaiah 1:13 and Habakkuk 3:2, the donkey and the ox knelt before the child. (See ASS, FEAST OF THE and PROPHECIES.) A host of legends sprang up around the supposed presence of other animals around the birth scene. The stork, for example, is said to have plucked out its own feathers to line the manger; for this reason the bird became the patron of babies everywhere. The robin, too, wanted to keep little Jesus warm, and in trying to fan a fire with its wings was singed by the flames, which explains why to this day it is marked by a red breast. (See ROBIN.) The nightingale that sang the baby to sleep was rewarded with a beautiful voice. The youngest of the camels in the caravan of the visiting Magi was said to have moaned with exhaustion and was blessed by the baby with immortality and the happy task of bringing presents to children in parts of the Middle East. The carol "THE FRIENDLY BEASTS" tells how all the animals contributed to the comfort of the infant and his parents.

Meanwhile, back in Jerusalem, King Herod was told of the birth of the Messiah but said he would not believe it unless the roast bird he was about to eat crowed three times. An old English carol relates how the cock, covered again in feathers, sprang to life and crowed. (See "THE CARNAL AND THE CRANE.")

Animal protection of the Holy Family continued on the FLIGHT INTO EGYPT. The spider wove a web to hide Mary, Joseph, and Jesus from soldiers. On board ship to Egypt the family was warned by birds that a storm was approaching;

Animals and Christmas *Livestock crowd the stable in this 19th-century engraving of the Nativity, from a painting by Alfred Fredericks.*

they went ashore and escaped the sinking of the vessel. As a reward Jesus blessed the ibis and ordained that its nests would henceforth be safe from marauding children.

Kindness to Animals

Given the record of kindness by animals to the Lord, it is not surprising that his birthday should be marked by acts of charity toward them. Saint Francis of Assisi, who loved the birds and fishes enough to preach the message of salvation to them just in case they had souls, was a leader in urging good treatment to the animal kingdom. He begged farmers to give their livestock extra food at Christmas in memory of the ox and ass between which the baby lay. "If I could see the Emperor," he said, "I would implore Him to issue a general decree that all people who are able to do so shall throw grain and corn upon the streets, so that on this great feast day the birds might have enough to eat, especially our sisters, the larks."

Scandinavians have long heeded the saint's message and constructed a birds' Christmas tree. In Norway the *julenek* is a sheaf of grain set on a pole for the birds; some farmers tramp down the snow around the pole so that smaller birds can feed on the grain that falls to the ground. In Hungary the last sheaf of the harvest is kept to be given on New Year's morning to the wild birds. Silesian farmers believed that grain kept in one's pocket during the Christmas service could be given to poultry to make them lay many eggs. In other parts of Europe livestock are given extra fodder at Christmastime; in England cattle were often wassailed and anointed with cider. (In Lithuania horses are excluded from the extra helping of food distributed to the livestock on Christmas Eve, either because the horse was not mentioned in scripture or because of the legend that the horse did not warm the baby Jesus with its breath as the ox and ass did that first night in Bethlehem.) Polish farmers give their cattle an *oplatek* wafer on Christmas Eve and bless them with the sign of the cross. In other places it is the custom on St. Thomas Eve, December 20, to sprinkle cows with holy water and scatter consecrated salt on the animals' heads with the words "St. Thomas preserve thee from all sickness." Horses are given special treatment on December 26, ST. STEPHEN'S DAY. They are bled to ensure health for the coming year and given more food.

Not all treatment of animals at Christmas was gentle. An Elizabethan Christmas feast held by lawyers of the Inner Temple involved a huntsman entering the hall with a fox and a cat, both bound at the end of a staff, followed by nine or ten dogs. To the blowing of hunting horns "then were the fox and cat set upon and killed by the dogs beneath the fire, to the no small pleasure of the spectators." The killing of the wren and a subsequent procession with the corpse of the tiny bird was long a custom of St. Stephen's Day celebrations in England, Ireland, and the Isle of Man. In Wokingham, Berkshire, a bull-baiting was customary on Boxing Day and the flesh of the tormented beast was distributed to the poor. Christmas Day foxhunts were long common in the southern United States.

Magical Christmas Eve

A number of folk beliefs assert that on Christmas Eve animals are gifted with special powers in commemoration of the birth of Jesus. One of the most popular of these is the notion that at midnight the animals in the stable fall on their knees in front of the manger, the subject of Thomas Hardy's 1915 poem "The Oxen" and this reminiscence of Old Christmas in Newfoundland:

The most important night of the year was Old Christmas Night. It was the night the cows prayed. The cows all got down on their knees and prayed at 12 o'clock midnight. The chores would have to be done, each cow given a little more hay that night, because they would have to be awake at twelve o'clock midnight to pray. . . . This was truly (supposed) to be the night of Jesus' birth and they prayed at the time of his birth, midnight.

The deer in the forest are said also to kneel and look up to heaven; an account of life in colonial Canada tells of a native trying to spy on the animals to see this happen.

On Christmas Eve it is said that the bees hum the 100th Psalm, but only the pure of heart can hear. Others say that animals on this night are gifted with speech. It is also said that the only animal that sleeps on Christmas Eve is the serpent. A medieval French mystery play describes how farmyard animals speak in Latin: the cock crows, "Christus natus est" (Christ is born); the cow says, "Ubi?" (Where?); the lamb answers, "Bethlehem"; and the ass proclaims, "Eamus!" (Let us go!). Poles claim that if a man without sin speaks to animals at midnight they will reply in a human voice, but in other countries it is bad luck to try to listen in; death within the year will be the punishment to the over-curious.

(For the role of animals in assisting the gift-bringer see REINDEER and REINDEER SUBSTITUTES.)

Annunciation to Mary   "And in the sixth month the angel Gabriel was sent from God unto a city of Galilee, named Nazareth, to a virgin espoused to a man whose name was Joseph of the house of David: and the virgin's name was Mary." The story of the angel's visit to Mary, and her agreement with the divine plan that she should conceive a child by the Holy Spirit, is the subject of Luke's gospel 1:26-38. It has been the inspiration for centuries of artists fascinated by the meeting between an angel of the Lord and a simple country girl. Among the more spectacular depictions are *The Cestello Annunciation* by Botticelli, with Gabriel kneeling before the Virgin, and Dante Gabriel Rossetti's *Ecce Ancilla Domini*, where Mary cowers on her bed. Common iconographic elements are a lily, a dove, or a ray of light.

The Feast of the Annunciation is celebrated on March 25. (See colour figs.2, 20.)

Annunciation to the Shepherds   "And there were in the same country shepherds abiding in the fields keeping watch over their flocks by night. And, lo, the angel of the Lord came upon them, and the glory of the Lord shone round about them: and they were sore afraid. And the angel said unto them, Fear not; for behold I bring you tidings of great joy, which shall be to all people. For unto you is born this day in the city of David a Saviour which is Christ the Lord. And this shall be a sign unto you: Ye shall find the babe wrapped in swaddling clothes and lying in a manger. And suddenly there was with the angel a multitude of the heavenly host praising God, and saying, Glory to God in the highest, and on earth peace, good will toward men." (Luke 2:8-14.)

The confrontation between the angelic host and the shepherds of Bethlehem has not been as popular a topic in Christian art as the ADORATION OF THE SHEPHERDS. In the 15th-century breviary of Martin of Tours we see a shepherd marching toward the Nativity as a bold bagpiper, but in Leon François Comerre's 1875 *L'Annonce aux bergers* the emphasis is on the stark dread of the shepherds as they are dazzled by the sudden appearance of the luminous angel.

The annunciation to the shepherds is retold in carols such as "Shepherd, Shake Off Your Drowsy Sleep" and "Campana sobre campana" and in medieval drama, where it is the occasion for a good deal of mirth and low humour – a tradition that continues to the present day in LOS PASTORES. The above passage from Luke is recited by Linus in *A Charlie Brown Christmas*.

Anoush Abour   A traditional Armenian Christmas porridge made with boiled wheat, dried fruits, nuts, and cinnamon. The dish is similar to other Christmas recipes involving grain, such as the English FRUMENTY and Ukrainian KUTYA.

The Anticks   Groups of mummers who formed in Boston in the second half of the 18th century (see MUMMING). During the Christmas season, men of the lower orders would go door-to-door in disguise and perform a version of the English mumming play that involves broad slapstick humour and a mock death and resurrection. They would expect a gratuity and hospitality for their efforts. By the 1790s their visits were arousing opposition from the middle class, who had come to resent their intrusions and the street violence that was part of their wanderings. One Bostonian complained,

> Their demands for entrance in house are insolent and clamourous; and should the peaceful citizen (not choosing to have the tranquility of his family interrupted) persevere in refusing them admittance, his windows are broke, or the latches and knockers wrenched from his door as the penalty. Or should they gain admittance, the delicate ear is oftentimes offended, children affrighted, or catch the phrases of their senseless ribaldry.

Misrule such as this helped lead to cries to make Christmas a more religious and domestic time, less given to riotousness in the streets. See CALLITHUMPIAN MUSIC and UNITED STATES.

"The Apple Tree"   An American carol first published in 1784 in Joshua Smith's *Divine Hymns or Spiritual Songs*.

> The tree of life, my soul hath seen,
> Laden with fruit and always green;
> The trees of nature fruitless be,
> Compar'd with Christ the apple tree.
>
> This beauty doth all things excel,
> By faith I know, but ne'er can tell,
> The glory which I now can see,
> In Jesus Christ the apple tree.
>
> For happiness I long have sought,
> And pleasure dearly I have bought;
> I miss'd of all, but now I see
> 'Tis found in Christ the apple tree.
>
> I'm weary'd with my former toil,
> Here I shall set and rest a while;
> Under the shadow I will be,
> Of Jesus Christ the apple tree.
>
> I'll sit and eat the fruit divine,
> It cheers my heart like spir'tual wine
> And now this fruit is sweet to me,
> That grows on Christ the apple tree.
>
> This fruit doth make my soul to thrive,
> It keeps my dying faith alive;

Which makes my soul in haste to be
With Jesus Christ the apple tree.

Argentina   Christmas in Argentina is a mixture of the old and the new, with traditional Catholic observances as well as those more akin to a secular North American holiday.

Like most Latin American countries the manger scene, the *pesebre*, is a common sight in homes and public places, and many neighbourhoods stage live pageants re-enacting the events of the Nativity. The midnight mass, the *misa de gallo*, is an important part of Christmas Eve, and after church the family returns home for a meal and a toast. Roast pig and turkey are central items on the table, along with *pan dulce*, a sweet Christmas bread. Highlights of the evening are the opening of gifts under the Christmas tree by the children, toasts with *sidra*, an alcoholic cider, and fireworks.

Christmas Day in Argentina occurs during summer, and it is not uncommon for families to spend the day at the beach or to barbecue their Christmas dinner.

On the evening of January 5, children place shoes by their bed and set out water and hay, expecting that the Three Kings, on their way to Bethlehem, will deposit gifts for them and use their offerings to refresh the camels. This custom is still observed, but exposure to the Americanized Santa Claus (represented in Argentina as Papá Noel) means that increasingly Christmas Eve is the delivery date for presents.

Armenia   Landlocked Armenia in the Caucasus mountains of western Asia has one of the longest traditions of Christianity in the world, having been converted by St. Gregory the Illuminator in 301 A.D. When the Church in Rome decided in the fourth century to celebrate Christmas on December 25, Armenian Christians clung to the earlier date of January 6, which marked both the Nativity of Jesus and his baptism in the River Jordan. This means that in areas that still mark time by the Julian calendar, Armenian Christmas takes place on January 18. Such is the case in Bethlehem, where the Armenian community shares responsibility with other denominations for the maintenance of the Church of the Nativity. Each January 17, the Armenian Patriarch and a flock of believers and clergy travel from Jerusalem to Bethlehem, where they are greeted with great ceremony and conduct services until the early hours of the 18th.

As well as religious services Armenians mark Christmas with the exchange of gifts, feasting, and visiting friends and family. The people of the far-flung Armenian diaspora tend to celebrate the holiday in the fashion of the countries in which they reside. In Armenia itself, which only recently gained its independence from the break-up of the Soviet Union, Christmas observances have been influenced by the Russian occupation; the gift-bringer, for example, is GRANDFATHER FROST.

Art and Christmas   See ADORATION OF THE CHILD, ADORATION OF THE MAGI, ADORATION OF THE SHEPHERDS, ANNUNCIATION TO MARY, ANNUNCIATION TO THE SHEPHERDS, CURRIER AND IVES, FLIGHT INTO EGYPT, THOMAS NAST, and HADDON SUNDBLOM.

"As With Gladness Men of Old"   This carol was written on Epiphany 1860 by the bedridden William Chatterton Dix (1837-98), who also wrote "What Child Is This?" and 40 other hymns. The tune is from an 1838 German collection of chorales by Conrad Kocher (1786-1872), adapted in 1861 by W.H. Monk for Dix's words and called "Dix" henceforth. Dix was not pleased by the music, saying, "I dislike it, but now nothing will displace it."

As with gladness men of old
Did the guiding star behold.
As with joy they hailed its light,
Leading onward, beaming bright.
So most gracious God may we
Evermore be led by Thee.

As with joyful steps they sped
To that lowly manger bed,
There to bend the knee before
Him whom heaven and earth adore;
So may we with willing feet
Ever seek Thy mercy seat.

As they offered gifts most rare
At that manger rude and bare,
So may we with holy joy,
Pure and free from sin's alloy,
All our costliest treasures bring
Christ to Thee, our heav'nly King.

Holy Jesus ev'ry day
Keep us in the narrow way
And when earthly things are past,
Bring our ransomed souls at last
Where they need no star to guide,
Where no clouds Thy glory hide.

In the heavenly country bright,
Need they know created light;
Thou its Light, its Joy, its Crown,
Thou its Sun, which goes not down;
There forever may we sing
Alleluias to our King

Asalto   Literally, "invasion." In Puerto Rico during the Christmas season, guests arrive unannounced at a home for the purposes of feasting, fellowship, and carol singing. The surprised host climbs out of bed and opens his house to the invaders for an hour of merriment until they hurry off to visit noisily another home, often accompanied by the people they have awakened at the first house.

Ashen Faggot   A southwestern English variant on the Yule log, the ashen faggot (also known as the ashton faggot) was a bundle of ash sticks tied together with bark bands. It was burnt on one of the Twelve Nights, and it was customary that a fresh round of drinks was served every time one of the bands broke in the fire. The faggot could be quite large (the biggest seem to have been 12 feet long) and the bands could number over a dozen. Like the Yule log, the faggot must traditionally be lit with a piece of last year's wood. In a Devonshire custom, the unmarried women of the household each choose a band and the girl whose band is the first to catch fire is the next one to be married.

Though many of the ceremonies surrounding the bringing in of the Yule log have disappeared, the burning of the ashen faggot is preserved in England, especially in pubs, where the conviviality and drinks now come at a price.

Ass, Feast of the   A part of the celebration of Christmas in medieval French churches when parody of sacred services and social inversion were allowed and when clergymen were given licence for light-hearted behaviour that was unthinkable during the rest of the year.

The Feast of the Ass celebrated the role played in the Nativity by the humble donkey, the beast that carried Mary to

Ashen Faggot *English countryfolk cut and bind the ashen faggot.*

Bethlehem, that stood over the baby Jesus in the stable, and that carried the Holy Family to safety in Egypt when King Herod was bent on killing the infant. As the clergy or students paraded toward the church where the ass was to be honoured they sang a "hymn of praise":

> From Oriental country came
> A lordly ass of highest fame,
> So beautiful, so strong and trim,
> No burden was too great for him.
> Hail, Sir Donkey, hail!

For the ceremony itself a donkey was often brought into the church, and during the Mass that ended the service the priest and the congregation made donkey noises. Like the Feast of FOOLS, with which the Feast of the Ass was linked, this sort of behaviour eventually grew too outrageous to be tolerated and the Church moved to suppress it. By the 16th century it had almost entirely disappeared from the Christmas scene.

"At the Bottom of the Snow Ocean"   "Tonight there is no mercy. Everything that is out and about must die." In "Paa bunden af snehauet," a 1929 story by Gunnar Gunnarsson (1889-1975), an Icelandic writer working in Danish, the winter storm enforces a sense of coming evil. A little family fears for the father absent at sea but they themselves are snowed in at Christmas and the house is submerged for 18 days.

Audley, John   (or Awdelay) English carol writer/collector of Haumond Abbey, Shropshire (fl. 1426). He described himself as deaf and blind, but he managed to assemble a collection of

25 English carols that he urged readers to sing at Christmas: "I pray you, sirus boothe moore and lase / Sing these caroles in Cristèmas."

Australia   At one time the Australian Christmas was simply a traditional British holiday set in the heat of Down Under, but over the years Australians have managed to keep what they valued in the Christmases they inherited from British and European immigrants and add to them colourful indigenous customs to make a unique blend.

During December Australian families can be found at activities similar to those engaged in around the world: children are writing letters to Father Christmas and opening Advent calendars; parents are selecting a Christmas tree (often pine boughs from native varieties), buying presents, and decorating the house with seasonal plants such as the Christmas Bush and Christmas Bell. Communities hold Christmas parades, and houses and businesses are decorated with festive lights. Schools stage Christmas pageants and carol programs just before closing for the summer vacation.

All over the continent late on Christmas Eve Australians gather to take part in CAROLS BY CANDLELIGHT. Begun in 1938 in Melbourne, this beautiful custom sees hundreds of thousands gather in parks and outdoor stadiums to sing carols, listen to professional performers, and hold candles in the balmy night. Though the biggest of these songfests take place in Sydney's Domain Gardens and Melbourne's Sidney Myer Music Bowl, towns and cities across the continent hold similar events, with the money raised going to charity. The traditional carols are sung, along with an increasing number

Australia *In Australia Christmas is a summer festival, allowing for much outdoor celebration.*

of Australian origin, such as "The Three Drovers," "The Melbourne Carol," and "Six White Boomers." At midnight all hold hands and sing "Auld Lang Syne." Those who cannot attend can follow the proceedings on television or radio. Many Australians also attend a Christmas Eve church service.

Back at home children put out at the foot of the bed their version of the Christmas stocking, the Christmas pillow slip, which will hold the candies and small gifts; the larger presents are left under the tree. Snacks are left out for Father Christmas (cookies and milk, or perhaps beer) and water for the kangaroos that pull his sleigh while he is in Australian airspace. As chimneys are rare Father Christmas is expected to make his entrance through a window.

The next morning presents are opened and the family prepares for the Christmas lunch. The hot summer weather leads many to expect a cold meal or a barbecue at the beach, but others cling to the habits of their British ancestors and sit down to a feast of roast turkey and plum pudding, with perhaps a pavlova for native colour. The queen's Christmas broadcast in the afternoon is a fixture for those Australians who are not of the republican persuasion. Those who insist on a cold Christmas may have gotten their wish months earlier by taking part in a "Christmas in July" trek to the mountains, where all the trappings of a northern celebration can be enjoyed around a roaring outdoor fire.

December 26 is Boxing Day in Australia, a holiday often dedicated to the enjoyment of sporting events, either attending a local fixture or watching the opening day of the test match at the Melbourne Cricket Ground or the start of the Sydney-to-Hobart Yacht Race.

Australian Christmas Tree *Nuytsia floribunda*, a Western Australian parasitic mistletoe. The tree grows 20 to 30 feet and produces clusters of bright yellow flowers during the Christmas season.

Austria For a country of such small size Austria crams a lot into its Christmas season, with bizarre folk customs, beautiful music, rich foods, and snowy Alpine settings.

In late November the Christmas markets of Austria open for business. In Salzburg the *Christkindlmarkt* (Christ Child Market) is set up in front of the cathedral; in Vienna it is in front of the town hall. Children begin to open their Advent calendars on December 1, and some pluck branches on ST. BARBARA'S DAY, December 4, but Christmas really gets underway on December 6, St. Nicholas Day. Children set out their shoes by the window in hope that the saint will fill them

full of good things, and they are seldom disappointed. On his day, the saint, in his bishop's garb, visits homes, schools, and public places to greet children and take part in the many St. Nicholas processions that wind their way through Austrian towns and villages. He is often accompanied by the devilish figure of KRAMPUS, who makes a show of scaring the children while good Nicholas hands out treats. This is also the time for some villages to stage *Krampus* or PERCHTEN-LAUFEN processions, where grotesquely costumed characters parade about, making noise and frightening passersby.

As Christmas approaches Advent candles are lit and children hurry to complete their letters to the Christ Child, who is believed to bring the presents on Christmas Eve. The Austrian postal service operates a special office for such letters in Christkindl in upper Austria. The glorious heritage of Austrian music is given full scope in the many concerts that precede Christmas, and other art forms are also on display: the carving and painting of manger scenes for which Tyrolean craftsmen are famous and the dramas that re-enact the search of Mary and Joseph for shelter. In Igls, near Innsbruck, the costumed children of the village take part in a torch-lit procession on December 23 to a stage where they perform a Nativity play.

Shops close at noon on Christmas Eve and people hurry home for last-minute preparations. Some spend the afternoon visiting the graves of family members, placing flowers and lighting candles. The Christmas tree must be decorated – many Austrian homes still favour real candles as a decoration and place a manger scene at its foot – and the Christmas Eve meal made. Carp and goose are traditional favourites, but turkey is making inroads. For the children the best part of the evening comes when a bell is rung to announce that the Christ Child and his angels have descended from heaven to bring the gifts. They are admitted to the room where the tree has been set up, the Nativity story is read from the Bible, carols are sung, and presents are opened. Midnight church services are widely attended; few are more popular with tourists than that in Oberndorf's chapel, where the carol "Silent Night" was first sung.

Christmas Day is spent receiving friends and eating. Austrians are devoted to the arts of Christmas baking; there are dozens of types of cookies available, including gingery *Lebkuchen*, crescent-shaped *Vanillekipferl*, or the *Zimtsterne* cinnamon stars, not to mention the *Christstollen* bread and *Sachertorte* or *Linzertorte* cakes. Sekt wine or *Glühwein* punch will wash it all down.

The Twelve Nights in Austria are the *Rauhnächte* ("Rough Nights" or "Smoke Nights"), a time of increased demonic activity and thus a time to purge the house and farm of evil spirits. Processions of masked figures armed with brooms parade about sweeping away the bad influences, while some homes are purged using holy smoke from a censer.

On January 6 the Christmas season ends with Epiphany, or the day of the Three Kings. Homes are visited by men dressed as Magi and a ceremony takes place: carrying a representation of the crib and accompanied by a servant with a censer, the Kings move through the house, blessing it and its inhabitants. As they leave they chalk a mark on a door post with the year of their visit and their initials, as in "19 K+M+B 99."

Autry, Gene (1907-98) The quintessential "singing cowboy," who made a career in radio, television, and the movie screen and a vast fortune in real estate and the communications industry. In the late 1940s and early 1950s he contributed greatly to the popular culture of the North American Christmas with three hit recordings: "Here Comes Santa Claus (Right Down

Santa Claus Lane)," which he wrote himself in 1946 after having ridden in the Hollywood Santa Claus parade, "Rudolph, the Red-Nosed Reindeer" (1949), and "Frosty the Snowman," the best-selling Christmas record of 1951. Autry retired from performing in 1956 having made 95 movies and 635 records, one of which was nominated for a Best Song Oscar. The jewel of his business holdings was the California Angels professional baseball team.

"Away in a Manger"   For a long time this Christmas song was attributed to Martin Luther, but its first two verses initially appeared anonymously in an 1885 American collection of Lutheran hymns. In 1887 James R. Murray, a Cincinnati music editor, set the text to his own tune and published it in *Dainty Songs for Little Lads and Lasses, for Use in the Kindergarten, School and Home*. He called it "Luther's Cradle Hymn (Composed by Martin Luther and still sung by German mothers to

their little ones)." A third verse was anonymously added before 1892. A different melody, popular in Britain, is by William James Kirkpatrick.

Away in a manger, no crib for a bed,
The little Lord Jesus laid down his sweet head.
The stars in the sky looked down where he lay,
The little Lord Jesus asleep in the hay.

The cattle are lowing, the baby awakes,
But little Lord Jesus no crying he makes.
I love Thee, Lord Jesus, look down from the sky
And stay by my cradle til morning is nigh.

Be near me, Lord Jesus, I ask Thee to stay
Close by me forever, and love me, I pray.
Bless all the dear children in thy tender care,
And take us to heaven, to live with Thee there.

Baba Noel The name for Santa Claus or Father Christmas in much of the Middle East and among the Christians of Israel. In 1988, in protest over the Israeli occupation, Palestinians began a boycott of Christmas in Bethlehem, which disappointed children expecting the usual visit from Baba Noel. The boycott ended in 1993 and a spokesman for the Palestinian Fatah faction called Jesus the first Palestinian martyr.

Babar and Father Christmas Jean de Brunhoff's favourite animal king meets Father Christmas in this children's book from the 1930s. When Zéphir, Arthur, and the rest hear the story of what Father Christmas does for the children in Man's country, they decide to write him a letter asking him to come to Elephants' country too. After their letter receives no reply, Babar decides to pay a visit to Father Christmas, whom he tracks down after a series of adventures. A happy ending results and the gift-bringer vows to visit the land of the Elephants every year.

Babar and Father Christmas (1986) Fans of the original book may be startled to find that the nasty rhinoceros Rataxes has made his way into this 1986 children's video of de Brunhoff's gentle tale. It appears that Babar's arch-enemy wants all Christmas toys for himself.

Babbo Natale An Italian Santa Claus figure that in some areas has replaced the Befana as the principal gift-bringer.

Babes in Toyland (1934) The evil Barnaby (Henry Brandon) has designs on blonde beauty Little Bo Peep (Charlotte Henry) and threatens to foreclose on the mortgage he holds on Mother Peep's Shoe, but his evil plans are thwarted by Ollie Dee and Stanley Dum (Laurel and Hardy). The outraged villain unleashes his army of bogeymen on Toyland and an epic battle results. This film, directed by Gus Meins and Charlie Rogers, from the Hal Roach studio, is still the most enjoyable of the three versions made and is favourite holiday movie fare on television.

Based on Victor Herbert's 1903 operetta, much of the original music, including "The March of the Wooden Soldiers," is woven into the score, along with a Walt Disney ditty "Who's Afraid of the Big Bad Wolf." Also known as *March of the Wooden Soldiers*, *Laurel and Hardy in Toyland*, *Toyland*, *March of the Toys*, and *Revenge Is Sweet*, recent releases of the film have been colourized.

Babes in Toyland (1961) The Disney studios and director Jack Donohue remade the 1934 Laurel and Hardy masterpiece with Annette Funicello and Tommy Sands as the young lovers and Ray Bolger as the villain. They needn't have bothered.

Babes in Toyland (TV) (1986) Richard Mulligan's scenery-chewing portrayal of the villainous Barnaby provides an interesting contrast to the wooden minimalism of Keanu Reeves as Jack-Be-Nimble in this Clive Donner remake of the 1934 classic. Drew Barrymore plays the lovely Lisa, and Pat Morita is the Toymaster. Leslie Bricusse provided a new score but retained the old favourites "Toyland" and "March of the Wooden Soldiers."

Baboushka A Russian gift-bringer and the equivalent of Italy's BEFANA. Like the Befana she is an old woman who refused to go with the Magi to visit the baby Jesus (and according to some variations even gave the Wise Men the wrong directions). She later repented, and to this day seeks the baby. Every Epiphany Eve she enters the rooms of sleeping children and leaves them gifts.

The Baddeley Bequest Echoes of the BEAN KING and TWELFTH NIGHT celebrations of old England still linger. Robert Baddeley, an English actor who died in 1794, left £100 in his will for the provision of a Twelfth Night cake for his fellow actors. It is served to this day in the green room of the Theatre Royal, Drury Lane, after the evening performance on Twelfth Day. His legacy also provides wine with which the performers drink to his memory.

Badnjak The Yule log in Serbo-Croatia, usually oak and brought into the home on Christmas Eve with great ceremony.

Baboushka *The Russian gift-bringer, depicted on a Guernsey Christmas stamp.*

As in other nations the log is not allowed to burn out completely; a remnant is always saved. If placed on a branch in the orchard it will bring a good harvest of fruit in the coming year.

In Croatia "*badnjak*" is also used to refer to Christmas Eve.

The Bahamas The highlight of Christmas in the Bahamas – aside from the delicious native seafood – is the *Junkanoo* tradition (see JOHN CANOE). Derived from a custom in the colonial period, when slaves were allowed a period of Christmastime liberty and celebration, *Junkanoo* has evolved into a bright and noisy carnival. Starting at 2 a.m. on Boxing Day, wildly costumed bands and groups of dancers parade through Nassau, filling it with the sounds of drums, bells, whistles, and horns. Businesses stay open until dawn to accommodate the thousands of tourists and locals who line the streets to applaud the troupes, who have spent months preparing their costumes, musical numbers, and dances in order to win the prize money offered every year.

Bairn Bishop See BOY BISHOP.

Baker, Theodore (1851-1934) American musicologist and carol translator. Known chiefly for his reference works such as *Baker's Biographical Dictionary of Musicians* and *Dictionary of Musical Terms*, Baker also produced English-language versions of German and Italian Christmas songs. His most famous renditions are "Carol of the Bagpipers," "Lo, How a Rose E'er Blooming," and "While by My Sheep I Watch at Night."

Baking Baking has become an essential part of the celebration of Christmas for a number of reasons. Historically it relates to the midwinter veneration of grain and grain products in hope that the next year's harvest will be bountiful. We can see this in the Eastern European custom of placing wheat and hay about the house, even under the tablecloth, on Christmas Eve, and in the widespread practice of preparing a grain porridge, such as *kutya* or frumenty, at Christmastime. This notion carries over to baked goods, especially bread. In the 19th century German peasants believed there was particular power in bread baked at Christmas: thrown into a fire, it would quench the flames; given to cattle, it would keep them healthy. Similar beliefs attached to the *oplatek* wafer in Slavic Europe and Christmas cake in Flanders. As a result special breads and other baked goods became identified with Christmas in many countries: the German *Christstollen* and the Romanian *turte*, which were said to represent the swaddling clothes of the baby Jesus; the Greek *Christopsomo*, which is often decorated with a cross; the medieval English mince pies, which were made in the shape of a crib and adorned with a dough figure of the Holy Child; the Belgian *cougnou* or *pain de Jesus* in the shape of the baby Jesus; and the Ukrainian *kolach*, which is sometimes stacked in threes as a reminder of the Trinity. Many cakes are baked in the shape of wreaths and circles to symbolize everlasting life.

Christmastide is a feast, and a feast means food and abundance. Christmas baking is therefore an expression of indulgence and the celebration of a full pantry after a year's hard work. This is a time when the richest ingredients and most costly spices can be employed with a guilt-free conscience; the effort and expense lavished on Christmas baking is unmatched at any other time of year. The weeks of Advent are scarcely time enough for the marshalling of resources and the preparation of the cakes, cookies, breads, and pies that are consumed in such quantities. It is little wonder that an Irish term for Christmas Eve is *Oidhche na ceapairi* ("Night of Cakes"). In Norway no fewer than seven kinds of cookies must be prepared.

Baking at Christmas is also a community activity. Most families prepare at least some goodies together, as in the custom of the STIR UP SUNDAY pudding, and on many occasions members of a whole village, church, or other group are involved. In Latin America, for example, the work of preparing *pasteles* is shared among women, some of whom stuff the leaves with the delicious filling while others chop, steam, or wrap. Eating Christmas baking is, of course, a communal activity as well, binding the family together in present enjoyment and often linking them to those who are dead or absent. The *oplatek* wafers of Poland are shared ritually with those around the table, but some are reserved for those away from home, and in many countries families leave bread out for the spirits of those departed or for the Holy Family. Sharing with those less fortunate is often part of the Christmas tradition, either by setting a place for the unexpected visitor or by giving baked goods away. The "soul cakes" of England and the French *pain calendeau* are examples of charity foods.

See GÂTEAU DES ROIS and KING CAKE.

Balthazar *The Wise Man who brought the gift of myrrh, depicted on a Guernsey Christmas stamp.*

Balthasar One of the three Magi who visited the baby Jesus. In legend and art he is often depicted as dark-skinned or African and is said to have been the Wise Man who brought the gift of myrrh.

Bambino Italian for "baby," but at Christmas the term refers to the figure of the infant Jesus placed in family and church manger scenes. The most famous is the medieval doll in the Church of Santa Maria in Ara Coeli, Rome, carved from wood from the Mount of Olives in Jerusalem. Ceremonies attend its placing every Christmas Eve; children preach before it and miracles are attributed to it, including one where it returned itself home after a kidnapping.

In the Church of San Domenico in Naples, a crèche is set up in a grotto. It contains every figure of the Nativity scene except the bambino, until on Christmas Eve a procession emerges from the church and a woman from the crowd places the missing baby in the hands of the Dominican priest, who places it in the crib. All then kneel and sing the old lullaby "Dormi, Benigne Jesu, in dulci somno." After Christmas the bambino is kept by a family in the congregation.

A similar ceremony is held in New Mexico at the Jemez Indian pueblo. A pious couple is chosen as "*padrino*" or godparents to the baby Jesus. On Christmas Eve at 11:30 the *padrino* and a procession go to church, where the padre emerges with the statue and gives it to the godmother. They process home while guns fire in salute and place the baby on a small altar. Candles are lit, prayers are said, and the godmother then leads the procession to return the baby to the church, reciting the Hail Mary in the native dialect. The crowd enters the church for midnight mass, after which the baby is venerated on the altar and then given to the seated godmother. All pass by her and kiss the "Bethlehem Babe" while hymns are sung. After the ceremony the baby is placed in its crib until Three Kings' Day.

Bank Holidays   Until the early 19th century, England had suffered no shortage of days free from work – before 1830, for example, banks were closed for approximately 40 saints' days and anniversaries. But under the pressures of the Industrial Revolution English government and business soon embarked on a ruthless campaign against holidays. Under the Factory Act of 1833, only Christmas and Good Friday along with Sundays were days on which workers had a statutory right to be absent from their duties. This reduction of holidays seriously curtailed Christmas celebrations in those areas that had kept the Twelve Days in traditional ways. William Sandys, a lawyer and carol collector, noted the decline of Christmas in 1833: "In many parts of the kingdom, especially in the northern and western parts, this festival is still kept up with spirit among the middling and lower classes, though its influence is on the wane even with them; the genius of the present age requires work and not play, and since the commencement of this century a great change may be traced. The modern instructors of mankind do not think it necessary to provide for popular amusements." Only later in the century did Bank Holiday legislation permit the number of non-working days to increase and come to include Boxing Day, thus extending the Christmas holiday.

Barbara's Day, St.   A virgin martyr slain by her father for converting to Christianity, St. Barbara is honoured on December 4, the start of the Christmas season in Syria and Lebanon and the occasion for European traditions involving blossoms. In Germany, Austria, the Czech lands, and Slovakia a "Barbara twig" is cut from a cherry tree and placed in water. If it blooms on or before Christmas Eve the family will see a marriage in the year to come. In Provence and parts of the Middle East, wheat and lentils are sown on St. Barbara's Day and if they germinate are served on Christmas.

When her father chopped off Barbara's head, he was instantly struck dead by a bolt of lightning. For this explosive reason, Barbara is the patron saint of miners and artillery men.

Barring-out   A Christmastime ritual and example of social inversion or "topsy-turvy." In Britain schoolboys would bar the door and refuse the master entrance until ritual verses were exchanged and a holiday was granted. The usual pattern

Barring-out *A schoolboy rebellion against a tyrannical headmaster as depicted in* Nicholas Nickleby, *by Charles Dickens.*

was for boys to gather weapons and provisions as Christmas drew near and then seize the school or, more often, a single classroom; if they could hold out for a set period, usually three days, they were allowed an extension of the usual Christmas holidays or a relaxation of the normal rate of flogging. If the master broke in they were generally beaten severely. The first mention of it comes in 1558, where it is treated as already being an old custom. Charles Hode's 1660 manual *A New Discovery of the Old Art of Teaching Schools* suggested that a set of rules be drawn up whereby masters were given warning and formal demands agreed on by head boys. The tradition was known in Scotland from 1580, and there are some 17th-century Irish examples. The growing tendency to spell out students' rights in school charters rendered it obsolete, and by the 19th century it had virtually disappeared in England. The last recorded barring-out of the schoolmaster seems to have been in 1938 in Derbyshire.

The custom can also be seen among the Pennsylvania Dutch and in Belgium, Denmark, and Holland, where St. Thomas's Day was a time for students to bar out the master until he treated them to a drink.

Baseball Bats for Christmas   A popular Canadian children's story about how Christmas was celebrated by an Inuit village on the Arctic Circle. Written in 1990 by Michael Kusugak, it tells of how the children of Repulse Bay, Northwest Territories (now Nunavut), reacted to "standing-ups" – Christmas trees they had only ever seen in books – when they were brought in by airplane.

Basil's Day, St.   St. Basil the Great (c. 329-79) was Bishop of Caesarea and a Doctor of the Church. His feast is celebrated on January 1, an important day in the seasonal celebrations of southeastern Europe. It is the day of the "Renewal of the Waters," exchanging gifts, and eating the Basil cake. In Greece he sometimes acts as the gift-bringer. See GREECE.

The Basques   Christmas is enthusiastically celebrated by the Basques of northern Spain. Most of the customs are common to Spain, but two aspects of the Basque celebrations stand out:

the many Christmas songs in their unique language, and the legendary figure of the Olentzero.

The Olentzero is usually portrayed as a charcoal burner or a shepherd who comes down from the mountains at Christmastime to announce the coming of the joyful season, to partake in its festivities, and to hand out gifts. He is not a handsome figure, but a vigorous one dressed in a beret and typical Basque garb, capable of prodigious feats of celebrating. In many villages his image is carried through the streets on the shoulders of folk who take it from house to house singing carols.

Carols have been composed in the Basque tongue since at least the 16th century, and since then the region has produced a number whose fame has reached beyond its borders. They include "OI! BETLEHEM" ("O Bethlehem"), "Aur txiki" ("Lovely Baby Mary Bore Him"), "Belen'en sortu zaigu" ("In Mid-winter They Set Out"), and "Birjinia gaztettotbat zegoen" ("The Angel Gabriel From Heaven Came"). Basque tunes were used by the English composer Sabine Baring-Gould for three of his carols: "Gabriel's Message," "The Infant King," and "Lullay My Liking."

Numerous fiestas are held in the Basque country during the Christmas season, beginning on St. Nicholas Day, December 6, when parades of children process through the streets singing songs about the saint and telling the stories of his amazing career. St. Lucia fairs (December 13) and St. Thomas fairs (December 21) bring farmers into towns to show their produce. On Christmas Eve in the village of Labastida, groups of shepherds draped in pelts recite ancient verses and perform dances that are likely remnants of medieval pastoral drama.

The Battle of Life   The fourth Christmas book by Charles Dickens appeared in December 1846 and is the only one that does not involve ghosts, spirits, or the supernatural. The subtitle speaks of it as a love story, and the tale involves an emotional sacrifice of one sister for another that leads to the conversion of their father from a cynical view of life to one of sentiment, as well as a happy ending for everyone else.

Bean King   In the Middle Ages it was customary on Twelfth Night for a cake to be served called the *gâteau des roi* or the "Bean Cake" from the practice of placing within it a bean or

Bean King *A somewhat more riotous view of the Twelfth Night festivities.*

pea. (The practice is said to have originated at Mont-St-Michel in the 13th century.) The person who found the bean became the king and would preside over the evening's festivities. A queen was often chosen as well, as indicated by this poem from the 17th century by Robert Herrick:

> Now, now, the mirth comes
> With the cake full of plums,
> Where bean is the king of the sport here;
> Beside we must know,
> The pea also
> Must revel as queen in the court here.
>
> Begin then to choose
> This night as ye use,
> Who shall for the present delight here;
> Be a king by the lot,
> And who shall not
> Be Twelfth-day Queen for the night here.

In 16th-century France the cake was cut into as many pieces as there were guests, and a child sitting under the table chose who was to be given each piece until the portion with the bean in it was discovered.

Beatings at Christmas   There are a number of different types of thrashings connected with the Christmas season. The first is the threat of chastisement embodied by the switches and rods carried by gift-bringers and their helpers. In 16th-century Germany the Christmas bundle of presents included "things that belong to teaching, obedience, chastisement, and discipline, as A.B.C. tablets, Bibles, and handsome books,

Bean King *The finder of the lucky bean in the Epiphany cake presides over the feast.*

Beatings at Christmas *Two 19th-century tots are confronted by the switch-bearing side of Santa Claus in this Thomas Nast drawing.*

writing materials, paper, etc., and the Christ-rod." The first book in the United States to include a picture of Santa Claus, the 1821 *Children's Friend*, has the gift-giver state that he was happy to reward good girls and boys, but

> Where I found the children naughty,
> In manners rude, in temper haughty,
> Thankless to parents, liars, swearers,
> Boxers, or cheats, or base tale-bearers,
>
> I left a long, black birchen rod,
> Such as the dread command of GOD
> Directs a parent's hand to use
> When virtue's path his sons refuse.

The threat of corporal punishment was inherent in the role played by such figures as Black Pete, Krampus, Cert, or Père Fouettard (Father Switch), who accompany the gift-giver.

On CHILDERMAS, December 28, which commemorates the Massacre of the Innocents by King Herod, it was once customary in England to beat children. The explanation given in the 17th century was that the memory of Herod's crime "might stick the closer; and, in a moderate proportion, to act over the crueltie again in kind," but anthropologists have noted that ritual beatings are more likely descended from pagan rituals of good luck than from punishment. An old German custom called "peppering" saw children beating their parents, and servants beating their masters, with sticks while asking in verse form for a treat. An equally venerable tradition in Normandy allowed children to give a thrashing to those

who stayed too long in bed on December 28. In Wales on St. Stephen's Day, the practice was called "HOLMING" or "holly-beating"; the last person to get out of bed was hit with holly sprigs and made to act as servant to the rest of the family. Sometimes the purpose of the holming was to draw blood. In parts of Scotland on New Year's Eve, boys beat each other with holly branches in the belief that for every drop of blood shed, a year of life was saved for the victim. In Sweden it was once customary for the first to rise on Christmas Eve to give other family members small bundles of twigs that they would use to beat each other in the spirit of imparting vitality.

It is worth noting that fruit trees also came in for ritual beatings at Christmas. See WASSAIL.

Beavis and Butthead Do Christmas (TV) (1996)   These two cartoon characters crawl out from under the rock of American popular culture to give their peculiar twist to Christmas classics. In the first segment, based on Dickens's *A Christmas Carol*, Beavis encounters the Ghosts on his television set, where he is trying to watch a pornographic movie. They fail in their attempt to get him to change his low-down ways even when he is shown his tombstone, which reads: "Here Lies Beavis. He Never Scored." Butthead is the subject of a parody of *It's a Wonderful Life* in which God sends an angel to convince the boys to commit suicide for the good of the entire human race. Created by Mike Judge.

La Befana   The principal gift-bringer in Italy. She was asked by the Magi to join them on their journey to worship the new-born king but delayed because she wanted to put her house in order before the journey and consequently missed seeing the Christ Child. Ever since she has wandered the globe seeking him, and on Epiphany ("*Befana*" is a corruption of "*Epiphania*") she brings presents to children, though she occasionally leaves a bag of ashes for bad kids. January 6 is also the time of Befana fairs in Italy.

La Befana *The Italian gift-bringer who slips down chimneys on Epiphany Eve, depicted on a Christmas stamp from Canada.*

She has her counterparts in Russia, where the Baboushka's history is almost identical to hers, and in Germany in some manifestations of Frau Berchta, who will steal into bedrooms and rock infants to sleep.

Begging Visits Ever since the Middle Ages people have used the Christmas season to go door-to-door soliciting charity in return for a song or good wishes for the coming year. In Alsace in 1462, visitors dressed as the Magi are recorded as having gone about on the eve of Epiphany. Sixteenth-century English sources noted the custom of the WASSAIL WENCHES on TWELFTH NIGHT. In Yorkshire lads used to go "Christmas ceshing," knocking on the door and shouting "Wish you a Merry Christmas, mistress and master." Similar English begging visits were called "gooding," "doling," or "mumping" and often took place on St. Thomas's Day. Plough Boys go begging on PLOUGH MONDAY, while the SILVESTERKLÄUSE tradition in Switzerland takes place on New Year's Eve. *Klopfelngehen* occurs in south Germany throughout Advent. In North America, BELSNICKLING and Newfoundland MUMMING sought hospitality more than charity. In Brazil the *Reisados* solicit donations for the celebration of Epiphany.

In return for their blessing the visitors always received money or hospitality. In those cases where a gift was not forthcoming, curses were often uttered. In pre-revolutionary Russia, carollers sang *kolyadki*, songs of blessing that could turn into wishes for a bad harvest or sick cattle if little gifts were not handed out. On the Greek island of Chios, groups of children revile the housewife who has run out of treats to pass out on Christmas Eve; they make uncomplimentary remarks and wish her cloven feet. Their remarks would be hard-pressed to surpass the venom of this malediction found on the Scottish island of South Uist:

> The curse of God and the New Year be on you
> And the scath of the plaintive buzzard,
> Of the hen-harrier, of the raven, of the eagle,
> And the scath of the sneaking fox.
> The scath of the dog and cat be on you,
> Of the boar, of the badger and of the ghoul,
> Of the hipped bear and of the wild wolf,
> And the scath of the foul polecat.

In central and eastern Europe the STAR BOYS still parade, though now the money collected is often directed toward Third World development. In the Austrian village of Oberndorf, where "Silent Night" was first written, boatmen, who were unable to work during the winter months, used to go about at Christmas soliciting donations to see them through until spring. The custom died for a time when social welfare was adopted by the government, but it was revived in the 20th century in a different form. Now groups of men walk around with their lanterns, bells, and a Christmas crib atop a pole, collecting money for charity. Even though the true begging visit has declined, Christmas is still the season for encouraging charity, as shown by the example of the Salvation Army with its street-corner kettles.

Some social historians distinguish between those visitors who are seeking charity – such as the WASSAIL WENCHES or those doling or MUMPING on ST. THOMAS'S DAY – and those after only a spot of hospitality in return for good wishes. These latter they call "luck visits." Customs such as wassailing (see WASSAIL) or Newfoundland MUMMING would fall into this category.

Belen The name, meaning "Bethlehem," for the crèche in Spain. The Italian tradition of making an elaborate manger scene – often set in an entire village, depicting the inhabitants as well as the adoring angels, shepherds, and Magi – penetrated Spain in the 18th century and flourished there. Spectacular examples from the 18th and 19th centuries are now valuable museum pieces and collectors' items. In many parts of Spain live *Belenes* are presented, with real people representing the Holy Family and the Three Kings.

Belgium The first week in December sees the beginning of the Christmas season in Belgium. All across the country Christmas markets are set up in medieval town squares, with booths full of seasonal offerings of food, drink, decorations, and gifts. The markets in the Grand' Place of Brussels, the Place du Marché of Liège, and the cobblestone streets of Bruges are particularly spectacular. Shoppers are entertained by wandering musicians, carollers, or jugglers and visit living Nativity scenes, sip hot punch, or skate on ice rinks. On December 6, St. Nicholas Day, the saintly gift-bringer arrives to deposit his offerings in the shoes children have left out for him to fill.

As Advent proceeds, Nativity plays are staged, Christmas trees erected, and wreaths hung. It is a time for specialty Belgian beers to appear and for baking Christmas goods such as the sweet bread known as *cougnou*, shaped like the baby Jesus, or the spiced *speculoos* cookies shaped like Saint Nicholas, as well as marzipan and the flat hard cakes called *klaasjes*. Belgian carols include "De drie koningen" ("The Three Kings"), "Sing, Good Company," and "De nederige geboorte" ("The Simple Birth").

On Christmas Eve the *réveillon*, common to French-speaking countries, is eaten: turkey is the usual main course, with the traditional BÛCHE DE NOÈL for dessert. Children have come to expect additional gifts on the night of December 24, brought by Santa Claus, Père Noël, or Le Petit Jésus and placed under the tree or in their stockings. While they wait for their presents, some of their fellow citizens now make an anti-consumptionist statement. Since 1970 marchers have walked in silence on Christmas Eve from Antwerp to Viesel, where a priest washes their feet and a simple meal of bread and cheese is eaten. Attendance at midnight mass is a must for many Belgians, and a large dinner on Christmas Day is also traditional.

January 6 is Epiphany or *Dreikonigendag*. Bands of children go door-to-door singing songs about the Three Kings in anticipation of treats. The Belgian version of the Twelfth Night Cake or bean cake is the *gâteau des rois*.

In January Belgians exchange New Year's cards, which have become more popular in that country than Christmas cards.

Belize Belize celebrates Christmas in a variety of ways, depending on the ethno-linguistic heritage of the people. Roman Catholic Belizeans of mixed Mayan and Spanish blood observe customs much like those in other Latin American countries. These *Mestizo* place manger scenes in their homes and take part in the nine days of the POSADA, neighbourhood families accompanied by musicians going door-to-door searching for a house that will shelter the Holy Family.

For the Garifuna people the high point of Christmas is the Wanaragua or JOHN CANOE celebrations, which involve brightly costumed processions of masked men going from house to house singing, dancing, telling stories, and receiving hospitality in return. The Garifuna, of mixed African and Carib ancestry, were expelled to the Caribbean coast from the island of St. Vincent in the late 18th century and since then have preserved their unique culture in Belize, Honduras, and Guatemala.

Both Catholics and Protestants attend church in large numbers on Christmas Eve and Christmas Day. The big Christmas dinner is held on the afternoon of December 25, the dishes depending on the ethnic background of the hosts. Ham, rice, and beans are common on most tables, but those of Spanish descent also eat tamales or bollos, ground corn with chicken wrapped inside palm leaves and steamed. Turkey is also a popular dish, with sweet cakes for dessert.

The poor economy of the country has forced thousands of Belizeans to migrate to the United States, where they have encountered the North American Christmas culture. Returning exiles have brought back English-language carols, Santa Claus, and decorations that imitate a northern winter.

Bells   Bells became part of Christian worship around the year 400, and their sound as they summon the faithful to worship was their first link with Christmas, an association that continues to this day. From this comes the notion of "ringing in" Christmas with a peal of bells; in parts of England, for example, Christmas is rung in starting on December 21, St. Thomas's Day. In Scandinavia bells ring to announce the end of work and the beginning of the festive season. English folklore also states that when Christ was born the devil died, and bells are rung for Lucifer's death-knell; in parts of Yorkshire the church bell is rung once for every year since Christ's birth, with the last stroke timed for midnight on Christmas Eve.

The sound of bells is heard when gift-bringers arrive. St. Nicholas has been known to carry a handbell on his visits; the Befana rings a bell as she descends Italian chimneys; and in Hungary, angel bells are rung to announce that the children's presents have been delivered.

Numerous carols use bells as a metaphor for Christmas joy and hope: "Silver Bells," "I Heard the Bells on Christmas Day," "Jingle Bells," and, of course, "The Carol of the Bells." Less melodious is the use of bells at Christmas to drive away evil

Belsnickel *A 19th century Christmas ornament in the shape of Belsnickel.*

spirits (as in the German *schreckläuten* or "fright ringing"), or perhaps just to give a shock to onlookers during one of the many European parades of hideously costumed figures during the festive season.

The very silhouette of bells is enough to convey a Christmas meaning. On gift wrap, ornaments, and decorations, in the shape of cookies, or on greeting cards, bells and Christmas are inseparable.

The Bells of St. Mary's (1945)   A sequel to the Oscar-winning *Going My Way*, in which Bing Crosby continues the role of Father Chuck O'Malley, singing priest. He and Sister Benedict (Ingrid Bergman) struggle to save an imperilled school and find time to warble "Aren't You Glad You're You?" A highlight is a children's Christmas pageant where the kids sing "Happy Birthday" to baby Jesus. Directed by Leo McCarey. The film was remade for television by CBS in 1959, starring Claudette Colbert and Robert Preston.

Belsnickel   One of the gift-bringer's HELPERS, derived from the German Pelznickel, or Nicholas in Furs. In German immigrant communities in 19th-century North America, Belsnickel served as the intimidating figure who, alone or in the company of St. Nicholas, quizzed children on their behaviour during the previous year. In full regalia, as in Baltimore

Bells *This allegory on Christmas bells appeared in an* Illustrated London News *of 1872.*

where German Catholic newcomers staged Christmas parades led by St. Nicholas, Belsnickel appeared carrying a switch and wearing a cape, fur cap, bells, and a chain. In frontier settlements the man playing him would be disguised in any way possible: with a sheet, a mask, or a blackened face. German-manufactured Belsnickels – showing the character as a bearded man in a long robe with a pointed hood and carrying a basket with tree branches – were imported into the United States as toys, decorations, or candy holders. These are now collectors' items.

Belsnickling   The custom of going about at Christmas in disguise, akin to mumming, especially in Pennsylvania Dutch communities and in parts of Nova Scotia. When the costumed figures go door-to-door they are received with hospitality and, in return, often sing or play musical instruments. Gratuities were occasionally paid; sometimes the money went to charity, and sometimes the performers kept it.

Children who accompanied the belsnicklers in Nova Scotia were expected to kneel and say their prayers before being allowed to see the Christmas tree or given a treat. Women who disguised themselves as Wise Men were known as Kris Kringles.

Berchta   A Nordic goddess, wife of Odin, who over the centuries mutated into a number of female figures with connections to Christmas in Germany and Austria. She can assume a friendly aspect or a terrible one and is known variously as Bertha, Berchtel, Budelfrau, Buzebergt, FRAU HOLLE, or Percht. Like the Befana she is sometimes depicted as an old woman who steals into the rooms of children whom she rocks to sleep; sometimes she is the leader of the Wild Hunt, a train of demons and doomed souls who rush about at night during the Christmas season. At one time in Styria she was a gift-bringer who heard children repeat their prayers and rewarded them with treats. See PERCHTENLAUFEN.

"Berger, secoue ton sommeil profond!"   A French traditional carol from Besançon, probably from the 17th century. The English translation is "SHEPHERDS, SHAKE OFF YOUR DROWSY SLEEP."

The Best Christmas Pageant Ever (TV) (1983)   Based on Barbara Robinson's best-selling kids' book, *The Best Christmas Pageant Ever* tells the story of the horrible Herdman children and their effect on the school play. Directed by George Schaefer and starring Loretta Swit and the wonderful Canadian actress Janet Wright.

Bethlehem   Today Bethlehem is a town of 35,000 people on the Israeli-held West Bank (though under the aegis of the Palestinian Authority), some five miles south of Jerusalem. Two thousand years ago it was a hillside village in the domain of Herod the Great, King of Judaea. Joseph of Nazareth came to Bethlehem with his wife, Mary, in answer to a bureaucratic summons; finding no room at the inn she gave birth to the infant Jesus in a nearby cave which served as an animal shelter. There the male children of the area were murdered on the order of Herod (see MASSACRE OF THE INNOCENTS).

Long before Christmas was an official celebration of the church, Christians had identified the place where Jesus was born. In order to discourage the new religion, Roman officials ordered that a pagan shrine be erected on the spot. When in the fourth century Christianity was allowed to be practised openly, the mother of the Roman emperor Constantine had a

magnificent church built over the site, a church that was rebuilt by the sixth-century Byzantine emperor Justinian. The fortress-like Church of the NATIVITY, which exists today, preserves much of Justinian's work. Beneath ground level a star of silver marks the exact spot of the birth with the inscription *Hic De Virgine Maria Jesus Christus Natus Est* ("Here Jesus Christ Was Born of the Virgin Mary"). Nearby is the manger where the baby was laid and where he was worshipped by shepherds and Wise Men. Though the Church of the Nativity belongs to the Orthodox faith, other Christians are accorded rights of worship in the grotto. (See colour fig. 3.)

Three times a year Christmas is celebrated in Bethlehem, depending on the ecclesiastical calendar used by each church. Roman Catholics and Protestants mark the Nativity on December 24. On Christmas Eve the Catholic Patriarch of Jerusalem leads a great procession from the ancient capital to Bethlehem, through the crowds filling Manger Square to St. Catherine's Church, where he celebrates midnight mass. Following this ceremony the procession wends its way to the nearby Church of the Nativity and the small subterranean grotto. There, with great solemnity, the Patriarch places an image of the Christ Child on the spot that marks the place of his birth. Meanwhile Protestants celebrate the Nativity in a field near the town. This area, maintained by the YMCA, is known as the SHEPHERDS' FIELD and is reputed to be where the angels announced the birth of Jesus to the astonished shepherds. On January 7 it is the turn of the Orthodox churches; and on January 18 Armenian Christians keep the feast.

Beyond Tomorrow (1940)   Three rich and hitherto selfish men (Harry Carey Sr., C. Aubrey Smith, and Charles Winninger) decide to invite two strangers to a Christmas Eve dinner. The young couple (Richard Carlson and Jean Parker) fall in love, but the three old bachelors soon die in a plane crash. When, in the afterlife, they observe that all is not well with their young friends, they return to set things right. Directed by A. Edward Sutherland.

Bird Count, Christmas   Begun in 1900 by American Museum of Natural History curator Frank Chapman, the Christmas Bird Count is a high point in the birdwatcher's calendar. Tens of thousands of observers in North, Central, and South America annually list the birds they encounter in specified areas. The records produced are invaluable in tracking species distribution, population trends, and alerting conservationists to the need to protect those birds whose numbers have declined.

"The Birds' Christmas Carol"   A sentimental story of 1887 by Kate Douglas Wiggin of a rich little girl's last Christmas spent being kind to the poor neighbour children. The death scene of Carol Bird, who expires during the singing of "My Ain Countrie" ("Like a bairn to its mither / A wee birdy to its nest / I fain would be gangin' noo unto my faether's breast; / For He gathers in His arms / Helpless, worthless lambs like me / An' carries them Himsel' / To his ain countrie"), must surely rival the passing of Little Nell in the annals of 19th-century literary pathos.

Wiggin (1856-1923) was a prominent American educator, leader of the kindergarten movement, and author of *Rebecca of Sunnybrook Farm*.

"The Birthday of a King"   Written by American conductor William Harold Neidlinger (1863-1924), c. 1890.

In the little village of Bethlehem,
There lay a Child one day;
And the sky was bright with a holy light
Over the place where Jesus lay.

Alleluia! O how the angels sang.
Alleluia! How it rang!
And the sky was bright with a holy light
'Twas the birthday of a King.

'Twas a humble birthplace, but O how much
God gave to us that day,
From the manger bed what a path has led,
What a perfect, holy way.

Bishop "... and we will discuss your affairs this very afternoon, over a Christmas bowl of smoking bishop, Bob!" Ebenezer Scrooge's promise to Bob Cratchit in Charles Dickens's *A Christmas Carol* refers to a traditional English Christmas drink made by pouring red wine on ripe, bitter oranges. The mixture is mulled over a fire and flavoured with sugar and spices such as cloves, cinnamon, and anise. The name comes from the deep-red colour of the drink, which resembles a bishop's robes.

The Bishop's Wife (1947) David Niven plays Henry Brougham, an Episcopalian bishop who is so obsessed with building a grand new church that he neglects his wife (Loretta Young) and daughter (Karolyn Grimes, who played little Zuzu in *It's a Wonderful Life*) even as Christmas approaches. The family encounters Dudley (Cary Grant), an angel sent to Earth to set things right. Miracles occur, jealousy is kindled, and love is restored. Directed by Henry Koster and written by Robert E. Sherwood and Leonardo Barcovici, the film is based on Robert Nathan's 1928 novel. Though the film works superbly, shooting began on it with the two main roles reversed: Grant was cast as the bishop and Niven as the angel. After weeks of production Samuel Goldwyn fired the original director, rebuilt the sets, and had the stars switch roles. The film was remade in 1996 as *The Preacher's Wife*.

Black Bun The Scottish version of the Twelfth Night Cake. The Black Bun is a rich dark cake packed with fruit, almonds, and often laced with whisky or brandy, baked inside a shortcrust pastry. It is now traditional to serve this at New Year's.

Black Christmas (1975) Thanks to generous government grants, Canadian filmmakers cranked out this sort of second-rate horror film by the trainload in the 1970s. Sorority girls are terrorized by a crazed killer over the Christmas holidays. The fun lies in spotting actresses like Margot Kidder and Andrea Martin, who went on to better things. Also called *Silent Night, Evil Night* and *Stranger in the House*, it was directed by Bob Clark (who gave us the wonderful *A Christmas Story* and the wretched *Porky's*).

Black Fast The traditional Irish Christmas Eve dinner of boiled salt cod and potatoes. The name derives from the Catholic custom (now largely disappeared) of a particularly rigorous abstention from eating more than one meal a day during Advent and a prohibition on meat, eggs, butter, cheese, milk, and wine.

Black Peter A gift-bringer's HELPER. See ZWARTE PIET.

Blackadder's Christmas Carol (TV) (1988) The comical Blackadder series delighted television watchers in the 1980s with the antics of various members of this nasty family throughout the centuries. At the courts of Richard IV (sic), Elizabeth I, Charles I, and the Prince Regent, as well as in the trenches of the First World War, these Blackadders have consistently been the most cowardly, treacherous, and greedy men in England. In this television special we meet an exception: Ebenezer Blackadder, the kindliest and most generous of Queen Victoria's subjects. A visit from a drunken Father Christmas and a glimpse into the future bring interesting changes into Ebenezer's life. Starring Rowan Atkinson as Blackadder, Tony Robinson as his dogsbody, Baldrick, and Robbie Coltrane as Father Christmas.

"Blessed Be That Maid Marie" The folk verses of this carol appeared in the 1600 *Lute Book* by William Ballet, who may have been responsible for the tune. Ballet also wrote "Sweet Was the Song the Virgin Sang."

Blessed be that maid Marie;
Born he was of her body;
Very God ere time began,
Born in time the Son of Man.

Eya! Jesus hodie Natus est de Virgine.
In a manger of an ass
Jesu lay and lullèd was;
Born to die upon the Tree
Pro peccante homine.

Refrain

Sweet and blissful was the song
Chanted of the angel throng:
"Peace on earth, alleluya!
In excelsis gloria."

Refrain

Fare three kings from far-off land,
Incense, gold and myrrh in hand;
In Bethlehem the Babe they see,
Stelle ducti lumine.

Refrain

Make we merry on this fest,
In quo Christus natus est,
On this Child I pray you call,
To assoil and save us all.

Refrain

"The Blessings of Mary" A traditional American folk carol sung in North Carolina.

The very first blessing Mary had, it was the blessing of one:
To think that her Son, Jesus, was God's eternal son;
Was God's eternal son, like th'Emmanuel in glory,
Father, Son, and the Holy Ghost, through all eternity.

The very next blessing Mary had, it was the blessing of two:
To think that her Son, Jesus, could read the Scriptures through;
Could read the Scriptures through, like th'Emmanuel in glory,
Father, Son, and the Holy Ghost, through all eternity.

The very next blessing Mary had, it was the blessing of three:

Blindman's Buff *The popular Christmas game in an 19th-century English setting, from the* Illustrated London News.

To think that her Son, Jesus, could set the sinner free;
Could set the sinner free, like th'Emmanuel in glory,
Father, Son, and the Holy Ghost, through all eternity.

The very next blessing Mary had, it was the blessing
    of four:
To think that her Son, Jesus, could live for evermore.
Could live for evermore, like th'Emmanuel in glory,
Father, Son, and the Holy Ghost, through all eternity.

The very next blessing Mary had, it was the blessing
    of five:
To think that her Son, Jesus, could bring the dead to live;
Could bring the dead to live, like th'Emmanuel in glory,
Father, Son, and the Holy Ghost, through all eternity.

The very next blessing Mary had, it was the blessing of six:
To think that her Son, Jesus, could heal and cure the sick;
Could heal and cure the sick, like th'Emmanuel in glory,
Father, Son, and the Holy Ghost, through all eternity.

The very next blessing Mary had, it was the blessing
    of seven:
To think that her Son, Jesus, could conquer hell and
    heaven;
Could conquer hell and heaven, like th'Emmanuel in glory,
Father, Son, and the Holy Ghost, through all eternity.

The very next blessing Mary had, it was the blessing
    of eight:
To think that her Son, Jesus, could make the crooked
    straight;
Could make the crooked straight, like th'Emmanuel
    in glory,
Father, Son, and the Holy Ghost, through all eternity.

The very next blessing Mary had, it was the blessing
    of nine:
To think that her Son, Jesus, could turn water into wine;
Could turn water into wine, like th'Emmanuel in glory,
Father, Son, and the Holy Ghost, through all eternity.

The very next blessing Mary had, it was the blessing of ten:
To think that her Son, Jesus, could write without a pen;
Could write without a pen, like th'Emmanuel in glory,
Father, Son, and the Holy Ghost, through all eternity.

The very next blessing Mary had, it was the blessing
    of eleven:
To think that her son, Jesus, could turn the world to heaven;
Could turn the world to heaven, like th'Emmanuel in glory,
Father, Son, and the Holy Ghost, through all eternity.

The very next blessing Mary had, it was the blessing
    of twelve:
To think that her son, Jesus, could turn the sick to well;
Could turn the sick to well, like th'Emmanuel in glory,
Father, Son, and the Holy Ghost, through all eternity.

See also "THE SEVEN JOYS OF MARY."

Blindman's Buff A popular English Christmas game in which a blindfolded player must catch someone and identify him or her. The fun lies in coming tantalizingly close to the player without getting caught. In *A Christmas Carol* by Charles Dickens, the guests of Scrooge's nephew Fred play the game in such a way as to further the possibilities of romance:

There was first a game at blind-man's buff. Of course there was. And I no more believe Topper was really blind than I believe he had eyes in his boots. My opinion is, that it was a done thing between him and Scrooge's nephew; and that the Ghost of Christmas Present knew it. The way he went after that plump sister in the lace tucker, was an outrage on the credulity of human nature. Knocking down the fire-irons, tumbling over the chairs, bumping against the piano, smothering himself among the curtains, wherever she went, there went he. He always knew where the plump sister was. He wouldn't catch anybody else. If you had fallen up against him (as some of them did), on purpose, he would have made a feint of endeavouring to seize you, which would have been an affront to your understanding, and would instantly have sidled off in the direction of the plump sister. She often cried out that it wasn't fair; and it really was not. But when at last, he caught her; when, in spite of all her silken rustlings, and her rapid flutterings past him, he got her into a corner whence there was no escape; then his conduct was the most execrable. For his pretending not to know her; his pretending that it was necessary to touch her head-dress, and further to assure himself of her identity by pressing a certain ring upon her finger, and a certain chain about her neck; was vile, monstrous. No doubt she told him her opinion of it, when, another blind-man being in office, they were so very confidential together, behind the curtains.

An 18th-century description reveals a darker side of the game: "[T]hen it is lawful to set any thing in the way for Folks to tumble over, whether it be to break Arms, Legs, or Heads, 'tis no matter, for Neck-or nothing, the Devil loves no Cripples. – This Play, I am told, was first set on foot by the Country Bone-setters."

A less boisterous variation was called Shadow-Buff. A "blind man" would sit on one side of a white sheet or table-cloth with a bright light shining on the other side. He would attempt to guess the identity of other players as they walked past the sheet casting shadows.

Blowing the Pudding An old custom in Newfoundland was to celebrate with gunfire the successful lifting of the Christmas pudding from the pot. One account of a surprised observer reads:

> On Christmas Day I was astonished to hear so many gun shots and ran quickly about to see what was wrong. There they have a fashion of blowin' the Christmas puddin' out of the pot. As the wife or woman of the house is lifting the pudding from the pot, the husband or man of the house is standing outside the back door with the gun. As soon as the pudding rises out, the shot is fired into the air.

"Blue Christmas" A big hit for Elvis Presley in the 1950s, the song was written in 1945 by B. Hayes and J. Johnson. Others who had successful recordings include Hugo Winterhalter and Ernest Tubb.

Blues, Christmas (1) The Swiss have a word for it, *Weihnachtscholer*; psychiatrists have a word for it too, Post-Christmas Traumatic Syndrome. Most people just call it the Christmas blues, a feeling of sadness that overcomes those for whom the holiday period is a time of dysfunction instead of joy.

It must not be thought that this ailment affects only jaded moderns. An American woman's diary from 1858 notes, "As these days come round our hearts are made Sad; we miss our loved Mother, now gone to her rest." On Christmas Eve, 1872, a widow wrote, "These days are sad indeed to me. I try to conceal my feelings for the sake of those I am with." On Christmas Day she wrote, "There are many sad hearts, as well as merry ones." In the 1901 Norwegian short story "Before the Candles Go Out," a couple struggles to be happier and to see the holiday through the eyes of their child, but the wife says of her melancholy: "Do I need to tell you all over again that there's something called Christmas Eve memories?"

Here are some causes of the Christmas blues:

– loss of a loved one
– resentment of the commercialism of the season
– a sense of not belonging, stemming from membership in a religion that does not celebrate Christmas
– anger over not being able to afford gifts for one's family
– anger at seasonally induced weight gain or increase in indebtedness
– homelessness, friendlessness, or alienation from family or ethnic group
– guilt at not being as happy as the ideal family depicted on television
– spouse saturation syndrome (too much of one's mate underfoot)
– separation at holiday-times from one's lover who is married to someone else.

Popular music, quick to spot trends, has cashed in on the sentiment with a plethora of songs emphasizing Yuletide depression, led by Elvis Presley's 1957 hit "Blue Christmas." One might add "What Do the Lonely Do at Christmas?" by The Emotions, "Christmas Eve Can Kill You" by The Everly Brothers, and "Who Took the Merry Out of Christmas?" by The Staple Singers.

Though Christmas is not a time of increased suicide (in fact, for women suicide declines in December and January), doctors do report a rush of depressed patients after the holidays. A number of churches hold "Blue Christmas" services to assure the faithful that God continues to be present even in the midst of sadness, and the Hallmark greeting-card company has introduced a line of Christmas cards for the grieving, called "Messages of Comfort."

(2) In the African-American musical tradition known as the blues, Christmas plays an important part. "Santa Claus" and "Christmas" were once code words referring to a separated mate; Christmastime often saw liberty for slaves to travel to different plantations to visit loved ones. More recently the words have added the connotation of sex or sensual pleasure. "I Want a Present for Christmas," sang J.R. Summer, "you can fill up my stockings with any girl." Count Basie's "Good Morning Blues (I Want to See Santa Claus)" implored the gift-bringer not to bring him anything but his baby back.

Boar's Head A staple of the medieval English Christmas banquet was the presentation of the boar's head, accompanied by no little spectacle. The killing of pigs was customary in northern Europe in November and December, when the beasts could not be fed over winter. Frey, the Norse fertility god, used to ride about on the boar Gullinbursti and was honoured by the sacrifice of pigs at Yule.

According to legend, a student of Queen's College, Oxford, was reading a book of Aristotle when he was attacked by a boar in Shotover Forest. With a shout of "*Graecum est*," he thrust the

Boar's Head *The ceremonial entry of the boar's head.*

book down the boar's throat and choked it to death. Lest he lose his Aristotle, he cut off the head and brought it back to the college, where it was served for dinner. To this day the college holds a procession including a decorated boar's head and students singing the "BOAR'S HEAD CAROL." A less decorous custom was held annually well into the 19th century in Hornchurch, Essex, where a local landlord was required to furnish a decorated boar's head every Christmas. The head was taken on a pitchfork to a local field and wrestled over, with the winner carrying it to a local inn and eating it with his friends.

"Boar's Head Carol"   This macaronic carol (containing a mixture of Latin and the vernacular) is sung every Christmas season at Queen's College on the presentation of the boar's head and was allegedly written by a student of that college.

> The boar's head in hand bear I,
> Bedecked with bays and rosemary;
> And I pray you my masters be merry,
> *Quot estis in convivio* ["All who are dining together"].
>
> *Caput apri defero*
> *Reddens laudes Domino,*
> *laudes Domino, laudes Domino, Domino.*
> ["I bring in the boar's head; sing praises to the Lord."]
>
> The boar's head, as I understand,
> Is the bravest dish in all the land
> When thus bedecked with a gay garland;
> Let us *servire cantico* ["Serve it while singing"].
>
> Our steward hath provided this
> In honour of the King of Bliss,
> Which on this day to be served is
> *In Reginensi Atrio* ["In the Queen's hall"].

Boniface, St.   (680-754) Missionary, martyr, and legendary inventor of the Christmas tree. Born Wynfrith in Anglo-Saxon Devon, he became a Benedictine monk, changed his name, and dedicated his life to the conversion of Germany to the Christian faith. With the co-operation of the papacy he founded the monastery of Fulda, which became a centre of missions activity, and as Archbishop of Mainz he supervised the evangelizing of vast areas and winning their obedience to Rome.

His destruction in the 720s of the pagan Oak of Thor at Geismar was woven into legend as the origin of the evergreen Christmas tree. According to this story, after defying the heathen gods by chopping down the sacred oak, Boniface pointed to a young fir tree as the new symbol to which the German people should look, a sign of life and growth even in the midst of winter darkness.

In his old age Boniface resigned his archbishopric but continued his missionary work in Frisia, where he and dozens of companions were murdered by pirates; his relics include the sword-slashed book he was carrying. He is the patron saint of Prussia, of Germany, and of tailors, file-cutters, and brewers. See "THE FIRST CHRISTMAS TREE."

Bonus, Christmas   The practice of employers giving a bonus in the form of goods or money at Christmas has its origins in the English Boxing Day, when it was customary for employees to go about soliciting tips from the business's clients. During the 19th century in Britain and North America, many workers came to expect it as part of their normal remuneration. A turkey was a customary gift from American and Canadian business owners. In Denmark servants and employees were given special Christmas baking, while in Iceland the Christmas bonus came in the form of shoes.

Since the 1960s in Brazil, a law has obliged employers to pay a "13th salary" – an extra month's pay – as a Christmas bonus. In other parts of Latin America this compulsory bonus is known as the *aguinaldo*.

Book, Christmas   (1) In 17th-century England it was the custom to keep a "Christmas book" to record presents given and received.

(2) In the 18th century publishers began to produce books and magazines for the Christmas season, a profitable practice that has continued to this day.

"The Boots of the Holly-tree Inn"   A Christmas tale by Charles Dickens that appeared in *Household Words* in 1855. "Boots" at an English inn was a servant whose duty it was to clean the footwear. This story of a strange elopement was a favourite of audiences when Dickens did reading tours. He records that after finishing his performance of the tale in Washington, "the audience rose, great people and all, standing and cheering until I went back to the table and made them a little speech."

Born on Christmas Day   Having one's birthday on Christmas Day is a lucky or unlucky coincidence depending on where one is born. In Eastern Europe it was generally considered bad luck to be born on the birthday of the Saviour. The Greeks traditionally believed that this was an affront to the Virgin Mother and Child, and therefore children born on Christmas were likely to turn into monstrous KALLIKANTZAROI. To prevent this from happening, parents were obliged to singe the toenails of the newborn, lest they turn into claws, and bind the baby with tresses of straw or garlic. In parts of Poland and Germany it was feared that being born on December 25 made a child more likely to become a werewolf, Christmas being the season of increased demonic power. In Silesia a Christmas birthday meant the child would be either a lawyer or a thief.

In Ireland, on the other hand, birth on Christmas allowed one to see the Little People and even to command spirits (a privilege also granted to those born on Good Friday). In England it was lucky to be born on Christmas – one would

Boxing Day *An 1836 illustration of soliciting gratuities amidst a host of puns on Boxing Day.*

never be hanged, drowned, or troubled by spirits – and extra lucky if that day fell on a Sunday, as the child would become a great lord. To the Pennsylvania Dutch, being born on Christmas Eve conveyed the power to understand the language of animals, for on that night beasts could speak and even predict the future. In the Vosges area of France, a baby born on Christmas Eve would be a smooth talker, but the baby born on Christmas would be a better thinker.

Some early-modern English almanacs, however, were more ambiguous. They seemed to agree that being born on Christmas was lucky if that day were a Sunday (lordship beckoned), a Wednesday (valour, nimbleness, and wisdom were attributes), a Thursday (wise and persuasive speech were in store), or a Friday (a long and lecherous life lay ahead), but being born on a Christmas Day that fell on a Tuesday would lead to a life of covetousness and an evil end, and a Saturday birth would result in death within half a year.

Modern scientists agree that being born on or near Christmas produces a basking-in-reflected-glory effect. Studies in California and Israel have shown that a disproportionate number of famous people were born during the Christmas season, and some have speculated that being born on Christmas might render a child special in his own eyes and those of his parents, with consequent high expectations and the chance of a self-fulfilling prophecy. It also seems that more high-ranking Christian clergy than low-ranking were born on December 25, thus linking a Christmas birth with increased chance of success in the church hierarchy.

Box, Christmas A box in which gratuities were given first to apprentices and later to certain kinds of workers: carmen, porters, clerks, etc., who went about on Boxing Day soliciting payment.

Boxing Day In Britain and many Commonwealth countries Boxing Day, December 26, is kept as a legal holiday. Some historians attribute the name to the parish church alms box, which was opened on Christmas and distributed to the poor, but most believe that the origin of the term lies in the earthenware boxes for gratuities kept by medieval servants and apprentices. Since the Middle Ages it was the custom during the Christmas season for English employees to solicit tips from those people with whom their employer did business. As early as the 15th century this had become a nuisance, as the following regulation shows:

> Forasmuch as it is not becoming or agreeable to propriety that those who are in the service of reverend men, and from them, or through them, have the advantage of befitting food and raiment, as also of reward, or remuneration, in a competent degree, should, after a perverse custom, be begging aught of people, like paupers; and seeing that in times past, every year at the feast of our Lord's Nativity, according to a certain custom, which has grown to be an abuse, the valets of the Mayor, the Sheriffs and the Chamber of the said city – persons who have food, raiment, and appropriate advantages, resulting from their office – under colour of asking for an oblation, have begged many sums of money of brewers, bakers, cooks, and other victuallers; and, in some instances, have, more than once, threatened wrongfully to do them an injury if they should refuse to give them something; and have frequently made promises to others that, in return for a present, they would pass over their unlawful doings in mute silence; to the great dishonour of their masters, and to the common loss of all the city: therefore,

on Wednesday, the last day of April, in the 7th year of King Henry the Fifth, by William Sevenok, the Mayor, and the Aldermen of London, it was ordered and established that no valet, or other sergeant of the Mayor, Sheriffs, or City, should in future beg or require of any person, of any rank, degree, or condition whatsoever, any moneys, under colour of an oblation, or in any other way, on pain of losing his office.

Despite such laws the practice continued unabated. Samuel Pepys in the 17th century speaks of voluntarily stopping at various places on Christmas to make a donation, but in 1710 Jonathan Swift complained, "By the Lord Harry, I shall be undone here with Christmas boxes. The rogues of the coffee house have raised their taxes, every one giving a crown, and I gave mine for shame, besides a great many half-crowns to great men's porters." The practice diminished somewhat in the 19th century as public attitudes to licensed begging changed and salaries rose, but it endured into the 20th century where some delivery professions still maintained a moral claim on their customers' generosity at Christmas.

During the 1800s it became customary for servants to be given the day off on Boxing Day while the employer's family contented themselves with eating leftovers and arranged a party or ball for the servants. Attending a pantomime remains popular on Boxing Day in England, while in Canada the day is marked by fighting through crowds of shoppers at post-Christmas sales. In Australia it is a day given over to the enjoyment of sport, particularly the cricket test in Melbourne and the beginning of the Sydney-to-Hobart Yacht Race.

The Scottish equivalent of Boxing Day is Hansel Monday, the Monday after New Year's Day, when "hansels," or gifts, were given to servants and children. The French are accustomed to giving gifts to tradespeople on the *Fête des Rois*, January 6.

A related custom in Holland and some parts of Germany saw children taught to put their little savings in a pig-shaped earthenware box. This box, called the "feast pig," was not to be opened until Christmas. In late 19th-century Newfoundland, the custom for children on the street was to cry "Christmas Box on you!" and be rewarded with treats such as fruit, coins, or "figgy" bread.

For other December 26 customs see ST. STEPHEN'S DAY.

Boy Bishop   In many medieval churches it was the custom on December 6, St. Nicholas's Day, to elect a choirboy as a mock bishop. During his tenure (which lasted until Holy Innocents' Day, December 28), he would wear a bishop's robes, go about in procession, take offerings, preach, and give his blessing. This practice grew partly out of Jesus' teachings on the special relationship of children to the Kingdom of Heaven and partly out of the spirit of social inversion that marked Christmas celebrations in the Middle Ages. This custom was not restricted to boys – in the 13th century, English nunneries allowed prayers and ceremonies to be performed by girls on Innocents' Day. At Carrow Abbey the female equivalent of the Nicholas Bishop was the Christmas Abbess.

Like those other examples of misrule and social inversion, the Feast of Fools and the Feast of the Ass, the Boy Bishop was eventually suppressed. Henry VII of England had his own St. Nicholas Bishop, chosen from the choristers of the Chapel Royal, but his son, Henry VIII, forbade the custom in 1541, complaining that "children be strangely decked and appareled to counterfeit priests, bishops and women, and so be led with songs and dances from house to house, blessing the people

Boy Bishop *The medieval custom of electing a child bishop for the Christmas season is celebrated in this British stamp.*

and gathering of money and boys do sing mass and preach in the pulpit, with such other unfitting and inconvenient usages." The Boy Bishop was briefly resurrected by Bloody Mary in 1555 but disappeared on her death in 1558. Vestiges remain in the Italian custom of children preaching before the BAMBINO and in some English churches and schools that have revived the custom in the 20th century.

"A Boy Is Born in Bethlehem"   An anonymous 13th-century Latin carol written in Central Europe, perhaps Germany or Bohemia, as "Puer natus in Bethlehem" and found in PIÆ CANTIONES. Its lyrics were widely copied in European languages: German, Danish, Dutch, and English, where it appears as "A Boy [or A Child] Is Born in Bethlehem." J.S. Bach used the tune for harmonization. By the 16th century the original melody had been supplanted by its descant, which is still used today.

> A Boy is born in Bethlehem,
> Rejoice, therefore, Jerusalem!
> Alleluya!
>
> Our human flesh doth he take on,
> High Word of God, the eternal Son.
> Alleluya!
>
> When Mary Gabriel's words received,
> Within her was her Son conceived.
> Alleluya!
>
> From virgin's womb doth he proceed
> No human father doth he need.
> Alleluya!
>
> 'Tis flesh like ours he's clothed in,
> Though free from man's primeval sin.
> Alleluya!
>
> As from his chamber strides the groom,
> So comes he from his mother's womb.
> Alleluya!
>
> Within the manger doth he lie,
> Who reigns eternally on high.
> Alleluya!
>
> The ox and ass that Child adored
> And knew him for their heavenly Lord.
> Alleluya!

To the shepherds did an angel come
To tell them there was born a Son.
Alleluya!

The wise men came from lands afar
To offer incense, gold and myrrh.
Alleluya!

They stooped to enter, one by one,
To greet in turn the new-born Son.
Alleluya!

At this glad birth, with one accord
Let us rejoice and bless the Lord.

To Holy Trinity be praise,
And thanks be given to God always.

Bramley, Henry Ramsden (1831-1917) English clergyman and church musician. With John Stainer he edited the very influential 1871 collection *Christmas Carols, New and Old*, which, along with a later edition, presented 70 carols for use in British homes and churches.

Brawn The most common Christmas fare in Elizabethan times, the recipe for brawn is found in Harrison's *Description of England*:

> Of our tame boars we make brawn, which is a kind of meat not usually known to strangers (as I take it), otherwise would not the swart Rutters and French cooks, at the loss of Calais (where they found great store of this provision almost in every house), have attempted with ridiculous success to roast, bake, broil, and fry the same for their masters, till they were better informed. . . . With us it is accounted a great piece of service at the table from November until February be ended, but chiefly in the Christmas time. With the same also we begin our dinners each day after other; and, because it is somewhat hard of digestion, draught of malvesey, bastard, or muscadel, is usually drank after it, where either of them are conveniently to be had; otherwise the meaner sort content themselves with their own drink, which at that season is generally very strong, and stronger indeed than it is all the year beside. It is made commonly of the fore part of a tame boar, set up for the purpose by the space of a whole year or two, especially in gentlemen's houses (for the husbandmen and farmers never frank them for their own use above three or four months, or half a year at the most), in which time he is dieted with oats and peason, and lodged on the bare planks of an uneasy cot, till his fat be hardened sufficiently for their purpose: afterward he is killed, scalded, and cut out, and then of his former parts is our brawn made. The rest is nothing so fat, and therefore it beareth the name of sowse only, and is commonly reserved for the serving-man and hind, except it please the owner to have any part thereof baked, which are then handled of custom after this manner: the hinder parts being cut off, they are first drawn with lard, and then sodden; being sodden, they are soused in claret wine and vinegar a certain space, and afterward baked in pasties, and eaten of many instead of the wild boar, and truly it is very good meat: the pestles may be hanged up a while to dry before they are drawn with lard, if you will, and thereby prove the better. But hereof enough, and there-fore to come again unto our brawn. The neck pieces, being cut off round, are called collars of brawn, the shoulders are named shilds, only the ribs retain the former denomination, so that these aforesaid pieces deserve the name of brawn: the bowels of the beast are commonly cast away because of their rankness, and so were likewise his stones, till a foolish fantasy got hold of late amongst some delicate dames, who have now found the means to dress them also with great cost for a dainty dish, and bring them to the board as a service among other of like sort, though not without note of their desire to the provocation of fleshly lust which by this their fond curiosity is not a little revealed. When the boar is thus cut out each piece is wrapped up, either with bulrushes, ozier, peels, tape inkle, or such like, and then sodden in a lead or caldron together, till they be so tender that a man may thrust a bruised rush or straw clean through the fat: which being done, they take it up and lay it abroad to cool. Afterward, putting it into close vessels, they pour either good small ale or beer mingled with verjuice and salt thereto till it be covered, and so let it lie (now and then altering and changing the sousing drink lest it should wax sour) till occasion serve to spend it out of way. Some use to make brawn of great barrow hogs, and seethe them, and souse the whole as they do that of the boar; and in my judgment it is the better of both, and more easy of digestion. But of brawn thus much, and so much may seem sufficient.

Brazil Christmas in Brazil is an expression of the blend of the many races and nationalities that make up the national mosaic. The season begins in early December, as it does in industrial nations around the world, when stores and malls begin erecting their Christmas decorations, lights, and displays, a signal to Brazilians to begin their shopping for the gifts, food, and paraphernalia with which to enjoy the holiday. The *presépio*, or Nativity scene, which is found in most Roman Catholic houses, is set out and additions to the figures that populate it are made at home or bought. Those families who erect their Christmas trees early (there are many who set them up only on Christmas Eve) are busy selecting the tree and decorating it; artificial trees are used in the north of the country, where there are no native conifers.

The preparations accelerate in mid-December, when Papai Noel, Brazil's gift-bringer, arrives in various cities by helicopter – the biggest manifestation is in Rio's huge Maracanã Stadium, where he is greeted by thousands of children who join him in singing carols. Despite the heat of the tropical summer Papai Noel dresses exactly like his Arctic cousin Santa Claus in a red suit, black boots, and fur trim.

Christmas Eve is the high point of the season. Parents adorn the Christmas tree behind closed doors and reveal it to awestruck children. Children set out their shoes by the door for Papai Noel. Unlike Santa Claus, he does not drop down a chimney on Christmas Eve (chimneys are rare in Brazil) but enters through the door. Very often families arrange for a friend or relative to pose as Papai Noel and deliver the gifts personally to the children. Evening visits are exchanged between families and final preparations are made for the big supper. Turkey stuffed with *farofa* (made of manioc) is a customary dish, but there are many regional variations in cuisine – roast suckling pig is popular, as is seafood. Those who cling to the Portuguese heritage eat the traditional *bolinho de bacalhau*, made of dried cod. The meal is accompanied by an abundance of fruit, especially grapes, and desserts such as cookies, ice cream, and *rabanada*, which resembles a cinnamon French toast. Poor families make their meal of chicken, rice, and beans.

The midnight mass, the *Missa do Galo*, is widely attended, though some prefer to watch it on television from the Vatican. Afterward families return home, where the children are put to bed and the adults party all night while bells ring and fireworks explode. Christmas Day itself is usually spent with family, though many Brazilians go to the beach or arrange a barbecue or pig roast.

A notable feature of the Brazilian Christmas season is the extended attention paid to the Three Kings. Their festival, the *Folia de Reis*, begins on December 24 and continues until Epiphany on January 6 (in some areas it lasts a month). The *Reisado* custom in the rural areas honours the Magi with spectacular door-to-door processions of costumed musicians and dancers, who solicit hospitality and alms for charities.

Brazilians love spectacle, and the Christmas season is marked by a number of dramatic presentations and festivities. In Rio de Janeiro the *Auto de Natal* is an annual play about children and the meaning of Christmas. In the rural northeast the *Bumba Meu-Boi* ("Beating of the Bull") resembles the mummers' plays of 18th-century England with its theme of death and resurrection at the hands of a folk doctor. A figure in the costume of a bull leaps and dances about but is killed by a cowboy for the sake of his love. A *curado*, or folk doctor, however, is able to revive the beast and the dance can continue. Pastoral drama abounds in Brazil in the form of the colourful *pastoril*, where the story of shepherdesses on their way to see the baby Jesus is recounted by troupes of dancers and actors, who find a spot in their play for butterflies, stars, clowns, farmers, and gypsies.

Despite the energy they invest in Christmas celebrations, Brazilians find time for plenty of revelry at New Year's Eve, or *réveillon*. After a night of partying, Brazilians along the coast take part in or observe two water-related events: the boat parade that honours Our Lady of Sailors, *Nossa Senhora dos Navegantes*, and the festival of Iemanjá, where believers plunge into the waves to bring offerings to the Afro-Catholic goddess of the sea.

The Christmas season ends with Epiphany and the Feast of the Three Kings. Children leave out shoes on January 5 to be filled by the Magi with chocolates or small gifts. Manger scenes are packed away, Christmas trees are taken down, and the country prepares for the next excuse for a party, Carnival.

Bread and Christmas   See BAKING.

"Break Forth, O Beauteous Heavenly Light"   This 17th-century German carol was written as "Brich an, du schönes Morgenlicht" by Johann Rist (1607-67) and Johann Schop (d. 1664) and was harmonized a century later by J.S. Bach. The translation is by Englishman John Troutbeck (1833-89).

> Break forth, O beauteous heav'nly light,
> And usher in the morning;
> Ye shepherds, shrink not with affright,
> But hear the angel's warning.
>
> This Child, now weak in infancy,
> Our confidence and joy shall be,
> The pow'r of Satan breaking,
> Our peace eternal making.

Breaking the New Year's Cake   In Ireland a number of curious customs were enacted on New Year's Eve to ensure prosperity

Breaking the New Year's Cake *The Irish custom of breaking a cake against a door would ensure a lucky year to come.*

for the family in the coming year. There was the necessity of eating a huge meal, which resulted in December 31 being known as the NIGHT OF THE BIG PORTION. In some parts of Ireland a loaf of bread or a cake was used to strike the door three times, while a ritual verse was chanted in which misfortune was bidden to be off and happiness to enter. A variation on this called for a cake to be smashed against the door of the house or barn.

Breaking the Witch   In many countries the question of who would be the first person across the threshold of the house on Christmas or New Year's Day was of great importance. The "first-footer" considered to bestow the most luck was usually a dark-haired male, and the unluckiest were often women. (See FIRST-FOOTING.) In Wales if a woman was the first to enter the house in the New Year, little boys were assembled (sometimes hired) to parade through the house to counteract the evil effects. This process was called "breaking the witch."

Brébeuf, Jean, St.   (1593-1649) French Jesuit missionary, martyr, and carol writer. Brébeuf was ordained a priest in 1623, and two years later he was sent to New France. There he lived and worked with the natives, first the Montagnais and then the Huron of present-day Ontario, for whom he produced a grammar, a dictionary, and, it is claimed, "Jesous Ahatonhia," the song that has come down to us as "THE HURON CAROL" or "Twas in the Moon of Wintertime."

Taken prisoner with his companion Gabriel Lalemant during the Iroquois campaign of extermination against the Hurons, Brébeuf was tortured to death and cannibalized. He was canonized in 1930 and, as one of the "Martyrs of North America," he is a patron saint of Canada.

Breton, Nicholas   (c. 1555-1626) English poet and satirist. We see in some of his work, such as this quote, how Elizabethans viewed Christmas, and can get a clear sense of the connection between the merry and the sacred:

> It is now Christmas, and not a cup of drink must pass without a carol; the beasts, fowl, and fish come to a general execution, and the corn is ground to dust for the bakehouse and the pastry: cards and dice purge many a purse, and the youth show their agility in shoeing of the wild mare: now, good cheer, and welcome, and God be with you, and I thank you: – and against the New Year provide for the presents: – The Lord of Misrule is no mean man for his time, and the guests of the high table must lack no wine: the lusty bloods must look about them like men, and piping and dancing puts away much melancholy: stolen venison is sweet, and a fat coney is worth money: pit-falls are now set for small birds, and a woodcock hangs himself in a gin: a good fire heats all the house, and a full alms-basket makes the beggar's prayers: – the maskers and the mummers make the merry sport, but if they lose their money their drum goes dead: swearers and swaggerers are sent away to the ale-house, and unruly wenches go in danger of judgment; musicians now make their instruments speak out, and a good song is worth the hearing. In sum it is a holy time, a duty in Christians for the remembrance of Christ and custom among friends for the maintenance of good fellowship. In brief I thus conclude it: I hold it a memory of the Heaven's love and the world's peace, the mirth of the honest, and the meeting of the friendly. Farewell.

Bride's Tree   A type of Christmas tree in Bavaria on which a dozen special ornaments are hung in token of those things necessary for a good marriage. They include an angel (representing God's guidance), a bird (joy), a fish (Christ's blessing), a flower basket (good wishes), a fruit basket (generosity), a heart (true love), a house (protection), a pine cone (fruitfulness), a rabbit (hope), a rose (affection), a Santa figure (goodwill), and a teapot (hospitality).

Bridget of Sweden, St.   (1303-73) A Swedish mystic and saint, patron of Sweden, founder of the Brigittine Order, and a visionary whose revelations about the Nativity were highly influential in the way it was artistically depicted during the Middle Ages.

After the death of her aristocratic husband, Bridget entered a convent and began to have a series of visions, some political, some personal, and some of which dealt with the birth of Jesus. Until Bridget's revelations it was believed that Mary had given birth in the normal fashion, but after she announced that it had been revealed to her that Mary had given birth standing in prayer, without pain or effort, medieval art changed its portrayal of the Nativity.

Bridget was canonized in 1391 and her *Revelations* were printed in 1492.

"Brightest and Best of the Sons of the Morning"   An Epiphany carol from the English hymn writer and Bishop of Calcutta Reginald Heber (1783-1826), who also wrote "Holy, Holy, Holy," "The Son of God Goes Forth to War," and "From Greenland's Icy Mountains." This hymn was written for Epiphany Sunday, 1811, to complement the reading from the Gospel of Matthew in which the Wise Men pursued the star. The hymn, however, was criticized for bordering on star-worshipping and being too "dancelike."

There have been almost 20 different tunes written for Heber's words, the most common being an 1892 melody by James Proktor Harding (1850-1911).

> Brightest and best of the sons of the morning,
> Dawn on our darkness and lend us thine aid;
> Star in the East, the horizon adorning,
> Guide where our infant Redeemer was laid!
>
> Cold on his cradle the dewdrops are shining,
> Low lies his bed with the beasts of the stall;
> Angels adore him, in slumber reclining,
> Wise men and shepherds before him do fall.
>
> Say, shall we yield him, in costly devotion,
> Odours of Edom and off'rings divine,
> Gems from the mountain and pearls from the ocean,
> Myrrh from the forest and gold from the mine?
>
> Vainly we offer each ample oblation,
> Vainly with gold would his favour secure;
> Richer by far is the heart's adoration,
> Dearer to God are the prayers of the poor.

"Bring a Torch, Jeanette, Isabella"   Written in 17th-century Provence, perhaps by Nicholas Saboly (1614-75), this carol first appeared as "Un flambeau, Jeannette, Isabelle." The song refers to the custom of torch-lit processions at midnight on Christmas Eve. The translation below by English composer Edward Cuthbert Nunn (1868-1914) is one of a number of renditions.

> Bring a torch, Jeanetta Isabella
> Bring a torch, to the cradle, run

It is Jesus, good folk of the village
Christ is born and Mary's calling
Ah! Ah! beautiful is the Mother
Ah! Ah! beautiful is her Son!

It is wrong when the Child is sleeping,
It is wrong to talk so loud;
Silence, all, as you gather 'round,
Lest your noise should waken Jesus;
Hush! Hush! see how fast He slumbers;
Hush! Hush! see how fast He sleeps!

Softly to the little stable,
Softly for a moment come;
Look and see how charming is Jesus
How He is white, His cheeks are rosy!
Hush! Hush! see how the Child is sleeping;
Hush! Hush! see how He smiles in dreams.

"Broncho Billy and the Baby" and the Movies "Broncho Billy and the Baby" was a short Christmas allegory by Peter B. Kayne that appeared in *The Saturday Evening Post* in 1910 and that spawned seven motion pictures. The story is of three bandits who rob the bank at New Jerusalem and head out into the desert to escape. There they encounter a dying woman who extracts a promise from them that they will save her newborn baby. The outlaws battle thirst and the elements, and finally one of them makes it back to New Jerusalem with the infant just in time for the Christmas Eve service.

The first cinematic version appeared in 1911, a one-reeler called *The Outlaw and the Child*. It was followed by three more silent films, in 1913, 1916, and 1919. The first sound version (and Universal Studio's first outdoor talkie) was *Hell's Heroes* in 1930, filmed by William Wyler in the Mojave Desert. Charles Bickford, Raymond Hatton, and Fred Kohler Sr. play three genuinely hard men, and the movie is uncompromisingly harsh. Two more-sentimental renditions, both called *Three Godfathers*, appeared in 1936 and, more memorably, in 1948. The latter was a John Ford western starring John Wayne, Harry Carey Jr., and Pedro Armendariz; it was the only one to dare a happy ending. In 1974 the made-for-television *The Godchild* moved the plot to three Civil War escapees, played by Jack Palance, Jack Warden, and Keith Carradine.

Bûche de Noèl French for "YULE LOG." It now commonly refers to the jelly roll cake, in the shape of a log and covered with icing, which is served at Christmas in France and French Canada.

Bulgaria Christmas in Bulgaria shares many of the customs found among its Eastern European neighbours, such as the 12-course meatless meal on Christmas Eve (which always includes the cheese pastry *banitza*), the central spot on the table for the large loaf of bread, and the ancient customs of the Yule log and the ritual beatings with switches on New Year's Day.

Unique to Bulgaria is the notion of celebrating Christmas twice, on December 25 and 26. During the Communist regime imposed after the Second World War, religious holidays like Christmas were suppressed, so the people cleverly invented a secular holiday that resembled Christmas and was celebrated on December 26. With the fall of the Iron Curtain, Christmas festivities were once again held openly, but the newer holiday has not been discarded.

Bulgarians are great supporters of choral traditions, and the custom of the *koleduvane*, Christmas Eve carol-singing by troupes of boys, has been lovingly preserved. Dressed in colourful native costumes with embroidered shirts, fur hats, and hooded cloaks, the *koledari* go door-to-door singing wishes of prosperity for the coming year. They are rewarded by homeowners with treats of pastry, fruit, and other delicacies.

Bull Week In 19th-century Sheffield "Bull Week" was the name given to the week before Christmas in which labourers pushed themselves to the limit to earn extra money for the expenses of the holiday to come. An account of an 1890 football match noted, "As it was 'Bull Week' in the town, the local artizans wanted to get in as much time as possible to be sure of a good wage for Christmas; but still more than 10,000 turned up at Olive Grove on a miserable, gloomy-grey Monday afternoon to witness the first clash between the Sheffield clubs."

"The Burning Babe" A poem by the Elizabethan Jesuit and martyr Robert Southwell, d. 1595.

As I in hoary winter's night stood shivering in the snow,
Surprised I was with sudden heat which made my heart
    to glow;
And lifting up a fearful eye to view what fire was near,
A pretty babe all burning bright did in the air appear;
Who, though scorched with excessive heat, such floods
    of tears did shed,
As though his floods should quench his flames, which with
    his tears were fed.
"Alas," quoth he, "but newly born, in fiery heats I fry,
Yet none approach to warm their hearts, or feel my fire
    but I!
My faultless breast the furnace is, the fuel wounding
    thorns,
Love is the fire, and sighs the smoke, the ashes shame and
    scorns;
The fuel justice layeth on, and mercy blows the coals,
The metal in this furnace wrought are men's defiled souls,
For which, as now on fire I am to work them to their good,
So will I melt into a bath to wash them in my blood."
With this he vanished out of sight and swiftly shrunk
    away,
And straight I called unto mind that it was Christmas Day.

Burning the Bush A custom in rural Herefordshire, England, wherein a large globe of twisted hawthorn and mistletoe was ceremonially burned in the fields early in the morning every New Year's Day. The purpose of the ritual was to drive the devil out of the area and purify the fields; without this ceremony folk believed that crops would be bad and the year an unlucky one. After the ceremony the participants were rewarded by farmers with cider and cakes.

The hawthorn was supposed to represent Christ's Crown of Thorns. As the old bush was being burnt a new bush was woven and hung up in the kitchen until it was needed the next January.

See SAINING.

Bush Christmas (1947) Veteran actor Chips Rafferty stars as horse-thief Long Bill in this Australian story of five children who head off into the wilderness in pursuit of stolen horses. Filmed in the Warrigal Hills, *Bush Christmas*, by director-writer Ralph Smart, is full of lovingly depicted local scenery. Its 1983 remake (with the young Nicole Kidman) was also known as *Prince and the Great Race*.

Buttenmandelhaut See RIDDLE-RADDLE MEN.

Byrom, John (1692-1763) English poet, hymnist, and inventor of an influential system of shorthand. He wrote the poem "Christians Awake, Salute the Happy Morn" as a 1749 Christmas present for his 11-year-old daughter Dolly. The piece was set to music in 1750 by John Wainwright.

Cake, Christmas The origin of Christmas cake lies in the TWELFTH NIGHT CAKE with its baked-in surprises, which were used either to prognosticate for the coming year or to choose a king and queen of the evening's festivities (see BEAN KING). When Twelfth Night ceremonies declined in the 19th century, the little charms made their way into the Christmas pudding and Christmas cake replaced the Twelfth Night Cake. In England the term has come to mean a fruitcake covered with marzipan and "royal icing" and sometimes decorated with a Father Christmas figure and snow scene. In Japan it is a gorgeously iced creation purchased for the holiday.

Calennig In Wales *calennig* means a little gift at New Year's. Boys used to go door-to-door at that time of year, exchanging a song or a rhyme for gifts of food or money. They often carried with them a curiously decorated apple or orange that also came to be called a *calennig*. The fruit was set on three legs made of sticks, topped with thyme, a fragrant herb, or other greenery, and oats, wheat or nuts were stuck in its skin. These three elements – fruit, grain or nuts, and herbs – represent the gifts of the Wise Men as well as sweetness, wealth, and immortality. Sometimes the *calennig* is kept in the house for good luck in the coming year.

Callithumpian Music Derived from the Greek for "beautiful," Callithumpian music refers to clangorous noise made by revellers during the Christmas season in 18th-century England and the early United States. "Music" was made by banging on pans, shouting, blowing horns, and making rude noises. Not only did it disturb the sleep of the honest middle class, it was also often associated with attacks on the church services or celebrations of the upper classes. This behaviour was one reason the middle class sought to domesticate Christmas early in the 19th century and bring celebrations indoors. See ANTICKS and UNITED STATES.

Canada Christmas in Canada may have been celebrated as long ago as 1,000 A.D. The Viking settlers who inhabited Newfoundland 1,000 years ago were Christians, and so might well have marked the Feast of the Nativity. Certainly the Roman Catholic immigrants who first came from France in the 16th and 17th centuries brought Christmas with them, and we know a good deal about how they kept the holiday. For them Christmas was a deeply religious occasion, centred on the midnight mass and the household Nativity scene. From this pious tradition came their conversion of the native

Callithumpian Music *The noise of boisterous lower-class celebrants helped convince the middle class to domesticate Christmas observances and bring them indoors.*

population and Christmas music such as "THE HURON CAROL" and "D'OÙ VIENS-TU BERGÈRE?"

But Christmas was also a time of festivity and frolic. From the customary taffy-pull ("*la tire*," an excellent time for young unmarried men and women to become better acquainted), which took place every St. Catherine's Day, to the telling of ghost tales, to the fiddling and dance parties, *Noël* in French Canada was a season to enjoy. French-Canadian folklore is rich in tales of the supernatural, with stories of werewolves, ghost-canoes, and phantom lovers being exchanged around the fire. In Quebec they adhered to the notion that Christmas Eve is the most supernaturally charged of all nights. On that night the Earth opened up and revealed its treasures, and animals spoke in human languages or knelt in homage to the baby Jesus. According to a popular legend, the dead of the parish return to hear mass at midnight on Christmas Eve and to look again on their old homes.

The centrepiece of the season was the *réveillon* or Christmas Eve feast, for which preparations had begun weeks before: pies and cakes were baked, meats cured, and drinks brewed. Children were put to bed early and then wakened for the trip to the midnight mass. After the church service, families hurried home to begin the meal. The main dish was usually the *tourtière* or meat pie, accompanied by homemade ketchups or chutney, but diners also had a choice of turkey, ham, stew, or goose. Desserts included sugar doughnuts, fruitcake, *bûche de noël*, or maple-syrup tarts. Children received gifts from Père Noël, but often the Christmas Eve presents were only small treats, with the bigger ones opened at New Year's in the French tradition.

Even today, when French-Canadian culture is much more urban than rural, Christmas remains a special part of Quebec life with the *réveillon* and its traditional foods, midnight mass, LA GUIGNOLÉE, Père Noël, and the spirit of celebration still alive.

English, German, and American immigrants brought their own traditions to the Canadian Christmas in the 18th and 19th centuries. From England came decorating the house with greens, the mistletoe and kissing ball, Christmas carols, parlour games, and MUMMING. From Germany came the Christmas tree, cookies and gingerbread men, and BELSNICKLING. From the United States came Santa Claus and his elves.

By the 20th century the English-Canadian Christmas had come in many ways to resemble the American celebration: a secular Advent marked by shopping more than the observance of saints' days or other religious observances, the decoration of the Christmas tree, the exchange of Christmas cards, Santa Claus appearing in shopping centres and Christmas parades (the world's first took place in Toronto in 1905) before his Christmas Eve descent down the nation's chimneys, and the opening of presents on December 25. Christmas dinner is a family affair, with a menu of turkey, dressing, and vegetables, and a dessert of mince pie. The season is a time of increased charitable giving, as seen in Salvation Army collections. Even the complaints about Christmas echo those heard in the United States: its over-commercialism, its political incorrectness (and the subsequent removal of Christian references and songs from schools' "Winter Concerts"), and its alleged marginalization of many voices (see BLUES, CHRISTMAS).

But there are also many ways in which the Canadian Christmas is distinct from that of its southern neighbour. Some Canadians of British origin maintain customs from the old country, such as plum pudding, watching the royal broadcast on Christmas afternoon, or keeping *hogmanay* in the Scottish

fashion. In the Maritime provinces and Newfoundland, raucous Christmas visits such as mumming and belsnickling persist, as do New Year's gift-bringers such as MOTHER GOODY. Acadians have kept their love of RAPEE PIE and Maritime children cling to Christmas treats called "barley toys" (animal-shaped hard candy on a stick) and "chicken bones" (hard candy pieces filled with chocolate). Aboriginal Canadians mark Christmas with community feasts, church-going, pow-wows, and, in the far north, winter games such as snowmobile races, dogsled races, and traditional Inuit contests like the two-foot high kick or the blanket toss. In the western provinces the large Ukrainian-Canadian community prolongs the Christmas season through its traditional use of the Julian calendar, which places Christmas Day on January 7 and Epiphany on January 19. (To honour the Eastern churches' observances, the Christmas lights on the national parliament building are left on until January 8.)

Visitors to Canada would find delight in the Carols by Candlelight ceremony held on the waters off Vancouver, British Columbia, or in viewing the spectacular light displays of Winnipeg, Manitoba, Canada's Christmas capital. In Ontario they could participate in a 19th-century Christmas at Black Creek Pioneer Village or watch the inauguration of the annual Christmas Lights Across Canada in Ottawa. They might try ice-skating outdoors in Montreal and then attending midnight mass in the beautiful Notre Dame Basilica with its interior created by French-Canadian woodcarvers, or seeing the collection of nativity scenes from around the world in St Joseph's Oratory. Eastern Canada offers visitors the spectacle of the janneys, ownshooks, and fools of Newfoundland.

Candlemas February 2; since the sixth century, the day of the Feast of the Purification of the Blessed Virgin Mary, and now known as the Feast of the Presentation, marking the ritual in the Temple required by Jewish law 40 days after the birth of a male child.

When the infant Jesus was brought to the Temple, Simeon spoke of him as "a light to lighten the Gentiles" (Luke 2:32), and so light is the theme of the day. Believers bring a candle to

Candlemas *In many countries it was important that Christmas greenery be taken down and burnt. Candlemas was often the date chosen for this task.*

the church to be blessed; these candles are thought to possess magical powers against sickness and thunder storms. Across many cultures it is the last day of the Christmas season, when all ornaments must be taken down and greenery burnt. In England the Yule log for the next Christmas was selected and set to dry; in Mexico it is the *Dia de Candelaria*, when the image of the baby Jesus is removed from the cradle. On Candlemas, Scottish schoolchildren used to bring money to their teacher to buy candles to light the schoolroom, a practice that turned into simply bringing gifts to the master. The boy who brought the most money (the term for this gratuity was "bleeze-money") was named Candlemas King. His reign would last six weeks, during which time he was allowed to remit punishments.

The custom of predicting the weather based on conditions on Candlemas has turned into Groundhog Day, wherein North Americans watch the emergence of particular groundhogs from their hibernation; if the rodents see their shadows on February 2, six more weeks of winter will follow. (Americans scrutinize the reaction of the Pennsylvania groundhog named Punxsutawney Phil, while Canadians observe Ontario's Wiarton Willie.) Candlemas was also believed to be a time when the soul of Judas was temporarily allowed out of Hell to ease his torment in the sea.

Candles The image of Jesus as the light of the world and the midwinter longing for the return of the sun have led to the candle being associated inextricably with Christmas. This can be seen in church ceremonies such as CANDLEMAS, CHRIST-INGLE, or candle-lit carol services, and in numerous home devotions. In countries such as Ireland it is the custom to place a candle in the window during the Christmas season; in Eastern Europe a large candle is placed in the centre of the table, sometimes stuck in a loaf of bread. In Germany the Advent wreath, the *Lichstock*, or Christmas pyramid, and the Christmas tree all employ candles, while in the southwestern United States and Mexico *luminaria* and *farolitas* light up the night. Australians flock in the hundreds of thousands to CAROLS BY CANDLELIGHT, while Filipinos place candles in their *parols*.

A beautiful custom is carried on in France's Auvergne on Christmas Eve. A candle is lit by the oldest member of the family and used to make the sign of the cross. It is then extinguished and passed on to the eldest son, who does the same and who then passes the candle to his wife, and so on. When the candle finally reaches the youngest, it is lit and placed in the middle of the table, a signal for the feast to begin. In Norway the thick Christmas candle must burn all night long on Christmas Eve or, it is believed, a family member will die that year.

Gouda, the centre of the Dutch candle industry, turns off all electrical lights in the city centre on Christmas Eve, while the mayor, by candlelight, reads the Nativity story to the crowd.

Canes, Candy The candy cane, a stick of striped, hard candy bent into a hook at one end, has been associated with Christmas for over three centuries. Legend attributes the origins of the candy cane to the choirmaster of Cologne Cathedral in the 1670s. Bothered by the noise of children attending the church's crèche scene, he had candies made up in the shape of a shepherd's crook and distributed to the young people to encourage their silence. The shape of the cane soon led to them being hung from German Christmas trees, where sweets were a common decoration.

The notions that the red stripes symbolized the blood of

Christ, or the mint flavour was a reference to the Biblical herb hyssop, or the shape was an inverted "J" for Jesus, seem to be pious retrojections dating from the modern period.

Cards, Christmas The origins of the Christmas card lie in the handwritten "Christmas pieces" produced during the first half of the 19th century by schoolboys demonstrating to their parents their growing skills in penmanship; in the production of decorative notepaper that was used to write to family and friends at Christmas and holidays by the 1830s; and in the Valentine's Day card craze that began in England in the 1820s and spread to North America in the 1840s. By 1840 it was recognized as socially acceptable to buy a printed card to express a personal sentiment.

The first to test this in the Christmas setting was Englishman HENRY COLE in 1843, who commissioned artist JOHN CALCOTT HORSLEY to produce 1,000 cards he could send to his friends. These hand-tinted lithographs featured a multi-generational family enjoying a glass of punch, flanked on either side by depictions of seasonal charity: clothing and feeding the poor. The inscription read "Merry Christmas and a Happy New Year to You." Such cards were too expensive (one shilling each) to be widely adopted, and it was not until the 1850s that the advent of mass-produced cards and a cheap postal rate combined to make the sending of Christmas greetings a widespread seasonal activity. So popular did the Christmas card become that editorials complained of "legitimate correspondence" being delayed by "cartloads of children's cards." Postmasters began to urge a policy of early mailing.

Though R.H. PEASE of Albany pioneered Christmas cards in the United States in the early 1850s, widespread acceptance in that country had to wait until 1875 and the first of LOUIS PRANG's highly attractive creations. For Prang, the Christmas card was a form of art, and his rather costly products elevated the genre until he was driven out of the business by cheap German imports and, in the 1890s, by the "GIMCRACK" fad.

In the 19th century, traditional Christmas themes made their first appearance: winter landscapes, Santa Claus, robins (a favourite on English cards since the 1850s), Nativity scenes, etc., but this was also a period of floral patterns, jewelled cards, fringed borders, seascapes, painted porcelain, and other fancies that did not survive the test of time. Many were ornate enough to be used as tree ornaments. By the end of the century, the original flat card had given way to the folded card with a graphic on the outside and a greeting on the inside.

The First World War put an end to German domination of the market and opened the door for companies like Hallmark to establish a presence. It also introduced cards with military and patriotic themes, regimental cards, and ones intended to boost the morale of the men in the trenches.

Throughout the 20th century the demand for cards did not slacken, even during the Great Depression. The sending of Christmas cards had come to be an important part of year-end sociability; businesses used them to connect with customers, family members to keep in touch with distant relatives, and friends to express a seasonal sentiment without the expense or complication of purchasing a gift. By the 1990s Americans alone were sending 2.6 billion each year.

This is not just a North American phenomenon; Christmas cards have become popular in non-Christian countries such as China. (In Brazil cards can be sent at any time during the holiday season, and it is not unusual to receive them in early January.) As with ornaments, eclecticism became the watchword in the late 20th century; religious and nostalgic themes abounded, but now they had to compete with humorous

Christmas Cards *The earliest known Christmas card, which appeared in 1843.*

cards, cards with political messages, and those suitable for agnostics or pagans.

"The Carnal and the Crane" A traditional English carol arranged by Ralph Vaughan Williams. The "carnal" is a crow (from the French *corneille*).

As I passed by a river-side,
And there as I did rein,
In argument I chanced to hear
A carnal and a crane.

The carnal said unto the crane,
"If all the world should turn,
Before we had the Father,
But now we have the Son."

"From whence does the Son come
From where and from what place?"
He said: "In a manger,
Between an ox and ass."

"I pray thee," said the carnal,
"Tell me before thou go,
Was not the mother of Jesus
Conceived by the Holy Ghost?"

"She was the purest virgin,
And the cleanest from sin;
She was the handmaid of our Lord,
And mother of our King."

"Where is the golden cradle
That Christ was rockèd in?
Where are the silken sheets
That Jesus was wrapt in?"

"A manger was the cradle
That Christ was rocked in;
The provender the asses left,
So sweetly He slept on."

Carol A song celebrating the events of the Nativity or the people involved in it.

There have been Nativity hymns since the fourth century, such as "Jesus refulsit omnium" by Hilary of Poitiers, "Veni redemptor gentium" by Ambrose of Milan, and "Corde natus ex parentis" by Prudentius. These were on the solemn side, expressing rather lofty theological truths; only Ephraem of Syria seems to have had an eye for the human dimension of the sacred events.

The term "carol" appears to be derived from *choros*, a Greek word for a circle dance with singing. The Church was wary of its pagan connections and legislated against carols in a number of medieval councils, a prejudice illustrated by the legend of those men and women who were caught circle-dancing in a churchyard on Christmas Eve and refused to stop at the priest's request. The outraged patron saint of the church appeared and condemned them to dance without ceasing until a year had passed. After a year's carolling the victims died or fled trembling.

In the 13th century Christian teaching shifted away from a vengeful God to the more human aspects of Jesus, and with this came an interest in the details of the Incarnation and Nativity. St. Francis of Assisi's assembly of a living crèche is an expression of this, as was the new type of sacred song popularized by the Franciscans, the use of carol music with poetry, such as that by the monk JACOPONE DA TODI celebrating the birth of Jesus. The new carol form spread from Italy with the help of the Franciscans and Dominicans and soon found favour all across Europe. Examples from this period include the macaronic "In dulci jubilo" from Germany and the Polish "W zlobie lezy."

The 15th and 16th centuries were in some ways a golden age of carols. They were sung in homes and on the street, used in church services and religious drama (e.g., "The Coventry Carol"), and were spread by the newly invented printing press. From England came "Adam Lay Ybounden," "I Saw Three Ships," and "The Boar's Head Carol," from France the *noèl*, from Spain the *villancico*, and from Germany carols like "O Tannenbaum" and "Es ist ein Ros entsprungen."

The Reformation put a halt to the religious use of carols in some Protestant countries, such as England and Scotland, which replaced most church singing with the chanting of metrical psalms. (Carols remained popular in Protestant Germany, where Martin Luther himself wrote "Von Himmel Hoch" and translated other Christmas songs from Latin.) Though carols were banned from the church, they continued to be sung at home and by door-to-door carollers on BEGGING VISITS during the Christmas season, but even this was frowned upon in the 17th century with the PURITAN revolution in England in the 1640s.

Carol *A group of English street carollers, as depicted in the* Illustrated London News.

Though the Restoration ended most Puritan anti-Christmas innovations, the Church of England remained opposed to the use of carols in worship. From 1660 to the 19th century, the only carols to receive official approval were Nahum Tate's "While Shepherds Watched Their Flocks by Night" and Charles Wesley's "Hark the Herald Angels Sing." Carolling was confined to churches in the north and west of England and to Dissenting and Catholic congregations, and many were prepared to declare the carol dead in the early 19th century. It was saved from extinction through the efforts of carol collectors such as William Sandys, John Stainer, and J.M. Neale, and the general renewal of interest in Christmas. In addition to collections of antique carols, new songs began to appear, with American composers leading the way, such as Phillips Brooks ("O Little Town of Bethlehem") and Edmund Hamilton Sears ("It Came Upon the Midnight Clear"). The Church of England renewed its interest in carols, particularly after the 1878 invention by Bishop Benson in Truro Cathedral of the form of service called Lessons and Carols, which combined scripture reading with songs.

The 20th century saw a continued interest in carols. While the host of secular Christmas songs that appeared cannot

Carol *Christmas carols began as a way for the Church to spread the news of the Nativity.*

properly be included in the term (e.g., "Jingle Bell Rock" or "White Christmas"), there were a number of notable additions to the canon, some new, some revived by collectors, and some through translation. Among these are "Do You Hear What I Hear?" "The Huron Carol," "Carol of the Bells," "I Wonder as I Wander," "Angels and Shepherds," and "Caroling, Caroling." The relentless use of carols in advertising or as shopping-mall music has robbed some of this music of its original charm; who can hear "The Little Drummer Boy" for the thousandth time without wincing? Carols have also been appropriated for use by atheists, pagans, and neo-Puritans (see OPPOSITION TO CHRISTMAS) and subject to revision for purposes of "inclusive language" (e.g., "Good Christian Folk Rejoice" replaces "Good Christian Men Rejoice").

Carol for Another Christmas (TV) (1964) Appearing on CBS in December 1964, this movie is a dark variant of Dickens's *A Christmas Carol*. Three spirits of Christmas appear to a man mourning the death of his son in the Second World War. Directed by Joseph L. Mankiewicz, written by Rod Serling, and starring Ben Gazzara and Sterling Hayden, this was the American television debut of Peter Sellers, who appeared as King of the Individualists.

"Carol of the Bagpipers" From the Sicilian song "Canzone d'i zampognari," "The Carol of the Bagpipers" has for centuries been played by carollers strolling in the streets the nine days before Christmas. Handel borrowed the air to use in one section of his *Messiah*, "He shall feed his flock."

> When Christ our Lord was born in Bethlehem afar,
> Although 'twas night,
> There shone as bright as noon, a star.
> Never so brightly, never so whitely,
> Shone the stars,

As on that night!
The Brightest star went
Away to call the Wise Men from the Orient.

"Carol of the Bells"   The music to this very popular carol was written by the Ukrainian composer Mykola Leontovych (1877-1921) as part of a choral work entitled *Shchedryk*, performed first in Kiev in 1916. It was translated into English as "Carol of the Bells" by the American composer and lyricist Peter Wilhousky (1902-78) in 1936. Three other English songs have made use of the music: M.L. Holman's "Ring, Christmas Bells" of 1947; the anonymous "Come, Dance and Sing" of 1957; and the anonymous "Carol of the Bells" of 1972.

In Ukraine the song is sung as a New Year's carol. The original words concern a swallow calling on a farmer and make no reference to Christmas.

"Carol of the Birds"   **(1)** "El cant dels ocells," a medieval Catalonian carol from northeastern Spain.

Upon this holy night,
When God's great star appears,
And floods the earth with brightness,
Birds' voices rise in song,
And, warbling all night long,
Express their glad hearts' lightness.

The nightingale is first
To bring his song of cheer,
And tell us of his gladness:

"Jesus, our Lord, is born
To free us from all sin
And banish ev'ry sadness."

The answ'ring Sparrow cries:
"God comes to earth this day
Amid the angels flying."
Trilling in sweetest tones,
The Finch his Lord now owns:
"To Him be all thanksgiving."

The Partridge adds his note:
"To Bethlehem I'll fly,
Where in the stall He's lying.
There, near the manger blest,
I'll build myself a nest,
And sing my love undying."

(2) A contemporary Australian carol using native wildlife to express the joy of Christmas.

Carols by Candlelight   At Christmas 1937, Melbourne radio announcer Norman Banks saw an old woman sitting alone in the dark, holding a candle, and singing along to carols on the radio. Inspired by this he arranged a sing-along concert for the next Christmas Eve in a Melbourne park. In return for a donation to the Royal Victoria Institute of the Blind, people were given candles, rather like in the CHRISTINGLE custom. The concert proved to be such a success that it began to attract tens of thousands of participants and millions of listeners, first on radio and then on television. The idea spread to other cities in Australia and from there to other countries. "Carols by Candlelight" can now be found in New Zealand, South Africa, and Canada. On the Pacific coast of Canada the spectacular setting is Vancouver Harbour, where boatloads of carollers sing across the water.

Carval y Nollick   Christmas carols from the Isle of Man off the west coast of England. Derived from the native ballad tradition, they were usually sung by individuals in church on Christmas Eve.

Ceppo   The term in Italian for both the Yule log and, later, the Italian Christmas pyramid, a structure decorated with greenery and holding a manger scene, small presents, or ornaments.

A Ceremony of Carols   Benjamin Britten's 1942 choral setting, opus 28, of a number of medieval English carols including "Wolcum Yole!" "There Is No Rose," and "Adam Lay Ybounden," begun on a wartime voyage across the Atlantic.

Cert   A black-clad Czech demon, who, along with a good angel dressed in white, accompanies Svaty Mikalas (St. Nicholas) as he drops from heaven on a gold cord on December 6 to bring gifts. Cert carries a whip and chains to symbolize punishment for bad kids.

Charity   In what might be termed the very first Christmas, we see evidence of a lack of charity on the part of an innkeeper toward a desperate family searching for a place for their child to be born. Since then Christmas has been associated with identifying the needy and making provision for them. During the Middle Ages Christmas charity flowed from the monarchy and the Church: in 1248 Henry III fed thousands of poor folk at his palace, and in 1283 his son Edward I fed 500 London beggars; medieval monasteries and nunneries made special allowance for the giving of extra food and clothing at Christmas. In Spain confraternities, groups of devout laymen, made particular efforts at Christmas to feed the poor and pay the debts of those in prison.

Landlords were also expected to show generosity during the Christmas season. Lord Robert Cecil always budgeted for £30-40 in money, beef, or bread as donations to his parishes at Christmas during the reign of Elizabeth I, and his contemporary Sir William Petrie's hospitality for those on his estates involved the roasting of 17 oxen, 14 steers, 5 hogs, 13 bucks, 29 calves, 54 lambs, and 129 sheep, plus a ton of cheese. This sort of feudal *noblesse oblige* is well expressed by Joseph Addison and his account of Sir Roger de Coverley, a rustic landowner:

He afterwards fell into an Account of the Diversions which had passed in his House during the Holidays; for Sir *Roger*, after the laudable Custom of his Ancestors, always keeps open House at Christmas. I learned from him that he had killed eight Fat Hogs for this Season, that he had dealt about his Chines very liberally amongst his Neighbours, and that in particular he had sent a String of Hogs'-puddings with a Pack of Cards to every poor Family in the Parish. I have often thought, says Sir *Roger*, it happens very well that Christmas should fall out in the Middle of Winter. It is the most dead uncomfortable Time of the Year, when the poor People would suffer very much from their Poverty and Cold, if they had not good Chear, warm Fires, and Christmas Gambols to support them. I love to rejoice their poor Hearts at this Season, and to see the whole Village merry in my great Hall. I allow a double Quantity of Malt to my Small Beer, and set it a-running for twelve Days to every one that calls for it, I have always a Piece of Cold Beef and Mince-pye upon the Table. . . .

Christmas was also a time in which begging by the poor was allowed. In many places the season was the occasion for individuals or groups to go door-to-door soliciting food or money in return for good wishes or a song. These BEGGING VISITS include mumping and wassail wenches in England, *Klopfelgehen* in Germany, and *la guignolée* in Quebec. As the feudal system declined and the rural economy changed so did Christmas charity, and numerous complaints were made in the 17th and 18th centuries of the selfishness that had crept into the hearts of the well-to-do; a 1624 poem lamented that "Christmas bread and beef is turned into stones."

Charity *This 1883 illustration by John Tenniel from* Punch *makes clear the traditional link between Christmas and charity. The caption quotes Father Christmas: "What! Not know me! Oh, this must be altered!"*

It was the genius of Charles Dickens and the philanthropic spirit of the Victorian age that once more linked Christmas and charity. In Dickens's *A Christmas Carol*, Ebenezer Scrooge is converted from a flinty-hearted capitalist, who hopes the poor will die and so reduce the surplus population, to a generous employer and donor to the poor. The 19th century produced numberless private charities for seasonal aid, such as the Christmas Letter Mission – a group that sent personal Christmas greetings (some 30,000) to every inmate in English hospitals, workhouses, and prisons – and the Christmas Clubs in the United States, which concentrated on providing a dinner and a present for the poor. Children in Burgundy, France, put alms for the poor in little paper bags on the street and set the corners of the bags on fire so the poor could find their way to the offering. Moreover, governments were moved to increase social welfare benefits, to such an extent that the old-fashioned begging visits became unnecessary and were gradually converted to quaint customs that were maintained to gather money to donate to charity.

The connection between charity and the Christmas season continued into the 20th century. For the Salvation Army, Christmas is a prime time for soliciting funds, a fact not lost

on numerous other charities such as UNICEF, which raises money through the sale of Christmas cards, or European groups that raise money for Third World development through the collections by Star Boys. A recent addition to these charitable efforts is the gathering of rock music performers to make Christmas albums, a trend started by Band Aid's "Do They Know It's Christmas?" in 1984.

A Charlie Brown Christmas (TV) (1965)   "All I want is what I have coming to me. All I want is my fair share," says Lucy in this little animated film on the dangers of a materialistic view of Christmas. Though there are some chuckles over Charlie Brown's direction of the school pageant and his search for a suitable tree, *A Charlie Brown Christmas* is more a morality play than a light-hearted romp.

CBS apparently had misgivings about the religious content of the show – one of the few explicitly Christian animated films about Christmas – but this Charles Schulz creation won an Emmy for best children's program and went on to become an enduring holiday favourite.

The score was written by Vince Guaraldi, who boldly chose to do a jazz-flavoured set of compositions instead of the more juvenile music that usually accompanied children's cartoons. The show was produced by Bill Melendez and Lee Mendelson, who were to collaborate on further Charlie Brown specials. A sequel, less profound but more amusing, was the 1992 television special *It's Christmastime Again, Charlie Brown*.

"Cherry Tree Carol"   There are a number of carols with the theme of the cherry tree bowing down to Mary when she expresses a desire for fruit. The original kernel of the tale can be found in the *Gospel of Pseudo-Matthew*, which dates from the sixth century. These carols were collected in England and the United States in the 19th century and were set to different tunes. The mention of the birthday of Jesus on January 6 refers to OLD CHRISTMAS.

> When Joseph was an old man,
> An old man was he,
> When he courted Virgin Mary,
> The Queen of Galilee,
> When he courted Virgin Mary,
> The Queen of Galilee.
>
> As Joseph and Mary
> Were walking one day,
> "Here are apples and cherries,"
> O Mary did say . . .
> Then Mary spoke to Joseph,
> So meek and so mild,
> "Joseph, gather me some cherries
> For I am with child."
>
> Then Joseph flew in anger –
> In anger flew he,
> "Let the father of the baby
> Gather cherries for thee!"
>
> Then Jesus spoke a few words,
> A few words spoke he,
> "Let my mother have some cherries;
> Bow low down, cherry tree!
> Bow down, O cherry tree!
> Bow low down to the ground!"
> Then Mary gathered cherries
> While Joseph stood around.

Then Joseph took Mary
All on his left knee;
Saying: "What have I done? Lord,
Have mercy on me!"
Then Joseph took Mary
All on his right knee,
"Pray tell me, little baby,
When your birthday shall be . . ."

"On the sixth day of January
My birthday shall be,
When the stars and the elements
Shall tremble with glee."

As Joseph was a-walking,
He heard an angel sing,
"Tonight shall be the birth-time
Of Christ, our heavenly king."

"He neither shall be born
In house nor in hall,
Nor in the place of paradise,
But in an ox's stall."

"He neither shall be clothed
In purple nor in pall
But in the bare white linen
That useth babies all."

As Joseph was a-walking,
Then did an angel sing,
And Mary's child at midnight
Was born to be our king.

Childermas   December 28, the Feast of the Holy Innocents, commemorates the murder of the male babies of Bethlehem by King Herod. (See HEROD THE GREAT.) In England the day was known as Childermas (or Dyzemas) and was considered a time of ill omen. Not only was no business conducted on that day, but the day of the week on which it fell was deemed unlucky for the rest of the year. In Ireland it was *Lá Crostna na Bliana*, the "cross day of the year," when no new enterprise was begun. Many sailors would not sail on that day; on the Aran Islands no one was buried on Childermas (or the day of the week on which it occurred); and in Cornwall to wash on that day was to doom one of your relatives to death.

Childermas was also a day for ritual beatings. The 17th-century writer Gregorie notes the custom of whipping children in the morning of that day so that Herod's murderousness "might stick the closer; and, in a moderate proportion, to act over the crueltie again in kind." See BEATINGS AT CHRISTMAS and INNOCENTS, FEAST OF THE HOLY.

"A Child's Christmas in Wales"   Dylan Thomas's poetic hymn of nostalgia was originally written as a BBC radio script for a Welsh regional station and was published only after the author's death in 1954. It recounts the memories of a boy's Christmas in a Welsh seacoast town, complete with snowball fights, house fires, presents (useless and useful), sleepy uncles, and maudlin aunts.

A Child's Christmas in Wales (TV) (1973)   A CBS production from December 1973 with narrator Michael Redgrave and the National Theatre of the Deaf.

A Child's Christmas in Wales (TV) (1986)   A gorgeous television version of Dylan Thomas's famous poem, directed by Don McBrearty. Denholm Elliott plays an old man telling the story of his youthful Christmases to his grandson Thomas (Mathonway Reeves).

The Children's Friend   The first book to print a picture of Santa Claus and the first to mention a reindeer and sleigh. Published in the United States in 1821, *The Children's Friend: A New Year's Present, to Little Ones From Five to Twelve* included eight colour plates and eight verses about the American gift-bringer's activities. The poem reads:

Old Santeclaus with much delight
His reindeer drives this frosty night.
O'er chimney tops, and tracks of snow,
To bring his yearly gifts to you.

The steady friend of virtuous youth,
The friend of duty and of truth,
Each Christmas eve he joys to come
Where peace and love have made their home.

Through many houses he has been,
And various beds and stockings seen,
Some, white as snow, and neatly mended,
Others, that seem'd for pigs intended.

Where e'er I found good girls or boys,
That hated quarrels, strife and noise,
I left an apple, or a tart,
Or wooden gun, or painted cart;

To some I gave a pretty doll.
To some a peg-top, or a ball;
No crackers, cannons, squibs or rockets,
To blow their eyes up, or their pockets.

No drums to stir their Mother's ear,
Nor swords to make their sisters fear;
But pretty books to store their mind
With Knowledge of each various kind.

But where I found the children naughty,
In manners rude, in tempers haughty,
Thankless to parents, liars, swearers,
Boxers or cheats, or base tale-bearers,

I left a long, black, birchen rod,
Such, as the dread command of God
Directs a Parent's hand to use
When virtue's path his sons refuse.

Authorship of the poem is uncertain (historians have suggested either James K. Paulding or Arthur J. Stansbury, a Presbyterian minister), but no one doubts its influence in shaping the American view of Santa Claus. It is this little piece of poetry that introduces to the world the notion of Santa Claus's connection with the northern winter, the reindeer and sleigh, and his visits coming not on his saint's day (as in Europe) but on Christmas Eve.

Chile   As in most Latin American countries, Christmas in Chile centres on the church and the family. Chilean Catholics observe the novena, nine days of prayer and preparation before Christmas, attend midnight mass, and tens of thousands of the faithful make pilgrimage to the 17th-century statue of the Virgin del Rosario in Andacollo, a small mining town in the Andes. There they pay their respects to the image, take part in religious processions, and witness the remarkable *Chinos*, brightly costumed teams of dancers with Asian-flavoured music. Catering to the masses of pilgrims, most of whom camp out in the hills surrounding the town, are cockfights, horse races, food stands, and gambling booths.

At home Chilean children await the Christmas Eve arrival of the gift-bringer, Viejo Pascuero, who looks very much like Santa Claus and comes complete with reindeer, but who climbs in a window instead of using the chimney. Dinner is eaten late in the evening, perhaps after church, and consists of turkey and a host of salads, seafood, and olives, accompanied by a local wine. Desserts always include *Pan de Pascua*, the sweet Christmas bread, and fruit, cookies, and cakes. Chileans are also fond of alcoholic punches such as Cola de Mono and Rompón. At midnight presents are exchanged, after which the children go to bed and adults continue to party.

Christmas Day is spent eating and drinking with the immediate family. A special treat is *Chirimoya alegre*, a sweet dessert made from a native fruit.

This holiday season ends January 6, Epiphany, which Chileans call *La Pascua de Los Negros*, the "Black Passover," after the Three Kings, one of whom is thought to be African.

The Chimes   The second of five Christmas books written by Charles Dickens, appearing in 1844, a year after *A Christmas Carol*. All of these books involve a conversion of some sort. Like Scrooge in the first book, Trotty Veck, a poor but decent porter, undergoes a change of heart at the hands of spirits,

Chimneys and Other Means of Ingress *Santa Claus, as imagined by Thomas Nast, prepares to descend the chimney with Christmas gifts.*

this time emanating from the bells of a church. *The Chimes*, like its predecessor, is an attack on selfishness, but here it takes on more overtly political tones as Dickens skewers politicians and the middle class for their indifference to the poor. Though Dickens thought the book "knocked the *Carol* out of the field," it was not as well received as its predecessor.

Chimneys and Other Means of Ingress   In the influential poem "A VISIT FROM ST. NICHOLAS," which taught North America much of what it knows about Santa Claus, the author, Clement Moore, notes that "down the chimney St. Nicholas came with a bound." That is how generations of Canadian and American children have expected the gift-bringer to arrive, so much so that many fathers have been moved to clomp around on the roof or in the attic to imitate the noise of reindeer standing by the chimney. The chimney is also the mode of entrance for a number of other of the world's Christmas gift-bringers. In Italy the Befana comes down the chimney (and in true chimney-sweep fashion carries a broom with her); in the same way Father Christmas enters homes in England and Père Noël or Le Petit Jésus in France. In Holland the gift-bringer's helper Black Pete goes down the chimney to keep St. Nicholas from getting his clothes dirty. The chimney also serves to carry messages to the gift-bringer: in England children write letters to Father Christmas and burn them in the fireplace, sending their smoky wishes via the chimney; in Scotland children "cry up the lum," shouting their wishes up the chimney on Christmas Eve.

But the chimney is not just a way in for the gift-bringer. To psychiatrists it represents the birth canal (see PSYCHIATRY AND CHRISTMAS), and it also admits unpleasant creatures. Norwegians feared that witches would come down the chimney and, to prevent this, would burn dry spruce which emits sparks, or put salt in the fire. In Greece the *skarkatzalos* log is burned over the Twelve Days of Christmas to keep out the KALLIKANTZAROI, who slip down the chimney; and in Scotland they use a similar trick to keep the elves out.

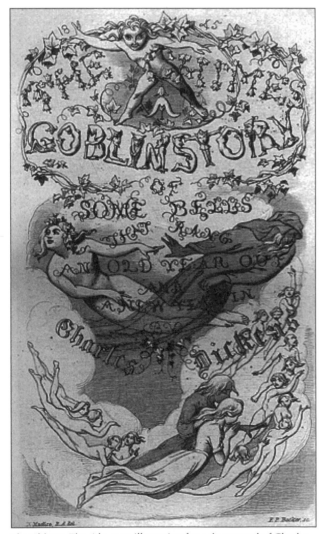

The Chimes *The title-page illustration from the second of Charles Dickens's Christmas books.*

There are other ways in for gift-bringers besides the chimney. In Brazil, where the tropical heat renders chimneys few and far between, Papai Noel comes through the front door. The direct method is also used in Sweden (where gifts are often thrown in through the door), Finland, and Australia. In Hungary the baby Jesus brings presents through the window and, like the Befana, rings a little bell when the deed is done. Germany's Weihnachtsmann has been known to use both the window and the chimney, while Chile's Viejo Pascuero prefers the window.

China   Though the People's Republic of China officially espouses an atheist ideology, interest in Christmas is quite evident, especially in the cities. In Beijing, Shanghai, and Hong Kong, stores are decorated with images of Santa Claus (known in China as Dun Che Lao Ren, "Old Man Christmas"), snowmen, and angels. People throng shopping areas looking for presents, as many among the prosperous classes have adopted gift-giving as a way of marking the season. It is also recognized as a time for parties, dining out, dancing, fireworks, and holiday concerts – the Beijing Opera has staged an all-night "Silent Night" program on Christmas Eve. The exchange of Christmas cards is widespread, perhaps almost at North American levels for some sections of the population. The industrial city of Changchun recently opened a multi-million dollar Christmas theme park, the Clear Moon Lake Santa Claus Paradise, based on a Finnish model and employing workers wearing traditional Lapp costumes.

Much of the popularity of Christmas can be explained as an interest in things Western and as an excuse for consumption by the more well-off. There is also the problem of a shortage of holidays and times of celebration for a population increasingly concerned with leisure time and quality of life. Many of the traditional festivals of China have been abolished by the Communist government but, as in England in the early Industrial Revolution, when rampant capitalism had swept away the old feast days, people still feel a need to mark the rhythms of the year with occasional bursts of celebration.

China, however, does not lack a spiritual component in its fascination with Christmas. Despite decades of persecution, Christianity is the faith of millions of Chinese, who flock to churches at Christmas. Services at Beijing's two cathedrals are so full of believers and the curious that police are used for crowd control and tickets are issued well in advance. (Even so, a thriving black market in passes has sprung up.) This is a phenomenon that troubles Communist officialdom, which has complained about youth celebrating foreign holidays and emulating a bourgeois lifestyle. A party newspaper has asked what a religious and romanticized Western festival has to do with an atheist nation. The future of Christmas in China remains uncertain.

"The Chipmunk Song"   Ross Bagdasarian as "David Seville" won a Grammy for best children's song for this 1958 version of "Christmas Don't Be Late" as sung by Alvin, Simon, and Theodore. Though Bagdasarian could neither read nor write music, he produced other novelty songs such as "Come On-a My House" (written with the Pulitzer Prize-winning playwright William Saroyan, his cousin) and "The Witch Doctor." The Chipmunks were named for three Liberty record executives. "The Chipmunk Song" is the only Christmas tune that has ever been Number One in the United States on Christmas Day.

Chrismon Tree   A Christmas tree decorated only with "Chrismons" ("Christ monograms"), such as the cross, the Chi-Rho (a Greek symbol for Christ), the lamb, the anchor, etc., conceived by Frances Kipps Spencer in the 1950s. Most Chrismons are white with gold trim, and the tree is lit only with white lights. They appeared first in an American Lutheran church, but the custom has since spread to other denominations, where it is seen as a more truly religious version of the Christmas tree. See JESSE TREE.

"Christians, Awake"   An English Christmas song, music by John Wainwright (d. 1768), lyrics by John Byrom (1692-1763).

> Christians, awake, salute the happy morn,
> Whereon the Saviour of the world was born,
> Rise to adore the mystery of love,
> Which hosts of angels chanted from above;
> With them the joyful tidings first begun
> Of God incarnate and the Virgin's Son.
>
> Then to the watchful shepherds it was told,
> Who heard the angelic herald's voice, "Behold,
> I bring good tidings of a Saviour's birth
> To you and all the nations upon earth;
> This day hath God fulfilled His promised word;
> This day is born a Saviour, Christ the Lord."
>
> He spake; and straightway the celestial choir
> In hymns of joy, unknown before, conspire;
> The praises of redeeming love they sang,
> And heaven's whole orb with Hallelujahs rang;
> God's highest glory was their anthem still,
> Peace upon earth, and unto men good will.
>
> To Bethlehem straight the enlightened shepherds ran,
> To see the wonder God had wrought for man,
> And found, with Joseph and the blessed Maid,
> Her Son, the Saviour, in a manger laid;
> They to their flocks, still praising God, return,
> And their glad hearts within their bosoms burn.

Christingle   Also known as a "Christ-light" service, it is a ceremony popular in English Protestant churches, often involving children. Originating with the Moravian church in the 18th century, these services are held during the Advent season and combine collecting money for charity with the image of Christ as the light of the world. A feature of the service is the Christingle or Christ-light, a candle placed in the top of an orange decorated with a red ribbon and four sticks, on which are placed fruit or candy, symbolic of the blood shed by Christ for all the peoples of the world.

Christkindl   "The Christ Child," a.k.a. Christkindli or Christkindlein. The replacement of St. Nicholas as the gift-bringer led to the belief in parts of Germany, Austria, Switzerland, and among the Pennsylvania Dutch that Christmas presents were brought by the Christ Child himself. Imagined at first as the baby Jesus, the Christkindl mutated over time into an angelic figure in a white robe, with a veil, jewelled crown, gold wings, and often carrying a wand. The Christkindl is thought to make an entrance through a window rather than the chimney and to ring a bell when the presents have been delivered. In North America the name became KRIS KRINGLE, which by the middle of the 19th century was just an alias for Santa Claus.

Christmas at Camp 119 (1948)   An Italian film, *Natale al campo 119*, directed by Pietro Francisci, about Christmas in a California prisoner-of-war camp. Seven Italians, taken captive in the Second World War, reminisce about earlier Christmases

Christkindl *Thomas Nast's depiction of the Christkindl.*

back home. Each is from a different part of the country, and the soundtrack contains folk songs from the various regions.

Christmas at Moose Factory (1971) A cleverly animated short by the National Film Board of Canada about a child's view of winter life in the remote North. Written and directed by Alanis Obomsawin.

Christmas Atoll Now called Kiritimati Atoll, the island, the largest coral formation in the world, was first sighted on Christmas Eve 1777 by English explorer Captain Cook. It became a British dependency in 1888, and from 1957 to 1962 it was the site of British and American nuclear tests. The island now forms part of the republic of Kiribati. See GEOGRAPHY AND CHRISTMAS.

Christmas Beetle A brightly coloured Australian scarablike insect of the genus *Anoplognathus*, the subject of much agricultural research aimed at curtailing its attacks on eucalyptus trees. It is also a term used in South Africa for the cicada.

Christmas Bell An Australian plant, *Blandifordia nobilis*, its red flowers are bell-shaped with yellow tips. It blooms in December and has become a popular symbol of Christmas, appearing on cards and decorations.

Christmas Berry *Heteromeles arbutifolia*, also known as Toyon, the Christmas Berry bush is found in the southwestern United States and California. The berries have been used by natives for dyes, food, and medicine. Nowadays it is common to see wreaths and decorations made with the berries at Christmas.

The Christmas Box A best-selling short novel of 1993 by Richard Paul Evans about a married couple and their child who take a job as caregivers for a wealthy widow. The husband is drawn to an antique box carved with a Nativity scene and containing letters from the old woman's past. By seeking the meaning of the question "What was the first Christmas gift?" he will learn lessons about love, Christmas, God, and family.

The story was written in six weeks and was originally self-published, meant only for a small circle of the author's friends. The writing style is earnest and pedestrian, but the publishing house Simon and Schuster detected in it a potential blockbuster and paid Evans $4.2 million for rights to the book and its successor. Their faith was rewarded with massive sales as the little volume became a publishing phenomenon. Evans has since followed it up with *Timepiece*, a "prequel" to *The Christmas Box*, and *The Letter*.

Those who prefer their Christmas reading to be more satirical than saccharine may favour the 1996 *Revenge of the Christmas Box: A Parody* by Cathy Crimmins and Tom Maeder.

The Christmas Box (TV) (1995) A CBS television movie of the sentimental Christmas best-seller by Richard Paul Evans. Shot on location in Salt Lake City, the film, starring Richard Thomas and Maureen O'Hara and directed by Marcus Cole, gained few friends on its release.

Christmas Bull The wearing of animal disguises at midwinter festivals was an old pagan practice that never died out after the Christianization of Europe, as the practice at Christmas of the MARI LWYD or HODENING HORSE or Schimmel attest. In the west of England the Christmas Bull was a man covered in a sheet or an animal hide, wearing the head of a bull, and guided from door to door by a keeper and a group of followers. He was allowed entry in homes, would prance about threatening folk with his horns, and be given some drink or food. In some areas a group carrying a wooden bull's head and a Christmas tree conducted a BEGGING VISIT, displaying the head to householders in return for a donation.

Christmas Bush *Ceratopetalum gummiferum*, a flowering Australian bush whose red blossoms appear among its green leaves around Christmas, making it a national favourite for the holidays.

Christmas Cactus A plant from the Brazilian rainforest, *Schlumbergera bridgesii*, whose purple or red blooms appear around Christmas.

A Christmas Carol A short novel by Charles Dickens that proved highly influential in reviving interest in Christmas in England and in shaping the themes attached to the holiday in the Victorian period. It tells the story of the moral redemption of the miser Ebenezer Scrooge at the hands of ghosts and spirits on Christmas Eve and of the importance of charity and reconciliation.

Dickens wrote the book in October and November 1843, when he was disappointed by the sales of *Martin Chuzzlewit*. The story came easily to him as he walked at night through London streets, and it delighted him as it came; for the rest of his life he was eager to spread what he called "*Carol* philosophy." The book was a great popular success and inspired Dickens to produce a series of Christmas books, essays, and stories, which came out every year (except 1847) until 1867. These were instrumental in persuading the English-speaking

A Christmas Carol *Mr. Fezziwig's Christmas ball.*

world to take Christmas seriously and to combine its celebrations with generosity to others. William Makepeace Thackeray called *A Christmas Carol* "a national benefit, and to every man and woman who reads it a personal kindness."

The book spawned a host of imitations and outright plagiarisms (eight unauthorized plays of *A Christmas Carol* had been produced by February 1844) and has been an inspiration to composers, moviemakers, and playwrights ever since.

"A Christmas Carol"   The only Christmas song that Charles Dickens wrote appeared in Chapter 28 of THE PICKWICK PAPERS, where it is sung to much applause by Mr. Wardle. Dickens's lyrics were later set to the tune of "Old King Cole."

> I care not for Spring; on his fickle wing
> Let the blossoms and buds be borne:
> He woos them amain with his treacherous rain,
> And he scatters them ere the morn.
> An inconstant elf, he knows not himself,
> Nor his own changing mind an hour,
> He'll smile in your face, and, with wry grimace,
> He'll wither your youngest flower.
>
> Let the Summer sun to his bright home run,
> He shall never be sought by me;
> When he's dimmed by a cloud I can laugh aloud,
> And care not how sulky he be!
> For his darling child is the madness wild
> That sports in fierce fever's train;
> And when love is too strong, it don't last long,
> As many have found to their pain.
>
> A mild harvest night, by the tranquil light
> Of the modest and gentle moon,
> Has a far sweeter sheen, for me, I ween,
> Than the broad and unblushing noon.
> But every leaf awakens my grief,
> As it lieth beneath the tree;

> So let Autumn air be never so fair,
> It by no means agrees with me.
>
> But my song I troll out, for CHRISTMAS stout,
> The hearty, the true, and the bold;
> A bumper I drain, and with might and main
> Give three cheers for this Christmas old!
> We'll usher him in with a merry din
> That shall gladden his joyous heart,
> And we'll keep him up, while there's bite or sup,
> And in fellowship good, we'll part.
>
> In his fine honest pride, he scorns to hide,
> One jot of his hard-weather scars;
> They're no disgrace, for there's much the same trace
> On the cheeks of our bravest tars.
> Then again I sing 'till the roof doth ring,
> And it echoes from wall to wall –
> To the stout old wight, fair welcome to-night,
> As the King of the Seasons all!

A Christmas Carol in the Movies   Moviemakers in Hollywood and Britain have made *A Christmas Carol*, the Charles Dickens masterpiece, the most frequently filmed story in Christmas history. It has been rendered in every conceivable variation, from ghost story to parody to porn flick, in black and white, colour, and animation, from one-man shows to the most lavish productions.

The earliest known attempt to do justice to Scrooge and the Cratchits on film occurred in November 1901 with *Christmas Carol – Scrooge: or Marley's Ghost*, a 10-minute film of 12 tableaux. This was followed in 1908 by the Essenay Company's 15-minute *A Christmas Carol* with Thomas Ricketts as Scrooge, and in 1910 by an Edison Company version starring Charles Ogle (who had been the first Frankenstein monster in movie history) as Scrooge. A number of British and American silent versions were made – including the oddly named *The Right to Be Happy*, which was assailed by critics for being a bit too clearly filmed in sunny California – before the first talking *Christmas Carol*, a nine-minute, one-man performance in 1928.

The 1930s saw *A Christmas Carol* attract big-money productions, notably a 1935 English *Scrooge* with Seymour Hicks in the title role, and a Hollywood extravaganza in 1938 starring Reginald Owen. These remained the landmark efforts until 1951, when they were eclipsed by Alastair Sim's definitive portrayal of the miser, against which a number of fine actors have measured themselves and been found wanting.

What followed was a series of attempts to update the approach or to try a novel twist. *Mr. Magoo's Christmas Carol* (1962) and *Mickey's Christmas Carol* (1983) used already popular animated characters in a Dickensian setting, while *A Muppet Christmas Carol* (1992) mixed humans with puppets. Translating the figure of Scrooge to a woman's form seemed a natural step, and so we got the pornographic *Passions of Carol* (1975) and the more earnest *Ebbie* (1995) and *Ms. Scrooge* (1997), all of them, incidentally, set in the United States, as were *An American Christmas Carol* (1979) and *A Carol for Another Christmas* (1964). A musical *Scrooge* in 1970 and *Scrooged*, a dark 1988 comedy set in a modern television station, bracketed the only recent attempt at a traditional portrayal, Clive Donner's 1984 televised version starring George C. Scott and a collection of veteran British actors, including Frank Finlay, Edward Woodward, and Susannah York.

There is clearly life left in Dickens's creation, and the 21st century will doubtless produce many more Scrooges, Ghosts, and Tiny Tims.

A Christmas Carol (1938) Edward L. Marin directed this version of *A Christmas Carol*, starring Reginald Owen as Scrooge. It is a film well-regarded by critics and can still be seen on television over the holiday season, but Owen is much too sprightly to make a convincing Scrooge; there is not much difference in his personality before and after the visitation by the Spirits. Lionel Barrymore, who had won vast audiences with his regular radio portrayals of Scrooge, had been scheduled to play the part in the MGM movie, but the arthritis that would confine him to a wheelchair for the rest of his life kept him from taking the role. Other noteworthy casting choices are blonde starlet Anne Rutherford as the Ghost of Christmas Present (a part usually played by jolly fat men) and future television star June Lockhart as one of the Cratchit children.

A Christmas Carol (1951) They don't get any better than this. Alastair Sim is the definitive Scrooge, and anyone else who attempts the part should be boiled with his own pudding and buried with a stake of holly through his heart. Sim's Scrooge is a grim and shrivelled miser, abject in his petty economies and cruel to those who imagine that generosity is anything but a form of weakness. His experiences at the hands of the Spirits of Christmas are harrowing – this is, after all, a ghost story; they wrench the emotions and lead to changes that redeem the old sinner and lift the hearts of audiences.

Director Brian Desmond-Hurst's settings in foggy and candle-lit London are masterful and the best argument for leaving black-and-white films in their original state. (Avoid the garishly tinted colourized version that appears too frequently on television screens.) This motion picture was titled *Scrooge* in Britain.

Sim and Michael Hordern (Marley's ghost) repeated their roles in a 1972 animated version directed by Chuck Jones and narrated by Michael Redgrave, which won an Oscar for best short animation.

A Christmas Carol (TV) (1954) Directed by Ralph Levy and written by Maxwell Anderson, this was the first attempt at a televised rendition of the Dickens classic.

A Christmas Carol (TV) (1984) It's seldom pleasant watching an American play an English character surrounded by a bevy of superb British actors. George C. Scott as Scrooge tries to overcome his inability to deliver a convincing London accent by incessantly growling his lines. He's no Alastair Sim, but the Shrewsbury setting and the supporting cast make up for it in part.

"A Christmas Carol" A 1935 Charles Ives piece for piano and voice.

Christmas Cat The pet of the ogre Gryla in Icelandic folklore. According to a rather peculiar piece of folk wisdom, those who do not get an item of new clothing for Christmas are liable to be eaten by this monstrous feline. The explanation is that all those who helped get the year's spinning and knitting done would be rewarded with clothing but the lazy would not. The Christmas Cat was therefore an inducement to hard work and co-operation.

Christmas Cherry *Solanum pseudocapiscum*, also known as Jerusalem cherry or Cleveland cherry, bearing orange-red poisonous fruit.

Christmas Club (1) In 19th- and early 20th-century England, Christmas clubs were established in pubs or markets. Working people would contribute their weekly pence and by Christmas would have saved up enough to pay for a holiday feast. Raffle prizes were also associated with the custom. "Goose clubs" provided a goose and a bottle of spirits. "Pudding clubs" provided a way to save for the Christmas pudding.

(2) A term for a number of 19th-century American charities that gathered money to distribute to the poor at Christmas or to provide Christmas meals and gifts.

(3) A 20th-century American custom begun in 1905 when a Pennsylvania shoe manufacturer encouraged workers to set aside a percentage of their salary for Christmas, with the money being returned to them two weeks before the holiday. This practice grew more widespread after 1910 when a ledger salesman, Herbert F. Rawll, looking to increase sales of his product, convinced banks to begin the practice. By the late 1920s, 8,000 banks had set up such savings clubs with 6,000,000 depositors, but the idea fell into disfavour during the Depression. The clubs allowed banks to reach new potential depositors and to disprove their image of heartlessness. They also paid very little, and in many cases no, interest. This was certainly good business for the banks, but it also allowed depositors to "decontaminate" the money from the market economy and dedicate it to Christmas. The idea was revived in the 1960s.

Christmas Comes to Willow Creek (TV) (1987) And it's coming by truck. Fans of the *Dukes of Hazzard* will enjoy seeing John Schneider and Tom Wopat as feuding kinfolk in this snoozer about transporting toys to Alaska.

Christmas Concerto A 17th-century orchestral piece by Arcangelo Corelli, often called Concerto Grosso in G Minor.

Christmas Daisy A variety of aster, *Aster grandiflorus*, which blooms in December.

Christmas Eve The day before Christmas, known variously as the Vigil of Our Lord, *Noche Buena* ("The Good Night" in Spanish), *Wigilia* in Poland, and *Heilig Abend* in Germany. In Eastern Europe it is marked by meatless meals (Advent being a fasting period), and in other countries it is the occasion of heavy feasting and drinking. In Catholic lands many faithful stay up for midnight mass, and in most places children anticipating the arrival of Santa Claus or another gift-bringer find it hard to sleep. In Provence, Christmas Eve is the Day of Reconciliation, when one goes to neighbours to beg or offer forgiveness for wrongdoings during the past year.

It is the most supernaturally powerful of the Twelve Days of Christmas. Animals speak or kneel in homage to the birth of Jesus, bees sing a psalm, etc. (See ANIMALS AND CHRISTMAS.) In Russia and France it was believed that water turned to wine at midnight, while on the isle of Sark this was the time water turned to blood. It was a time for treasure to be revealed, for the Star of Bethlehem to be seen in the WELL OF THE MAGI, and to remember the dead, for on Christmas Eve spirits revisit houses where a place is left for them at the table, or in a bed, or a bath is drawn for them.

"Christmas Eve" A fairy story by Nikolai Gogol (1809-52) about love, the Devil, and a blacksmith, it was the basis of a number of Russian operas: Peter Tchaikovsky's 1876 *Vakula the Smith*; Nikolai Siloviev's 1880 *Christmas Eve*; and Nicolai Rimsky-Korsakov's 1896 *Christmas Eve*.

Christmas Eve *A movie poster for this sentimental 1947 production in which George Raft saves Christmas.*

Christmas Eve (1947) *Sinner's Holiday* was the other title for this loosely knit series of tales about a little old lady whose greedy nephew is out to steal her property. Her only hope is to reconnect on Christmas Eve with the three foster children she helped raise and who are now men with problems of their own: Randolph Scott, an alcoholic cowboy; George Brent, a weakling in the sway of the evil nephew; and George Raft, on the run for a crime he didn't commit.

Christmas Eve (TV) (1986) Loretta Young plays Amanda Kingsley, a dying widow trying to locate her three grandchildren before her greedy son can steal her estate.

Christmas Eve and Easter Day A double poem of 1850 by Robert Browning (1812-89) under a single title. The first section, "Christmas Eve," deals with an attempt to understand which religious denomination might have the best understanding of God.

Christmas Fern *Polystichum arostichoides*, a fern of eastern North America, found as far south as Florida, Texas, and Mexico.

Christmas Fish Dried and salted cod eaten on St. Stephen's Day in Newfoundland. For a long time Catholic families in that Canadian province would eat no meat on December 26, and treasured their recipes for the preparation of the "Christmas Fish."

Christmas Gift A 19th-century American custom prevalent in the antebellum South. When two people met on Christmas Day, the first to shout "Christmas Gift!" merited a present from the other. Slave owners were traditionally expected to

lose this game and provide gifts for their domestic slaves, as parents were expected to lose to their children. The wife of Confederate President Jefferson Davis recalled the Christmas of 1864 in the midst of the Civil War:

> On Christmas morning the children awoke early and came in to see their toys. They were followed by the negro women, who one after another "caught" us by wishing us a merry Christmas before we could say it to them, which gave them a right to a gift. Of course, there was a present for every one, small though it might be, and one who had been born and brought up at our plantation was vocal in her admiration of a gay handkerchief.

In a similar vein, 19th-century Newfoundland children would shout "Christmas Box on you!" and expect a treat in return.

"Christmas Goose" An ode by the Scottish poet William McGonagall (1830-1902), who fancied, in a long and deluded career, that he and Shakespeare were on a par artistically, and whose work has found favour with lovers of things truly dreadful. The last two verses of this holiday ditty are somewhat at odds with the usual spirit of Christmas charity:

> Peggy, it is Christmas time,
> So let us drive dull care away,
> For we have got our Christmas goose,
> So cook it well, I pray.
>
> No matter how the poor are clothed,
> Or if they starve at home,
> We'll drink our wine, and eat our goose,
> Aye and pick it to the bone.

In fairness it must be said that McGonagall does take a more sentimental view of Christmas in another poem entitled "A Christmas Carol."

Christmas His Masque *Playwright Ben Jonson wrote Christmas entertainments for King James I.*

Christmas His Masque A brief dramatic presentation written by Ben Jonson for King James I and played at court on Christmas Day, 1616. It is a politically charged defence of the traditional English Christmas and an attack on Puritans and the government of the City of London, who have slighted the old-fashioned ways. In the masque, Old Christmas defends his Protestant leanings from the accusation that he is a popish innovation and intimates that Londoners have insulted their king and abandoned their national traditions by their Calvinist opposition to mirth and the celebration of Christmas. The 10 children of Old Christmas appear – Mis-Rule, Carol, Minc'd Pie, Gamboll, Post and Paire (a card game), New-Yeares-Gift, Mumming, Wassail, Offering, and Babie-Cake (the Epiphany cake) – all much-loved aspects of the holiday season.

Christmas Holiday (1944)   Despite the presence of Deanna Durbin, this is no light-hearted Christmastime romp. In this *film noir* rendition of Somerset Maugham's dark story, Durbin is a good girl married to a murderous rotter (smoothly played by Gene Kelly). One Christmas Eve she tells her story to a stranger – and then the husband returns. Directed by Robert Siodmak.

Christmas in Connecticut (1945)   Barbara Stanwyck stars as journalist Elizabeth Lane, who has made her reputation as an expert on food and family, a hard-working farm woman with children who still finds time to write advice on home-making. In fact she is a single city girl with no culinary skills whatsoever. Her real identity is in danger of being exposed when her magazine decides that she will entertain a war hero (Dennis Morgan) and her employer (Sidney Greenstreet) for an old-fashioned Christmas. Directed by Peter Godfrey.

Christmas in Connecticut (TV) (1992)   A made-for-television remake of the 1945 classic, starring Dyan Cannon as Elizabeth (in this version the host of a television show), Kris Kristofferson (the war hero's part now having become a heroic forest ranger), Tony Curtis, and Richard Roundtree. Arnold Schwarzenegger chose this as the vehicle for his directorial debut and appears briefly.

Christmas in French Canada   A collection of short stories published in 1899 by the Québécois writer Louis Frechette, all with a Christmasy theme. Some stories, such as "Santa Claus's Violin" and "Jeanette," are variations on the sick-child-at-Christmas theme. Others have the quality of ghost stories told around a fireplace. In "Loup Garou" a werewolf attacks a miller who has the impious notion of operating his business on Christmas Day. In "Christmas Log" a Breton nobleman attempts to interfere with the burning of the Yule log, which has already been consecrated, and he suffers the supernatural consequences. The collection is known in French as *La Noèl au Canada*.

Christmas in July (1940)   Christmas in this Preston Sturges comedy is a metaphor for the good life. Jimmy MacDonald (Dick Powell) is convinced by joking co-workers that he has won $25,000 in a jingle-writing contest and he goes on a spending spree. He proposes marriage, buys gifts for all, and wangles himself a promotion before the truth is revealed. A happy ending? Of course.

Christmas in July   December 25 is the height of summer in Australia. For those Australians who long for a wintry setting for Christmas, a recent custom has been to celebrate the

Christmas Island *Father Christmas travels by frigate bird on this stamp from Christmas Island.*

holiday in June or July by heading into the cool mountains, camping out, and singing carols around a fire.

Christmas Island   An island dependency of Australia, located south of Java, it was named on Christmas Day 1643 by a captain in the service of the British East India Company. The island was annexed by Great Britain in 1888 and was linked politically for a time to Malaya. During the Second World War the island was occupied by the Japanese, but it was transferred to Australian administration in 1958. See GEOGRAPHY AND CHRISTMAS.

The Christmas Kid   In this 1964 movie Jeffrey Hunter plays Joe Novack, a gunfighter with a mysterious past, born on Christmas Eve to a dying woman and raised by kindly townsfolk. He must now choose his destiny in this Spanish-made western also known as *Joe Navidad*. Directed by Sidney Pink.

   Hunter, though handsome enough in a matinee-idol sort of way, died young and never achieved real stardom, coming closest to greatness as Jesus in *King of Kings* (1961) and as the actor first chosen to command the USS *Enterprise* in the original *Star Trek* television series.

Christmas Lilies of the Field (TV) (1979)   Billy Dee Williams plays the Homer Smith role pioneered 16 years earlier by Oscar-winning Sidney Poitier in the original *Lilies of the Field*. Having learned nothing from his previous encounter with nuns, Smith is tricked once again into helping; this time he must build an orphanage and kindergarten. Director Ralph Nelson was nominated for an Academy Award for the original.

Christmas Markets   Open-air markets or fairs selling goods for the Christmas season. The oldest may well be the *Striezelmarkt* in Dresden, which is first mentioned in 1434; carved figurines are a specialty there. The Nuremberg *Christkindlmarkt* dates back to at least 1559, when it was called the Children's Market. Today the Nuremberg market is probably the world's largest, drawing a million visitors each year to its many booths, where one can buy trees, toys, seasonal food such as smoked sausages, marzipan, gingerbread, roast chestnuts, and *Glühwein*, decorations and crafts, all the while being serenaded by carollers or bands. Every year it is opened with great ceremony by Das Christkind, a teenage girl who is chosen to represent the Christ Child. Many other cities in Germany, such as Munich, Bremen, and Hamburg, also have large fairs. Austria holds Christmas markets: Vienna's is in

Christmas Markets *A 19th-century engraving of a German Christmas market.*

front of the town hall, Salzburg's is in front of the cathedral, while in Innsbruck the *Tiroler Heimatwerk* on the Meranerstrasse specializes in hand-carved wooden decorations. In the east of France, Strasbourg and Alsatian towns hold *marchés de Noël*, while in Belgium visitors flock to the markets in Brussels and the medieval section of Bruges. In Copenhagen, Denmark, the fair is held in the Tivoli Gardens, where visitors can drink *glögg* and go ice-skating. Rome's Piazza Navona hosts a market whose highlight is a huge Nativity scene, created each year by a different artist.

Some markets specialize in materials for the family crèche. In Aix and Marseilles, the *Foires aux santons*, fairs offering SANTON figurines for the crèche, have operated since 1803. In Barcelona's Cathedral district, the Christmas market opens every St. Lucia Day and offers Nativity figures as well as cork and other materials to make the backdrops for the crèche. In Central America, where the PESEBRE is an institution, markets in December sell *santero* carvings and coloured sawdust for the scenery.

Jamaican Christmas markets are noteworthy for being held on Christmas Day itself so that children can buy toys and treats.

In recent years in Germany, a new kind of Christmas market has developed, one held after Christmas to divest oneself of unwanted gifts. These swap markets allow disgruntled recipients to pass their hideous or inappropriate gifts along to someone with different tastes.

"A Christmas Memory" A sad little story from 1956 by Truman Capote about a boy and an elderly female friend who save all year to accumulate the money necessary to buy ingredients for the host of Christmas cakes they bake and give away.

The 1966 ABC television version won Emmy awards for Geraldine Page for her role as Sookie and for Truman Capote

and Eleanor Perry for their adaptation of the story for television. Remade in 1997 with Patty Duke.

Christmas Miracle in Caulfield, U.S.A. (TV) (1977) There's trouble at the mine as striking workers are trapped by an underground explosion and must hope for a miracle. Based on a true story.

John Carradine, one of the great voices in Hollywood history and brilliant as the preacher in *The Grapes of Wrath*, plays Grandpa.

Christmas on Division Street (TV) (1991) Rich young Trevor Atwood (Fred Savage, child star of television's *The Wonder Years*) encounters a derelict (the great Canadian actor Hume Cronyn) and together they learn about the value of home, Christmas, and friendship. Directed by George Kaczender.

Christmas Oratorio Johann Sebastian Bach's *Christmas Oratorio*, BWV 248, is one of the undoubted masterpieces of classical music. Written in 1734, it is not an oratorio in the usual baroque sense but rather a set of six cantatas, each 25 to 30 minutes in length, which portray the events of the Nativity, from the birth of Jesus to the arrival of the Magi at the Epiphany. It was not at first performed as a whole, but rather one cantata at a time in Leipzig churches on specific feast days from December 25 to January 6, 1734-35.

"Christmas Phantoms" A Maxim Gorki story about a writer who has blithely continued to write his annual Christmas tales about freezing beggars and orphan children and who is visited by the ghosts of these creations. He insists that his stories were meant to inspire readers to acts of charity, but the phantoms deride his theory; if cruel reality will not move men to kindness, fiction will not work either.

Christmas Seals *Emily Bissell, shown here on a U.S. stamp, helped spread the popularity of Christmas seals in the United States.*

Christmas Pride *Ruellia*, Caribbean and South American perennials, including *R. devosiana*, with its mauve-striped white flowers, *R. graecizans*, with small red flowers, and *R. squarrosa*, with blue blossoms.

Christmas Rose Two flowers go by this name: *Anastatica hierochuntica*, also known as Rose of Jericho, a small annual whose dried leaves and flowers open up when moistened and is thus said to resemble the Virgin Mary's womb; and *Helleborus niger*, or black hellebore, bearing white and green flowers and poisonous roots.

Christmas Seals Stamps whose revenue is directed toward the eradication of tuberculosis. They were invented by Danish postmaster Einar Holbøll and were first printed in 1904 with a portrait of Queen Louise. Jacob Riis, a Danish immigrant who had lost six brothers to TB, took the notion to the United States, where it was popularized in 1907 by Delaware social worker Emily Bissell, who was in need of money to keep a TB clinic alive. She designed her own stamp to raise the funds, and the success led to the National Tuberculosis Association. The familiar symbol of the double-barred cross of Lorraine was chosen in 1919; it had been the sign of Godfrey of Lorraine, a leader of the First Crusade, and thus symbolic of a holy war against a deadly disease. Holbøll died in 1927, knighted and decorated by several kings, having lived long enough to see dozens of countries adopt Christmas seals.

"The Christmas Song" This vision of chestnuts roasting on an open fire and Jack Frost engaged in nose-nipping was written in 1946 by Mel "The Velvet Fog" Tormé (1925-98) and Robert Wells. The most popular rendition was that done by Nat "King" Cole.

A **Christmas Story** (1983) A comedy about a boy's fervent Christmas wish for an air rifle. Not just any air rifle, but a Genuine Red Ryder Carbine Action Two Hundred Shot Lightning Loader Range Model Air Rifle with a Shock-Proof High Adventure Combination Trail Compass and Sundial set in the stock. This 1983 film directed by Bob Clark starred Peter Billingsley as young Ralphie Parker, Darren McGavin as his harried father, and Melinda Dillon as his mother. Narration was provided by novelist Jean Shepherd, who based it on a chapter in his book *In God We Trust – All Others Pay Cash*. It has become a favourite on video and on television during the Christmas season.

The **Christmas That Almost Wasn't** (1966) This is a very peculiar Italian-American musical fantasy directed by veteran actor Rosanno Brazzi, who must have had a bad childhood experience with Christmas. It seems that Santa Claus (Alberto Rabagliatti) is depressed because an evil businessman, Phineas T. Prune (Brazzi himself), has bought the North Pole and will soon evict St. Nick and his elves. In order to pay his back rent, Santa takes a job as a department store Santa Claus but discovers he doesn't relate well to children.

Writer Paul Tripp must share some of the infamy, as it is his book that was the basis of his script. The theme song is sung by Glenn Yarborough of The Limelighters folk group.

The **Christmas Tree** (1969) William Holden plays a rich French father trying to make his radiation-poisoned son's last days enjoyable. Directed by Terence Young and co-starring the lovely Virna Lisi. Also known as *L'Arbre de Noël* and *When Wolves Cry*.

The **Christmas Tree** (TV) (1996) Sally Field, former Flying Nun, adapted and directed this lovely story about an elderly nun (Julie Harris) and the evergreen tree she has loved for years. Based on the book by writer Julie Salamon and illustrator Jill Weber.

"Christmas Tree Suite" *Weihnachtsbaum*, a suite of carols and dances arranged as a piano solo by Franz Liszt, written in 1874-76 and published in 1882. There are 12 movements, some with distinctly Christmas themes, such as "The Shepherds at the Crib" as well as a Hungarian dance and a Polish mazurka. The suite was dedicated to Liszt's granddaughter Daniela.

"Christmas Tree" Virus A computer virus that attacked IBM's 350,000-terminal network in December 1987. Since then a number of computer viruses have been linked by name to Christmas, such as "Japanese Christmas #2" and "Christmas-600," usually because they become active on December 25.

The **Christmas Visitor** (TV) (1987) A very good children's film about Christmas in the Australian outback in the Victorian period by George Miller, the director of the successful *Man From Snowy River*. A family farm suffers from drought; Christmas hopes look dim until a mysterious stranger arrives. Also known as *Bushfire Moon*.

The **Christmas Wife** (TV) (1988) Jason Robards plays John Tanner, a lonely man who hires a companion, Iris (Julie Harris), to spend Christmas with him in the mountains. He falls in love, but his rent-a-wife has a guilty secret. Directed by David Jones and based on a story by Helen Norris.

A Christmas Without Snow (TV) (1980)   Michael Learned (Olivia in *The Waltons*) plays a newly divorced woman in autocratic director John Houseman's choir as he prepares his singers for a Christmas performance of Handel's *Messiah*. Did John Houseman (who played himself in the dire Christmas comedy *Scrooged*) ever play a character who wasn't autocratic?

Christopsomo   Greek Christmas bread sometimes served with a coin in the middle, as in the New Year *Vasilopitta* custom.

Chrysanthemum   A star-shaped flower which, in Christmas legend, was discovered by the Magi as they arrived in Bethlehem and found themselves lost in the dark. When Melchior picked it, the door of the stable opened by itself, revealing the Holy Family.

Chrysostom, St. John   (c. 347-407) Patriarch of Constantinople and supporter of Christmas. He is responsible for introducing the celebration of Christmas into the church at Antioch in the 380s, arguing that it was a feast of great antiquity in the West and that Jesus was born on December 25. In opposition to the pagan celebrations of the Unconquered Sun, he asked, "Who is so unconquered as our Lord?" He believed that the Magi numbered 12.

Church, Francis Pharcellus   (1839-1906) American journalist and defender of Santa Claus. The son of a Baptist clergyman and magazine publisher, Church began his writing career with the *New York Chronicle*, moving on eventually to found several magazines himself, report on the Civil War for the *New York Times*, and join the *New York Sun* in 1874.

In September 1897 the *Sun* received a letter from little Virginia O'Hanlon asking if there really was a Santa Claus. At the behest of editor Edward Mitchell, the childless Frank Church reluctantly took up the challenge and gave the famous reply "Yes, Virginia, there is a Santa Claus," which the newspaper ran each Christmas season until it folded in 1950. Church died in New York in 1906, and it was only then that the *Sun*, which routinely never bylined its editorials, revealed that he had been the author of the piece.

See "YES, VIRGINIA, THERE IS A SANTA CLAUS" and VIRGINIA O'HANLON.

Cipaille   Cipaille, also known as cipâte, is a type of meat pie served in French-Canadian homes on Christmas at the *réveillon* traditionally held after midnight mass. There are many variations on the name of this dish: cipâte, six-pâtes, cipaille, si-paille, and sea-pie. Some believe the word comes from the number of layers of crust used to make the pie (six pâtes). Others say that the word "cipaille" comes from "sea pie," a pastry dish of seafood made by people on the Atlantic coast. Sea pie was transformed to cipaille, then cipâte, when people had left the coast and learned to prepare the dish with poultry and game.

Circumcision, Feast of the   The infant Jesus was circumcised, according to Jewish custom, on the eighth day after his birth. This falls on New Year's Day, which is also the Feast of St. Basil, an important figure in the Christmas celebrations of the Eastern churches.

Clare of Assisi, Saint   (1194-1253) Saint Clare was the companion of medieval Saint Francis of Assisi and the founder of the order of nuns known as the Poor Clares. Her miraculous vision of a Christmas mass being held many miles away led to her being named the patron saint of television.

Coca-Cola and Christmas   In an attempt to encourage the purchase of soft drinks during the winter months, The Coca-Cola Company commissioned artist HADDON SUNDBLOM to portray Santa Claus consuming its product. From 1931 to 1964 these annual advertisements became part of the Christmas landscape in North America and have led some to credit Coca-Cola with creating the image of Santa Claus as he is now known. It would be fairer to say that the Coke ads used a view of Santa (red costume with white fur trim, black boots, and black belt) that had already become standardized in books, advertisements, and movies, but that after these Sundblom paintings had become popular it was impossible to think of the gift-bringer looking any other way.

Cole, Sir Henry   (1808-82) English businessman and patron of the arts. The driving force behind the Great Exhibition of 1851 at the Crystal Palace and the Victoria and Albert Museum, Cole laboured all his life to unite industry and the arts. In 1843 he commissioned JOHN CALCOTT HORSLEY to produce the first printed Christmas cards.

Colombia   Piety, colour, and noise mark Christmas in Colombia. The season begins on December 7 with the celebration of the eve of the Feast of the Immaculate Conception. It is a time for religious processions and for homes and sidewalks to be decorated with candles and lanterns; family and friends spend the night partying. On December 16 the novena begins nine days of prayer and spiritual preparation. During this time families prepare the *pesebre*, or crèche – prizes are offered in many communities for the best representation of the manger scene in Bethlehem – and decorate the home and Christmas tree with lights and garlands. Children go about playing tambourines or maracas and singing Christmas carols, hoping to raise money to buy fireworks.

On Christmas Eve the image of the baby Jesus is placed in the crèche as families gather to eat and dance. Dinner is likely to include chicken, roast pork, salads, *tamales*, corn, and rice cakes. Dessert is sure to include *natilla* custard as well as fruit, cookies, *buñuelos*, and cakes. Though the North American Santa Claus is increasingly common as gift-bringer, the Colombian tradition is for the Christ Child, El Niño, to put the presents under the tree on Christmas Eve. (In Barranquilla, in the northern part of the country, gifts are placed under the children's beds.) At midnight the country erupts in noisy celebration, as fireworks explode, guns are fired, and sparklers lit. In the Cali area, a Christmas tradition (despite the danger and illegality of the practice) is the construction of *globos*, hot air balloons up to 5 feet in diameter fuelled by burning gas-soaked rags and released into the sky.

From Christmas Day until the New Year, Colombians indulge in a round of festivals, including bull fights, concerts, beauty pageants, and horse shows. The season ends on Epiphany, when children receive more small gifts and the family *pesebre* is taken down.

Conference, The Christmas   The meeting held in Baltimore in 1784 among American followers of John Wesley which resulted in the formation of the Methodist Episcopal Church, separate from the Church of England.

Consumerism   Modern critics of the season have vociferously protested the excessive consumerism involved in the celebration of Christmas (see OPPOSITION TO CHRISTMAS). It may be some comfort to such well-meaning folk to learn that their criticisms are nothing new. Listen to the fourth-century pagan sophist Libanius on the December holiday of Saturnalia: "The impulse to spend seizes everyone. He who the whole year through has taken pleasure in saving and piling up his money becomes suddenly extravagant."

In fact the very psychology of a midwinter festival demands consumption in excess; it is the time of year when short days are countered by a flourish of candles and lights and when the barrenness of the earth is offset by decorations with greenery and by conspicuous feasting. The Christian Middle Ages marked Christmas with the consumption of food and drink in great quantities. In 1213 King John of England ordered 3,000 capons, 1,000 salted eels, 400 hogs, 100 pounds of almonds, and 24 casks of wine for his Christmas festivities. This sort of excess eventually helped lead to the abolition of Christmas under the PURITANS, but the people's love of holiday consumption outlasted such reforms. Christmas came back and festive dissipation came with it. In 1861 the Reverend J.P. Gardiner, in a northern Canadian trading post, noted that 105 gallons of rum and brandy had been consumed during one week by the fort's 50 inhabitants.

With the Industrial Revolution came a shift in Christmas consumerism; riotous eating and drinking gave way to expending wealth on manufactured presents, especially for children. Merchants were quick to urge that Christmas was the time to express sentiment by spending money and relaxing accustomed economic restraints. Social historians have pointed out that this nakedly commercial appeal was disguised as an expression of family values and the elevation of childhood as a time of privilege. The 19th-century middle class may have realized this; certainly they were aware of the moral ambiguities and dangers of celebrating the Nativity in acts of consumerism, and mitigated them to some extent by ensuring that Christmas was also a time of CHARITY and generosity to those outside the family circle.

These ethical tensions remained throughout the 20th cen-

Consumerism *For centuries Christmas has meant indulgence and consumerism.*

tury, leading to reform movements (see SOCIETY TO CURTAIL RIDICULOUS, OUTRAGEOUS AND OSTENTATIOUS GIFT EXCHANGES) and widespread annual misgivings. The American writer Bill McKibben noted, "Christmas is a school for consumerism – in it we learn to equate delight with materialism. We celebrate the birth of the One who told us to give everything to the poor by giving each other motorized tie racks." Nonetheless there are ironies: social historians have detected that religious resistance to the commercialization of Christmas has itself become a consumer product. Bumper stickers and coffee mugs reading "Put Christ Back Into Christmas" and "Jesus is the Reason for the Season" are big sellers in Christian bookstores.

A British study in 1999 claimed that Christmas shopping could damage men's health and that peak stress levels for men in crowded shops reached levels experienced by fighter pilots or police going into dangerous situations. The same study found that stress in women was less when they took their children shopping than when they took their partners. The psychologist who conducted the research said, "I urge women to listen to their partners this year and consider the long-term benefits of not forcing them to help. Not only will their men be less stressed at Christmas, but they will be too."

Costa Rica   A visitor to Costa Rica around the beginning of December would note that it was beginning to look a lot like Christmas; lights are hung on houses and in windows, Santa decorations appear, store displays urge consumption, and Christmas carols are played on the radio. The law mandating that employers pay an "AGUINALDO" to their employees at the beginning of December means working Costa Ricans have one-twelfth of a year's pay in their pockets with which to enjoy the holidays.

An important part of the preparation for Christmas is the assembly of the *portal*, or crèche, to which many Costa Rican families devote much effort. Some examples of these manger scenes are quite large, often occupying a whole room in the house. The figures of Mary and Joseph are placed there first, and the baby Jesus is laid in his manger only on Christmas Eve. Pious families gather around the crèche and say prayers, after which they may temporarily cover the scene so that they might party and dance.

On Christmas Eve El Niño brings presents for the children (though, as in many Latin American countries, the Christ Child is being gradually displaced as the gift-bringer by Santa Claus), fireworks light up the sky, and people feast. Essential to the meal are *tamales* – made of corn dough, mashed potatoes, chicken, and pork wrapped in plantain leaves and boiled – accompanied by eggnog, local alcoholic punches, and rum.

The Christmas season is a time for parades, such as the Festival of Lights, bull runs (the Costa Rican equivalent of bull fights), fairs, choral festivals, dance festivals, and rodeos. It all ends on February 2, CANDLEMAS, when processions of candle-holding believers honour the Virgin.

"The Coventry Carol"   The Shearmen and Tailors' Guild of Coventry took part in the famous cycle of mystery plays staged annually in the late-medieval period at the feast of Corpus Christi. The Bible stories they were responsible for portraying included the Annunciation, the Nativity, the Adoration of the Magi, and the Massacre of the Innocents. It is the latter tale for which the song known as "The Coventry Carol" was written, sung in the pageant by women of Bethlehem trying to keep their children quiet lest their crying betray them to the murderous soldiers of King Herod.

Christmas Cracker *This 1847 depiction in the* Illustrated London News *of an explosive Christmas cracker was probably the first ever published.*

Robert Croo appears to have written at least part of the play in 1534, and the 16th-century music was edited by Thomas Sharp in 1825.

> Lullay, Thou little tiny Child,
> By, by, lully, lullay.
> Lullay, Thou little tiny Child,
> By, by, lully, lullay.
>
> O sisters too, how may we do,
> For to preserve this day?
> This poor youngling for whom we sing,
> "By, by, lully, lullay."
>
> Herod the king, in his raging,
> Charged he hath this day.
> His men of might, in his own sight,
> All young children to slay.
>
> That woe is me, poor child for Thee!
> And ever mourn and say,
> For thy parting neither say nor sing,
> "By, by, lully, lullay."

Cowboys' Christmas Ball An annual dance, first put on by M.G. Rhodes at his Morning Star Hotel in Anson, Texas, in 1885 to entertain the cowboys who patronized the establishment. The original hotel burned down early in the 20th century, but the custom has grown so popular that it is now held for several nights in a row, with hundreds attending in the required traditional western dress. The ball begins with a Grand March led by a newly wed couple in honour of a cowboy and his bride who attended the dance early in its history. See DANCING AND CHRISTMAS.

Cracker, Christmas A Christmas novelty popular in Britain and countries of the Commonwealth. A Christmas cracker takes the form of a small cardboard tube covered in decorative wrap and containing a strip of chemically impregnated paper which, when pulled, creates a miniature explosive snap. When opened, the cracker reveals a paper hat, a motto or joke, and a small prize.

The cracker was invented in 1847 by a London confectioner named Tom Smith. The idea began with the *bon bon*, a French candy in a twist of paper. To this Smith added a small motto and then conceived the idea of incorporating the noise made when throwing a log on a crackling fire. After much experiment Smith came up with the right chemical formula and the cracker was born. He soon discarded the candy and

began to call his invention "*cosaques*," after the crack of the Cossack whip.

Since the 1840s the Christmas cracker has contained mottos humorous, romantic, artistic, and puzzling, with prizes ranging from inexpensive plastic toys to decorated boxes to real musical instruments and expensive jewellery, with special lines prepared annually for the British royal family. It is now an indispensable part of Christmas dinner in millions of homes around the world.

Cradle-rocking To honour the presentation of the baby Jesus in the Temple, a ceremony is held at Blidworth, England, on the Sunday nearest CANDLEMAS. The male baby most recently baptized is placed in an antique rocking cradle decorated with flowers and greenery. The child is blessed, and the priest rocks him for a few moments in the cradle before restoring him to his parents. The service ends with the singing of the *Nunc dimittis*, "Now lettest thou thy servant depart in peace," which are the words of Simeon, who encountered the Holy Family at the Temple (Luke 2:25-35).

This ceremony is thought to have been performed at Blidworth during the Middle Ages, but was suppressed by the Protestant Reformation in the 16th century. Its revival dates from 1923.

For a German variation on cradle-rocking, see KINDELWIEGEN.

Crèche A representation of the Nativity scene with manger and attendant figures such as the Holy Family, Magi, shepherds, and animals.

The earliest-known depiction of the Nativity dates from about 380 A.D. in the burial chamber of a Christian family in Rome's St. Sebastian's Catacombs, though there are indications from the fourth century that a crèche had been placed in the church in front of the spot where the priest delivered his homily. Certainly there was a jewelled image of the Virgin and Child in the Church of Santa Maria Maggiore in the eighth century – the pope would celebrate Christmas mass here in the Middle Ages with the crèche functioning as an altar. By the 11th century the liturgical drama "*Officium Pastorum*" required a crèche as a prop. To this manger scene came five cantors representing the shepherds seeking the baby Jesus; they were met by two priests, who asked them in song who they sought. The drama ends with the shepherds kneeling beside the manger.

It was ST. FRANCIS OF ASSISI who popularized the use of the crib, when on Christmas Eve in 1223 he restaged the original

Bethlehem scene at Greccio, complete with a peasant family laying a baby in the hay of the manger, surrounded by a real ox, ass, and shepherds. A medieval biography of Francis recounts:

> The manger is ready, hay is brought, the ox and ass are led in. Simplicity is honoured there, poverty is exalted, humility is commended and a new Bethlehem, as it were, is made from Greccio. Night is illuminated like the day, delighting men and beasts. The people come and joyfully celebrate the new mystery. The forest resounds with voices and the rocks respond to their rejoicing. The brothers sing, discharging their debt of praise to the Lord, and the whole night echoes with jubilation. The holy man of God stands before the manger full of sighs, consumed by devotion and filled with a marvelous joy. The solemnities of the mass are performed over the manger and the priest experiences a new consolation.

St. Francis's intention was to emphasize the humanity of the Nativity and make the miracle real to his illiterate audience. It succeeded brilliantly. Before long the crèche was an institution across Europe, and since the late Middle Ages a crèche has been displayed in Catholic churches all around the world. In 1953, worried that the spread of the Christmas tree (originally of Protestant origin) was supplanting the crèche in Catholic homes, Pope Pius XII began an institution to promote the crib, an association that has grown internationally.

The crèche is known variously as the *presepio*, *pesebre*, *portal*, or *Kripp*. These scenes can be simple homemade efforts or vastly expensive collections assembled over centuries and taking up several rooms in a museum or palace. It is of particular importance in the Christmas devotions of Latin America, but it has its supporters everywhere. The Franciscan church of Ara Coeli in Rome possesses one of the largest and most beautiful crèches in the world; this crib hosts the famous jewelled BAMBINO carved from wood from the Mount of Olives. The Church of Santa Maria Maggiore claims to possess pieces of the original Bethlehem crib – five wooden slats of sycamore brought from the Holy Land in the seventh century, which are exposed on the high altar every Christmas Eve.

Cricket on the Hearth   Dickens's third Christmas book, published in December 1845, *The Cricket on the Hearth* has scarcely any of the supernatural apparatus that underlies *A Christmas Carol* and *The Chimes*. The cheery spirits of a resident insect and the house fairies pale beside the mighty ghosts in the first two books, but they are enough to bring about reconciliation and conversion in the tangled affairs of a carrier and his wife, an old toymaker and his blind daughter, a mysterious stranger, an unwelcome suitor, and an unwilling bride.

Cripples Go Christmas (1989)   In *Das Mädchen mit den Feuerzeugen* ("The Girl With the Cigarette Lighter"), director Ralf Huettner produced an unusual holiday story – a film about four paraplegics who escape from their group home to spend Christmas Eve in a fancy München restaurant. There they encounter a bit of magic in the form of a cigarette girl and are granted three wishes: motorized wheelchairs, women, and a third wish that takes them on an adventure.

Croatia   Christmas in Croatia is a fascinating blend of ancient Eastern and Western European customs with modern North American accretions. This can be seen early in the season: where once Croatian children would have expected to receive

their gifts on December 6 at the hands of St. Nicholas, for whom well-polished shoes are put out, or on December 13 from St. Lucy (depending on the part of the country in which they lived), many now look to Christmas Eve and the arrival of Santa Claus.

As Christmas approaches preparations are laid. Baking is done; the house is decorated with greenery. On St. Lucy's Day Croatians plant wheat grains in a plate and wait for them to germinate. The green shoots are then bound with a red-white-and-blue ribbon with a candle in the middle. In some regions a floating wick substitutes for the candle, its flame representing the soul.

In rural areas men go to the woods on Christmas Eve at dawn to fetch the *badnjak*, or Yule log, and drag it home, where it is wreathed in garlands and received with great ceremony, passing through rows of candles and sprinkled with corn and wine. After it is lit with a remnant of the previous year's log, it is struck sharply to produce sparks as wishes are made for the family's prosperity in the coming year. Later in the day the Christmas tree is decorated, often with red hearts made of baked dough, and straw is laid under the tablecloth. On the table are placed candles, Christmas bread, and bowls of fruit and nuts as well as bottles of wine and brandy. The evening meal on December 24 is traditionally meatless, and in coastal areas consists of dried cod, smelt, or sardines. During supper Santa Claus (or the baby Jesus) arrives secretly at some homes and puts presents under the tree, ringing a bell as he leaves so that the children can rush in and open their gifts. In other places he comes in the night after the family has returned from midnight mass, and children discover the results of his visit on Christmas morning. (During the Communist regime, religion was discouraged and gift-giving was shifted to New Year's, when presents were said to be brought by Grandfather Frost.)

Christmas Day is a time for family and feasting. The main meal is based on turkey, suckling pig, or Dalmatian pot roast with stuffed cabbage and noodles. Desserts include cookies, fritters, walnut and poppy seed rolls, plus the essential fruit bread. Some families place a candle in a loaf of braided bread and use it as a centrepiece for the table, where it will remain until January 6. On Epiphany Christmas officially ends; the braided bread is cut and eaten, the tree and ornaments are taken down, and a priest visits to bless the home.

Crosby, Bing   (1904-77) Pop singer and actor whose renditions of seasonal music have made him a part of American Christmas culture. He sang "White Christmas" in *Holiday Inn*, *Blue Skies*, and *White Christmas*; "Silent Night" in *Going My Way*; "Adeste Fideles" in *The Bells of St. Mary's*; "It Came Upon the Midnight Clear" in *High Times*, and "The Secret of Christmas" in *Say One for Me*.

Cross-dressing and Christmas   A clear signal that social inversion is in effect and that festive misrule and licence will be tolerated is for one sex to assume the dress of another. This has its origins in the Roman feast of Saturnalia held in late December, and continued after the Christianization of Europe. Numerous edicts exist from the Middle Ages in which authorities decry transvestism at Christmas among the lower clergy and in popular folk customs. In 1445 the Paris Faculty of Theology complained, "Priests and clerks may be seen wearing masks and monstrous visages at the hours of office. They dance in the choir dressed as women, panders, or minstrels." The Staffordshire Horn Dance has a cross-dressing cast member called Maid Marian, while GUISING on the

Scottish borders provides comic relief with the figure of Bessie the Besom, a man dressed as an old woman. In Newfoundland MUMMING, each sex participates dressed as the other, with young women disguised as sailors and men known as "ownshooks" clad as women. In Nova Scotia the females who went BELSNICKLING dressed as Wise Men were called Kris Kringles.

Cuba   Before the imposition of Fidel Castro's Communist regime, Christmas in Cuba was celebrated in a typically colourful Latin American Catholic way. Nativity scenes decorated homes, processions honoured the Virgin, and families went to midnight mass. Seasonal foods included roast pork, *congrí* rice, yucca, plantains, and black beans, with nougat, *buñuelos*, marzipan, and fruits for dessert. Gifts came to children at Epiphany from the Three Kings, who were in return left tobacco, grass for the camels, and coffee beans to sustain them on their journey to Bethlehem.

In 1969 the government abolished the Christmas holiday, ostensibly not to deprive the economy of a working day during the sugar cane harvest, but really as part of a drive against religious observances in general. Festivities and gift-giving were moved to a new "Children's Day" in July. However in 1998, in honour of the visit of Pope John Paul II, the regime reintroduced a Christmas holiday. While tens of thousands flocked to midnight mass, many treated December 25 as just another day off work. The future of Christmas in Cuba remains uncertain.

Currier and Ives   A New York publishing firm whose lithographic prints achieved widespread popularity from 1857 to 1907. As purveyors of "Colored Engravings for the People," they chronicled every aspect of social life in 19th-century America. Their portrayal of winter scenes made their name synonymous with an old-fashioned Christmas. (See colour fig. 4.)

Cyprian, St.   (d. 258) Bishop of Carthage and martyr who calculated that December 25 was the date of Nativity and who, noting that this was (according to his calendar) the winter solstice, said, "How wonderfully acted Divine Providence that on the day that the Sun was born – Christ should be born."

The Czech Republic   Christmas in the Czech Republic used to get underway with two saints' days, though they are not now much observed: St. Andrew's Day on November 30, which was a great time of prognostication and fortune-telling, and December 4, St. Barbara's Day, when cherry twigs were taken indoors to see if they would bloom before Christmas.

Nowadays it is December 5, the eve of St. Nicholas's Day, which sees the beginning of Christmas activities. The saint himself, Mikulaç, as he is known in the Czech Republic, appears in bishop's robes accompanied by an angel and a devil.

Mickulaç quizzes children on their behaviour, whereupon the angel hands out treats to the good kids while the devil rattles his chains and rewards the bad with lumps of coal.

Advent preparations are not just spiritual. They also include a thorough house-cleaning before the decorations and greenery are put up. Children write letters to the baby Jesus telling him their wishes, and their parents scour the Christmas markets and department stores. Baking takes much of the month, with the *vánocka*, braided Christmas bread, being an essential part of the preparations. The tree is bought and left untrimmed until Christmas Eve, and finally there is the acquisition of the carp.

In late October fishermen hold the carp harvest, dragging tons of the fish live out of lakes and ponds and transporting them to holding tanks, where the fish will purge themselves over a period of weeks of the muddy taste that comes of their bottom-feeding existence. From the middle of December, carp are available for sale on the streets of the Czech Republic; they can be killed and cleaned on the spot, but most are taken home to live in the bathtub so that the flesh is as fresh as possible for the Christmas Eve meal. The carp's scales are said to bring good luck.

On Christmas Eve the tree is decorated – the fashion is for ornaments to be natural, such as apples, gingerbread, and real candles – preferably out of sight of the children, and presents and a Nativity scene are placed under it. Then it is time for the traditional meatless dinner: perhaps a fish soup to begin with, certainly followed by deep-fried carp, potato salad, and dumplings, with strudels, vanilla rolls, cake, and cookies for dessert.

After dinner a bell is rung to signal that the baby Jesus has come and left gifts. (The Soviet-imposed gift bringer, Grandfather Frost, was swept away with the fall of Communism.) The tree and presents are revealed to the children, and all sit down to unwrap their gifts. The rest of the evening is spent singing carols, watching television, and perhaps going to a midnight mass.

Both December 25 and 26 are national holidays, "Big Christmas" and "Little Christmas." Christmas is a family day, with relatives dropping by to visit and share the desserts. December 26 used to be a day for carolling and begging visits in the rural areas, but is now a day for attending concerts, skating parties, skiing trips, or viewing the elaborate crèche in Prague's old town square.

Attending a New Year's Eve party, called a *Silvestr* after the saint whose day it is, is very common. The Christmas season ends on January 6 with Epiphany. Groups of boys go door-to-door dressed as the Three Kings (one will have his face blackened in honour of Balthazar) and sing carols. In the countryside many cling to the custom of chalking the initials of the Magi (K+M+B) on the doors of barns and houses.

Daidí na Nollag Father Christmas in Ireland.

Dancing and Christmas People have been inspired to dance in celebration of Christmas for a long time, judging by the numerous prohibitions issued against it by Church authorities through the centuries. Dancing in churches was prohibited by the Council at Toledo in 590; in 692 another council in Byzantium warned against dancing during the Twelve Nights, as did the Faculty of Theology in Paris in 1445 – and in both cases they linked dancing to cross-dressing. In 16th-century Iceland, Church decrees were issued against dancing on Yule Eve, and in Scotland in 1574 14 women were arrested for "playing, dancing, and singing filthy carols on Yule Day." Despite these strictures Christmas and dancing continue to be linked.

In 1325, Church authorities in Paris forbade clerics under pain of excommunication from participating in dances *except* at Christmas and the feasts of Saint Nicholas and Saint Catherine, when certain round dances were part of the liturgy. Nowadays, in Spain, the "Dance of the Six" in the cathedral of Seville opens the Christmas season; in front of the altar, 10 boys dance through a series of postures and movements that symbolize the mysteries of the Incarnation and Nativity. (In a rather less solemn manner in Cordoba, other Spaniards engage in *El baile de los locos*, "The Dance of the Madmen." Led by El Loco Mayor, the chief madman, a mob of folk pretending to be demented dance through people's houses. Dancing opens the Christmas season in Honduras as well; the Warini, the Christmas Herald, is a masked dancer who goes from house to house accompanied by singers and drummers. In Lalibela, Ethiopia, Christmas Day ceremonies include a dance by some of the priests who have accompanied the procession of the Coptic Ark of the Covenant. The *Matachine* dancers perform during Christmas in Mexico, while in Canada numerous aboriginal tribes hold competitive powwows. In Tirol men dressed as bears dance in the streets, while in northeastern Brazil the *Bumba Meu-Boi* involves dancers guised as bulls and donkeys. In Scotland "guisers" went door-to-door dancing and singing; in Cornwall such folk were called "geese dancers."

In Provence, at special Christmas services to honour their profession and its connection to the original Nativity, traditionally clad shepherds and shepherdesses sing and dance behind a ram pulling a cart with a lamb. Scandinavian families link hands on Christmas Eve and dance around the tree singing carols. In the United States there are few cities without a ballet company who will perform *The Nutcracker* over the Christmas holidays, while in the rural west of the country those with a yen to dance can attend the Texas Cowboys' Christmas Ball or the Sheepherders' Overall Dance. (See colour fig. 5.)

The Dangerous Christmas of Red Riding Hood (TV) (1965) A November ABC TV musical special with Liza Minnelli as Lillian Hood, Cyril Ritchard as Lone T. Wolf, Vic Damone, and the English rock group The Animals.

Dating Christmas Despite the fact that the Western world reckons its dates "Anno Domini" fashion, based on an ancient computation that the year of the Nativity was the 31st of the reign of Caesar Augustus, no one now supposes that Jesus was actually born in the year 1 A.D. The sixth-century estimate by the monk Dionysius Exiguus has long been known to be off by several years, and the date of the first Christmas has remained a matter of debate for almost 2,000 years.

Christian scriptures give a number of clues to those seeking to establish a date. Luke tells us that Jesus was born when Caesar Augustus ruled in Rome, when Publius Sulpicius Quirinius was governor of Syria, and when an empire-wide census was decreed. Matthew notes that this occurred during the reign of Herod the Great in Judaea, and also tells us that Eastern Magi had followed a star to find the baby. Unfortunately these statements immediately cause confusion. Herod is said to have died in 4 B.C., and Quirinius was governor in Syria only in 6 A.D., 10 years after that. Moreover there is doubt over whether Joseph, a Jew of Nazareth, would have been forced to take part in a census of Roman citizens.

Some historians have concluded from this that the New Testament accounts of the Nativity are untrustworthy. Others have tried to harmonize these seemingly contradictory facts by allowing Herod to rule two years longer, positing a temporary period of deputy governorship for Quirinius while his superior was away in Rome, and explaining the enforced registration as the oath of loyalty known to have been conducted on the occasion of the 25th anniversary of Caesar receiving the title of Augustus. This, they claim, would allow a date of late 3 B.C. for the birth of Jesus. (This accords with the consensus of early Christian theologians, such as Clement of Alexandria, that 2 or 3 B.C. was the most likely date for the Nativity.)

The notion of a census being an enforced demonstration of loyalty to the Roman regime has been buttressed by scholars using an alternative reading of Luke 2:15. Based on a medieval gospel harmony using second-century texts, their version now reads, "At that time Caesar Augustus ordered that all men should come to their own town and bring the governor a silver coin as a sign of subjection to the empire." Disturbances in Palestine in the year 3 B.C., they say, might have prompted this.

But what of the star: can astronomical records help us here? Though different kinds of astral phenomena have been examined as candidates for the STAR OF BETHLEHEM – planetary conjunctions, comets, astrologically significant planetary movements, and novae – none so far is conclusive. Some that have attracted attention are: a comet (or nova) noted by the Chinese in 5 B.C.; a retrograde motion by Jupiter in 5 B.C.; a conjunction of Venus and Jupiter in August 3 B.C. and June 2 B.C.; a conjunction of Jupiter with Regulus in Leo; a retrograde loop by Jupiter in 2 B.C. in which it appeared to be stationary on December 25.

If the year of the Nativity remains problematic, is there any evidence as to the day that Jesus was born? The present date of December 25 is recognized by all Christians except the Armenian Church, which has clung to January 6 (January 18 on the Gregorian calendar) since the fourth century. But December 25 has problems with it as well, chiefly that it was not until over 300 years after Christ's birth that the Church used that day to celebrate the Nativity.

The earliest semi-official notice of December 25 as the anniversary of the Nativity is a document called the Philocalian calendar of 354, which may refer back to circumstances in 336. Scholars are not certain that Christmas was ever marked before that date. Celebrating birthdays was uncommon in the ancient world, except perhaps for emperors and other rulers, and even then the exact date was not considered important. Christians were more likely to note the death-date of a martyr as his entrance into heaven – a new birthday in a way. There was no pre-existing Jewish ceremony that was parallel to Christmas as Passover was to Easter or Pentecost. Early Christians were more concerned with Christ's return than details of his earthly birth; only two gospels even mention the Nativity. Finally, January 6, Epiphany, already had a birth component to it – the baptism of Jesus.

So the evidence of Christmas as a pre-fourth century celebration is slight. There are a couple of references that may have been placed in sources after the fact: one document speaks of a group of believers in the late third century who when found to be celebrating the Nativity were massacred; the early Church in Gaul was said in another source to have fixed a date in December.

But this doesn't mean that Christians weren't curious about the date, particularly when Gnostic heretics began denying that Jesus had a mortal birth at all. By the second century, Christian writers were debating the date. Clement of Alexandria (c. 190) picked December 18, but he also thought it might be November 17; Hippolytus (c. 202) was the first to pick December 25; Julius Africanus (221) agreed with that estimate; an African tract on calculating Easter said December 28; Eastern theologians were keen on January 6; and a wide variety of other dates, especially in the spring, were also advanced.

When the persecutions of Christianity stopped after 313 and it became legal to practise their religion openly, the Christian leadership in Rome chose to fix on December 25 as the date of the Feast of the Nativity. It is often said that this was an arbitrary date chosen to pre-empt pagan celebrations and the cult of the Unconquered Sun, and there is some reason to think that this played a part in the decision. Late December was a time of festivals in Rome: Saturnalia on December 17 to 24; Sol Invictus on December 25; the Kalends on January 1. Though the December 25 celebrations were not grand, they were highly symbolic for imperial sun-god worship. Placing Christmas on December 25 would co-opt the day for Christian sun symbolism and also allow Christians to worship under the cover of general pagan festivities.

However, as we have seen, December 25 had been suggested as the date of the Nativity long before the emperor Aurelian chose that day, in 273, to celebrate the sun god. The chief reason for this was a series of symbolic calculations. Theologians believed that the Earth had been created on March 25 (the beginning of spring) and that it was fitting that the Annunciation had taken place on that day as well; nine months of pregnancy would then yield December 25 as the birthdate of Jesus. Other theologians posited March 25 as the date of the crucifixion; its mirror image was again the Annunciation on that date with the Nativity nine months later. Still others, using solar imagery, noted that Jesus as the Messiah was the Sun of Justice and his birthday should logically be at the rebirth of the sun – the winter solstice, or December 25 according to their calendar.

Once December 25 had been chosen in Rome, it was necessary to convince other churches of the rightness of the choice. The Western churches had no difficulty with the date, but in the East many were reluctant to abandon January 6, Epiphany. They were persuaded, in part, by claims that the date was of long standing in Spain and Gaul and also by the claim (almost certainly untrue) that Rome possessed a copy of Joseph's census records which indicated that he had registered in Bethlehem on December 25. It was not until early in the 400s when that date became nearly universal.

December 25 Events

273 – Establishment of Roman imperial cult of Sol Invictus
336 – Earliest recorded celebration of Christmas in Rome
354 – Pope Liberius makes December 25 the official date of Christmas
379 – Christmas observed in Constantinople
386 – Christmas inaugurated in Antioch over much objection
390 – Ambrose, bishop of Milan, forces Emperor Theodosius I to do penance for Thessalonican massacre
395 – St. Augustine celebrates first Christmas as Bishop of Hippo
425 – Theodosius II forbids circus games on Christmas
428 – Nestorius, bishop of Constantinople, preaches against use of term "Theotokos" as applicable to Mary
438 – Emperor Theodosius II issues the Theodosian Code
496 – Baptism of Clovis and 3,000 Franks
529 – Emperor Justinian makes Christmas a civic holiday
537 – Hagia Sophia church dedicated in Constantinople
567 – Beginning of the "Twelve Days of Christmas" as decreed by Council of Tours
597 – Augustine of Canterbury baptizes thousands of Saxons in Kent
598 – England adopts the Julian calendar
604 – Burgundians defeat Neustrians at Etampes
634 – Sophronius, Patriarch of Jerusalem, warns of Islamic menace
780 – Charlemagne and family pause in Pavia on way to Rome

December 25, 597 *Saint Augustine of Canterbury baptizes King Ethelbert in this British stamp.*

December 25, 1100 *Baldwin of Edessa is crowned king of Jerusalem.*

786 – Charlemagne spends Christmas in Florence on way to Rome

795 – Pope Hadrian I dies

800 – Pope Leo III crowns Charlemagne emperor in Rome

820 – Leo the Armenian, Byzantine Emperor, murdered in Hagia Sophia church

858 – Photius crowned as Patriarch of Constantinople

875 – Charles the Bald crowned Emperor by Pope John VIII

877 – English servants begin 12-day Christmas holiday ordered by law code of Alfred the Great

878 – Alfred the Great celebrates Christmas at Chippenham but will be surprised by Danish attack

961 – King Edgar of England celebrates Christmas with great splendour at York

967 – Otto II crowned Holy Roman Emperor by Pope John XIII

969 – Johannes I Tzimisces crowned Byzantine emperor

983 – Otto III crowned German king at Aachen, age three

989 – Empress Theophano celebrates Christmas in newly subdued Rome

995 – Christmas observed for first time in Norway by King Olaf

999 – Heribertus becomes bishop of Cologne

1000 – St. Stephen crowned king of Hungary

1003 – John Phasanus named Pope John XVII

1013 – King Ethelred of England keeps Christmas in London while besieged by Danes

1016 – Edward the Confessor begins his exile from England

1017 – Eadric, Earl of Mercia, slain by King Canute

1021 – English bishop Elfgar, "the abundant giver of alms," dies

1038 – *Cristes maessan* ("Christmas") first used in *Anglo-Saxon Chronicle* to refer to December 25

1042 – Gebhard, later Pope Victor II, presented as candidate for bishopric of Eichstatt

1046 – Suidger crowned as Pope Clement II; Henry III crowned as Holy Roman Emperor in Rome by Clement II

1048 – Bruno van Egisheim elected Pope Leo IX; Emperor Henry III attends at Diet of Worms

1050 – German nobles swear fidelity and allegiance to Henry III and his infant son Henry

1053 – Edward the Confessor orders Welsh prince Rhys put to death

1056 – Pope Victor II attends at Diet of Ratisbon; Peter Venerabilis, French theologian and abbot of Cluny, dies

1057 – Pope Stephen IX orders monks of Monte Cassino to choose a new abbot

1059 – Malcolm of Scotland spends Christmas with Edward the Confessor

1062 – Earl Harold raids Rhuddlan

1065 – Consecration of Westminster Abbey

1066 – Coronation of William I, "the Conqueror" of England

1069 – William I spends Christmas in York after devastating the north of England

1075 – Pope Gregory VII kidnapped in middle of mass; German princes swear to uphold the succession rights of Conrad, son of Henry IV

1084 – Emperor Henry IV captures Rome from Pope Gregory VII

1085 – William I holds court at Gloucester and decides on Domesday Book

1089 – Anti-pope Guibert celebrates Christmas in Rome while Pope Urban II anathematizes him from outside the city

1094 – King William II of England receives envoys from Duke Robert of Normandy

1095 – St. Anselm, Archbishop of Canterbury, stops at monastery of Cluny on way to Rome to protest against King William II

1099 – Arnulf of Rohea is superseded as Latin patriarch of Jerusalem by papal legate Daimbert

1100 – Baldwin of Edessa crowned king of Jerusalem in Bethlehem

1111 – English King Henry I "bare not his crown at Christmas"

1115 – Henry I in Normandy to persuade nobles to do homage to Prince William

1116 – Henry I at St. Alban's for consecration of abbey

1120 – St. Norbert of Xanten founds Premonstratensian order; Henry I in mourning for the loss of the White Ship and the death of his son William

1121 – Strong windstorm shakes England

1123 – Henry I receives Angevin embassy at Dunstable

1124 – Henry I summons English mint-men to Windsor to be mutilated in punishment for debasing the coinage

1127 – King David of Scotland, "and all the head men that were in England, learned and lewd," assemble in Windsor to swear allegiance to Matilda as Henry I's successor

1130 – Anti-pope Anacletus crowns Roger II King of Sicily

1131 – *Anglo-Saxon Chronicle* uses "Cristemesse" for first time as one word

1154 – Henry II of England spends Christmas at Bermondsey and orders foreign mercenaries expelled

1156 – Peter Venerabilis, abbot of Cluny, dies

1158 – Henry II, spending Christmas at Worcester, removes his crown, places it on an altar, and never wears it again

1161 – Byzantine Emperor Manuel marries Mary, daughter of the prince of Antioch

1170 – Archbishop Thomas Becket preaches in Canterbury Cathedral and prophesies his own murder (he is killed four days later)

1171 – Henry II spends Christmas in Ireland and persuades reluctant Irish guests to feast on crane

1176 – Welsh prince Rhys ap Gruffudd holds the first *eisteddfod* at Cardigan Castle

1183 – Peter de Marcy holds controversial Christmas mass in Glastonbury Abbey

1190 – Richard I (the Lionheart) of England on way to Crusade holds tournament in Sicily

1191 – French king Philip Augustus returns to Paris from Third Crusade

1194 – Emperor Henry VI crowned King of Sicily in Palermo

1202 – King John of England spends Christmas at Caen "faring sumptuously every day and prolonging his morning slumbers until dinner time"

1213 – King John provided with 3,000 capons, 1,000 salted eels, 400 hogs, 100 pounds of almonds, and 24 casks of wine for his Christmas feasting

1214 – King John spends Christmas alone at Worcester while English barons discuss the list of demands they will present to him

1223 – St. Francis of Assisi assembles first live Nativity crèche at Greccio, Italy

1236 – Henry III of England receives a live elephant as Christmas gift from St. Louis, King of France

1239 – Henry III opens a hall of Windsor Castle to feed and clothe the poor

1241 – Henry III angers nobility by giving papal legate best seat at Christmas banquet

1248 – Henry III feasts thousands of poor at Westminster Hall

1249 – Saint Peter Nolasco, Spanish monastery founder, dies; forces of the Seventh Crusade attacked by Turks at Damietta

1252 – Henry III entertains 1,000 knights and nobles at York – 600 oxen are consumed; King Alexander of Scotland marries Henry's daughter Margaret

1277 – Edward I of England entertains Welsh prince Llewellyn at Kenilworth

1281 – Viciously cold weather in England, with "such a frost and snow as no man living could remember the like"

1282 – German King Rudolf of Habsburg invests sons Albert I and Rudolf II with Austria and Styria

1283 – Edward I feeds 500 London beggars

1286 – Edward I keeps Christmas at Oxford, where he will order the hanging of the mayor

1289 – Bishop of Hereford orders boar's head as centrepiece for Christmas feast

1290 – Edward I mourns death of wife in a monastic retreat

1299 – Thousands of pilgrims flood Rome, causing Pope Boniface VIII to proclaim a jubilee

1306 – Jacopone da Todi, Franciscan monk and carol writer, dies

1311 – Edward II spends Christmas with his favourite, Piers Gaveston, despite the order of exile against him

1317 – Few English nobles attend Edward II's Christmas at Westminster because of "discord betwixt them and the king"

1326 – Edward II spends Christmas as a prisoner of his rebellious nobles at Kenilworth

1328 – Emperor Louis the Bavarian spends Christmas in Trent

1347 – Edward III introduces mumming into royal English Christmas entertainments

1348 – Edward III of England orders 80 masks, mantles with embroidered dragons, and tunics decorated with head and wings of peacocks for Christmas mumming

1357 – Geoffrey Chaucer and John of Gaunt spend Christmas at Countess of Ulster's manor

December 25, 1377 *A royal banquet from around the time of Richard II.*

1358 – Edward III entertains the kings of France and Scotland as his prisoners

1375 – Bernese militia defeats French raiders at Jens

1377 – In England, Richard II's Christmas feast consumes 300 sheep and 28 oxen

1386 – Richard II entertains King Leon of Armenia

1389 – Paris crowds welcome Queen Isabel of Bavaria with shouts of "*Noël!*"

1392 – Richard II and Queen Anne hold court at Langley; a dolphin "came foorth of the Sea and played himselfe in the Thames at London to the bridge"

1396 – French court receives news of defeat of crusaders at Nicopolis

1398 – Richard II keeps Christmas at Westminster, where daily jousts are held

1400 – Henry IV keeps Christmas at Eltham, where 12 aldermen of London and their sons ride in a mumming for the entertainment of the king and the visiting Byzantine emperor

1406 – Castille's Enrique III (El Doliente, the Sufferer) dies at age 27

1413 – Lollard plot to capture King Henry V fails

1414 – Emperor Sigismund arrives at the Council of Constance and demands the release of John Hus

1415 – Henry V of England orders food distributed to citizens of Rouen trapped by his siege; he himself dines on roast porpoise garnished with figures of angels

1418 – Lollard rebel Lord Cobham executed in London

1420 – Henry V spends Christmas in Paris with Queen Katherine, the king of France, and the duke of Burgundy

December 25, 1414 *Despite Emperor Sigismund's demands, reformer John Hus is burnt by the Council of Constance.*

1421 – Henry V besieges Meaux

1426 – During feast for Queen Katherine, the Earl of Worcester rides his horse indoors to keep order

1428 – Henry VI of England pays £4 for Jack Travail and his company of actors for seasonal entertainment; the French and English armies declare a Christmas truce at the siege of Orléans

1429 – Joan of Arc spends Christmas at Jargeau

1430 – Joan of Arc imprisoned in a tower at Rouen

1436 – King James I of Scotland spends Christmas with monks of Perth; en route he hears prophecy of his imminent death (he is assassinated in February 1437)

1454 – Henry VI recovers from a long illness

1461 – A law of Edward IV of England permits card-playing and dice games at Christmas

1482 – Edward IV entertains 2,000 at Eltham Palace

1483 – Henry, Earl of Richmond (later Henry VII), swears to marry Elizabeth of York when he wins English throne

1484 – Richard III spends 200 marks on Christmas presents

1489 – Henry VII and English court spend Christmas at Greenwich, because "ther wer the Meazellis 500 strong" in London; no disguisings and few plays but an active Abbot of Misrule

1492 – Christopher Columbus's ship *Santa Maria* runs aground on Hispaniola and has to be abandoned

1496 – James IV of Scotland receives money from his treasurer with which to play cards

1497 – Vasco da Gama sights African east coast and names it Natal

1499 – Christopher Columbus writes complaining about his enemies and his fate

1502 – Portuguese court entertained by Vicente's *Castillian Pastoral Play*

1509 – Henry VIII marks first Christmas as king with three plays and a concert

1512 – Henry VIII keeps Christmas at Greenwich, "where was such abundance of viands served to all comers of anie honest behaviour, as hath beene few times seene"; the Duke of Northumberland is served five swans for Christmas dinner

1513 – Johannes Amerbach, Swiss publisher/printer, dies

1515 – Francis I of France spends Christmas in newly conquered Milan

1519 – Magellan's expedition renews supplies on the Brazilian coast; Alessandro Farnese, later Paul III, says first mass

December 25, 1512 *Henry VIII of England keeps Christmas at Greenwich in great splendour.*

1520 – Spanish conquistador Hernan Cortes begins his march on the Aztec capital, Tenochtitlan

1521 – Protestant reformer Andreas von Carlstadt shocks Wittenberg by performing mass in German

1522 – Turks invade Rhodes

1525 – Francis I of France spends Christmas in captivity in Madrid

1526 – Plague rages in London, causing Henry VIII and court to keep a quiet Christmas

1527 – First play performed at London's Inns of Court lands authors in trouble with authorities

1529 – Henry VIII spends Christmas at Greenwich designing a new palace at Whitehall

1530 – Babur the Tiger, Mughal emperor of India, dies

1535 – Jacques Cartier and crew celebrate first Christmas in Canada at Stadacona

1538 – First Christmas mass in Mexico, celebrated by Fray Pedro de Gante; Saint Ignatius Loyola, founder of the Society of Jesus, celebrates first mass

1539 – Bad weather keeps Ann of Cleves, future bride of Henry VIII, from leaving Calais for England

1540 – Coronado expedition to American interior spends Christmas in winter camp near present-day Albuquerque, New Mexico

1542 – Ruy Lopez de Villalobos on voyage from Spain to Spice Islands reaches Marshall Islands

1543 – Henry VIII feasts 23 captured Scottish nobles and releases them without ransom

1551 – Edward VI postpones the execution of the Duke of Somerset

1552 – Jesuits celebrate first Christmas mass in Japan; Charles V besieges Metz

1557 – Princess Elizabeth, no longer under suspicion of treason, spends Christmas with English Queen Mary at Hampton Court

1558 – Queen Elizabeth I walks out of mass when bishop refuses her demand to omit elevating the Host

1559 – Gian Angelo Medici crowned Pope Pius IV

1561 – London Inns of Court stage political drama *Gorbuduc*

1564 – Abraham Bloemaert, Dutch painter, born; a "hard frost" in England; the Thames freezes over

1565 – Miguel Lopez de Legazpi celebrates first Christmas in the Philippines

1568 – Plague in London forces Queen Elizabeth I to spend Christmas at Hampton Court; Spanish Moriscos rise against government of Philip II

1580 – The Christmas hospitality of Sir William Petrie requires 17 oxen, 14 steers, 5 hogs, 13 bucks, 29 calves, 54 lambs, 129 sheep, and one ton of cheese

1582 – Parts of the Netherlands accept the Gregorian calendar

1583 – Glasgow churchmen forbid Christmas observances; English composer Orlando Gibbons baptized

1585 – Francis Drake's fleet spends Christmas on St. Christopher's Island in the Caribbean to "refresh our sick people and cleanse and air our ship"

1588 – Haddington, Scotland, presbytery forbids singing of carols

1589 – English gentry spend Christmas on their estates "to keep hospitality among their neighbours," by order of Queen Elizabeth I

1594 – Fugger agent reports uproar in Silesia over eruption of a mountain and the rising of the dead

1599 – Founding of Natal, Brazil

1601 – Ernest I, Duke of Saxe-Gotha-Altenburg, born; Jose Ximenez, composer, born

1603 – Mohammed III, Turkish emperor, dies of plague

1604 – French settlers on islands off Maine observe first American Christmas

1605 – Lancelot Andrewes preaches the first of 17 Nativity sermons for King James I of England

1607 – King James ignores custom and demands a play for Christmas evening; he knights Robert Carr, his favourite, and makes him a Gentleman of the Bedchamber

1608 – John Smith of Jamestown colony boasts of finer food and more warmth in Virginia than at home in England

1611 – Settlers and natives battle in Virginia

1613 – Johan Sigismund of Brandenburg converts to Protestantism

1615 – King James languishes in bed with gout

1616 – Ben Jonson's *Christmas His Masque* performed for King James I; Englishman Nathaniel Couthorpe begins attempt to end Dutch nutmeg monopoly in Spice Islands

1619 – Lancelot Andrewes, bishop of Winchester, preaches on the use of Christmas carols in the home and anthems in the church

1620 – Mayflower colonists ignore festivities and build their first common house; Jens Eriksen Munk manages to return to Copenhagen with only two surviving crew members after horrifying winter ordeal in Hudson Bay

1621 – Game playing on Christmas Day is banned in Plymouth colony by Governor William Bradford; King James vows on his sword to aid the distressed Queen of Bohemia

1622 – Bishop Lancelot Andrewes preaches before King James I on the journey of the Magi

1624 – Dutch traders go ashore on Manhattan island

1625 – Jules Mazarin, later Cardinal, undergoes a mystical experience

1626 – Duke of Buckingham complains that sailors in English fleet neglect their duties in order to attend Christmas revels

1630 – John Milton is inspired to write his poem "On the Morning of Christ's Nativity" as a "birthday gift to Christ"

1631 – Gustavus Adolphus's Swedish army reaches Mainz in the Thirty Years' War

1633 – Maryland-bound passengers on board the *Ark* die of drinking spoiled Christmas wine; Jacques Hertel becomes the first settler at Three Rivers, Quebec

1635 – French explorer Samuel de Champlain dies in Quebec City

1640 – Pierre de Fermat writes to philosopher Marin Mersenne

1642 – Isaac Newton born; the settlement of Montreal in New France is hit by floods

1643 – Saint Isaac Jogues (Jesuit, later martyred) reaches France after captivity by Iroquois; Hudson River Valley natives are massacred by the Dutch when they seek refuge from the Mohawk; Christmas Island named by Captain William Mynors of the British East India Company

1644 – English Parliament meets on Christmas Day to set example for neglecting seasonal celebrations

1645 – Fire breaks out in the chapel at Quebec

1646 – London mobs abuse merchants who remain open on Christmas Day

1647 – English Parliament declares Christmas a day of penance, not feasting; London shops are closed, but lord mayor's men ride about burning evergreen decorations

1648 – Riots break out in Canterbury over attempts to suppress Christmas; King Charles I spends his last Christmas under guard at Windsor Castle

1651 – Massachusetts General Court ordered a fine of five shillings for "observing any such day as Christmas"

1656 – English members of Parliament complain that too many of their countrymen are observing Christmas

1657 – Puritan troops raid English churches holding Christmas services; diarist John Evelyn is among those detained for questioning

1660 – Christmas celebrated openly again in England; Samuel Pepys falls asleep during "a dull sermon by a stranger"

1661 – Samuel Pepys quarrels with his wife and dines with William Penn, father of founder of Pennsylvania

1662 – Pepys attends service where courtiers laugh at the sermon preached against their behaviour; later he sends out for a mince pie, a dish that his wife was too ill to make herself

1664 – Pepys's wife is still bedridden from the beating he gave her – he admires "a very fine store of fine women" in church; Heinrich Schütz's *Christmas Oratorio* performed in Dresden

1665 – Pepys attends a wedding and finds it strange "to see what delight we married people have to see these poor fools decoyed into our position"; Lady Grizel Baillie, Scottish poet, born; Charles II spends Christmas at Oxford to avoid the plague in London.

1667 – Pepys watches the queen take Christmas mass – on the way home "round the City . . . stopped and dropped money at five or six places, which I was the willinger to do, it being Christmas"; Kateri Tekakwitha, Iroquois mystic, has her first communion at the church in Kahnawake, Quebec

1676 – Sir Matthew Hale, English chief justice and law reformer, dies

1678 – Huron converts perform a Christmas play at Michilimackinac

1681 – Massachusetts General Court revokes laws against celebration of Christmas

1683 – English rebel Duke of Monmouth flees to Netherlands; Kara Mustapha, Turkish vizier, executed; Spanish expedition under Juan Dominguez de Mendoza crosses the Rio Grande river and plants a "holy cross" on Texas soil

1686 – Governor of Massachusetts requires escort of soldiers to get to Christmas service; John Evelyn attends Whitehall Palace chapel to listen to the singing of "a Eunuch"

1688 – Expelled English King James II lands in France

1689 – French expedition under de la Salle celebrates Christmas in Texas

1690 – Scotland celebrates Christmas officially for the last time until 1958

1697 – Russian Czar Peter the Great spends Christmas in England close to Deptford dockyards, where he studies shipbuilding

1698 – Jacobus Houbraken, Dutch engraver, born

1706 – Boston mob smashes windows of a church celebrating Christmas

1711 – Jean-Joseph Cassenea de Mondonville, composer, born

1712 – Puritan preacher Cotton Mather lashes out at Christmas excesses; William King, English poet, dies

1714 – George I of England tastes his first Christmas pudding, made with five pounds of suet and a pound of plums

1716 – Johann Jakob Reiske, German scholar of Arabic, born

1717 – Giovanni a Braschi (Pius VI) born; floods ravage Netherlands, killing thousands

1721 – William Collins, lyric poet, born

1728 – Johann Adam Hiller, German composer and conductor, born

1730 – The Great Frost of London begins, temperatures reach minus 17 degrees Fahrenheit

1734 – J.S. Bach's "Christmas Oratorio" first performed at Leipzig, with Bach conducting

1737 – John Wesley, founder of Methodism, sails from Georgia for England

1741 – Swedish astronomer Anders Celsius invents Centigrade temperature scale

1742 – David Garrick stars in the play *Fop's Fortune* in London

1745 – Treaty of Dresden between Prussia and Austria lets Prussia keep Silesia

1747 – The Hudson's Bay Company supervisor at Moose Factory reads to his hard-drinking employees from a book the company had sent "as a Diswasive from the Sin of Drunkenness"

1750 – John "Christmas" Beckwith, English composer, born; Ohio Company explorer George Gist and his dog spend Christmas at the trading post of George Croghan

1752 – Thousands gather in England to see whether a remnant of the Glastonbury Thorn will bloom, and when it does not, all conclude that December 25 New Style (after Gregorian calendar reform) is not "the right Christmas Day"; Philip Embury, one of the founders of Methodism in the United States, is converted

1754 – Edward Gibbon re-admitted to Protestant communion

1758 – Sixteen years after Edmund Halley's death, his prediction of return of Halley's Comet comes true

1759 – Christmas hymns sung for first time in Boston's Old North Church; Richard Porson, English classicist, born

1760 – Jupiter Hammon, New York slave and first black American poet, publishes "An Evening Thought: Salvation by Christ, with Penitential Cries"

1761 – Empress Elizabeth of Russia dies

1762 – Thomas Jefferson writes John Page to complain about his troubles; James Boswell discusses modern poetry with Oliver Goldsmith

1763 – Claude Chappe, French engineer, born; James Boswell takes first Anglican communion in English ambassador's chapel at The Hague

1764 – Foundation of the Royal Society of Friends of the Basque Country

1765 – Antonio Tonelli, composer, born

1766 – Tobias Smollett spends Christmas at Bath, where he begins *The Expedition of Humphrey Clinker*

1769 – The crew of Captain Cook's *Endeavour* celebrates Christmas in the Pacific with a goose pie and "all hands as drunk as our forefathers used to be upon like occasion"; first Christmas mass celebrated in Upper California

1770 – Samuel Hearne's expedition in northwest Canada traversing "empty, barren ground, on empty bellies"

1771 – Dorothy Wordsworth, sister of William, born

1772 – First recorded celebration of Christmas by New England Baptists

1773 – Ottoman sultan Mustapha III dies; Massachusetts Assembly petitions the English Crown for removal of Governor Thomas Hutchinson

1774 – English officer in Boston notes that the only thing done to observe Christmas is the execution of a soldier for desertion

1775 – Pius VI issues encyclical "Inscrutabile" on problems of pontificate

1776 – Washington crosses Delaware to attack Hessians in Trenton, New Jersey; Captain Cook's expedition spends Christmas on Kerguelen Island in Indian Ocean

1777 – Washington and men spend a cold Christmas at Valley Forge

1779 – George Washington writes to Thomas Jefferson with news of a British fleet

1780 – Nashville, Tennessee, founded

1783 – Washington, just retired as commander-in-chief, spends Christmas at Mount Vernon

1787 – Alexander Hamilton issues Federal Paper no. 27 on states and defence

1788 – John Logan, Scottish conductor, dies; first Christmas celebrated in Australia in Sydney Cove

1789 – Washington and wife worship at St. Paul's church in Manhattan

1791 – Constitutional Act divides province of Quebec into Upper and Lower Canada

1793 – Boston police forbid "the Anticks," groups involved in boisterous Christmas celebrations; in France, where the Revolution has abolished Christian holidays, December 25 is Décade I, Quintidi de Nivôse de l'Année II de la Révolution

1794 – Reverend James Woodforde suffers epileptic fit just before administering communion

1797 – Pope Pius VII praises democracy

1798 – George Washington writes to the Marquis de Lafayette on the state of politics in the United States and on relations with France

1799 – Napoleonic Constitution of the Year VIII issued

1800 – First English Christmas tree erected at Queen's Lodge by Queen Charlotte; French police scour Paris for those responsible for assassination attempt on Napoleon

1804 – Lewis and Clark expedition at its winter camp in North Dakota fires three cannons and drinks rum in celebration of Christmas

1805 – The khanate of Shirvan is included in the Russian Empire; American explorer Zebulon Pike gives his men "two pounds extra of meat, two pounds extra of flour, one gill of whiskey, and some tobacco, to each man, in order to distinguish Christmas Day"

1809 – First successful operation for ovarian cancer performed in Kentucky

1810 – Bare-knuckles prize-fight in London – champion Tom Cribb defeats American challenger Tom Molineaux in the 39th round

1811 – Wilhelm Emmanuel Kettler, German social reformer and clergyman, born

1814 – Jan de Liefde II, Dutch reformer, born; English missionary Samuel Marsden preaches first Christian sermon in New Zealand

1815 – Temistocle Solera, composer, born

1818 – Clara Barton, founder of American Red Cross, born; "Silent Night" sung for first time in Oberndorf, Austria

1820 – Joseph Fouché, Napoleonic police minister, dies

1822 – London police arrest street musicians for performing on Christmas Day

1823 – Preston Smith, Confederate general, born

1824 – Barbara Krudener, mystic visionary who renounced nobility, dies

1825 – Pope Leo XII encyclical "Charitate Christi" extends jubilee of 1825

1826 – First performance of American Christmas carol "Shout the Glad Tidings" by William Augustus Mühlenberg; West Point cleans up after "Grog Mutiny" or "Eggnog Riot" – 70 cadets will be court-martialled

1829 – Heinrich Schliemann receives a history book as a child that he later says inspired him to seek Troy

1830 – Premiere of Berlioz's *Symphonie Fantastique*; the locomotive *Best Friend of Charleston* begins first regularly scheduled passenger train service in the United States

1831 – Charles Darwin spends Christmas at Plymouth before setting out on H.M.S. *Beagle*

1832 – Charles Darwin spends Christmas at Wigwam Cove, Tierra del Fuego; Ralph Waldo Emerson sails from Boston for the Mediterranean; John Henry Newman writes "Christmas Without Christ"

1833 – Charles Darwin spends Christmas at Port Desire in Patagonia

1834 – Charles Darwin spends Christmas "at anchor in a wild harbour in the peninsula of Tres Montes"; Texan separatist Stephen F. Austin released from prison in Mexico City

1835 – Charles Darwin spends Christmas in New Zealand, goes to chapel of Pahia; Texan separatists hold meetings to promote independence from Mexico

1836 – Princess Victoria receives two Dresden china dolls on the last Christmas before she becomes queen; Alabama becomes first U.S. state to recognize Christmas as a legal holiday; Sam Houston's Texan rebels celebrate Christmas at Washington-on-the-Bravos

1837 – Cosima Liszt, wife of Wagner, born; Seminole Indian force defeated by American troops at Battle of Okeechobee; *Mirror of Liberty*, pioneer African-American magazine, published in New York City by abolitionist David Ruggles

1838 – Arkansas and Louisiana recognize Christmas as holiday

1842 – Texan irregulars raid town of Mier and battle Mexican army; Anglo-British Treaty of Nanking first to be reproduced photographically

1843 – First New York theatre matinée

1845 – Fremont expedition to California dines on one of their pack mules

1846 – Missouri Mounted Volunteers defeat Mexicans at the battle of Brazito

1847 – English poorhouses granted extra funds for Christmas dinners

1848 – Artist Paul Kane dines on moose nose and beaver tails at Fort Edmonton on Canadian frontier; Johann Erik Nordblom, composer, dies

1849 – Mormon leader Brigham Young entertains 150 in the new Utah settlement

1850 – Taiping rebels defeat an Imperial Chinese force and rescue leader Hong Xiuquan; Isabella Valancy Crawford, Canadian poet, born

1851 – English royal family dines for first time on turkey instead of swan

1852 – The Christmas baron of beef served cold to the English royal family weighs 446 pounds

1853 – Clipper ship *Great Republic* ravaged by fire in New York harbour

1855 – Earliest recorded ice hockey game in Canada at Kingston, Ontario; James Galvin, American baseball pitcher, born

1856 – King Kamehameha IV of Hawaii orders both Christmas and Thanksgiving to be celebrated on December 25

1859 – Raoul Gunsbourg, composer, born

1860 – American Major Anderson's Union forces evacuate Fort Moulton; barque *George Henry*, part of expedition to discover fate of Franklin expedition, is trapped in Arctic ice – local Inuit Tookoolito is given a Bible for a Christmas present by the captain, Charles Francis Hall

1861 – Robert E. Lee writes his wife about fears for their house; President Lincoln meets with Cabinet and entertains at a White House dinner

1862 – John Hunt Morgan leads Kentucky raid in U.S. Civil War; crowd of 40,000 watch Union soldiers play baseball at Hilton Head, South Carolina; President and Mrs. Lincoln visit hospitals in the Washington, D.C., area; Sherman's Federal troops spend the day tearing up the Vicksburg, Shreveport, and Texas Railroad; Christmas a holiday in Hawaii by order of King Kamehameha IV

1863 – Charles Pathé, French filmmaker, born; Federal forces bombard Charleston, South Carolina

1864 – First Christmas Day swim in the Serpentine in Hyde Park; Federals abandon first attack on Fort Fisher, North Carolina

1865 – Evangeline Cory Booth, Salvation Army general, born; Chicago's Union Stock Yards opens

1866 – First transatlantic yacht race won by the American *Henrietta*, which sails into Cowes, Isle of Wight; Georgia governor John Slaton, born

1867 – Christmas a holiday in Canada for federal workers

1868 – Linus Yale, locksmith, dies; Chang Ping-lin, Chinese revolutionary and Confucian scholar, born; President Andrew Johnson grants an unconditional pardon to all who took part in the 1861-65 rebellion

1869 – Friedrich Nietzsche spends Christmas with Richard and Cosima Wagner

1870 – Helena Rubinstein, cosmetician, born; Paris starves in 98th day of its siege; German polar expedition trapped in Greenland ice

1871 – Bank Holiday Act makes Boxing Day a day of rest in U.K.; Alexander Scriabin, composer who thought he was God, born; first steam locomotive in Austin, Texas

1872 – William Conklin, American silent movie actor, born

1874 – First Christmas window, a doll collection at R.H. Macy & Co.; Charles Caldwell, black state senator, assassinated in Clinton, Mississippi

1875 – Walter Lees, English cricketer, born; Nietzsche suffers physical collapse; Thomas Morris, English golfer, dies

1876 – Mohammed Ali Jinnah, founder of Pakistan, born

1878 – Louis Chevrolet, automobile designer and racer, born; Francis Kilvert presides over burial of "little Davie"

1879 – Grace George, American actress, born

1880 – French actress Sara Bernhardt stranded by snowstorm in Urania, Michigan

1881 – Joseph V. McCarthy, American baseball manager, born

1883 – Maurice Utrillo, French painter, born

1884 – Evelyn Nesbit, "The Girl on the Velvet Swing," born; Samuel Berger, American Olympic boxing champion, born

1885 – U.S. federal workers get first Christmas holiday by order of President Arthur; Paul Manship, American sculptor, born

1886 – Franz Rosenzweig, German-Jewish religious existentialist, born; Kid Ory, trombonist, born

1887 – Conrad Hilton, hotel magnate, born; Maxim Gorky attempts suicide

1888 – First indoor baseball game played, Philadelphia fairgrounds; Pope Leo XIII "Exeunte Iam Anno," On the Right Ordering of Christian Life

1889 – Lila Bell Acheson Wallace, Canadian philanthropist and editor, born

1890 – Hugo Bolander, Swedish filmmaker, born

1891 – Clarrie Grimmett, Australian leg-spinner, born; Alex Thomas, Canadian native writer, born

1892 – Rebecca West, English author, born; John Sparrow David Thompson sworn in as Prime Minister of Canada

1893 – Belle Baker, American vaudevillian, born; Bert Bertram, Australian-American actor and writer, born

1894 – University of Chicago becomes first Midwestern football team to play on west coast as it defeats Stanford 24-4 at Palo Alto; San Francisco's Cliff House Hotel destroyed by fire

1895 – Raul d'Avila Pompeia, Brazilian writer, dies

1896 – John Philip Sousa writes "The Stars and Stripes Forever"

1897 – Noël Delberghe, French Olympic water polo player, born

1898 – Pope Leo XIII, "Quum Diuturnum" on the Latin American bishops' Plenary Council; British Imperial penny postage introduced

1899 – Humphrey Bogart born; Elliott Coues, American naturalist, dies; George O'Brien murders three men in Yukon Gold Rush

1900 – Barton Maclane, American actor, born; Polish mathematician Antoni Zygmund, born

1901 – Battle at Tweefontein Orange-Free State: Boers surprise attack British; Princess Alice, Duchess of Gloucester, born

1902 – Pope Leo XIII endorses European Christian Democratic movement as alternative to socialism

1903 – J. Edward Bromberg, actor, born; first Peter Pan Cup swimming race in Hyde Park

1904 – Gerald Herzberg, awarded 1971 Nobel Prize for Chemistry, born; Upton Sinclair begins to write *The Jungle*

1905 – Lewis Allen, American director, born

1906 – Lew Grade, entertainment mogul, born; race riots in Mississippi kill 12 blacks, two whites; Ernst Ruska invents electron microscope

1907 – Cab Calloway, jazz singer, born; Andrew Cruikshank, Scottish actor (*Dr. Finlay's Casebook*), born

1908 – Quentin Crisp, author, born; actress Helen Twelvetrees (née Helen Jurgens), born; American Jack Johnson KOs Canadian Tommy Burns in Sydney, Australia, to become first black to win heavyweight boxing championship

1909 – Shohei Ooka, Japanese novelist, dies; Mike Mazurki, American actor, born

1910 – David Lichine (Lichtenstein), Russian/US dancer, born; dynamite attack on strike-bound Llewellyn iron works in Los Angeles

1911 – Noel Langley, American screen/scriptwriter, co-wrote *Wizard of Oz*, born; premiere of *Kismet*, by Edward Knoblock; Sun Yat-sen returns to China to lead revolution against the Manchu dynasty

1912 – Italy invades Albania; Donald McRae, New Zealand cricketer, born

1913 – Mieczyslaw Moczar, Polish Communist leader, born; Tony Martin, singer, born

1914 – Allies end 10-day attack on German trenches; one million casualties for each side after five months of war; RNAS float planes attack a Zeppelin base in northern Germany; widespread fraternization and unofficial truces on western front

1915 – Nora Dunfee, actress, born; far less fraternization or truce-making along western front

1916 – Daniel Devoto, composer, born; Baron Noel Annan, English scholar and vice-chancellor of University of London, born

1917 – *Why Marry?*, by Jesse Lynch Williams, first play to win Pulitzer prize, opens; independence declared by Ukrainian People's Republic

1918 – Anwar Sadat, Egyptian president, born; Ahmed Ben Bella, Algerian leader, born

1919 – IWW begins organizing in Chile

1920 – Artur Agostinho, Portuguese actor, born

1921 – Steve Allen born; Eugene Debs released from sedition sentence in prison by Harding

1922 – Mohammed Aziz Lahbabi, Moroccan writer, born; Lenin dictates his "Political Testament"

1923 – Louis Lane, American conductor, born

1924 – Rod Serling born; Moktar Ould Daddah, Mauritania's first president, born

1925 – American Admiral Latimer disarms Nicaraguan insurgents; Carlos Castenada, mystic, born

1926 – Hirohito becomes emperor of Japan; Kenhiro Takayanagi of Japan successfully transmits a 40-line electronic television picture

1927 – Nellie Fox, baseball player, born; Mexico opens land to foreign investors; anarchists attack bank in Buenos Aires

1928 – Dick Miller, American character actor whose first credited role was Tall Tree (native wearing hat), born

1929 – Irish McCalla, actress (Sheena Queen of the Jungle), born; Ginger Rogers debuts on Broadway in *Top Speed*

1930 – Robert Joffrey, born; *Charley's Aunt* released

1931 – Metropolitan Opera broadcasts an entire opera over radio for the first time; "Hansel & Gretel," by Engelbert Humperdinck, featuring Lawrence Tibbett, heard on NBC; Pope Pius XI, "LUX VERITATIS" on the 1500th anniversary of the Council of Ephesus

1932 – Mabel King, American actress, born; King George V makes the first royal broadcast to the peoples of the British Empire

1933 – Franco Pastorino, Italian actor, born

1934 – John Ashley, American actor, born

1935 – Movie version of *A Tale of Two Cities*, starring Ronald Colman, premieres; rock-and-roll pioneer Little Richard born Richard Penniman; Paul Borget, French poet and critic, dies

1936 – Chiang Kai-Shek released from captivity by warlord Chang Hsueh-liang; 82 anti-fascists board S.S. *Normandie* for Spanish Civil War; Belgian bishops condemn communism and fascism

1937 – Arturo Toscanini conducts first Symphony of the Air on NBC radio; O'Kelly Isley (The Isley Brothers), born; first Christmas broadcast by George VI

1938 – George Cukor announces Vivien Leigh will play Scarlett O'Hara in *Gone With the Wind*; Karel Capek, Czech writer who coined the word "robot," dies; Hitchcock's *The Lady Vanishes* is released

1939 – *Wizard of Oz* is released; Finnish troops enter U.S.S.R.

1940 – Phil Spector born; *The Thief of Baghdad* released; First Canadian Corps organized in England under General A.G.L. McNaughton

1941 – Japanese take Hong Kong and Wake Island; Free French take St Pierre-Miquelon; Pius XII defends neutrality of small states

1942 – Russians at Stalingrad unleash tank attack on Germans, who are eating the last of their horsemeat; Pius XII Christmas message on human rights; Françoise Durr, French tennis player, born

1943 – Eduard Benes calls for increased Slovakian resistance to Nazis; U.S. President Franklin D. Roosevelt warns American public during a fireside chat that World War II will soon turn bloody for America; Hedley Howarth, New Zealand cricketer, born

1944 – Red Army reaches Budapest; Americans secure Leyte; Churchill visits Greece to seek halt to civil unrest; Canadian Army captures Adriatic coast city of Ravenna

1945 – Gary Sandy, American actor, born; Noel Redding (Jimi Hendrix Experience), born

1946 – W.C. Fields dies; Larry Csonka born; Chiang Kai-Shek offers China new constitution with universal suffrage; Jimmy Buffet, American songwriter, born

1947 – Connie Petracek, American Olympic swimmer, born

1948 – Barbara Mandrell born; Bulgarian Communist party outlaws anarchists

1949 – Sissy Spacek born; Cary Grant marries Betsy Blake

1950 – Stone of Scone is stolen from Westminster Abbey by Scottish nationalists; American general Matthew Bunker Ridgway takes command of retreating UN forces in Korea; "One Hour in Wonderland," Walt Disney's first TV show, airs

1951 – Florida NAACP secretary Harry Moore and wife, Harriet, killed by bomb in their house; first Christmas Day play in Test Cricket; West Indies defeat Australia at Adelaide

1952 – Police hunt Mau Mau terrorists in Kenya; *Captains Courageous* released in U.S.; *Jungle Jim in the Forbidden Land* released in Finland

1953 – New Zealand Ruapahu volcano erupts, killing 150; Pope Pius XII praises technological progress as a gift from God

1954 – Annie Lennox, Scottish pop singer, born; The Penguins release "Earth Angel"; Johnny Ace, rock star, dies

1955 – Pius XII encyclical *Musicae sacrae disciplina* on sacred music

1956 – Home of Rev. F.L. Shuttlesworth, Birmingham protest leader, destroyed by bomb; *Old Yeller* opens in theatres; Robert Walser, Swiss writer, dies; Mansoor Akhtar, Pakistani cricketer, born

1957 – Frederick Law Olmsted, U.S. architect, dies; Shane MacGowan, pop singer, born

1958 – Rickey Henderson born; Alan Freed's Christmas Rock and Roll Spectacular opens in New York, featuring Bo Diddley, Chuck Berry, and Jackie Wilson; Scotland celebrates Christmas officially for first time since 1690

1959 – Richard Starkey (Ringo Starr) receives first drum set for Christmas; Sony introduces a transistor television set

1960 – Amy Grant, American pop singer, born; Mary Wells makes her debut on the R&B chart with "Bye Bye Baby"

1961 – Rheinbold Rudenberg, physicist, dies; Otto Loewi, German Nobel Prize winner in Medicine, dies

1962 – Bay of Pigs captives who were ransomed vow to return and topple Castro; Serge Gregoire, French pacifist, dies

1963 – Disney releases *The Sword in the Stone*; Tristan Tzara, French Dadaist poet, dies

1964 – Hurricane kills 7,000 in India and Ceylon; American premiere of *Goldfinger*; George Harrison's girlfriend (and later wife), Patti Boyd, attacked by female Beatle fans

1965 – Dmitri Mironov, Russian hockey player, born; George Harrison proposes to Patti Boyd; Beatles release "Day Tripper"; The Dave Clark Five hit Number One on the U.S. pop chart with "Over and Over"

1966 – Craig Veasey, American football player, born; Javier Frana, Argentine tennis player, born

1967 – Beatle Paul McCartney engaged to Jane Asher

1968 – Helena Christensen, Danish model, born; Apollo 8 spacecraft leaves lunar orbit to return to Earth

1969 – Five Israeli gunboats escape from Cherbourg harbour; Castro condemns Christmas as a luxury Cuba cannot afford

1970 – Stu Barnes, NHL centre, born

1971 – Reverend Jesse Jackson organizes Operation PUSH (People United to Save Humanity); hotel fire in Seoul kills 163; Neil Hogan, guitar/vocalist of The Cranberries, born; Terry Vaughn, CFL receiver, born

1972 – Earthquake devastates Managua, Nicaragua, killing over 10,000; North Korean communist leader Kim-il Sung announces the party is superior to the state

1973 – U.S. Skylab III, seven-hour spacewalk, photography of comet Kohoutek; Tommy Chambers finishes 51-year, 800,000-mile bicycle tour; Ismet Inonu, Turkish president, dies

1974 – Cyclone hits Darwin, Australia

1975 – Gaston Gallimard, French publisher, dies; Bernard Herrmann, composer, dies

1976 – Egyptian ship *Patria* sinks in Red Sea, 100 die; Eagles release "New Kid in Town"; an Egyptair 707 explodes and crashes at Bangkok, killing 81

1977 – Sir Charlie Chaplin dies; Israeli PM Begin meets Egyptian President Sadat in Egypt

1978 – Vietnam invades Cambodia; Science-fiction classic *The Hitchhiker's Guide to the Galaxy* premieres on British TV; four members of "Reindeer Alliance" dressed as Santa Claus are arrested climbing a fence at Pilgrim Nuclear Plant, Massachusetts; Venera 11 probe lands on Venus

1979 – Joan Blondell dies; U.S.S.R. invades Afghanistan; Egypt begins renovation of the Sphinx

1980 – Archbishop Oscar Romero of El Salvador murdered

1981 – Blues guitarist Eddie Taylor dies

1982 – Helen Foster, American actress, dies; Jack Pearl, American radio and film actor, dies

1983 – Joan Miró, Spanish painter, dies

1984 – Three abortion clinics bombed in Pensacola; the first man-made comet is visible in the sky – the ball of chemicals from a West German satellite appears to be yellowish-green, and in the constellation Virgo

1985 – Tribal fighting in South Africa claims several dozen lives

1986 – Hijacked Iraqi jetliner crashes in Saudi Arabia, killing 60

1987 – Authorities recapture Lynette "Squeaky" Fromme, who had escaped two days earlier from the federal prison in Alderson, West Virginia, where she was serving a life sentence for her attempt on the life of President Ford

1989 – Nicolae Ceausescu, Romanian dictator, and wife, Elena, are executed; Billy Martin, baseball manager, dies; Vaclav Havel elected president of Czechoslovakia; Japanese scientists achieve coldest temperature ever recorded, minus 271.8°C

1990 – Former King Michael of Romania returns to homeland but is quickly expelled; Pope John Paul II appeals for peace in the Persian Gulf; Soviet President Gorbachev wins sweeping new powers from Congress of People's Deputies

1991 – Soviet President Mikhail Gorbachev resigns; U.S.S.R. to be replaced by a Commonwealth of Independent States

1992 – Monica Dickens, English writer, dies; Bishops of Albania appointed by Pope John Paul II

1993 – Typhoon Nell pummels the Philippines, killing 47; Emma Samms marries Tim Dillon; release of *Schindler's List*

1994 – Zail Singh, first Sikh president of India, dies; Jerusalem suicide bomber kills himself and wounds 13 people

1995 – Dean Martin dies; flash floods kill at least 130 people in Natal, South Africa; papal Christmas message and blessing issued on the Internet

1996 – 17 killed in Saudi Arabia bus accident; up to 280 die when ship carrying illegal migrants sinks off Malta; JonBenet Ramsey, child beauty queen, murdered in Boulder, Colorado; bomb explodes near government offices in Lhasa, Tibet

1997 – Denver Pyle, American actor, dies; Toshiro Mifune, Japanese actor, dies; former Zambian President Kenneth Kaunda is arrested

1998 – Richard Branson's attempt to circle the world by balloon ends in failure off coast of Hawaii; Pope John Paul II calls for end to death penalty; militant Hindus attack Christians in India

1999 – Russian troops fight in streets of Grozny; John Paul II declares a jubilee; Kashmiri militants hold an Air India jet hostage

"Deck the Halls With Boughs of Holly"

A secular carol of Welsh origin; Mozart uses a bit of it as the theme of a composition for violin and piano. "Follow me in merry measure" suggests that the singers would dance about as they sang, much as they would in a ring dance, the original meaning of "carol."

Deck the halls with boughs of holly,
Fa la la la la, la la la la.
Tis the season to be jolly,
Fa la la la la, la la la la.

Don we now our gay apparel,
Fa la la la la, la la la la.
Troll the ancient Yuletide carol,
Fa la la la la, la la la la.

See the blazing Yule before us,
Fa la la la la, la la la la.
Strike the harp and join the chorus,
Fa la la la la, la la la la.

Follow me in merry measure,
Fa la la la la, la la la la.
While I tell of Yuletide treasure,
Fa la la la la, la la la la.

Fast away the old year passes,
Fa la la la la, la la la la.
Hail the new, ye lads and lasses,
Fa la la la la, la la la la.

Sing we joyous, all together,
Fa la la la la, la la la la.
Heedless of the wind and weather,
Fa la la la la, la la la la.

"Deileg er den himmel blaa"　A traditional Danish carol translated into English by Nicolai F.S. Grundtvig as "Lovely Is the Dark Blue Sky."

Lovely is the dark blue sky,
Beautiful to ev'ry eye,
Where the golden stars are blinking,
See them smiling, see them winking
Beck'ning us to Heav'n on high,
Beck'ning us to Heav'n on high.

On the earliest Christmas night,
All the stars were shining bright,
When, among them, burst in brilliance
One lone star whose streaming radiance
Far surpassed the sun's own light,
Far surpassed the sun's own light.

Wise men from the East afar,
Led to Jesus by the star,
There adoring Heav'n's elected,
Found within his eyes reflected
God's great Light, and Love, and Pow'r,
God's great Light, and Love, and Pow'r.

Denmark　It would be difficult to be unaware of the approach of Christmas in Denmark. Every child has an Advent calendar which when opened reveals a candy or a picture, and most families have an Advent candle or wreath. Charitable Danes buy Children's Developing-Country Calendars, with the profits going to a Third World project. Danish television broadcasts the *Children's Christmas Calendar* starting on December 1, with a different puppet show or fairy tale every day until Christmas. At the beginning of the month, Christmas lights adorn buildings and Christmas trees and displays are set up outdoors.

Danes spend December preparing for the celebrations to come: gift buying and wrapping, Christmas card sending, with each card marked by a Christmas Seal (a Danish invention), and baking. Among the cookie favourites are *pebbernødder* (like the German *pfeffernüsse*), vanilla cookies, deep-fried *klejne*, and honey-cakes. Danes also like to make homemade candies and cakes, such as marzipan, rum balls, and apple cake. Many decorations are homemade, especially the red-and-white Christmas heart. A custom recently imported (since 1945) from Sweden is the St. Lucia procession, which takes place in schools and public institutions on December 13 and features a girl dressed in white with a wreath of fir and candles leading children in singing. Some families cling to the tradition of erecting the Christmas tree at the last moment to surprise the children, but other families decorate the tree together, with Christmas hearts, Danish flags, tinsel, candles, and a star at the top.

The Christmas lunch – usually in the form of an office party – is a popular custom which, despite the name, can be held at any time of the day. The menu includes herring, liver paté, ham, sausage, cheese, and biscuits, with plenty of beer (often a Christmas beer brewed only for that time of year) and schnapps. These parties have a reputation for being on the wild side, but most are in fact quite tame. On December 23, Little Christmas Eve, it is common to invite guests to drink *glögg*, a spiced red wine.

The high point of Danish Christmas celebrations is *Juleaften*, Christmas Eve, when shops close early and people rush home to be with their families. Some spend the afternoon in church, others in trimming the tree, but all look forward to the traditional dinner. Roast goose is the main course, accompanied by potatoes and red cabbage, but the meal must also contain, either as a starter or dessert, rice porridge. Hidden in the porridge is an almond, and the one who finds it is considered lucky for the coming year and gets a small prize, often a marzipan pig. When dinner is over and the washing up done, the tree is revealed and presents are opened. Many Danish families preserve the lovely custom of walking, with joined hands, around the tree singing a Christmas carol. Another centuries-old Christmas Eve custom is the setting out of the *juleneg*, a sheaf of grain for the birds.

In Denmark gifts are brought by a Santa Claus figure called the Julemanden, who is reputed to live in Greenland, a Danish possession, and travel by reindeer sleigh. He is assisted in his efforts by native sprites known as *Nisser*. These are elves dressed in red and grey with pointed red hats who live in attics and barns; they have a mischievous side and need to be placated, preferably by leaving out a bowl of rice porridge for them.

The next two days, Christmas Day and Second Christmas, are official holidays, spent visiting, relaxing with family and friends, and eating *smørrebrod*, open-faced sandwiches, and drinking *aquavit*.

Like the British, the Danes sit down for a few minutes to listen to a CHRISTMAS MESSAGE, which the monarch gives at 6 p.m. on December 31. New Year's Eve is a time of parties, dining out, and pranks; the Danish sense of humour finds great pleasure in the practical jokes played on *Nytaarsaften*.

On January 6, Epiphany, or Three Kings' Day, the tree is taken down and disposed of; sometimes it is turned into firewood and sometimes it is hung with suet and seeds for the birds. Candles are lit in the house in honour of the Magi, and the Christmas season is over for another year.

Department Store Santas　In 1841 the first department store Santa Claus appeared in Philadelphia. J.W. Parkinson's store arranged for a real "Criscringle" to come down a chimney and astonish the assembled children. The stunt was so successful that Parkinson began to advertise his business as "Kriss Kringle's Headquarters." Strangely, Parkinson had no imitators until 1890, when the Boston Store in Brockton, Massachusetts, hired a rotund Santa who came with his own white beard. Before too long, lines of children had formed waiting to visit Santa and other stores had copied the idea. By 1900 dozens of stores were to ensconce a Santa Claus in his own grotto or on a throne and encourage kids to sit on his lap and tell him their Christmas wishes.

Since then numerous schools have opened up to train department store Santas, who have formed their own professional associations. In the United States they have been the targets of bomb threats and irate parents and have asked for police protection; they have gone on strike in tropical countries to protest their hot clothing.

The ideal department store Santa is described as middle-aged, plump, red-faced, and possessing his own beard, with an ability to charm children and pass a police background check. Such candidates are rare and getting more so, according to those responsible for recruiting them. Modern healthy lifestyles have apparently reduced the number of suitably obese men.

Department store Santas have been immortalized in films such as *Miracle on 34th Street* and *Christmas Story*.

Devils and Evil Spirits at Christmas In *Hamlet*, Marcellus, referring to the royal ghost, says, "It faded on the crowing of the cock. Some say that ever gainst that season comes wherein our Saviour's birth is celebrated, This bird of dawning singeth all night long, and then, they say, no spirit dare walk abroad, The nights are wholesome, then no planets strike, No fairy takes, nor witch hath power to charm, So hallowed and so gracious is that time." However, despite Shakespeare's understanding of the weakness of demonic power during Christmas, most European countries have thought the season to be one of increased menace from supernatural forces. In Germany and parts of northeastern Europe, WEREWOLVES are active during the Twelve Nights; in Greece the KALLIKANTZAROI slip down chimneys to torment people. In Iceland the JÓLASVEINAR and the CHRISTMAS CAT are seasonal dangers, and the Yule Host, the souls of the unbaptized and the cursed or murdered dead, roam the night.

To safeguard humans and livestock against these evil spirits, certain Christmastime precautions are taken. The ringing of church bells drives them away, as does holy water, which is sprinkled in corners of houses and barns; incense has a similar effect. Logs are left burning in fireplaces at night. In much of Central Europe it is believed that loud noises will deter the forces of darkness, and a number of ceremonies revolve around the firing of guns, the cracking of whips, the ringing of cowbells, and noisy processions of grotesquely costumed figures to drive demons away.

In fairness it must be noted that sometimes devils such as KRAMPUS, KLAUBAUF, or CERT accompany the gift-bringer and serve to frighten bad children.

(See WEREWOLVES AND CHRISTMAS and WITCHES AT CHRISTMAS.)

Devils and Evil Spirits *An 18th-century woodcut portrays the popular fear of supernatural visitors.*

The Devil's Knell *This British stamp shows the Christmas Eve custom commemorating an ancient murder.*

Devil's Knell A Christmas Eve custom in Dewsbury, Yorkshire, is the tolling of the "Devil's Knell," or "The Old Lad's Passing Bell," which some say has been carried out in the village for the past 700 years. The knell is rung once for each year that has passed since the birth of Jesus (and thus the departure of the Devil from the Earth) by a team of ringers who time the last stroke to fall precisely at midnight. Local legend attributes the custom to a 13th-century baron, Sir Thomas de Soothill, who killed a servant and then gave the bell to the church to be rung each Christmas as a reminder of his crime.

Dickens, Charles (1812-70) English novelist and popularizer of Christmas. After a childhood of poverty, Dickens turned to writing, and by 1843, with *The Pickwick Papers*, *Oliver Twist*, and *Nicholas Nickleby* under his belt, he was already an established literary star. This did not relieve him of financial worries, however, and in October 1843, with the sales of *Martin Chuzzlewit* failing to meet his expectations, he conceived of a short book that would recoup his fortunes. This was *A Christmas Carol*, and it became an overnight sensation with the public, who were enthralled by the story of the moral resurrection of the miser Scrooge and the importance of Christmas as an agency of social good. He followed this up with a stream of stories and Christmas books that helped revive national interest in the Christmas season and link it in the minds of his readers with charity and reconciliation. Dickens and the example of the royal family did much to change ideas of Christmas in 19th-century Britain and to make it into a family-centred festival.

Didukh Literally, "grandfather" or "forefather spirit," this is a sheaf of grain brought into the house at Christmas Eve to symbolize the unity of the family, including the dead, the living, and those to come. It is a remnant of a pagan belief that the spirits of the ancestors guarded the fields in the summer and entered the house in the winter when the *didukh* was brought in. Made of the best grain of the harvest, the sheaf was often decorated with flowers or ribbons or tied around the middle with an embroidered cloth called a *rushnyk*. Once inside, the *didukh* (perhaps about four feet in height) was given a place of honour near the icons. It remained in the home until the eve of Epiphany, when it was taken out and burnt and its ashes scattered over the fields or orchard to induce fertility in the coming year and free the spirits within.

*Fig. 1: **Adoration of the Child** The Florentine painter Filippino Lippi shows a very plump baby Jesus being worshipped by his mother, Mary, and an angel. The painting dates from c. 1485.*

*Fig. 2: **Annunciation to Mary** In Fra Carnevale's* The Annunciation *(c. 1448) the angel Gabriel kneels before Mary holding a lily.*

Fig. 3: **Bethlehem** *The grotto in the Church of the Nativity marks the spot of the birth of Christ.*

Fig. 4: **Currier and Ives** *A print of a horse-drawn cutter by Currier and Ives.*

Fig. 5: **Dancing and Christmas** *For centuries people have danced to celebrate Christmas.*

Fig. 6: **Flight into Egypt** *In Vittore Carpaccio's painting (c. 1500), St. Joseph leads a donkey bearing Mary and the young Jesus toward the safety of Egypt.*

Fig. 7: **Homecoming** *Since the middle of the 19th century, families have become increasingly scattered, making the modern Christmas the principal time for family reunion (except in the United States, where it is edged out by Thanksgiving). Norman Rockwell's painting dates from 1948.*

Fig. 8: **John Canoe** *A junkanoo dancer from the Bahamas.*

Fig. 9: **Joseph** *The Rest on the Flight into Egypt, by the Flemish artist Gerard David (c. 1510), shows the Madonna feeding grapes to Jesus while in the background Joseph beats at a tree to get fruit for his family. In Nativity art, Joseph is often portrayed somewhat apart from Jesus – a sign that he is not the child's true father.*

Fig. 10: **Letters to Santa Claus** *In this 1935 illustration, Norman Rockwell helps standardize the modern portrayal of a jolly, bearded Santa Claus as a kindly old friend to children.*

Fig. 11: **Luxembourg** *Outdoor Christmas markets packed with seasonal goods herald the arrival of Christmas in Luxembourg.*

Fig. 12: **Madonna and Child** *One of the Venetian Giovanni Bellini's favourite topics was that of the Madonna and Child. His* Madonna and Child with Saints *dates from c. 1490.*

Fig. 13: **Massacre of the Innocents** Pieter Brueghel's depiction of the murder of the boy babies of Bethlehem is set in a 16th-century Dutch village occupied by foreign troops. The dark figure at the centre is thought by some to represent the Spanish general the Duke of Alva, whose cruelty became legendary in the Netherlands.

Fig. 14: **Melchior** In The Adoration of the Magi, by Juan de Flandes, (c. 1508-19) the Magi represent the three ages of man. Elderly Melchior presents his gold, watched by the middle-aged Gaspar and the young African Balthazar. The stable is set among classical ruins, symbolizing the death of the old dispensation.

Charles Dickens The young author of A Christmas Carol.

"Ding Dong! Merrily on High"   This Christmas carol matches a 16th-century tune with more modern lyrics. The French folk melody was printed first by Thoinot Arbeau, the *nom de plume* of French priest Jehan Tabourot (1520-95), in his *Orchésographie*, a treatise on dancing in 1588, where it was called "Branle de l'officiel" ("Dance of the Official"). George Ratcliffe Woodward (1848-1934), an English carol writer and collector, added verses early in the 20th century.

> Ding! dong! merrily on high
> In heav'n the bells are ringing;
> Ding! dong! verily the sky
> Is riv'n with angel singing.
>
> *Gloria! Hosanna in excelsis!*
>
> E'en so here below, below,
> Let steeple bells be swungen,
> And "Io, io io!"
> By priest and people sungen.
>
> *Refrain*
>
> Pray you, dutifully prime
> Your matin chime, ye ringers!
> May you beautifully rime
> Your evetime song, ye singers!
>
> *Refrain*

Disguysing   A custom at Christmas among medieval English aristocracy and nobility was the wearing of costumes for the performance of extravagant masques and MUMMING. The disguises provided licence for a certain amount of loose speech and indecent behaviour, which prompted Henry VIII, himself an enthusiastic masquer, to enact a law against wearing masks in public. See GUISING and MASKING.

Distaff's Day, St.   January 7, so called because the Christmas season in the United Kingdom ended on Epiphany, and on the following day women returned to their distaffs, or daily work.

It is also called Rock Day, after the antique term for a distaff. A 17th-century poem states:

> Give St. Distaff all the right,
> Then give Christmas sport good night,
> And next morrow every one
> To his own vocation.

Divination at Christmas   Two sorts of divination, or telling the future, were popular at Christmas: predicting the weather and discerning one's intended spouse.

One way of determining the weather in the year to come was based on the day of the week on which Christmas fell. Should it fall on a Sunday, it meant a year of peace and good weather, a good year for sheep and beans, and the speedy capture of thieves. Christmas Day on Monday produces a stormy and windy year; the sick will survive, although many beasts will die, and thieves be taken. It is bad luck when Christmas Day falls on a Tuesday: women, sheep, lords, kings, and thieves will die, yet the sick will recover. Wednesday presages a harsh winter with danger to the young and to sailors. Thursday gives mixed predictions, but when Christmas falls on a Friday, "you may sow in ashes," meaning crops will be so good they will spring up anywhere. Saturday's indications are dire: "What woman that day of childe travaille / They shall bothe be in gret peraile." Another means of weather prediction was to assign each of the Twelve Days of Christmas to a particular month; the conditions on that day would prevail in the corresponding month. In New Zealand the Maoris say that if the pohutukawa flowers before Christmas, it will be a long hot summer; if it doesn't, then a sultry, wet Christmas season is in store. A Scottish proverb that a "black Christmas makes a fat kirkyard" means that a snowless Christmas will result in many people dying in the coming year, a common saying all across Europe. The Romanian proverbs "Christmas in mud, Easter in snow" and "Green Christmas brings white Easter" are similarly widespread. German farmers say, "If the crow is standing in clover at Christmas, she'll be sitting in snow at Easter." A windy Christmas, however, and a calm Candlemas are signs of a good year.

There are countless ways for a young woman to determine the identity or character of her future husband, as this 16th-century poem indicates:

> In these same dayes yong wanton Gyrles that meete for mariage bee,

St Distaff's Day Medieval women spin using a distaff.

Doe search to know the names of them that shall their
    husbandes bee.
Foure Onyons, five, or eight, they take and make in
    every one,
Such names as they do fansie most and best do thinke
    upon.
Thus neere the Chimney them they set, and that same
    Onyon than,
That first doth sproute, doth surely beare the name of their
    good man.
Their husbandes nature eke they seeke to know, and all
    his guise,
When as the Sunne hath hid himselfe and left the starrie
    skies,
Unto some woodstacke do they go, and while they there
    do stande,
Eche one drawes out a faggot sticke, the next that commes
    to hande,
Which if it streight and even be, and have no knots at all,
A gentle husband then they thinke shall surely to them fall.
But if it fowle and crooked be, and knottie here and theare
A crabbed churlish husband then, they earnestly do feare.

Should none of these methods work, the girl might tap on
the henhouse door on Christmas Eve: if a hen cackles, her
marital prospects are bad; cock crows are good. She might
place her name and those of her friends on the bands of the
ASHEN FAGGOT; the first to burn through will be the first to
marry. In Germany it was the custom to form a circle of girls
and trust in the powers of a blindfolded goose; the first to be
touched by the bird will be the next to be wed. In Denmark
young women could induce dreams of their future mates by
reciting, just before bedtime on St. Lucia's Eve,

Sweet St. Lucy, let me know
Whose cloth I shall lay,
Whose bed I shall make,
Whose child I shall bear,
Whose darling I shall be,
Whose arms I shall lie in.

See PODBLYUDNUIYA.

"Do They Know It's Christmas?" To raise money for famine
relief in Africa, a number of British rock stars, led by Bob
Geldof, formed Band Aid and recorded "Do They Know It's
Christmas?" in November 1984. This raised millions of dollars
and set an example for other charitable vocal events, such as
Live Aid, Farm Aid, and Net Aid.

"D'où viens-tu bergère?" A traditional French-Canadian carol
with an 1866 English translation by William McLennan, who
chose to render *bergère*, or "shepherdess," as "my maiden."

"D'où viens-tu bergère?
"D'où viens-tu?"
"Je viens de l'étable
De m'y promener.
J'ai vu un miracle
Ce soir arrivé."

"Whence art thou, my maiden
Whence art thou?"
"I come from the stable,
Where this very night,
I, a shepherd maiden,
Saw a wondrous sight."

"What saw'st thou, my maiden
What saw'st thou?
What saw'st thou, my maiden
What saw'st thou?"
"There within a manger,
A little Child I saw,
Lying, softly sleeping
On a bed of straw."

"Nothing more, my maiden
Nothing more?
Nothing more my maiden
Nothing more?"
"There I saw the mother
Her sweet baby hold,
And the father, Joseph,
Trembling with the cold."

"Nothing more, my maiden
Nothing more?
Nothing more my maiden
Nothing more?"
"I saw an ass and oxen,
Kneeling meek and mild,
With their gentle breathing
Warm the holy Child."

"Nothing more, my maiden
Nothing more?
Nothing more my maiden
Nothing more?"
"There were three bright angels
Come down from the sky,
Singing forth sweet praises
To our God on high."

Dr. Seuss's How the Grinch Stole Christmas (TV) (1966) Dr.
Seuss's much-loved book is given a brilliant film version by
the animating genius Chuck Jones. This cartoon, which
debuted on CBS television December 18, 1966, is narrated by
Boris Karloff with the voice of June Foray as Cindy-Lou Who
and Thurl Ravenscroft as the singer of "You're a Mean One,
Mister Grinch." Albert Hague, a Tony-winning composer,
wrote the score. Karloff's recording of the book *How the
Grinch Stole Christmas* won a Grammy in 1967 for best children's record.

The Grinch character appeared in other, less memorable,
television specials: *Hallowe'en Is Grinch Night* (ABC, 1977), and
The Grinch Grinches the Cat in the Hat (ABC, 1982). Ironically,
both of these shows won an Emmy award, which the original
failed to do. In 1993 the animated sitcom *The Simpsons* parodied the story in the episode "Last Exit to Springfield," where
the evil tycoon Mr. Burns is drawn to resemble the Grinch
straining to hear the sounds of a doleful Who-ville.

Dodekameron The term used in the Eastern churches for the
Twelve Days following Christmas.

"A Dog of Flanders" A sentimental tale of 1872 about a boy and
his dog, both mistreated by an uncaring society, who meet the
fate that is reserved for 19th-century fictional outcasts on
Christmas: freezing to death. The story by Ouida (1839-1908)
has been made into a movie six times, almost always with a
happier ending than its author intended.

Dominican Republic Despite the large cultural and economic
role that the United States plays in the Caribbean region, the

Dominican Republic has been successful in maintaining its Christmas traditions largely untouched.

The country shares many of its Christmas customs with its Latin American cousins. There is the Christmas bonus that comes in December and provides spending money for the season. Churches (mainly Catholic) are well attended, particularly for the early morning services, where the *aguinaldos navideños*, Christmas carols, are sung to the accompaniment of instruments such as the accordions, guiras, guitars, maracas, and tambourines that the parishioners themselves bring. As in Puerto Rico, groups of carollers go from house to house on surprise visits looking for hospitality in return for a song. The manger scene is found in churches, homes, and in public places, and churches stage Nativity pageants during Advent.

The Christmas tree has made its way into many homes, but has yet to supplant the crèche as the focal point of family attentions. In order to make it look snow-covered in the tropical heat, Dominicans cover the tree with tinsel or angel hair. Wreaths, garlands, homemade decorations, and lights are all used to make the newly cleaned house look ready for Christmas.

On Christmas Eve, or *Noche Buena*, the festivities reach their height. It's the time for the big meal where the main dish is almost always roast pork (occasionally turkey), with tamales, pastelitos, and salads; cake, fruit, and rice pudding are common desserts. After dinner the family goes to midnight mass and then returns home for more merry-making and noisy fireworks. Christmas itself is a quiet day, perhaps spent recovering from the previous night's excesses and visiting with family members. Many visit church for a Christmas Day service.

Though some families open gifts on Christmas Eve, most Dominicans wait until *Dia de los Reyes* ("Kings' Day"), January 6; the gift-bringers are the Magi on their way to see the baby Jesus. A lovely custom, reminiscent of the Italian Befana, is the Vieja Belén, the Old Lady of Bethlehem, who gives presents to poor children who might not otherwise have received any.

Don't Open 'til Christmas (1984)   Pity Father Christmas in this British holiday horror picture. Someone with unresolved issues in his emotional life is going around killing department store Santas in particularly nasty ways. Directed by (and starring) Edmund Purdom.

Doppa y Grytan   The seasonal ritual in Sweden where family and friends gather in the kitchen on Christmas Eve when the meat for dinner is simmering and with pieces of rye bread "dip in the pot" to soak up the drippings. So popular is this tradition that Christmas Eve used to be known as "dipping day."

Dot and Santa Claus (1979)   Dot goes in search of her missing kangaroo and persuades Santa Claus to help her find him in this full-length Australian holiday feature that employs some clever animation techniques.

Drama and Christmas   Christmas drama began in ninth-century church services when additional words and melodies were added to the mass. The choir sang questions about the coming of Jesus with the congregation responding. This led to clergy singing the part of shepherds and angels and, as time went on, Old Testament prophets and characters connected to the Nativity, such as the heavenly host and midwives. As the stories being enacted became more complex, costumes and props, particularly the Star, were added. The dramatic impact

of these plays, the *Officium Stellae*, the *Prophetae*, and the *Officium Pastorum*, was limited by their performance in Latin and their confinement to the church. By the 11th century, Christmas drama was appearing in the vernacular and in the open air (though the liturgical drama continued for centuries to be performed in churches and monasteries).

With the language of the common people came developments in the plays that would not have been tolerated in the liturgy: broad comedy – thieving shepherds, bad puns in the local dialect, and slapstick – folk religion, and characters not in the officially sanctioned body of Nativity legend. The climate of Western Europe discouraged the open-air performance of Christmas drama in December, and most of them were performed in the spring or summer as part of town festivals. A remarkable exception was put on in Rouen in the winter of 1474, when a play about the Incarnation and Nativity was performed out of doors on 24 stages around the city over a two-day period. These mystery plays, which first appeared in the 13th century, were often staged by town guilds such as the Shearmen and Tailors' Guild of Coventry, which enacted the story of the Nativity as part of a cycle of plays at the feast of Corpus Christi, a drama that gave us the "COVENTRY CAROL." Such drama became unfashionable in the 16th century, and these plays virtually disappeared under the pressures of the Reformation and Counter Reformation.

The subject of Christmas does not seem to have produced great drama in the Renaissance. William Shakespeare scarcely mentions Christmas except as a date, and Ben Jonson was content to rent out his genius by crafting expensive and gaudy Christmas masques for the court of James I. Of the great dramatists, only Spain's Lope de Vega seems to have taken Christmas in earnest, as in his *Birth of Christ* and *Shepherds of Bethlehem* (1612).

However absent Christmas might have been on the urban stage, it was nonetheless a flourishing part of folk drama. Catholic missionaries around the world educated their newly converted flocks in the Nativity story by writing plays about

Drama and Christmas *Before the invention of theatres, plays were usually performed outdoors.*

the events of the birth of Jesus. To this day the faithful from the Philippines, the southwest United States, the Caribbean, and South America stage dramas re-enacting the search of the Holy Family for shelter, or the tale of the angels and the shepherds, or the rage of Herod. Sometimes this takes the form of street theatre, such as the Mexican *posadas* or the Filipino *panuluyan*; sometimes, as in the Dominican Republic's *Veladas*, they are held in churches. A different line of Nativity folk drama in Eastern Europe has produced the Romanian play called *Vicleim* (from "Bethlehem") and, in Moldavia and Transylvania, *Irozi* (from "Herod"). In this latter play, Herod encounters the Magi and orders them arrested, but all ends in repentance.

Like many Eastern European plays of this sort, the action is often performed by puppets. Puppet drama was particularly popular in Poland, Naples, and Provence, where performances of such Nativity drama are still staged. In England puppet drama took the form of Punch and Judy shows which, though they lacked overtly Christmas content, were very popular during the holiday season. The same can be said about PANTOMIME, a form of play that evolved from the Italian *commedia dell'arte* in the 18th century and that still dominates the English stage at Christmastime. Another form of Christmastime drama with a low Christmas content is the mummers' play. Though they often contain a character named Father Christmas, these folk plays, which emerged in the 18th century, have puzzled ethnologists with their plots about ritual combat, death, and resurrection at the hands of a healer. Similar plays are performed in Brazil and Wallachia.

In the 20th century the dramatization of Christmas has largely been seen in motion pictures. See MOVIES AND CHRISTMAS.

Dresdens   Embossed cardboard Christmas tree ornaments originating in 19th-century Dresden, Germany. These colourful decorations used gold or silver accents to enhance the image and are now prized collectors' items.

Drink and Christmas   One of the earliest English carols says:

Lordings, Christmas loves good drinking,
Wines of Gascoigne, France, Anjou,
English ale that drives out thinking,
Prince of liquors old or new.
Every neighbour shares the bowl,
Drinks of the spicy liquor deep,
Drinks his fill without control,
Till he drowns his care in sleep.

And now – by Christmas, jolly soul!
By this mansion's generous sire!
By this wine, and by this bowl,
And all the joys they both inspire!
Here I'll drink a health to all,
The glorious task shall first be mine:
And ever may foul luck befall
Him that to pledge me shall decline!

Drink and Christmas *A rather wild Father Christmas figure toasts the holiday season.*

Christmas has been associated with festive drinking since the time of the late Roman Empire, and every nation that celebrates Christmas brings to it its own favourite Christmas beverage. In England the wassail bowl was full at Christmas with ale, roasted apples, and spices, served hot. Ale was once referred to as "nog," and when the Americans adopted the French *lait de poule*, a drink with eggs, sugar, and milk, they added liquor to make the modern eggnog. Christmas in Scandinavia is fuelled by *glögg*, a spiced wine similar to the *glühwein* that warms Germans and Austrians. In Ecuador they drink *canelazo*, a hot drink made of spiced tea and an anise-flavoured brandy. Sorrel is the basis of the Jamaican Christmas drink. Rum punches gladden the heart of the Caribbean and Central America, while in Denmark drinkers reach for special Christmas varieties of beer and *schnapps*. Champagne is drunk on holiday occasions around the world (though Spaniards seem to prefer their own sparkling wine called *cava*).

Whatever the beverage of choice, drinking at Christmas symbolizes conviviality, hospitality, and a celebration of relaxation from work. It also means that drinking to excess is a Yule-time problem, and police forces around the world have special holiday enforcement of drinking-and-driving laws.

Ebbie (TV) (1995) Some Christmas ideas are better than others. Whose stroke of genius was it to cast a gender-reversed *A Christmas Carol*? Fingers may be pointed at George Kaczender for directing it and the soap-opera world's Susan Lucci for accepting the role of Elizabeth "Ebbie" Scrooge, employer of Wendy Crewson playing Roberta "Robbie" Cratchit.

Ecuador   Like most of Latin America, Ecuador is deeply Catholic, and the approach of Christmas is marked by religious observances. Manger scenes are erected in homes and churches; these are not only admired for their workmanship and ingenuity but are also scenes of family devotions and prayers. Advent candles are lit, and Christmas trees, which have infiltrated from North America, are erected. Processions honouring the Holy Family and the Magi wind through the streets accompanied by musicians. On the Sunday before Christmas, food is delivered to shut-ins as a way of honouring the Wise Men who brought gifts to the baby Jesus.

The *aguinaldo*, or compulsory Christmas bonus, is distributed by employers in December so that workers have plenty of money to spend on their celebrations. Office parties are plentiful, as are impromptu neighbourhood gatherings as Christmas approaches.

Midnight mass is a must for most families on Christmas Eve. Some children receive their presents on Christmas Eve or the following morning, while other families wait for the Three Kings on January 6. Christmas dinner is based on chicken, roast pork, or turkey, with *capritoda*, a sweet bread, fruit, and *pristiños*, pastries. On the highland farms and ranches, fiestas are held with musicians, dancing, and feasting.

On December 28, in keeping with their Spanish heritage, Ecuadorians mark the Feast of the Holy INNOCENTS with pranks and practical jokes, or *inocentadas*. To honour the mothers of Bethlehem, who disguised their children to hide them from Herod's soldiers, the day is also one of costume parties.

The burning of Mr. Old Year, *La Quema de los Años Viejos*, is the highlight of New Year's Eve in Ecuador. Carefully prepared effigies, some resembling popular (or unpopular) public figures, are dressed and set up on the street for passersby to laugh at before they are put on a bonfire.

In January the image of the baby Jesus is taken from his manger and paraded to the church for the *Paso del Niño*, a service of blessing. The Christmas season ends on Epiphany or the Day of the Kings.

Eggnog   A popular holiday drink, it takes its name from an old term for ale, "nog." When 19th-century Americans discovered the French drink *lait de poule*, made of eggs, milk, and spices, they added liquor (usually rum) and topped it with nutmeg to create eggnog. The threat of salmonella has forced commercial producers to treat the concoction with high heat before packaging.

Eggnog Riot   Also known as the "Grog Mutiny." In 1826 cadets at West Point military academy rioted when the superintendent declared an alcohol-free Christmas season. Nineteen cadets were court-martialled after the disturbances were quelled. The disorders were led by cadets from the southern states (including future Confederate President Jefferson Davis), who were used to a more spirited celebration of the holiday.

Egypt   Though Egypt is an overwhelmingly Muslim country, millions of Copts celebrate Christmas there every year. The Coptic church is one of the oldest Christian denominations in the world. They note that Jesus spent his infancy in Egypt, where the Holy Family fled Herod, and claim their spiritual descent from St. Mark, one of the original disciples. Copts have survived over 1,300 years of Islamic rule by clinging to customs such as their unique Christmas, which is far more a religious holiday than a time for conspicuous consumption.

Copts are great fasters; in fact most of the Coptic calendar is occupied by one fast or another. Christmas is preceded by a 43-day fast in which food and drink is shunned from midnight to 3 p.m. and all meals are vegetarian or fish. Prayer meetings and special Advent hymns are part of the pre-Christmas ritual, as is increased charitable giving.

Because Copts also cling to their ancient calendar, Christmas itself is held on the 29th day of the Egyptian month of Kiakh, which is January 7 to that part of the world that uses the Gregorian system. The celebration begins on the night of Christmas Eve, when families go to church for the midnight service. *Qurban* bread, marked with the cross and 12 dots representing the apostles, is distributed to the congregation. Because tensions often exist between Muslims and Copts, the Egyptian government and church officials are at pains to promote toleration and communal dialogue at Christmas. This is one reason why state television broadcasts the celebration of the midnight mass from the cathedral in Cairo.

After church, people return home to break their fast and open gifts; Christmas Eve is an especially good time to receive new clothes. Christmas food includes a kind of shortbread or sweet biscuit known as *kahk*. Christmas Day is a holiday for Christians, who spend it visiting friends and relatives and eating.

In Egypt tourists can visit the Virgin's Tree, an ancient sycamore in Mataria that supposedly sheltered the Holy Family, and the Church of Abu Sergah (St. Sergius), whose basilica is built on the cave in which the Holy Family is believed to have stayed.

Eisteddfod   A much-loved Welsh artistic festival, the *eisteddfod* had its origins in Christmas 1176. A medieval chronicle noted, "At Christmas in that year the Lord Rhys ap Gruffudd held court in splendour at Cardigan. . . . And he set two kinds of contests there: one between bards and poets, another between harpists . . . and pipers and various classes of music-craft. And he had two chairs set for the victors." These festivals continue to this day and are an essential part of Welsh cultural life, though the larger ones are no longer held at Christmas.

El Salvador   In El Salvador Christmas literally begins with a bang. Fireworks are an inescapable part of festivities in that country, and at the beginning of December rockets light up the sky to signal the start of the Christmas season. Celebrations accelerate on December 8, the festival of the Immaculate Conception of Mary, and on December 12, when the Virgin of Guadeloupe is celebrated. Fireworks are set off, religious processions and bands wind their way through the streets with images of the Virgin, and innumerable parties are held. (These festivities are financed, as in much of Latin America, by the *aguinaldo*, or compulsory Christmas bonus. Unfortunately in recent years, unscrupulous employers have taken to laying off many workers in December to avoid having to make this payment.)

In mid-December Salvadoreans stage POSADAS, re-enactments of the search of Mary and Joseph for shelter, and *pastorelas*, plays about the events of the Nativity, with costumed shepherds, musicians, singing, and dancing in celebration of the birth of Jesus. Carols include not only traditional Spanish-language songs, but also popular North American carols which, like the Christmas tree in Salvadorean homes, have made their way south through the globalization of American Christmas customs. The North American figure of Santa Claus has replaced the baby Jesus and the Three Kings as the gift-bringer in many parts of Latin America. He comes on Christmas Eve and brings presents mainly to children. The gifts are left under the tree, or sometimes under the children's beds to be opened on Christmas Day.

Christmas dinner is based on chicken or roast pork and *tamales*, though turkey has become increasingly popular. Fruit, sweets, and pies are dessert; wine and punch are in plentiful supply. Those Salvadoreans close to the coast may well choose to celebrate Christmas on the beach.

Though the Christmas tree has made its appearance it has not driven out the *nacimiento*, or manger scene, which is still a feature in churches and homes. Unique to El Salvador is the miniature scale of the crèche, many of which are homemade. These will remain in place until Epiphany, January 6, when the Christmas season ends.

Elmo Saves Christmas (1992) The entire Sesame Street gang shows up in this straight-to-video tale of a Christmas wish gone wrong. Harvey Fierstein as the singing Easter Bunny is worth the price of the tape all by himself, but look for references to *It's a Wonderful Life* throughout. Directed by Emily Squires. Writers Tony Geiss and Christine Ferraro won a Writers Guild of America award for the script.

Elves Small supernatural creatures who are now associated with Christmas through the notion that they work as Santa's helpers at the North Pole.

They were not always so benign. They originated in the Scandinavian *nissen* and *tomten*, farm- or house-elves, who could be helpful if bribed but malicious if they were slighted, especially at Christmas when, as in Denmark, a bowl of milk must be left out for them. In the second half of the 19th century, the reputation of elves began to change for the better as part of a drive to make Christmas more child-centred. An 1859 poem in *Harper's Weekly* speaks of Santa Claus keeping "a great many elves at work, / All working with all their might, / To make a million of pretty things . . ." (See colour fig. 21.)

Perhaps no country is as mindful of elves at Christmas than Iceland, where there is a rich folklore tradition about these supernatural creatures and how to keep on their good side during the long winter nights. It is believed that elves move house every New Year's. It is possible, though dangerous, to obtain gold from them at this time by interrupting them, but most choose merely to pacify them. Housewives on Christmas could obtain their goodwill by chanting on New Year's Eve

Let those who want to, arrive;
Let those who want to, leave;
Let those who want to, stay
Without harm to me or mine.

Elves (1990) A love-hungry Nazi elf is part of a fiendish plan to breed a super-race and bring back a Hitlerian Fourth Reich in this nasty piece of low-budget horror. Can a department store Santa Claus, played by Dan Haggerty of *Grizzly Adams* fame, save the world (or at least the virgin who is destined to be mated to the elf on Christmas Eve)? Directed and written by Jeff Mandel, who had difficulty finding work in show business after this.

L'Enfance du Christ *The Childhood of Christ*, an 1854 oratorio by Hector Berlioz that tells the story of the aftermath of the Nativity in three parts: Herod's Dream, the Flight into Egypt, and the Arrival at Saïs.

England Our knowledge of Christmas in England begins in the year 597, when Augustine of Canterbury used the day to baptize thousands of Anglo-Saxons. For Augustine, December 25 represented an immensely sacred day in the Christian calendar, while for the pagans it was the beginning of their new year and the middle of their midwinter feasting. His decision to use the festival as a tool in his drive to convert the

England *Seasonal charity, the Yule log, feasting, music, and mumming are some of the English Christmas traditions depicted here.*

island to Christianity fits in with the instructions given to him by Pope GREGORY the year before: to adapt local customs and patterns of worship where they could be given a Christian interpretation.

By doing so Augustine helped create an English Christmas that was both sacred and secular in flavour. Throughout the Anglo-Saxon period, the two aspects were blended. Late in the seventh century, Archbishop Theodore granted that Christmas was a legitimate excuse in the confessional for having over-indulged. King Alfred decreed that the Twelve Days of Christmas were holidays and were to be free of labour (his reluctance to fight during the period caused him to lose the battle of Chippenham to the Vikings in 878). The unfortunate King Ethelred (reigned 991-1016) ordered that the season of the Nativity should be a time of peace and goodwill, when all strife was to cease. Historians assume that during these years the customs of the YULE LOG were observed, as well as wassailing (see WASSAIL), midwinter feasting, and perhaps MUMMING. By the time of the Norman Conquest in 1066, the season held elements of the Nativity as well as being a time of vacation and merriment, and a new word "Christmas" had been coined to describe the festival.

The religious side of Christmas appears to grow in England during the High Middle Ages. New legends entered into national folklore, such as the stories of the GLASTONBURY THORN, the MAGI, ST. NICHOLAS, and animals kneeling at midnight. Church drama and its secular successors told audiences of the miracles of the Nativity and especially the role of the humble shepherds. The Franciscan invention of Christmas carols spread to England, and songs in Latin and English made the Incarnation seem a homely and a joyous thing. The celebration of the birth of Christ demanded merriment of medieval believers. The Boy Bishop became a fixture at a number of English churches, and shows that though Christmas had yet to become the child-centred holiday it would be in the 19th century, the Church recognized the connection between children and Christmas.

In the Middle Ages, Christmas was regarded as a season, not just one day. Gifts exchanged on New Year's Day were called Christmas gifts; TWELFTH NIGHT celebrations were part of Christmas-tide mirth. This was a time when feasting on a massive scale became a feature of English royal Christmases and when masquing and mumming become popular courtly entertainments. A LORD OF MISRULE directed festivities at courts and rich men's houses. Christmas gifts were exchanged between feudal lords and their inferiors, and the demands for BOXING DAY gratuities were denounced as having grown to the point of extortion. Nonetheless, Christmas was also recognized as a prime season for charity, when tenants or the poor could expect hospitality from their landlords or social superiors.

The Protestant Reformation had a small effect on the English Christmas. The Boy Bishop and Lord of Misrule were discouraged in the 16th century, and fewer parents referred to St. Nicholas as the gift-bringer for children, but unlike Scotland, where Christmas was legislated almost out of existence, the holiday itself survived. George Wither, an English poet (1588-1667), wrote "A Christmas Carol" in 1622, and the work tells us much about the Jacobean attitude to the season. He stresses themes of merriment, charity, reconciliation, and social inversion.

So, now is come our joyfull'st feast;
Let every man be jolly;
Each room with ivy leaves is drest,
And every post with holly.
Though some churls at our mirth repine,
Round your foreheads garlands twine;
Drown sorrow in a cup of wine,
And let us all be merry.

Now all our neighbours' chimneys smoke,
And Christmas blocks are burning;
Their ovens they with baked meats choke,
And all their spits are turning.
Without the door let sorrow lie;
And if for cold it hap to die,
We'll bury 'tin a Christmas pie,
And ever more be merry.

Now every lad is wondrous trim,
And no man minds his labour;
Our lasses have provided them
A bag-pipe and a tabour;
Young men and maids, and girls and boys
Give life to one another's joys;
And you anon shall by their noise
Perceive that they are merry.

Ned Squash hath fetched his bands from pawn,
And all his best apparel;
Brisk Nell hath brought a ruff of lawn
With droppings of the barrel;
And those that hardly all the year
Have bread to eat, or rags to wear,
Will have both clothes and dainty fare,
And all the day be merry.

Now poor men to the justices
With capons make their errants;
And if they hap to fail of these,
They plague them with their warrants:
But now they feed them with good cheer,
And what they want they take in beer;
For Christmas comes but once a year,
And then they shall be merry.

Good farmers in the country nurse
The poor that else were undone;
Some landlords spend their money worse,
On lust and pride at London.
There the roysters they do play,
Drab and dice their lands away,
Which may be ours another day;
And therefore let's be merry.

The client now his suit forbears,
The prisoner's heart is eased:
The debter drinks away his cares,
And for the time is pleased.
Though other purses be more fat,
Why should we pine or grieve at that?
Hang sorrow! care will kill a cat,
And therefore let's be merry.

Hark! how the wags abroad do call
Each other forth to rambling:
Anon you'll see them in the hall
For nuts and apples scrambling.
Hark! how the roofs with laughter sound!
Anon they'll think the house goes round;
For they the cellar's depth have found,
And there they will be merry.

The wenches with the wassail bowls
About the streets are singing;
The boys are come to catch the owls,
The wild mare in is bringing.
Our kitchen-boy hath broke his box,
And to the dealing of the ox
Our honest neighbours come by flocks,
And here they will be merry.

Now kings and queens poor sheep cotes have,
And mate with every body;
The honest now may play the knave,
And wise men play the noddy.
Some youths will now a mumming go,
Some others play at Rowland-ho,
And twenty other gambles mo,
Because they will be merry.

Then wherefore in these merry days
Should we, I pray, be duller?
No, let us sing some roundelays,
To make our mirth the fuller.
And, whilst thus inspired we sing,
Let all the streets with echoes ring,
Woods and hills, and every thing,
Bear witness we are merry.

But we do hear two, rather opposite, complaints emerge during these years. Social conservatives remarked (as Wither does in the sixth verse above) that hospitality and charity had declined, that landlords were ignoring their old obligations to their tenants and spending the holiday season in London. (Both Queen Elizabeth I and King James I would react by ordering the nobility to spend Christmas on their estates fulfilling their traditional roles.) Social radicals, like the ultra-Protestant PURITANS, complained of the riotousness of the season and wished to wipe Christmas off the religious calendar altogether.

The Puritans got their wish in the 1640s and 1650s after their victory in the English Civil War: the observance of Christmas was outlawed, and those who attended church on December 25 or who made mince pies or plum pudding or put up seasonal greenery were subject to arrest. Even when the English monarchy was restored in 1660, many felt that much of Christmas had been lost forever. The aristocracy continued their neglect of traditional charity; many riotous popular customs associated with Christmas were never revived; carolling fell into disfavour; and, in fact, for the next century or more, Christmas fell into a long, slow decline.

Much of the blame for this can be placed on the Industrial Revolution, which disrupted rural ways of life and worked against such non-productive notions as an extended Christmas break. By the late 1700s, government and business had stripped the calendar of holidays, rendering Christmas Day and Good Friday the only statutory days off work and thus abolishing the traditional 12 days of leisure and merry-making. The *Times* of London scarcely mentioned the word "Christmas" at all in its December issues, and many educated people had come to regard the day as an anachronistic bore. It had been replaced in Scotland by New Year's revelry and in the west of England by lingering affection for Twelfth Night merriment.

Christmas was saved in 19th-century England by a number of developments. The first was the Oxford Movement, an ecclesiastical campaign that aimed at restoring High Church notions inside the Church of England and promoted an enhanced appreciation of ritual, decoration, and the festive year. John Keble's 1827 book of poems, *The Christian Year*, celebrated the whole Christian calendar, including Christmas. Tied in with this movement was the work of a number of collectors of English carols, such as Sir JOHN STAINER and JOHN MASON NEALE, who succeeded in rescuing older carols and encouraged the writing of new ones. Also helping to revive Christmas was a shift in certain middle-class sensibilities: a new emphasis on family ties; love of children and childhood as a time of innocence; fear of a rift between rich and poor; and yearning for an idealized pre-industrial England. In 1840 and 1841, *Punch*'s Christmas issues decried lack of charity and the rule of miserliness.

The resurrection of Christmas also owes much to the example of the British royal family as celebrators of a family-centred (as opposed to a traditionally riotous) Christmas. This is greatly due to Prince Albert's German background. His importation of the Christmas tree, the family's adoption of turkey as the seasonal meal, and their emphasis on family togetherness proved an enormously attractive model for middle-class English folk, who now sought to emulate their monarch.

Finally, we can ascribe a great deal to CHARLES DICKENS, whose 1843 *Christmas Carol* turned Christmas into a crusade against selfishness and greed. In this book and his other seasonal stories, he revived the lost medieval link between worship and feasting, the Nativity and Yule, and emphasized the holiday as a time of personal and social reconciliation.

By 1847 the Poor Law Board permitted a special Christmas dinner in the grim workhouses. Magazines were quick to take up the new celebratory mood, and authors started churning out special Christmas stories with freezing orphans, kindly middle-class families, and misers undergoing redemption at the hands of the Christmas spirit. The 1843 invention of the Christmas card, which had failed to take immediate hold because it was too expensive, began to boom in the 1860s with the introduction of cheaper postal rates and less-expensive cards. Children looked forward to the visit of Father Christmas on Christmas Eve, and PANTOMIME became the wildly popular Boxing Day activity. The 1871 Bank Holidays Act expanded to include Boxing Day as a holiday.

Though Christmas had been revived and rejuvenated, many of its charms were still too expensive for working-class English families; the tree, the stuffed stockings, the visit to the panto were still beyond the reach of many until the mid-20th century. Since the end of the Second World War, however, Christmas has become a part of life for most English families.

The contemporary English Christmas cultivates an appreciation of tradition. The 20th century saw a revival of, or renewed interest in, antique customs and games. All around England during the Christmas season, visitors can see remnants of old English folk rituals: the ASHEN FAGGOT, the HAXEY HOOD GAME, wassailing (see WASSAIL), morris dancing, sword dancing, MUMMING, the HODENING HORSE, and the GLASTONBURY THORN.

Outdoor lights at Christmas are an English tradition, not so much on private homes (as in North America), but along the streets and on public buildings. This dates back to the Victorian practice of lighting up and decorating shopping arcades. In November and early December, ceremonies mark the beginning of the illumination of retail areas such as London's Oxford Street or the huge Norwegian Christmas tree in Trafalgar Square. Often these displays are given a Christmasy or fairy tale theme.

England *The visit of carollers going door-to-door has long been part of an English Christmas.*

The English gift-bringer – a unique blend of the North American Santa Claus and the traditional figure of OLD CHRISTMAS – is Father Christmas. His outfit is similar to Santa's (red with white fir trim) but he is distinguished by his unbelted robe with a pointed hood. In the past he was also not quite as obese as Santa, and was always a little more solemn, but in recent years the old gentleman has put on weight and become jollier. His imitators can be seen in department stores or on television during the shopping season, but his true arrival is on Christmas Eve, when he places presents under the tree or in children's stockings.

Carolling is inextricably linked with the English Christmas. As well as local groups going door-to-door to entertain their neighbours and hoping for a little hospitality in return, the season also features wonderful programs of Christmas music in churches and on television. The most famous of the latter is probably the Festival of Nine Lessons and Carols, based on readings of the Nativity story, and glorious songs broadcast around the world on Christmas Eve from King's College Chapel, Cambridge.

An English Christmas dinner cannot be mistaken for any other. Turkey (with a sausage-sage-and-onion stuffing) has edged out goose as the festive dish, but no other country would accompany it with Brussels sprouts and bread sauce along with roast potatoes and peas. Dessert is equally traditional: mince pies, plum pudding aflame in brandy, or heavily iced fruit cake. The pudding may contain coins or lucky tokens and will have been prepared by the family weeks in advance, perhaps on STIR UP SUNDAY. Christmas crackers have been

pulled at English Christmas tables since the middle of the 19th century, and the comic paper hat contained within must be worn for a time at least. On Christmas Day, while the family is digesting its dinner, many will turn on the television set to watch the Royal Broadcast, a custom in England since 1932.

December 26 is known in England and the British Commonwealth as BOXING DAY, which takes its name from the custom of giving a "Christmas Box," a gratuity, to certain tradespeople with whom one has dealt during the year. This tradition lingers in the custom of tipping the milkman, postman, and dustmen. Boxing Day is also a day for the family visit to the pantomime. All across the country, theatres present fairy tale plays such as "Jack and the Beanstalk," "Mother Goose," "Puss in Boots," or "Aladdin." The heroes, or principal boys, are played by young women, and hideous old Dames are played by men. The costumes are spectacular and the audience always has a part to play in the fun. Boxing Day is also the time for sporting events: soccer matches, fox-hunts, and races are all well-attended.

The traditional end to Christmas in most of England was Twelfth Night, January 5, a time for parties, disorder, misrule, masquing, and the Epiphany cake. Most of that has disappeared, but thanks to a bequest by actor ROBERT BADDELEY, a Twelfth Night Cake is part of the evening's proceedings at a theatre in Drury Lane.

Ephraem Syrus, St. (c. 306-73) Ephraim the Syrian, author of "The Hymns on the Nativity of Christ in the Flesh," some of the earliest poetry on the Nativity.

Epiphany   From the Greek *epiphania*, or manifestation. Celebrated in both Eastern and Western churches on January 6, Epiphany marks a number of important appearances or manifestations: the arrival of the Magi, the baptism of Jesus, the miracle at Cana, and the Feeding of the 5,000.

Its first instance seems to have been in the second century A.D. among the Basilidean heretics of Alexandria, who believed that Jesus did not become divine until his baptism, which they claim had taken place on January 6. Though this idea of a late-acquired divinity was rejected by orthodox Christianity, some churches seem to have used the date to celebrate Christ's earthly birth, an epiphany of a different kind. When in the fourth century Rome adopted December 25 as the day to celebrate the Nativity, the Western churches' Epiphany shifted in focus to the Magi, while in the East stress was placed on the baptism. The period between these two important holy dates became known as the Twelve Days of Christmas.

Epiphany became an official holiday in the Eastern Roman Empire, marked by a ban on chariot racing and attending games in the arena, and by ceremonies of blessing the waters. At these ceremonies the emperor would drink the waters three times to the cry of "The emperor drinks!" The blessing of the waters takes place even today in Orthodox denominations. A priest blesses a body of water, either inside, or by a lake, river, or sea, and the faithful take the water home to sprinkle it on houses, barns, and fields and so ensure prosperity for the coming year. In some places the priest throws a cross into the water and divers race to be the one to recover it.

In the West, Epiphany was a day to celebrate the visitation of the MAGI, or the Three Kings as they became known. Religious services honouring the Magi gradually turned into dramas held outside of the church, such as *The Play of Herod*. As returning Crusaders in the 12th and 13th centuries brought back stories of the fabulous East, fascination with the Magi grew; cities held processions honouring the Kings, and carols retelling their journeys were sung. (The remnants of these customs are the STAR BOYS and their January pilgrimages from door to door.) Epiphany came to be a time all across Europe for popular celebrations marked by eating a cake and gift-giving.

The custom of the King's Cake, Twelfth Night Cake, *Dreikonigskuchen, gâteau des rois*, etc., can be traced back to the 13th century. A bean or pea or coin was baked into the cake, and the lucky finder was named king or queen of the party and could direct others to do his or her bidding for the evening. Though the tradition lingers in much of Europe (as well as French America), the custom of the cake was displaced in England to December 25, where it became the Christmas cake. In medieval France it was customary to put a piece of the cake aside for the poor, or to collect money from the rich for their share of the cake and use the money for charity.

Because the Christmas season ends in many parts of the world on January 6, Twelfth Night became a time of raucous celebration, associated with masking, mumming, drinking, and social inversion. This misrule may have been a carry-over to some extent from the riotousness of the pagan KALENDS. In Byzantium, for example, church councils had to legislate against the dancing and transvestism that went on in early January; during the reign of Michael III (842-67), the emperor and his court went so far as to use the occasion to mock the Patriarch of Constantinople and the mass itself. Mock coronations and consecrations became common in medieval Europe, with clerical hijinks, cross-dressing, noise, and laughter prevailing on Twelfth Night.

To commemorate the visit of the Magi, who brought gold, frankincense, and myrrh to the infant Jesus, Epiphany became the day for giving gifts, especially to children. In the Spanish-speaking world, the eve of the day of *Los Tres Rejes Magos* is when the Three Wise Men pass through on their way to Bethlehem and leave presents for kids who, in turn, leave out snacks for the kings and their camels. In Spain their Majesties and their attendants can be seen processing in great splendour through the city streets on January 5. In Italy the night of January 5 sees the visit of the Befana (the name itself is a corruption of *Epiphania*), an old woman who refused to spare time from her housekeeping to accompany the Three Kings on their journey. She soon repented of her decision and tried to join the Magi, but has never succeeded to this day. Her fate is to visit each home in search of the Christ Child and leave presents for the little ones she finds sleeping there.

In parts of the Middle East there is a charming story about this night. On the Night of Destiny, when the Magi first journeyed to Bethlehem, the palm trees bent down to show them the way – as they have done, says legend, every January 5 since. Once, a mule was tied to a tree on such a night, and when the trees sprang back to their ordinary posture the beast was whipped high into the branches. To mark this miracle, the Mule was made the gift-bringer in Lebanon, where doors are left open for him to bring in the presents and where hay and water are set out to refresh him.

Epiphany is also the time for houses to be blessed for the coming year. A priest recites a prayer, sprinkles the house with holy water, and censes the home and barn. The initials of the Magi and the number of the year are chalked on the door frame, as in "19 K+M+B 99." Even the chalk can be first consecrated with a Ceremonial Blessing of the Chalk.

Epiphany also serves as a time for driving demons out of the whole town. In parts of Switzerland boys go about on Twelfth Night making noise with horns and whips to drive away nasty wood spirits. In the eastern Alps, the *Berchtenlaufen* ceremony sees 200 to 300 boys with masks, cowbells, whips, and weapons shoot up into the sky and make as much noise as possible. In Eschenloe, in Upper Bavaria, three women with bags over their heads go from house to house carrying a chain, a rake, and a broom. They knock on doors with the chain, rake the ground, and sweep with the broom, all to clear away evil.

In England it has been the custom since the Middle Ages for the reigning monarch to imitate the Magi. On January 6, during the Epiphany service in the Chapel Royal at Saint James's Palace, two Gentleman Ushers, acting on behalf of the monarch, bring forth silken bags containing gold, frankincense, and myrrh. The gold is in the form of 25 gold sovereigns which, after the service, is changed into ordinary currency and donated to the poor. This presentation used to be carried out by the ruler himself until the madness of King George III prevented his participation; since then servants have acted as proxies.

Because of the disparity between the older Julian calendar and the reformed Gregorian calendar, what was once December 25 is now January 6, and for this reason the day of Epiphany is sometimes referred to as OLD CHRISTMAS.

Ernest Saves Christmas (1988)   Jim Varney first created his low-browed but big-hearted character Ernest P. Worrell for a series of "Hey Vern" commercials, then rode him to big-screen success. In this, the second of the Ernest movies, the incumbent Santa Claus is retiring and wishes to pass on his magic sack to a successor, kids' show host Joe Carruthers (Oliver Clark). Despite incessant bumbling, Ernest saves the day. Along the way director John Cherry takes a poke at Christmas horror movies when we are taken onto the set of the violent, alien-infested *Christmas Slay.*

"Es ist ein' Ros' entsprungen"   "LO, HOW A ROSE 'ER BLOOMING" A 16th-century German folk tune set by Michael Praetorius in 1609. Brahms used it for an 1896 choral prelude.

Estonia   Estonian Christmas is a fascinating blend of Orthodox, Lutheran, and pagan elements, with influences from Scandinavia, North America, and Russia also playing their part. The holiday was banned, along with many other religious observances, during the era of post-war Soviet domination; as in the U.S.S.R., New Year's was promoted as the replacement winter holiday. Since 1989 and the collapse of the Iron Curtain, Estonians have been rediscovering Christmas and reformulating it according to their new circumstances.

Like their Nordic cousins, Estonians mark the approach of Christmas with Advent calendars and the lighting of Advent candles. Children believe that if they place their shoes out on the windowsill during the month of December, the elves will fill them with little treats. Though baking, cleaning, and shopping occupy much of Advent, the Christmas season officially begins on December 21, St. Thomas's Day, when in the Middle Ages it was customary for work to cease for the holiday. One recent Scandinavian import has been the Christmas office party, or "little Christmas."

Though some say that the Christmas tree is a German import that became popular only in the 19th century, others say that the custom has a longer history. According to some, the earliest record of an evergreen tree playing a part in Christmas celebrations was in Tallinn, Estonia, in 1441. There is no doubt, however, that the tree, almost always a fir, is a big part of Christmas today in most Estonian homes. Those who live in the country make it a family practice to go into the woods and harvest the tree themselves. Commercial decorations, folk art, and candles are traditional ways to adorn the tree.

On Christmas Eve the president of Estonia follows a 350-year-old tradition and declares a Christmas Peace. That evening Estonians, having made all the preparations for the evening meal, traditionally head for the sauna to be steamed clean. Then they step into new clothes and attend church, after which it is time for dinner. Though turkey has become popular, many families retain an older menu: roast pork or goose with sauerkraut and blood sausage. For dessert there is a special Christmas bread and ginger cookies. Some families leave the remains of the Christmas meal on the table that night for the spirits of the family dead who will visit the home for Christmas Eve.

Estonians have adopted the Finnish vision of the gift-bringer, a Santa Claus figure who lives in Lappland and who travels by reindeer-drawn sleigh. Once the gifts are delivered, Estonians gather about the tree and have to earn the right to open them by performing a song or reciting a poem. Other Christmas Eve activities might include attending a fireworks display or visiting the graves of family members and lighting a candle – an activity that was a tacit pro-Christian demonstration in the days of Soviet occupation.

Since independence, Christmas Day is once again a holiday and is generally spent at home. December 26 is a little more active and involves visiting family and friends. The Christmas season ends on Epiphany, by which time most people will have taken their tree down, unless they are of the Orthodox persuasion, in which case January 6 is Christmas Eve and they still have more festive days ahead.

Ethiopia   Having been converted in 330 A.D., Ethiopia is one of the oldest Christian nations in the world, and Christmas there is quite unlike anywhere else. It is primarily a religious observance, largely untouched by the commercialization and emphasis on gift-giving that has spread elsewhere. The season begins with a 40-day fast, which, though not as strict as the Lenten period that precedes Easter, is still a time for physical and spiritual disciplines that prepare the body and soul for Christmas.

Ethiopians, following the Coptic calendar, celebrate Christmas on January 7. In churches around the country, candle-lit processions take place and people stand (there are no pews in an Ethiopian church) for a mass that may last up to three hours. Thousands come every year in pilgrimage to the country's spiritual capital, Lalibela, home to ancient churches. They spend the night before Christmas in a vigil of prayer, singing, and dancing. In the morning a great procession carries the Ark of the Covenant to the top of a nearby hill, where the liturgy is celebrated. After the service there is more dancing, feasting, and, for the men and boys, a game of *genna*, a kind of hockey played only on Christmas. This game is said to date from the time of Jesus' birth, when the shepherds, who had just heard the good news from the angels, waved their staffs in joy.

Food served at Christmas includes *injera*, a spongy flat bread, on which *doro wat*, a chicken stew (spicy like every other Ethiopian dish) or other main course, will be spread. A piece of the *injera* is then broken off to scoop up the stew. Gift-giving is a very small part of Christmas in Ethiopia and is usually directed only toward children, who receive something simple such as new clothes.

One foreign custom that has crept into Ethiopian Christmas celebrations is the Christmas tree. Such is the demand for the trees in the area of the capital, Addis Ababa, that the government has had to impose conservation measures to save the local juniper trees from extinction.

Two weeks after Christmas is Timket, or Epiphany, which is an even greater festival, lasting three days in honour of the baptism of Jesus and St. Michael. More gift-giving takes place and more feasting.

Étrennes   French term for holiday gifts, from the Latin word for presents, *strenæ*. The word is said to derive from the Roman goddess Strenia, from whose sacred grove branches were plucked at the KALENDS of January. These gifts are generally exchanged between adults at New Year festivities.

"Everywhere, Everywhere, Christmas Tonight"   A Christmas carol by the 19th-century American duo who collaborated on "O Little Town of Bethlehem," Philips Brooks (1835-93) and Lewis Redner (1831-1908).

> Christmas in lands of the fir tree and pine,
> Christmas in lands of the palm tree and vine;
> Christmas where snow peaks stand solemn and white,
> Christmas where cornfields lie sunny and bright;
> Everywhere, everywhere Christmas to-night!
>
> Christmas where children are hopeful and gay,
> Christmas where old men are patient and gray;
> Christmas where peace, like a dove in its flight;
> Broods o'er brave men in the thick of the fight;
> Everywhere, everywhere Christmas to-night!
>
> For the Christ child who comes is the Master of all;
> No palace too great – no cottage too small.
> The angels who welcome Him sing from the height,
> "In the city of David, a King in His might!"
> Everywhere, everywhere Christmas to-night!
>
> Then let every heart keep its Christmas within,
> Christ's pity for sorrow, Christ's hatred of sin,
> Christ's care for the weakest, Christ's courage for right,
> Christ's dread of the darkness, Christ's love of the light;
> Everywhere, everywhere Christmas to-night!
>
> So the stars of the midnight which compass us round,
> Shall see a strange glory and hear a sweet sound,
> And cry, "Look! the earth is aflame with delight.
> O sons of the morning rejoice at the sight!"
> Everywhere, everywhere Christmas to-night!

The Examination and Tryal of Old Father Christmas   When Christmas was restored with the English monarchy in 1660, there remained widespread prejudice against the excesses of its celebration, accusations that were expressed in the 1678 book *The Examination and Tryal of Old Father Christmas*, where Christmas, portrayed as an old man, is put on trial for encouraging social inversion, drunkenness, wasting, etc. He replies in his own defence:

> And first my lord, I am wronged in being indicted by a wrong name. I am corruptly called Christmas but my name is truly Christ-tide, or time. And though I generally come at a set time, yet I am with him every day that knows how to use me. My Lord, let the records be searched and you shall find that the Angels rejoiced at my coming and sang *Gloria in Excelsis*; the patriarchs and prophets longed to see me. The Church Fathers have sweetly embraced me, our modern divines all comfortably cherished me, O let me be not despised

now that I am old. Is there not an injunction in *Magna Carta* that commands men to inquire for the old way, which is the good way; many good deeds do I do, O why do the people hate me? We are commanded to be given to hospitality, & this hath been my practice from my youth upward: I come to put men to mind of their redemption, to have them love one the other, to impart with something here below, that they may receive more and better things above: the wise man saith, *There is a time for all things*, & why not for thankfulness?

Families at Christmas Before the 19th century, Christmas in the English-speaking world was not a family-centred festival. The emphasis was rather on hospitality, community, and feasting. The activities associated with it were often held outside the home (e.g., wassailing and mumming) and could involve raucous behaviour fuelled by alcohol and marked by the use of firearms. For reasons of commerce, and because of a growing sense of propriety in the culture, Christmas was eventually domesticated in the 1800s and the rowdiness was suppressed, leaving a holiday in which the family became central. Increased mobility through the advent of the railway contributed to this, in combination with those things that enforced separation: boarding schools, war (especially the American Civil War), and industrial employment. By the 20th century, reconciliation and reunion were overwhelming themes in Christmas literature, drama, and (later) cinema.

Family Day, "Dia da Familia" Portuguese term for Christmas.

Fantasia on Christmas Carols A work by English composer Ralph Vaughan Williams for baritone, chorus, and orchestra composed in 1912.

Fantasticals A term used in the 19th century for mumming at New Year's by Swedish immigrants in Pennsylvania. In Alabama there were Fantastic or Christmas Riders, who wore masks and costumes and spent Christmas morning riding from plantation to plantation, where they were received with a drink of liquor. In the South this custom was also known as Riding the Fantastic, Riding Ragamuffin, or the D.Q.I.s.

"Far, Far Away on Judea's Plains" An 1869 carol by John Menzies Macfarlane (1833–92), one of the few contributions to Christmas music by a member of the Mormon faith.

> Far, Far away on Judea's plains
> Shepherds of old heard the joyous strains:
>
> *Glory to God. Glory to God*
> *Glory to God in the highest*
> *Peace on earth, good will to men*
> *Peace on earth, good will to men!*
>
> Sweet are these strains of redeeming love
> Message of mercy from heav'n above:
>
> *Chorus*

> Lord with the angels we too rejoice
> Help us to sing with the heart and voice:
>
> *Chorus*
>
> Hasten the time when, from ev'ry clime
> Men shall unite in the strains sublime:
>
> *Chorus*

Farolitas Often confused with LUMINARIA, these are small lanterns used to decorate houses and walkways at Christmas in the southwestern United States and Mexico. *Farolitas* were originally Chinese paper lanterns but evolved into paper sacks lined with wax, with gravel or sand at the bottom into which a votive candle was stuck. Imitation *farolitas* are now plastic containers holding an electric bulb. In a reversal of cultural imperialism, this custom has now been adopted in Spain. See PAROL.

Father Christmas The personification of Christmas in the British Isles is Father Christmas. Some have pointed to a pagan origin (a perceived resemblance to Saturn, Neptune, and Odin), but the term comes into use only in the 15th century, when a carol addresses him: "Hail, Father Christmas, hail to thee!" He appears again in the 16th century, when social critics began to bemoan the loss of traditional Christmas hospitality. Ben Jonson's *Christmas His Masque*, written in 1616 for James I, opens with a parade of the sons and daughters of Father Christmas: Mis-Rule, Carol, Minc'd Pie, Gamboll, Post and Paire (a card game), New-Yeares-Gift, Mumming, Wassail, Roast Beef, Plum Pudding, Offering, and Babie-Cake.

After his children have been led in by Cupid, Father Christmas enters, despite attempts to bar him, and tries to establish his credentials as a native Englishman:

> "Why, gentlemen, do you know what you do? Ha! would you have kept me out? CHRISTMAS! – Old Christmas – Christmas of London and Captain Christmas! Pray let me be brought before my Lord Chamberlain; I'll not be answered else. *'Tis merry in hall, when beards wag all.'* I have seen the time you have wished for me, for a merry Christmas, and now you have me, they would not let me in: *I must come another time!* A good jest – as if I could come more than once a year. Why I am no dangerous person, and so I told my friends of the guard. I am old Gregory Christmas still, and though I come out of the Pope's Head-alley, as good a Protestant as any in my parish."

In Jonson's play Father Christmas is described as a man with a long, thin beard in a costume of round hose, long stockings, close doublet, high-crowned hat, with a brooch, a truncheon, little ruffs, white shoes, with his scarves and garters tied cross, and his drum beaten before him, but later 17th-century illustrations picture a more sedately distinguished bearded man in a long robe with a round cap. By the late 18th century he has grown quite fat, has holly in his hair, and is dressed in a fur-trimmed robe – the image that Dickens uses for the Ghost of Christmas Present.

Father Christmas was not associated with gift-bringing until the 19th century, when, under competitive pressure from the North American Santa Claus, he evolved into a friend of children rather than of feasting, drink, and merriment. His costume is similar to that of Santa Claus, but where his American counterpart has a short, belted jacket, he wears a longer, open robe with a pointed hood.

Father Christmas *Father Christmas makes an appearance at a 19th-century English children's party.*

Father Christmas A famous, perhaps even notorious, British children's book written and illustrated by Raymond Briggs and first published in 1973. In this irreverent portrayal of the daily life of Father Christmas, the old gentleman is shown to be very human, rather short-tempered, and fond of his comforts, particularly his brandy. Drawn in comic-strip form, Father Christmas carries out his activities constantly complaining about the weather, his cold feet, and the sooty chimneys he has to negotiate. After a hard night of delivering presents he wishes his readers a "Happy Blooming Christmas."

A 1991 animated cartoon version of the book was directed by Dave Unwin.

Father Christmas Goes on Holiday This 1975 sequel to *Father Christmas* by Raymond Briggs shows our hero trying to find a bit of peace and quiet on a vacation where he can go unrecognized. After unsuccessfully sampling the charms of France and Scotland, Father Christmas finds bliss in Las Vegas, where the heat, cold drinks, and leggy waitresses refresh his soul. Those readers who were amused to see Father Christmas on the toilet in the first book will note that his bowels suffer from French cooking in this story. "Blooming diarrhoea!" he complains as he rushes to the men's room.

The Father Christmas Letters A children's book by J.R.R. Tolkien. Based on letters supposedly written by Father Christmas to the Tolkien children every year from 1920 for over two decades, the book tells the story of life at the North Pole, where Father Christmas is aided by elves and the North Polar Bear and opposed by evil goblins.

Feather Tree A 19th-century artificial Christmas tree made with feathers to imitate evergreen branches. Some were dyed green, but many used natural colours.

Fête des Rois The French name for Epiphany, January 6, a time to dine out and give gifts to tradespeople, as in the English Boxing Day.

Finland Christmas in Finland is a mix of the modern and the ancient, with the Finns showing a genius for taking up new customs and making them their own. This can be seen, for example, in their adoption of St. Lucia, the Sicilian saint whose cult was popularized in Sweden, whence the Finns borrowed the custom. On St. Lucia's Day, December 13, girls dress in white, and one of them, wearing a crown of greenery and lit candles, leads her companions in a song and distributes gifts and snacks. The greatest act of cultural appropriation, however, was the Finnish takeover of Santa Claus.

Until the 20th century the Finnish version of the gift-bringer was the Joulupukki (Yule Buck or Christmas Goat), a rather crude and frightening figure out of folklore who was more likely to demand gifts than deliver them. From an icon of menace, his image was gradually softened until he came to resemble Santa Claus; from a figure that terrified children into good behaviour he became a benevolent dispenser of presents. The American notion that Santa travels by reindeer-drawn sleigh fit in nicely in Finland, where Lapps have domesticated the deer, but the idea that he lived at the North Pole was not a welcome one. Instead, Markus Rautio, a Finnish radio personality of the 1920s known as Uncle Markus, propagated the belief that Santa Claus was a resident of Finland and that his workshop, complete with wife and *tontut* (elves), was on Korvatunturi (Mount Ear). So convincing a job did Uncle Markus do on the Christmas consciousness of Finnish children that when Russia proposed annexing the territory around Mount Ear as part of war reparations in the 1940s, the outcry and possibility of a public relations disaster convinced the Soviets to let the Finns keep the now-sacred ground. Since then the Finns have been rather successful at persuading other nations that Finland is the true home of Santa (for more on this hotly contested claim, see SANTA CLAUS and SANTA CLAUS WORLD CONGRESS). The country receives over a million letters a year addressed to Santa Claus, and Finnish entrepreneurs have built a Santa complex near the Arctic Circle complete with a Santa Claus University and indoor amusement park.

A Finnish custom that has spread to neighbouring countries is *Pikkijoulu*, or "Little Christmas," a round of pre-Christmas parties at work or home, often including skits and songs and always including food and drink. Other Advent customs are a thorough house-cleaning and decorating the home with hand-crafted wood and straw decorations such as the *himmeli*, a mobile that hangs from the ceiling.

On Christmas Eve in Turku, the ancient capital, the mayor pronounces the annual Christmas Peace, a custom uninterrupted for over 500 years. The ceremony is televised and marks the country's official opening of the Christmas season. Shops close early and folk head for the sauna or to the cemetery to place candles on the graves of the family dead. The traditional meal for Christmas Eve is a ham with casseroles, stockfish, and herring salad. A rice pudding is the traditional dessert, with an almond in it that will bring luck to the finder. Even the birds are given a special meal of grain. That night children are visited by the Joulupukki (in the form of a family member dressed as Santa Claus), who brings gifts and quizzes them about their behaviour.

The next two days, December 25 and 26, are holidays, spent in visiting, relaxing, and outdoor activities. The season comes to an end on January 13, St. Knut's Day, when the Christmas tree is thrown out.

"The Fir Tree"   A typically depressing tale of Christmas by Hans Christian Andersen, 1844. The Fir Tree is impatient to grow up and does not appreciate his youth, fresh air, or sunlight. He yearns first to be a ship's mast and then a Christmas tree, decorated in pomp and glory. He gets his wish when he is cut down, set in a tub of sand on Christmas Eve, and trimmed

"The Fir Tree" Hans Christian Andersen's little fir tree is harvested for Christmas.

with nets full of candy, gold apples, and walnuts, 100 red, blue, and white candles, dolls, and other presents, with a gold star on top. His moment of glory is short-lived; he is taken down the next day and put in the attic, where he entertains mice with his single story and yearns for the forest. In the spring he is taken out, chopped up, and thrown on the fire:

> But at every crack, which was a deep sigh, the tree was thinking about a summer's day in the woods, a winter night out there when the stars were shining; it was thinking about Christmas Eve and Clumpy-Dumpy, the only tale it had ever heard and knew how to tell . . . and then the tree was all burnt up.

Fireworks, Firearms, and Christmas   In many parts of the world Christmas is associated with gunpowder: fireworks and firearms have been "shooting in" the holiday for centuries.

One reason for this is the belief that demonic forces can be driven away with loud noises. Ringing bells, snapping whips, and shouting are all very well, but for real devil-dispersing noise many Germans rely on rifles. In southern Germany marksmen's clubs in traditional costume gather on Christmas Eve to fire off antique rifles at midnight. In Berchtesgaden, in the Bavarian Alps, before midnight mass, 60,000 shots are fired in the space of one hour. In the southwestern United States, the parishioners of the Church of San Geronimo at Taos Pueblo carry a statue of the Virgin in a procession accompanied by an honour guard of men in ceremonial dress who periodically fire into the air in order to protect the Virgin and chase away evil spirits. In rural areas of Norway, shooting-in Christmas takes the form of young men sneaking up to farm houses and discharging their guns to give the inhabitants a shock before being invited in for a drink. Every December 8 in Torrejoncillo, Caceres, in Spain, the youth of the town wrap themselves in sheets, carry the banner of the Virgin, and ride through the streets shooting off shotguns to the cheers of the populace. In Ireland it was once the custom to fire a salute from a shotgun at noon on Christmas Eve.

An account of Labrador in 1770 reads, "At sunset the people ushered in Christmas, according to the Newfoundland custom. In the first place, they built up a prodigious large fire in their house; all hands then assembled before the door, and one of them fired a gun, loaded with powder; afterwards, each of them drank a dram of rum; concluding the ceremony with three cheers. These formalities being performed with great solemnity, they retired into their house, got drunk as fast as they could, and spent the whole night in drinking, quarrelling, and fighting." A similar Newfoundland custom was BLOWING THE PUDDING.

Christmas in the southern United States is a more popular time for fireworks than July 4, as can be seen from the numerous displays south of the Mason-Dixon line. The most spectacular are probably in Louisiana, where the *feux de joie* ("fires of joy") are a traditional part of Cajun Christmas Eve. Huge wooden structures in the form of riverboats, houses, and teepees are set on fire, ostensibly to light Papa Noël's way to the bayous. In the days of slavery, slaves would inflate a pig bladder and then explode it in lieu of firecrackers.

Fireworks are a part of Christmas celebrations all through Latin America, but who would have thought they were once a part of the holiday in Switzerland? One worshipper complained in the 19th century about a church service where the Christmas tree was decorated with "serpent squibs" and where it was "difficult for the minister to conduct the service, for at all times, except during the prayers, the people were letting off fireworks."

The First Christmas An opera written for television by Australian composer John Antill (1904-86). It was commissioned by the New South Wales government in 1966 with libretto by Pat Flower and was aired by the Australian Broadcasting Corporation on Christmas Day, 1969, and repeated in 1970, conducted by Verdun Williams.

"The First Christmas Tree" The legendary story of St. Boniface and his replacement of the pagan oak with the fir tree, retold by American writer Henry van Dyke, author of "The Other Wise Man." When the itinerant missionary Boniface encounters a pagan ceremony that is to include sacrificing a human child, he interferes to rescue the boy and destroys the shrine, replacing it with a young evergreen. The saint proclaims,

> For this is the birth-night of the White Christ, son of the All-Father and Saviour of mankind. Fairer is He than Baldur the Beautiful, greater than Odin the Wise, kinder than Freya. Since He has come to earth the bloody sacrifice must cease. . . . Here is the living tree, with no stain of blood upon it, that shall be the sign of your new worship. . . . The thunder-oak has fallen and I think the day is coming when there shall not be a home in all Germany where the children are not gathered around the green fir tree to rejoice in the birth night of Christ.

First-footing In parts of Europe the question of who shall be the first person to set foot in the home at Christmas or the New Year is very important; certain classes of people are considered lucky and will bring good fortune to the house, while some are unlucky. In the British Isles, in general, welcome first-footers were dark, male, handsome, and unmarried. A high arch on the foot was preferred, a foot that "water flowed under." In some areas of England, the best effect of all came from a "footling," a man known to have been born feet-first. Generally unwelcome were women, fair- or red-haired people of either sex, and those with flat feet or eyebrows that met above the nose. In some places women were unwanted, not just as first-footers, but at any time on the morning of January 1; should one appear she could be blamed for birth

First-footing *First-footers in the streets of Edinburgh.*

defects or deaths in the family during the coming year. Exceptions were widespread: on the Anglo-Scottish border, light-haired males were acceptable, while various places in Scotland specified women, especially barefoot, or children. In Yorkshire's West Riding, a red-haired man (rejected as a first-footer everywhere else) was welcome, as were fair-haired visitors.

Rather than leave such an important arrival to chance, the wise householder arranged for a suitable friend to be the first across the threshold or actually hired someone to "let in" Christmas or the New Year. In 19th-century Lancashire, a dark-haired man could make 10 shillings in the wealthy neighbourhoods by calling after midnight. Some folk hired troops of boys to be first-footers. In Acadian Canada, little boys made the rounds late December 31 to let in the New Year in return for treats; in Acadian parts of Cape Breton, older boys travelled about hitting the corners of houses to "beat the New Year in."

Some first-footers were expected to bring a gift, make a toast, or stir the fire; some were expected to go in the front door and out the back to let the new year in. In County Durham, the first-footer had to bring a drink of liquor and some bread and recite, "Happy New Year to you! God send ye plenty! Where ye have one pound note I wish ye may have twenty."

In Slavic Eastern Europe, the *polaznik* is the first-footer who brings a handful of wheat at dawn on Christmas Eve. He sprinkles the grain on the family and wishes them a Merry Christmas. He beats on the fire log until it throws sparks and stays for the family's pre-Christmas feast, departing in the evening with a gift. This custom ensures prosperity for the coming year. In Greece the first-footer should take care to enter with his right foot first.

"The First Nowell" A traditional song (perhaps from 16th-century Cornwall) first published in the influential 1833 collection *Christmas Carols New and Old* by William Sandys. John Stainer wrote the arrangement most commonly used today.

> The first Nowell the Angel did say
> Was to certain poor Shepherds in the fields as they lay;
> In fields where they lay keeping their sheep
> In a cold winter's night that was so deep.
> Nowell, Nowell, Nowell, Nowell,
> Born is the King of Israel.
>
> They looked up and saw a Star
> Shining in the East beyond them far,
> And to the earth it gave great light,
> And so it continued both day and night.
> Nowell, Nowell, Nowell, Nowell,
> Born is the King of Israel.
>
> And by the light of that same Star,
> Three Wise Men came from country far;
> To seek for a King was their intent,
> And to follow the Star wherever it went.
> Nowell, Nowell, Nowell, Nowell,
> Born is the King of Israel.
>
> This Star drew nigh to the North West,
> O'er Bethlehem it took its rest,
> And there it did both stop and stay
> Right over the place where Jesus lay.
> Nowell, Nowell, Nowell, Nowell,
> Born is the King of Israel.
>
> Then did they know assuredly
> Within the house the King did lie:

One entered in then for to see,
And found the Babe in poverty.
Nowell, Nowell, Nowell, Nowell,
Born is the King of Israel.

Then enter'd in those Wise Men three
Most reverently upon their knee,
And offer'd there in his presence,
Both gold, and myrrh, and frankincense.
Nowell, Nowell, Nowell, Nowell,
Born is the King of Israel.

Between an ox stall and an ass,
This Child truly there born he was;
For want of clothing they did him lay
All in the manger, among the hay.
Nowell, Nowell, Nowell, Nowell,
Born is the King of Israel.

Then let us all with one accord
Sing praises to our heavenly Lord,
That hath made heaven and earth of nought,
And with his blood mankind hath bought.
Nowell, Nowell, Nowell, Nowell,
Born is the King of Israel.

If we in our time shall do well,
We shall be free from death and Hell,
For God hath prepared for us all
A resting place in general.
Nowell, Nowell, Nowell, Nowell,
Born is the King of Israel.

Flight Into Egypt   In order to escape the rage of King Herod, the Holy Family fled into Egypt. Their flight is the setting for artistic depictions by such painters as Giotto and Vitori Carpaccio. The Rest on the Flight into Egypt is often treated as a separate theme in religious art. (See ANIMALS AND CHRISTMAS.)

Pious legends tell us much that scripture has omitted. The most famous story of the Flight concerns a farmer planting his field as Mary, Joseph, and the baby pass by. A few hours later, Herod's soldiers, hot on the trail, ask him if he has seen a family on the road. Yes, he replies, when he was planting his crop. The soldiers see that his field is now fully ripened (thanks to a miracle) and conclude they are too far behind to continue the chase. (See colour figs. 6, 9.)

Flower of the Well   It was once the custom in Scotland and parts of England to prize the first water drawn from the well on New Year's morning. Known as the Flower of the Well or the Cream of the Well, it would bring luck to the one who drew it; if it was a young woman she could expect to be married within the year. The water caused cows to produce more milk or, if kept in a bottle, preserved the house from harm. See WATER.

Food and Christmas   Food at Christmas is a topic loaded with meaning. What is eaten, what is not eaten, when to eat, when not to eat, and whom to eat with are all important issues and help illuminate the different ways the festival is celebrated around the world.

Food, for example, symbolizes the solidarity of the group. One's presence at a Christmas dinner indicates one is part of a particular family, admitted to one of the most important feasts on the calendar. Food also ties the generations together; making sure that distant relatives or those on the periphery of everyday life are invited to the festival is a means of binding the extended family closer. In many cultures this is carried even beyond the boundaries of life itself when food is left out on Christmas Eve for the spirits of dead family members, who are believed to return to the ancestral home on that night.

Food is also a way of reaching out. Ensuring that others have food or drink during the festival is not only an expression of hospitality and Christian charity, but also a way of demonstrating that one's own group has food to excess. In the Middle Ages it was also a token of social responsibility built into many feudal contracts, whereby the lord had to provide Christmas hospitality for his followers. The decline of this custom in the 16th and 17th centuries resulted in the rise of BEGGING VISITS and complaints about the death of Christmas as a time of charity. This is also the season of providing extra food for animals, not just one's own livestock but also the birds of the air.

Christmas feasting is a celebration of plenty, a sign that one can eat not just to satisfy the day's hunger. When techniques of food preservation were primitive, and when farm animals had to be slaughtered rather than wintered over, feasting at Christmas only made good sense; the food might well be wasted otherwise. In modern times celebrants have tended to manifest their possession of plenty by concentrating less on sheer quantity than on quality and expense of the menu; expensive dainties, drinks, or cuts of meat are indulged in at Christmas more than at other times of the year.

The food one eats is also a celebration of loyalty, a sign of belonging to a particular people, place, and set of traditions. By eating the same food every year one declares membership in a particular denomination or tribe. The *lutefisk* of the Norwegians, the rapee pie of the Acadians, and the turkey of the Americans are parts of Christmas not just for reasons of taste but because they are symbols of community.

Fools, Feast of   During the Christmas season in the Middle Ages it was the custom in many large churches, particularly in France, to allow the clergy certain days in which to celebrate and behave in ways not normally allowed. This period of licensed misbehaviour was partly a carry-over from similar midwinter festivals in ancient Rome, Saturnalia and the Kalends, as well as an attempt by Church authorities to maintain long-term order by sanctioning a time of temporary disorder. From this emerged the FEAST OF THE ASS, the BOY BISHOP, and the Feast of Fools.

The Feast of Fools was usually held on January 1, when the lower clergy elected a Bishop of Fools or Fools' Pope and carried on outrageously, making fun of sacred ceremonies and revelling in a hierarchy turned upside down. However, what began as an exercise in social relaxation eventually turned into burlesque and excess. Church leaders complained in 1445 that

> Priests and clerks may be seen wearing masks and monstrous visages at the hours of office. They dance in the choir dressed as women, panders or minstrels. They sing wanton songs. They eat black puddings at the horn of the altar while the celebrant is saying Mass. They play at dice there. They cense with stinking smoke from the soles of old shoes. They run and leap through the church, without a blush at their own shame. Finally they drive about the town and its theatres in shabby traps and carts, and rouse the laughter of their fellows and the bystanders in infamous

performances, with indecent gesture and verses scurrilous and unchaste.

Such behaviour was legislated against by king and Church but proved very hard to eradicate; records of the Feast of Fools endured into the 18th century.

Fouettard, Père, or Père Fouchette   Father Switch, from the French *fouet* ("birch rod"). A companion to the gift-bringer in France, he carries switches with which to threaten bad children and advises on which children to reward. His usual costume is a dark-coloured robe and a scraggly grey beard.

The Fourth Wise Man (TV) (1985)   Directed by Michael Ray Rhodes, this movie is based on the story "The Other Wise Man" about a magus who searches his whole life for the infant king only to meet him in Jerusalem when all hope has gone. Martin Sheen plays Artaban, his son Charlie Sheen plays a captain of Herod's soldiers, while the other father-son duo of Alan and Adam Arkin portrays Orontes and Joseph.

France   There is much to be done in France to prepare for Christmas. There are the saints' days at the beginning of the month to observe, depending on one's locality. In Provence, for example, December 4, St. Barbara's Day, is a time to sow buckwheat or lentils in a shallow dish or in cotton batting; it's good luck if they germinate before Christmas. On St. Nicholas's Day, December 6, the saint makes his appearance in towns in the north and west of France. (In Lorraine, where St. Nicholas walks through the streets, he is sometimes accompanied by a cart with a barrel out of which stick three boys – a reminder of his miraculous revival of the murdered and pickled kids. See ST. NICHOLAS.)

In Paris from the end of October, the large department stores have been preparing for Christmas with spectacular window displays; Christmas markets, such as the *marché de Noël* in Strasbourg, have opened up; and the markets in Aix and Marseilles feature *santons*, realistic clay figures for the family crèche. Throughout France this is a time for religious pageants: in Paris's Notre Dame Cathedral, the Nativity story is presented; and in the provinces the *pastorales* enact the Christmas story with musical accompaniment and often in the local dialect. A long-running *pastorale* in Provence has all the characters speaking in Provençal except the Virgin Mary, who speaks perfect Parisian French.

In homes families assemble their crèche, set up the *sapin de Noël*, the Christmas tree, and give the premises a good house-cleaning. Children address letters to the gift-bringer (usually Père Noël, though there are regional variations) and place them in their shoes or drop them in the mailbox or in department stores, where they will either be sent on to a special Danish postal station for delivery to the elves in Greenland or returned to the child's parents to inform them of the gifts desired.

Christmas Eve is the focal point of the season, with remarkable ceremonies all over the country. In Alpine regions torch-carrying skiers wind their way down the mountains in the dark to go to midnight mass. In Champagne, at the 16th-century château Braux-Ste-Cohière, there is a dinner for the shepherds of the region and their families and a performance of classical music. After the concert, the audience joins a torch-lit procession through the village, featuring a local teenager as the Virgin Mary, on a donkey, and another as Joseph. At midnight, the couple attempts to gain access to the château but finds the doors barred against them, just as in

Bethlehem. After Joseph knocks three times with his staff, the doors are opened and the Holy Family, followed by shepherds, proceeds to a manger scene overlooking an altar and mass begins. In parts of Provence a lamb on a carved wooden cart is pulled into church by a magnificent ram; behind them come traditionally clad shepherds and shepherdesses, singing and dancing. Carols are sung in dialect with medieval instruments. Beside the altar is a living crèche with animals and a real baby, if one can be found. After the mass and sermon, the shepherds pay their homage to the baby Jesus, with the last shepherd bearing the lamb as his offering. The post-mass meal is *le grand souper* and lasts for hours: there are seven courses, served on white octagonal plates, 13 loaves of bread (representing Christ and the disciples) and the famous THIRTEEN DESSERTS.

The meal eaten after midnight mass is called *le réveillon* and varies regionally. *Foie gras*, sausages, and oysters are traditional in Paris; goose is favoured in Alsace; and turkey stuffed with chestnuts in Burgundy. The most popular dessert is the BÛCHE DE NOËL, a chocolate cake in the form of a Yule log. In Provence the table must be set with three tablecloths representing the events of the season: Nativity, Circumcision, and Epiphany.

On Christmas Eve French children set out their shoes by the chimney or window and go to sleep expecting that the gift-bringer will come in the night. For most French children this means a visit from Père Noël, a tall, rather gaunt gentleman in a red, fur-trimmed, hooded robe. He is closer in appearance to the English Father Christmas than the North American Santa Claus, but he is not without rivals in various parts of the country. The baby Jesus, or Le Petit Jésus, the CHRISTKINDL in Alsace, Saint Nicholas, and TANTE ARIE in Franche-Comté all have their devotees. Sometimes the gift-bringer makes appearances before Christmas in the company

France A Guernsey stamp showing a shepherd of southern France with his Christmas ram.

of a frightening figure such as Hans Trapp or PÈRE FOUET-TARD. Christmas is not the day for adult gift exchanges; grown-ups tend to wait until New Year's. Surveys in the 1990s revealed that the French were generous givers of presents, with their children receiving more gifts than in any other European nation. (Also see YULE LOG.)

Francis of Assisi, Saint   Francesco di Pietro di Bernardone (c. 1181-1226), saint and popularizer of Christmas. The son of a prosperous merchant of Assisi, Francis underwent a religious conversion as a young man and became a wandering ascetic before asking papal permission to found a new order of monks who would emphasize poverty and preaching. In 1223 he staged a *presepio*, a living representation of the Nativity scene, at the church in Greccio as a means of making the Incarnation and humanity of Jesus real to the ordinary people. Francis was not the first to do this, as is sometimes claimed, but his example inspired a new attitude to Christmas and helped spread the idea of the crèche. After his death his Franciscan order propagated the CAROL as a spiritual song and attached its lively music to pious words for Christmas.

Frankincense   The gift of the Wise Man GASPAR to the baby Jesus, a symbol of Christ's divinity and worship. Also known as olibanum, it is a fragrant gum resin from African trees of genus *boswellia* long used as incense in religious services.

Frau Holle   Also Hullefrau, Hulda, or Holda, a German female gift-bringer. Frau Holle ("Mother Frost") is among the kindest and least frightening of the various female figures of Christmas in the German-speaking lands. She is the subject of a Grimm brothers' fairy tale, and it is said that when she shakes her feather bed it snows.

"The Friendly Beasts"   An interesting combination of a medieval tune (the Latin hymn "Orientis Partibus"), which was used in the FEAST OF THE ASS and a 20th-century lyric. The author was the otherwise unknown American Robert Davis. The text seems to have appeared first in 1934.

> Jesus our brother, kind and good
> Was humbly born in a stable rude
> And the friendly beasts around Him stood,
> Jesus our brother, kind and good.
>
> "I," said the donkey, shaggy and brown,
> "I carried His mother up hill and down;
> I carried her safely to Bethlehem town."
> "I," said the donkey, shaggy and brown.
>
> "I," said the cow all white and red
> "I gave Him my manger for His bed;
> I gave him my hay to pillow his head."
> "I," said the cow all white and red.
>
> "I," said the sheep with curly horn,
> "I gave Him my wool for His blanket warm;
> He wore my coat on Christmas morn."
> "I," said the sheep with curly horn.
>
> "I," said the dove from the rafters high,
> "I cooed Him to sleep so He would not cry;
> We cooed him to sleep, my mate and I."
> "I," said the dove from the rafters high.
>
> Thus every beast by some good spell,
> In the stable dark was glad to tell

> Of the gift he gave Immanuel,
> The gift he gave Immanuel.

The Burgundian writer Bernard De La Monnoye noted, "When in the time of frost Jesus Christ came into the world the ass and ox warmed him with their breath in the stable. How many asses and oxen I know in this kingdom of Gaul! How many asses and oxen I know who would not have done as much."

"From Heaven Above to Earth I Come"   A translation by CATHERINE WINKWORTH of Martin Luther's "VON HIMMEL HOCH." It is said that Luther wrote the song for his family's celebration of Christmas Eve in 1534. He eventually produced a carol of 15 verses; the first seven verses were to be sung by someone dressed as an angel and the remainder sung by children who would then dance. J.S. Bach would later use the tune in his *Christmas Oratorio*.

> From heav'n above to earth I come,
> To bear good news to ev'ry home,
> Glad tidings of great joy I bring,
> Whereof I now will gladly sing.
>
> To you this night is born a Child
> Of Mary, chosen mother mild;
> This little Child, of lowly birth,
> Shall be the joy of all the earth.
>
> Glory to God in the highest heav'n,
> Who unto us his Son hath giv'n!
> While angels sing with pious mirth,
> A glad New Year to all the earth.

"Frosty the Snowman"   Written in 1950 by Steve Nelson (1907-) and Jack Rollins (1906-73); recorded by Gene Autry, who made it the best-selling Christmas record of 1951. (Nelson and Rollins were also the creators of another holiday character, "Peter Cottontail," who first hopped down the bunny trail in 1949.) The song gave rise to an album and an animated film.

Frosty the Snowman (TV) (1969)   The snowman of song becomes a movie star in this animated film narrated by Jimmy Durante. The plot centres on the silk hat that brings Frosty to life, the magician who wants his hat back, and the school kids who want to protect their icy friend. Deadpan comedian Jackie Vernon is the voice of Frosty. Directors Jules Bass and Arthur Rankin Jr. were also responsible for a sequel, *Rudolph and Frosty's Christmas in July*, and a number of other Christmas-themed animations, including *Nestor the Long-Eared Christmas Donkey* and *Pinocchio's Christmas*.

Frumenty   From the Latin *frumentum*, meaning "grain," frumenty, made of wheat and milk, was a customary dish in northern England at Christmas. Also known as furment or furmenty, in Yorkshire it was the first thing eaten Christmas morning. A recipe from around the year 1400 reads,

> Take clene qwete [wheat] and bray hit wele in morter, that the holles gone alle of, and then seth hit that hit breke in faire watur, and then do thereto gode brothe and cowe mylk, or mylk of almondes, and colour hit wythe saffron, and take raw yolkes of eyren [eggs] and bete hom wel in a vessell, and do in the pot, but let hit not boyle aftur; and serve hit forthe.

Games For centuries it has been customary to play games at Christmas. An early 16th-century poem makes it clear that a forfeit is to be paid by anyone who is unwilling to help provide entertainment suitable to the season.

> Lett no man cum into this hall,
> Grome, page, nor yet marshall,
> But that sum sport he bryng withall;
> For now ys the tyme of Crystymas!
>
> Yff that he say he can not sing
> Some oder sport then let him bring,
> That yt may please at thys festyng;
> For now ys the tyme of Crystymas!
>
> Yff he say he can nowght do,
> Then for my love aske hym no mo,
> But to the stokkis then lett hym go;
> For now ys the tyme of Crystymas!

Late medieval English law allowed servants and commoners to play games at Christmas that were forbidden the rest of the year, provided this was done in the master's home with his permission. Such games were specified in a law of Henry VIII to include tables, tennis, dice, cards, and bowls. Thomas Burton's 1621 *Anatomy of Melancholy* says, "The ordinary recreations which we have in winter are cards, tables and dice, shovelboard, chess-play, the philosopher's game, small trucks,

Games *This 19th-century illustration contains a whimsical interpretation of hunt the slipper.*

billiards, music, masks, singing, dancing, Yule games, catches, purposes, questions; merry tales of errant knights, kings, queens, lovers, lords, ladies, giants, dwarfs, thieves, fairies, goblins, friars, witches, and the rest."

Other games associated with Christmas in the early-modern period were BLINDMAN'S BUFF, Feed the Dove, HOT COCKLES, and YAWNING FOR A CHESHIRE CHEESE. This poem lists a number popular in England:

> Young Men and Maidens, now
> At *Feed the Dove* (with laurel leaf in mouth)
> Or *Blindmans Buff*; or *Hunt the Slipper* play,
> Replete with glee. Some, haply, *Cards* adopt;
> Of it to *Forfeits* they the Sport confine,
> The happy Folk, adjacent to the fire,
> Their Stations take; excepting one alone.
> (Sometimes the social Mistress of the house)
> Who sits within the centre of the room,
> To cry the pawns; much is the laughter, now,
> Of such as can't the Christmas Catch repeat,
> And who, perchance, are sentenc'd to salute
> The jetty beauties of the chimney black,
> Or Lady's shoe others, more lucky far,
> By hap or favour, meet a sweeter doom,
> And on each fair-one's lovely lips imprint
> The ardent kiss.

Gambling was always popular with the aristocracy. In the 1520s Princess Mary was given an allowance of £20 for her Christmas gaming; Elizabeth I was alleged to have used loaded dice. Gamblers laid very high stakes in James I's court; over Christmas 1603 the queen lost £300 one evening and Robert Cecil lost £800. (In Iceland, on the other hand, the government tried to keep Christmas a solemn time and forbade "all chess, games, running, card games, loose talk, and entertainment.")

The common people were often more robust in their Christmas games. At Haxey, Lincolnshire, they played the HAXEY HOOD GAME, a struggle between towns for possession of a leather roll called the "hood." The game begins with a formal speech that includes the exhortation: "Hoose agin hoose, town agin town, and if you meet a man knock him down." In Ireland it was once customary to hold a village hurling match immediately after church on Christmas Day. Ethiopian men have traditionally played a form of field hockey on Christmas.

In *A Christmas Carol*, Charles Dickens lovingly portrays a Christmas party at Fred Scrooge's home that involved singing, but noted that the guests "didn't devote the whole evening to music. After a while they played at forfeits; for it is good to be children sometimes, and never better than at Christmas, when its mighty Founder was a child himself." The Victorian period emphasized nonviolent indoor games, including ones that permitted the sexes to come into closer contact than they otherwise might. "Squeak, Piggy, Squeak," for example, involved a blindfolded person sitting on someone's lap and trying to guess who they were from the squeaks they emitted. In "SNAP DRAGON" people tried to snatch raisins out of a bowl of burning brandy.

The 19th century saw the rise of the board game (see TOYS AND CHRISTMAS), which then came to dominate Christmas entertainment until the last half of the 20th century, when television began to intrude.

Gaspar Also known as Caspar, Kaspar, or Jasper, he is one of the Magi who visited the baby Jesus. Described most often as

Gaspar *The Wise Man who brought frankincense, as depicted on a Guernsey stamp.*

the young and beardless King of Tarsus, he is usually depicted as bearing the gift of frankincense in a jar or censer.

Gâteau des Rois The "Kings' Cake," so called because it was traditionally served at Epiphany, the celebration of the Three Kings or Magi who visited the baby Jesus. It is first mentioned in the early 1300s in France, from which it spread to Germany and then much of the rest of Europe.

In 1792 French revolutionaries tried to suppress the selling of "king cakes" as irreconcilable with the republican sentiment they wished to foster; in Bourdeaux they were called instead "cakes of liberty." Epiphany was stripped of its religious connections and celebrated as part of *la fête des sansculottes* (the festival of the revolutionary working class). In Paris on Christmas Eve 1794 (4 Nivôse III in the new republican calendar), the mayor ordered the arrest of pastry cooks for their "liberticidal tendencies." Taverns named after the Three Kings, who had come to be regarded as the patron saints of inns, changed their names to avoid incurring the wrath of radicals.

It was sometimes the custom in France for the first two pieces of the cake to be set aside for the *bon Dieu* and the Virgin and for these pieces to be given to the poor who came knocking on Epiphany.

The custom crossed the Atlantic to New Orleans, where the KING CAKE now contains a bean or plastic baby. The person who finds the prize must host the next King Cake party, hundreds of which are held every Epiphany. One Mardi Gras organization even uses the King Cake tradition to choose the queen of its annual ball.

The Gathering (TV) (1977) Adam Thornton (Ed Asner) is a bad father and husband who learns he has not long to live and who wishes for one last Christmas with his estranged family.

Good acting by Jean Stapleton and Asner lift this hackneyed plot above the ordinary made-for-television fare. *The Gathering*, directed by Randal Kleiser, won an Emmy for best special. A sequel, *The Gathering, Part II*, appeared in 1979.

General Grant The name given to an enormous sequoia in California that since 1926 has been the "NATION'S CHRISTMAS TREE." It is over 267 feet tall, 40 feet across its base, and over 107 feet around. Estimates of its age range up to 2,000 years old. Ceremonies are held at its base every Christmas season.

General Lee and Santa Claus A children's book of 1867 written by Louise Clack. It is set in the post-Civil War American South, where three little girls, Lutie, Birdie, and Minnie (the latter still a hardened rebel because of the memory of her father, who died in the Confederate army), wonder at the absence of Santa Claus during the war years. They write to General Robert E. Lee as "the goodest man who ever lived" to ask him "whether Santa Claus loves the little rebel children, for we think that he don't; because he has not come to see us for four Christmas Eves." General Lee favours them with the following reply: in fact Santa Claus does love the children of the South, but in 1861 Lee himself stopped Santa from delivering any toys to the Confederacy. He said, "Santa Claus, take every one of the toys you have back as far as Baltimore, sell them, and with the money you get buy medicines, bandages, ointments and delicacies for our sick and wounded men; do it and do it quickly – it will be all right with the children." And Santa did so for the duration of the war.

General Lee and Santa Claus is remarkable for its very early connection of American politics and Christmas and as a

General Lee and Santa Claus *The Confederate warrior greets the Giftbringer.*

Southern counterpoint to the Civil War cartoons of Thomas Nast, who had made Santa Claus into a firm supporter of the Union. Clack's depiction of little rebel girls desolate at their desertion by Santa Claus shows how important a figure he had become in the imaginations of American children. The American Civil War did much to accelerate the reception of Christmas in the United States as a holiday representing homecoming and family.

Gentle Camel of Jesus   Legend says that when the youngest of the camels in the caravan of the Three Wise Men moaned with exhaustion, the baby Jesus took pity on it and gave it eternal life and the mission of delivering presents every Christmas to the children of the Middle East.

"Gentle Mary Laid Her Child"   A carol by American Joseph S. Cook, 1919.

> Gentle Mary laid her Child
> lowly in a manger.
> There He lay, the Undefiled,
> to the world a stranger.
> Such a Babe in such a place,
> can He be the Savior?
> Ask the saved of all the race
> who have found His favor.
>
> Angels sang about His birth,
> wise men sought and found Him.
> Heaven's star shone brightly forth
> glory all around Him.
> Shepherds saw the wondrous sight,
> heard the angels singing.
> All the plains were lit that night,
> all the hills were ringing.
>
> Gentle Mary laid her Child
> lowly in a manger.
> He is still the Undefiled,
> but no more a stranger.
> Son of God of humble birth,
> beautiful the story.
> Praise His name in all the earth.
> Hail! The King of Glory!

Geography and Christmas   The Christmas season has given names to various parts of the world. Here are a few of the places with Yule-related names:

- Advent: WV
- Angel City: FL
- Bells: TN, TX
- Bethlehem: CT, GA, IN, IO, KY, MD, NH, NC, PA, SD, TX, South Africa, Virgin Islands, Wales. (Portuguese and Spanish versions of "Bethlehem" have been attached to the following places. Belém: Brazil, Mozambique, Portugal; Belén: Argentina, Colombia, Nicaragua, Paraguay
- Carol City: FL
- Christkindl: Austria
- Christmas: FL, MI
- Christmas Atoll: Pacific Ocean
- Christmas Bay: TX
- Christmas Cove: Maine
- Christmas Creek: Western Australia; TX
- Christmas Island: Indian Ocean
- Christmas Lake: OR
- Christmas Mountain: Alaska

- Christmas Pass: Zimbabwe
- Christmas Ridge: undersea Pacific
- Christmas Valley: OR
- Eggnog: UT
- Eggnog Branch: TX
- Epiphany: SD
- Evergreen: AL, CO, LA, NC, VA
- Holly: CO, MI, WV
- Joseph City: AZ
- Mistletoe: KY
- Natal: BC, South Africa, and Brazil
- Navidad: NM, Mexico, and Chile
- Nazareth: KY, MI, PA, TX
- Noel: MO, VA
- North Pole: AK, NY
- Partridge: KS, KY
- Reindeer Island: SK
- Reindeer River: SK
- Reindeer Lake: NWT
- Reindeer Station: NWT
- Rudolph: OH, WI
- Saint Mary's City: MD
- Saint-Nicholas: Belgium, France, and Quebec
- Santa: ID, Peru
- Santa Claus: GA, IN, ID
- Shepherd: MI, TX
- Silver Bell: AZ
- Snow: OK
- Snow Hill: MD
- Snowflake: AZ
- Star City: SK, WV
- Three Wise Men Peaks: UT
- Virgin: UT
- Winter: WI
- Wiseman, AZ
- Wreath Hill, WY
- Yule Bay: Antarctica
- Yule Island: Papua New Guinea
- Yule River: Western Australia

Germany   The approach of Christmas in Germany is signalled by the observance of traditions associated with a number of saints' days. ST. MARTIN'S DAY, on November 11, provides a warm-up for the gift-giving and festivities to come. St. Andrew's Day, November 30, marks the real beginning of the Christmas season in Germany. It is when many CHRISTMAS MARKETS open for business; it is the first of the *klopfelnächte*; and its eve is popular in German folklore for divination, especially to identify one's future spouse. One way of fortune-telling was to throw a shoe at a door at midnight – if the shoe pointed toward the door the young woman would marry within the year – or to toss an apple peel over the shoulder in the hope that its shape would reveal the initial of a future husband.

On December 1 Germans put up Advent calendars (a German invention) and the first of the 24 windows are opened to reveal a picture, verse, or piece of candy. The family's Advent wreath is taken out in preparation for lighting the first candle on the first Sunday of Advent.

St. Barbara's Day is December 4, when many bring in the branch of a fruit tree, the *Barbarazweig*, and encourage it to bloom before Christmas. In some areas it is also the day to bake *Kletzenbrot* (a fruit cake).

December 6, the feast of St. Nicholas, is when most of the gift-giving used to be carried out in Germany. Though much of that has been shifted to Christmas Eve, St. Nicholas's visit is still looked forward to by German children. The saint will often appear in person, clad in his bishop's robes, and ask how the little ones have behaved during the previous year. The children may also be called upon to perform a little song or say a prayer before being given their small gift. Nicholas will often be accompanied by a menacing figure, often called KNECHT RUPRECHT, but who also might go by the name of Hans Muff, Pelzebock, Krampus, or countless regional variations. His job is to threaten the children with a switch or the possibility of being stuffed into his sack and spirited away to wherever it is that bad children go. Those children who do not get to meet St. Nicholas by day will leave out their shoes at night to be filled with treats.

In Catholic parts of Germany, the nine days before Christmas is a time to honour the Virgin Mary and the search of the Holy Family for lodging. In the *Frauentragen* ("Carrying the Virgin"), the torch-bearing faithful carry an image of Mary through the village to the home of a family who will host it for that night. The *Herbergsuche* ("Searching for Lodging") re-enacts the story of Mary and Joseph seeking a room at the inn in Bethlehem as statues of the holy couple are carried from house to house. In some places children dress up as Joseph and Mary or carry a Nativity scene and go from door to door collecting money for charity.

Germans have produced some of the most beautiful Christmas music ever written, and visitors to the country can hear such masterpieces as J.S. Bach's *Christmas Oratorio* or sing such German-language carols as "Es ist ein' Ros' entsprungen," "Von Himmel Hoch," "Wie schön Leuchtet der Morgenstern," or "Stille Nacht" (written in Austria). Groups of carollers still go door-to-door in various parts of the country, and where the custom was once a BEGGING VISIT they now raise money for charity.

Christmas Eve is traditionally when the family's Christmas tree is set up and decorated away from the prying eyes of the children. Though other countries lay claim to the invention of the Christmas tree, it is generally accepted that it was in Germany that the custom took hold and then spread to the rest of the world. The idea that the 16th-century reformer

Martin Luther was the first to put lights on the tree is not now given much credence, but there is no doubt that Germans still love to decorate their trees with real candles. When all is ready a bell is rung and the tree and the presents under it are revealed to the young ones, who are told that the gift-bringer has just come. (Protestant areas tend to be visited by the Weihnachtsmann, a Santa Claus figure, while Catholic families are served by the Christkind, the Christ Child, who is envisaged as a white-clad maiden.) In addition to the gifts under the tree, each family member receives a plate of goodies. A church service, carol singing, and a feast are also on the Christmas Eve agenda. The large meal is centred on goose or turkey, with many regional variations such as sausage, red cabbage, noodles, and carp. Desserts are legion: the most famous ones are *stollen*, a rich Christmas bread; *lebkuchen*, gingerbread; marzipan; cinnamon stars; and *springerle* cookies. Eating to excess is encouraged; a nickname for Christmas Eve is *Dickbauch*, or fat stomach, because of the tradition that those who do not eat their fill on Christmas Eve will be haunted by demons in the night.

Many Germans spend part of Christmas Eve visiting family graves and placing candles over the resting places of the dead.

December 25 and 26 are both holidays in Germany and are spent in more feasting, relaxing, and visiting friends. This is also the beginning of the *Rauhnächte*, smoke nights or rough nights, a time to combat the forces of evil and cleanse the home of their influence. The house is smoked with incense, and numerous ceremonies take place in the streets with wildly costumed characters shouting and making noise.

Festivities in Germany continue through *Silvester*, New Year's Eve, which folk celebrate with great gusto, throwing parties and enjoying fireworks, to Epiphany. While some Germans are taking down their Christmas trees, others celebrate January 6 with parades of STAR BOYS imitating the Magi and collecting money for charity or safeguarding the house and farm for the coming year by chalking each home with the initials of the Wise Men. They might also attend Three Kings parties, where the Bean King and Queen are chosen by lot.

Gift-bringers   Though North Americans are familiar with the figure of Santa Claus, he is just one of a number of gift-bringers around the world, and Christmas Eve, the night of his descent down the chimney, is just one of a number of days on which the gift-bringer arrives during the Christmas season.

The original gift-bringer, the founder of the feast, was ST. NICHOLAS. Though displaced from many of the countries he used to visit, he is still a welcome sight in the Netherlands and other parts of Europe on December 5 and 6. He can be recognized by his bishop's attire, and he tends to travel by white horse or mule accompanied by such helpers as Black Peter.

Secularized descendants of St. Nicholas, who for the most part appeared first in the 19th century, include Santa Claus (who was a North American manifestation before his franchise went global), Father Christmas (popular in Great Britain and parts of the British Commonwealth), Père Noël (francophone lands), the Weihnachtsmann of parts of Germany, Baba Noel in the Middle East, and the Scandinavian gift-bringers, such as Joulupukki, Julemand, and Jultomten. The appearance of these gentlemen is rather similar – red-clad, fur-trimmed, bearded fellows of a portly build – and they all tend to work on the night of December 24-25. Most secular of all is Grandfather Frost, a Communist version of Santa Claus, who was offered by Soviet authorities as a New Year's replacement for the Christmas givers the state wished to suppress. He has been

Germany *A medieval representation of the Adoration of the Magi is depicted on this German Christmas stamp.*

evicted from most of Eastern Europe since the fall of the Iron Curtain, but maintains a presence in Russia.

The notion that the baby Jesus himself brings gifts is a widespread one. He is called El Niño in Spanish America, the Christkind in Germany, or Le Petit Noël in France, and has other names in Central Europe. In some places he is depicted as a small child, in others as a kind of teenage, female angel or fairy. Christmas Eve is the usual time of gift-bringing for this figure, but his saints appear on various days during the season; saints Basil, Barbara, Peter, Martin, and Lucia all have their own regions to service.

In Spanish-speaking lands, the Magi or Three Kings make their appearance on the night of January 5; as they journey to Bethlehem they stop off and deliver gifts to children. In Syria the legend of the Magi's youngest camel has made the Gentle Camel of Jesus into the local gift-bringer. In parts of Lebanon another legendary animal, the Mule, carries out these duties.

There are a number of female gift-bringers around the globe, though most of them work other times than Christmas Eve. In Italy the Befana, who has been searching for the Christ Child ever since that night she refused to join the Magi on their trek, comes down the chimney on the night of January 5. (Her Russian counterpart is the Baboushka.) In eastern Canada Mother Goody (also known as Aunt Nancy or Mother New Year) distributes small gifts to children on New Year's Eve, while in the Dominican Republic the Vieja Belén, the Old Lady of Bethlehem, gives presents to poor children at Epiphany. Tante Arie, of the Franche-Comté area of France, is the only female gift-bringer who is active on the night of December 24.

Gifts Gift-giving has been associated with Christmas ever since the Magi arrived to worship the baby Jesus and present him with gold, frankincense, and myrrh, but the practice has not always been so universal or all-consuming as it has become.

The midwinter festivals in Rome, which preceded the establishment of Christmas on December 25, were marked by gift-giving. During the celebration of Saturnalia and the Kalends, friends presented each other with *strenæ*, small tokens of goodwill and best wishes for the coming year (echoes of this custom linger in the French name for Christmas gifts, *étrennes*). At what point Christians decided to mark the Nativity with gift-giving is unclear, but a sermon from around the year 400 complains that the practice was making children selfish and that gifts were too often exchanged out of base sentiments rather than real friendship.

For much of the Middle Ages it seems gift-giving was confined to the upper classes and particularly the monarchy. Kings expected to be given Christmas gifts and could be quite testy if these were not forthcoming. Henry III ordered London shops closed until the city's merchants came up with £2,000 for his Christmas present. The value of gifts to English royalty was meticulously recorded so that the worth of a suitable return gift could be calculated. These gift exchanges often occurred at the New Year but were always referred to as "Christmas presents."

By the 13th century we begin to see evidence of gifts to children, often given on St. Nicholas's Day as the cult of that saint rose in popularity. A medieval French song says:

Nicholas patron of good children,
I kneel for you to intercede.
Hear my voice through the clouds
And this night give me some toys.
I want most of all a playhouse
With some flowers and little birds.

Nuns in Italian convents left out gifts for poor children in imitation of Nicholas's gifts to the three daughters of the poor man (see ST. NICHOLAS). In Germany in 1531 Martin Luther noted that children put out their stockings in hope that St. Nicholas would fill them with good things. A 16th-century list of Christmas presents for German children included money, sweets, fruit, dolls, clothes, books, Bibles, and writing paper – little wonder that at this time the Nuremberg Christmas fair was called the Children's Market. In England children were told that St. Nicholas brought them gifts on his feast day by coming in through the window,

In the 18th century Christmas had yet to become commercially driven, but we begin to see for the first time advertisements for Christmas gifts. They seem to suggest that gifts were bought largely for children and dependents (including servants) but that as the century progressed adult gift-exchanges were a growing part of Christmas spending. In the 19th century the Industrial Revolution and changing attitudes toward children accelerated gift-giving and hastened the commercialization of the holiday. It was considered increasingly intolerable that poorer children should be deprived of gifts, and numerous charities in Europe and North America sprang up to remedy this.

People now began to wrestle with the problem of to whom to give presents and the cost of these gifts. For a time GIM-CRACKS were the answer, but they were replaced early in the 20th century by Christmas cards as a way to acknowledge a relationship that was not so intimate as to demand a gift. As prosperity increased throughout the century, gift-giving spread to countries (for example, Central America) that had hitherto not made it a part of Christmas celebrations. The amount that families in industrialized countries spend on Christmas gifts has become a moral issue and the subject of public debate. (See SOCIETY TO CURTAIL RIDICULOUS, OUTRAGEOUS AND OSTENTATIOUS GIFT EXCHANGES and OPPOSITION TO CHRISTMAS.)

"The Gifts of the Magi" In probably the most famous of modern Christmas short stories, American author O. Henry (1862-1910; real name William Sydney Porter) tells the tale of the young married couple Jim and Della. Money is short for presents and economies have to be made, but the love each bears for the other produces willing sacrifices. Della sells her gorgeous hair to buy Jim a watch fob while, in sad irony, Jim sells his watch to buy combs for his wife.

It is said that O. Henry's love of alcohol often made him late in submitting his stories, and that in 1906 his Christmas story was badly behind schedule. In desperation the artist whose job it was to illustrate O. Henry's work went to the author to be given at least an idea of what to draw. O. Henry replied that he had not got a word of the story written, let alone completed it, but that he did have a vision of a poorly furnished room with a man and a woman talking about Christmas. The man had a watch in his hand while the woman's principal feature was long beautiful hair. The illustrator began to draw, and within a few hours O. Henry had produced a classic.

In the 1990s Mark St. Germain and Randy Curtis produced a Christmas musical combining the plots of two O. Henry stories, "The Gifts of the Magi" and "The Cop and the Anthem."

Gigantes These huge wood and cardboard figures, representing kings, queens, and historical or mythological characters, are part of street processions after midnight mass on Christmas Eve in the Catalonian area of Spain.

Gimcracks Low-priced gifts, remarkable for their tackiness and useless nature. From 1880 to 1910 gimcracks were the most common type of Christmas gift between friends in the United States. Examples include cheap novelties, Christmas spoons, and decorative figurines. Gimcracks were replaced by Christmas cards.

Gingerbread Ginger seems to have reached Europe by the 11th century, brought back by those who traded with the Middle East. Its attractions were quickly recognized: it could be used medicinally (to treat flatulence, hangovers, and stomach disorders), as a preservative, and to flavour food, and the root was soon traded at fairs across the continent. The centre of the medieval ginger trade, however, was Nuremberg, which became famous for its gingerbread cakes and cookies baked by a special guild of *Lebkuchler*. At Christmastime gingerbread was a well-loved feature of Nuremberg's *Christkindl-market*, as it is to this day.

Gingerbread can be soft or hard, dark or light, heavily spiced or mild. It can be cut into various shapes, the most famous of which are "gingerbread men" (the invention of which some attribute to Queen Elizabeth I of England) and gingerbread houses, which the Germans call *Hexenhäusle*, or "witches' houses," after the abode of the cannibal confectioner in "Hansel and Gretel." Gingerbread can also be cut into shapes suitable for ornaments and hung from Christmas trees.

Glastonbury Thorn A hawthorn tree, *Crategus oxyacantha præcox*, found at Glastonbury in Somerset, England, which is legendary for blooming on Christmas Day. The original tree is said to have sprouted on Weary-All Hill when Joseph of Arimathea, the man who gave his tomb for the burial of Jesus and who brought the Holy Grail to Britain, thrust his staff into the ground whereupon it miraculously produced white blossoms.

It was the custom for young people to gather under the tree on Christmas Eve and listen for the crackle of the buds as they burst into flower. The original was cut down in the 17th century by Puritans during Cromwell's regime (legend says the axe-man was killed by a splinter that flew into his eye), but survivors exist, having grown from shoots.

In 1752 crowds came to observe whether the thorn would bloom on the date of the New Style Christmas or on January 5, OLD CHRISTMAS. When the blossoms emerged on the latter date resistance to the new dating of Christmas grew stronger. Local ministers thought it wise to "give notice that

Glastonbury Thorn *A British stamp showing the miraculous thorn tree that blooms at Christmas.*

the old Christmas Day should be kept as holy as before." Every year since 1929, blossoms from the Thorn have been sent to the monarch for the Royal Table on Christmas Day.

Gloucester Wassail An 18th-century carol from the west of England reflecting the custom of wassailing the farm animals at Christmas.

> Wassail, wassail all over the town
> Our toast it is white and our ale it is brown
> Our bowl it is made of the white maple tree
> With the wassailing bowl, we'll drink to thee
>
> So here is to Cherry and to his right cheek
> Pray God send our master a good piece of beef
> And a good piece of beef that may we all see
> With the wassailing bowl, we'll drink to thee
>
> And here is to Dobbin and to his right eye
> Pray God send our master a good Christmas pie
> A good Christmas pie that may we all see
> With the wassailing bowl, we'll drink to thee
>
> So here is to Broad Mary and to her broad horn
> May God send our master a good crop of corn
> And a good crop of corn that may we all see
> With the wassailing bowl, we'll drink to thee
>
> And here is to Fillpail and to her left ear
> Pray God send our master a happy New Year
> And a happy New Year as e'er he did see
> With the wassailing bowl, we'll drink to thee
>
> And here is to Colly and to her long tail
> Pray God send our master he never may fail
> A bowl of strong beer! I pray you draw near
> And our jolly wassail it's then you shall hear
>
> Come butler, come fill us a bowl of the best
> Then we hope that your soul in heaven may rest
> But if you do draw us a bowl of the small
> Then down shall go butler, bowl and all
>
> Then here's to the maid in the lily white smock
> Who tripped to the door and slipped back the lock
> Who tripped to the door and pulled back the pin
> For to let these jolly wassailers in.

Gnomes See ELVES.

"Go Tell It on the Mountain" A traditional African-American song collected by black American composer and scholar Frederick Jerome Work (1880-1942) with a setting by his nephew John Wesley Work (1901-67).

> While shepherds kept their watching
> O'er silent flocks by night,
> Behold throughout the heavens
> There shone a holy light
>
> *Go, tell it on the mountain*
> *Over the hills and everywhere*
> *Go, tell it on the mountain*
> *That Jesus Christ is born.*
>
> The shepherds feared and trembled
> When lo! above the earth
> Rang out the angel chorus
> That hailed our Saviour's birth;
>
> *Chorus*

Down in a lowly manger
Our humble Christ was born;
And God sent us salvation
That blessed Christmas morn

Chorus

When I was a seeker
I sought both night and day
I sought the Lord to help me
And He showed me the way.

Chorus

He made me a watchman
Upon the city wall
And if I am a Christian
I am the least of all.

"God Rest Ye Merry, Gentlemen" Though most likely written in the 16th century or earlier, this popular carol was published first in the 18th century and has been sung to a number of tunes. It is mentioned in Dickens's *A Christmas Carol* when Scrooge frightens away a group of carollers.

An alternative ending to the last two lines of each verse reads, "O tidings of comfort and joy, / For Jesus Christ our Saviour was born on Christmas day."

God rest ye merry, gentlemen,
Let nothing you dismay,
For Jesus Christ our Saviour
Was born upon this day,
To save us all from Satan's power
When we were gone astray.
O tidings of comfort and joy, comfort and joy,
O tidings of comfort and joy.

In Bethlehem in Jewry
This blessed babe was born,
And laid within a manger
Upon this blessed morn;
The which his mother Mary
Did nothing take in scorn.
O tidings of comfort and joy, comfort and joy,
O tidings of comfort and joy.

From God our Heavenly Father
A blessed Angel came,
And unto certain Shepherds
Brought tidings of the same,
How that in Bethlehem was born
The Son of God by name.
O tidings of comfort and joy, comfort and joy,
O tidings of comfort and joy.

Fear not, then said the Angel,
Let nothing you affright,
This day is born a Saviour
Of virtue, power and might;
So frequently to vanquish all
The friends of Satan quite.
O tidings of comfort and joy, comfort and joy,
O tidings of comfort and joy.

The Shepherds at those tidings
Rejoiced much in mind,
And left their flocks a feeding
In tempest, storm and wind,
And went to Bethlehem straightway,

This blessed babe to find.
O tidings of comfort and joy, comfort and joy,
O tidings of comfort and joy.

But when to Bethlehem they came,
Whereas this infant lay,
They found him in a manger
Where oxen feed on hay,
His mother Mary kneeling
Unto the Lord did pray.
O tidings of comfort and joy, comfort and joy,
O tidings of comfort and joy.

Now to the Lord sing praises,
All you within this place,
And with true love and brotherhood
Each other now embrace;
This holy tide of Christmas
All others doth deface.
O tidings of comfort and joy, comfort and joy,
O tidings of comfort and joy.

"Godchild of the Highwayman" A story from the Netherlands by Anton Coolen. A poor shoemaker (in Christmas stories there is no other kind) can't find a godfather for his newly born 12th child until a mysterious stranger volunteers and gives the family a purse heavy with gold. The benefactor turns out to be a violent highwayman, and the mother is consumed with guilt about where the money might have come from.

The always-sickly child dies one Christmas Eve and is conducted to Heaven by his guardian angel, but he refuses to enter when he learns that his godfather is doomed to Hell for his life of crime. Finally Jesus relents and says that if the thief can fill a jar with tears of repentance he too may enter. The little child then returns to Earth to see if he can accomplish his rescue.

Gold The first gift offered by the Magi (usually by Melchior, though some sources name Gaspar) to the baby Jesus, it symbolized Christ's royalty (see colour fig. 14).

According to a legend recounted by JOHN OF HILDESHEIM, the gift was in the form of a golden apple once owned by Alexander the Great and 30 gold coins minted by Thara, the father of Abraham. Abraham used these coins to buy his burial place; Joseph was sold into Egypt for them. They were later sent to buy spices in Sheba for Joseph's burial, and the queen of Sheba deposited them in Solomon's temple. After the destruction of Jerusalem they made their way into the king of Arabye's treasury, whence the Magi took them. Mary lost the money on the flight into Egypt, but it was found by a shepherd. Judas would sell Christ for the coins, and finally, half of them would buy the burial field and the other half would be given to the guards who kept watch over Christ's tomb.

"Good Christian Men Rejoice" A rendition of the macaronic carol "In Dulci Jubilo" by the 13th-century German mystic Henry Suso, who dreamed of being invited by the angels to join in a dance whose tune he wrote down when he awoke. The earliest English translation dates from around 1540. In 1853 JOHN MASON NEALE, remembered for "Good King Wenceslas," made the current translation from the 16th-century collection PIÆ CANTIONES.

Good Christian men, rejoice
With heart and soul and voice!
Give ye heed to what we say:

News! news!
Jesus Christ is born today!
Ox and ass before him bow,
And he is in the manger now:
Christ is born today!

Good Christian men, rejoice
With heart and soul and voice!
Now ye hear of endless bliss:
Joy! joy!
Jesus Christ was born for this!
He hath oped the heavenly door,
And man is blessed evermore:
Christ was born for this!

Good Christian men, rejoice
With heart and soul and voice!
Now ye need not fear the grave:
Peace! peace!
Jesus Christ was born to save!
Calls you one and calls you all,
To gain his everlasting hall:
Christ was born to save!

"Good King Wenceslas"   Though music critics have complained for over a century about the awkward combination of words and music, this St. Stephen's Day carol by J.M. Neale has proven to be an enduring favourite. Neale's words, written in 1853 about the 10th-century Bohemian Duke Wenceslas, were matched to a spring carol from the 16th-century collection *Piæ Cantiones* with an 1871 arrangement by John Stainer.

"Good King Wenceslas" The king and his page set out on a mission of charity on this Bristish stamp.

Why Neale should have chosen Wenceslas to embody the call to Christmas charity remains a mystery. Some claim that there was a longstanding legend about his generosity, which English soldiers who fought during the Thirty Years War in Bohemia brought home, but, if there was, no trace of it remains. Neale would most likely have used "the feast of Stephen" because December 26 (St. Stephen's Day) was Boxing Day in England, a customary time for seasonal charity.

Good King Wenceslas looked out
On the feast of Stephen,
When the snow lay round about,
Deep and crisp and even.
Brightly shown the moon that night,
Though the frost was cruel,

When a poor man came in sight,
Gathering winter fuel.

Hither, page, and stand by me.
If thou know it telling:
Yonder peasant, who is he?
Where and what his dwelling?
Sire, he lives a good league hence,
Underneath the mountain,
Right against the forest fence
By Saint Agnes fountain.

Bring me flesh, and bring me wine.
Bring me pine logs hither.
Thou and I will see him dine
When we bear them thither.
Page and monarch, forth they went,
Forth they went together
Through the rude wind's wild lament
And the bitter weather.

Sire, the night is darker now,
And the wind blows stronger.
Fails my heart, I know not how,
I can go no longer.
Mark my footsteps my good page,
Tread thou in them boldly:
Thou shalt find the winter's rage
Freeze thy blood less coldly.

In his master's step he trod,
Where the snow lay dented.
Heat was in the very sod
Which the saint had printed.
Therefore, Christian men, be sure,
Wealth or rank possessing,
Ye who now will bless the poor
Shall yourselves find blessing.

Good Star/Father Star   Alternative terms for the Polish Santa figure, the Star Man, who brings gifts on Christmas Eve.

Goose   A traditional Christmas meat in England (it's what the Cratchit family eats in *A Christmas Carol*), Alsace, and Denmark, also popular in Germany on Martinmas.
 "Goose clubs" were a way of saving money throughout the year for Christmas dinner and were also lotteries for the poor, providing geese of various sizes and alcohol as prizes.
 In Arthur Conan Doyle's "The Adventure of the Blue Carbuncle," Sherlock Holmes solves a mystery of the Christmas goose who swallowed a jewel.

El Gordo   Every December 22 Spaniards are held in suspense by the *Loteria de Navidad*, the Christmas Lottery, also known as *El Gordo*, "The Fat One," because of the hundreds of millions of dollars to be won in prizes. Most Spaniards buy a ticket and it is covered live by the national media.

Grain   As a sign of fertility and hope for prosperity for the coming year, grain is an important part of the Christmas observances in Eastern Europe: it appears in dishes for the meatless Christmas Eve suppers; it is tucked under the tablecloth; or placed in a sheaf in the corner. In Scandinavia grain is set out for the birds at Christmas (see JULENEK). In Ireland a pan of oats is placed as high as possible in the room, with 12 candles representing the apostles and a large candle in the centre representing Christ. Grain porridges and puddings,

Goose *Goose clubs like the one in operation here were a way of saving for Christmas necessities in 19th-century England.*

such as frumenty, *Jólagrautur*, and *kutya*, appear at Christmas all over Europe.

Grandfather Frost   The Soviet version of Santa Claus – meant to replace Father Christmas, or Kolyáda, at Christmas and

Grandfather Frost *This Canadian stamp shows the Russian gift-bringer Grandfather Frost, also known as Ded Moroz.*

Baboushka at Epiphany – Grandfather Frost ("Ded Moroz") was depicted as an elderly white-bearded man in a long coat and winter furs. As part of the Communist campaign against the old religion and all its customs, Grandfather Frost was said to bring presents at New Year's. He was accompanied on his rounds by an attractive young woman, alleged to be his niece, called Snegurochka, the Snow Maiden. His survival in the post-Communist world is still uncertain.

In Soviet-dominated Eastern Europe, attempts by officials to eradicate the Christmas legends of local gift-bringers was met with resistance, and Grandfather Frost was perceived as a symbol of Russian oppression.

"Grandma Got Run Over by a Reindeer"   A novelty song written in 1979 by veterinarian Elmo Shropshire and popularized by Elmo and Patsy. In it Grandma, who had been drinking too much eggnog, is found dead under circumstances that suggest she has been hit by Santa's sleigh. The song achieved notoriety in Canada when complaints were lodged with politicians, women's groups, and seniors' organizations that it was offensive to elderly women and that the death of a matriarch was no laughing matter. Though nothing was done to limit its airplay, the song was voted one of the "Three Most Dreaded Christmas Songs Ever" and an American disc jockey was fired for playing it (by request) 27 times in a row. A parody followed entitled "Grandpa Got Runned Over by a John Deere."

"A Great and Mighty Wonder"   J.M. Neale's translation of St. Germanus's (634-733) liturgical hymn for Christmas Day. The melody can be traced to a Christmas or Twelfth Night folk carol from the diocese of Trier in the 15th or early 16th century.

A great and mighty wonder,
A full and holy cure!

The Virgin bears the Infant
With virgin-honour pure.

Repeat the hymn again:
"To God on high be glory,
And peace on earth to men."

The Word becomes incarnate
And yet remains on high!
And cherubim sing anthems
To shepherds, from the sky.

Refrain

While thus they sing your Monarch,
Those bright angelic bands,
Rejoice, ye vales and mountains,
Ye oceans, clap your hands!

Refrain

Since all he comes to ransom,
By all is he adored,
The Infant born in Bethlehem,
The Saviour and the Lord.

Refrain

And idol forms shall perish,
And error shall decay,
And Christ shall wield his sceptre,
Our Lord and God, for ay.

Refrain

Greece Christmas in Greece is entering a new era. The decorations, food, and customs increasingly resemble those in Western Europe or North America, and where once Christmas was a quiet, spiritual time with little commercialization, it is now more hectic and flashy, at least in the urban centres. Despite this Greece retains many unique customs.

A penitential Advent season in Greece, the Fast of the Nativity begins on November 17, but preparations for Christmas accelerate on December 6, the feast of St. Nicholas. Nicholas in many countries is a quaint gift-giver; in Greece he is the national patron saint and the special protector of sailors, who perform devotional ceremonies to him on his day. Christmas trees, which were once rare in Greece, are now becoming more common (though often artificial) and are set up in mid-December. (Before the popularity of the tree, many Greeks decorated model ships at Christmastime or kept a sprig of basil wrapped around a wooden cross.)

Christmas baking is important in Greece, and a number of productions are indispensable: *loukoumathes* (honey dough balls); *kourabiedes* (sugar-coated shortbread); *melomakarona* (biscuits dipped in honey or syrup and rolled in ground nuts); and *Christopsomo* (the round Christmas bread that is the centrepiece of the Christmas Eve meal). *Kouloures* are Christmas breads made to indicate the family's profession: a plough shape for a farming family, a sheep for shepherds, etc. (Some of these cookies are saved for the children, who go door-to-door singing *kalandas*, the beautiful Greek carols that are often accompanied by the sound of the triangle and drum.)

Where it was once customary for most Greeks to open their presents at the New Year, many are now following the Western custom of doing so on Christmas Eve or Christmas morning. The main course at the Christmas meal is changing as well. Roast pork was once the invariable highlight, with many rural families raising the pig themselves for just this purpose, but nowadays turkeys are appearing on Greek tables. Disappearing

too are the rituals of the pig slaughter and the marking of a cross on the children's foreheads with the animal's blood. The *Christopsomo* bread, though, remains an unchanged and essential element of the meal.

On New Year's Eve children sing hymns to St. Basil (whose feast is January 1) and are rewarded with treats and money. St. Basil's cake, the spongy *Vasilopitta*, is eaten after a ceremonial division in which portions are ritually allocated to the saint, various family members, and the poor. A coin is baked into the cake, and the finder is considered lucky for the coming year; if it is found in the piece for the poor, the coin is given to charity. The next day gifts are distributed, a sumptuous meal is served, and the Renewing of the Waters takes place when new St. Basil's Water replaces the old year's water in jugs.

January 6 is the last major celebration of the Christmas season in Greece and marks the Theophany of Jesus, the descent of the Holy Spirit upon him at his baptism. Greek bishops perform the Great Blessing of the Waters by carrying a cross, tied with a sprig of basil, and throwing it into a river, lake, or the sea in token of Christ's birth and baptism. The cross will be retrieved by a diver; sometimes there is competition for the honour of finding the cross, as luck accrues to the one who returns it to the bishop.

No account of Christmas in Greece would be complete without a mention of the folk belief in the *kallikantzaroi*. These are subterranean monsters that emerge during the Twelve Days of Christmas to torment humans. They are angry that their year-long work to gnaw away at the tree that supports the world is thwarted by the birth of Jesus at Christmas. In their rage they come down the chimney and perform little acts of nastiness, such as souring the milk, urinating in the fire, or forcing folk to dance to exhaustion. They can be deterred by keeping the Yule log burning through the season, burning old shoes, or hanging up hyssop and a pig's jaw. The Blessing of the Waters finally drives them back underground for another year.

Greenery Social historians tell us that one essential part of every midwinter festival is the presence of greenery as a token of the hope that the earth, now cold and barren, will once more be fruitful. Certainly green plants and branches were so much a part of the Roman and Egyptian feasts that predated Christmas that early Christian leaders were reluctant to see their followers use them. Tertullian said, "Let them kindle lamps, they who have no light; let them fix on doorposts laurels which shall afterwards be burnt, they for whom the fire is close at hand. . . . But thou art a light of the world and a tree that is ever green; if thou hast renounced the temple make not a temple of thy own house door." Church councils also condemned greenery, but the syncretic approach of Pope GREGORY won out in the end and all manner of plants once used by pagans were put to a Christian purpose.

Among the first to be used for Christmas decoration was laurel, the symbol of victory in the ancient world and a sign to Christians of Jesus' victory over sin and death. A wreath of laurel was often hung on doors in Rome; though laurel has been replaced for this purpose by evergreens, the wreath is still a popular Christmas decoration.

In the Middle Ages rosemary was often used in church decoration at Christmas and was welcomed for its fragrance and its part in the legend that Mary hung the baby's swaddling clothes (or her cloak) on the plant to dry during the Flight into Egypt. For some reason rosemary fell out of favour as a church decoration in the 19th century.

"Holly and ivy, box and bay put in the church on Christmas day," says the English rhyme. Holly with its sharp-edged leaves and red berries was a symbol of Christ's crown of thorns and the blood he shed. It is the subject of Christmas carols such as "The Holly and the Ivy" and the "Sans Day Carol." Ivy was said to be a female plant and a symbol of the human weakness that clings to divine strength.

By the 15th century greenery was inseparable from the notion of an English Christmas. John Stowe says in his *Survey of London*:

> Against the feast of Christmas every man's house, as also the parish churches, were decked with holm, ivy, bays, and whatsoever the season of the year afforded to be green. The conduits and standards in the streets were likewise garnished; amongst the which I read, in the year 1444 that by tempest of thunder and lightning, on the first of February, at night, Powle's steeple was fired, but with great labour quenched; and towards the morning of Candlemas day, at the Leaden hall in Cornhill, a standard of tree being set up in midst of the pavement, fast in the ground, nailed full of holm and ivy, for disport of Christmas to the people, was torn up, and cast down by the malignant spirit (as was thought), and the stones of the pavement all about were cast in the streets, and into divers houses, so that the people were sore aghast of the great tempests.

Greenery *A family prepares its Christmas greenery in this 1880 illustration from* Harper's Weekly.

When the Puritan government of England in the 1640s wished to suppress Christmas they made it a point to tear down such street greenery as Stowe describes above. This prejudice endured in some places well into the 19th century. In 1881 in Newfoundland, members of the ultra-Protestant Orange Lodge opposed putting evergreen boughs in their church on the excuse that it was a Roman Catholic practice and that green was the Fenian (Irish nationalist) colour. The pastor was able to defuse their objections by pointing to Isaiah 60: "The glory of Lebanon shall come unto thee, the fir tree, the pine tree, and the box together, to beautify the place of My sanctuary."

Mistletoe, with its pagan associations, was once thought to have been banned from church decoration, but records from the 17th century show that it was common to bring the parasitic plant into the church. In the home, the custom of kissing under the mistletoe (or under the kissing bough), which began in the 18th century, seems to have been a practice exclusive to the servant class until about 1850, when it became popular among the better-off as well.

When Europeans began to colonize the globe they found they missed their accustomed greenery at Christmas. They solved this either by importing their native plants to their new lands or by adopting indigenous plants. A settler in the backwoods of Canada in 1838 wrote, "That it might look more like an English Christmas Day, I dispatched Martin the boy and old Malachi, the hired man, to bring a sleigh load of evergreens, from the swamp to dress the house with, but when all our green garlands were put up, we missed the bright varnished holly and its gay joy-inspiring red berries." So these hardy pioneers made do with local cranberries instead. In Australia various bushes have been used to replace the Christmas tree, while in New Zealand the native pohutukawa, with its deep green leaves and red flowers, has been taken to heart as the symbol of Christmas.

When to take the greenery down and how to dispose of it have been the subjects of many superstitions. The 17th-century poet Robert Herrick claimed it should be done by Twelfth Night, and said,

> Down with the rosemary and so
> Down with the bay and mistletoe,
> Down with the holly, ivy, all
> Wherewith ye deck'd the Christmas hall;
> That so the superstitious find
> No one least branch there left behind:
> For look! how many leaves there be
> Neglected there, Maids, trust to me,
> So many goblins you shall see.

In other areas it was January 13, and in others it was Candlemas, February 2. Many of the plants, especially holly, had to be burned rather than just thrown away. The miracle of modern plastics has now made this a negligible issue; artificial holly, ivy, and mistletoe can be popped back in the box for use again next Christmas.

Gregory I, St. (c. 540-604) The pope who advised Augustine, missionary to the Germanic peoples of Britain, to allow the newly converted to keep old customs if they could be given a Christian interpretation. This policy helped ensure that Christmas celebrations over the ages would be syncretic, varied with many local flavours. His advice is contained in a letter to Abbot Mellitus, who was travelling to join Augustine:

> By no means destroy the temples of the gods but rather the idols within those temples. Let him, after he has purified them with holy water, place altars and relics of the saints in them. For, if those temples are well built, they should be converted from the worship of demons to the service of the true God. Thus, seeing that their places of worship are not destroyed, the people will banish error from their hearts and come to places familiar and dear to them in acknowledgement and worship of the true God. Further, since it has been their custom to slaughter oxen in sacrifice, they should receive some solemnity in exchange. Let them therefore, on the day of the dedication of their churches, or

on the feast of the martyrs whose relics are preserved in them, build themselves huts around their one-time temples and celebrate the occasion with religious feasting. They will sacrifice and eat the animals not any more as an offering to the devil, but for the glory of God to whom, as the giver of all things, they will give thanks for having been satiated. Thus, if they are not deprived of all exterior joys, they will more easily taste the interior ones. For surely it is impossible to efface all at once everything from their strong minds, just as, when one wishes to reach the top of a mountain, he must climb by stages and step by step, not by leaps and bounds.

Gremlins (1984)   A black comedy about a Christmas gift gone bad. A father (Hoyt Axton) buys a loveable furry creature called a Mogwai for his son Billy (Zach Galligan) and is given three instructions for the pet: keep it out of bright lights, keep it away from water, and never feed it after midnight. All the rules are soon broken and the cute pet reproduces a host of destructive monsters who wreak mayhem on the little town. Director Joe Dante filled the picture with countless movie references and inside jokes.

Grinch   A term that has entered the language from Dr. Seuss's famous children's book *How the Grinch Stole Christmas* to denote one who despises Christmas and all it implies. No better example of the spirit can be found than the following 1995 "Credo" by "Anonymous Grinch":

> I repudiate the Christmas traditions which I remember and know about.
>
> I reject and dedicate energy to oppose and weaken and discredit the belief system which underlies these traditions.
>
> I do not believe that Jesus was born of a Virgin on Christmas and died on the cross and was raised on the third day to save believers in him from sin and damnation. I believe that that idea is both stupid and immoral.
>
> I do not believe that Santa Claus brings gifts to good children.
>
> I believe we should try an economy which does not depend on the exchange of gifts at the end of the year. The invention, distribution and sale of items that do not correspond to what humans need or want amounts to waste and stupidity.
>
> I do not believe that trees should be killed in honor of any of these beliefs. I do not believe that farmland should be used to plant and harvest such a useless crop. If corn or wheat isn't needed, the trees should be allowed to mature.
>
> I do not believe that mythology should be burdened with the task of teaching the young, and the old, that altruism should be given a one-day annual try-out, because it is so sentimentally "nice."
>
> Ecology, human solidarity and planetary unity all indicate that we should get rid of Christmas. I intend to weaken it a little, by withdrawing my emotional involvement.

Grotto of the Milk   Bethlehem possesses remarkable religious sites connected with the Nativity. One such is the Grotto of the Milk, a cave of milky-white stone in which, according to legend, the Holy Family sought refuge from Herod's soldiers, who were carrying out the Massacre of the Innocents. Drops of the Virgin's milk are said to have fallen onto the rock and were responsible for the unusual colour of the cave. Franciscan monks in the 15th century built a chapel on the spot, and it has become a site of pilgrimage for women seeking miracles and a healthy flow of breast milk. See BETHLEHEM.

Gruber, Franz Xaver   (1787-1863) Austrian teacher and musician, composer of the melody of "Silent Night." As the organist of the St. Nicholas church in Oberndorf, Gruber was asked in December 1818 by parish priest Josef Mohr to set a poem of his to music for the Christmas Eve midnight mass. The result of this collaboration was "Stille Nacht," which became the world's most famous Christmas song. Gruber continued to compose after he left Oberndorf, and some of his hymns and masses are still sung in Austria.

Gryla   A monster of Icelandic folklore, her 13 children are known collectively as the JÓLASVEINAR or Yule Lads. She and her husband, Leppaludi, were regarded for centuries as cannibal ogres, particularly fond of the flesh of children. Parents used fear of her and her CHRISTMAS CAT as a way of keeping children well-behaved.

Guatemala   In 15th-century Florence, a religious revival led by the monk Savonarola resulted in the famous "Bonfire of the Vanities," a public burning of luxuries that were deemed to distract believers from God and salvation. A similar spectacle occurs every year at the beginning of the Christmas season in Guatemala. On December 7 (also the day to celebrate the Immaculate Conception), Guatemalans haul out of their homes the things they think they don't need any more and set them on fire in a ceremony called "The Burning of the Evil." With their homes thus purged of unnecessary encumbrances, people can prepare for the coming of Christmas. Homes are then cleaned and decorated and the household crèche, or *nacimiento*, is placed out. In Guatemala these Nativity scenes can be quite elaborate; models of Bethlehem and the figures hurrying to see the birth of Jesus sometimes occupy an entire room. (Only on Christmas Eve is the figure of the baby added.)

Nine days before Christmas, Guatemalans begin the season of the *posadas*, processions recreating the search of the Virgin and Joseph for lodging. Each night a different couple plays the part of the Holy Family and knocks on doors, being ritually rebuffed before finding a home that will take them in. On the ninth night all the couples who have played Mary and Joseph, plus musicians, friends, and neighbours, gather at the final home to welcome them and have a grand party.

The native pine, the pinabete (*Abies guatemalensis*), is an endangered species because the growing demand of urban residents for a Western-style Christmas tree has pushed it to the brink of extinction and threatened an ecological disaster in the countryside. As a result it is illegal to cut or sell the tree, and patrols of police and conservation officers prowl the hills looking for poachers and cruise city streets confiscating trees and branches. Artificial trees have filled the gap for those wishing to have something to decorate and put presents from El Niño under.

After the children open their presents on Christmas Eve, the midnight mass, or the *Misa de Gallo*, is a must for most Guatemalan families. Afterwards fireworks are set off to celebrate the Nativity and folk sit down to a dinner of *tamales*, meat and salsa-filled corn dough wrapped in plantain leaves. Christmas Day is marked by visiting, a noon-time church service, and more fireworks.

La Guignolée *The French-Canadian custom of soliciting charity during the Christmas season.*

La Guignolée The custom in the province of Quebec, Canada, of going door-to-door during the Advent season to raise money and collect food for charity. It began in the Middle Ages as a noisy BEGGING VISIT at New Year's, and was transported to North America during the French settlement of the continent in the 17th century. To the refrain "*La ignolée, la ignoloche*," a traditional song is sung in which admittance is craved and threats made if a donation is not forthcoming.

> Good day to you master and mistress,
> And all the people of the house.
> We have made a promise to come and see you once a year,
> Once a year is not much.
> Just a little piece of pork,
> A little piece of pork,
> If you like.
> If you have nothing to give us
> Just say so.
>
> We will take the eldest girl,
> And roast her feet for her,
> The Ignolée, the Ignoloche,
> To grease our pockets,
> We do not ask for much
> For our visit.
> 25 or 30 feet of pigs' tails
> If you like.
> We are five or six good fellows,
> And if our song does not please you
> We will make a fire in the wood
> To hear the song of the cuckoo
> And the dove.

The cry "*La ignolée, la ignoloche*" is thought to be derived from a demand for New Year's mistletoe. The menacing reference to roasting the eldest daughter's feet has been explained by some as an allusion to an ancient Druidic practice of human sacrifice at the midwinter festival.

Guising The custom of going about in fancy dress or disguise at Christmas, particularly as practised in the United Kingdom. In the Shetland Islands, the Skeklers or Gulicks – young men in straw costumes with conical hats, and handkerchiefs covering their faces – went abroad during the Twelve Nights. On approaching a farm they would fire a gun, and if they were welcome an answering shot would be fired. Once inside they would dance and be rewarded with refreshments and a little money. In Allendale, Northumberland, guisers carried flaming barrels of tar on their heads, which they tossed onto a bonfire. Guising was a New Year's custom across much of eastern Scotland, with disguised young people, both males and females, going door-to-door singing songs or dancing. In Cornwall the term "guise-dancers" was sometimes corrupted to "goose-dancers."

This custom was part merry-making and part a typical 19th-century means of making money or earning hospitality. Like most of these BEGGING VISITS it declined in the 20th century with the introduction of state welfare and year-round employment and, because of increased labour mobility, the intrusion into the community of strangers. See BEGGING VISITS and PEERIE GUIZERS.

"Hark! The Herald Angels Sing" A stamp from Christmas Island illustrates the famous carol.

Hackin An early name for plum pudding. A 1740 account of a traditional Christmas claims, "In these Times all the Spits were sparkling, the Hackin must be boil'd by Day-break, or else two young Men took the Maiden by the Arms, and run her round the Market-place, 'till she was ashamed of her Laziness." Probably related to "HAULKIN."

Hansel Monday In Scotland the equivalent of the English Boxing Day was Hansel Monday, the first Monday after New Year's Day. It was the day on which employees expected a "hansel," or money gift, from their employers, poor folk expected to receive a gratuity from their more prosperous neighbours, and school masters anticipated a gift from their students. Until the end of the 19th century, it was a holiday for agricultural workers and a time of community feasting.

"Hark! The Herald Angels Sing" On Christmas morning 1739, Charles Wesley, poet and clergyman, was walking to church when he was struck by the beauty of the ringing bells. He was thus inspired to create a piece he called "For Christmas Day," which began "Hark, how all the welkin rings," "welkin"

"Hark! The Herald Angels Sing" Charles Wesley, the Methodist hymn writer.

being an antique term for the heavens. Over the years a number of authors, including Wesley's fellow Methodists George Whitefield and Martin Madan, revised the poem until it gradually assumed the form of the hymn we now know as "Hark! The Herald Angels Sing." Among those who changed the words was one author, offended by the notion of the virgin birth, who amended "Late in time behold Him come, Offspring of the Virgin's womb" to "Long desired behold Him come, Finding here his humble home."

Various tunes have been attached to Wesley's amended words, but the most popular for years was "Hendon" or "Take My Life and Let It Be." The currently popular tune is by Felix Mendelssohn from his 1840 *Festgesang no. 7* in honour of Gutenberg's invention of the printing press. Mendelssohn didn't think it suitable for a sacred text: "I am sure that piece will be liked very much by the singers and hearers," he said, "but it will *never* do to sacred words. There must be a national or merry subject found out, something to which the soldier-like and buxom motion of the piece has some relation, and the words must express something gay and popular, as the music tries to do it." Despite these misgivings, English church musician William Cummings adapted it successfully in 1857 for Wesley's words.

> Hark! the herald angels sing,
> Glory to the newborn king;
> Peace on earth, and mercy mild,
> God and sinners reconcil'd!
> Joyful, all ye nations, rise,
> Join the triumph of the skies;
> With th'angelic host proclaim,
> Christ is born in Bethlehem!
>
> *Hark! the herald angels sing,*
> *Glory to the newborn king!*
>
> Christ, by highest Heaven ador'd,
> Christ, the everlasting Lord:

Late in time behold him come,
Offspring of the Virgin's womb!
Veil'd in flesh, the Godhead see,
Hail th' incarnate Deity!
Pleas'd as man with man to dwell,
Jesus, our Immanuel.

Refrain

Hail, the heaven-born Prince of Peace,
Hail, the Sun of Righteousness!
Light and life to all he brings,
Risen with healing in his wings.
Mild he lays his glory by,
Born that man no more may die;
Born to raise the sons of earth;
Born to give them second birth.

Refrain

Haulkin   The monster sausage brought in on Christmas Day in English homes of the 18th century was called a haulkin or haukin.

"The Haunted House"   The 1859 Christmas issue of the magazine *All the Year Round* centring on ghostly tales and a supposedly haunted house. Charles Dickens contributed two of the eight chapters of "The Haunted House," which was partly a satire on popular credulity toward the supernatural and partly a nod to the English tradition of ghost stories told around the Christmas fire. Here, in a conversation between two strangers on a train, Dickens takes a gentle poke at those who believe in messages dictated by the spirits:

> "You will excuse me," said the gentleman contemptuously, "if I am too much in advance of common humanity to trouble myself at all about it. I have passed the night – as indeed I pass the whole of my time now – in spiritual intercourse."
> "O!" said I, somewhat snappishly.
> "The conferences of the night began," continued the gentleman, turning several leaves of his notebook, "with this message: 'Evil communications corrupt good manners.'"
> "Sound," said I; "but, absolutely new?"
> "New from spirits," returned the gentleman.
> I could only repeat my rather snappish "O!" and ask if I might be favoured with the last communication.
> "'A bird in the hand,'" said the gentleman, reading his last entry with great solemnity, "'is worth two in the Bosh.'"
> "Truly I am of the same opinion," said I; "but shouldn't it be Bush?"
> "It came to me, Bosh," returned the gentleman.
> The gentleman then informed me that the spirit of Socrates had delivered this special revelation in the course of the night. "My friend, I hope you are pretty well. There are two in this railway carriage. How do you do? There are seventeen thousand four hundred and seventy-nine spirits here, but you cannot see them. Pythagoras is here. He is not at liberty to mention it, but hopes you like travelling." Galileo likewise had dropped in, with this scientific intelligence. "I am glad to see you, AMICO. COME STA? Water will freeze when it is cold enough. ADDIO!" In the course of the night, also, the following phenomena had occurred. Bishop Butler had insisted on spelling his name, "Bubler," for

which offence against orthography and good manners he had been dismissed as out of temper. John Milton (suspected of wilful mystification) had repudiated the authorship of *Paradise Lost*, and had introduced, as joint authors of that poem, two Unknown gentlemen, respectively named Grungers and Scadgingtone. And Prince Arthur, nephew of King John of England, had described himself as tolerably comfortable in the seventh circle, where he was learning to paint on velvet, under the direction of Mrs. Trimmer and Mary Queen of Scots.

The Haunted Man   The fifth and final Christmas book by Charles Dickens, appearing in December 1848. The haunted man is Redlaw, a professor of chemistry made miserable by memories of past injustices. He strikes a ghostly bargain that rids him of his painful thoughts but turns him into a monster of selfishness and ingratitude, hurting those around him. He is rescued from his condition on Christmas Day by Milly Swidge. Though ignored by most readers of Dickens, *The Haunted Man* is an interesting reflection on the relationship between memory and morality.

Der Haus-Christ   Literally "The House Christ," a 16th-century German term for the gift-bringer. German Protestants, who wished to abolish the Catholic cult of saints, needed a replacement for St. Nicholas as the traditional bearer of presents at Christmas. Clergymen chose to speak of Christ himself as the bringer of good things at Christmas and his collection of gifts as the "Christ-bundle." From this developed the belief in the Christkindl, a childlike figure dressed in white representing the Christ Child as bringer of Christmas gifts.

"Have Yourself a Merry Little Christmas"   Written by Hugh Martin and Ralph Blane and sung by Judy Garland in the 1944 film *Meet Me in St. Louis*.

Haxey Hood Game   Every year on Old Christmas Day, January 6, a strange game is played in Haxey, Lincolnshire. A Fool dressed in red rags, his face smeared with soot and ochre, opens the proceedings by welcoming all present and declaring that the order of the day is

> Hoose agin hoose, town agin town,
> And if you meet a man knock him down,
> But don't hurt him.

(While he says this he is being ritually fumigated by a bonfire.) He then conducts his team of red-clad Boggans led by King Boggan, or Lord of the Hood, to a nearby field, where for the next several hours the men of the parish will contest for the possession of a series of "hoods" or rolls of canvas, rope, and leather. The game is said to have links to pre-Christian ritual combats performed as a fertility rite.

He That Should Come   A one-act radio play about the Nativity written by English mystery novelist Dorothy Sayers and broadcast on the BBC Christmas Day 1938. It received popular acclaim for setting the birth of Jesus among ordinary people. Sayers, creator of the Lord Peter Wimsey stories, would go on to write a 12-play radio series on the life of Jesus, *The Man Born to Be King*. The first in the series was *Kings in Judea*, a Nativity play broadcast on December 21, 1941.

"The Heavenly Christmas Tree"   An 1876 story by Feodor Dostoevsky in which a poor orphan child freezes to death on

Santa's Helpers *Hans Trapp makes a frightening entrance accompanied by the Christkindl.*

Christmas Eve and goes to heaven, where he encounters other children:

> And he discovered that these boys and girls were all children like himself; that some had frozen to death in the baskets in which they had been deposited on doorsteps; others had died in wretched hovels, whither they had been sent from the Foundlings' Hospital; others again had starved to death at their mothers' dried-up breasts; had been suffocated in the foul air of third-class railroad carriages. And now, here they were all angels, Christ's guests, and He Himself was in their midst, extending His hands to them, blessing them and their poor, sinful mothers. . . . And the mothers stand there, a little apart, weeping; each one knows her little boy or girl; and the children fly up to them, and kiss them, and wipe away their tears with their tiny hands, and beg them not to weep, for they, the children, are so happy.

See "CHRISTMAS PHANTOMS," "KAREN'S CHRISTMAS," and "THE LITTLE MATCH GIRL."

Heligh-monat   "Holy-month," the name given by the Anglo-Saxons to December, in reference to Christmas Day.

Helpers, Santa's and Other Gift-bringers'   With all the work that Santa Claus and other gift-bringers have to accomplish, it is little wonder that, over the years, they have accumulated an army of helpers, both back at the North Pole (or Mount Ear, etc.) or on their rounds.

The Dark Side

The first category of helper is the companion of the gift-bringer, who evolved in Europe (particularly in German-speaking territories) after the Protestant Reformation of the 16th century. Some of these characters seem to represent the darker side of St. Nicholas, as can be seen by the names given them: Aschenklas ("Nicholas in Ashes"), Ru-Klaus ("Rough Nicholas"), or Pelznickel ("Furry Nicholas"). Others take the form of a demonic companion to St. Nicholas. Their job is to be a mean, intimidating figure, threatening children with a beating or the possibility of abduction; they may often be seen with a handful of switches or a basket in which to pop a disobedient child. Grim sidekicks who can be classified by their overwhelming shagginess include PELZNICKEL, KLAUBAUF, Hans Trapp from Alsace, and Bartel; those best described as devilish are Krampus (Austria) and Cert (Czech). Those named for their dark complexion are the Swiss Schmutzli and the Dutch Black Peter.

The Distaff Side

Not all the gift-bringer's helpers are male. There is, of course, MRS. CLAUS, the wife of Santa, who is known as Lucy in Switzerland. This name derives from ST. LUCIA, whose day is celebrated in Scandinavia with much ceremony on December 13; in the Tyrol she once brought presents for girls while St. Nicholas brought them only to boys. In some areas the figure of the Christ Child as gift-bringer has evolved over the years into that of a young female angel. In Alsace the girl representing the Child appears with her face whitened by flour, wearing a crown with lights, and carrying a bell in one hand and a basket of goodies in another. In Russia, Kolyáda is a beautiful maiden who goes about on Christmas Eve on a sleigh with carol singers.

Less attractive are those female characters of Central Europe derived from pagan mythology, such as Berchta or Holda. They can be either terrifying or kind, handing out gifts or making the most blood-curdling threats. Variations on these names include Buzebergt (who wears black rags, has a blackened face and wild hair, and carries a pot of starch, which she smears on people's faces), Budelfrau, and Berchtel.

The Short Side
Today youngsters believe that in his North Pole home Santa Claus is assisted in the manufacture of toys by a workforce of elves. These elves also assist department store Santas in crowd control and handing out candy canes. Scandinavian folklore was first to associate elves with the Christmas season, but usually in mischievous, not helpful, ways; it was not until the early 20th century that elves in Denmark, Norway, and Iceland were seen as well-intentioned.

In America Santa Claus himself was first portrayed (in Clement Clarke Moore's "A Visit From St. Nicholas") as a "right jolly old elf," but before too long he had grown in stature and acquired small helpers, as in an 1873 engraving in *Godey's* magazine called "The Workshop of Santa Claus." (See also colour fig. 21.) In Hawaii Santa is often helped by the *menehunes*, the legendary little people who were the first inhabitants of the island.

"Here Comes Santa Claus (Right Down Santa Claus Lane)" A popular music hit written in 1946 by Gene Autry and Oakey Haldeman and recorded by Autry. The song was inspired by Autry's ride in the Los Angeles Santa Claus parade.

Herod "The Great" (73-04 B.C.) King of Judaea at the time of the birth of Christ and rebuilder of the Temple in Jerusalem. His murderousness was legendary; he killed many of his children and wives and the Massacre of the Innocents, which the Bible ascribes to him, is very much in keeping with what we know of his personality. He is the subject of a number of Christmas carols and ballads (see COVENTRY CAROL, "THE CARNAL AND THE CRANE," and "ST. STEPHEN AND HEROD") and appears in seasonal dramas as a raging tyrant.

In Christmas art, he was portrayed as a rather big old man, crowned and sitting on a throne. He is always bearded, with long dark hair, and wears royal garments.

Herod, the Play of The 12th-century abbey of Fleury in France staged a dramatic presentation that has come to be known as *The Play of Herod*. It describes the Nativity, with its attendant angels, midwives, and shepherds; the encounter between King Herod and the Magi, and the Massacre of the Innocents, which the king orders. Of the surviving medieval plays with these themes, the Fleury *Herod* is considered the most artistically satisfying.

Herrick, Robert (1591-1674) Church of England clergyman and the greatest of the Cavalier poets. During his time as a country priest in Devon, he learned the ways 17th-century rural Englishmen celebrated Christmas and wrote a number of poems to illustrate these folk customs and to add his voice to the celebration of the Nativity. The following example he called "A Carol":

What sweeter music can we bring
Than a carol for to sing
The birth of this our heav'nly King.
Awake the voice! Awake the string!
Dark and dull night fly hence away,
And give the honour of this day,
That sees December turned to May.

Hertha Norse goddess of the hearth, who arrived in fireplaces during midwinter. Some ethnologists believe that the method of Santa's entry into houses through the chimney is derived from her practice.

Het Pint A Scottish version of wassailing (see WASSAIL). The Het Pint – hot spiced ale, sugar, and whisky – was traditionally drunk after midnight on New Year's Eve. In Scottish cities kettles of the Het Pint were carried through streets on New Year's Eve and offered to passersby in order to toast the new year.

Hildesheim, John of A 13th-century German Carmelite friar who wrote a book about the Magi that helped to spread legends about their journey to worship the new-born king and how their bodies came to rest in Cologne Cathedral. The book was known in England from 1499, when Wynkyn de Worde printed a translation as *The moost excellent treatise of the three kynges of Coleyne*.

"Ho Ho Ho!" The traditional exclamation of Santa Claus, though department store Santas are told not to utter it lest it frighten little children. However, at least one folklorist points out the shout's earlier pagan origins and the many examples of it being uttered by mythological wild men, such as Robin Goodfellow and members of the Wild Hunt, which rages through the night between Christmas and Epiphany. It was also said to be the devil's entry line in medieval mystery plays.

Hodening Horse A 19th-century custom from Kent, England, in which a man was draped in a hood and carried a wooden horse's head on a pole. Accompanied by others – one acting as a "rider," another leading the horse and carrying a whip, another a cross-dresser known as the Mollie, and, occasionally, musicians – the Hodening Horse would go door-to-door on Christmas Eve and beg a gratuity. The head was constructed so that the jaws could snap, and sometimes lighted candles were put in the eye holes for even more dramatic effect. The custom has been revived since the 1950s as a means of raising money for charity.

"Hodie Christus natus est" "Today Christ Is Born," a seventh-century Gregorian chant, sung at vespers on Christmas Day.

Hodie Christus natus est. Alleluja!
Hodie salvator apparuit. Alleluja!
Hodie in terra canunt angeli,
laetantur archangeli. Alleluja!
Hodie exultant justi dicentes:
Gloria in excelsis Deo et in
Terra pax hominibus voluntatis.

Today Christ was born. Alleluya!
Today the Saviour hath appeared. Alleluya!
Today angels rejoice on earth
And archangels rejoice. Alleluya!
Today the righteous rejoice, saying:
Glory to God on high and on earth
Peace to men of goodwill. Alleluya!

Hoesecker   One of the gift-bringer's HELPERS (also called Hoùseker), he accompanies St. Nicholas on his visits to the children of Luxembourg. Like his French counterpart, Père Fouettard, he carries switches to intimidate the bad children.

Hoffmann, Heinrich   (1809–94), German physician and writer who, looking for a Christmas gift for his three-year-old son in 1844, could find no book that was both entertaining and instructive. He bought instead a blank notebook and wrote the stories that would become the classic *Struwwelpeter*, or "Slovenly Peter," tales. Mark Twain was one of a number who have translated these cautionary stories into English.

Hogmanay   Hogmanay is New Year's Eve in Scotland, the focus of most holiday revelry.

> Get up, good wife, and shake your feathers,
> And dinna think that we are beggars;
> For we are bairns come out to play,
> Get up and gie'us our Hogmanay.

When Calvinist governments in the 16th and 17th centuries succeeded in suppressing the celebration of Christmas, seasonal merriment shifted to New Year's Eve and New Year's Day. It is the time for gift-giving, FIRST-FOOTING, drinking the HET PINT, and numerous customs to bring in good luck for the coming year, such as the FLOWER OF THE WELL.

The name is a mystery. Some say it is derived from the Anglo-Saxon *Heligh-monat* ("Holy Month"), or the Gaelic *oge maidne* ("New Morning"). Others claim it comes from the French phrase *Homme est né* ("Man is born"), a reference to the birth of Jesus. Still others propose that it commemorates an alleged solar deity, Hogmagog, while the more learned suggest a derivation from the French *aguillanneuf*, meaning either New Year or a New Year's gift.

Holiday   In 877, in the midst of defending England from the Viking onslaught, Alfred the Great decreed the Twelve Days of Christmas to be a holiday for servants. Ever since then, Christmas has been a season in which hard-working people have taken time off from their labours to celebrate the Nativity with their family and neighbours. This 15th-century verse gives a sense of how this leisure time was spent:

> And caroles singen everi craiste messe tyde
> Not with schamfastenes bot jocondle
> And holey bowghes aboute, and al asydde
> The brenning fyre hem eten, and hem drinke
> And laughen mereli, and maken route,
> And pype, and dansen, and hem rage; ne swinke [work],
> Ne noethynge else, twalve days thei wolde not.

Contrast that with the observation by William Sandys, an English lawyer and carol collector, in 1833:

> In many parts of the kingdom, especially in the northern and western parts, this festival is still kept up with spirit among the middling and lower classes, though its influence is on the wane even with them; the genius of the present age requires work and not play, and since the commencement of this century a great change may be traced. The modern instructors of mankind do not think it necessary to provide for popular amusements.

The Industrial Revolution had no place for any such thing as a 12-day break from work, and across Europe and North America holidays gradually disappeared from the calendar.

The revival of Christmas customs after 1840 led to the revival of midwinter holidays such as BOXING DAY and a renewed interest in the season as a time for recreation and a break from paid employment.

Holiday Affair (1949)   A romantic comedy set at Christmas about Connie Ennis (Janet Leigh), a war widow with a young son, courted by unemployed Steve Mason (Robert Mitchum) and lawyer Carl Davis (Wendell Corey). Though not a hit when originally released, like *It's a Wonderful Life*, it has gained a loyal following from its television appearances. Remade for television in 1996.

Holiday Inn (1942)   If you can suspend your disbelief about anyone investing in a country inn that only opens on national holidays to stage holiday-related song-and-dance numbers, you will enjoy this musical comedy starring Bing Crosby and Fred Astaire. There's the usual snappy patter, great dancing, and obligatory romance, but the highlight is the music, especially Irving Berlin's "White Christmas," which won an Oscar for best song.

Holly   *Illex aquifolium*, a plant whose greenery has long been associated with Christmas and magical powers.

During bleak Decembers the red berries and green leaves of the holly make the plant a natural choice for decorating homes and churches for the Christmas season. Holly can be found in wreaths, on altars and tables, in doorways, and accompanying the mistletoe or KISSING BUNCH; its image can be seen on Christmas cards, gift wrap, and seasonal art.

Holly reminded medieval Christians of both the Incarnation and the Passion, its berries seeming to be drops of blood and its prickles reminiscent of the Crown of Thorns that circled Christ's brow at his crucifixion. In fact, in one legend, holly was the tree that was used for the cross, a dubious distinction given in other legends to the MISTLETOE.

In many countries holly is thought to have supernatural qualities, among them the power to divine the future. A ritual for determining one's future mate calls for the curious to pick nine berries in silence at Friday midnight, tie the berries with nine knots in a three-cornered handkerchief, and place them under the pillow. If one can remain silent until next morning one will dream of one's future spouse. Holly is a weapon against witchcraft, and English girls used to tie the plant to their beds to ward off demons. In Louisiana berries were said to protect folk from the evil eye and lightning, a belief that was echoed in Germany as long as the holly had previously been used in decorating a church. Tossing a sprig of holly on the Christmas fire would guarantee an end to troubles, and the plant also helped to cure rheumatism, asthma, bad dreams, coughing, and the gout.

In folklore the prickly-leafed holly is considered "male" and the smooth-leafed variety "female." Which type was brought first into the house at Christmas would determine who ruled the roost that year, the husband or the wife. Moreover, while ivy was considered a female plant that brought luck to women, holly was said to bring good fortune to men.

"The Holly and the Ivy"   This song made its first appearance in an English broadside of 1710 and was published in a collection in 1861. Note that the carol refers only to the holly. The tune is a traditional French melody.

> The holly and the ivy,
> When they are both full grown,

Holly *The evergreen with its bright red berries has long been a popular image on Christmas cards.*

Of all the trees that are in the wood,
The holly bears the crown.

O the rising of the sun,
And the running of the deer,
The playing of the merry organ,
Sweet singing in the choir.

The holly bears a blossom
As white as lily flower;
And Mary bore sweet Jesus Christ
To be our sweet Savior.

The holly bears a berry
As red as any blood;
Any Mary bore sweet Jesus Christ
To do poor sinners good.

The holly bears a prickle
As sharp as any thorn;
And Mary bore sweet Jesus Christ
On Christmas day in the morn.

The holly bears a bark
As bitter as any gall;
And Mary bore sweet Jesus Christ
For to redeem us all.

The holly and the ivy,
When they are both full grown,
Of all the trees that are in the wood,
The holly bears the crown.

The Holly and the Ivy (1953) A wonderfully acted movie about the Christmas reunion of the troubled family of rural English clergyman Martin Gregory (Ralph Richardson). There are conflicts and anxiety galore before all is resolved in a suitable fashion and harmony is restored. Based on a play by Wynard Browne and directed by George More O'Ferrall.

"The Holly Bears a Berry" See the "SANS DAY CAROL."

"A Holly Jolly Christmas" A Johnny Marks song sung by Burl Ives as part of the 1964 animated television special "Rudolph, the Red-Nosed Reindeer."

Holly Riders A custom of carolling in Exmoor, England, where groups of singers went from farm to farm carrying lanterns and wearing sprigs of holly on their coats and holly wreaths on their hats. They were given coins or cakes and cider after each performance.

Holming Also known as Holly Beating. In Wales on St. Stephen's Day (December 26), it was once the custom for men to thrash each other with holly leaves until blood was drawn. They also attacked young servant women on the bare arms.

Holy Bough A 16th-century English Christmas decoration. A willow or hazel hoop was trimmed with evergreens and ribbons, and inside it hung a representation of the crib or the Holy Family. The decoration was hung in a doorway and folk embraced beneath it. See KISSING BUNCH.

Holy Family, Feast of the A Roman Catholic religious festival in honour of Mary, Joseph, and the infant Jesus. Though the Coptic church had long had a feast of the Holy Family, it did not become a part of Catholic observance until the 17th century and was officially recognized only in 1921. Originally celebrated on the Sunday after Epiphany, the feast was moved in 1969 to the Sunday after Christmas to bring it within the Christmas season.

Home Alone (1990)   Eight-year-old Kevin (Macaulay Culkin) is mistakenly left behind when his family leaves town for a Christmas vacation and finds he must defend his home against invasion by two bumbling thieves (Joe Pesci and Daniel Stern). Director Christopher Columbus showed he has a good eye for slapstick violence. The mandatory Christmas sentiment is added by a neighbour with the Dickensian name of Marley (Roberts Blossom) and Kevin's desperate mom (Catherine O'Hara).

Home Alone 2: Lost in New York (1992)   Director Chris Columbus and writer John Hughes, who teamed up for the original *Home Alone*, succumbed to sequel fever and produced this shabby effort. Kevin again ends up separated from his family and spends Christmas in New York's Plaza Hotel (where owner Donald Trump makes himself available as a human product placement). Joe Pesci and Daniel Stern are once more subject to frightfully violent acts, and Tim Curry is the hotel concierge.

Home for Christmas (TV) (1990)   Amanda (Chantellese Kent) wants a grandfather for the holidays and Elmer (Mickey Rooney) is chosen. Elmer is a vagrant ex-con, but he still knows something about Christmas. Directed and written by Peter McCubbin.

"Home for the Holidays"   Popular since its 1954 composition, this song expresses a near-universal sentiment. Written by Al Stillman (1906-79) and music by Robert Allen.

Home for the Holidays (TV) (1972)   This Christmas movie has it all: an aged Walter Brennan (78 years old in this, his last movie), convinced that his second wife is out to kill him; four daughters (including the young Sally Field), who gather to protect him; and a pitchfork-wielding maniac. Also known as *Deadly Desires*.

Homecoming   It is now widely accepted that Christmas is a time of homecoming. Songs such as "Home for the Holidays" and "I'll Be Home for Christmas" testify to the place the season holds in the life of modern, scattered families. It was only in the 19th century, however, when industrialization and (in England) the rise in popularity of boarding schools took millions away from their homes, that the tradition arose. The sentiment was strengthened with a renewed emphasis on the humanity of Jesus in the Nativity and the notion of the original Christmas as a family event.

Expansion of the railway and cheap fares made it possible for those away from home to consider returning for the holidays, and more and more countries legislated Christmas as a holiday time. By the 20th century Christmas was the principal time for family reunion (except in the United States, where it is edged out by Thanksgiving). (See colour fig. 7.)

The Homecoming – A Christmas Story (TV) (1971)   It's Christmas 1933 at the Walton family's mountain home. This television special, adapted from Earl Hamner's novel, was such a hit that a long-running series emerged. Patricia Neal played Olivia, Andrew Duggan played her husband, John, and ventriloquist Edgar Bergen played Grandpa. Those familiar with the series will recognize Richard Thomas as John-Boy, Ellen Corby as Grandma, Mary Beth McDonough as Erin, and sundry other long-serving Waltons.

Honduras   Christmas in Honduras begins with the appearance of the Warini, the Christmas Herald, a masked dancer who goes house-to-house accompanied by singers and drummers. His dance on January 6 signals an end to the season. In fact dancing is an integral part of Christmas celebrations in this Central American country: the aboriginal Garifuna people perform costumed dances such as *Pijamanadi*, *Dona Amidi*, *Coreopatea*, and John Canoe; in early December the women of certain tribal groups dance from door to door in groups; neighbourhoods stage *tambakus*; and on Christmas morning children and their families dance *rondas* and play games.

As in most Latin American countries, the manger scene, or *nacimiento*, is central to home devotions at Christmas. The entire family takes part in putting together the scene, which can be quite ornate and detailed. Other activities during Advent include participating in or watching the *pastorelas*, costumed shepherd dramas whose rehearsals start in October, and enjoying office parties, where workers may be matched in *cochombros*, a kind of SECRET SANTA present exchange.

A major part of getting ready for Christmas is the preparation of holiday food and drink. The Christmas Eve meal is often centred on turkey or roast piglet, but there are many other traditional Honduran dishes, such as meat pie filled with vegetables, raisins, fried plantain, and peppers; and *nactamales*, or *sartén*, green peppers filled with sour cream, cottage cheese, milk, and corn dough, slow-cooked in an earthenware pot. The seasonal Honduran Christmas drink is eggnog, made from milk, eggs, sugar, cinnamon, cloves, and *guaro* liquor.

With much of the Honduran population living in the United States, it is no surprise that American Christmas customs have penetrated the country. Presents are often exchanged on December 25 instead of on January 6, and Santa Claus has been edging out the Magi as gift-bringer. But most traditions linger. The nine days of the POSADAS processions are still observed, and Christmas mass is still a major attraction in this intensely Catholic land. Christmas trees have still not displaced the *nacimiento*, and Three Kings Day still sees festive parades and the burning of Mr. Old Year as the Christmas season comes to a close.

"Hoodoo McFiggin's Christmas"   A wise and funny short story by Canadian humorist Stephen Leacock (1869-1944) published in his 1910 *Literary Lapses*. It concerns a boy who yearns to find a puppy, an air rifle, and a drum under the Christmas tree but is given only sensible presents, such as a toothbrush, Bible, and pants.

Hoop and Hide   An 18th-century Christmas game. "As for the Game of *Hoop and Hide*, the Parties have the Liberty of hiding where they will, in any Part of the House and if they happen to be caught, the Dispute ends in Kissing, etc."

Hope, Bob   (1903-) British-born American star of vaudeville, radio, movies, and television. His chief contribution to Christmas was his volunteer work entertaining American and Allied troops abroad during the holiday season from 1942 to 1975. From his first Christmas show in Alaska, through stops on every war front, including the Pacific islands, North Africa, Berlin, Korea, Vietnam, and Lebanon, Hope brought the boys in uniform laughs, a touch of home, and a chance to see a bevy of starlets and Miss World contestants. For his services Bob Hope was granted numerous awards from the American government and was knighted by Queen Elizabeth in 1998.

Horses Yule was the time among the pagan Teutons for the sacrifice of a white horse. Christmas, too, has ceremonies that focus on horses, though not in such a fatal way.

For reasons that remain unclear, St. Stephen has come to be regarded as the patron saint of horses, and therefore his day, December 26, is given over to horse parades, races, and special treatment for the animals. See ST. STEPHEN'S DAY.

In Wales the *Mari Llwyd* ("Grey Mare") ceremony involves a man capering about under a white sheet trimmed with bells carrying a pole topped by a horse's head with snapping jaws. Anyone the horse seizes in its mouth must pay a forfeit to be released. According to legend, the *Mari Lwyd* is the animal turned out of its stable to make room for the Holy Family; it has been looking for shelter ever since. Accompanied by a group of men, often in mummers' costumes or bearing bells, the *Mari Lwyd* approaches a house during the Christmas season and the group begs admittance. After a ritual negotiation that may involve the exchange of humorous verses they are let inside, where the horse darts about while hospitality is shared.

In England similar horse figures are Old Hob, who went about with a group of men, singing and ringing hand bells for a gratuity, and the HODENING HORSE of Kent. On the Isle of Man it is the *Laare Vane* ("White Mare") that appeared on New Year's Eve.

In Germany the hobby-horse is called *Schimmel* (or, in some places, *Schimmelreiter* to emphasize the rider). Like the *Mari Lwyd* it takes part in house visits, jumping about to entertain the children and dancing with pretty girls.

Horsley, John Callcott (1817-1903) English artist and designer of the first Christmas CARD. In 1843, at the request of his friend Sir Henry Cole, Horsley produced a hand-coloured lithograph of a family party with the message, "A Merry Christmas and a Happy New Year to You." A thousand of these were manufactured and sent out, causing a minor scandal, because the family on the card appeared to be drinking.

Because he objected to nudes in painting, the artist was known as "Mr. J.C(lothes) Horsley."

Hot Cockles A traditional English Christmas game in which a blindfolded person kneels down and has to guess who hit him. A whimsical entry in the *Spectator* asks, "Friday, 28 December 1711. Mr Spectator, I am a Footman in a great Family, and am in Love with the House-maid. We were all at Hot Cockles last Night in the Hall these Holidays; when I lay down and was blinded, she pulled off her Shoe, and hit me with the Heel such a Rap, as almost broke my Head to Pieces. Pray, Sir, was this Love or Spite?"

The name is said to derive from the French *Hautes-Coquilles*. The game is mentioned in Rabelais' *Gargantua and Pantagruel*, and is the subject of a painting by Jean Honoré Fragonard.

"The House of Christmas" A collection of four carols, music by Canadian composer Robert Turner, based on poems by G.K. Chesterton: "The House of Christmas," "The Wise Men," "A Child of the Snows," and "The Nativity."

"How Brightly Shines the Morning Star" Written in the midst of a deadly plague, "Wie Schön Leuchtet der Morgenstern," by Philipp Nicolai (1556-1608), quickly became a beloved German Christmas hymn. J.S. Bach and Mendelssohn both used the tune in their compositions. It was translated as "How Brightly Shines the Morning Star" by William Mercer, 1859, and "O Morning Star, How Fair and Bright" by CATHERINE WINKWORTH.

How brightly shines the Morning Star,
With mercy beaming from afar;
The host of heav'n rejoices;
O righteous Branch, O Jesse's Rod!
Thou Son of Man and Son of God!
We, too, will lift our voices;
Jesus, Jesus!
Holy holy,
Yet most lowly,
Draw Thou near us;
Great Emmanuel, come and hear us.

Though circled by the hosts on high,
He deigned to cast a pitying eye
Upon his helpless creature;
The whole creation's Head and Lord,
By highest Seraphim adored,
Assumed our very nature;
Jesus, grant us,
Through Thy merit,
To inherit
Thy salvation;
Hear, O hear our supplication.

Rejoice, ye heav'ns; thou earth, reply;
With praise, ye sinners, fill the sky,
For this His Incarnation.
Incarnate God, put forth Thy power,
Ride on, ride on, great Conqueror,
Till all know thy salvation.
Amen, amen!
Alleluia,
Alleluia!
Praise be given
Evermore, by earth and heaven.

"How Santa Claus Came to Simpson's Bar" A sentimental story of the American West set in 1862 by Francis Bret Harte (1836-1902). The local low-lifes of Simpson's Bar, California, are moved to make a decent Christmas for a sick little boy, and one of their number undertakes a dangerous ride to bring back toys.

"And even so, bedraggled, ragged, unshaven, and unshorn, with one arm hanging helplessly at his side, Santa Claus came to Simpson's Bar and fell fainting on the first threshold. The Christmas dawn came slowly after, touching the remoter peaks with the rosy warmth of ineffable love. And it looked so tenderly on Simpson's Bar that the whole mountain, as if caught in a generous action, blushed to the skies."

How the Grinch Stole Christmas "While every Who down in Who-ville liked Christmas a lot, the Grinch who lived just north of Who-ville, did not." So begins the beloved 1957 story by Dr. Seuss (Theodore Seuss Geisel, 1904-91) of a Christmas-hating creature with a heart two sizes too small.

The Grinch decides he will put an end to Christmas by stealing all the Christmas presents, decorations, and food for the feast. Once he has stolen everything, including the ice in the ice box and the log for the fire, he brings it all to the top of Mt. Crumpit to dump it off the other side. However, as he waits to hear the gratifying sounds of a sorrowful Who-ville when the town realizes Christmas is not coming, he hears instead the beautiful singing of all the Whos undaunted by the loss of their gifts. The Grinch realizes that "Maybe Christmas doesn't come from a store. Maybe Christmas . . . perhaps . . . means a little bit more." This endearing tale ends

Hungary *The Flight into Egypt is depicted on this Hungarian Christmas stamp.*

with a Grinch whose heart has grown three sizes, who has brought all the loot back and has become the merriest Who of them all. He even carves the roast beast.

A Latin translation, entitled *Quomodo Invidiosulus Nomine Grinchus Christi Natalem Abrogaverit*, appeared in 1998.

For the animated version, see DR. SEUSS'S HOW THE GRINCH STOLE CHRISTMAS.

Howling "Howling" is an antique term in the West Country of England for the ceremony of wassailing (see WASSAIL) the fruit trees. On Twelfth Night (January 5), men "howl" an orchard by going out with the wassail-bowl and blessing the trees by sprinkling ale on them and placing a piece of toast on their branches and roots. A traditional rhyme is chanted to ensure the fertility of the trees in the coming year.

An Hue and Cry After Christmas A 17th-century English tract, written as part of the intense debate on the propriety of celebrating Christmas. The devout Protestants known as Puritans argued that Christmas was a popish and heathen invention and spoke against the feasting, merriment, and revelry of the holiday. For a time under the Commonwealth of the 1650s, they succeeded in making it illegal. The author of *An Hue and Cry After Christmas* uses Old Christmas as the personification of the season and asks, "Any man or woman, that can give any knowledge or tell any tidings of an old, old, very old grey-bearded gentleman, called Christmas, who was wont to be a very familiar guest and visit all sorts of people, both poor and rich, and used to appear in glittering gold, silk and silver, in the court, and in all shapes in the theatre in White Hall, and had ringing, feasts and jollity in all places, both in the city and the country for his coming – whoever can tell what is become of him, or where he may be found, let him bring him back again into England."

Hungary For centuries Hungary has been a cultural crossroads. Situated between Eastern and Western Europe and the Balkans, rich in ethnic identity, and a land where Protestantism and Catholicism each claim many followers, Hungary shows its mixed heritage in the celebration of Christmas.

On his feast day of December 6, St. Nicholas (Mikolás to Hungarians), in his traditional bishop's attire, arrives to deliver small presents and candy to good girls and boys and switches to the bad ones. Children leave out their neatly polished shoes for Nicholas to fill. On his travels to shopping areas and schools and in parades he is often accompanied by an angel and a devilish companion named Krampusz.

But the saint's appearance is only a prelude to the Christmas celebrations, which get into full swing on December 24. Adults hurry home from work, children are sent off to play, and the tree is decorated in their absence. After a visit from the gift-bringer (which on Christmas Eve is the baby Jesus or his angels), a bell is rung and children are allowed to see the tree and open their presents. Following supper the family might sing carols or attend midnight mass. The next two days are national holidays. Christmas Day itself tends to be reserved for immediate family and a large mid-afternoon meal, often of turkey; visiting friends and family takes place on December 26.

Seasonal delights include the *szalon cukor*, brightly wrapped chocolate candies with a marzipan or jelly centre, and *baigli*, traditional walnut and poppy-seed cakes.

"The Huron Carol" The Christmas song we now know as "The Huron Carol" began life as "Estennialon de tsonoué Iesous ahatonnia," a retelling of the Nativity story in the Huron tongue, attributed to the murdered Jesuit missionary JEAN DE BRÉBEUF. The tune is based on a 16th-century French folk song, "Une jeune pucelle." It has had a number of arrangements and translations, but the version below entitled "Twas in the Moon of Winter Time" by Jesse Edgar Middleton (1926) has become the standard.

"The Huron Carol" may well be the first Christmas song written in North America and is certainly the only internationally known carol taken from a native American language. It is especially well-loved in Canada, where it is used annually as the leading song in a series of Christmas concerts that raise money for Salvation Army charities.

> Twas in the moon of winter time,
> When all the birds had fled,
> That mighty Gitchi-Manitou
> Sent angel choirs instead;
> Before their light the stars grew dim,
> And wondering hunters heard the hymn:
> Jesus your King is born, Jesus is born,
> *In excelsis gloria.*
>
> Within a lodge of broken bark
> The tender babe was found,
> A ragged robe of rabbit skin
> Enwrapped his beauty round;
> But as the hunter braves drew nigh,
> The angel song rang loud and high:
> Jesus your King is born, Jesus is born,
> *In excelsis gloria.*
>
> O children of the forest free,
> O sons of Manitou,
> The holy child of earth and heaven
> Is born today for you.

CHRISTMAS NOËL   JESOUS AHATONHIA

CANADA 25

*"**The Huron Carol**" This postage stamp depicts the Nativity as seen through the eyes of aboriginal Canadians.*

Come, kneel before the radiant boy,
Who brings you beauty, peace and joy:
Jesus your King is born, Jesus is born,
In excelsis gloria.

Hutterites The remarkable early Anabaptist sect known as the Hutterian Brethren began to migrate to North America in the 18th century, and since then they have established numerous colonies across the Canadian and American prairies. Though they cling to long-standing customs such as communal living and plain dress, the Hutterites have adopted modern agricultural technology and have prospered.

On the Hutterite colonies, Christmas is a four-day event with church services every morning and evening beginning December 24. All work stops and the time is devoted to prayer and meditation. No secular carols are sung; only religious hymns are part of the Hutterite canon, and these will be sung by children's choirs in old folks' homes, hospitals, and at other colonies. Nativity plays are often prepared by school children. Bread is baked and taken to town to sell as a means of raising money for Christmas charities; colony members also work in soup kitchens or food banks. Presents are given to children – one from the colony itself and some from parents – but there is no pretence made of the existence of Santa Claus or any other supernatural gift-bringer.

"A Hymn on the Nativity of My Saviour" A poem by Englishman Ben Jonson (1572-1637), whose best known contributions to Christmas are the seasonal masques he prepared for the court of James I.

I sing the birth was born tonight,
The Author both of life and light;
The angels so did sound it,
And like the ravished shepherds said,
Who saw the light, and were afraid,
Yet searched, and true they found it.

The Son of God, the eternal King,
That did us all salvation bring,
And freed the soul from danger;
He whom the whole world could not take,
The Word, which heaven and earth did make,
Was now laid in a manger.

The Father's wisdom willed it so,
The Son's obedience knew no "No,"
Both wills were in one stature;
And as that wisdom had decreed,
The Word was now made Flesh indeed,
And took on Him our nature.

What comfort by Him do we win?
Who made Himself the Prince of sin,
To make us heirs of glory?
To see this Babe, all innocence,
A Martyr born in our defense,
Can man forget this story?

World War hit "Lili Marlene") and recorded by 13-year-old Jimmy Boyd, this was the most popular Christmas record of 1952. Molly Bee, Spike Jones, and Perry Como also did well with the song.

"I Saw Three Ships" An enigmatic English carol from the 15th century with a 19th-century arrangement by Sir John Stainer. The meaning of those three ships sailing into land-locked Bethlehem has puzzled listeners for centuries. Some link this carol with the arrival in Cologne in 1162 of the bodies of the Three Magi after Holy Roman Emperor Frederick Barbarossa razed the city of Milan, where the remains of the Magi had rested. There are a number of variant lyrics, including "Our Saviour Christ and his lady" instead of "The Virgin Mary and Christ were there" in verse three, and a line that speaks about Mary and Joseph with "O, he did whistle and she did sing."

"I Saw Three Ships" This carol, commemorated here on a British postage stamp, may refer to the arrival in Cologne of the bodies of the Three Wise Men.

"I Heard the Bells on Christmas Day" A poem written by Henry Wadsworth Longfellow (1807-82) in 1863 while the American Civil War raged and his son, a lieutenant in the Union Army, lay wounded. In 1872 the words were joined to a processional by the English organist John Baptiste Calkin (1827-1905), though other tunes have been tried.

> I heard the bells on Christmas day
> Their old familiar carols play
> And mild and sweet the words repeat,
> Of peace on earth, good will to men.
>
> I thought how as the day had come,
> The belfries of all Christendom
> Had roll'd along th' unbroken song
> Of peace on earth, good will to men.
>
> 'Til ringing, singing on its way,
> The world revolved from night to day,
> A voice, a chime, a chant sublime,
> Of peace on earth, good will to men!
>
> And in despair I bow'd my head:
> "There is no peace on earth," I said,
> "For hate is strong, and mocks the song
> Of peace on earth, good will to men."
>
> Then pealed the bells more loud and deep:
> "God is not dead, nor doth He sleep;
> The wrong shall fail, the right prevail,
> With peace on earth, good will to men."

The five verses above were joined in the original anti-war poem by two more stanzas, seldom used today because of their Civil War context, which would have been verses four and five:

> Then from each black accursed mouth
> The cannon thundered in the South,
> And with the sound
> The carols drowned
> Of peace on earth, good will to men.
>
> It was as if an earthquake rent
> The hearth-stones of a continent,
> And made forlorn
> The households born
> Of peace on earth, good will to men.

"I Saw Mommy Kissing Santa Claus" Written by Tommie Connor (who also wrote the English words to the Second

> I saw three ships come sailing in,
> On Christmas Day, on Christmas Day;
> I saw three ships come sailing in
> On Christmas Day in the morning.
>
> And what was in those ships all three,
> On Christmas Day, on Christmas Day?
> And what was in those ships all three,
> On Christmas Day in the morning?
>
> The Virgin Mary and Christ were there,
> On Christmas Day, on Christmas Day;
> The Virgin Mary and Christ were there,
> On Christmas Day in the morning.
>
> Pray, whither sailed those ships all three,
> On Christmas Day, on Christmas Day;
> Pray whither sailed those ships all three,
> On Christmas Day in the morning?
>
> O they sailed into Bethlehem,
> On Christmas Day, on Christmas Day;
> O they sailed into Bethlehem,
> On Christmas Day in the morning.
>
> And all the bells on earth shall ring,
> On Christmas Day, on Christmas Day;
> And all the bells on earth shall ring,
> On Christmas Day in the morning.

And all the Angels in Heaven shall sing,
On Christmas Day, on Christmas Day;
And all the Angels in Heaven shall sing,
On Christmas Day in the morning.

And all the souls on Earth shall sing,
On Christmas Day, on Christmas Day;
And all the souls on Earth shall sing,
On Christmas Day in the morning.

Then let us all rejoice amain,
On Christmas Day, on Christmas Day;
Then let us all rejoice amain,
On Christmas Day in the morning.

"I Sing of a Maiden That Is Makeles" A 15th-century English carol, also called "As Dew in Aprille," which has attracted modern settings from Benjamin Britten, Lennox Berkely, and Martin Shaw. "Makeles" means "matchless."

I sing of a maiden
That is makeles.
King of all kinges
To her son she chose.

He came all so stille
There his mother was
As dew in Aprille
That falleth on the grass.

He came all so stille
To his mother's bower,
As dew in Aprille,
That falleth on the flower.

He came all so stille
To his mother's lay,
As dew in Aprille,
That falleth on the spray.

Mother and maiden
Was never none but she;
Well may such a lady
Godes mother be.

"I Wonder as I Wander" An adaptation of a North Carolina folk tune by John Jacob Niles (1892-1980), the American balladeer and collector of folk music. Niles is said to have paid the young girl whom he first heard singing this song 25 cents to repeat it until he had written it down. Among his other songs are "Black Is the Color of My True Love's Hair" and "Jesus, Jesus Rest Your Head." Late in life he turned to art song, writing oratorio and music based on the poetry of the mystic and monk Thomas Merton.

I wonder as I wander out under the sky,
How Jesus the Savior did come for to die
For poor or'n'ry people like you and like I.
I wonder as I wander out under the sky.

When Mary birthed Jesus, 'twas in a cow's stall,
With wise men and farmers and shepherds and all;
But high from God's heaven, a star's light did fall
And the promise of ages it then did recall.

If Jesus had wanted for any wee thing,
A star in the sky or a bird on a wing
Or all of God's angels in heav'n for to sing –
He surely could have it, 'cause He was the King.

I wonder as I wander out under the sky,
How Jesus the Savior did come for to die
For poor or'n'ry people like you and like I.
I wonder as I wander out under the sky.

Iceland Christmas in Iceland is a unique event, the product of a tiny island nation whose pagan Viking past, physical isolation, and long northern nights have combined with Christianity to produce traditions and a holiday unlike those anywhere else.

In the beginning was Yule, that midwinter time of animal slaughter and feasting in pagan Northern Europe. Then, after the Viking settlers of Iceland were converted to Christianity, Christmas and Yule became synonymous. When Iceland joined the Protestant Reformation in the 16th century, the Lutheran church took a dimmer view of midwinter feasting and superstition, and customs were again amended. "All chess, games, running, card games, loose talk and entertainment" were forbidden, and dancing during the Christmas season was frowned on, with the result that Iceland lost many of its traditional folk dances.

The island's poverty meant that Advent and Christmas could not be times of excess and consumption. December was a time when families were hard at work producing woollen goods to be bartered for Christmas supplies, a situation that gave rise to some unique customs. Stories were told of cruel employers propping their exhausted workers' eyes open with sticks to keep them at their labours, so that the last week before Christmas became known as "Stick Week" and a hasty snack was called a "stick bite." Folk also said that he who did not receive an article of clothing for Christmas would be prey to the monstrous CHRISTMAS CAT; since clothing was a reward to those who worked hard at spinning and knitting, this threat was a spur to work harder.

From these hard times, when resources were scarce and nights were at their longest, came tales of cannibal ogres and their offspring threatening isolated farmhouses during the Christmas season. Not only was the landscape haunted by GRYLA and her mate Leppaludi, monsters with a taste for human flesh, but their 13 offspring were prone to invade the house and make life miserable for its inhabitants. The JÓLASVEINAR, or Yule Lads, had names such as Meat Hook, Doorway Sniffer, and Door Slammer, which suggest their particular malicious specialties. They came down from the mountains one by one in the 13 days before Christmas, practised their nasty deeds, and left one by one in the days after Christmas.

Nowadays Icelanders are much more prosperous. Christmas is a merrier season, and the Yule Lads have been softened by time to become welcome, if occasionally mischievous, guests in December. In fact, starting on December 12, the eve of St. Lucia, children put out their shoes at night believing that each of the Lads as they arrive will leave them little treats. Other Advent customs include "Little Christmas" (office and school parties), decorating the Christmas tree (a recent addition to the season on an island with few trees), and cleaning the house on December 23, St. Thorlak's Day. On this day a special pre-Christmas meal is also traditional: a kind of skate hash so unappetizing that it makes subsequent dining seem all the more delicious.

Christmas Eve is spent attending an evening church service and eating a family dinner. The meal is usually based around *hangikjöt*, smoked mutton, or the traditional native bird, rock ptarmigan. *Jólagrautur*, a grain porridge with raisins and a lucky almond in it, and *laufabraud*, leaf-bread – an intricately cut thin biscuit – are also a part of the meal. After dinner the children open their presents. In a practice unheard of anywhere else, Icelandic television stops broadcasting from 5 p.m. to 10 p.m. to encourage families to spend their Christmas Eve together.

Icelanders enjoy imported Christmas music such as "Silent Night" and "White Christmas," which they sing both in Icelandic and English, but they have also produced their own carols. "The Night Was Such a Splendid One" and "Soon the Blessed Yule Will Arrive" have both been honoured on Icelandic Christmas stamps. The poverty of earlier days can be glimpsed in the words of the latter song, which says that Christmas is anticipated by children hoping to receive something nice – "at least a candle and cards."

Christmas Day (*Jóladagur*) and Boxing Day (*Annar Jóladagur*) bring more eating, visiting, and parties. New Year's Eve was believed to be a magically charged night, much as Christmas Eve is seen in other lands: ELVES move about, cattle speak, seals take on human form, and the dead rise from their graves. Farm folk who wished to stay on the good side of supernatural creatures would leave out lights and food to assure the elves they could come in without fear. It was also a time for "elf dances" and bonfires, and to this day New Year's Eve in Iceland is marked by fireworks, dancing, and merriment.

Christmas ends on January 6. Bonfires burn Christmas refuse, more fireworks are set off, folk dress up as the Yule Lads and their monstrous parents, and the last parties of the season are held.

"Ihr Kinderlein kommet"   A German carol with words by Christoph von Schmid (1768-1854) and music from an earlier tune by Abraham Peter Schultz. Translated as "O Come Little Children."

> O come, little children;
> O come one and all,
> Who lies in the manger
> In Bethlehem's stall;
> For there, little children
> On this holiest night,
> Our God sends from Heaven
> His Son, your delight.
>
> He lies there, before you,
> Asleep in the hay,
> With Mary and Joseph
> To guard Him and pray.
> The wondering shepherds
> Look in at the door,
> And seeing the Infant
> They kneel and adore.
>
> Adore like the shepherds!
> Your glad voices raise
> With those of the angels
> Who sing in his praise.
> Your chorus will echo
> From earth to the sky,
> With "Glory to God
> In His Heaven most high!"

"Il est né, le divin Enfant"   An 18th-century French folk carol, translated as "He Is Born, the Holy Child."

> *He is born, the holy Child,*
> *Play the oboe and bagpipes merrily!*
> *He is born, the holy Child,*
> *Sing we all of the Savior Mild.*

> Through long ages of the past,
> Prophets have foretold His coming;
> Through long ages of the past;
> Now the time has come at last.

Refrain

> O how lovely, O how pure,
> Is the perfect Child of Heaven;
> O how lovely, O how pure,
> Gracious gift of God to man!

Refrain

> Jesus, Lord of all the world,
> Coming as a Child among us,
> Jesus, Lord of all the world,
> Grant to us Thy heav'nly peace.

Refrain

"I'll Be Home for Christmas"   Written by Walter Kent (1911-) and James Kimball "Kim" Cannon (1900-74), this song appeared in 1943 in the midst of the Second World War, when its hopeful sentiments were felt by people around the world. Bing Crosby's recording sold over a million copies and reached Number 3 on the hit parade. Kent had also written the music for that other great wartime ballad "The White Cliffs of Dover."

I'll Be Home for Christmas (1998)   Teen heart-throb Jason Taylor Thomas plays Jake, a potty-mouthed young man in need of some lessons in life. Instead he finds himself in the middle of a desert in a Santa Claus suit trying to get to New York by Christmas Eve. Neither Thomas nor the Disney studio won any friends with this lame and unlikeable effort. Directed by Arlene Sanford, for whom this was a first movie after years of more successful work in television.

I'll Be Seeing You (1944)   Ginger Rogers, Joseph Cotten, Shirley Temple, and Spring Byington give it all they've got in this melodrama about a mentally disturbed soldier and the beautiful paroled murderer he meets on the train at Christmas. Based on the play *Double Furlough* by Charles Martin and directed by William Dieterle.

"I'm Gettin' Nuttin' for Christmas"   A 1955 novelty song by Robert Tepper and Roy C. Bennett. Five different recording artists made it onto the pop charts with this song in 1955, the most successful being Barry Gordon and Art Mooney, who reached Number 6. The least successful version, which was by Stan Freberg and reached only Number 55, is the one whose fame has endured.

"In the Bleak Midwinter"   An 1872 poem by the devout English poet Christina Rossetti, who also wrote "Love Came Down at Christmas." The most popular musical setting for her words came in 1906 from English composer Gustav Holst (1874-1934).

> In the bleak midwinter
> Frosty wind made moan.
> Earth stood hard as iron,
> Water like a stone;
> Snow had fallen, snow on snow,
> Snow on snow,
> In the bleak midwinter
> Long ago.

"In the Bleak Midwinter" The English poet and carol writer
Christina Rossetti.

Our God, Heaven cannot hold Him,
Nor earth sustain;
Heaven and earth shall flee away
When He comes to reign:
In the bleak midwinter
A stable-place sufficed
The Lord God Almighty
Jesus Christ.

Enough for Him whom cherubim
Worship night and day,
A breastful of milk,
And a manger of hay;
Enough for him whom angels
Fall down before,
The ox and ass and camel
Which adore.

Angels and Archangels
May have gathered there,
Cherubim and Seraphim
Throng'd the air;
But only his Mother,
In Her maiden bliss,
Worshipped the Beloved
With a kiss.

What can I give Him,
Poor as I am?
If I were a shepherd,
I would bring a lamb;
If I were a wise man,

I would do my part.
Yet what can I give him?
Give my heart.

"In the Workhouse, Christmas Day"   A longish poem, much
parodied, by George R. Sims (1847-1922), often referred to as
"Christmas Day in the Workhouse." A poor man in the midst
of a Christmas feast brought by wealthy do-gooders to the
parish workhouse angrily refuses to eat his pudding because
of the memory of his wife, who the year before had starved to
death after the parish had refused them "relief" and said the
workhouse was the only option. Its penultimate verse gives a
taste of the bathos the poem invokes:

Yes there, in the land of plenty,
Lay a loving woman dead,
Cruelly starved and murdered
For a loaf of parish bread.
At yonder gate, last Christmas,
I craved for a human life.
You who would feast us paupers,
What of my murdered wife!

"Infant Holy, Infant Lowly"   One of the English translations
of the beloved Polish carol "w zlobie lezy."

Innocents, Feast of the Holy   Since the fifth century the
church has commemorated the death of the boy babies of
Bethlehem at the hands of King HEROD. In many countries
this feast day, December 28, is the time for customs surrounding children. In German folklore it was a time for the ghosts
of unbaptized children to wander the world; if one of these
spirits was seen and addressed by a Christian name, it would
be free to enter paradise. It also was a time of social inversion
in religious communities in the Middle Ages, when the young
were able to temporarily lord it over the old, such as in the
ceremonies of the BOY BISHOP.

In Spanish-speaking countries, December 28 is Innocents'
Day, a time for pranks on friends. When the joke is revealed
the cry is "*inocente, inocente!*" In England the day is known as
CHILDERMAS. See also BEATINGS AT CHRISTMAS.
see: massacre of the innocents

Inspector Gadget Saves Christmas (TV) (1992)   To the list of
those who have saved Christmas add Inspector Gadget in this
NBC animated special. Don Adams did the voice of the aug-
mented agent. See ELMO SAVES CHRISTMAS and ERNEST
SAVES CHRISTMAS.

Iran   The connection between Iran and Christmas is as old as
can be. The Magi who visited the baby Jesus and brought him
gifts of gold, frankincense, and myrrh are thought to have
been Persian astrologers. Though Iran (formerly Persia) has
been Muslim since the seventh-century Arab invasions,
Christian minorities of three churches – the Armenian,
Assyrian, and Chaldean – have lived here and celebrated
Christmas since at least the fourth and fifth centuries.

Christmas is not a very public festival in Iran, given the
minority status of the Christian communities, but it is enthusiastically kept in churches and homes. Visitors looking for
evidence of Christmas in the shops must go to the Christian
sections of town, such as the Armenian quarter in Tehran,
where Nativity scenes are placed in store windows to attract
Christian holiday shoppers. Every year Iranian Muslim leaders send greetings at Christmas to show their respect for
Christianity and for Christians living in Iran.

The season begins with what is known as the Little Fast (the

Great Fast being Lent), a time for spiritual preparation and abstaining from meat and dairy products. Western influences brought the Christmas tree to Iran in the 20th century, and under it are put the gifts delivered by Santa Claus or Baba Noel for the children of the house, as well as little packages of sweets and treats for children of friends who will be visiting the home on Christmas Day. At one time gift-giving was not a large part of the festivities – children might have expected to receive one homemade gift tucked under their pillows on Christmas Eve – but now it is much more a child-centred time. Adults exchange gifts too, but usually only among family members.

On Christmas Eve Christian families attend church, where they see a re-enactment of the Nativity, complete with Holy Family, shepherds, angels, and Magi. On Christmas Day they attend church again and then return home for the traditional dinner of *harisa*, chicken stew, and a sweet pastry called *kada*. Christmas is called the Little Feast (the Great Feast being Easter).

Iraq Iraqi Christians are a minority in this overwhelmingly Muslim country, but Christmas is a more public affair here than in many other Islamic states. Many non-Christians now put up Christmas trees as a way to share in the festive fun and to use as a decoration for New Year's. This tradition seems to have developed in the 1990s, when Iraq was subject to an international economic embargo and the government was more eager to have its domestic policies seen in a positive light.

There are many varieties of Christians in Iraq – Latin, Syrian, Armenian and Chaldean, Syrian and Greek Orthodox, Assyrians, Copts, and evangelicals – and each tends to celebrate the Nativity of Jesus in a slightly different way. Armenians and some Orthodox, for example, mark January 6 as their Christmas. All, however, attend church on Christmas Eve and Christmas Day, feast with family and friends, and await the arrival of Baba Noel.

Christmas tends to blur the denominational barriers, and all Christians of one's neighbourhood are included in the relentless hospitality that is part of Christmas in Iraq. In rural areas the Christmas feast, usually of lamb, is a communal one, with the entire village sitting down together as a single family. In Baghdad Christian homes fill up with well-wishers who go house-to-house in a complex round of reciprocal partying that goes on until the New Year.

Ireland In Ireland Advent is taken seriously as a time of preparation, domestically and spiritually, for the coming of Christmas. The house and farmyard must be rigorously cleaned, sometimes even given a coat of whitewash; greenery is gathered for decorations (particularly holly), and in rural areas the Yule log, the *bloc na Nollag*, is chosen and brought in. Extra prayers are added to usual religious devotions, a trip to the confessional is encouraged, and some aspect of penitential fasting observed. Shopping for seasonal requirements is called "bringing home the Christmas," and shopkeepers traditionally gave their customers a holiday treat. The Christmas tree is a recent addition to Irish homes, but is now widespread on the island. It is purchased a few days before Christmas and is usually decorated on Christmas Eve.

Christmas Eve is a day for final preparations. The seasonal puddings are readied for boiling the next day, Christmas pies are baked in the traditional medieval shape to resemble the cradle the baby Jesus was laid in, and candles are decorated with holly and lit. The Christmas Eve meal is traditionally a fasting one – sometimes called the black fast – containing no meat and consisting of cod and potatoes. Some lovely Irish traditions include leaving a candle in the window to light the way for the Holy Family or strangers, and leaving bread and milk on the table on Christmas Eve with the door unlocked in case the Holy Family should require a snack. The Irish also believe that on Christmas Eve no prayer goes unanswered and that the gates of Paradise are left open – those who die that night will go straight to Heaven instead of having to spend time in Purgatory. Folk often visit the graves of the family dead, light candles, and leave some greenery. Cattle are given extra food on Christmas Eve, and stalls in the barn are decorated. In the cities midnight mass is a relatively recent innovation, but one growing in popularity.

On Christmas morning presents brought by Father Christmas are opened, and the family, especially if it lives in the countryside, goes off to an early-morning church service. Some pluck a piece of straw from the Nativity scene in the church in the belief that it will bring good luck for the coming year. While the women hurry home to prepare a big meal, the men and boys often amuse themselves in some sporting activity – a game of hurley, a hunt, or a Gaelic football match.

Christmas lunch is a family affair, with all expected to return home if possible for the meal. Beef and goose were long-time favourites as the main course, but the turkey has won itself a spot as well on Irish Christmas tables, along with potatoes, boiled vegetables, and bread sauce. The dessert is most likely to be a plum pudding, with its flaming brandy topping, and mincemeat tarts.

The Irish musical genius, so evident in other genres, does not seem to have expended itself much on Christmas carols. Probably the best known of Irish Christmas songs is "THE WEXFORD CAROL."

The day following Christmas is St. Stephen's Day, marked in Ireland by "hunting the wren." For centuries costumed Irish boys went out on December 26, killed an inoffensive little wren, protected by custom all the rest of the year, and paraded about with the body on a pole chanting a song beginning:

***Ireland** A scene depicting the old Irish custom of hunting the wren on St. Stephen's Day.*

The wren, the wren, the king of birds,
St. Stephen's Day, was killed in the furze.
Although he is little, his honour is great,
And so good people, give us a treat.

The purpose of this ceremony was for the Wren Boys to solicit drinks or money from each house they stopped at and use the proceeds toward a party that night. Those who contributed were given a feather from the bird and allowed free admission to the night's festivities. Those who failed to tip the Boys would be ritually cursed or have the wren's body buried on their property – an act sure to bring ill fortune. Nowadays animal welfare sentiment has persuaded most that a replica of the wren will suffice, and the real birds are spared. The purpose of the ceremony has changed as well; no longer a BEGGING VISIT, it is an excuse to collect money for charity and dress up in costume for a community event.

Other St. Stephen's Day activities include mumming plays by Christmas Rhymers, Dublin's annual dog show, sporting events, fox hunts, and countless community dances.

New Year's Eve in Ireland is marked by the parties, fireworks, and drinking that are worldwide reactions to the passing of the old year and the beginning of the new, but there are also antique traditions that speak of a culture used to surviving in a subsistence economy. To assure the family of plenty in the coming year, it was considered important to end the old year with a huge meal. New Year's Eve thus became known as *Oiche na Coda Móire*, the NIGHT OF THE BIG PORTION.

The Christmas season ends on Epiphany, January 6. It is a time for all trees and greenery to come down and be burnt, and a time in some areas for "WOMEN'S CHRISTMAS," when tea and dainties are served and women relax as others do the work. The Magi are also honoured that day with three candles placed in the window.

Irmgard, August A German immigrant who is reputed to have introduced the Christmas tree to the United States in 1847 at Wooster, Ohio. Others point to Hessian mercenaries who fought on the side of the British during the American Revolution of the 1770s.

Irving, Washington (1783-1859) American writer and popularizer of Christmas traditions. Although trained as a lawyer, Irving made a name for himself as the first great American writer. His 1809 mock-historical *Diedrich Knickerbocker's History of New York From the Beginning of the World to the End of the Dutch Dynasty* introduced Americans to Saint Nicholas as a Christmas gift-bringer, featuring the saint winging his way over treetops in a wagon, smoking a pipe and "laying his finger beside his nose" before flying off – all extremely influential images in the development of the figure of Santa Claus. *The Sketch Book of Geoffrey Crayon, Gent.* (1819-20) contained "The Legend of Sleepy Hollow" and "Rip Van Winkle," two beloved short stories, but also five sketches about Christmas at Bracebridge Manor in England. His account of the Squire of Bracebridge's attempts to recreate an old-fashioned Christmas, complete with feudal hospitality and a procession with a boar's head, fascinated both Americans and Englishmen and helped lead to a revival of interest in Christmas at a time when the holiday was under attack from public indifference and the Industrial Revolution.

"It Came Upon the Midnight Clear" An American carol written in 1859 by Unitarian clergyman Edmund Hamilton

"It Came Upon the Midnight Clear" The American composer and journalist Richard Storrs Willis.

Sears (1810-76), noteworthy for containing no reference to the Nativity or to Jesus at all. The music is an 1850 tune, "Carol," by the music journalist Richard Storrs Willis (1819-1900) and was originally written for the hymn "See Israel's Gentle Shepherds Stand."

It came upon the midnight clear,
That glorious song of old,
From angels bending near the earth
To touch their harps of gold!
"Peace on the earth, good will to men,
From heaven's all gracious King!"
The world in solemn stillness lay
To hear the angels sing.

Still through the cloven skies they come
With peaceful wings unfurled
And still their heavenly music floats
O'er all the weary world;
Above its sad and lowly plains
They bend on hovering wing.
And ever o'er its Babel sounds
The blessed angels sing.

Yet with the woes of sin and strife
The world hath suffered long;
Beneath the angel-strain have rolled
Two thousand years of wrong;
And man, at war with man, hears not
The love song which they bring:
O hush the noise, ye men of strife,
And hear the angels sing.

For lo! the days are hastening on,
By prophet bards foretold,
When, with the ever-circling years,
Shall come the Age of Gold;
When peace shall over all the earth
Its ancient splendors fling,
And all the world give back the song
Which now the angels sing.

It Came Upon the Midnight Clear (TV) (1984)   Policeman Mike Halligan (Mickey Rooney) promised that he would spend a Christmas with his grandson, and the fact that he's dead is not going to stop him. Heaven allows him to return for one last holiday. Directed by Peter Hunt.

It Happened One Christmas (TV) (1977)   Remakes of classic movies are seldom worth the effort, and switching the sex of the protagonist only increases the likelihood of disaster. This earnest flop is a trans-gendered version of *It's a Wonderful Life*, starring Marlo Thomas in the role pioneered by Jimmy Stewart. Cloris Leachman was nominated for an Emmy, and Orson Welles plays a mean Mr. Potter.

It Nearly Wasn't Christmas (TV) (1989)   Charles Durning plays a Santa Claus at the end of his patience with an ungrateful humankind and ready to give up the Christmas business entirely. Only a little girl (Risa Schiffman) wishing to reunite her parents, and a loyal elf (Bruce Vilanch) can show him he is still needed. Directed by Burt Brinckerhoff with the assistance of various members of the Osmond Family, who can be blamed for the title song as well.

Italy   There are plenty of signs that Christmas is coming in Italy. Supermarkets and other large stores fill their aisles with advertising and all the luxuries and necessities of the holiday season. Christmas markets open up in town squares across the country, offering foods – particularly the essential *panettone* cake – toys, balloons, and figures for the family *presepio* (see below). In Bari, on the southeast coast, December 6 is a special place to be on St. Nicholas Day. This is where the saint's bones have been interred since their kidnapping over 900 years ago. Thousands of pilgrims flock to his tomb, some receiving the coveted MANNA DI SAN NICOLA, but all taking part in the processions that honour his patronage of sailors and children. In Sicily on December 13, Saint Lucia is celebrated on her native soil. A girl representing the saint goes about distributing presents, and children leave out their shoes at night believing she will fill them with little gifts.

In the middle of December market squares in some cities are filled with bagpipe music as the ZAMPOGNARI come down from the hills to play their pipes. These shepherd musicians claim that it was bagpipe music that soothed the Virgin in her labour pains and lulled the baby Jesus to sleep in Bethlehem. It was once their custom to play before manger scenes and shrines of the Madonna and to drop in on carpentry shops to pay their respects to Joseph. They now play in public places or hire themselves out to households or community organizations to serenade them in the approach to Christmas.

Preparations accelerate eight days before Christmas, when a novena of prayers and church services begins. Churches and homes erect *presepi*, or Nativity scenes, some of great complexity and antiquity, particularly in Naples where the tradition of carving *presepi* figures goes back centuries. The most elaborate, now preserved in palaces and museums, were those produced for Neapolitan rulers and aristocrats in the 18th century. Living manger scenes are also staged across the country, many of them using traditional regional peasant costumes to clothe the participants. On the Sunday before Christmas, thousands of children bring images from their

It's a Wonderful Life *George Bailey (Jimmy Stewart) confronts the nasty Mr. Potter (played by Lionel Barrymore).*

manger scenes to the Vatican, where the pope will bless them in St. Peter's Square.

On Christmas Eve at the papal Castel St. Angelo in Rome, a cannon is fired to announce the beginning of the holiday season. The Christmas Eve dinner is delicious but still technically part of the pre-Christmas fast, as it contains no meat. Some families make eel the centre of the meal; in other places it is customary to prepare seven fish dishes in different ways in honour of the Seven Sacraments. Pasta, salads, fruits, and breads accompany the fish along with plenty of Italian wine. Desserts usually include the *panettone* fruit cake, *torrone* (nougat), spicy cookies, and nuts. A charming Italian custom was for children to write poems or letters expressing their love for their parents and hide them on the table before Christmas dinner. During the meal the parents would discover these missives under a plate or in a napkin and read them aloud.

Though many Italian families have adopted the Christmas tree, it is still customary to have a *presepio* on display or a *ceppo*, the Italian Christmas pyramid on which a manger scene might be set. Some families have adopted Christmas Eve as the time to exchange gifts to go along with the emergence of Babbo Natale, the Italian Santa Claus, as the gift-bringer.

Christmas Eve is most likely to include a visit to church for midnight mass. Rome's churches have long been a showcase for Christmas and contain not only gorgeous Nativity scenes but also the BAMBINO of Ara Coeli, before whom little children are encouraged to give sermons and speeches, and relics of the original manger of Bethlehem, housed in the Church of Santa Maria Maggiore. The spectacular midnight mass conducted by the pope is broadcast around the planet. He also uses Christmas as the occasion for a speech to the world,

usually urging an end to war, violence, or some contemporary injustice.

The Italian Christmas season ends on January 6, Epiphany, but it goes out with a bang, because during the night the Italian gift-bringer, the BEFANA, descends chimneys to reward good children with presents and leave lumps of coal for the naughty.

It's a Wonderful Life (1946) "Merry Christmas, you beautiful old savings and loan! Merry Christmas, you beautiful beat-up old house!" So shouts George Bailey (Jimmy Stewart), who has just been saved from suicide by an apprentice angel who convinced him of his life's worth by showing what the town of Bedford Falls would have looked like without his influence.

This enormously popular Christmastime movie was not a success when first released in 1946, and when its copyright expired in 1974 no one bothered to renew it, allowing television stations to broadcast it without charge. This allowed new generations to discover this finely crafted Frank Capra film, which also features Donna Reed as Mary Bailey, Lionel Barrymore as nasty Mr. Potter, and Ward Bond and Frank Faylen as the original Bert and Ernie. (Republic Entertainment assumed control of the copyright in 1993 and broadcast fees are once again in effect.)

There is another Christmas connection to *It's a Wonderful Life*. Philip Van Doren Stern, the author of "The Greatest Gift," the short story on which the movie was based, could not interest a publisher in his work, so he printed up the story as a Christmas card and sent it to 200 friends. Among the recipients was a Hollywood agent, who convinced RKO studio that it would make a great movie.

See IT HAPPENED ONE CHRISTMAS and MERRY CHRISTMAS, GEORGE BAILEY.

Ivy *A 17th-century Englishman suffers the penalty for not providing the house with ivy.*

"It's Beginning to Look Like Christmas" A 1951 song by Meredith Willson, composer of *Music Man* and *The Unsinkable Molly Brown*. He included it in the 1963 Broadway musical *Here's Love*, based on the film *Miracle on 34th Street*. The popular show also included such songs as "Pine Cones and Holly Berries," and "Dear Mister Santa Claus."

Ivy In ancient Rome, ivy, *Hedera helix*, was a symbol of wine and merriment – it was worn as an antidote to drunkenness – but was adopted by Christians as a symbol of human weakness and the need to cling to divine strength. In England the vine was frequently used to decorate churches at Christmas, particularly in company with holly, with which it is celebrated in song. In Scotland it was useful in DIVINATION. Young women would pluck an ivy leaf, hold it to their hearts, and say, "Ivy, Ivy, I love you; / In my bosom I put you, / The first young man who speaks to me / My future husband shall be."

An Oxfordshire custom of the 17th century held that if maidservants asked a man to bring ivy for Christmas decoration and he did not, they were allowed to nail a pair of his breeches to the gate and to deny him the "well-known privilege of the mistletoe."

The plant, when hung in milksheds, was said to prevent souring, and it was also a preventative for baldness and corns. Its other medicinal uses can be read in this early-modern account:

> The juice of the berries or leaves snuffed up into the nose, purges the head and brain of thin rheum that makes defluxions into the eyes and nose, and curing the ulcers and stench therein; the same dropped into the ears helps the old and running sores of them; those that are troubled with the spleen shall find much ease by continual drinking out of a cup made of Ivy, so as the drink may stand some small time therein before it be drank.

Jack Frost (TV) (1979)   Harmless animated fluff by Jules Bass and Arthur Rankin Jr. Buddy Hackett as The Groundhog tells the life story of Jack Frost (voice of Robert Morse).

Jack Frost (1996)   The convicted murderer Jack Frost, played by Scott MacDonald, is on his way to his execution when he is involved in a snowy chemical accident and becomes a genetic mutant able to melt and refreeze at will. This does not improve his personality; rather he seeks icy revenge for past wrongs. A nasty but somewhat stylish holiday chiller by director/writer Michael Cooney.

Jack Frost (1998)   A sentimental sort of Christmas story. Michael Keaton plays Jack Frost, a father feeling guilty about not spending enough time with his family. On his way home he is killed in a car crash, but despite his death he manages to return to his family for one last Christmas. The problem is that he comes back as a snowman. Directed by Troy Miller.

J'ai rencontre le Père Noèl (1984)   Seven-year-old Simon (Emeric Chapuis) has a dilemma: his parents are lost in Africa and he wants them back. Naturally he searches for Santa Claus, whom he finds in Finland, and convinces the old gentleman (Armand Philoxene Meffre) to rescue Mom and Dad from the evil guerrillas. This French production by director Christian Gion was released in the English-speaking world as *Here Comes Santa Claus*.

Jamaica   Preparations for a Jamaican Christmas begin with the fruit cake – the ingredients are set to soak in wine and rum – and cleaning up the house and yard. Even the stones lining the walk are whitewashed. Cakes and puddings are baked in abundance; they will be served at home or taken as gifts to neighbours. Schools and churches stage Christmas pageants, carols celebrating a snowy holiday play on the radio, and businesses and homes put up lights and decorations. SORREL is bought and the petals made into the quintessential Jamaican Christmas drink.

Christmas in Jamaica is an intensely social affair. The night of Christmas Eve is the time for partying – "touring" groups go from house to house intent on taking part in as much hospitality as possible. Christmas Day is much quieter. After attending church in the morning, families might visit a Christmas market to buy toys before settling down to lunch, which is primarily a family affair. Ham, chicken, goat, turkey, and roast beef are all possibilities for the main dish, along with gunga peas, salads, cassava, rice, pastelles, corn pudding,

and the essential Christmas cake. At night the drinking and partying continues.

On Boxing Day friends will drop over to exchange small gifts and taste the Christmas cake. There may be a picnic planned or a beach party. What is certain is that there will be more partying and house-visiting. Boxing Day is also a day for JOHN CANOE. Groups of wildly costumed male dancers accompanied by musicians parade down streets and go door-to-door to amaze onlookers and solicit money and hospitality. Each character will have a name: Horse, Actor Boy, Belly-woman, Devil, Pitchy-Patchy, Policeman. As in Europe, this is the time of year for ghosts and ghost stories. When the sun goes down, chilling tales of duppies, the Rolling Calf dragging its chains, or the Three-Footed horse are told.

The holiday season is rounded out by the appearance of "Coney Islands" – impromptu gambling booths – and New Year's Eve parties. On January 2 the Christmas trees and decorations are taken down and thoughts turn to the next holiday, Carnival.

James I   (1566-1625) King of Scotland (1567-1625) and England (1603-25), defender of Christmas.

Raised as King James VI of Scotland, where the Calvinist church had forbidden Christmas celebrations, James was believed to be an opponent of the feast when he travelled south to assume the throne of England in 1603. Instead he proved a stout advocate of Christmas customs, commissioning holiday entertainments from Ben Jonson and Richard Middleton and ordering the English nobility to leave London for their country estates so that they could keep Christmas and its traditional hospitality as in days of old. In the Puritan opposition to Christmas and to religious ceremonial in general, King James perceived a kind of sedition and opposition to royal authority. He defended "the freedom to be merry," commanding dour Scotland in the Five Articles of Perth to keep Christmas in the English manner and issuing the *Book of Sports*, which prescribed the activities that could lawfully be enjoyed after church on Sundays.

Janny   The disguised house visitors during the Twelve Days of Christmas in Newfoundland and Labrador are called jannies. The origin of the word continues to mystify scholars, but folks in Newfoundland claim it is derived from Janus, the Roman god of the New Year, when the festivities of the Kalends were held. See MUMMING.

Japan   The celebration of Christmas in Japan is an interesting study in cultural appropriation. The Japanese have adopted many Western notions of the holiday, but in ways that would strike foreigners as unique and curious. Though Christianity was introduced to Japan in the 16th century, violent persecution for hundreds of years kept it a forbidden, underground religion with little effect on the mind of the nation. Consequently Japanese Christmas is almost devoid of the religious overtones it carries in much of the rest of the world. In Japan, Christmas, or *Kurisimasu*, is observed because of its connection to the exotic West, and because it serves a valuable commercial function, stimulating consumption in the midst of the traditional year-end gift-giving season, just before the New Year holiday.

Most Japanese grew acquainted with Christmas only after the Second World War, when they observed it being celebrated by American occupation forces and when the country began manufacturing toys for the global market. Its popularity has grown, and Christmas, known as "Holy Night" or just

"Eve," has become a very visible phenomenon in Japanese cities in December. Carols sung in English play in department stores; Christmas lights appear in stores and shopping malls (but seldom on houses); and in more and more homes artificial Christmas trees are decorated with lights, origami, fans, and small ornaments. Commercially sold Christmas cakes are a popular item to accompany a dinner of turkey after the exchange of gifts. Instead of Handel's *Messiah* as the great work of Christmas music, the Japanese prefer attending a performance of Beethoven's Ninth Symphony.

Japanese folklore has a figure resembling Santa Claus – Hoteiosho, an old man with a pack on his back and the ability to see behind himself – but the Western gift-bringer (sometimes called Uncle Chimney) is the one featured in advertising. Some advertisements might cause an observer to marvel at how meanings shift across cultural planes: one ad for a novelty store chain features a childlike angel standing on a red rose with the caption "'Oh! My God.' God Save the Christmas." A possibly apocryphal story claims that a Tokyo department store in the post-war years displayed a crucified Santa Claus with the motto "Happy Shopping" above the cross.

Though the Japanese love giving presents to children, Christmas is also a time for adults to indulge in heavy-duty consumption. Christmas Eve is considered the prime time of the year for buying diamonds and other jewellery. It is also the season of sensual love and assignations in hotels and restaurants, which advertise themselves as places of romance.

Christmas does not linger in Japan. On December 26, Christmas ads disappear, decorations are taken down, and the Japanese prepare themselves for the fast-approaching New Year's holiday.

"Jeg er så glad hver julekveld" A Norwegian carol by Peter Knudsen (1819-63), translated to English as "I Am So Glad on Christmas Eve" by Marie Wexelsen (1832-1911).

Jeg er så glad hver julekveld
Ti da blev Jesus fodt,
Da ilyte stjernen som en sol,
Og engle sang så sodt.

Jer er så glad hver julekveld
Da synger vi hans pris,
Da aapner han for alle smaa
Sit sode paradis.

I am so glad on Christmas Eve,
The night of Jesus' birth;
The night the Star shone like the sun,
And angels sang on earth.

I am so glad on Christmas Eve.
Our grateful praises rise
To Jesus, who has opened wide
His own sweet Paradise.

The little Child in Bethlehem,
He was a King indeed!
For He came down from heaven above
To help a world in need.

He dwells again in heaven's realm,
The Son of God today;
And still He loves His little ones
And hears them when they pray.

I am so glad on Christmas Eve!
His praises then I sing;

He opens then for every child
The palace of the King.

When mother trims the Christmas tree
Which fills the room with light
She tells me of the wondrous star
That made the dark world bright.

And so I love each Christmas Eve,
And I love Jesus too;
And that He loves me every day
I know so well is true.

"Jesous Ahatonhia" See "THE HURON CAROL."

Jesse Tree A popular motif in medieval art, particularly in stained glass, was the depiction of the earthly ancestry of Jesus as a tree growing from Jesse, the father of David. A spectacular example of this is the 12th-century Jesse Tree window from the Benedictine abbey of St. Denis in France. In the 20th century the notion of a Jesse tree as a symbol of Advent attracted a number of American artists and craftspeople. Many churches and homes now contain a tree or tree branch, decorated with ornaments symbolic of Messianic prophecies or a banner adorned with Bible verses prophesying the coming of Jesus.

Sometimes the Jesse Tree is decorated piece by piece like an Advent calendar, and in some churches a Jesse tree is used to collect winter clothing for the poor, with members attaching hats, scarves, or mittens.

"Jesus' bloemhof" A 15th-century Dutch carol, published first in 1689 and translated as "The Garden of Jesus," "Lord Jesus Has a Garden," or "King Jesus Hath a Garden."

King Jesus hath a garden, full of divers flow'rs,
Where I go culling posies gay, all times and hours.

There naught is heard but paradise bird,
Harp, dulcimer, lute,
With cymbal, trump and tymbal,
And the tender soothing flute.
With cymbal, trump and tymbal,
And the tender soothing flute.

Yet, 'mid the brave, the bravest prize of all may claim.
The Star of Bethlehem Jesus blessed be His name!

Chorus

Jesus of Nazareth (1976) A very lengthy treatment (over six hours) of the entire life of Jesus, this Franco Zeffirelli film was made for television. With its sterling production values, it transcended the mini-series genre to become an instant classic.

The luminous Olivia Hussey played Mary, and Yorgo Voyagis, Joseph; Donald Pleasence, James Earl Jones, and Fernando Rey were the Magi. Robert Powell played the adult Jesus. The English screenplay was written by English novelist Anthony Burgess.

"Jesus refulsit omnium" Often credited as the earliest Christmas hymn, these Latin verses are by St. Hilary of Poitiers (d. 368).

Jesus refulsit omnium
Pius redemptor gentium;
Totum genus fidelium
Laudes celebret dramatum,

Quem stella natum fulgida
Monstrat micans per aethera,
Magosque duxit praevia
Ipsius ad cunabula.

Illi cadentes parvulum
Pannis adorant obsitum,
Verum fatentur ut Deum
Munus fruendo mysticum.

Jingle All the Way (1996)   A film for any parent who has tried to supply his or her children with the latest in-demand toy for Christmas only to find that they are all sold out (or deliberately kept in short supply to fuel the craze). Howard Langston (played by Arnold Schwarzenegger) is a busy father whose guilt over neglecting his family leads him to promise his son a Turbo Man action figure. Naturally these have long since disappeared from toy shelves, and Langston finds himself in a desperate hunt that leads him into a duel with Myron Larabee (Sinbad), who is on a similar mission, and a shady rendezvous with an evil department store Santa who promises a bootleg version of the toy. Directed by Brian Levant, the film includes footage shot in the cavernous Mall of America.

"Jingle Bell Rock"   A 1957 popular music hit, written by Joe Beal and Jim Boothe and recorded by Bobby Helms.

"Jingle Bells"   A winter carol by James L. Pierpoint (1827-93) originally entitled "One Horse Open Sleigh" and meant for an 1857 Sunday school program in New York City. Pierpoint served with the Confederate cavalry in the American Civil War and was the uncle of financier J.P. Morgan.

> Dashing through the snow
> In a one-horse open sleigh,
> Over the fields we go,
> Laughing all the way;
> Bells on bob-tail ring, making spirits bright,
> What fun it is to ride and sing
> A sleighing song tonight
> Jingle bells, jingle bells, jingle all the way!
> O what fun it is to ride
> In a one-horse open sleigh
>
> A day or two ago,
> I thought I'd take a ride,
> And soon Miss Fanny Bright
> Was seated by my side;
> The horse was lean and lank;
> Misfortune seemed his lot;
> He got into a drifted bank,
> And we, we got upsot.
> Jingle bells, jingle bells, jingle all the way!
> What fun it is to ride
> In a one-horse open sleigh.
>
> A day or two ago, the story I must tell
> I went out on the snow
> And on my back I fell;
> A gent was riding by
> In a one-horse open sleigh,
> He laughed as there I sprawling lie,
> But quickly drove away.
> Jingle bells, jingle bells, jingle all the way!
> What fun it is to ride
> In a one-horse open sleigh.

> Now the ground is white
> Go it while you're young,
> Take the girls tonight
> And sing this sleighing song;
> Just get a bob-tailed bay two-forty as his speed
> Hitch him to an open sleigh
> And crack! you'll take the lead.
> Jingle bells, jingle bells, jingle all the way!
> What fun it is to ride
> In a one-horse open sleigh.

"Job Warner's Christmas"   An 1863 short story by American rags-to-riches author Horatio Alger, Jr. (1832-99). Humble clerk Job Warner is denied a raise in pay on Christmas Eve, but his employer undergoes a change of heart when he notices Warner's kindness to an orphan girl. He resolves almost to double his clerk's salary and explains, "Prosperity had begun to harden my heart. At any rate, it had made me thoughtless of the multitudes who are struggling with ills which my wealth could alleviate. To-night I was an unseen witness of your kindness to the poor girl who crossed your path. I felt rebuked by the contrast between your conduct and mine, and I resolved, God helping me, to become hereafter a better steward of His bounty."

John Canoe   "John Canoe," *Junkanoo*, *Jonkonnu*, and *Koonering* are just some of the terms for carnival-like celebrations held in the Caribbean, Honduras, Belize, and North Carolina derived from a holiday and period of social inversion for slaves during Christmas in the 18th and 19th centuries. Slave owners used the custom as a safety valve, much like Saturnalia in the Roman empire; slaves used it to subvert and mock the established order.

There is no agreement on the origins of the name John Canoe. Some hold it to be derived from African deities, others from Mayan ritual, others from the name of a slave owner, and still others assert it was the name of a slave. Today participants dance and parade in elaborate costume, and the spectacle attracts thousands of tourists. (See colour fig. 8.)

John Grin's Christmas (TV) (1986)   An African-American adaptation of *A Christmas Carol*, produced, directed, and starring Robert Guillaume as the Scrooge-like toymaker who will not give toys to children of the poor.

John the Baptist, Saint   The miraculous son of ZACHARIAS and Elizabeth and kin to Jesus, John is frequently portrayed in art of the Nativity cycle, where he is depicted as a slightly older infant, already clothed in the skins he will wear as an adult and often pointing to Jesus as the Messiah. Later in life John will live as a hermit, call the people of Israel to repentance and baptism, and be executed by Herod.

John's Day, St.   December 27 is the feast day of Saint John the Evangelist, the son of Zebedee, companion of Jesus and reputed author of the Fourth Gospel. In the Middle Ages the day was marked by a blessing of the wine, derived from the legend that John drank poisoned wine and was not harmed. As Barnaby Googe in the 16th century related:

> Nexte John, the sonne of Zebedee
> hath his appointed day,
> Who once by cruell tyraunts will,
> constrayned was they say
> Strong poison up to drinke, therefore
> the papistes doe beleeve

That whoso puts their trust in him,
no poyson them can greeve.
The wine beside that halowed is
in worship of his name,
The prestes doe give the people
that bring money for the same.
And after with the self same wine
are little manchets made
Agaynst the boysterous winter stormes
and sundrie such like trade.
The men upon this solemne day
do take this holy wine
To make them strong. So do the maydes
to make them faire and fine.

It was also a custom for people to bring wine or cider to the church on December 27 to be blessed. This "St. John's Wine" was considered a protection for travellers setting out on a journey or for those near death. Because the Gospel of John proclaims Jesus as the light of the world, a German custom allowed children named John or Joan to be the first to light the Advent candle.

Jólasveinar   The Yule Lads, Yule Swains, or Yule Goblins of Icelandic Christmas lore. The sons of the monstrous child-eaters Gryla and Leppaludi, they were once feared as malicious visitors in the holiday season. The tales of these ogres were so blood-chilling that the Danish government, which ruled Iceland in the 18th century, legislated in 1746 against using them to frighten children.

Though the number of Yule Lads has varied over the years, 13 is the presently accepted figure. They were wont to descend, one by one, from their mountain home in the interior of Iceland, the first arriving on December 12, the Eve of St. Lucia, and the last showing up on Christmas Eve. Each is known by a separate name (which can also vary) and a particular prank he is fond of playing.

The first is Stekkjarstaur – otherwise known as Fence Post, Sheep-Cot Clod, or Stiff-Legged Sheep Chaser. (His stiff legs come from kneeling on the hard ground to steal the sheep's milk.) The next is Giljagaur, the Crevice Imp or Gully-Gawk. The smallest is Stúfur, also known as Stumpy or Itty Bitty. Then comes Thvörusleikir, the Spoon Licker, followed by Pottasleikir, Pot Licker, and Askasleikir, Bowl Licker. Hurdarskellir, the Door Slammer, is the noisiest of the lads, while Skyrgámur is so named because he gobbles up the local yogourt. The crimes of the next two are self-explanatory: Bjúgnakrækir, the Sausage Snatcher, and Gluggagægir, the Window Peeper. They are followed by Gattathefur, the Doorway Sniffer, Ketkrókur, the Meat Hook (prone to take to the rafters and steal the meat hanging there to cure), and Kertasnikir, the Candle Beggar. They are all rather ugly and boorish in behaviour, dressed as peasants of centuries ago.

Where once they were feared, and used by parents as a threat to keep children in line during the winter, they are now beloved characters whose arrival is welcomed and who have been woven into the commercial culture, making appearances on radio and television. Children leave out their shoes for the Yule Lads to deposit in them a treat or small present in the days leading up to Christmas. (Bad kids often receive only a rotten piece of fruit or potato as a sign that they should amend their behaviour.) After December 25 the Lads depart as they came, one by one, until Twelfth Night, January 6, when the Christmas season comes to an end.

The softening of their character is in keeping with a trend, which began in the 19th century, to make Christmas figures less frightening and more child-friendly. The same phenomenon can be seen in Scandinavia, where figures such as the *nisse* and Joulupukki have become much milder, and in the gradual disappearance of those helpers of the gift-bringer who were menacing embodiments of punishment for children. The survival of the *Jólasveinar* in a century when local customs have often been submerged or homogenized by the North American Santa Claus is a tribute to Icelandic nationalism and love of folklore.

"Jolly Old St. Nicholas"   An anonymous American secular Christmas song, whose style has led at least one musicologist to attribute it to the 19th-century author of "Up on the Housetop," Benjamin R. Hanby.

Jolly old Saint Nicholas,
Lean your ear this way!
Don't you tell a single soul
What I'm going to say;
Christmas Eve is coming soon;
Now, you dear old man,
Whisper what you'll bring to me;
Tell me if you can.

When the clock is striking twelve,
When I'm fast asleep,
Down the chimney broad and black,
With your pack you'll creep;
All the stockings you will find
Hanging in a row;
Mine will be the shortest one,
You'll be sure to know.

Jólasveinár Ketkrókur, or Meat Hook, is one of the Jólasveinar *of Iceland.*

Johnny wants a pair of skates;
Susy wants a dolly;
Nellie wants a story book;
She thinks dolls are folly;
As for me, my little brain
Isn't very bright;
Choose for me, old Santa Claus,
What you think is right

Joseph A carpenter of Nazareth and the earthly father of Jesus, Joseph appears first in the gospels as Mary's betrothed. When he learns she is pregnant he is dissuaded from abandoning her by an angelic visit that tells him the child has been conceived by the Holy Spirit. He takes Mary, late in her pregnancy, to Bethlehem to be enumerated, and there she gives birth to Jesus. Warned in a vision to flee Herod, Joseph takes his wife and child to Egypt and then back to Nazareth. The last glimpse we have of him in the canonical scriptures is on a visit to Jerusalem when Jesus is 12 and eludes his anxious parents to stay and talk with learned men in the Temple.

Legend and apocryphal scripture treat Joseph in much more detail. There, he is always depicted as an older man, a widower with sons, who won Mary as a bride after supernatural intervention. In Nativity art he appears in depictions of his encounters with the angels, the Journey to Bethlehem, the manger scene, and the Flight into Egypt. In these settings he is often portrayed somewhat apart from Jesus – a sign that he is not the child's true father – and often looking bemused or thoughtful at the amazing turn of events. (See colour figs. 9, 18.)

Joseph is patron of Austria, Belgium, and Canada, and of fathers, carpenters, house hunters, social justice, and the universal Church. In the West his feast is March 19, and in the Eastern churches it is the first Sunday after Christmas. As Joseph the Worker, he is also celebrated on May 1.

"Joseph, Dearest Joseph Mine" This song is a translation by Neville Stuart Talbot (1879-1943) of the German carol "Joseph, lieber Joseph mein," which originated in a late-medieval mystery play. Brahms borrowed part of the melody for his "Spiritual Cradle Song."

"Joseph dearest, Joseph mine,
Help me cradle the child divine;
God reward thee and all that's thine
In paradise," so prays the mother Mary.

He came among us at Christmastide,
At Christmastide, in Bethlehem;
Men shall bring Him from far and wide
Love's diadem: Jesus, Jesus,
Lo, He comes, and loves, and saves, and frees us!

"Gladly, dear one, lady mine,
Help I cradle this child of thine;
God's own light on us both shall shine
In paradise, as prays the mother Mary."

Refrain

Peace to all that have good will!
God who heaven and earth doth fill,
Comes to turn us away from ill
And lies so still, within the crib of Mary.

Refrain

All shall come and bow the knee,
Wise and happy their souls shall be,

Loving such a divinity,
As all may see, in Jesus, son of Mary.

Joulupukki The Santa Claus figure of Finland. Originally depicted as a man in goatskins, this "Yule Buck" gradually mutated into a less frightening character in the course of the 19th and early-20th centuries. From 1927 a radio broadcaster spun stories claiming the gift-bringer lived in Finland on Korvatunturi (Mount Ear), and from these stories came a whole Finnish Christmas industry.

"Journey of the Magi" A poem by T.S. Eliot based on the account in the Gospel of Matthew of the visit of Eastern Magi to the baby Jesus. Eliot takes as his starting point a passage from the 1622 Nativity sermon of LANCELOT ANDREWES:

"A cold coming we had of it,
Just the worst time of the year
For a journey, and such a long journey:
The ways deep and the weather sharp,
The very dead of winter."

"Joy to the World" An adaptation of Psalm 98 by the prolific English hymnist Isaac Watts (1674-1748), who in his youth wrote the words for a hymn each week for 222 consecutive weeks. In all, he produced 50 volumes of published works, including *Hymns and Spiritual Songs*, 1707, and the 1719 *Psalms of David in the Language of the New Testament*, from which "Joy to the World" is taken.

The hymn has been extremely popular over the centuries, though various denominations have seen fit to alter some lyrics to suit their theological preoccupations. Some Unitarians, for example, took umbrage at the notion of Original Sin contained in the fourth line of the third verse, and Adventists, looking to an imminent return of Christ, felt more comfortable singing, "Joy to the world! the Lord *will* come." There is even a 19th-century adaptation to let atheists sing with a clear conscience.

Musicologists still debate the origins of the tune, and some assert a similarity to a portion of Handel's *Messiah*. The American Lowell Mason (1792-1872) combined Watts's poetry with the mystery music in 1836.

"Joy to the World" Isaac Watts, the prolific hymn writer.

Joy to the world! the Lord is come;
Let earth receive her King;
Let every heart prepare Him room,
and heaven and nature sing,
and heaven and nature sing,
and heaven, and heaven and nature sing.

Joy to the earth! the Savior reigns;
Let men their songs employ;
while fields and floods,
rocks, hills and plains
Repeat the sounding joy,
Repeat the sounding joy,
Repeat, repeat the sounding joy.

No more let sins and sorrows grow,
nor thorns infest the ground;
He comes to make His blessing flow
far as the curse is found,
far as the curse is found,
far as, far as the curse is found.

He rules the world with truth and grace,
and makes the nations prove
the glories of His righteousness,
and wonders of His love,
and wonders of His love,
and wonders, wonders of His love.

Julafred   The Norwegian Christmas peace in which custom decreed no wheel must turn and no bird, animal, or fish be hunted. Quarrels were to cease and folk were to go about unarmed. See TRUCE, CHRISTMAS.

Julbock   The Swedish "Christmas goat," probably a descendant of a devilish companion of St. Nicholas, the *Julbock* became for a time after the Protestant Reformation the gift-bringer. He was displaced from that occupation in the 19th century by a Santa Claus figure called JULTOMTEN, but found new employment pulling Jultomten about on his travels. He is often represented by straw ornaments and cookies made in his form.

Julebaal   The Danish Christmas fire, started with remnants of the previous year's Yule log and dispelling lurking evil spirits.

Julebukk   Literally, "Yule Buck." A custom in rural Norway and areas of Norwegian settlement in the American Midwest where folk go door-to-door in disguise during the Christmas season. When done by adults it resembles Newfoundland MUMMING, where a key element of the fun is trying to guess the identity of the visitors. When performed by children it more closely resembles Halloween soliciting of treats while in costume. In Norwegian immigrant communities in the United States it is also known as Christmas Fooling.

Julehalm   In the old days Norwegian householders would carry "Christmas hay," or *julehalm*, into the house and spread it on the floor of the front room. On Christmas Eve the master and his servants would sleep there together, partly for mutual support on that night of the year when demonic forces outside were at their strongest, and partly in remembrance of the baby Jesus and his bed in the hay-filled manger. The custom was also observed in Sweden in the belief that the beds should be left empty for the spirits of the family dead who had returned for the holiday.

Julenek *A swedish postage stamp depicting the Scandinavian custom of leaving out a sheaf of grain for the birds on Christmas.*

Julekake   Norwegian sweet Christmas bread made with raisins.

Julemand   The Santa Claus figure of Denmark.

Julenek   A sheaf of grain erected on a pole for birds to eat. This Norwegian custom reflects the desire to share Christmas hospitality even with the animal kingdom. Some clear away the snow beneath the pole in the belief that birds dance around the circle before eating the grain. *Juleneks* can be seen in city yards and apartment balconies of urban Norway as well as in the countryside. In Denmark it is the *juleneg*.

Julenisse   The Danish gnome of house or farm, dressed in grey, with a red cap, red stockings, and white clogs; he must be bribed with the customary Christmas Eve rice pudding or

Julenisse *The Christmas elf on a Guernsey Christmas stamp.*

mischief results. The *Julenisse* is very popular in Danish advertising as a Christmas symbol.

Julesvenn   The Norwegian Santa, derived from a pagan Yule figure who used to come and hide lucky barley stalks about the house for a good harvest.

Julklapp   The Yule box custom of Scandinavia, where a present is thrown in from the doorway by a mysterious giver. Great effort is made to tantalize the recipient; the gift is disguised by being wrapped very comprehensively, or perhaps after much unwrapping the recipient finds only directions on how to find the real gift.

Julskinka   The Swedish Christmas ham, which, if done in the traditional manner, takes a great deal of preparation. First salt-cured, it is then boiled on December 23 and left in its broth overnight to cool. On Christmas Eve the ham is dried, coated in beaten egg, mustard, sugar, and bread crumbs, and baked for the late afternoon meal.

Jultomten   The Swedish Santa Claus figure, once a gnome, clad in a red cap and with a long white beard, who guarded the farm in return for bribes. He rides in a sleigh pulled by the JULBOCK.

Jumanji   Released in 1995, this is not really a movie about Christmas, but one whose ending shows what Christmas has come to mean to North American cinema and popular culture in general.

Alan Parrish and Sarah Whittle played an evil game in their childhood and their inability to finish it ruined their lives. When two new children begin to play the game there comes a chance for broken lives to mend. The final scene is set at a Christmas party with "Hark! The Herald Angels Sing" sung in the background – a signal to the audience that all is now well, that harmony has been restored, and God and sinners are reconciled. In a movie without any overt religious reference, Christmas stands as a metaphor for healing and fresh beginnings.

The movie stars Robin Williams and Bonnie Hunt; it was directed by Joe Johnston and based on a book by Chris Van Allsburg, author of *The Polar Express*.

Kalends The first day of a Roman month. The Kalends of January signalled a New Year celebration in ancient Rome. It was a time for festive lights and greenery, presents (*strenæ*) – at least for the emperor – extravagance, generosity, and merry-making while disguised in masks or animal skins or wearing clothes of the opposite sex. All these elements became attached at one time or another to Christmas, partly because they were common to most midwinter festivals and partly because they were hard to eradicate.

At first the Church set its face against such carryings-on during the season of the Nativity, but ultimately it decided to turn people away from the pagan connotations of the Kalends by sanctifying the time. The Council of Tours in 567 ordered that January 1 become the feast of the Circumcision, while it denounced excesses such as transvestism and the wearing of animal skins.

As the Middle Ages progressed, however, the notion of merriment crept back into Christmas as it gradually lost its purely theological flavour and became the celebration of the birth of Jesus as a real human child. In this a little touch of the Kalends survives, as it does in Russia, where the equivalent of the Christkindl is Kolyáda, a white-robed maiden who goes about on a sleigh on Christmas Eve. *Kolyáda* is the Russian term for Christmas, and is derived from Kalends.

Kallikantzaroi Evil monsters of Greek Christmas folklore whose description varies; in some places they are viewed as half-human with hooves and claws, in others they are wolflike or simian. They spend most of the year in the underworld, chopping away at the tree that supports the Earth. This tree is renewed at Christmas by the birth of Christ, so the demons come to Earth for revenge; they urinate on fires, ride on folks' backs, force them to dance to exhaustion, and commit other enormities. They may be kept out of the chimney (through which they enter) by keeping the Christmas log alight or by burning salt or old shoes, the smoke of which repels them; the lower jaw of a pig or certain herbs, such as hyssop, hung behind the door or inside the chimney will also keep them out. They roam the Earth until January 6, when the Blessing of the Waters drives them underground.

Any child born during Christmas is in danger of becoming one of the *kallikantzaroi*; to prevent this the child must be bound in tresses of garlic or straw or have his toenails singed.

"Karen's Christmas" "Karens Jul," an 1885 story by Amalie Skran, a Norwegian writer interested in the plight of society's less fortunate. A policeman discovers an unwed mother and new baby in an unheated shack at Christmas. He allows her to remain there, but she dies of exposure. The device of freezing a pathetic character to death on Christmas can be found in other stories, such as Hans Christian Andersen's "THE LITTLE MATCH GIRL," and is parodied by Maxim Gorki in "CHRISTMAS PHANTOMS."

Kindelwiegen The veneration of the crèche, which began in the Middle Ages, led in Germany to the custom of *Kindelwiegen* or "Cradle Rocking." At first the rocking was performed by priests, who sang a duet about the Virgin and the baby Jesus; the choir and congregation then joined in, singing and dancing around the crib. Later the people were allowed to rock the cradle themselves. In the 16th century, Protestants abandoned the custom, and even to Catholics the rocking seemed like an irreverent act, so the image of the Christ Child was removed to the altar and folk danced around it there:

> Three Maisses every Priest doth sing upon that solemne day,
> With offrings unto every one, that so the more may play.
> This done, a woodden childe in clowtes is on the aultar set
> About the which both boyes and gyrles do daunce and trymly jet,
> And Carrols sing in prayse of Christ, and for to helpe them heare,
> The Organs aunswere every verse, with sweete and solemne cheare.
> The Priestes doe rore aloude, and round about the parentes stande,
> To see the sport, and with their voyce do helpe them and their hande.

In the 18th century it was performed every day between Christmas and Candlemas by boy-acolytes of Brixen Cathedral in Tyrol. The rowdiness of the scene may be inferred from the printed instructions to the sacristan: "Be sure to take a stick or a thong of ox hide, for the boys are often misbehaved." The custom continued in Germany until the 19th century.

King Cake The French Epiphany cake, *le gâteau des rois*, as found in New Orleans. Between January 6 (Three Kings' Day) and Mardi Gras, New Orleans bakers produce thousands of King Cakes, decorated in the Mardi Gras colours of purple, green, and gold. Hidden in each cake is a bean or plastic baby, and the person who finds the prize must host the next party.

King, Christmas A version of the LORD OF MISRULE. In 15th-century Norfolk, a Christmas King rode in state through the streets clad in silk and tinsel, preceded by 12 costumed folk dressed as the months of the year and followed by a figure representing Lent, who is "clothed in white garments, trimmed with herring skins, on horseback, the horse being decorated with trappings of oyster-shells, being indicative that sadness and a holy time should follow Christmas revelling."

"King Herod and the Cock" A late-medieval English ballad.

> There was a star in David's land,
> In David's land did appear:
> And in King Herod's chamber
> So bright did it shine there.
>
> The Wise men they soon spied it,
> And told the King a-nigh
> That a princely babe was born that night,
> No king shall e'er destroy.

"If this be the truth," King Herod said,
"That thou hast told to me,
The roasted cock that lies in the dish
Shall crow full sense [times] three."

O the cock soon thrustened [came to life] and feathered
well,
By the work of God's own hand,
And he did crow full senses three,
In the dish where he did stand.

Kissing Bunch or Bough   Here is an account from 19th-century Derbyshire:

The "kissing bunch" is always an elaborate affair. The size depends upon the couple of hoops – one thrust through the other which form its skeleton. Each of the ribs is garlanded with holly, ivy, and sprigs of other greens, with bits of coloured ribbons and paper roses, rosy-cheeked apples, specially reserved for this occasion, and oranges. Three small dolls are also prepared, often with much taste, and these represent our Saviour, the mother of Jesus, and Joseph. These dolls generally hang within the kissing bunch by strings from the top, and are surrounded by apples, oranges tied to strings, and various brightly coloured ornaments. Occasionally, however, the dolls are arranged in the kissing bunch to represent a manger-scene.

Mistletoe is not very plentiful in Derbyshire; but, generally, a bit is obtainable, and this is carefully tied to the bottom of the kissing bunch, which is then hung in the middle of the house-place, the centre of attention during Christmastide.

Klapparbock   In Danish Christmas folklore, the "Goat with Yule Gifts," probably derived from Thor's goat and related to the Finnish JOULUPUKKI.

Klaubauf   When St. Nicholas visits Austria on December 5, he may be accompanied by Klaubauf, a rather frightening assistant with a dark shaggy hide, goat horns, a long red tongue, dressed in rags and clanking chains. His name seems to be derived from the order "*Klaub auf!*" ("Pick them up!") when nuts and apples are scattered in front of the children.

Klopfelngehen   Literally, to "go knocking," an old Christmas-time custom in Bavaria. Poor folk would go door-to-door in evenings during Advent, singing songs in return for food, which they would stuff into a sack. Today the tradition is being revived, with the proceeds now going to charity.

Knecht Ruprecht   A gift-bringer's HELPER who first appeared in a 1668 German play and was condemned as a manifestation of the devil by the Catholic Church in 1680. Knecht Ruprecht is an intimidating figure who carries a switch and is dressed like a monk, with a long dark coat of animal skins and a dark filthy beard that reaches the floor. He quizzes children about their behaviour. He is sometimes identified with BELSNICKEL, or Pelznickel ("Nicholas in Furs"), and Ru-Klas ("Rough Nicholas"), indicating that he was originally a darker version of St. Nicholas rather than just his companion.

The English poet Thomas Coleridge witnessed local Christmas ceremonies in north Germany in the early 19th century and noted that it was the custom in smaller centres for presents to be given by Knecht Ruprecht

in high buskins, a white robe, a mask, and an enormous flax wig. . . . On Christmas-night he goes round to every house, and says that Jesus Christ, his master, sent him hither. The parents and elder children receive him with great pomp and reverence while the little ones are most terribly frightened. He then inquires for the children, and, according to the character which he hears from the parents, he gives them the intended present as if they came out of heaven from Jesus Christ. Or, if they should have been bad children, he gives the parents a rod and, in the name of his master, recommends them to use it frequently. About seven or eight years old the children are let into the secret, and it is curious how faithfully they keep it.

Knickerbockers   A group of writers and amateur historians of early 19th-century New York who were extremely influential in shaping the modern American view of Christmas. Taking their name from Washington Irving's *Diedrich Knickerbocker's History of New York*, the group included Irving, John Pintard, president of the New York Historical Society, novelist James Fenimore Cooper, and Clement Clarke Moore, author of "A Visit From St. Nicholas." Their goal seems to have been to carve out a distinctively American, and at times consciously anti-British, culture for their new country. In doing so they virtually invented the figure of Santa Claus, whom they alleged was part of the Dutch heritage of New York. Their works changed Christmas from a rowdy communal celebration to a private, domestic, child-centred one, and they changed Santa Claus from a Catholic bishop to a non-denominational elf, one who was seized on by Yankee merchants as the front-man for their commercial exploitation of Christmas. See SANTA CLAUS.

Knocking Nights   Nights during Advent in south Germany when groups go from house to house singing hymns and knocking on doors and windows. See KLOPFELNGEHEN.

Knut's Day, St.   On January 13, known as St. Knut's Day or Hilarymas, Swedish and Norwegian children enjoy one last party before the decorations and trees are taken down. The folk saying is "Twentieth day Knut, Driveth Yule out." There are records of two medieval saints named Knut (or Canute): one was a martyred Danish king of the 11th century, the other a martyred duke of the 12th century.

Kolacky   Czech sweet bread served at Christmas in a variety of shapes: rolls (with fruit or poppy seed fillings), or cookies or tarts with a preserved-fruit centre.

Kolyáda   A Russian Santa figure in the form of a white-robed girl who travelled in a sleigh accompanied by carol singers. The name is derived ultimately from KALENDS. She was suppressed under the Soviet Union and replaced by Grandfather Frost and his niece the Snow Maiden.

Korvatunturi   Mount Ear, the Finnish home of Santa Claus according to an influential series of children's radio programs in the 1920s.

Krampus   Also known as Krampusz, Krumpus, or Grampus, a gift-bringer's helper in Central Europe, especially lower Austria. A devil carrying a rod or a whip, he accompanies St. Nicholas and intimidates children; he wears a wooden basket on his back in which to throw bad kids, but always the saint kindly intercedes.

Krampus *The demonic Krampus accompanies St. Nicholas on this early-20th-century Christmas card.*

In the 1990s Macy's department store was forced to pull two Czech-made ornaments in the shape of Krampus from their stores when customers complained. "It left me with an ill feeling," said one. "Macy's always pushes the theme of being a family store – and if they are, then they should stick to family things. Even if you're not Christian, it doesn't make sense to hang the devil on your tree at Christmas."

Kringle, Kris Now just a synonym of Santa Claus, "Kris Kringle" shows an interesting linguistic evolution. The name originates from *Christkindl*, the German term for the Christ Child, who was thought to bring gifts. From the 17th to the 19th century, from its European origins to North America, where it was brought by immigrants, the name mutated to Krischkindel to Kriss Kindle to Kriss Kinkle and, by 1842 in Philadelphia, to Kriss Kringle. We see in American children's books such as *Kriss Kringle's Christmas Tree* and department store advertisements that the name was being applied in the 1850s to a Santa Claus figure far from the original notion of the Christ Child. In the 20th century the name was spelled both "Kris" and "Kriss" Kringle. The original *Miracle on 34th Street*, for example, uses the former, and the 1994 remake uses the latter.

Female BELSNICKLERS in German settlements in the Canadian province of Nova Scotia who disguised themselves as Wise Men were known as Kris Kringles.

Kutya A Christmas dish of cooked grain with honey, sesame seed, and sometimes nuts. Eating it is an important part of the ritual of Christmas dinner in Ukrainian and other Eastern European households. Traditionally the father of the house takes the first spoonful, invokes the presence of God, and utters the ritual Christmas greeting "*Khrystos Rhodyvsya!*" ("Christ is Born!"). All reply "*Slavim Yoho!*" ("Let us glorify him!"). Following this, all get a taste of *kutya*. It was once customary for a spoonful to be thrown on the ceiling and one to be thrown out the window.

In Old Russia there were always three bowls of *kutya* – white, amber, and black – to remember the Three Kings.

Lamb The birth of Jesus in a stable, the appearance of adoring shepherds soon after, and the role of Jesus as the sacrificial Lamb of God have combined to make the lamb a powerful Christian symbol. In Nativity art shepherds are often seen bearing a lamb toward the cradle. They frequently appear in Christmas carols and in seasonal animated films, such as *The Little Drummer Boy*. Two remarkable folk ceremonies also made use of the lamb at Christmas. In the Outer Hebrides groups of carollers once performed a blessing rite by putting the household's youngest child on a lambskin and carrying it three times around the fire as a token of Jesus as the Lamb of God. In Provence on New Year's Eve, a lamb is pulled into the church on a cart by a ram and later offered as a gift by a shepherd.

Lambswool A traditional English Christmas drink made of hot spiced ale with roasted apples floating in it; sometimes cream and eggs are added to thicken the beverage. The white flesh of the apples gives the drink its name. It is also known as "old man's beard." In the 17th century the poet Robert Herrick wrote:

> Now crowne the bowle full
> With gentle lamb's wooll;
> Adde sugar, nutmeg and ginger,
> With store of ale too;
> And thus ye must doe
> To make the wassaile a swinger.

"The Last Month of the Year" Also known as "What Month Was Jesus Born In?", this song was written by Vera Hall (1905-64), an African-American domestic servant and musician, and recorded by folk song collector John Avery Lomax. It was first published in 1953 but was probably written in the 1920s or 1930s.

Latvia After years of anti-religious persecution by the Soviet government, Christians in Latvia can once again freely celebrate Christmas. As December begins, Advent wreaths and calendars appear in homes, the house is cleaned, shopping is undertaken, and Christmas baking gets underway. The Christmas tree has long been a part of Christmas on the Baltic coast, and presents are piled under it on Christmas Eve, a night divided between a big meal, attending church, and opening gifts.

A traditional Christmas meal in Latvia is sure to contain pork – perhaps as a roast or a pig's head or bacon or sausage – with peas, beans, and sauerkraut, followed by gingerbread, cookies, fruit, and pies for dessert, washed down with local beer. After dinner, presents are exchanged; in some homes Father Christmas pays a personal visit and quizzes children on their behaviour. It is customary when receiving a present to pay for the privilege by reciting a poem or singing a little song. In a country where Lutherans, Catholics, and Orthodox mix, there are plenty of church services on Christmas Eve.

Latvia has also retained some of the pagan practices that were once part of the midwinter festival *Ziemassvetki*. One of the most remarkable of these is the rolling of the log. An oak tree is cut down and chopped into sections. One of these logs is then dragged around the house and yard before being burnt that night. For some, the log represents eternal life and its burning calls back the sun and the longer days; for others, the log serves to absorb the ill luck in the vicinity, and its burning enables the household to start the new year afresh. The midwinter festival is also marked by mumming – masked characters, *Kekatnieki*, go door-to-door to receive hospitality in return for a song – and by telling fortunes using hot lead or wax poured into cold water and interpreting the shapes.

Laufabraud Icelandic for "leaf bread," a thin cake fried in oil or mutton fat in which designs are cut. Before Iceland had attained its present prosperity, many inhabitants lived lives of poverty in which items such as flour, sugar, and salt were in short supply, especially during the winter months. In order to make these ingredients go as far as possible at Christmas, it became the custom to roll out dough very thin and to decorate these plain cakes with intricate patterns. Today making *laufabraud* is not a necessity born of hardship but a treasured family activity.

Laughter, Christmas The seasonal equivalent of *risus paschalis*, or "Easter laughter," the notion that even a holy time such as Christmas may rightly be the occasion for merriment, especially by the clergy. From this sprang ceremonies such as the FESTIVAL OF FOOLS and the FESTIVAL OF THE ASS as well as many medieval carols. In 1522 Johannes Pauli, a German monk, published a book of jests "in order that the spiritual children cloistered in monasteries might have something to

Laufabraud *The Icelandic Christmas "leaf bread."*

read to amuse their minds and for relaxation's sake: it is not possible to always abide in a serious mood." The Protestant and Catholic reformations of the 16th century put an end to most of this sort of merry-making.

Law, Christmas and the Governments in the United Kingdom have been legislating Christmas behaviour for centuries, and often not bothering to repeal laws that may have become outdated. The following laws were still in effect in the 1990s:

- The Holy Days and Fasting Days Act of 1551 makes church attendance obligatory on "the Nativitie of our Lorde." The same law demands that everyone walk, not ride, to church and back. The police are empowered to confiscate any vehicle used for Christmas Day church-going, sell it, and distribute the proceeds to the poor.
- The Unlawful Games Act of 1541 forbids all sports on Christmas but archery, though leaping and vaulting have since been added as legitimate exercises.
- A law of 1625 specifies: "There shall be no meetings, asemblings or concourse of people out of their owne parishes for any sports or pastimes whatsoever."
- The Long Parliament of 1646 forbids Christmas dinners of more than three courses; it also bans the "abominable and idolatrous" dishes of mince pie and Christmas pudding.
- A 1667 act says, "Noe servant, artificer, workeman, labourer or other person whatsoever shall do or exercise any worldly labours, business or worke of their ordinary callings" on Christmas.
- An 1831 act forbids any hunting on Christmas.
- An 1847 law allows police to shut off roads around churches on Christmas and reroute vehicles seen to be approaching a church.
- The 1906 Act for the Better Prevention of Corruption limits the giving and receiving of presents by certain officials.

Also in Britain, one can't be served with a summons on Christmas or pressed for a legal time-limit expiring on Christmas, as it doesn't count in the calculation of days for most legal purposes.

Lebkuchen A spicy bar cookie, sometimes, but not always, made with ginger, very popular in the Nuremberg area of Germany, where it is a Christmas treat. Cut in seasonal shapes, it is often hung as a tree ornament.

Lectures, Christmas In the Christmas season of 1826, physicist Michael Faraday (1791-1867), inventor of the electric motor, arranged the first of a series of lectures on science at the Royal Institution. These talks were aimed at a juvenile audience and were meant to bring scientific discoveries to the popular mind. The lectures grew in popularity – 85,000 children are estimated to have attended Faraday's 19 series of lectures – and continue to this day. Since 1966 they have been televised by the BBC, drawing a million viewers every Christmas.

Lefse A Norwegian comfort food, these potato crêpes are often served at Christmas with meatballs or *lutefisk*. They can also be made with cinnamon and sugar and eaten for dessert.

"Legend of the Christmas Rose" A famous 1908 story by Swedish Nobel prize winner Selma Lagerlöf. The Robber Chief, his wife, and their young ones terrorize the neighbourhood. One day the mother and her children invade the grounds of an abbey. She boasts to the monks that every Christmas Eve the forest transforms itself into a flower garden to commemorate the hour of the Lord's birth. The Abbot wishes to see the miracle and makes a bargain with the Archbishop: a rose from this Christmas garden in return for a pardon for the robber family. The miracle occurs, animals emerge peacefully, angels with harps appear, but the lay-brother accompanying the Abbot is frightened and with a curse and a shout ends the miraculous display. The Abbot dies on the spot, but a cutting he had taken from a white rose bush is transplanted to the abbey garden. The next Christmas Eve the rose blossoms and pardon is given to the bandit family. The miracle in the forest never re-occurs, except for those white blooms at Christmas.

The Lemon Drop Kid (1951) Bob Hope plays Sidney Melbourne (the Lemon Drop Kid), a gambler in a Damon Runyan world where everyone has a nickname – Brainy, No Thumbs Charlie, Gloomy Willie. He has to come up with $10,000 to pay off a gangster by Christmas Eve and devises a scheme to defraud little old ladies before he has the predictable change of heart. The movie is memorable mostly for the holiday song "Silver Bells" by Jay Livingston and Ray Evans, which was nominated for an Oscar.

Leopard To the medieval mind the leopard was the offspring of a lion and a panther; consequently, in Christian art, such as depictions of the Adoration of the Magi, it came to represent the union of the humanity and the divinity of Jesus.

"Let It Snow! Let It Snow! Let It Snow!" A 1945 song by Sammy Cahn (1913-92) and Jule Styne (1905-94).

Letters to Santa Claus Of paramount importance to children around the world is how best to convey their Christmas wishes to the gift-bringer.

Letters to Santa Claus *Santa Claus reflects on the naughty and the nice, by Thomas Nast.*

For those who write letters (and millions do every year), the question is how to get them to the right address. Some children advocate putting them in a regular letter-box, and for them post offices around the world have made special arrangements. In the United States, the U.S. Postal Service's Operation Santa Claus takes charge, while for Canadian children Santa Claus or Père Noël can be reached at the North Pole, postal code HOH OHO. The Danes believe that Santa lives in Greenland and forward letters to him there through the Danish Tourist Association. In Norway Santa Claus lives in a town called Drøbak and has his own postal station to handle his mail. Germans use a "Celestial Post Office" in the city of Augsburg to reach the Christ Child, while Austrian kids direct their mail to the village of Christkindl, near Steyr, Upper Austria. Stamp collectors around the world use the Austrian facilities, as they have special postmarks: 70,000,000 letters are processed each year with either the mark of a crèche or the Three Kings, depending on whether the letter is mailed closer to Christmas or Epiphany. In Switzerland a December 6 postmark from the post office in the town of St. Niklaus is a collectible item. Any British child writing to Father Christmas at Christmas receives a reply from "Reindeer Land." Many of these services, plus countless electronic equivalents on the World Wide Web, arrange a reply from Santa Claus.

Other children resort to different means of getting their letters to the gift-bringer. In the United Kingdom children pen notes to Father Christmas, but instead of dropping them in the mailbox, they burn them in the fireplace. The smoke carries their wishes up the chimney and beyond, until they reach Father Christmas. Some Scottish children use a similar method called "crying up the lum." They simply stick their heads up the chimney and shout out their Christmas desires. In Latin America children know that a letter to the Christ Child or the Magi will reach its intended audience if left beside the crèche; angels will take the messages to heaven during the night. In much of Europe, leaving a note in one's shoe beside the chimney or Christmas tree is an accepted way of reaching the gift-bringer, be it the Befana, the Magi, St. Nicholas, or the Christ Child. Swiss children know that the letter they left on the windowsill for the Christkindli has been taken because of the chocolate left in its place.

Letters to Santa Claus have attracted scholarly attention. A recent study of hundreds of letters to Santa Claus from American children revealed that boys and girls request the same amount of gifts, but that girls write longer and more polite letters. (See colour fig. 10.)

Lichstock   The German Christmas pyramid of wooden rods on which small lighted candles are set. Sometimes they are topped by vanes or wooden umbrellas that rotate from the heat of the candles.

The Life and Adventures of Santa Claus (1985)   Based on a story by Frank L. Baum, author of *The Wizard of Oz*, who clearly had been reading Rudyard Kipling's *The Jungle Book*. This is the animated cartoon story of Claus, an abandoned child raised by a fairy and a lion. When he grows up, he dedicates his life to alleviating the suffering in the world and making children happy. Alfred Drake is the voice of the Great Ak, Earle Hyman is nasty King Awgwa, and Lynne Lipton is Queen Zurline. Directed by Jules Bass and Arthur Rankin Jr.

The Life of Brian (1979)   A film made by the Monty Python troupe about the life of Brian Cohen, a Jewish lad of 2,000 years ago, born in the manger next door to the infant Jesus,

and mistaken throughout his life for the Messiah. He is, for example, given gifts by the Three Wise Men, who angrily return for them when they discover their mistake. An attack on fanaticism, both religious and political, it was made in Tunisia by director Terry Jones, who used the sets created for Franco Zeffirelli's 1976 *Jesus of Nazareth*.

Lights, Christmas Tree   It is said, without much historical foundation, that Martin Luther was struck by the beauty of the winter sky as he walked home in the dark one Christmas Eve. Inspired by the sight, and trying to recreate the wonder of the heavens above Bethlehem on the night of the Nativity, he became the first person to place lit candles on the Christmas tree. Though our earliest reference to candles on trees comes from over a century later, there is no doubt that tree lights have been a big part of Christmas for hundreds of years.

Though lit candles on an evergreen tree make for a beautiful sight, they are a troublesome ornament. The first problem one faces is how to attach them safely to the tree. Earliest efforts involved melting wax onto the branches and sticking the candles to that, or piercing both branch and candle with a needle. There were attempts to wire the light to the tree, or to use thin, flexible candles that could be wrapped around the branch. A German invention of the 1700s was the "hoop of fire." A candle-holding wooden ring was slipped over the top of the tree to rest on the branches, but this required a tree with very symmetrical foliage. Candle-holders with long rods that could be screwed into the trunk appeared in the 1800s, as did socket-and-pin devices and a counter-weighted holder, but these were either unduly heavy or wobbly or both. It was not until Frederick Arzt invented a clip-on candle holder in 1878 that the problem was largely solved. (The mess created by dripping wax was overcome by the invention of the oil-cloth tree skirt.)

There were other ways of attaching lights to a tree, principally hanging oil lamps or lanterns. These contained oil with a floating wick and had the advantage of lasting longer than many candles. On the other hand they were heavy, which restricted their use to sturdy branches, and very hot. In 1878 an enterprising Englishman devised a metal Christmas tree with gas jets, but his invention attracted few buyers.

It was not just the safety issue that prompted folk to look for alternatives to the naked flame, though that was certainly an issue with the insurance industry. The fact was that candles and oil lamps were inconvenient, having always to be watched. The invention of the electric Christmas tree light in 1882 showed the way of the future.

Electric Christmas lights emerged from the Edison company labs, though the rights to produce them were soon bought up by General Electric. They were easy to set up and could be left on for hours unattended. For over 20 years after their introduction, however, they were still a plaything for the rich, beyond the reach of ordinary Americans. (They were first used in the White House under President Cleveland in 1895.) The earliest bulbs were round or pear-shaped, but in 1907 Europeans produced figural lights, hand-painted Viennese bulbs in the shape of Santa Claus, clowns, and animals. Americans loved this innovation, but the First World War cut off European supplies and forced buyers to look to Japan, which came to dominate the figural bulb industry until the Second World War.

After the war the craze for bulbs in the shape of Goofy or pine cones had passed, to be replaced by the bubble light. Invented in 1936 by Carl Otis, who found how to make lamps containing methaline chloride, these bulbs were a big post-war hit. Fashions in lights shifted quickly in the post-war world. Bubble lights were out and fluorescent bulbs were in; these were soon replaced by flashing strings of lights, or the rotating colour wheel and the mini-light. As soon as technology provided new styles in lighting, they were snapped up by the consumer.

Lights at Christmas   All over the world Christmas means Christmas lights, whether on a tree, in church, or decorating a house or public building, and whether as a candle, bonfire, or electric bulb. They are symbols of Jesus as the Light of the World, and of the hope, expressed in every midwinter festival, that the long nights will soon end and the sun and springtime will return.

See CANDLES, CANDLEMAS, FAROLITAS, FIREWORKS, LICHSTOCK, ST. LUCIA, LUMINARIA, ORNAMENTS, PAROL, PYRAMID, TREE, and YULE LOG.

Lily   A flower of great meaning in Christian symbology connected with purity and rebirth. According to legend the lily sprang from the tears of Eve as she and Adam were expelled from the Garden. In medieval art it is often associated with Mary and the Annunciation, possibly because its trumpet shape denotes an announcement. (See colour figs. 2, 20.)

Lithuania   Preparing for Christmas in Lithuania means cleaning: the house is cleaned, bed sheets are changed, and family members take a bath and wear new clothes. At one time even trees were wrapped in fresh straw. Though the days of a rigorous fast are over and people no longer have to be content with a handful of peas, many Lithuanians refrain from meat on Christmas Eve and will not sit down to dinner until the first star is visible in the evening sky.

A number of Eastern Christmas customs can be observed at the *Kucios*, or Christmas Eve, dinner: the straw on the table (a sign of fertility and a symbol of Christ's birth in a stable), the round wafers, a place set for dead or absent family members, and 12 meatless dishes. On the traditional menu is fish, potato pancakes, sauerkraut, beet soup, and mushrooms in sour cream, with fruit compote, grain pudding, poppy seed milk, and cookies for dessert. It was customary in some Lithuanian families to leave some food on the table after dinner in case the Holy Family passed by. Another lovely tradition is for each member of the family to place a straw for every gracious word or act that occurred at Christmas into a cradle set under the Christmas tree for the baby Jesus.

The Christmas tree is in fact a recent addition, first becoming popular in the 1920s and 1930s. The custom was to decorate the tree out of sight of the children, usually with real candles and homemade ornaments fashioned from straw, fruit, and candies. After dinner the tree and the gifts are revealed to the children, who then open the presents brought by Kaledu Senelis, Grandfather Christmas. Often the gift-bringer appears in person on Christmas Eve, and before handing over any presents he demands that each recipient earn his or her gift by reciting a poem, playing an instrument, or singing a song. After the excited kids are put to bed, adults go to the midnight church service called the Shepherds' Mass.

Epiphany marks the end of the Christmas season in Lithuania. The tree is stripped of its remaining candies and treats by the children and the decorations are put away for another year.

Lithuanian customs include many different means of DIVINATION, especially for determining one's future spouse. Unmarried females draw a piece of straw from under the Christmas Eve tablecloth: a long, thin stalk betokens a tall, thin husband; a short, thick stalk indicates a short, fat husband. If a married person draws a thin piece it means a bad year economically; a fat piece means a fat wallet. If a married woman pulls a straw that is thicker in the middle, she will have a baby that year. In a kind of Christmas Rorschach test, interpreting first impressions from a crumpled piece of paper or a blob of wax in cold water can also yield glimpses of the future: a form of transportation means travel in the new year; a house or building means a move; a flower points to a wedding; a cradle, a birth; and a coffin or burning candle, death. After supper on Christmas Eve, those with flexible young bodies were urged to go alone into a room, place a mirror against a door and, bending down, look at the mirror through their legs; in it would be revealed their future husband or wife.

Little Christmas   A term with a variety of meanings around the world. In Ireland and Spain it refers to the Feast of Epiphany on January 6. In New Brunswick, too, it is the Epiphany, but people once believed it was also the time by which all Christmas greenery had to be taken down and burnt or fed to the cattle lest bad luck ensue.

In Finland, Little Christmas, or *pikkijoulu*, means the round of pre-Christmas parties held in offices and homes; this custom has recently been adopted by Estonians. In the Scottish Highlands of the 18th century, *Latha na Bliadhn' Ur* ("New Year's Day") was also known as the Day of Little Christmas.

Le Petit Noël in France is the Christ Child gift-bringer, while in Scandinavia St. Lucia's Day was formerly known as Little Yule. In the last week of school before the Christmas vacation, Icelandic children hold a Little Christmas party, lighting candles, eating cookies, and exchanging small gifts or cards. In the Czech Republic it is December 26, St. Stephen's Day.

Little Christmas Eve   December 23 called "Little Christmas Eve" in Norway and Denmark.

"The Little Drummer Boy"   This popular Christmas song was written in 1941 as "Carol of the Drum" by Katherine Kennicott Davis (1892-1980), a composer of usually more serious music, including hymns and operettas. For some reason, however, she attributed it in a school book to "Czech" as if it were a traditional folk song. It was taken and slightly altered by another publisher and became a hit in 1959 under its now widely accepted title. Davis later sued and won authorship.

The Little Drummer Boy (TV) (1968)   The success of the song "The Little Drummer Boy" led to the idea for this animated story, narrated by Greer Garson. Aaron's family has been murdered, and his only friends are his drum, a donkey, a lamb, and a camel. When the camel is sold to three travelling kings, it leads Aaron to a manger and the chance to heal his life. Directed by Jules Bass and Arthur Rankin Jr., who teamed up once again with Greer Garson for a 1976 sequel, *The Little Drummer Boy Book II*.

Little Feast   Christmas to Iranian Christians, for whom Easter is the Great Feast.

"The Little Match Girl"   Written by Denmark's Hans Christian Andersen, this is one of a number of famous 19th-century short stories on the theme of children freezing to death over the Christmas season.

But in the corner, at the cold hour of dawn, sat the poor girl, with rosy cheeks and with a smiling mouth, leaning against the wall – frozen to death on the last evening of the old year. Stiff and stark sat the child there with her matches, of which one bundle had been burnt. "She wanted to warm herself," people said. No one had the slightest suspicion of what beautiful things she had seen; no one even dreamed of the splendor in which, with her grandmother she had entered on the joys of a new year.

"Little Saint Nick"   A 1963 hit for the Beach Boys, written by Brian Wilson and Mike Love. It appeared first as a single – with "The Lord's Prayer" on the B side – and then, in a slightly different form, on the Beach Boys' 1964 *Christmas Album* along with other seasonal gems such as "The Man With All the Toys" and "Santa's Beard."

The Littlest Angel   This very sad little animated 1969 movie is about a young shepherd who dies, goes to heaven, but is lonely and homesick. He is allowed to return to Earth for a short while to retrieve his treasures. The cast is great, with E.G. Marshall as God, Cab Calloway directing the celestial musicians, and Johnny Whitaker (Jodie of *Family Affair*) as the new angel.

Livingston Jr., Henry   American writer of light verse, believed by some to be the true author of "A Visit From St. Nicholas," better known as "The Night Before Christmas." According to his supporters, Livingston wrote the poem about 1804 or 1805, but the original manuscript was lost in a fire in the 1840s.

A woman who was later employed as a governess for Clement Moore's children allegedly heard Livingston recite the poem and asked for a copy of it. It was she who was supposedly the agent of transmission from the poem's true creator to the man who would come to take credit for it. See CLEMENT CLARKE MOORE and "A VISIT FROM ST. NICHOLAS."

"Lo, How a Rose E'er Blooming"   Based on Isaiah 11:1, the poem "Es ist ein' Ros' entsprungen" was published first in 1599 in the *Kölner Gesangbuch* but probably dates from the 15th century. The most popular of English translations was rendered in 1894 by the American musicologist Theodore Baker (1851-1934), who was the editor of *Baker's Biographical Dictionary of Musicians*. Other translations and alternative verses abound.

The musical setting is by the German composer Michael Praetorius (1571-1621), who based it on a folk tune. See "ES IST EIN' ROS' ENTSPRUNGEN."

Lo, how a Rose e'er blooming
From tender stem hath sprung!
Of Jesse's lineage coming,
As men of old have sung.
It came, a floweret bright,
Amid the cold of winter,
When half-spent was the night.

Isaiah 'twas foretold it,
The Rose I have in mind,
With Mary we behold it,
The Virgin Mother kind,
To show God's love aright,
She bore to men a Saviour
When half-spent was the night.

This Flower, whose fragrance tender
With sweetness fills the air,
Dispels with glorious splendor
The darkness everywhere.
True man, yet very God;
From sin and death He saves us,
And lightens every load.

Lord of Misrule   An official in late-medieval courts, colleges, or aristocratic households whose job it was to provide Christmas entertainment. John Stowe's 16th-century *Survey of London* makes this mention of the Lord of Misrule:

First, in the feast of Christmas, there was in the king's house, wheresoever he was lodged, a lord of misrule, or master of merry disports, and the like had ye in the house of every nobleman of honour or good worship, were he spiritual or temporal. Amongst the which the mayor of London, and either of the sheriffs, had their several lords of misrule, ever contending, without quarrel or offence, who should make the rarest pastimes to delight the beholders. These lords beginning their rule on Alhallow Eve, continued the same till the morrow after the Feast of the Purification, commonly called Candlemas day. In all which space there were fine and subtle disguisings, masks, and mummeries, with playing at cards for counters, nails, and points, in every house, more for pastime than for gain.

The Lord of Misrule had many other names – Christmas King or Prince, ABBOT OF MISRULE or Unreason, Prester John – but everywhere he appears, he seems to have had real power to direct his audience in merry practices or even real misrule and social inversion. His office probably derives from

Lord of Misrule *The master of merriment in the Christmas season.*

the Roman Magister Ludi, who presided during Saturnalia and is connected to the officer in charge of the Feast of Fools. During his term of office, he expended a considerable amount of money arranging the plays, feasts, mumming, masking, and games of the Christmas season, and often ruled over them with a mock court and signs of royal office. Lords of Misrule took their position seriously, as can be seen from the battles on Twelfth Night in 1627 fought between law students of the London Inns of Court and the Mayor and town watch. Riotous behaviour led to the custom being discouraged in many places and then suppressed. The English experience during the Civil War period seems to have left the nation with a distaste for social upheaval, and after the Restoration of the monarchy in 1660 the Lord of Misrule virtually disappeared, to be replaced by the more harmless Bean King or Queen of Epiphany.

"Love Came Down at Christmas"　The words of "Love Came Down at Christmas" are among the many devotional verses written by the pious English poet Christina Rossetti (1830-94).

The most popular musical setting is by Reginald Morris; other tunes have included an Irish folk melody and compositions by Sidney Hann, John Ernest Borland, and Edgar Pettman.

> Love came down at Christmas,
> Love all lovely, love divine;
> Love was born at Christmas,
> Star and angels gave the sign.
>
> Worship we the Godhead,
> Love incarnate, love divine;
> Worship we our Jesus –
> What shall be our sacred sign?
>
> Love shall be our token,
> Love be yours and love be mine;
> Love to God and neighbor,
> Love for prayer and gift and sign.

Lucia, St.　Saint Lucia, or Lucy, was a Christian virgin of Catania, Sicily, who was martyred in the persecutions of the late third century. After various travels, her relics ended up in Venice, where the song "Santa Lucia" is in the repertoire of singing gondoliers to this day. Because her feast day fell on December 13, the date of the winter solstice before calendar reform, her legend became entwined with the midwinter festivals of various parts of Europe. In Sweden the story is told of a terrible famine in the Middle Ages that was relieved when a ship bearing food arrived with a beautiful, radiant woman in white at the helm. In Syracuse, Sicily, they speak of a famine in the midst of which folk went to the church of St. Lucia to pray, whereupon a grain ship sailed into the harbour. In both Italy and Sweden she represents light and the promise of the renewal of spring. Some scholars say that the Swedish version of Lucia is actually a descendant of the Christ Child, who was the Protestant Reformation's replacement for St. Nicholas. The CHRISTKINDL in Germany, where many of Sweden's Christmas customs originated, was often depicted as a white-clad young girl, and it is said that this figure was adopted by Swedes in the west part of the country to personify the celebrations that traditionally began on December 13. By the early 20th century, Lucia was a popular figure all across the country.

In Sweden on December 13, a "Lucy Bride," a girl dressed in white with a red sash and a crown of candles and lingon berries, has ceremonial responsibilities. At home, she brings coffee and cakes to her parents; in schools or public institutions, she

St. Lucia The "Lucy Bride" on a Guernsey Christmas stamp, with her candles, coffee, and straw goat.

leads a parade of similarly clad young women and Star Boys. Across Europe, December 13 is a time of bonfires and torch-lit parades. In the Tyrol, Lucia is a gift-bringer who delivers presents to girls while St. Nicholas attends to the boys.

There is a dark side to the Lucia figure. Because the depths of midwinter are considered a time of great demonic activity, Lucia is sometimes identified with witches or monsters. In parts of Germany she is the Lutzelfrau, a witch who rides the winds and must be bribed with gifts; in some parts of central Europe, Lucy takes the form of a nanny goat rewarding good children and threatening to disembowel the bad. In Iceland she is identified as an ogre. The night before her feast day is therefore held to be a good time for ceremonies to drive away evil spirits with lights, noise, and incense. At midnight, Austrians believed that a special light, the *Luzieschein*, appeared outdoors and would reveal the future to those brave enough to seek it out. In Norway she is quick to punish those who dare to work on her day.

Lucky Stiff (1989)　Almost certainly the best movie ever made about cannibalism in the holiday season. Joe Alaskey plays a lonely man delighted to be asked home by a beautiful woman (Donna Dixon) for Christmas dinner, little suspecting that he is meant to be the main course. Anthony Perkins, of *Psycho* fame, directed.

Luke, Gospel of　One of the two gospels to include details of the Nativity. From Luke we learn of the angel announcing the miraculous conception by Elizabeth of John the Baptist; the annunciation of the angel to the Virgin Mary and her visit to Elizabeth; the Roman decree that sent Mary and Joseph to Bethlehem, where Jesus was born in a stable; the annunciation of the birth to the shepherds; and the presentation of the child in the Temple, where he was hailed by Simeon and Anna.

Little is known for certain about Luke. He is identified with the "beloved physician" mentioned by Paul, who accompanied Luke on his travels. Luke is also reputed to have been an artist, and according to legend created the first images of Mary and Jesus. He is said to have been martyred beside St. Andrew in his old age.

The gospel seems to have been written in excellent Greek, outside of Palestine, for a Gentile audience, and may date to some time in the 70s.

"Lulajze Jezuniu"   A late medieval Polish carol, adapted by Chopin for his Scherzo in B Minor. Translated variously as "Polish Lullaby," "Sleep Little Jesus," or "Rockabye Jesus."

Luminaria   Small bonfires lit in the American Southwest and Mexico at Christmas. There has been a debate in recent years as to whether those sand-filled paper bags with a candle inside can also be called *luminaria*; local experts call them *farolitas*.

Lussebocken   The "Lucia Buck" tamed by St. Nicholas to help him deliver Christmas gifts and the subject of Swedish straw decorations in the shape of goats. *Lussebocken* masqueraders also appeared on St. Lucia's Day.

Lussekatter   "Lucy Cats," saffron buns offered in Sweden on St. Lucia's Day by girls dressed as St. Lucia.

Lutefisk   The piece of cod that passeth all understanding. In Norway *lutefisk* is the quintessential Christmas dish; prepared from cod soaked in lye, it has a pungency that deters many outsiders from appreciating its delights.

A popular Norwegian-American song sung to the tune of "O Tannenbaum" has outlined the attractions of the dish:

> Lutefisk, O Lutefisk, how fragrant your aroma,
> Lutefisk, O Lutefisk, you put me in a coma.
> You smell so strong, you look like glue,
> You taste just like an overshoe,
> But lutefisk, come Saturday,
> I tink I eat you anyvay

> Lutefisk, O Lutefisk, I put you in the doorvay.
> I wanted you to ripen up just like they do in Norvay.
> A dog came by and sprinkled you.
> I hit him with my overshoe.
> O lutefisk, now I suppose
> I'll eat you while I hold my nose.

> Lutefisk, O Lutefisk, how well I do remember.
> On Christmas Eve how we'd receive our big treat of
>   December.
> It wasn't turkey or fried ham.
> It wasn't even pickled Spam.
> My mother knew there was no risk
> In serving buttered lutefisk.

> Lutefisk, O Lutefisk, now everyone discovers
> That lutefisk and lefse [a flat bread] make Norvegians
>   better lovers.
> Now all the world can have a ball.
> You're better than that Geritol.
> O lutefisk, with brennevin [a Norwegian brandy]
> You make me feel like Errol Flynn.

> Lutefisk, O Lutefisk, you have a special flavor.
> Lutefisk, O Lutefisk, all good Norvegians savor.

> That slimy slab we know so well
> Identified by ghastly smell.
> Lutefisk, O Lutefisk,
> Our loyalty won't waver.

Here is a light-hearted set of instructions for making this delicacy:

1. Get the *lutefisk*.
2. Lay it on a pine board.
3. Flatten with a meat cleaver.
4. Salt and pepper it and pour on butter.
5. Bake on board in oven for 30 minutes.
6. Remove from oven and allow to cool.
7. Throw out the *lutefisk* and eat the board.

Martin Luther *Religious reformer and Christmas carol writer.*

Luther, Martin   (1483-1546) German religious reformer who is credited with a number of Christmas innovations and who altered the course of Christmas history.

Legend says that Martin Luther, inspired by the starry sky on Christmas Eve, was the first to put lights on a Christmas tree. He is also said to have been the first to put a small crèche under the tree. The Christmas carol "Away in a Manger" was attributed to him. The first two of these claims are extremely unlikely, while the third is certainly false. Luther did, however, play an important role in the development of Christmas in other ways.

Unlike other Reformers who broke away from Rome in the 16th century, Luther was by no means willing to shed Christmas as a popish invention. He loved the holiday and continued to celebrate it all his life. He wrote five Christmas carols; the most famous, "FROM HEAVEN ABOVE," was probably written for his own children. Some of his finest sermons were delivered at Christmastime and were devoted to making the Nativity real in the eyes of his listeners. Luther described what Mary lacked at the birth in Palestine in terms of what might have been found in a German home; he described the distance from Nazareth to Bethlehem as being that from Saxony to Franconia. He spoke to his congregation of the predicament of the Holy Family in the stable:

> Think, women, there was no one there to bathe the baby. No warm water, nor even cold. No fire, no light. The mother was herself midwife and the maid. The cold manger was the bed and the bathtub. I am amazed that the little one did not freeze. Who showed the poor girl what to do? Do not make of Mary a stone. It must have gone straight to her heart that she was so abandoned. She was flesh and blood, and must have felt miserable – and Joseph too – that she was left in this way, all alone with no one to help, in a strange land in the middle of winter. Her eyes were moist even though she was happy, and aware that the baby was God's Son and Saviour of the world. She was not stone. For the higher people are in the favour of God, the more tender they are.
>
> There are some of us . . . who think to ourselves, "If I had only been there! How quick I would have been to help the Baby. I would have washed His linen. How happy I would have been to go with the shepherds to see the Lord lying in the manger!" Yes, we would. We say that because we know how great Christ is, but if we had been there at that time, we would have done no better than the people of Bethlehem. . . . Why don't we do it now? We have Christ in our neighbour.

Luther also played a destructive role in his attitudes toward Christmas. He criticized any veneration of the Magi and sneered at their relics in Cologne, which he had seen and declared fake. He was an opponent of the cult of saints at a time when Christmas was rife with saints and their holy days. As late as 1531 he mentioned St. Nicholas as the gift-bringer and the one to whom German children looked when putting out their stockings, but in the long run his attack on saints led to the replacement of Nicholas by the Christ Child and, later, the Weihnachtsmann as the nation's supplier of Christmas presents.

Lutzelfrau　A German version of St. Lucia, where she is cast as a witch. This appears to be a case of a saintly figure of folklore splitting into separate personalities, one good and the other evil. A similar Christmas transmogrification occurs with Saint Nicholas, who in the 16th and 17th centuries seems to have produced shadow images of himself, such as Belsnickel, Ru-Klaus, and Knecht Ruprecht.

Luxembourg　Christmas markets and the arrival of St. Nicholas herald the Advent season in the small Western European duchy of Luxembourg. Outdoor markets sell Christmas goods such as decorations, crèche figures, candles, wreaths, and trees, and local delicacies such as sausages, pancakes, cookies, and mulled wine to keep shoppers warm. Choirs, bands, strolling musicians and carollers add to the Christmas feeling. (See colour fig. 11.)

In Luxembourg St. Nicholas is referred to as the "Kleeschen." In a custom unique to this country, he drops in a week before his December 6 feast day to check up on children's behaviour and leave little treats in their shoes. In early December he and his grim companion, Hoùseker, the local equivalent of Holland's Black Peter or France's Père Fouettard, appear in public in stores and on the streets. The saint acts kindly but black-clad Hoùseker threatens kids with a bundle of switches. On the night of December 5, the Kleeschen secretly visits homes and leaves presents for deserving children. Many families also expect the Christ Child to come on Christmas Eve with yet more presents.

On Christmas Eve families sit down together for a big dinner, which in Luxembourg has traditionally included black pudding, sausage, cabbage, rabbit stew, and potatoes, but might now feature turkey. For dessert there is *stollen*, a German fruit bread, or the French-inspired *Bûche de Noël*, Christmas log. Midnight mass is popular; those who do not attend can watch it televised from the beautiful Benedictine abbey in Clervaux. Presents are placed under the tree, and families choose to open them either before or after the church service.

Christmas and Boxing Day are spent relaxing, visiting, or taking in a concert or charity auction. New Year's Eve is spent at a dance or party or watching a fireworks display. The Christmas season traditionally ends on Epiphany, January 6, when parties mark Three Kings' Day and decorations are taken down.

Mab, Queen A little-known eastern Canadian gift-bringer of the 19th century. In 1807 Lady Hunter wrote from Fredericton, New Brunswick, to an English friend, "Tomorrow is Christmas and the children are saying, 'Oh, Mama, what do you think the fairy will put into our stockings?' Queen Mab is a Dutch Fairy that I was never introduced to in England, or Scotland; but she is a great favourite of the little folks in this and the other province, and if they hang up a stocking on Christmas eve, she always pops something good into it, unless they are very naughty, and then she puts in a birch rod."

Madonna and Child *Madonna* is Italian for "My Lady" and refers to the Virgin Mary. In English, "Madonna" usually refers to Mary's painted image as the mother of the Christ Child – one of the most popular of all topics in Christian art. Some of the most famous representations are Leonardo da Vinci's *Madonna of the Rocks*, Raphael's *The Alba Madonna*, and Tintoretto's *The Madonna of the Stars*. (See colour fig. 12.)

Magi The Gospel of Matthew tells how Magi from the East arrived in Jerusalem during the reign of King Herod seeking a new-born king of the Jews. They were directed to Bethlehem, where they found the infant Jesus and his family. There they worshipped him and presented him with gifts of gold, frankincense, and myrrh. Warned in a dream about Herod's evil intentions, they returned to their country by a different route. Exactly who these men were, where they came from, and what they did after their appearance in the Nativity story has fascinated chroniclers ever since.

Who Were They?
Most historians agree that the term *magi* refers to a caste of Persian priests and astrologers, but after this has been said all else falls into the realm of legend and speculation. Though we are used to thinking of these travellers as three in number, the Bible is actually silent on how many Magi came to see the Holy Child. Some later accounts said two or four and others twelve, but three was the figure eventually settled on by chroniclers, probably because of the number of gifts mentioned.

The notion that the Magi were kings – as, for example, in the carol "We Three Kings" – is a long-standing but incorrect assumption originating in a belief that their coming was prophesied in Psalm 72: "The kings of Tarshish and the isles shall bring gifts; the kings of Sheba and Seba shall offer gifts." The second-century theologian Tertullian remarked that they were regarded as "almost kings." Western art and fable has certainly portrayed them as such – a popular medieval Magi theme is of three crowned figures sleeping in the same bed and being awoken by an angel – but in the East (which already had an emperor in Constantinople) they are never depicted as royalty.

Names were assigned to the Magi, but, again, these differed from account to account. The *Arabic Infancy Gospel*, which considered them royalty, named them Hormizdah, king of Persia, Yazdegard, king of Saba, and Perozadh, king of Sheba.

Magi In this 12th-century French carving, an angel wakes the sleeping Magi and points to the star they must follow to Bethlehem.

Other Middle Eastern chronicles termed them variously: Larvandad, Hormisdas, Gushnasaph, Kagba, or Badadilma. It was the sixth-century *Excerpta Latina Barbari* which gave them the names that have endured: Melchior, Gaspar (or Caspar or Kaspar or Jasper), and Balthasar.

Earliest depictions of them in Christian art (see ADORATION OF THE MAGI) show them looking alike and dressed as Persians, but eventually it became usual to treat the three as representatives of all parts of the Gentile world and make each one identifiable. Some sources assigned Europe, Asia, and Africa as their homelands; others referred to Persia, Arabia, and India. Another tradition saw them as descendants of Shem, Ham, and Japeth, the sons of Noah. From the sixth century onwards, one of the Magi was often depicted as a black man, and after the New World was discovered by Europeans in the late 15th century, Renaissance painters occasionally made one of the Magi into an Amerindian chief. Not only were they viewed as representing different races but as representing different ages as well: youth, maturity, and old age.

But which was which? Many artists and writers, such as Pseudo-Bede, identified Balthasar as the black king, but the influential medieval chronicler John of Hildesheim says Gaspar was "a black Ethiop, whereof is no doubt: for among all other the prophet seith 'before him shall fall down Ethiops, and his enemies shall lick the earth.'" For some, Melchior was the old king and Gaspar the youth, but for others Gaspar was the senior magus. Since there is no one authoritative source, the confusion continues to this day.

The Magi in Legend
Numerous apocryphal scriptures and medieval chroniclers have told stories of the wanderings of the Magi before and after their visit to the infant Jesus, each adding a particular episode or emphasis. Most agree that the Wise Men each saw the star separately and followed it by a different route before coming together outside Jerusalem. Some with a sense of irony have them meeting at Golgotha, where Jesus would later be crucified. According to some accounts, when they had presented their gifts to Mary they were given gifts in return: one of the baby's swaddling cloths, bread, a portrait or (according to the Venetian traveller Marco Polo) a box containing a magic stone. The cloth proved to be indestructible by fire and the stone burst into sacred flames, and so both were worshipped by the Persians who witnessed these miracles.

Though modern poets such as T.S. Eliot and W.B. Yeats have written of the Magi returning to their native lands as pagans, medieval writers were sure that the three eventually became Christians. The most widespread story is of the Magi journeying to India, where they were converted by St. Thomas. After becoming archbishops and leading lives of exemplary piety, they died and were buried together (having first designated the legendary Eastern king Prester John as their successor). In the fourth century their bodies were recovered by St. Helena, mother of the emperor Constantine, and taken first to Constantinople, the capital of the newly Christianized Roman empire, and then to Milan. When that city was conquered and razed by the German emperor Frederick Barbarossa in 1164, he ordered that the relics of the Magi be relocated to Cologne, where they were taken with great solemnity and placed in the mighty Gothic cathedral that is their home today (though in the 13th century Marco Polo says he was told their tombs were in Persia).

The Magi and the Celebration of Christmas
According to one legend, the last time the Magi met together was to celebrate Christmas in the year 54 A.D. – a charming tale but an anachronistic one, as Christians would not mark the Feast of the Nativity until many years later. But it is true that these "star-led wizards" (in the words of John Milton) have been part of Christmas almost from the beginning of the holiday. The Church chose January 6 as the day of Epiphany to commemorate, among other things, the manifestation of Jesus to the Gentiles (in the form of the Magi). In the Byzantine East, the date was marked with feasting, which often included riotous drinking, dancing, and cross-dressing that drew the reproof of clerical officials. In the West, church services began to include a place in the liturgy for dramatic re-enactment of the Magi's journey to Bethlehem. January 6 came to be known as Three Kings' Day, and the customs of the prize-laden cake, the Bean King, and Star Boys, among others, sprang up.

Today the Magi are an indispensable part of Christmas pageantry. No depiction of the Nativity scene is complete without them (unscriptural though that is). They are the gift-bringers in many Hispanic countries, and their arrival in Spain every January 5 is marked by celebration and elaborate processions. King cakes, Twelfth Night cakes, and *gâteaux des roi* are eaten in their honour around the world. In Switzerland bakers' associations sponsor Magi parades. Groups of Star Boys, clad as Wise Men and carrying a representation of the Star of Bethlehem, perambulate every Christmas season to sing carols and collect money. *Amahl and the Night Visitors,* by Gian Carlo Menotti, celebrates their arrival in operatic form, and their initials (K+M+B) are chalked on European homes and barns. (See colour figs. 14, 18.)

Malta A tiny island republic in the south Mediterranean, Malta has a long history as a crossroads between North Africa and Europe. It has been occupied by Carthaginians, Romans, Normans, Spaniards, the Knights of St. John, the French, the Italians, and the British, all of whom have left their mark on the culture. Christmas there is a deeply Catholic affair with influences from all around the world.

The Christmas tree, Christmas lights on buildings, a visit from Father Christmas, and turkey on the table would all be familiar to those who have experienced an English Christmas, but there are unique Maltese touches evident as well. One of those is the emphasis on the crèche, the representation of the original Nativity in Bethlehem, which can be seen in most homes and in many public places. The custom was imported from Italy and has been promoted by the Catholic Church as a way of focussing devotion on the Holy Family rather than on the more secular tree or gift-bringer. To emphasize this sentiment, processions of children carrying an image of the baby Jesus are common in December on Malta. These lantern-lit marches wind through the night streets, the participants singing carols and reciting poems. The midnight mass in Maltese churches features a young boy, dressed as an acolyte, recounting the Christmas story.

Many homes erect both a tree and a crèche. Presents are placed under the tree, while around the crib and the baby Jesus is placed sprouted wheat that has been nurtured in a pan for some weeks. It was once customary for the Christmas dinner to feature a boiled rooster, but that bird has been replaced by the turkey. Traditional foods that have survived include baked macaroni in pastry, chestnut soup, and *qaghaq tal-ghasel,* or honey rings.

Christmas on Malta is a time for concerts, street parties, military and historical displays, and, thanks to the years of

British occupation, pantomime, a tradition that continues to delight families.

The Man in the Santa Claus Suit (TV) (1979) The story of the men behind the fake beard: lonely men, divorced men, men running from the Mob. Bert Convy, Gary Burghoff, and John Byner play characters with different reasons for putting on the costume. Fred Astaire provides continuity and pops up as the owner of a costume shop, a taxi driver, a cop, a chauffeur, a jeweller, a choir director, a floor walker, and Santa Claus. He also sings the title song.

The Man Who Came to Dinner (1941) A wonderful, if somewhat stagey, film of a pompous writer whose broken leg forces him to spend the winter with an unsuspecting family. He meddles in their lives and makes a comedic nuisance of himself. Based on the hit play by George S. Kaufman and Moss Hart, the movie is full of parodies of show-biz figures. The stellar cast includes Betty Davis, Monty Woolley, Jimmy Durante, and Ann Sheridan. Directed by William Keighley.

Manger A box or trough in which food for livestock is placed. Luke's gospel relates how, when Jesus was born in a stable, his mother laid him in a manger; pious legend has it that the animals of the stable warmed him and watched over him. (See ANIMALS AND CHRISTMAS.) Representations of the manger can be seen in the near-universal CRÈCHE, in artwork depicting the Nativity, as well as in the lattice-work crust of the Christmas mince pie and the straw placed under the tablecloth in Eastern European homes. Carols celebrating the scene include "Away in a Manger," "O Holy Night," and "Tomorrow Shall Be My Dancing Day."

The Church of Santa Maria Maggiore in Rome claims to possess pieces of the original Bethlehem crib – five wooden slats of sycamore brought from the Holy Land in the seventh century, which are exposed on the high altar every Christmas Eve. These are believed to have formed part of an X-shaped support for the manger itself, which was probably made of the same limestone that formed the cave used as a stable where Jesus was born. In the 16th century, Frederick the Wise of Saxony, Martin Luther's patron, also had portions of the manger among his vast collection of relics, but the fate of these pieces is unknown.

See CRÈCHE and NATIVITY SCENE.

Manger, Preparing the A now-widespread custom, originating in medieval France, where, during Advent, children add wisps of straw to the crèche, each one representing a good deed or a prayer said that day. This is done so that when the baby Jesus is placed in the manger on Christmas Eve, he will have a soft bed on which to rest.

Manna di San Nicola The tomb of St. Nicholas in Bari, Italy, is beneath the ground, and water trickles into it from the living rock. This liquid is collected with sponges by priests, bottled, and sold or given as *manna di San Nicola* to pilgrims, who regard it as a cure for a number of ailments.

Mari Lwyd In Wales it was once the custom at Christmas for a horse's skull, or a carved replica, to be decorated with ribbons and fixed with a hinged jaw that allowed the mouth to open and snap shut. The skull was placed atop a pole and carried by a man covered in a white sheet. The *Mari Lwyd*, or "Grey Mare," as it was known, was then led from house to house by a team of men. In some areas the company included a Leader,

Mari Lwyd *A horse's skull atop a pole is led around from house to house in an ancient Welsh custom.*

who held the reins of the horse, Punch and Judy (played by a cross-dressed man who carried a broom), and a fiddler.

At each house the men would knock at the door and sing out in Welsh: "Well here we come, / Innocent friends, / To ask leave, to ask leave / To ask leave to sing." The group outside and the people within would then engage in an improvised battle of rhymes and insults. The first to run out of inspiration was deemed the loser; if it was the householder (and traditionally it was) he would admit the *Mari Lwyd* and his crew for a bit of noisy fun. The horse would caper and snap; the attendants might play a fiddle or kiss the girls; and hospitality would be provided until it was time to go along to the next house. The group would withdraw, singing, "Farewell, gentle folk, / We have been made welcome. / God's blessing be upon your house, / And upon all those who dwell there."

Folklorists have tried to trace the custom to a pagan fertility ceremony, a pre-historic animal cult, or a re-enactment of a medieval mystery play about the FLIGHT INTO EGYPT, but without much success. After disappearing from much of Wales, the *Mari Lwyd* is making a comeback as a symbol of Welsh distinctiveness in the midst of an increasingly globalized Christmas.

"Maria durch ein Dornwald ging" A 15th-century German folk carol in which thorns represent the world of sin which is regenerated by the birth of Jesus. This English translation is called "Blest Mary Wanders Through the Thorn."

Maria durch ein' Dornwald ging,
Kyrie eleison! [Lord have mercy!]
Maria durch ein' Dornwald ging,
der hatte in sieb'n Jahr'n kein Laub getrag'n!
Jesus und Maria!

Blest Mary wanders through the thorn,
Kyrie eleison!
Blest Mary wanders through the thorn,
That seven long years no bloom hath borne.
Jesu et Maria!

What clasps she to her breast so close?
Kyrie eleison!
An innocent child doth there repose,
Which to her breast she claspeth close.
Jesu et Maria!

Fair roses bloom on every tree,
Kyrie eleison!
As though the thorn-wood passeth she
Fair roses bloom on every tree.
Jesu et Maria!

What shall this Infant called be?
Kyrie eleison!
The Christ, he shall be called truly,
Which Name he hath borne from eternity,
Jesu et Maria!

This holy Name, who shall proclaim?
Kyrie eleison!
Saint John Baptist shall do the same,
This holy Name he shall proclaim.
Jesu et Maria!

What christening-gifts to him are given?
Kyrie eleison!
All things that be, the earth, the heaven,
As christening-gifts to him are given.
Jesu et Maria!

Who hath the world from sin set free?
Kyrie eleison!
This Child alone, and only he,
He hath the world from sin set free.
Jesu et Maria!

Marks, Johnny (1909-85) American composer of popular music whose Christmas tunes included a number of hits: "Rudolph, the Red-Nosed Reindeer" (1949), "When Santa Claus Gets Your Letter" (1950), "I Heard the Bells on Christmas Day" (1956), "A Merry, Merry Christmas to You" (1958), "Rockin' Around the Christmas Tree" (1960), "Silver and Gold" (1964), "A Caroling We Will Go" (1966), and "A Holly Jolly Christmas" (1966).

In 1973 the International Society of Santa Claus gave Marks and Irving Berlin the Spirit of Christmas award.

Marriage at Cana January 6, Epiphany, marks three "manifestations" of Jesus: the Adoration of the Magi, which notes his manifestation to the Gentiles; his baptism at the River Jordan; and the turning of water into wine at the marriage at Cana, his first miracle. Its significance as a symbol of the sacrament and of Mary's role as intercessor made it a popular theme in Christian art.

Le Martien de Noël (1971) *The Christmas Martian*, an easily forgettable children's Christmas movie from Quebec about a Martian who lands in the backwoods, gets lost, arouses the ire of adults, and is befriended by kids who help him escape. Directed by Bernard Gosselin and written by Roch Carrier, who became a famous writer despite this.

Martin's Day, Saint In Germany, Christmas for some begins with Martinmas on November 11, Saint Martin's Day, celebrated by Catholics and Protestants alike (Martin Luther was born on November 10, St. Martin's Eve). Children receive small gifts, eat goodies, and walk in colourful processions with homemade lanterns, some of which are hollowed-out turnips, while other, more elaborate ones show scenes of the saint's life. Kids and processing musicians sing St. Martin's songs. Some towns hold re-enactments of the story of Martin and the Beggar, which teaches kindness to the poor. Children are given currant buns in the shape of people, plants, or animals on St. Martin's Day. Bonfires are big items on Martinmas, with giant ones fuelled by wood scraps, boxes, and so on collected by kids for weeks ahead.

In Protestant areas, they sing songs to honour Luther; in Bohemia and Bavaria, it is a day dedicated to shepherds. The popular supper is the Martinmas goose.

Mary, the Blessed Virgin A young woman of Nazareth late in the first century B.C., Mary was informed by an angel that she had been chosen by God to bear Jesus, despite her virgin condition and her marriage to Joseph. Well-advanced in her pregnancy, she and her husband travelled to Bethlehem in answer to a Roman bureaucratic summons, and there she gave birth, in straitened circumstances, to a son and witnessed the Adoration of her child by the shepherds and the Magi. She is later depicted by the gospels presenting the child in the Temple and fleeing with her family to Egypt. Non-canonical accounts such as the PROTOEVANGELIUM OF JAMES, the GOSPEL OF PSEUDO-MATTHEW, and the *Golden Legend* give much more detail about her own birth and childhood as well as events of her later life and death.

Depictions of Mary in the early Church were rare, and it was not until the fifth century and the Council of Ephesus' designation of Mary as "Theotokos," or "God-Bearer," that her life really became a popular object of graphic art and stories. For more of her role in the story of the first Christmas, see ANNUNCIATION, ADORATION OF THE CHILD, ADORATION OF THE MAGI, ADORATION OF THE SHEPHERDS, ANIMALS AND CHRISTMAS, CANDLEMAS, FLIGHT INTO EGYPT, and MADONNA.

Mary is honoured by a number of festivals, including the Purification or Candlemas (February 2), the Annunciation (March 25), the Visitation (July 2), and the Assumption and the Immaculate Conception (December 8).

"Mary Had a Baby" An Afro-American carol also known as the Saint Helena Island Spiritual. Many other verses were added to this song, such as "Stars keep a-shinin'," "Movin' through the elements," and "Jesus went to Egypt."

Mary had a baby, oh, Lord,
Mary had a baby, oh my Lord,
Mary had a baby, oh Lord,
People keep a-comin' an' the train done gone.

What did she name him? oh, Lord,
What did she name him? oh my Lord,
What did she name him? oh Lord,
People keep a-comin' an' the train done gone.

She named him Jesus, oh, Lord,
She named him Jesus, oh my Lord,
She named him Jesus, oh Lord,
People keep a-comin' an' the train done gone.

Now where was he born? oh, Lord,
Where was he born? oh my Lord,
Where was he born? oh Lord,
People keep a-comin' an' the train done gone.

Born in a stable, oh, Lord,
Born in a stable, oh my Lord,

Masking *English King Charles II is entertained at Christmas by courtiers in masks and animal costumes in this scene from the* Illustrated London News.

Born in a stable, oh Lord,
People keep a-comin' an' the train done gone.

And where did she lay him? oh, Lord,
Where did she lay him? oh my Lord,
Where did she lay him? oh Lord,
People keep a-comin' an' the train done gone.

She laid him in a manger, oh, Lord,
Laid him in a manger, oh my Lord,
Laid him in a manger, oh Lord,
People keep a-comin' an' the train done gone.

Mary had a baby, oh, Lord,
Mary had a baby, oh my Lord,
Mary had a baby, oh Lord,
People keep a-comin' an' the train done gone.

Marzipan A mixture of ground almonds, egg whites, and sugar that has long been associated with Christmas. Though inhabitants of Lübeck (where the best European marzipan is still made) claim to have invented the treat, its true origins lie in the Middle East; it probably reached Europe through Moorish Spain by the 1300s.

Marzipan can be used in baking as an icing or as a filling for cakes, cookies, and breads such as *stollen*, German Christmas bread. It can also be coloured and fashioned into a myriad of shapes to resemble fruits, animals, vegetables, or flowers, which can be eaten or used as seasonal ornaments. Chocolate-covered marzipan candies are a Christmas delight in many countries.

There is some debate over the origins of the name. There are those who favour *Marci panis*, or "St. Martin's bread," as

the root word, while others point to the Arabic *mawtaban*, which later became the name of a Venetian coin and then the name for a box holding the coins and then the name of a box holding confections and then the confections in the box. In England marzipan is sometimes referred to as "marchpane."

Masking The custom of wearing disguises during Christmas revelries seems to have become common in royal circles in the 1300s. A notable tragedy occurred at the French court in 1393, when several costumed revellers caught fire when they came too close to flaming torches; they had covered themselves with highly flammable pitch and fur in order to look like forest savages. A number of young nobles were burnt to death, and King Charles barely escaped with his life.

In England, Edward Hall's *Chronicle* noted that in 1512 Henry VIII

kept his Christmasse at Greenewich, where was such abundance of viands served to all comers of anie honest behaviour, as hath beene few times seene. And against New Yeeres night was made in the hall a castell, gates, towers, and dungeon, garnished with artillerie and weapon, after the most warlike fashion: and on the front of the castell was written *Le fortresse dangereux*, and, within the castell were six ladies cloathed in russet satin, laid all over with leaves of gold, and everie one knit with laces of blew silke and gold. On their heads, coifs and caps all of gold. After this castell had beene carried about the hall, and the queene had beheld it, in came the king with five other, apparelled in coats, the one halfe of russet sattin, the other halfe of rich cloth

Masking Maskers, by Walter Crane, gambol at Christmas.

of gold; on their heads caps of russet sattin embrodered with works of fine gold bullion.

These six assaulted the castell. The ladies seeing them so lustie and courageous, were content to solace with them, and upon further communication to yeeld the castell, and so they came downe and dansed a long space. And after, the ladies led the knights into the castell, and then the castell suddenlie vanished out of their sights. On the daie of the Epiphanie at night, the king, with eleven other, were disguised, after the manner of Italie; called a maske, a thing not seene before, in England; they were apparelled in garments long and broad, wrought all with gold, with visors and caps of gold. And, after the banket done, these maskers came in, with six gentlemen disguised in silke, bearing staffe torches, and desired the ladies to danse: some were content, and some refused. And, after they had dansed, and communed togither, as the fashion of the maske is, they tooke their leave and departed, and so did the queene and all the ladies.

The potential for disorder when crowds of masked men came together led many areas to ban the custom. Henry VIII, himself a "lustie and courageouse" masker, passed a law against the "wearing of visors" because a "Company together naming themselves Mummers have come into dwelling places of divers men of honour and substantial persons; and so departed unknown." The custom, of course, survived and can be seen today in the mummers of Philadelphia, England, and Newfoundland, and in many masked Christmas processions in Europe and Latin America. In Greece, masked processions during the Twelve Days of Christmas seem linked to earlier fertility customs.

Mass   The most sacred of the celebrations of the Nativity of Jesus are the masses said at midnight on Christmas Eve and later on Christmas Day. In Rome, the custom of the triple mass developed in the fifth century, when popes set up a crèche in the Church of Santa Maria Maggiore and celebrated mass there at midnight, the supposed time of the birth of the Christ Child, with masses later in the morning at Sant' Anastasia's and St. Peter's. (These churches have varied over

time.) The first mass, the *missa nocte*, or "night mass," was held by St. Thomas Aquinas to signify the birth of the Word of God in the Father; the second, the *missa in aurora*, "dawn mass," to signify the birth of God in the flesh; and the third, the *missa in die*, "daytime mass," the spiritual birth in the hearts of the faithful. Others have claimed that the first mass represented humanity's dark condition before the law of Moses; the dawn mass, the time of the growing light of the Law and the prophets; and the daytime mass, the Christian era of light and grace.

Around the world the masses have different names and times. In Hispanic countries, the early mass is called the *Misa de Gallo*, the "Rooster Mass"; in Eastern Europe it is the "Shepherds' Mass"; in Puerto Rico and the Philippines, the early morning mass and carol service is called the *Misa de Aguinaldo*, the "Carol Mass."

Midnight masses from some of the most famous churches – St. Peter's in Rome, the Church of the Nativity in Bethlehem, or Notre Dame Cathedral in Montreal – are now televised, allowing vicarious participation for the faithful.

Massacre of the Innocents   "Then Herod, when he saw that he was mocked of the wise men, was exceeding wroth, and sent forth, and slew all the children that were in Bethlehem, and in all the coasts thereof, from two years old and under, according to the time which he had diligently enquired of the wise men. Then was fulfilled that which was spoken by Jeremy the prophet saying: In Rama was there a voice heard, lamentation and weeping, and great mourning, Rachel weeping for her children, and would not be comforted, because they are not." The gospel of Matthew, 2:16-18, describes the reaction of King HEROD to the flight of the Magi and the possibility of a rival king born in Bethlehem. He then ordered a massacre of all the male children under two so he could be sure of slaying his rival. December 28 has been designated by the Church as the Feast of the Holy Innocents to commemorate the death of these, the first martyrs of the Christian era. Though the medieval Church believed that as many as 144,000 children were slain, modern estimates, based on the projected size of Bethlehem at the time of Herod, place the number at less than a dozen.

The incident has long been a topic in Christian art; central to this iconography were images of mothers bewailing their dead children, Herod seated on a throne, soldiers with raised swords, and, occasionally, Elizabeth escaping with the young John the Baptist. A striking, but in many ways atypical, painting of the atrocity is Pieter Brueghel's 1566 *Massacre of the Innocents*, which he sets in a snowy village in the Netherlands overrun by Spanish troops (see colour fig. 13). Medieval mystery drama, such as the PLAY OF HEROD, took the Massacre as its theme. Carols mentioning it include the haunting "Coventry Carol."

The day is marked by many ceremonies and folk beliefs, many concerning children. See INNOCENTS, FEAST OF THE HOLY. For English customs see CHILDERMAS.

Mather, Cotton   American Puritan clergyman (1663-1728) who in 1712 inveighed against Christmas: "Can you in your Conscience think, that our Holy Saviour is honored, by Mad Mirth, by long Eating, by hard Drinking, by lewd Gaming, by rude Reveling: by a Mass fit for none but a Saturn or a Bacchus or the Night of a Mahometan Ramadam? You cannot possibly think so! At the Birth of our Saviour, we read, A Multitude of the Heavenly Host was heard Praising of God. But shall it be said, that at the birth of our Saviour for which we owe as high Praises to God as they can do, we take the

Cotton Mather *Puritan preacher and opponent of Christmas.*

Time to Please the Hellish Legions and to do Actions that have much more of Hell than of Heaven in them?"

Matthew, Gospel of   One of two gospels to include references to the Nativity (1:18-2:23). To Matthew we owe the accounts of Mary's virgin conception, the Adoration of the Magi, the Flight into Egypt, and the Massacre of the Innocents. Said to be written by one of the original disciples of Jesus, the gospel is believed by some New Testament scholars to be the oldest, dating from c. 60 A.D. Those who claim that the Book of Mark is the original gospel would date Matthew somewhat later, perhaps 75-85 A.D. (See LUKE, GOSPEL OF).

Meet John Doe (1941)   An unscrupulous reporter (Barbara Stanwyck) out to save her job fakes a series of letters from "John Doe," supposedly an ordinary citizen so fed up with corruption and cynicism that he vows to commit suicide on Christmas Eve. Her newspaper hires a homeless man (Gary Cooper) to pretend to be John Doe, who soon becomes a national hero and an unsuspecting pawn in a sinister politician's plans. Directed by Frank Capra, who would again combine social activism with a warm message in *It's a Wonderful Life*.

Meet Me in St. Louis (1944)   Judy Garland and Margaret O'Brian play a pair of enchanting sisters who live in St. Louis in 1904, when the city is preparing to stage the World's Fair. Judy sings "The Trolley Song," "The Boy Next Door," and, to cheer her sister up, "Have Yourself a Merry Little Christmas." Directed by Vincente Minnelli (whom Garland would marry) with music by Ralph Blane and Hugh Martin.

Melchior   The name traditionally given to one of the three Magi who visited the baby Jesus. Though accounts vary, he is usually depicted as the oldest of the Wise Men and the one

who brings the gift of gold. A South American chronicle of 1609 claims that one of Christ's original disciples, St. Bartholomew, had evangelized the Andes and that the magus Melchior was an Inca. (See colour fig. 14.)

"Mele Kalikimaka"   "Merry Christmas" in the Hawaiian language, "Mele Kalikimaka" was written by R. Alex Anderson and recorded by Bing Crosby and the Andrews Sisters in 1950.

Merry Christmas, George Bailey (TV) (1997)   In a postmodern twist, American public TV (PBS) staged a television production in 1997 of a live radio play based on a movie based on a short story that was published as a Christmas card. *Merry Christmas, George Bailey*, starring Bill Pullman, Penelope Ann Miller, Nathan Lane, Sally Field, and Martin Landau, was a reading of a 1947 Lux Radio script of the Frank Capra film *It's a Wonderful Life*. (It was customary in the 1940s to stage radio plays as a means of promoting current movies.) Republic Entertainment, which assumed the copyright of the film in 1993, allowed the television production to go ahead as a benefit for a pediatric AIDS foundation.

Matthew Diamond directed, and the producer of the show was Jimmy Hawkins, who as a child had played Tommy, one of the Bailey kids, in the original *It's a Wonderful Life*.

Merry Christmas in Different Languages
Afrikaans – *Geséende Kersfees*
Albanian – *Gèzur Krishlindyet*
Amharic – *Melkame Yeledet Beale*
Apache – *Gozhqq Késhmish*
Arabic – *Idah Saidan Wa Sanah Jadidah*
Argentine – *Felices Pasquas*

Melchior *A Guernsey postage stamp commemorating Melchoir, the oldest of the Wise Men and the one who brought gold to the baby Jesus.*

Armenian – *Shenorhavor Dzenount*
Azeri – *Tezze Iliniz Yahsi Olsun*
Bamoun – *Poket Kristmet*
Bengali – *Shuvo Boro Din*
Basque – *Zorionak eta Urte Berri On*
Belgian – *Vrolijke Kerstmis*
Bohemian – *Vesele Vanoce*
Brazilian – *Boas Festas; Feliz Natal*
Breton – *Nedeleg laouen*
Bulgarian – *Tchestita Koleda*
Chinese – (Cantonese) *Gun Tso Sun Tan'Gung Haw Sun;* (Mandarin) *Kong He Xin Xi*
Cornish – *Nadelik looan na looan blethen noweth*
Cree – *Mitho Makosi Kesikansi*
Croatian – *Srecan Bozic*
Czech – *Veselé Vánoce*
Danish – *Glædelig Jul*
Dutch – *Vrolijk Kerstfeest*
English – *Merry Christmas*
Esperanto – *Gajan Kristnaskon*
Eritrean – *Rehus-Beal-Ledeats*
Estonian – *Häid jõule*
Farsi – *Cristmas-e-shoma mobarak bashad*
Filipino – *Maligayang Pasko*
Finnish – *Hyvää joulua*
French – *Joyeux Noèl*
Frisian – *Goede Krystdagen*
Gaelic – *Nollaig Chridheil*
Georgian – *Gilotsavt Krist'es Shobas*
German – *Froehliche Weihnachten*
Greenland – *Juullimi pilluartsi*
Greek – *Kala Christouyenna*
Guarani – *V'ya pave mita tupara-pe*
Hausa – *Barka da Kirsìmatì*
Hawaiian – *Mele Kalikimaka*
Hindi – *Shub Naya Baras*
Hungarian – *Kellemes Karácsonyi ünnepeket*
Icelandic – *Gledileg Jól*
Indonesian – *Selamat Hari Natal*
Irish – *Nollaig Shona Dhuit*
Italian – *Buon Natale*
Japanese – *Kurisumasu Omedeto*
Korean – *Sung Tan Chuk Ha*
Lakota – *Wanikiya tonpi wowiyuskin*
Latin – *Felice Festa Navititas*
Latvian – *Prieci'gus Ziemsve'tkus*
Lithuanian – *Linksmu Kalédu*
Luxembourg – *Schéi Chrèschtdeeg*
Manx – *Nollick ghennal*
Malta – *Il-Milied It-Tajjeb*
Maori – *Meri Kirihimete*
Marathi – *Shub Naya Varsh*
Mayan – *Utzul mank'inal*
Navajo – *Yá'át'ééh Keshmish*
Norwegian – *God Jul*
Oromiffa – *Bagga Ayana Dhalehu Gofetatini Esenee gae*
Polish – *Wesolych Swiat*
Portuguese – *Boas Festas*
Rapa-Nui – *Mata-Ki-Te-Rangi*
Quechua – *Sumaj kausay kachun Navidad ch'sisipi*
Romanian – *Sarbatori vesele*
Romansh – *Bellas Festas*
Russian – *Hristos Razdajetsja*
Sami – *Buorre Juovllaid*
Samoan – *Ia manuia le Kerisimasi*

Serbian – *Hristos se rodi*
Singhalese – *Subha nath thalak Vewa*
Slovak – *Veselé Vianoce*
Slovene – *Vesele Bozicne*
Spanish – *Feliz Navidad*
Swedish – *God Jul*
Tahitian – *Ia ora i te Noera*
Tamil – *Nathar Puthu Varuda Valthukkal*
Thai – *Sawadee Pee Mai*
Turkish – *Noeliniz Ve Yeni Yiliniz Kutlu Olsun*
Ukrainian – *Srozhdestvom Kristovym*
Urdu – *Naya Saal Mubarak Ho*
Vietnamese – *Chung Mung Giang Sinh*
Welsh – *Nadolig Llawen*
Yoruba – *E ku odun, e ku iye'dun!*

Merry Christmas, Mr. Lawrence (1983)   Rock star David Bowie plays prisoner of war Major Jack "Strafer" Celliers, who is locked in a contest of wills with his Japanese captors in the Second World War. Japanese captain Yonoi (Ryuichi Sakamoto) has no respect for his prisoners, whom he believes have chosen the path of cowardice when they surrendered instead of the honourable death that a soldier should have sought. Haunted by a past episode of betrayal, Celliers refuses ever to back down and finds a tragic way to redeem himself.

The film features great performances by the two principals, as well as by Tom Conti as the one prisoner who can speak Japanese and by Takeshi Kitano as a brutal guard. Based on Laurens van der Post's three-part novel *The Seed and the Sower* (van der Post himself spent years as a POW), this was director Nagisha Oshima's first English-language film. In addition to his starring role, Ryuichi Sakamoto also wrote the haunting soundtrack of the movie, which won him a British Academy Award.

The Messiah   A 1741 oratorio (HWV 56) by Georg Frideric Handel about the birth, death, and resurrection of Jesus. Though only a part of it relates to the Nativity, and originally meant as an Easter piece, it is now most frequently performed during the Christmas season.

The Messiah *G.F. Handel, composer of* The Messiah.

The music was written by Handel, working without a commission, in a mere 24 days. The composer claimed that he was literally inspired: "I did think I did see all Heaven before me, and the great God Himself." His librettist, Charles Jennens, was less impressed, saying that Handel's treatment of his text was "not near so good as he might and ought to have done.... There are some passages far unworthy of Handel, but much more unworthy of the Messiah."

The first performance of *Messiah* was in Dublin, where it was meant to raise money for the benefit of "the Prisoners in several Gaols, and for the support of Mercer's Hospital in Stephen Street, and of the Charitable Infirmary on the Inn's Quay." The oratorio was extremely well-received by the audience. The contralto solo by the scandalous Susanna Cibber prompted the chancellor of St. Patrick's Cathedral to rise and shout, "Woman, for this all thy sins be forgiven thee." It met with less favour in London, but has come to be recognized around the world as the quintessential classical Christmas composition. Following an example set by King George II, the audience customarily rises during the "Hallelujah" chorus. It is also common for audiences to bring their own scores and sing along with the choir.

Mexico Christmas has been celebrated in Mexico since the 1520s, and few nations mark the season with as much spectacle, piety, and enthusiasm.

Early in December there are hints of the festivities to come. The Feast of the Virgin of Guadeloupe, the patron saint of Mexico, is celebrated on December 12 with great devotion. This fiesta marks the miraculous appearance in 1531 of the Virgin to the native Juan Diego. Christmas markets open up, with their stalls offering seasonal foods, PIÑATAS, and figures and materials for the family *nacimiento*, or crèche. In Mexico these home Nativity scenes can be quite painstaking productions, involving not only a replica of the stable where the baby Jesus was born, but an entire landscape complete with mountains, waterfalls, a village, and the host of angels, shepherds, Wise Men, and livestock that have gathered to adore the Christ Child.

December 16 is the first of nine nights of the POSADAS, a re-enactment of the Holy Family's search for lodgings in Bethlehem that was developed in Mexico in the 16th century by friars who wished to replace the native midwinter celebrations with a Christian alternative. In this custom a procession assembles after dark. Led by a child dressed as an angel and two more children carrying images of Mary and Joseph, they march through the streets, singing songs and playing musical instruments, to a house chosen for the night's ceremony. There they knock and beg admittance for two weary travellers, only to be ritually rebuffed. After an exchange of traditional phrases, the procession is invited inside, where they gather in front of the family Nativity scene and sing carols, and afterwards accept refreshments. On December 24 the *posadas* conclude with a big party for the families who have participated in the processions or played the innkeepers. *Piñatas* are smashed by the children, hospitality flows, and then all may go off to the midnight mass. This custom has spread throughout the American southwest and Central America.

On December 23 in the southern city of Oaxaca, inhabitants and visitors celebrate the famous *Noché del Rábano*, the NIGHT OF THE RADISHES. Giant radishes are carved into elaborate shapes depicting characters in the Nativity story, Aztec gods, or animals; prizes are awarded for the most creative, while dances, firework displays, and a huge Christmas fair take place.

All across Mexico this is a time for traditional dances and ceremonies. One of the oldest of these is *los matachines*, a dance-drama that has its origins in medieval Spain and the wars between the Moors and the Christians. Gorgeously costumed lines of dancers play roles such as the Grandfather, the Grandmother, la Malinche, the Captains, the Monarch, and the Bull, and enact the age-old struggle between good and evil, with good triumphant in the end. The *pastorelas*, or pastoral dramas, were also brought from Spain in the 16th century as part of that European-wide tradition of Advent drama featuring shepherds. The story is of the shepherds of Bethlehem, who have been informed by the angels of the birth of Jesus, and their attempts to find him despite the machinations of the Devil. A mixture of humour and piety, Spanish and native American influences, stereotyped scripts and improvisation, these dramas have proved immensely popular with the people.

Noche Bueno, Christmas Eve, sees the climax of the *posadas*, *pastorelas*, and parades known as *calendas*. It is the night to put the figure of the baby Jesus in the *nacimiento*, to attend the *Misa de Gallo*, the midnight mass, and return home for a feast. Turkey – which was domesticated by the Aztecs – chicken, or ham is often eaten, along with tamales, rice, and corn pudding. Fruit punches, sparkling cider, and eggnog are common beverages, while *buñuelos*, a deep-fried pastry, cakes, cookies, and fruits provide dessert. Fireworks, sparklers, and *piñatas* provide entertainment for the children. Some children believe Christmas is the night their presents will be delivered by El Niño Dios, the Christ Child, but the traditional time for gifts is Epiphany.

December 28 is the Day of the Holy Innocents, *Los Santos Inocentes*, commemorating the massacre of the boy children of Bethlehem by King Herod, who was attempting to murder the newborn Jesus. As in many Hispanic countries, it is a day of pranks and practical jokes akin to April Fool's Day in North America. It is a bad day to lend money or trust too much in another's goodwill.

Epiphany, on January 6, is also *Día de los Reyes*, Three Kings' Day, in Mexico. The night before, Mexican children put out their shoes and a morsel of hay and expect that the Magi, passing by on their way to Bethlehem, will leave them gifts while their horses and camels enjoy the hay. The Mexican equivalent of the King Cake, or *gâteau des rois*, is the *Rosca de Reyes* – a ring-shaped sweet bread decorated with candied fruits, which is served with hot chocolate on the afternoon of January 6. A figure of a baby is baked into the bread, and whoever gets the piece containing it is obliged to host another party at Candlemas.

February 2 is *El Dia de la Candelaria*, Candlemas, or the Feast of Purification. On this day the Christmas season in Mexico comes to an end. The baby-finder gives a final party, with plenty of *tamales*, and the family *nacimiento* is put away for another year.

Mickey's Christmas Carol (1984) Little is sacred to those folks at Disney. Here, they have set Dickens's masterpiece amidst a cast of cartoon mice and ducks. Alan Young is the voice of Scrooge McDuck. Directed by Burny Martinson.

A Midnight Clear (1991) A group of young American soldiers is sent on a fool's mission in the last winter of the Second World War. They encounter a group of Germans with whom they share Christmas and who wish to surrender. The Germans insist, however, on a fake skirmish to satisfy their honour before they are taken captive. Since the movie is an anti-war message, tragedy results. Beautifully directed by Keith Gordon

"Le Miracle du Grand St. Nicolas" St. Nicholas resurrects the murdered boys from their tub of brine.

and filmed by Tom Richmin, *A Midnight Clear* stars Ethan Hawke, Gary Sinise, Curt Lowens, and Kevin Dillon.

Milly Box Maids   A milly box (derived from "milady's box") was a decorated container holding a representation of Mary or the baby Jesus on a bed of moss or dried flowers. English girls in the 16th and 17th centuries carried the box from house to house as they sang Christmas songs. For an offering they would reveal the contents of the box. This derived from the VESSEL MAID custom of carrying about an image of the Holy Family.

Mince Pies   Now a popular Christmas dessert in England, Canada, and other Commonwealth countries, these were once meat pies with fruit added as a preservative, as can be seen in this 17th-century poem by ROBERT HERRICK:

> Drink now the strong beer,
> Cut the white loaf here,
> The while the meat is a-shredding;
> For the rare mince-pie
> And the plums stand by
> To fill the paste that's a-kneading.

The contents symbolized the gifts of the Magi, and at Christmastime the pie was traditionally made in an oblong shape like a crib with an image of the baby Jesus on top. The Puritans of the 1640s, who banned Christmas and all things related, found time to outlaw the mince pie as "idolatry in crust"; in order to avoid the detection of snoopy neighbours, English housewives began to make the pie in the conventional round shape. John Bunyan, author of *Pilgrim's Progress* and a Puritan sympathizer, refused to eat mince pie in his jail cell.

"Le Miracle du Grand St. Nicolas"   The legend of ST. NICHOLAS reviving the three slain children pickled in brine by an innkeeper inspired an ironic story by Anatole France (1844-1924). Nicholas adopts the three resurrected kids who, alas, turn out to be vile creatures, raping his niece, starting a war, and getting St. Nicholas himself excommunicated. The broken saint wanders and chances upon the murderous innkeeper, now a reformed and saintly man. Nicholas remarks to God: "*Votre sagesse est adorable; mais vos voies sont obscures et vos desseins mystérieux*" ("Your wisdom is wonderful, but your ways are dark and your designs mysterious").

Miracle of Morgan's Creek (1944)   It's the Second World War, and local beauty Trudy Kockenlocker just loves soldiers. So much so that she wakes up one morning after a party for the boys in uniform, and hazily remembers having married one. Her predicament gets worse when she discovers she is pregnant. Complications abound until she delivers sextuplets on Christmas Day.

     This film was considered scandalous in its time, but Betty Hutton as Trudy and Eddie Bracken as her stay-at-home boyfriend, Norval, keep this Preston Sturges comedy pretty sweet. Remade in 1958 for Jerry Lewis as *Rock-a-bye Baby*.

Miracle on Main Street (1934)   Maria is a strange heroine for a Christmas movie: a low-rent stripper with a violent thug for a husband. When she and her mate commit a crime on Christmas Eve and flee into a church, Maria discovers an abandoned baby in the Nativity scene and decides to keep it. Having a child turns her thoughts toward goodness, and she finds herself a decent boyfriend only to have her husband return. Steve Sekely directed, with the uni-named Margo as

Miracle on 34th Street *John Payne reassures the skeptical Natalie Wood in this Hollywood Christmas classic.*

Maria, Walter Abel as Jim, the boyfriend, and Lyle Talbot as Dick, the husband.

(Margo's real name was Maria Marguerita Guadalupe Teresa Estela Bolado Castilla y O'Donnell, which may explain why she chose a professional moniker that would fit on a theatre marquee.)

Miracle on 34th Street (1947)   A classic treatment of the necessity for faith and the importance of miracles in the Christmas season. Kris Kringle (Edmund Gwenn) believes he is Santa Claus, and is in fact hired by Macy's to work as a department store Santa. There he encounters a little girl (Natalie Wood), who is too worldly-wise to believe in him but whose desire for a complete home and family overcomes her doubts. Kringle's claim that he is the real Santa Claus are put to the test in a sanity hearing that is delightfully resolved by the American postal service. Also starring Maureen O'Hara, John Payne, and William Frawley, the movie won three Academy Awards, one for Gwenn and two for its writers, including Valentine Davies, who wrote the original story. Meredith Willson adapted the story in 1963 for the Broadway musical *Here's Love*.

Miracle on 34th Street (1994)   The two television remakes (1955 and 1973) of this Christmas favourite were negligible fluff, but the performances of Mara Walker as the girl who comes to believe in miracles and Richard Attenborough as Kriss Kringle make this Les Mayfield film worth watching.

Misa de Gallo   "Rooster" or "Cockcrow" Mass, an early-morning service on Christmas in Hispanic countries. See MASS.

Mistletoe   A parasitic shrub, *Viscum album*, mistletoe has a long history in folklore and legend. The Druids supposedly collected it around midwinter in a solemn rite, and it was deemed to have magical healing powers and be a token of peace, which is perhaps where the Christian use of it at Christmas originated. Like many evergreens, it was used as a church decoration (despite prejudice against it in some parts). At York Minster during the Middle Ages, a branch of mistletoe was laid on the altar during the Twelve Days of Christmas and a public peace proclaimed in the city for as long as it remained there.

The custom of kissing under the mistletoe was long in developing. Some medieval English homes hung an effigy of the Holy Family inside a wooden hoop decorated with winter greenery, under which it was customary to exchange an embrace or kiss. After the Reformation, when the image of the Holy Family disappeared, the kissing bunch or bough, a collection of greenery that often included mistletoe, remained as a Christmas custom. Kissing beneath it, or just a sprig of mistletoe, seems to have been a custom confined to the servant class until the 19th century, when it was more generally adopted. In the *Pickwick Papers*, Charles Dickens describes its use in the early 19th century:

> From the centre of the ceiling of this kitchen, old Wardle had just suspended with his own hands a huge branch of mistletoe, and this same branch of mistletoe instantaneously gave rise to a scene of general and most delightful struggling and confusion; in the midst of which, Mr. Pickwick, with a gallantry that would have done honour to a descendant of Lady Tollimglower herself, took the old lady by the hand, led her beneath the mystic branch, and saluted her in all courtesy and decorum.

Mistletoe *By the 19th century the custom of kissing under the mistletoe had spread from below stairs to the middle class.*

Each kiss necessitated the removal of a berry from the sprig, and when all berries were gone the merriment ceased. The custom was for a long time confined to the English-speaking world, though it has spread farther in recent years. The only similar European tradition is the Austrian New Year's custom in which the Sylvester figure is permitted a kiss under any sort of greenery. (See colour fig. 15.)

Mithra   An ancient Middle Eastern deity, associated with the sun god. His cult was very popular with the Roman military, and his birthday was celebrated on December 25, which by the fourth century A.D. was also linked to the worship of SOL INVICTUS, the Unconquered Sun. Some believe that it was in order to pre-empt the devotion to these solar deities that the Christian observation of the Nativity was assigned to this date.

Mock   In Devon and Cornwall, the YULE LOG is sometimes called the Mock, meaning a stump of wood. A toast is offered to it when it is placed on the fire on Christmas Eve.

Mohr, Josef   (1792-1848) Austrian priest and poet who wrote the words to "SILENT NIGHT." Ordained in 1815, his parish was the Alpine village of Mariapfarr, where he wrote a poem "Stille Nacht! Heilige Nacht!" Transferred to the St. Nicholas church in Oberndorf in 1817, he struck up a friendship with the organist Franz Gruber, whom he asked in December 1818 to set "Stille Nacht" to music. Gruber obliged, and the new work was first performed with guitar accompaniment at the midnight mass on Christmas Eve. Mohr spent the rest of his life as a parish priest in a number of Austrian villages, dying poor but well-loved at Wagrain in the Alps.

Mon Oncle Antoine   A beautifully filmed story of one Christmas Eve in rural Quebec during the 1940s. Young Jacques' uncle Antoine runs the general store, the centre of the social universe in the little mining town. Here, Jacques learns all the stories of people's lives and a thing or two about death as well. Directed by Claude Jutra, the 1971 movie won awards all around the world.

Moore, Clement Clarke   (1779-1863) American scholar and poet, credited by most historians with the authorship of "A Visit From St. Nicholas," better known as "The Night Before Christmas."

A professor of languages at a New York seminary, he is said to have written his famous poem for the enjoyment of his children in 1821. It was published anonymously in the Troy *Sentinel* in 1823, and it was not until 1837 that Moore took public credit for his creation, which by then had become a national sensation and the source of much of what America thought it knew about Santa Claus.

Another school of thought claims the poem was written by HENRY LIVINGSTON, JR.

Moros y Cristianos   "Moors and Christians," a Caribbean dish made of white rice and black beans, often served at Christmas in Spanish America. Also the name of a medieval morality play in which Christian Spaniards contend with Islamic Moors; it is believed to be the basis for the *matachine* Christmas drama in Mexico.

Mother Goody   On Campobello Island, New Brunswick, children set out their stockings on New Year's Eve and expect small gifts from a female personification of the New Year called Mother Goody. This is in addition to Santa Claus's visit at Christmas and is thought to have its origins in Scotland, from where many of the island families migrated.

Movies and Christmas   There have been movies made about Christmas ever since the late 19th century. The very brief 1897 *Santa Claus Filling Stockings* showed the hero coming down a chimney, placing toys in stockings, and going back up again – not much of a plot, but in those early days of the cinema the visual effect was almost everything. By the early 20th century Christmas movies were becoming longer and storylines were discernible. The need for charity and social justice at Christmas were popular themes, a carry-over from Victorian storytelling, where needy orphans and starving widows were succoured by well-meaning members of the middle class.

Given the startling and dramatic elements present in the story, it is perhaps surprising that the Nativity has not been made more often into a movie. It was once a popular topic: three film versions of the birth of Jesus appeared from 1903 to 1909, and an early spectacle, the 1912 *From the Manger to the Cross*, was filmed in the Holy Land itself. Various Hollywood epics, such as *Ben-Hur* (1959) and *King of Kings* (1961), have had Nativity scenes, but only Zeffirelli's 1977 *Jesus of Nazareth* went beyond conventional piety to put a little more life into the events. (It must be said that the Monty Python troupe's *Life of Brian* went *far* beyond conventional piety, but it only showed what was happening in the next stable over from the actual Nativity. There, the newly born Brian Cohen was given gifts by the Magi meant for Jesus, only to have them snatched back when the Wise Men realize their mistake. This 1979 film used the sets left behind in Tunisia by the makers of *Jesus of Nazareth*.)

It might be argued, however, that the Nativity shapes most Christmas filmmaking even though its actual events are usually ignored. It is the miraculous that dominates the original story – visits by angels, a virgin conceiving, Eastern sages led by a star, warnings in dreams, a god taking the shape of a human baby – and it is the possibility of the miraculous that informs the majority of Christmas movies. While society becomes increasingly secular and science ever more intrusive, Christmas remains the only time of the year when miracles are considered possible, if not inevitable. As Bart says to Homer in *The Simpsons' Christmas Special*: "Aw come on, Dad. This could be the miracle that saves the Simpsons' Christmas. If TV has taught me anything, it's that miracles always happen to poor kids at Christmas. It happened to Tiny Tim, it happened to Charlie Brown, it happened to the Smurfs, and it's going to happen to us!" Christmas movies chide those who cling only to reason. In *Miracle on 34th Street*, handsome attorney Fred Gailey tells the woman he loves (played by Maureen O'Hara): "Look, Doris, someday you're going to find that your way of facing this realistic world just doesn't work. And when you do, don't overlook those lovely intangibles. You'll discover those are the only things that are worthwhile."

And what miracles do we expect at Christmas in the movies? A chief one is that a bearded fat man will fly to one's house carrying presents. The fascination with Santa Claus and his Christmas Eve duties has remained a constant element in Yuletide moviemaking. In 1925, still in the silent era, a film by Frank E. Kleinschmidt called *Santa Claus* showed the polar landscape Santa lives in most of the year and explained how he watches the children of the world through a giant telescope; those who are caught doing bad things are stricken off the list of kids who will get presents that year. Santa's workshop and its labour force of elves was always a source of fascination for audiences. In the 1966 *The Christmas That Almost Wasn't*, the shop was run by a mere handful of elves, while in 1959's *Santa Claus*, a very peculiar film from Mexico, the toys are made by children from around the world. Things are much more industrial and high-tech in *Santa Claus: The Movie* (1985) and *Must Be Santa* (1999).

The question of how Santa came to be Santa has been tackled by a number of filmmakers. In *The Santa Clause* (1994) Tim Allen becomes the gift-bringer by putting on the costume of the previous incumbent, who has just perished, while in *Ernest Saves Christmas* (1988), the Santa successor is nominated by his predecessor. In *Santa Claus: The Movie* we are told that Mr. and Mrs. Claus began life as Claus and Anya, a medieval woodcutter and his spouse, who froze to death in a snow storm but were resurrected as immortal gift-bringers. In a novel twist, the Canadian *Must Be Santa* reveals that everyone at the North Pole is immortal except Santa, who must be replaced when it is time to "join the Santa Senate" by crossing over to the "angel side of the Pole."

There is also the miracle in Christmas movies of starting anew and of redeeming a wasted life. In *Miracle on Main St.* (1934) a fallen woman finds an abandoned baby in a church Nativity scene. She keeps the child and puts her wicked past behind her. There is the miracle of reconciliation, when estranged families are reunited and wounds are healed. This was the theme of *The Bishop's Wife* (1947) and its 1996 remake, *The Preacher's Wife*, where good, but ambitious, men have forgotten their families until reminded at Christmas by angelic intervention.

Miraculous interventions at Christmas are at the core of the two best Christmas movies ever made: Frank Capra's 1946 hymn to the importance of the ordinary life well lived, IT'S A WONDERFUL LIFE, and the finest of all versions of Charles Dickens's A CHRISTMAS CAROL, the 1951 version with Alastair Sim as Scrooge. In *It's a Wonderful Life*, George Bailey, played by Jimmy Stewart, is about to commit suicide; he has never achieved any of his life's ambitions, and now his reputation for integrity and his small business are threatened with ruin. Heaven sends him an angel to show him what life in his town would have been like without him, and he realizes that he has made a difference and that there remains much to live for. Capra's vision has been remade a number of times, but it has never been equalled. The same may be said of Brian Desmond-Hurst's *A Christmas Carol*. Ebenezer Scrooge, a cynical capitalist whose solution for the problem of poor people is prison, the workhouse, or a speedy death by starvation, is given a chance to mend his ways by the visit of four ghosts. The Spirits of Christmas fan the tiny spark of humanity left in Scrooge into a warm fire of generosity and repentance. The sight of the penitent old man seeking entrance to the house of the nephew he has spurned, while "Barbara Allen" plays in the background, has had audiences reaching for their hankies for decades.

Christmas in movies also means the importance of home and family, a theme not unrelated to the story of a young family in a strange town searching for a place to stay on a winter's night. In 1940's *Remember the Night*, prosecutor Fred MacMurray takes shoplifter Barbara Stanwyck back to her home for Christmas, where she is met with a cold welcome. He then resolves to take her to his hometown for the holiday, and there she finds a loving family and the acceptance that will help her begin her life anew. The 1948 Italian prisoner-of-war movie *Christmas at Camp 119* is all about homesickness, while the *Home Alone* movies are driven by the unnaturalness of a child without his family at Christmas. Movies also tell us that in the absence of a home of one's own, friendship will prove an adequate substitute. In *Cripples Go Christmas* (1989) and *Mixed Nuts* (1994) we are shown how even those at the margins of society can make a happy Christmas by banding together.

Mr. Magoo's Christmas Carol (1962)   Jim Backus is the voice of near-sighted Mr. Magoo in the days before political correctness made it impolite to have fun with vision disorders. Here Magoo doubles as Ebenezer Scrooge in an animated version of the Dickensian classic. Abe Levitow, who was a long-time Warner Brothers animator in the great days of the studio (he worked, for example, on the deathless "Robin Hood Daffy" and "What's Opera, Doc?"), directed.

Mrs. Claus   As a bishop, Saint Nicholas was, of course, celibate, but his spiritual descendant, Santa Claus, has at various times and places been blessed with a spouse. Katherine Lee Bates, author of "America the Beautiful," spoke of her in the 1889 story "Goody Santa Claus on a Sleigh Ride." In Finland she is known as Mother Christmas; in Austria she is the Nikolofrau and has the reputation of being a bit shrewish. In Switzerland she goes by the name of Lucy, while in the Netherlands she has been known to answer to Molly Grietja.

Mrs. Santa Claus (TV) (1996)   Charles Durning is Santa Claus (again) and his wife (Angela Lansbury) has a plan for him to save time on his Christmas Eve circumnavigations. When he won't listen, she determines to use the magic sleigh to test her

theory and winds up in New York in the year 1910. Here, her feminist proclivities are put to work for women's suffrage and improved labour conditions in toy workshops. She sets things to rights and returns to the present to a relieved and more attentive husband.

All of the above is accomplished to music provided by Broadway composer Jerry Herman (*Mame*) in the form of songs about women's rights, oppressed workers, and Christmas. Directed by Terry Hughes, and also starring Rosalind Harris and Terrence Mann, this television special won an Emmy for hair-styling.

Ms. Scrooge (TV) (1997)   *A Christmas Carol*, by Charles Dickens, is an irresistible lure for directors and actors, no matter how misguided, who wish to put their personal stamp on a classic. In this trans-gendered, trans-racial, cable-television version, Ebenita Scrooge (Cicely Tyson) is an African-American woman visited by the ghost of her dead partner, Maude Marley (Katherine Helmond), who has come to warn her to change her miserly ways. Michael Beach plays her nephew the Reverend Luke Scrooge.

Mule   Among the Christian families of Lebanon and northern Syria, the Mule was once regarded as the Christmas gift-bringer. Legend says that palm trees bowed down on the eve of Epiphany to show the Magi the way to Bethlehem; a mule was tied to one of these trees, and when it sprang back to its original posture the mule was thrown high up into its branches.

Mumming   A Christmas performance in disguise, related to MASKING and GUISING. It can be seen today in different forms in the English Mummers' Play, the Newfoundland house-visit tradition, and the Philadelphia Mummers' Parade.

One sort of mumming in early-modern England involved masked groups going to neighbouring houses for seasonal hospitality. A 17th-century ballad describes the intent of the activity:

> To maske and to mum kind neighbours will come with
>   Wassels of nut-browne Ale,
> To drinke and carouse to all in this house, as merry as
>   buck in the pale;
> Where cake, bread and cheese, is brought for your fees to
>   make you the longer stay;
> The fire to warme will do you no harme, to drive the cold
>   winter away.

Mumming in England also refers to a traditional play at Christmas involving a mock combat between two heroes. It often begins with an introduction by a character called Father Christmas, followed by the appearance of the protagonists, St. George or King George versus the Turk or the Slasher. They swagger and boast before the fighting begins; one falls, dead or wounded, but is revived by a Doctor. Minor characters, such as a Fool, Beelzebub, a poor man, and a sweeper do a spot of entertaining before collecting money from the audience and ending the show with a song. There are hundreds of regional variations on this theme and many folklorists have puzzled over the origin of the custom. It was once thought that the play was the descendant of a medieval morality play or even a pre-Christian fertility ritual, but there is no evidence that any such performance was given before the 18th century. It seems to have developed some time between 1700 and 1750.

The Mummers' Play was taken by settlers to Newfoundland, where it was performed until, in the 19th century, it was found

Mumming *Christmas mumming in the Middle Ages, from the* Illustrated London News.

too predictable and to have lost its charm. Newfoundlanders kept mumming alive, though, by adapting it to a formal parade of costumed figures and a Christmas-season house-visit. Elaborately costumed mummers wound their way through the streets of St. John's at Christmas as early as 1812; occasionally they might stop and perform a mock combat. Part of the spectacle was the presence of Fools and cross-dressing OWNSHOOKS. The Fool was a solitary mummer who chased people until they were caught and ritually tapped. Fools were disguised by masks or thick veils and wore triangular hats made of cardboard and wallpaper or cocked hats with spangles, plumes, and ribbons; sometimes a model ship rode on top of the hat. They wore white shirts and no coats, the shirts being decorated with ribbons. The ownshooks (also known as "owensooks" or "eunchucks") were men wearing veils and women's clothes and speaking in a falsetto. Both they and the Fools struck people using inflated bladders covered with canvas or a switch made from a cow's tail fastened to a stick.

The rowdiness of the occasion and the dangerous licence enjoyed by men wearing masks in public resulted in the legislature banning mumming in 1861. It continued nevertheless in the house-visits by mummers known as jannies. Small groups of disguised folk would appear at neighbours' houses and request permission to enter with cries of "Will ye let the mummers in?" or "Got anything for the jannies, ma'am?" The hoped-for reply was "Mummers is welcome!" Once inside, the jannies would try to keep their identities a secret by disguising their voices and normal behaviour. "Janny-talk" was the term for the distorted or ingressive speech used to conceal their identity. Some would carry a stick to drive away the over-curious, but if identified, custom would allow the janny to be

chased off with his own stick. At some point the visitors would unmask and refreshments would be served.

Modernization in Newfoundland seemed for a time to render the old merry-making ways obsolete; the opening of the island in the 20th century by road and rail meant that strangers in disguise might be admitted with unpredictable results. This was lamented by antiquarians, who said that the custom was psychologically rejuvenating for the hard-working men who took part:

> Phlegmatic and silent fishermen who had not a word to say all the year round, now blossomed into Grand Knights of St. Patrick, St. Michael and St. George, Hector, Alexander, etc., and gave out their heroic speeches in verse as they went in their fantastic costumes from one neighbour's house to another.

The practice has been revived, however, and continues joyfully across the province to this day. A similar tradition on the Canadian mainland is called BELSNICKLING.

In Philadelphia, Pennsylvania, every January 1, a 12-hour parade of over 10,000 marchers reminds people of the long mumming tradition. Marching and strutting in elaborate costumes replete with jewels, sequins, and feathers, dozens of mummers' clubs compete in four divisions – comics, fancies, fancy brigades, and string bands – for prizes and bragging rights. These are descendants of the masked rowdies of the 18th and early 19th centuries who would visit neighbours with the demand

> Here we stand before your door,
> As we stood the year before.

Mumming *Mummers, in this 1861 illustration from the* Illustrated London News, *perform the traditional combat and resurrection play.*

Give us whiskey, give us gin
Open the door and let us in.

The same kind of violence and raucous behaviour that prompted Newfoundland officials to ban mumming led the city of Philadelphia to suppress the custom. It survived in tamer form through the annual parade and competitions that developed in the late 1800s. Clubs grew up to compete for the prizes and foster community togetherness, and today the Philadelphia Mummers' Parade is a grand spectacle.

Mumping   Begging during the Christmas season was in some parts of England termed mumping, a word derived either from gypsy slang or from the mumbled speech of aged beggars. December 21, St. Thomas's Day, was called Mumping Day or Doleing Day. Other terms used for this seasonal begging were "going a-corning" – that is, getting gifts of grain – and, in Staffordshire, "a-gooding." National welfare reforms did away with this Christmas custom as well as other begging traditions of the season.

The Muppet Christmas Carol (1992)   If you can't have Alastair Sim you may as well have Michael Caine. Caine does a fine job as Ebenezer Scrooge, with Kermit the Frog as Bob Cratchit, Fozzie Bear as Fozziwig, and Miss Piggy as Emily Cratchit, with a guest appearance by the Great Gonzo as Charles Dickens. Directed by Brian Henson.

Must Be Santa (TV) (1999)   Rumoured to be the most expensive movie production ever by the Canadian Broadcasting Corporation, this earnest holiday epic directed by Brad Turner sank without a trace on its release. Arnold Pinnock plays a young African-American who, despite a less-than-savoury background and a strained relationship with his child, is chosen to be the next incarnation of Santa Claus; with Dabney Coleman as a crusty North Pole executive and Deanna Mulligan as his angelic assistant.

Myrrh   One of the gifts brought by the Wise Men to the baby Jesus, myrrh is a fragrant gum resin of the genus *commiphora*, found in east Africa and Arabia and used in making perfume, incense, medicines, and unguents. Because of its use in anointing dead bodies, the inclusion of myrrh as one of the gifts of the Magi is seen as a prophecy of Christ's death. Balthasar is the magus most often depicted carrying the container of myrrh.

Nacimiento A term used in Spain and parts of Latin America for the CRÈCHE. In these countries, the family Nativity scene is a more important part of the Christmas season than the evergreen tree.

Naluyuk A character in the Newfoundland tradition of MUMMING, particularly in the Labrador region, where he is seen as a costumed bogey-figure who helps to enforce community values both by intimidation and by handing out presents at Epiphany. The term is derived from the local Inuit language and means "unbeliever" or "pagan."

Naming Christmas The word Christmas is derived from the Anglo-Saxon *Christes Maessan*, an 11th-century term meaning "Christ's Mass." Though there is a similar Dutch word for Christmas, *Kersmis*, most languages have derived their name for the holiday from different roots. The original Latin term was *Festum Nativitatis Domini Nostri Jesu Christi*, the Feast of the Nativity of Our Lord Jesus Christ, which was shortened to *Dies Natali Domini*, the Birthday of the Lord. From this Latin phrase comes the name for Christmas in a number of European languages: *Il Natale* (Italian); *La Navidad* (Spanish); *Natal* (Portuguese); *Nadal* (Provençal); *Nollaig* (Irish); *Nadolig* (Welsh). The French *Noël* may be derived from this source or from *nowel*, meaning "news." In Eastern Europe the name for the season also refers to a birthday: *Karácsony* in Hungarian; *Boze Narodzenie* ("God's Birth") in Polish; and Greek, Russian, and Ukrainian terms for Christmas also refer to the birth of Jesus.

"Holy Night" is the meaning of the German *Weihnacht*, as well as the Czech *Veselé Vánoce* and the Slovak *Veselé Vianoce*. The Lithuanian *Kaledos* means "Day of Prayer." Yule, the ancient northern winter festival, lent its name to Christmas in the Scandinavian lands: *Jul* (Danish, Swedish, and Norwegian); *Jól* (Icelandic); *Joula* (Finnish); and even Estonian, *Jõule*. *Ziemassvetki* is the Latvian winter festival whose name has become synonymous with Christmas there. See also MERRY CHRISTMAS IN DIFFERENT LANGUAGES.

Narcissus In Greek myth Narcissus rejected the love of the nymph Echo and was condemned to fall in love with his own reflection. The flower that takes its name from this myth is usually a symbol of vanity, but in depictions of the ANNUNCIATION TO MARY or the Madonna it represents the triumph of divine love over death and self-love.

Nast, Thomas (1840-1902) German-born American cartoonist whose depictions of Santa Claus helped popularize a standard image of the North American gift-bringer and who added interesting details to Santa's biography. As an illustrator for *Harper's Illustrated Weekly*, Nast would become famous as a political cartoonist, inventing both the Republican elephant and Democratic donkey that are still used to represent the main American political parties. His zeal for reform helped bring down the corrupt rule of Boss Tweed in New York and elect Ulysses S. Grant as President.

But it is his drawings of Santa Claus that have made his reputation endure. Nast combined his memories of Christmas in Germany with an American sensibility to produce the prototype for the developing image of Santa, one that was to abide when rival images had long since been forgotten. For Nast the gift-bringer was kindly, fat, and jolly, clothed (as "A VISIT FROM ST. NICHOLAS" demanded) in furs from head to foot, and with a broad belt about his middle. Though Santa's clothes have changed over the years, the face and personality of all later depictions are derived from Nast. Nast also provided the notion of a North Pole workshop and the earliest depiction of children leaving out a snack for St. Nick. Many other conceptions of Santa were given expression by Nast: the ledger that recorded children's good and bad deeds; Santa's spying on their activities; the working conditions in his polar operation; and the piles of letters from around the globe.

During the American Civil War, Nast illustrated Santa in the Stars and Stripes of the Union cause and showed him bringing Christmas cheer to Federal troops at the front. This helped to spread the celebration of Christmas in the United States and to link it and Santa Claus with the idea of family reunion. It also prompted reaction from the South, where Santa's apparent partisanship had to be explained to the children. (See GENERAL LEE AND SANTA CLAUS.)

National Lampoon's Christmas Vacation (1989) Like all National Lampoon movie parodies, *Christmas Vacation* relies on tasteless humour to move things along, but this story of the hapless Griswold family's reunion has a few more touching moments as well. Directed by Jeremiah S. Chechik and written by John Hughes, it stars Chevy Chase as Clark Griswold and Beverly D'Angelo as his wife, with Randy Quaid, Diane Ladd, E.G. Marshall, and Juliette Lewis as the assorted relatives.

Nation's Christmas Tree A huge California sequoia (*Sequoiadendron giganteum*), some 267 feet high with a circumference of 107 feet, was named the "Nation's Christmas Tree" in 1926. Called The General Grant, this tree (the third-largest in existence) was once thought to be 4,000 years old, but recent estimates have now placed it at about 2,000 years of age, making it as old as Christmas itself.

Every year in December visitors flock to the Kings Canyon National Park and attend a "Trek to the Tree" ceremony while rangers lay a wreath at the foot of the giant sequoia.

Nativity, Church of the A large fortesslike church complex on Manger Square in Bethlehem, centred on the site where Jesus is said to have been born.

As early as the second century, local tradition claimed that the Nativity of Christ took place in a stable-cave, the location of which was sufficiently well-known that the Roman emperor Hadrian established a pagan grove there dedicated to Adonis in order to discourage Christian worship on the site. In the third century, Origen and other visitors were still being directed to the spot. The theologian reported, "In Bethlehem the cave is pointed out where He was born, and the manger in the cave where He was wrapped in swaddling clothes, and the rumor is in those places and among foreigners of the Faith that indeed Jesus was born in this cave."

The first Church of the Nativity was built over the cave by Saint Helena, mother of the emperor Constantine. This church was later damaged in an uprising and was rebuilt in the sixth century at the command of the Byzantine emperor Justinian. When the area was overrun by Persian invaders in 614, legend claims that the Church of the Nativity was spared because of depictions in a mosaic of Magi in Persian dress.

The cross-shaped Church of St. Mary of the Nativity, 170 feet long and 80 feet wide, stands above a small grotto where a silver star marks the spot where Jesus was born; the inscription reads *Hic De Virgine Maria Jesus Christus Natus Est*, "Here Jesus Christ was Born of the Virgin Mary." Nearby is a chapel where the manger stood in which the infant was placed. Surrounding the Church of the Nativity are other chapels and convents of the Catholic, Orthodox, and Armenian churches; these three denominations share the administration of various parts of the complex. Quarrels between the denominations in the 19th century took on dangerous overtones. The Russian government supported the Orthodox claims, while the French government backed the Catholics; these hard feelings were one of the reasons for the outbreak of the Crimean War in the 1850s.

See BETHLEHEM, GROTTO OF THE MILK, and SHEPHERDS' FIELD.

Nativity Scene   All around the world, an essential part of Christmas celebrations is the erection of a replica of the original birth site of Jesus. In miniature form in homes or churches, this is known as a crèche, *presipio, pesebre, nacimiento, portal, jeslicky, belen, szopka,* or *Krippe*. The carving of the figures and the preparation of the backgrounds and landscape have produced wonderful folk art. There are several vast collections of these Nativity scenes in palaces and museums, but the honour for the world's largest must go to a Swiss production, the Diorama Bethlehem in Einsiedeln, which reproduces the topography of Bethlehem and stocks it with hundreds of carved figures, illustrating not just the birth of Jesus, but also the Annunciation to the Shepherds, the Adoration of the Magi, and the Flight into Egypt.

Credit for the first live re-enactment of the Nativity outside of a church is given to St. Francis of Assisi for the scene he staged in Greccio, Italy, in 1223. Since then, the practice has spread around the world in neighbourhood rituals such as the *posada*, the school Christmas pageant, or the professionally staged equivalents of the Easter Passion Play, where huge casts, including animals, are marshalled. In a number of U.S. cities, thanks to churches and community groups, it is possible to experience the Nativity in a drive-through setting. Visitors can walk or ride through acres of scenery populated by camels, Roman centurions, Magi, shepherds, harlots, innkeepers, and the Holy Family. In Edmond, Oklahoma, for example, the Boys Ranch Town home for children annually stages 10 scenes from the life of Christ, with the kids as actors and a taped narration. Visitors need not leave the comfort of their cars to experience the Nativity anew.

Social historians have charted the rise of the school Nativity play from the 1920s, and see it as an indicator of the growing importance of Christmas and its link to the family. Its increasing popularity, they say, is due not to growing religious sentiment but rather to the use of the Christian Holy Family as a means to buttress the institution of the human family and give it spiritual legitimacy. In recent years in North America

John Mason Neale *English carol collector and author of "Good King Wenceslas."*

and Britain, school productions of the Nativity story have been attacked as insensitive to the feelings of non-Christian students; lawsuits and disruptions of the plays have resulted.

Neale, John Mason   (1818-66) English clergyman, antiquarian, and influential translator and popularizer of Christmas carols. Among the carols he is responsible for are "Good King Wenceslas," "O Come, O Come, Emmanuel," "Good Christian Men Rejoice," "Our Master Hath a Garden," and "Of the Father's Love Begotten."

Netherlands   In late November a vessel docks in a Dutch port and a stately bishop comes ashore accompanied by a dark-skinned Moorish servant. Christmas in the Netherlands has begun. The white-bearded Sinterklaas, as the locals call St. Nicholas, mounts a white horse and begins his round of appointments. He will be received by government dignitaries, greet television audiences, visit schools, take part in numerous parades, but most importantly he will meet the children of the Netherlands and quiz them on their behaviour in the past year. His companion ZWARTE PIET, Black Peter, hands out candy and treats but also threatens to stuff bad kids into his bag and take them back to Spain for the year. Those who receive a gift from Sinterklaas are often called upon to recite a poem or sing a little song. On the eve of his saint's day, December 5, Sinterklaas flies over Dutch rooftops on his horse and with Piet's assistance drops presents down chimneys into the shoes of children. His duty done, Sinterklaas then disappears until next year – but Christmas continues.

Advent in the Netherlands is the time to buy a Christmas tree (or rent a live one that can be planted after the holiday is over), put an Advent star in the window, and begin to clean and decorate the house. Among the noisier Advent ceremonies in the Netherlands is the *midwinterhoorn blazen*, in which horns are sounded to announce the beginning of the holy season. In Oldenzaal, trumpeters blow in Advent from the four corners of a medieval tower; elsewhere, horns carved out of young saplings are blown over wells to produce a deep, foghorn tone. This custom is carried out from the beginning of Advent to *Dreikoningen*, or Epiphany.

On Christmas Eve many families observe a second opportunity for gift-giving and children open the presents stacked under the tree. For many a church service is customary, either in the evening or on Christmas morning, as is singing carols or reading the Bible story of the Nativity. The Dutch enjoy wrapping presents in deceptive ways, such as a gift within a gift or a tiny present in a big box, often accompanied by a humorous rhyme.

December 25 and 26 are First and Second Christmas Day, holidays given over to feasting, relaxation, and visiting. The menu for Christmas dinner varies widely, but turkey is always popular. Sweets include puddings, cookies in the shape of an initial, marzipan, chocolates, and *kertstol* or *kerstbrot*, a fruity Christmas bread. December 26 is also a day for dining out or taking in a play or movie.

In a world where Christmas customs are becoming increasingly homogenized, the Dutch struggle to maintain their distinctive approach. The figure of Zwarte Piet is under fire from those who object to the black-face disguise and the perceived racial stereotyping. Sinterklaas is losing ground to the Kerstman, a more secular local Santa Claus with his reindeer and elves, just as December 5 is waning in importance as Christmas Eve becomes the time for gift exchange. Some blame German or American culture for these changes and are fighting back. In certain towns it is illegal to appear in the costume of Santa Claus or the Weihnachtsmann, while other towns post signs with Christmas trees and reindeer inside red circles with a slash across them.

New Year's Day In Rome it was customary to exchange gifts at the Kalends, the first day, of January. These presents were called *strenæ*, after the goddess Strenia, a term that survives in the French word for New Year's gift, *étrenne*. For most of the Middle Ages, New Year's Day was the time for giving gifts, especially to kings, nobles, and judges, but because Christmas is a whole season, not just a day, these were still called "Christmas presents." Even as late as the 18th and early 19th centuries, New Year's was the day of gift-giving in much of England, Canada, and the United States. The highly influential American poem "A VISIT FROM ST. NICHOLAS," better known as "The Night Before Christmas," was often amended to read as if the events took place on New Year's Eve, with Saint Nick exclaiming "A Happy New Year to all!"

This explains the survival in many parts of the easternmost Canadian provinces of different gift-bringers who arrive on New Year's Eve. Known variously as Mother Goody, Mother New Year, Father Time, Aunt Nancy, or the New Year's Baby, they place small presents or left-over Christmas candies in the stockings or shoes of children.

New Year's Day is still a day for the exchange of presents in parts of France, Greece, and Scotland.

New Zealand The first Christmas in New Zealand was celebrated in 1814, when the missionary Samuel Marsden preached on the text "Peace on Earth, Goodwill to All Men."

Many of the British trappings linger: plastic mistletoe and holly as decorations, a red-clad Father Christmas bringing gifts on Christmas Eve, and carols about snow and reindeer. The meal on many a table is still turkey, plum pudding, and mince pie, and many families watch the queen's Christmas broadcast to the Commonwealth. But alongside these salutes to tradition are native touches more suited to the southern hemisphere: beautiful POHUTUKAWA blossoms as decoration, a Christmas Day picnic or barbecue at the beach, and new carols by New Zealand composers. The Australian custom of Carols by Candlelight has spread to its Pacific neighbour, and all across the islands people gather in parks after dark to sing Christmas songs.

The spirit of a modern New Zealand Christmas is reflected in the words of the song "Christmas on the Beach":

We don't want no holly
Or mistletoe.
We don't want no Christmas tree
With artificial snow.
We don't want no snowman
Made of cotton wool.
We're not a bunch of fools

Christmas on the beach.
Christmas on the beach.
Pack your picnic hamper up,
We're gonna have a feast
Underneath the huge
Pohutukawa tree.
Christmas on the beach

We don't want no reindeer.
We don't want no sleigh.
We just want some sunshine
And a good old holiday.
We don't want to suffocate
In our shoes and socks.
We don't want to sit around the box.

Nicaragua The Christmas season in Nicaragua begins on December 7 with *La Purísima*, the national holiday that marks the Immaculate Conception of the Virgin Mary. It's a day of parades, songs, and such exuberance that the celebrations are called *La Noche de Gritería*, THE NIGHT OF THE SCREAMS. Fireworks called Volcanoes, Red Bombs, Roman Candles, Butterflies, and Bottle Rockets light up the sky all night. Another sign of the season is the Christmas goods in the markets (gifts, candles, seasonal food, and material for making or adding to the family *nacimiento*, or crèche). Houses are decorated with poinsettias (called *Flores de Pastor*, "shepherd's flowers," in Nicaragua), colourful paper decorations, and pictures of the Nativity, and the *nacimiento* is set up. Nine days before Christmas a novena, a special series of prayers, is said.

Christmas Eve sees the day-long preparation of a big dinner: making *nacatamal* (a meat and vegetable mixture wrapped in plantain leaves) takes a lot of work. Chicken is also likely on the menu, with rice and beans; fruit, biscuits, squash cooked in honey, *leche de burra* ("burro's milk"), and rum punch follow. After dinner people go to church for midnight mass, and many wait in line after the service to kiss a doll in the church's crèche representing the baby Jesus. At home again they open presents brought by El Niño, the Christ Child, and place his image in the family Nativity scene.

January 6 is Epiphany, or Three Kings' Day. The night before, children put out their shoes with a little grass in them for the Magi's camels, and in the morning they find treats and little presents. It's also a day for godparents to visit their godchildren and to bring them a small gift. That night, the Christmas season ends with yet more fireworks.

Nicholas, Saint Fourth-century bishop of Myra and a vastly popular medieval saint whose reputation for giving linked him forever with Christmas.

St. Nicholas *The saintly giftbringer portrayed in a 14th-century Russian icon.*

Though no evidence of his life and career exists, he is alleged to have been born in Patara in what is now Turkey and to have shown signs of his holiness very early, standing up to praise God the moment he was born and refusing his mother's milk on fast days. He is said to have been imprisoned under the persecuting emperor Diocletian, released under Constantine, and, as bishop of Myra in Asia Minor, to have attended the 325 Council of Nicaea, where he was alleged to have smacked the heretic Arius.

Many legends grew up around his celebrated generosity and miraculous powers. The two most enduring stories concern a trio of daughters and three murdered boys. The saint, having heard that a poor man's three daughters might have to become prostitutes, secretly provided three bags of gold so that each one might have a dowry and find a husband. (The three bags of gold are three gold balls in some legends, and, as Nicholas was patron saint of bankers and money-lenders, those three balls became the symbol of pawnbrokers.) In another story, Nicholas visits an inn where the evil innkeeper has murdered three students and pickled them in brine. Nicholas detects the crime and brings the boys back to life; for this and similar miracles he became the patron saint of students and children. (See "LE MIRACLE DU GRAND ST. NICOLAS.")

After his death, Nicholas became a well-loved saint, being named the patron, among other things, of Russia and Greece, and of Vikings, choirboys, thieves, perfumers, barrel makers, unmarried women, and sailors. (Medieval sailors on the Mediterranean would not venture aboard a ship without "Nicholas loaves," bread that could be thrown overboard to miraculously calm stormy seas.) Hymns were written to him as early as 527, and hundreds of churches were dedicated to him from the Middle East to Greenland – 45 in Rome alone, and more than 400 in England. He seems to have been, after

the Blessed Virgin Mary, the most widely venerated saint of the medieval period. In 1087 his remains in Myra – a town that had fallen into Islamic hands – were kidnapped from their resting place in an Orthodox church and taken to Bari, Italy, where they became the focus of a new Catholic basilica. His tomb still exudes a sweet-smelling liquid that is referred to as *Manna di San Nicola*.

The relocation of his body served to spur the Nicholas cult, and he became the subject of plays, hymns, sculptures, paintings, and more legends. By 1100 he was associated with the Christmas season. As patron of children and students, his feast day of December 6 became linked to the custom of the BOY BISHOP, who rules certain churches until the December 28 Feast of the Holy Innocents. It also became customary to give gifts to children on his day: this practice, which may have been started by Italian nuns, soon spread across Europe. From Artois comes this petition:

> St. Nicholas patron of good children,
> I kneel for you to intercede.
> Hear my voice through the clouds
> And this night give me some toys.
> I want most of all a playhouse
> With some flowers and little birds.

By the 16th century, German children were hanging out their stockings for him to drop presents in, just as he had left bags of gold with the poor man's daughters. At the same time in England, children were told that he came in through the window to deliver his gifts, but he didn't start depositing them in stockings there until the 19th century.

The 16th century also brought the Protestant Reformation and its war on the cult of saints. Nicholas was replaced as gift-bringer first by the Christ Child and then by secularized figures resembling a darker shadow of the saint, such as PELZNICKEL, BELSNICKEL, or KNECHT RUPRECHT. The gift-giving time was also moved from December 6 to either December 25 or New Year's Day. Among Protestant countries, only the Netherlands maintained its devotion to Nicholas, known there as Sinterklaas. This figure inspired early 19th-century Americans in New York City to develop a new gift-bringer, Santa Claus. It is Santa Claus who was exported back to Europe to provide the model for gift-bringers such as Father Christmas, the Weihnachtsmann, and Père Noèl. Today, Saint Nicholas, clad as a Catholic bishop complete with crozier and mitre, with companions such as Zwarte Piet, still brings gifts on the eve of his feast to children in the Netherlands and other areas of Europe.

In 1969 a revision of the Roman Catholic calendar of saints resulted in a demotion for Nicholas. His veneration was removed from the category of universal to optional, but the Vatican noted that all saints that had been objects of devotion before the new edition of the liturgical calendar were "still to be venerated as they were before the calendar's updating." In 1972 some relics of St. Nicholas were transferred from Bari to an Orthodox church in New York, and as the church in Myra (now Demre, Turkey) always claimed to have kept at least some of the original body, St. Nicholas can now be said to be resting on three continents.

"The Night Before Christmas"   See CLEMENT CLARKE MOORE.

Night of Cakes   *Oidhche na ceapairi*, an Irish term for Christmas Eve, referring to the baking of cakes and breads for the holiday.

Night of Destiny   January 5, Epiphany Eve, is important to Middle Eastern Christians, who call it *Lilat-al-kadr*, "Night of Destiny." It is the night when palm trees bend down in honour of the occasion when they bent before the Three Kings to guide them to Bethlehem.

Night of Good Tidings   A term for Christmas Eve in Spanish-speaking countries, *Noche Buena*.

Night of the Big Portion   New Year's Eve in Ireland is called the Night of the Big Portion, *Oiche na Coda Móire*, because in order to ensure prosperity for the home in the new year a huge meal must be eaten on December 31. In fact, in some areas it was once believed that all the food in the house had to be devoured.

Night of the Radishes   For over a century the town of Oaxaca, Mexico, has held the *Noché del Rábano*, or Night of the Radishes, a festival dedicated to the carving of large twisted radishes that are shaped by artists into Nativity scenes or images of the Virgin of Guadeloupe, Aztec gods, or local geography. Thousands of locals and tourists crowd the town square during the Christmas season to tour the stalls, visit the hundreds of vendors, and enjoy the music and fireworks that accompany this fiesta. Recently prizes have also been offered for works made from corn husks and dried flowers.

Night of the Screams   In Nicaragua Christmas begins December 7 with the Feast of the Immaculate Conception, known in Spanish as *La Purísima* ("The Most Pure"). The festivities are so loud and exuberant that it has also come to be called *La Noche de Gritería*, or the Night of the Screams. Songs are sung at maximum volume, fireworks are set off, and crowds shout out questions and responses: "*Quien causa tanta alegría?*" ("Why all this happiness?) "*La Concepción de María!*" ("The Conception of Mary!") "*Viva la Concepcio!*" ("Long live the Conception!") Homeowners hand out candies, fruit, and little treats to the crowds, and the party lasts until dawn.

The Nightmare Before Christmas (1993)   An instructive tale of what happens when two holidays collide. Pumpkin King Jack Skellington is ruler of the land of Halloween, where inhabitants do their best to be frightening, but when he stumbles into Christmas he begins having second thoughts. He resolves to kidnap Santa Claus and bring a bit of Christmas to his part of the holiday universe. Naturally things don't work out the way he hoped. This is a brilliantly animated piece of work by Tim Burton and Henry Selick, a bit too intense in parts for young children but certainly entertaining for adults.

El Niño   A warm surface current in the western Pacific Ocean that often appears around Christmas off the coast of Ecuador and Peru. (The name El Niño refers to the Spanish-language term for the Christ Child.) Though it usually ends by April 1, every three to seven years it persists, lingering up to 18 months and causing climatic changes in the western hemisphere. In South America, coastal fisheries suffer and rainfall increases along the coast. In North America El Niño usually means warmer temperatures along the west coast and more rain in the Gulf of Mexico.

Nisse   The Scandinavian house elf. See JULENISSE.

Nivôse, Fifth of   The radicals of the French Revolution were

Nisse *The Scandinavian Christmas elf and his bowl of rice pudding depicted on a Swedish postage stamp.*

eager to remake the calendar and seize control of the reckoning of time. Believing in the Enlightenment doctrine that evil traditions could warp the natural goodness of humanity, they set out to abolish the old months and days of the week, despising them for their irregularity and connection to religions of the past. The months were renamed after climatic conditions descriptive of seasonal life in the Paris region: July, for example, became *Thermidor*, the hot month. Months were divided into three 10-day *décades*, and these, along with the days, were most often referred to by number rather than name. In this system Christmas Day became the *Décade I, Quintidi de Nivôse*: the fifth day of the first decade of the snowy month. This calendar was in effect from 1793 until 1806, when it was abolished by Napoleon.

No Toys for Christmas (1967)   American actor and director John Derek was known more for the series of beautiful actresses he married than for his cinematic accomplishments. This dreadful Philippine-made film, also known as *Once Before I Die*, features Derek as an American officer and one of those wives, Ursula Andress, as his fiancée attempting to escape a Japanese attack during the Second World War.

Noche Buena   "The Good Night," Christmas Eve in Spain and Spanish America. This is the high point of the Christmas season in Latin America, marked by feasting, fireworks, and attendance at the midnight mass.

Noël   The French term for Christmas, which, like the English "Nowel," is derived from the Latin *natalis*. In the Middle Ages it was used as an expression of joy, as when cries of "*Noël!*" greeted the arrival of Queen Isabella of Bavaria in Paris in 1389. In the late 15th century, the term referred to strophic poetry dealing with the Nativity, often sung with "*Noël*" as the refrain. From this it came to refer to Christmas carols in general and now to the Christmas season.

"Noël des enfants qui n'ont plus de maison"   "A Christmas Carol for Homeless Children," text and music written by Claude Debussy in 1915 in the midst of the First World War. A denunciation of the German invasion, it is perhaps the bitterest Christmas song ever written. The children of France, whose towns have been burnt down and who have been orphaned, call on the Christ Child not to visit the homes of their enemies, but to punish them.

Nous n'avons plus de maisons!
Les ennemis ont tout pris,
Jusqu'à notre petit lit!
Ils ont brûlé l'école et notre maître aussi.
Ils ont brûlé l'église et monsieur Jésus-Christ!
Et le vieux pauvre qui n'est pas pu s'en aller!

Nous n'avons plus de maisons!
Les ennemis ont tout pris,
Jusqu'à notre petit lit!
Bien sûr! papa est à la guerre,
Pauvre maman est morte
Avant d'avoir vu tout ça.
Qu'est-ce que l'on va faire?
Noël! petit Noël! n'allez pas chez eux,
N'allez plus jamais chez eux,
Punissez-les!

Vengez les enfants de France!
Les petits Belges, les petits Serbes,
Et les petits Polonais aussi!
Si nous en oublions, pardonnez-nous.
Noël ! Noël! surtout, pas de joujoux,
Tâchez de nous redonner le pain quotidien.

Nous n'avons plus de maisons!
Les ennemis ont tout pris,
Jusqu'à notre petit lit!
Ils ont brûlé l'école et notre maître aussi.
Ils ont brûlé l'église et monsieur Jésus-Christ!
Et le vieux pauvre qui n'est pas pu s'en aller!
Noël ! écoutez-nous, nous n'avons plus de petits sabots:
Mais donnez la victoire aux enfants de France!

Nollaig Mhóhr "Big Christmas," the Irish term for December 25 to distinguish it from "Little Christmas" or EPIPHANY.

Nollaig na bhFear "Men's Christmas," Irish term for Christmas Eve, to contrast with "Women's Christmas" on January 6. It was customary for men of the village to visit each other for a drink.

North Pole Why should Santa Claus dwell at the North Pole? Though no one now doubts that Santa and his toy-making workshop are located at the North Pole (except the Finns, who maintain that he lives in their country), the idea took some time to develop. The first hint that it might be someplace cold came with the works in the 1820s of WASHINGTON IRVING and CLEMENT CLARKE MOORE, who pointed out his reindeer-drawn means of travel and his fur suit. The search for the lost Franklin expedition drew the attention of the world to the Arctic regions during the 1840s and may have helped fix the Pole as Santa's home. Horatio Alger's poem "St. Nicholas," published in 1875, begins

In the far-off Polar seas,
Far beyond the Hebrides,
Where the icebergs, towering high,
Seem to pierce the wintry sky,
And the fur-clad Esquimaux
Glides in sledges o'er the snow,
Dwells St. Nick, the merry wight,
Patron saint of Christmas night.

Solid walls of massive ice,
Bearing many a quaint device,
Flanked by graceful turrets twain,
Clear as clearest porcelain,

Bearing at a lofty height
Christ's pure cross in simple white,
Carven with surpassing art
From an iceberg's crystal heart.

Here St. Nick, in royal state,
Dwells, until December late
Clips the days at either end,
And the nights at each extend;
Then, with his attendant sprites,
Scours the earth on wintry nights,
Bringing home, in well-filled hands,
Children's gifts from many lands.

Here are whistles, tops and toys,
Meant to gladden little boys;
Skates and sleds that soon will glide
O'er the ice or steep hill-side.
Here are dolls with flaxen curls,
Sure to charm the little girls;
Christmas books, with pictures gay,
For this welcome holiday.

North Pole *Thomas Nast's drawings helped popularize the notion that Santa Claus lived at the North Pole.*

In the 1880s Thomas Nast's cartoons show Santa Claus at the North Pole, and Katherine Lee Bates's story "Goody Santa Claus on a Sleigh Ride" places him there with elves, workshop, and a Mrs. Claus. Since then movies have frequently depicted the icy surroundings, with his lodgings ranging from homey to high-tech.

Northern Nativity: Christmas Dreams of a Prairie Boy A marvellous book from 1976 by famed Canadian painter William Kurelek. He illustrates incidents in the Nativity story in terms of slices of Canadian life and includes, among other things, farmers, immigrants, Inuit, and a Salvation Army hostel.

Norway Among the preparations made for Christmas in Norway are the lighting of the candles on the Advent wreath;

office parties for employees and clients; massive amounts of baking (*julekake*, the Christmas bread, and seven varieties of cookies are essential); the brewing of *juleol*, Christmas beer; making crafts to decorate the tree and home; attending Christmas concerts; singing carols; and a thorough house-cleaning. Norwegians have also adopted the Swedish custom of marking December 13, St. Lucia's Day, with processions led by a girl in a white dress wearing a crown of lights on her head and carrying a candle in her hand.

In the 19th century, Norwegians, who had long used greenery such as holly and evergreen boughs in their seasonal decorating, adopted the Christmas tree. As in many European countries, the tree is bought ahead of time but not decorated until Christmas Eve, when it is revealed in all its glory to the children. National flags are a popular decoration, along with figures of the *nisse*, or house elf, and many families still prefer the light of real candles to strings of electric bulbs. Giant Norwegian trees are shipped every year to various cities around the world: Trafalgar Square in London erects a tree sent annually as a gift from Oslo in thanks for supporting Norway during the Second World War.

On the afternoon of Christmas Eve, all work ceases. It is a tradition at that time to take a bath and put on new clothes. Late in the afternoon church bells ring out, summoning the faithful to worship and announcing the peace of Christmas. After church families hurry home for the evening's festivities, a reading of the Bible's Christmas story and the Christmas Eve meal. A number of dishes are customary: roast pork, spareribs, the amazing cod dish known as LUTEFISK, and, for the very traditional, porridge with a lucky almond hidden in it. (Tradition also dictates that some food be left for the spirits of the family dead; that the JULENEK, the sheaf of oats, be placed out for the birds; and that the family *nisse*, the elf who lives in the barn or attic, be placated with a bowl of porridge.) Finally the moment that the children have been waiting for arrives: the door to the living room is opened and the tree with its mound of presents is revealed. Some families arrange for a visit by the JULESVENN, the Norwegian Santa figure who quizzes the children on their behaviour and hands out gifts. Those present then join hands in a custom known as "circling the Christmas tree," singing carols and walking around the tree in a display of love and solidarity.

Norway's Santa Claus is said to live in the town of Drøbak, south of Oslo, where he has his own post office and where thousands of tourists visit all year round. Road signs warn drivers to beware of the sudden appearance of elves.

On Christmas Day the family may attend church once more and return home for a well-stocked buffet meal. Diners can expect to see *lutefisk* again, as well as cold meats, herring, trout, and salmon dishes, head cheese, mutton, sausages, *lefse* (the traditional flat bread), cheese, fruit, cakes, and cookies. Cold aquavit (or *akevitt*, of which there are 16 kinds in Norway) and beer wash it all down.

Celebrations continue until Epiphany, or even until ST. KNUT'S DAY. It's a time for visiting, feasting, winter sports, New Year's Eve fireworks, and, for children, the season to "go JULEBUKK," a post-Christmas round of costumed visits to neighbours to collect little treats.

Like many other countries of Northern Europe, Norway has its legends of evil forces, which are most active during the Christmas season. The Wild Host, a gang of unclean spirits and demons, rages through the midwinter night. *Lussinatten*, the night of December 13, which before calendar reform was the longest of the year, was particularly full of creatures best avoided. Barn doors were marked with a cross to keep evil spirits away, dry spruce was burned in the fireplace so that its sparks would keep witches from descending the chimney, the Yule log and Christmas candle were kept burning all night long, and men would fire off guns to "shoot in" Christmas and warn away the forces of darkness.

Novena   A nine-day period of special religious devotion. Novenas occur around the world during the nine days before Christmas. In Latin America special church services are held in honour of El Niño, the Christ Child, with prayers, carol singing, and the playing of native instruments. The POSADAS are also held at this time: nine evenings of parades of the faithful re-enacting the search of the Holy Family for lodging in Bethlehem. In Europe pictures of Mary or statues of Joseph are carried from house to house accompanied by torches; prayers and hymns are said before the images.

The Nutcracker   The Nutcracker phenomenon began life in 1816 as a story by the German writer E.T.A. Hoffmann (1776-1822). Entitled "The Nutcracker and the Mouse King," it was a rather grim tale of an unhappy girl named Marie whose only love is a nutcracker doll. The story was adapted in 1845 by famed French novelist Alexandre Dumas, who made it more suitable for children. In 1891 the cheerier version was chosen as the basis of a Russian ballet to be scored by Piotr Ilyich Tchaikovsky and choreographed by Marius Petitpa and Lev Ivanov.

The *Nutcracker Suite* opened in St. Petersburg on December 17, 1892. It is the tale of a girl named Clara who is given a nutcracker doll for Christmas by her godfather, Drosselmaier. That night she falls asleep and is disturbed by an attack of mice led by the Mouse King, who wishes to take her away to his kingdom. She is rescued by soldiers and the Nutcracker who, as a prince, takes her to his land, a country full of sugarplums and waltzing flowers. She awakens the next morning with only the nutcracker doll and memories of her Christmas adventure.

The original production was not an overwhelming success. Though popular in Russia, it was never staged outside of that country until 1934, when a setting appeared in London. Since then numerous versions of the dance, long and short, have been attempted, with the most successful being that by George Balanchine in 1954. It is probably the world's favourite ballet, being seen by millions each year, especially during the Christmas season.

One curious consequence of the ballet's popularity has been to stimulate interest in the collection of nutcrackers. Though many types of metal and wood nutcrackers were made through the centuries, the commercial production of the popular wooden toy nutcracker dates only from the 1870s in Germany. The Leavenworth Nutcracker Museum in Washington State exhibits over 3,000 of these implements from around the world.

The Nutcracker and the Movies   There are dozens of motion pictures based on the *Nutcracker Suite*. Viewers have the following choices: the Bolshoi Ballet, the Royal Ballet, the Kiev Ballet, or the New York City Ballet; Mikhail Baryshnikov, Natalya Arhipova, Yekaterina Maximova, Vladimir Vasiliev, or Macaulay Culkin; sound or no sound; live or animated; on stage or on ice.

Two of the more popular versions are *Nutcracker, The Motion Picture* (1986), with the Pacific Northwest Ballet using stage settings by Maurice Sendak, and *The Nutcracker* (1993) by the New York City Ballet, narrated by Kevin Kline, with

Macaulay Culkin as the Nutcracker Prince (this production was also known as *George Balanchine's The Nutcracker*).

A good children's introduction to the story is the 1990 animation *The Nutcracker Prince*, with the voices of Kiefer Sutherland, Peter O'Toole, Megan Follows, and Phyllis Diller.

Beware *The Nutcracker* (1982) by director Anwar Kawadri. This is a sleazy drama about a defecting Russian ballerina who ends up in a company of dancer-prostitutes. Also known as *Nutcracker Sweet*.

Nuts   A symbol of fruitfulness long associated with midwinter festivals. During the early Roman empire, the poet Marcus Valerius Martialis sent a present of them to a fellow writer, saying, "From my small garden, behold, eloquent Juvenal, I send you Saturnalian nuts. The rest of the fruit the rakish Garden God has bestowed on frolicking girls." Romans believed each type of nut to be possessed of a special virtue: almonds were an antidote to drunkenness; walnuts counteracted poisons; hazelnuts prevented famine.

Christmastime in many countries sees bowls of nuts on the table and nuts used in desserts. They are an indispensable part of the THIRTEEN DESSERTS of Provence; St. Nicholas and his helpers throw them to children or put them with apples in their shoes. Boys and girls throw walnuts at each other in Poland on St. Stephen's Day. North American crooners sing of "Chestnuts roasting on an open fire," and nuts have long been used as edible decorations on Christmas trees.

O's, "The Great" or "The Christmas" On the seven evenings before Christmas Eve, the vespers (evening) service includes the singing of one of seven antiphons, or liturgical verse, each beginning with "O." Known as "The Great O's" or "The Christmas O's," they are: *O Sapientia* ("O Wisdom"), December 17; *O Adonai* ("O Lord"), December 18; *O Radix Jesse* ("O Root of Jesse"), December 19; *O Clavis David* ("O Key of David"), December 20; *O Oriens* ("O Day-Spring"), December 21; *O Rex* ("O King"), December 22; and *O Emmanuel*, December 23.

These musical pieces are sometimes attributed to Pope Gregory the Great himself (c. 540-604), and certainly predate the ninth century. If one takes the first letter of the key words in reverse order they form an acrostic in Latin suitable to the season of the coming birth of Jesus: ERO CRAS, "I shall be tomorrow."

"O Bethlehem" See "OI BETLEHEM."

"O Christmas Tree" One of several English versions of the German carol "O TANNENBAUM," author unknown.

> O Christmas tree, O Christmas tree!
> How are thy leaves so verdant!
> O Christmas tree, O Christmas tree,
> How are thy leaves so verdant!
>
> Not only in the summertime,
> But even in winter is thy prime.
> O Christmas tree, O Christmas tree,
> How are thy leaves so verdant!
>
> O Christmas tree, O Christmas tree,
> Much pleasure doth thou bring me!
> O Christmas tree, O Christmas tree,
> Much pleasure doth thou bring me!
>
> For every year the Christmas tree,
> Brings to us all both joy and glee.
> O Christmas tree, O Christmas tree,
> Much pleasure doth thou bring me!
>
> O Christmas tree, O Christmas tree,
> Thy candles shine out brightly!
> O Christmas tree, O Christmas tree,
> Thy candles shine out brightly!
>
> Each bough doth hold its tiny light,
> That makes each toy to sparkle bright.
> O Christmas tree, O Christmas tree,
> Thy candles shine out brightly!

"O Come All Ye Faithful" Debate about the authorship of this carol continues even today, but the name most frequently attached to it is that of John Francis Wade, an Englishman at the Catholic college at Douai. Written as "ADESTE FIDELES" about 1742, the carol was brought to England by returning Catholics and was often sung at the Portuguese embassy in London, thus becoming known for a time as "The Portuguese Hymn." It was translated in 1841 by a Church of England clergyman, Frederick Oakeley (1802-80), as "Ye Faithful, Approach Ye." After his conversion to Catholicism Oakeley made another translation in 1852, the now familiar "O Come All Ye Faithful." Additional verses have been added by W.T. Brooke (1848-1917), but these are seldom sung.

> O come, all ye faithful,
> Joyful and triumphant,
> O come ye, O come ye to Bethlehem.
> Come and behold Him,
> Born the King of Angels!
>
> *O come, let us adore Him,*
> *O come, let us adore Him,*
> *O come, let us adore Him,*
> *Christ the Lord.*
>
> God of God,
> Light of Light,
> Lo! He abhors not the Virgin's womb;
> Very God,
> Begotten, not created.
>
> *Chorus*
>
> Sing choirs of angels;
> Sing in exultation
> Sing, all ye citizens of heaven above:
> Glory to God –
> In the highest.
>
> *Chorus*
>
> Yea, Lord, we greet Thee,
> Born this happy morning;
> Jesus, to Thee be the glory giv'n;
> Word of the Father,
> Now in the flesh appearing,
>
> *Chorus*

"O Come, O Come, Emmanuel" An Advent carol based on "THE GREAT O'S," seven antiphons sung at vespers, one on each of the seven nights preceding Christmas Eve. The tune, adapted in 1854 by Victorian musicologists Thomas Helmore and John Mason Neale (1818-66), is probably from medieval France, and the words are translated from the Latin "*Veni, Veni Emanuel.*"

> O Come, O Come, Emmanuel
> And ransom captive Israel
> That mourns in lonely exile here
> Until the Son of God appears.
>
> *Rejoice! Rejoice! Emmanuel*
> *Shall come to thee O Israel*
>
> O come, thou rod of Jesse, free
> Thine own from Satan's tyranny.
> From depths of hell thy people save
> And give them vict'ry o'er the grave.
>
> *Chorus*

O come, O Dayspring, come and cheer
Our spirits by thine advent here,
And drive away the shades of night
And pierce the clouds and bring us light.

Chorus

O come, Thou Key of David, come
And open wide our heavenly home.
Make safe the way that leads on high
And close the path to misery.

Chorus

O come, O come, Thou Lord of might
Who to thy tribes, on Sinai's height
In ancient times did'st give the law
In cloud and majesty and awe.

Chorus

"O Little Town of Bethlehem" Organist Lewis Redner, who wrote the music for "O Little Town of Bethlehem."

With glowing hearts by His cradle we stand.
So led by light of a star sweetly gleaming
Here come the wise men from Orient land.
The King of Kings lay thus in lowly manger,
In all our trials born to be our friend.

Truly He taught us to love one another,
His law is love and His gospel is peace.
Chains shall He break for the slave is our brother,
And in His name all oppression shall cease.
Sweet hymns of joy in grateful chorus raise we,
Let all within us praise His holy name.

"O Little Town of Bethlehem"   Phillips Brooks (1835-93) was an American Episcopal bishop, famous for his preaching and liberal views. On Christmas Eve, 1865, he rode from Jerusalem to Bethlehem and is said to have viewed the town from the field where shepherds received the news of Christ's birth from the angels. Three years later he wrote the words of "O Little Town of Bethlehem"; his organist, Lewis Redner (with whom he had collaborated when writing the carol "Everywhere, Everywhere, Christmas Tonight"), wrote the music, which he said came to him in a dream "with an angel strain." It was first performed by the children of their Sunday school.

In England, Redner's tune has been overtaken in popularity by a 1906 Ralph Vaughan Williams version of the folk tune "The Ploughboy's Dream" or "Forest Green." Other tunes by Henry Walford Davies and Joseph Barnby have attracted less interest.

O little town of Bethlehem,
How still we see thee lie!
Above thy deep and dreamless sleep
The silent stars go by;
Yet in thy dark streets shineth
The everlasting Light;
The hopes and fears of all the years
Are met in thee to-night.

For Christ is born of Mary,
And gathered all above,
While mortals sleep, the angels keep
Their watch of wondering love.
O morning stars, together
Proclaim the holy birth!

"O Holy Night" The French composer Adolphe Adam.

"O Holy Night"   In its native French this song is known as "*Cantique de Noèl*" or "Minuit, Chrétiens," with music by Adolphe Adam (1803-56) and words by Placide Cappeau (1808-77). Adam was already celebrated as the composer of the ballet *Giselle* when he was asked in 1847 to set Cappeau's words to music. Cappeau was a rural commissioner of wines and a writer of verse who later in life became a political radical and asked to be buried standing up. The English words are by the American journalist John Dwight (1818-93).

Oh holy night! The stars are brightly shining
It is the night of the dear Savior's birth!
Long lay the world in sin and error pining
Till he appear'd and the soul felt its worth.
A thrill of hope the weary world rejoices
For yonder breaks a new and glorious morn!

Fall on your knees,
Oh hear the angel voices.
Oh night divine,
Oh night when Christ was born,
Oh night divine,
Oh night divine.

Led by the light of Faith serenely beaming,

And praises sing to God the King,
And peace to men on earth.

How silently, how silently,
The wondrous gift is given!
So God imparts to human hearts
The blessings of his heaven.
No ear may hear his coming,
But in this world of sin,
Where meek souls will receive him, still
The dear Christ enters in.

Where children pure and happy
Pray to the blessed Child,
Where misery cries out to thee,
Son of the mother mild;
Where charity stands watching
And faith holds wide the door,
The dark night wakes, the glory breaks,
And Christmas comes once more.

O holy Child of Bethlehem!
Descend to us, we pray;
Cast out our sin and enter in,
Be born in us to-day.
We hear the Christmas angels
The great glad tidings tell;
O come to us, abide with us,
Our Lord Emmanuel!

"O Tannenbaum"   Supposedly of medieval origin, this German carol is more likely a product of the 16th or 17th century. The tune was first published in 1799; verse one appeared in 1820, while the second and third verses were added by the poet Ernst Gebhard Anschütz (1800-61). In 1861 the tune was borrowed for "Maryland, My Maryland." For an English translation, see "O CHRISTMAS TREE."

O Tannenbaum, o Tannenbaum,
Wie treu sind deine Blätter!
Du grünst nicht nur zur Sommerszeit,
Nein auch im Winter, wenn es schneit.
O Tannenbaum, o Tannenbaum,
Wie treu sind deine Blätter!

Oberndorf *The Silent Night Chapel in Oberndorf, Austria.*

Oberndorf   The Austrian village where "SILENT NIGHT" was first played in 1818 in the St. Nicholas church. The church was torn down after it was damaged in a flood early in the 20th century, but a memorial Silent Night Chapel has been erected in its place, and every Christmas it attracts tourists for an atmospheric performance of the carol. After the reading of the Christmas story and a short sermon, the lights are extinguished and in the dark two men with a guitar sing the first verses of "Silent Night," just as it was sung in 1818. Next to the chapel is a museum of local history with a number of "Silent Night" exhibits. (See colour fig. 25.)

"Of the Father's Love Begotten"   Based on the Latin hymn "Corde Natus ex Parentis," written in the early fifth century by Aurelius Clemens Prudentius (348-c. 413), lawyer, head of Emperor Honorius's bodyguard, and, late in life, a monk who spent his last years writing hymns. The English translation is by John Mason Neale (1818-66), revised by Henry William Baker (1821-77). The tune is derived from 13th-century plainsong.

Of the Father's love begotten
Ere the worlds began to be,
He is Alpha and Omega,
He the Source, the Ending he
Of the things that are, that have been,
And that future years shall see,
Evermore and evermore.

At his word was all created;
He commanded, it was done:
Earth, and heaven and depths of ocean,
In their threefold order one;
All that grows beneath the shining
Of the orbs of moon and sun
Saeculorum saeculis.

He assumed this mortal body,
Frail and feeble, doomed to die,
That the race from dust created
Might not perish utterly,
Which the dreadful Law had sentenced
In the depths of hell to lie.

O that birth, for ever blessed!
When the Virgin, full of grace,
By the Holy Ghost conceiving,
Bore the Saviour of our race,
And the Child, the world's Redeemer,
First revealed his sacred face.

O ye heights of heaven, adore him!
Angel-hosts, his praises sing!
Powers, dominions, bow before him,
And extol your God and King!
Let no tongue today be silent,
Every voice in concert ring.

This is he whom once the sibyls
With united voice foretold,
His the birth that faithful prophets
In their pages did unfold;
Let the world unite to praise him,
Long-desired, foreseen of old.

Hail, thou Judge of souls departed!
Hail, thou King of them that thrive!
On the Father's throne exalted
None in might with thee may strive,

Old Christmas *An allegory of Old Christmas as the* Illustrated London News *envisioned it in 1858.*

Who at last, to judge returning,
Sinners from thy face shall drive.

O ye elders, lead the anthems:
Laud your God in ancient lays!
Youths and maidens, hymn his glory!
Infants, bring your songs of praise!
Guileless voices, in sweet concord
Unto all the length of days,

Let the storm and summer sunshine,
Gliding stream and sounding shore,
Sea and forest, frost and zephyr,
Night and day their Lord adore;
All Creation joined to praise thee
Through the ages evermore,

Christ, to thee, with God the Father,
And, O Holy Ghost, to thee,
High thanksgiving, endless praises,
And eternal glory be;
Honour, power and all dominion,
And eternal victory.

O'Hanlon, Virginia As the eight-year-old daughter of a New York coroner's assistant, Laura Virginia O'Hanlon (1889-1971) disagreed with her friends over the reality of Santa Claus. Taking her father's advice, she wrote to ask the *New York Sun* about the existence of St. Nick. The paper, through editorial writer Francis Church, replied on September 21, 1897, in the famous editorial "YES, VIRGINIA, THERE IS A SANTA CLAUS."

Virginia O'Hanlon grew up to achieve a doctorate and work as a teacher and principal in the New York school system. She died in 1971 at age 81 in a nursing home in Valatie, New York, still professing a belief in the power of Santa Claus.

"Oi Betlehem" The best known of the Basque carols.

O Bethlehem,
O'er you a brilliant star is shining,
O Bethlehem.
Heavenly choirs of angels bring
To the world glad news of an infant King;
Round you the hills and valleys are echoing!
O Bethlehem,
O Bethlehem.

Oie'l Verrey "The Eve of the Feast of Mary," a Christmas Eve service on the Isle of Man in which people attended midnight services bearing lighted candles decorated with ribbons. It was the custom for the priest to go home after the mass, leaving the congregation in the church singing carols, or "carvals," reminiscent of the Welsh PLYGAIN. These songs were sung not in unison but by one person at a time, and the singer had to stop if his candle went out.

One 19th-century source records that, like *plygain*, the long service could get unruly, "as it was the custom for the female part of the congregation to provide themselves with peas, which they flung at their bachelor friends."

Old Christmas (1) A pre-Father Christmas figure of medieval and early-modern England. He is a symbol of revelry, not gift-giving, and stands for the hospitality and neighbourliness of the season, especially in contrast to those opposed to celebrating Christmas. The 17th-century ballad "Old Christmas

Fig. 15: **Mistletoe** The custom of kissing under a sprig of mistletoe was until the 19th century confined to the servant class. For a long time it was also limited to the English-speaking world, though it has spread farther in recent years. This Saturday Evening Post *cover by Norman Rockwell is from 1936.*

Fig. 16: **Opposition to Christmas** *Before the 19th century, Christmas usually meant feasting and carousing, a fact which stirred up opposition to the holiday.*

Fig. 17: **Pastoral Drama** *A 19th-century French advertisement for a Christmas play.*

Fig. 18: **Peacock** *Fra Angelico and Filippo Lippi have crowded a lot of action into this depiction of the Adoration of the Magi (c. 1445). The peacock perched on the roof of the stable symbolizes eternal life, based on the belief that the bird's flesh never rotted and its tail could renew itself. The pheasant symbolizes loyalty.*

Fig. 19: **Pohutukawa** *The Christmas tree of New Zealand.*

Fig. 20: **Rainbow** *Jan van Eyck's 1435 The Annunciation shows Mary being greeted by a rainbow-winged angel with the Holy Spirit about to descend upon her in the form of a dove. In Christian art, a rainbow is the symbol of God's peace. Note also the lilies, a frequent motif in Annunciation art, and the light streaming through the window, symbolic of the virgin conception.*

Fig. 21: **Santa Claus** In America, Santa Claus himself was first portrayed as a "right jolly old elf" (by Clement Clark Moore in "A Visit From St. Nicholas"), but by the 1870s he had grown in stature and acquired small helpers. This Norman Rockwell illustration dates from 1922.

Fig. 22: **Shepherds** The Adoration of the Shepherds by the Venetian artist Giorgione (c. 1505) shows the stable as a cave in a rural Italian landscape.

Fig. 23: **Shop Early Campaign** Begun in 1906, this campaign hoped to persuade shoppers to finish their purchasing weeks ahead of time. The purpose was not to begin the Christmas shopping season early but to prevent the abuse of shop workers with a last-minute rush. Norman Rockwell's illustration dates from 1947.

Fig. 24: **Sibyls** The Tiburtine Sibyl prophesies the birth of Christ.

Fig. 25: *"**Silent Night**" A painting of the old St. Nicholas church in Oberndorf, where the carol "Silent Night" was sung for the very first time. The church was torn down early in the 20th century.*

Fig. 26: **Stockings** *Saint Nicholas's act of charity led to the tradition of Christmas stockings.*

Fig. 27: **Turkey** A Victorian Christmas card. Turkey has been associated with Christmas since the 16th century.

Fig. 28: **Ukraine** Evening carollers in 19th-century Ukraine.

Returned" points out the plight of the poor at Christmas and blames the uncharitable.

> All you that to feasting and mirth are inclined,
> Come, here is good news for to pleasure your mind;
> Old Christmas is come for to keep open house,
> He scorns to be guilty of starving a mouse;
> Then come, boys and welcome, for diet the chief,
> Plum-pudding, goose, capon, minc'd pies and roast beef.

An Hue and Cry After Christmas, 1645, expresses the desire of most Englishmen who wished to retain Christmas celebrations despite Puritan legislation enacted against them: "But is old, old, good old Christmas gone? Nothing but the Hair of his good, gray, old Head and Beard left? Well, I will have that, seeing I cannot have more of him."

Sir Walter Scott (1771-1832) praises the twin aspects of an old English Christmas, merriment and charity: "England was merry England, when / Old Christmas brought his sports again / 'Twas Christmas broached the mightiest ale; / 'Twas Christmas told the merriest tale; / A Christmas gambol oft could cheer / The poor man's heart through half the year."

And Charles Lamb (1775-1834) rejoices that extreme Protestants have not succeeded in killing off the Englishman's love of Christmas: "Old Christmas is a-coming to the confusion of Puritans, Muggletonians, Anabaptists, Quakers and that unwassailing Crew. He cometh not with his wonted gait; he is shrunk nine inches in his girth, but is yet a lusty fellow."

(2) By the 16th century, the Julian calendar, introduced in Rome in the first century B.C., was noticeably out of step with the heavens. The built-in inaccuracy was on the order of 11 minutes and 14 seconds a year, meaning that 10 extra days had accumulated. In order that the calendar year accord with the solar year and the equinoxes and solstices appear on their correct days, Pope Gregory XIII ordered that October 5 to October 14 be entirely stricken from 1582. This, along with other adjustments to make sure the problem never reoccurred, solved the calendrical disparities only in those countries that acknowledged the supremacy of the pope. England (and most of Eastern Europe) did not, and so for almost two centuries afterwards English and European dates did not coincide.

The New Style was finally introduced into England in 1752, during the reign of George II, when Wednesday, September 2, was followed by Thursday, September 14. The day that had previously been celebrated as Christmas now appeared on January 5, which came to be known as "Old Christmas." (Since 1800 further calendrical changes have made Old Christmas coincide with present-day January 6.) There was widespread reluctance among the people to accept this new scheme of things, and many continued to observe Old Christmas as the true date, especially after it was rumoured that the GLASTON-BURY THORN continued to bloom on that date.

In the United States, there are still said to be remote areas of Appalachia where "Old Christmas" is adhered to and where January 6, not December 25, is the proper day to celebrate the birth of Christ. An old mountain ballad maintains:

> On the Sixth Day of January
> His birthday shall be,
> When the stars and the mountains
> Shall tremble with glee.

Much of the folklore that attached to Christmas in 16th- and 17th-century England still endures in reference to January 6 in Appalachia: animals kneel on the anniversary of Christ's birth, bees sing in their hives, and so on. In the district of North Carolina's Great Dismal Swamp, inhabitants mark the Old Christmas Frights, a custom during which a black goat and a hobby horse seek out wayward children.

"An Old Fashioned Christmas Eve" "En gammel dags Juleaften," an 1843 story by Peter Christian Asbjørnsen (1812-85), a Norwegian folklorist. It is set in Christiania (now Oslo), where a convalescing officer spends Christmas in an old house with kind old women. Stories are told round the fire about brownies and their tricks in the kitchen, attic, and barn, and about a Christmas morning service held by the dead.

Old Hob The English Old Hob custom, in which a horse's head is carried about from All Souls' Day to Boxing Day by a man enveloped in a sheet, seems a hold-over from animal sacrifices of pagan times. The German equivalent is the *Schimmel*, and the Welsh counterpart is the MARI LWYD. See HORSES.

"Old Peabody Pew" A short story by Kate Douglas Wiggin, published in 1907, about the Christmas reunion of a couple long separated. It dwells lovingly on the strength of women who can keep an old church looking presentable and who can make a success out of a man with seemingly little to offer.

"The Olden Days Coat" A 1979 children's Christmas story by Canadian author Margaret Laurence. A bored young girl, visiting her grandparents, discovers an old coat and is wafted back in time to when her grandmother was young. Illustrated by Muriel Wood.

Olentzero A legendary figure of Christmas among the Basque people. A charcoal burner, he is believed to come down from the mountains every Christmas Eve to tell the good news of the birth of the baby Jesus, take part in the feasting, and hand out gifts. In many villages a representation of the Olentzero is carried from house to house while Christmas carols are sung.

Olive Branch In Christian iconography a symbol for martyrdom, faith, and peace, the olive branch takes on a special meaning in paintings of the ANNUNCIATION TO MARY done by artists from the Italian city of Siena. In such paintings the angel Gabriel holds out to Mary an olive branch (the emblem of Siena) instead of the traditional lily, which was the symbol of its hated rival, Florence.

Olive, the Other Reindeer Olive, a dog, mishears a line from "Rudolph, the Red-Nosed Reindeer" and concludes that she is to be one of Santa's helpers too. This popular children's book of 1997 by Vivian Walsh with illustrations by J. Otto Seibold was made into a 1999 animated television movie. The film starred Drew Barrymore as the voice of Olive, backed up by Matt Groening, creator of *The Simpsons*, and regular *Simpsons* contributors Dan Castellaneta and Tress MacNeille.

"On the Morning of Christ's Nativity" A long poem written in 1630 by John Milton (1608-74), which begins:

> This is the month, and this the happy morn,
> Wherein the Son of heaven's eternal king,
> Of wedded maid and virgin mother born,
> Our great redemption from above did bring –
> For so the holy sages once did sing –
> That He our deadly forfeit should release,
> And with His Father work us a perpetual peace.
> That glorious form, that light unsufferable,
> And that far-beaming blaze of majesty

Wherewith He wont at heaven's high council table
To sit in the midst of Trinal Unity,
He laid aside; and here with us to be,
Forsook the courts of everlasting day,
And chose with us darksome house of mortal clay.

The first of Milton's great works, the poem took shape on Christmas Day, and the author claimed that it was his birthday gift to Christ. It describes the peace that descended upon the world when the baby was born, a peace that will return at the end of time, when God institutes an age of truth, justice, and mercy. But for now the infant Jesus sleeps, watched by nature and all the angels.

"On This Day the Earth Shall Ring" The English version by Jane M. Joseph (1894-1929) of the Latin hymn "PERSONENT HODIE."

> On this day earth shall ring
> With the song children sing
> To the Son, Christ the King,
> Born on earth to save us:
> Him the father gave us.
> *Ideo gloria in excelsis Deo*
>
> His the doom, ours the mirth,
> When he came down to earth;
> Bethlehem saw his birth;
> Ox and ass, beside him,
> From the cold would hide him.
>
> *Refrain*
>
> God's bright star, o'er his head,
> Wise men three to him led;
> Kneel they low by his bed,
> Lay their gifts before him,
> Praise him and adore him.
>
> *Refrain*
>
> On this day angels sing;
> With their song earth shall ring,
> Praising Christ, heaven's King,
> Born on earth to save us;
> Peace and love he gave us.
>
> *Refrain*

"Once in Royal David's City" Published in 1848 as part of *Hymns for Little Children* by Mrs. Cecil Frances Alexander (1832-95), wife of the Anglican primate of Ireland, who also wrote the lyrics for "All Things Bright and Beautiful." The music is by hymnist Henry Gauntlett (1805-76), the author of 10,000 hymn tunes.

> Once in royal David's city,
> Stood a lowly cattle shed
> Where a mother laid her baby
> In a manger for his bed.
> Mary was that mother mild,
> Jesus Christ her only child.
>
> He came down to earth from heaven
> Who is God and Lord of all,
> And his shelter was a stable,
> And his cradle was a stall.
> With the poor and mean and lowly
> Lived on earth our Saviour holy.

And through all his wondrous childhood
He would honour and obey,
Love and watch the lowly maiden
In whose gentle arms he lay;
Christian children all must be
Mild, obedient, good as he.

For he is our childhood pattern:
Day by day like us he grew;
He was little, weak and helpless
Tears and smiles like us he knew;
And he feeleth for our sadness,
And he shareth in our gladness.

And our eyes at last shall see him
Through his own redeeming love,
For that Child, so dear and gentle,
Is our Lord in heaven above;
And he leads his children on
To the place where he is gone.

Not in that poor, lowly stable
With the oxen standing by
We shall see him, but in heaven
Set at God's right hand on high,
When like stars, his children, crowned,
All in white shall wait around.

One Magic Christmas (1985) One of the darkest movies ever made about the redemptive power of Christmas. Ginny Grainger (Mary Steenburgen) is worn down by poverty and hard circumstances, and it takes an angel (Harry Dean Stanton) to show her how well off she really is. The Christmas virtues of charity, faith, and love are reaffirmed, but only after some grim demonstrations of how life would be without them.

This Canadian film is directed by Philip Borsos; Jan Rubes plays Santa Claus, and Ginny's children are played by Elizabeth Harnois and Robbie Magwood. Twenty thousand real letters to Santa Claus were donated by Canada Post to make Santa's mailroom look busy.

Operation Red Nose Operation Red Nose, or *Opération Nez Rouge* in French-speaking countries, is a service that originated in Quebec, Canada, in 1984 as a way of making the streets safer at Christmas. Volunteers drive home those who have imbibed too much holiday cheer and who might otherwise be tempted to get behind the wheel themselves. This campaign has spread from Canada to Europe.

Operation Santa Claus An annual campaign by American postal workers to answer children's letters to Santa Claus. Since the 1920s volunteers in the U.S. Postal Service have taken time each Christmas to write replies to children, raise money to provide gifts for thousands of deserving cases, or deliver presents.

Oplatek In Poland, a large round wafer, often stamped with a picture of the Nativity and blessed by the local priest. The breaking of the *oplatek* by the head of the house on Christmas Eve signals the end of the Advent fast.

The custom of baking wafers in stamped metal forms dates back to the Middle Ages, and the tradition of sharing a wafer on Christmas Eve dates to the end of the 1700s. Clergy started the practice of sharing unconsecrated bread in the church as an expression of fellowship, and this practice eventually spread throughout the country. Families with members living abroad often mail the wafers to their loved ones so that they too can share in this aspect of the celebration of Polish Christmas.

In Slovakia the wafer is known as the *oplatki* and in Lithuania they are *plotkeles*.

Opposition to Christmas Opposition to Christmas has a long history and has taken different forms over the centuries. The earliest Christians were too focused on Christ's imminent return to concern themselves with marking his human birth in Bethlehem. Only when Gnostic heretics began to assert that Jesus had really not taken earthly form did Christians seek to emphasize the Incarnation and the details of his Nativity. As a result, speculation began about when the birth had taken place and whether it should be celebrated. The Alexandrian theologian ORIGEN in the third century opposed observing the anniversary of Christ's birth as if he were some sort of "King Pharaoh," worldly rulers being the ones most likely to have their births celebrated. Such opposition almost disappeared after the Roman Church in the early fourth century began to celebrate the Feast of the Lord's Nativity on December 25 (the Armenian Church held out against it for centuries, preferring to emphasize EPIPHANY).

In the Middle Ages opposition to Christmas took the form of decrying the excesses of the festivities. Various church councils denounced dancing, cross-dressing, social inversion, and the near-blasphemy that manifested itself in such ceremonies as the FEAST OF THE ASS, the FEAST OF FOOLS, and the BOY BISHOP. By the early-modern period, the Church had succeeded in purging most of these elements from the Christmas season, but the holiday faced further challenges from some proponents of the Protestant Reformation.

The Anglican and Lutheran churches wanted to reform certain aspects of Christmas, but not to abolish its celebration. The Calvinist Reformation, on the other hand, strong in Switzerland, the Netherlands, and Scotland, wanted to do just that. Believing that the observance of Christmas smacked of Catholicism, and clinging to the principle that whatever the Bible did not specify as proper worship could only be man-made idolatry, Calvinists attempted to suppress the holiday. In Scotland it was outlawed in 1583, and in England native Calvinists, known as PURITANS, campaigned against it for decades. Philip Stubbes, in his 1583 *Anatomy of Abuses*, complained that "especially in Christmas time there is nothing else but cards, dice, tables, masking, mumming, bowling and suchlike fooleries; and the reason is that they think they have a commission and prerogative that time to do what they list, and to follow what vanity they will. But (alas!) do they think that they are privileged that time to do evil? The holier the time (if one time were holier than another, which it is not) the holier their exercises ought to be . . . [but] who knoweth that more mischief is that time committed than in all the year besides?" When they emigrated in the 17th century to the American colonies, Puritans succeeded in outlawing Christmas there, and when they took power in England in the late 1640s after a bloody civil war, Christmas celebrations were forbidden there, too, along with mince pies, decorating with greenery, and taking the day off from work.

The restoration of the English monarchy in 1660 saw the return of Christmas celebrations, but in a muted key. Christmas observances went into a decline in England, from which they recovered only in the 1840s, when Charles Dickens, Queen Victoria, and the Christmas card brought the holiday back into wider favour (see colour fig. 16). But as Christmas revived, so did the criticisms. For some North Americans, too many of the old excesses lingered: the noise, the carousing, and the riotous drunken behaviour were unsuitable for what was thought to be a celebration of middle-class family life.

"Christmas," said one 19th-century Quaker newspaper, "tended more to open licentiousness of manners, than to the increase and encouragement of sound morality and religion . . . [and its observance was] wonderfully calculated to enlarge the sphere of stupidity, and to increase the shades of moral darkness over the minds of mankind." This behaviour would have to be eliminated if the celebration of Christmas were to become domesticated and universal, and so legislation and social pressure gradually tamed the wilder elements. In Newfoundland, for example, the tradition of Christmas mumming was banned in 1861 as it led to disorder and violence; in 1868 the raucous Philadelphia Christmas Eve Carnival was outlawed.

The 19th century saw Christmas gift-giving become the central part of the holiday, and many began to complain of excessive commercialism. The Irish playwright George Bernard Shaw was one of those. In 1898 he wrote, "I am sorry to have to introduce the subject of Christmas. . . . It is an indecent subject; a cruel, gluttonous subject; a drunken, disorderly subject; a wasteful, disastrous subject; a wicked, cadging, lying, filthy, blasphemous and demoralizing subject. Christmas is forced on a reluctant and disgusted nation by the shopkeepers and the press; in its own merits it would wither and shrivel in the fiery breath of a universal hatred; and anyone who looked back to it would be turned into a pillar of greasy sausages."

Such misgivings persisted into the 20th century. Clergy implored the faithful to "put Christ back into Christmas" and to "remember the reason for the season"; charity and worship were to be held more important than gift-giving. The American writer Bill McKibben noted, "Christmas is a school for consumerism – in it we learn to equate delight with materialism. We celebrate the birth of the One who told us to give everything to the poor by giving each other motorized tie racks." Critics also pointed to the stress the Christmas season generated, particularly in women, who bore the brunt of shopping, baking, and household preparation. Then there was fat: Christmas was decried as the national eating season, where weight gained in holiday feasting was never lost. Various movements sprang up in the late 20th century to reform Christmas, to pare back the spending, promote good works instead of gifts, and to simplify it all.

Some ultra-conservative Protestant ministers went so far as to urge Christians to abandon the holiday altogether. Such exhortations not only revived the Puritan complaint against excess, but also included anti-Catholic and anti-pagan messages. For them Christmas was the "Christ-mass," too drenched in its popish and Babylonian origins to be worth reforming. One neo-Calvinist penned the following ditty to be sung to the tune of "White Christmas":

I'm dreaming there'll be no Christmas
Just like those Scottish days of yore
When the people listened,
Reformed truth glistened
And they laid low the Romish whore.

In this they were echoed by atheists, who used Christmas songs, such as this rewrite of "God Rest Ye Merry, Gentlemen," to ridicule the historical basis of the Nativity:

There was no star of Bethlehem, there was no angel song,
There could have been no wise men, for the journey was
   too long,
The stories in the Bible are historically wrong.
Glad tidings of reason and fact, reason and fact,
Glad tidings of reason and fact.

The globalization of an American-style Christmas has aroused nationalist resentment around the world. In 1951 French Catholic priests burnt an effigy of Santa Claus outside of Dijon Cathedral; in 1972 Peru banned Santa Claus from the nation's radio and television, because he was alleged to be an anti-Christian myth and part of a merchants' conspiracy that reflected Peru's shameful cultural dependency on foreign customs. In some Dutch towns eager to preserve the supremacy of the native Sinterklaas, police are under orders to arrest and expel anyone wearing a Santa Claus suit. This is milder treatment than that dealt out in Bosnia. In 1996 a Muslim gang with connections to the ruling party beat up a man dressed as Santa Claus in Sarajevo; President Izetbegovic had condemned Santa Claus as something alien to Bosnians and linked him to "European vices" such as pornography, alcohol, and drugs.

Opposition to Christmas *The American idea of the separation of Church and State has led to conflict over public displays of Christmas symbols.*

In some places multiculturalism and political correctness have arisen as forces in opposition to Christmas celebrations. Canadian schools have been under pressure to replace Christmas concerts with "winter concerts" and to avoid the singing of religious carols. In the United States the vexed question of the separation of church and state has led to conflicts over the appearance of Christmas decorations on public property and the promulgation by the Supreme Court of the REINDEER RULES. In Birmingham, England, a city with a large Asian population, the city council renamed the Christmas season "Winterval" and dubbed Christmas lights "festive lights," while in the Netherlands the figure of "Black Pete," who accompanies St. Nicholas, has been the focus of accusations of racism.

See BLUES, CHRISTMAS.

Oratorio de Noël An 1858 oratio for the Christmas season by French composer Camille Saint-Saëns (1835-1927). Written in 10 sections, it begins with a pastoral prelude imitative of J.S. Bach and ends with a Hallelujah chorus that recalls both Handel and the French carol tradition. The text is in Latin, drawn from Nativity narratives and other Old and New Testament scripture.

Origen (185-254) Christian theologian of Alexandria, a vastly learned apologist for his faith, martyred in the Decian persecutions. He opposed marking the anniversary of Christ's Nativity as resembling the birthday celebrations of pagan secular rulers. Origen was also the first to suggest, probably on the basis of the number of gifts mentioned in Scripture, that there were three MAGI.

Ornaments The earliest decorations on trees connected with Christmas appear to have been the apples and cookies hung on the PARADISE TREE in the medieval dramas about Adam and Eve in the Garden of Eden. There are also accounts of this Paradise Tree being hung with wafers symbolizing the host in the ceremony of the mass. In Riga, Latvia, in 1510, a fir tree was carried about in a Christmas procession and was decorated with roses, a flower associated with the Virgin Mary. Roses made of paper decorated a tree brought indoors in Strasbourg in 1605, along with nuts, wafers, and sweets. Despite the story of MARTIN LUTHER decorating a Christmas tree with candles, the earliest use of lights dates to the mid-17th century.

Tree ornaments were largely homemade until after 1850. Before then, most trees were either undecorated (set on tables or hung from the rafters) or adorned with edibles, such as cookies, marzipan, egg-shell baskets full of candles, popcorn chains, and chains of raisins, nuts, or pretzels. An 1868 book of household advice urged women to eschew store-bought candies and decorate the tree with fruits, nuts, and homemade sweets. The tops of trees were often adorned with flags, angels, or stars. In the later 19th century, small unwrapped toys began to be hung from the tree, along with bells, garlands, and paper decorations. As the taste for large, free-standing trees developed so did the need for more ornaments, and an industry grew up in Germany to serve this demand. Charles Dickens in the 1850s gave this description of Victorian tree ornamentation:

> I have been looking on, this evening, at a merry company of children assembled round that pretty German toy, a Christmas Tree. The tree was planted in the middle of a great round table, and towered high above their heads. It was brilliantly lighted by a multitude of little tapers; and everywhere sparkled and glittered with bright objects. There were rosy-cheeked dolls, hiding behind the green leaves; and there were real watches (with movable hands, at least, and an endless capacity of being wound up) dangling from innumerable twigs; there were French-polished tables, chairs, bedsteads, wardrobes, eight-day clocks, and various other articles of domestic furniture (wonderfully made, in tin, at Wolverhampton) perched among the boughs, as if in preparation for some fairy housekeeping; there were jolly, broad-faced little men, much more agreeable in appearance than many real men – and no wonder, for their heads took off, and showed them to be full of sugar-plums; there were fiddles and drums; there were tambourines, books, work-boxes, paint-boxes, sweetmeat boxes, peep-show boxes, and all kinds of boxes; there were trinkets for the elder girls, far brighter than any grownup gold and jewels; there were baskets and pincushions in all devices; there were guns, swords, and banners; there were witches standing in enchanted rings of pasteboard, to tell fortunes; there were teetotums, humming-tops, needle-cases, pen-wipers, smellingbottles, conversation-cards, bouquet-holders; real fruit, made artificially dazzling with gold leaf, imitation apples, pears and walnuts; crammed with surprises in short, as a pretty child before me delightedly whispered to another pretty child, her bosom friend, "There was everything, and more."

Despite Dickens's reference to Wolverhampton, it was Germany that provided the bulk of the world's tree ornaments.

Nuremberg in Bavaria produced many imaginative metal objects for export – butterflies, stars, miniature musical instruments, and "icicles" of silver foil – while a cottage industry based in Lauscha in eastern Germany concentrated on blown-glass ornaments: chains of beads, colourful balls known as *kugeln*, and tree-topping pointed *piken*. Woolworth's department store popularized Lauscha glass and imported cheaper examples by the millions. In Dresden and Leipzig, manufacturers produced embossed paper or cardboard ornaments known as Dresdens. "Angel hair" of spun glass was also a German invention.

The problem of securing candles safely on a Christmas tree challenged numerous inventors. In 1867 an American named Charles Krichholf patented a device to counterweight the candle holder, but the heavy device caused branches to droop. The problem was finally solved by Frederick Arzt in 1879, when he invented a decorative spring-loaded clip. Within three years, however, people were using electric lights on trees, and the use of candles would eventually all but disappear, in large part due to pressure from insurance companies fearful of paying out for fire damage. In 1895 the Christmas tree in President Grover Cleveland's White House was decorated with electric lights, and as North American homes were increasingly electrified they switched to the convenience and safety of artificial lighting. President Warren Harding stuck with the traditional candles until a fire broke out in the White House on Christmas Eve.

The First World War and its disruption of normal commerce ended German dominance of the Christmas tree ornament industry as British and American companies began to produce home-grown, cheaper alternatives and develop new technologies. The problem of silver-foil tarnishing was solved first by lead-foil icicles in the 1920s and later by mylar ornaments. In 1939 Corning showed that mass production of glass ornaments was possible. Japan emerged as the major producer of electric lights in the 1920s and eventually overcame the challenge of paint flaking off bulbs by using milk glass. New techniques enabled manufacturers in Japan and the United States to produce glass bulbs in different shapes: Santa Claus figures, nursery rhyme characters, flowers, and so on. Innovations accelerated as the public seized on one fad after the next, including bubble lights, miniature lights, and revolving colours. In 1973 Hallmark entered the ornament business and since then has produced hundreds of designs, popularizing a new kind of tree decoration: the novelty collectible. Families can choose from ornaments in the shape of rock stars, sports figures, cars, Barbie dolls, or dated items to mark a particular event such as "Baby's First Christmas." Items considered suitable for tree decoration have come to include the political, such as red AIDS awareness ribbons, and the invented religious traditions of the "Christmas Nail" or the "CHRISMON TREE." By 2000 the keyword in tree decoration was eclectic.

Oskorei   Mischievous Norwegian spirits who became troublesome at Christmastime. Unless deterred by a cross painted on the barn they would ride horses to exhaustion, defile the beer supply, or attack humans foolish enough to go abroad alone at night. The name is derived from *Asgårdsreien*, a term for the Wild Hunt.

"The Other Wise Man"   An 1896 story by the American preacher and writer Henry van Dyke (1852-1933). It concerns a magus who sets out to seek the baby Jesus but who spends a lifetime searching in vain, caring for the poor and sick he finds on his way. Finally he arrives in Jerusalem on the day of the crucifixion and dies having at last met the Lord he sought for so long. See THE FOURTH WISE MAN.

Our-Lady's-Bedstraw   The herb *Gallium verum*, whose flowers, said to have originally been white, were turned bright yellow when Mary laid the baby Jesus on them in the cradle. The Protestant Reformation effected a name change for this plant, as for so many other botanical terms associated with the Virgin Mary, and the herb is now also known as "Lady's Bedstraw," "Maid's Hair," "Yellow Bedstraw," "Petty Mugget," and "Cheese Rennet" from its use in cheese-making. The plant serves as a floral symbol for both the Nativity of Jesus and the humility of Mary and her baby.

Ownshook   A fool in the Newfoundland Christmas MUMMING tradition, dressed as a woman and often armed with an inflated bladder used to flail at spectators and to clear a path. Also known as an oonchook, eunchook, or owenschook, the character was reputedly the most boisterous of the parading mummers and shrieked in a falsetto voice. The name seems to be derived from the Irish *oonshugh*, a foolish woman.

Ox and Ass   Two animals that, according to legend, were in the stable where the baby Jesus was laid. The Gospel of PSEUDO-MATTHEW claims that they knelt in adoration at the manger. They are frequently depicted in Nativity art and symbolically represent Jews and Christians or the sacrificial and the redemptive aspects of Jesus. Isaiah 1:3 is held to be a prophecy of the ox and ass. A mistranslation of the Greek version of Habakkuk 3:2 led some to read "between two beasts thou art made known" instead of "in the midst of the years make (it) known."

The notion that oxen (and other animals) go down on their knees at midnight on Christmas Eve in memory of the Nativity is a widespread legend, but it has its regional variations. In some places folk insist that tears run down the cheeks of their cattle as they kneel, while others claim that only the three-year-old (or seven-year-old) oxen bend low, as this was the age of the animals in the Bethlehem stable.

"The Oxen"   A Thomas Hardy poem describing the legend that animals kneel in their stalls on Christmas Eve to commemorate the birth of Christ. See ANIMALS AND CHRISTMAS.

Paganism and Christmas Social historians have noted a connection between the Christian calendar and the cycle of the seasons. Christmas occurring near the winter solstice, and Easter in spring, meant that religious observances could mingle with those activities that were not in themselves Christian but which could be adapted to the Church's way of thinking. Ever since Pope GREGORY gave St. Augustine of Canterbury licence to Christianize pagan ceremonies, there have been pre-Christian influences in the origins of observances such as Christmas.

Pagan origins have been cited for almost every aspect of the Christmas season: Saint Nicholas is said to resemble Odin or Neptune, both bearded figures who travel about and protect sailors; Romans and Egyptians used greenery in the home and exchanged gifts at midwinter. The Yule log, wassailing the fruit trees, the use of sheaves of wheat in the Slavic holiday celebrations, mumming, mistletoe, and many more are all customs that have been linked to a pre-Christian origin. Most of these pagan connections are grossly exaggerated, and anthropologists have pointed out that many ceremonies that supposedly date to an animist past are of comparatively recent origin. Sir James George Frazer's influential *The Golden Bough* popularized a theory that ancient pagan religion lay at the root of modern folk rituals, such as the Mummers' Play. However, English records contain not a single reference to such a play before 1700; this combat and resurrection drama, and other seemingly antique survivals of paganism, appear to be fairly recent innovations.

It is interesting to note that neo-pagan cults of the 20th century have tried to appropriate Christmas customs and tie them to an imagined pagan past in order to acquire some of the respectability that the Christmas season confers. Thus it is insisted that Yule and Christmas are synonymous and that Christian seasonal rites have been stolen from pagans. In this attempt to reclaim Christmas, neo-pagans have also adapted traditional holiday clichés to their own ends; they sing of "Walking in a Wiccan Wonderland" or wish friends "Goddess bless us, everyone."

Pageant See NATIVITY SCENE.

Paignton Pudding Disaster In 1819 the English town of Paignton produced a 900-pound Christmas pudding in honour of the anniversary of their town charter. Despite being boiled in a brewer's furnace for four days, the pudding was still raw on the inside. The townsfolk attempted an even more massive pudding in 1859 as part of a celebration of the arrival of the railway. This time it was cooked to perfection. Made of 500 pounds of flour, 190 pounds of bread, 400 pounds of raisins, 184 pounds of currants, 400 pounds of suet, 96 pounds of sugar, 320 lemons, 150 nutmeg seeds, and 360 quarts of milk, the Monster Pudding (as newspapers referred to it) was over 13 feet in circumference and rested on a wagon pulled by eight horses. It was meant to feed 850 poor of the parish as well as 300 railway labourers, but before that could happen a crowd of 18,000 sightseers, well-lubricated by the local cider, rushed the pudding, swept aside its police escort, and demolished the dessert in a scene of riotous disorder.

As monstrous as the Paignton Pudding was, it would have been dwarfed by the giant Christmas pudding of over three tons made in Aughton, Lancashire in 1992.

Palm Tree A symbol of immortality and paradise that appears in depictions of the Rest on the Flight into Egypt. Middle Eastern Christmas legends also tell of palm trees bending down on Christmas Eve in honour of the Nativity (or on Epiphany Eve to show the Magi the way to Bethlehem) and a mule, tied to a bowing palm tree, being flung up high into the tree when it resumed its normal posture.

Panama Like many Latin American countries, Panama celebrates Christmas with a mixture of traditions from its Spanish Catholic heritage and customs from the United States; the latter influence is particularly acute, because of the long American occupation of the Panama Canal Zone, which ended only in 1999.

In Panamanian homes, for example, the family Nativity scene, always important to Catholic families, shares space with that northern import, the Christmas tree. For many years the country had to import tens of thousands of evergreens from the United States – they would arrive in mid-December on ships – but now Panama has its own tree-farming industry and they are much more widespread. The mix of cultures can also be heard in the Christmas music on radio and television: traditional songs, the Spanish-influenced *villancicos* and *gaitas*, coexist with American English-language carols.

The approach of Christmas is marked by novenas, nine days of religious services involving special Christmas prayers, songs, and devotions, which take place in both churches and homes. It is also a time of parties, little treats from godparents to godchildren, Christmas markets, home decoration, and parades. The climax is the family dinner on Christmas Eve: on the menu is sure to be *tamales* (cornmeal stuffed with chicken, onions, and sauce and wrapped in plantain), beans, *Arroz con Pollo* (chicken and rice), and seafood, especially shrimp. To drink there is rum punch, piña colada, wine, and beer, with soft drinks for the kids. For Catholic families the *Misa de Gallo*, the midnight "rooster" mass, is not to be missed.

Influenced by the American example, many Panamanian children now expect to find presents under the tree on Christmas, brought either by Santa Claus or the Christ Child. In other families children have to wait until the more traditional Epiphany, January 6, when on *Dia de los Reyes*, or Kings' Day, the Magi bring them gifts and the Christmas season comes to an end with another round of parties.

Panettone The most popular Italian Christmas dessert, a light, high cake made with yeast and studded with currants and candied fruit. Most *panettoni* are bought commercially rather than made in the home and are often given as gifts.

Pantomime A traditional English form of holiday entertainment, particularly associated with Boxing Day, December 26. Pantomime, or "panto," developed in the 18th century out of the *commedia dell'arte* harlequin plays popular at the time. Such plays were usually preceded by scenes of mimed and danced action. The first true pantomime is said to have been the 1717 "Harlequin Executed," presented by John Rich. Gradually, as words, comic turns, and stage effects were added, pantomime grew more popular than the plays that gave it birth, emerging as colourful, costumed spectacles based on fairy tales.

Popular throughout the 18th and 19th centuries, pantomime remains a customary part of the English Christmas season despite, or perhaps because of, its predictability. In plays such as "Cinderella," "Jack and the Beanstalk," and "Aladdin," the hero or "principal boy" is always played by an attractive actress in a form-fitting costume, while the "Dame," an ugly old woman, is played by a male comedian. Other features of the pantomime include atrocious puns, ritual shouted exchanges between the actors and the audience, appearances by celebrities, and references to current events.

Here is an early 19th-century account of a family in attendance: "But oh, the rapture when the pantomime commences! Ready to leap out of the box, they joy in the mischief of the clown, laugh at the thwacks he gets for his meddling, and feel no small portion of contempt for his ignorance in not knowing that hot water will scald and gunpowder explode; while with head aside to give fresh energy to the strokes, they ring their little palms against each other in testimony of exuberant delight."

Papa Noel A name sometimes given to Santa Claus in Spain, Latin America, and Louisiana.

Papai Noel The Brazilian name for Santa Claus or Father Christmas. In Brazil he is dressed in the traditional red suit with fur trim and high boots, despite the fact that Christmas there falls in the hot tropical summer. He arrives yearly at Rio de Janeiro's Maracanã Stadium (and other urban sites) in a helicopter and brings gifts to children on Christmas Eve, entering through the door since chimneys are rare in Brazil.

Papparkakor A small wooden tree in Sweden for displaying cookie ornaments, like the Canadian "cookie tree" or the German Christmas pyramid.

Parades Parades and Christmas are inextricably linked. From the earliest liturgical processions in honour of the Nativity, to the massive commercial pageants of present-day North America, the celebration of Christmas has virtually always been marked by parades of one kind or another.

Two noteworthy parades of the Middle Ages involved social inversion, turning the world upside down. These are the FEAST OF THE ASS and the antics of the LORD OF MISRULE. The former ceremony in medieval France was meant to honour the flight of the Holy Family into Egypt. After staging

Pantomime Cross-dressing is an important part of Christmas pantomime in England.

a play in celebration of the role of donkeys in the Bible, a procession of students and priests sang songs on the way to mass, praising the ass who carried Mary and the baby Jesus. In some places a donkey was actually led into the church. The custom eventually degenerated into indecorous behaviour, which included people braying like donkeys during the service, and the ceremony had to be suppressed by religious authorities in the 15th century. In England it was customary in the Middle Ages and early modern period to elect a Lord of Misrule to preside over Christmas festivities. He would often be clad in gaudy clothes and lead a wild procession about the parish. Here is the description of one such impromptu parade taken from Philip Stubbes's 1583 *Anatomy of Abuses*:

First all the wild heads of the parish conventing together choose a grand Captain (of mischief) whom they ennoble with the title of my Lord of Misrule and him they crown with great solemnity, and adopt for their king. This king anointed chooseth twenty, forty, three-score or a hundred lusty-guts like to himself, to wait upon his lordly majesty, and to guard his noble person. Then every one of these his men he investeth with his liveries of green, yellow or some other light wanton colour. And as though that were not bawdy enough I should say, they bedeck themselves with scarves, ribbons, and laces, hanged all over with gold rings, precious stones, and other jewels: this done, they tie about either leg twenty or forty bells with rich handkerchiefs in their hands, and sometimes laid across over their shoulders and necks, borrowed for the most part of their pretty Mopsies and loving Bessies, for bussing them in the dark.

Thus things set in order, they have their hobbyhorses, dragons, and other antiques, together with their bawdy pipers, and thundering drummers to strike up the Devil's Dance withal, and march this heathen company towards the church and church yard, their pipers piping, drummers thundering, their stumps dancing, their bells jingling, their handkerchiefs swinging about their heads like madmen, their hobby-horses and other monsters skirmishing amongst the throng: and in this sort they go to the church (though the minister be at prayer or preaching) dancing and swinging their handkerchiefs over their heads, in the church, like devils incarnate, with such a confused noise that no can hear his own voice. Then the foolish people, they look, they stare, they laugh, they fleer, and mount upon forms and pews, to see these goodly pageants, solemnized in this sort.

This sort of behaviour has its echoes today in processions of MUMMERS; the largest such parade is held annually in Philadelphia, where 10,000 costumed and musical marchers strut every January 1 in a continuation of tradition brought to Pennsylvania by European settlers in the 18th century.

Another popular North American custom is the Santa Claus parade. Every year as Christmas approaches, most cities in the United States and Canada witness a procession of floats, marching bands, waving celebrities, and a jolly Saint Nicholas figure, often sponsored by a local department store. The oldest of these parades, dating from 1905, is held in Toronto; the first in the United States was probably put on by Goldsmith's department store in Memphis in 1913. The most famous are held in the United States. Macy's Thanksgiving Parade in New York, which is famous for its giant balloons in the shape of cartoon characters, has since 1925 marked

Parades *For centuries Christmas has meant colourful processions. This Canadian stamp celebrates the Santa Claus Parade.*

the start of the Christmas shopping season. Hollywood's Christmas Parade dates from 1928, when merchants rented two live reindeer to pull a cart upon which were Santa Claus and a movie starlet. Since that modest beginning, Hollywood Boulevard has come to be renamed Santa Claus Lane every December, the route for a parade notable for the number of film stars, sports heroes, politicians, and other luminaries who take part. In 1946 the singing cowboy GENE AUTRY rode his horse, Champion, in the parade, and the experience led him to write the Christmas favourite "Here Comes Santa Claus (Right Down Santa Claus Lane)."

Christmas parades also take place on the water. In Florida and Alaska, boat-owners decorate their craft with lights and take part in night-time processions along the waterways. In the Philippines, on Anauayan Island, fishermen festoon their boats with garlands of flowers and create a lively "sea parade." Each boat has a queen who throws flowers and fruit to those on shore. Brazilians honour Our Lady of Sailors every January 1 with a naval parade.

Parades with more overtly religious content are also part of the Christmas season. The POSADAS, with their parades of believers re-enacting the search of the Holy Family for lodging, fill the streets of Mexico every night for the nine evenings before December 25. In the Philippines the equivalent is the *panuluyan*, believed to have been introduced from Mexico during the 18th century. A couple dressed in native costume and their followers wander through the streets to dramatize the plight of Mary and Joseph in Bethlehem. They stop at four of five pre-arranged balconies to plead in poetry for a place to stay the night. At each stop they are refused, and they eventually proceed to the church plaza, where a symbolic cave has been erected. In the Austrian Alps an old custom called the *Josephstragen* ("Carrying Joseph") called for a parade of boys to carry a statue of St. Joseph from one house to another on the evenings before Christmas. In Alaska, young boys from the Orthodox churches take part in processions called "Carrying the Star." One boy carries a star mounted on a pole, followed by two lantern-bearers, and a crowd goes with them from house to house, sometimes stopping in for refreshments. On some nights they might be chased by costumed "Herod's men," representing the attempt by King Herod to kill the baby Jesus and the children of Bethlehem.

In Switzerland Christmas begins with the *Klausjagen*, the "pursuit of Saint Nicholas." On St. Nicholas Eve, December 5, in the village of Kussnacht, hundreds of marchers carry huge bishops' mitres made of cardboard and containing a lighted candle. They, along with bands, bell-carriers, and men cracking whips in front of the loud procession, escort the saint through the town. In Scandinavia the ST. LUCIA processions take place on December 13, St. Lucia's Day, which begins the Christmas season. The Lucia bride, wearing a crown of fir with lit candles, leads a train of schoolchildren dressed in white and carrying candles. December 26 is the feast of ST. STEPHEN, a day on which special attention is paid to HORSES in keeping with the tradition that Stephen was a stable-boy. In some rural areas of Sweden, horses are brought out to be blessed and ridden three times around the church. "Staffan Riders" parade through villages singing carols in honour of the patron saint of horses. The THREE KINGS and their servants lead the parades in Spain and parts of Spanish America on Epiphany Eve, January 5, the day that marks the appearance of the Magi before the baby Jesus and his earthly parents.

In Congo, it is sometimes the custom to present a "love offering" to the Christ Child on his birthday. Congregation members gather in the morning to listen to carols sung by special musical groups. The most important part of the service is the "March Around Offering," in which everyone takes part: all parade around the altar, each one laying his or her birthday gift of money or produce on a raised platform.

Paradise Tree   The central prop in the medieval Paradise Play, staged on December 24, the feast of SAINTS ADAM AND EVE. It represented the Garden of Eden, and particularly the tree from which Eve plucked the fruit for Adam, the act that led to the fall of humanity and the expulsion from Paradise. Hung with apples, or sometimes wafers representing the host of the mass, the Paradise Tree was the precursor of the Christmas tree. When such medieval mystery plays fell into disfavour with church authorities, it became the custom in some German homes to decorate a wooden PYRAMID with greenery and ornamentation in imitation of the Paradise tree. In Bavaria *Paradeis* was for a long time the term used for the Christmas tree.

Parol   A star-shaped lantern used in Philippine Christmas decoration and processions, representing the Star of Bethlehem. Originally made of bamboo and paper, they are now often quite large and elaborate.

Parrandas   The Puerto Rican tradition of singers going from house to house at Christmas. Their songs are less religious than they are celebrations of the island's holiday culture and the foods prepared for the season. At the end of their performance the *parrandistas* are rewarded with food and drink.

"The Parson Has Lost His Cloak"   A traditional English Christmas game whose rules are now lost to us. A passage from *The Spectator* of 1712 refers to it:

> Mr Spectator
>   I desire to know in your Next, if the merry Game of the Parson has lost his Cloke, is not mightily in Vogue amongst the fine Ladies this Christmas; because I see they wear Hoods of all Colours, which I suppose is for that Purpose; if it is, and you think it proper, I will carry some of those Hoods with me to our Ladies in Yorkshire; because they injoined me to bring them something from London that was very new. If you can

> tell any Thing in which I can obey their Commands more agreeably, be pleas'd to inform me, and you will extreamly oblige,
> Your humble Servant

The Passions of Carol (1975)   There have been many variations on Charles Dickens's *A Christmas Carol*: it has been set in London, in the American Midwest, in black ghettoes, and in modern television studios; Scrooge has been played by men, women, Muppets, puppets, and cartoon ducks. Few versions, however, have stretched the genre as much as *The Passions of Carol*, a 1975 pornographic movie starring Merrie Holiday. Directed by Warren Evans, the movie examines the change of heart Christmas brings to Carol Screwge, a cruel editor of a skin magazine.

Pasteles   Traditional Spanish Caribbean Christmas food. Similar to *tamales*, they are banana or plantain leaves filled with a variety of stuffings, tied up, and steamed. They are often made communally by groups of women, some chopping, some stuffing, some wrapping. A Venezuelan dish that resembles *pasteles* is *hallacas*; in Nicaragua the equivalent is *nacatamales*.

A Puerto Rican song proclaims:

> If you serve pasteles
> Bring them steaming hot.
> I'll end up with heartburn
> If steaming hot they're not.

Pastoral Drama   Christmas drama grew out of medieval Easter-time tropes (phrases or verses introduced as embellishments into the mass). By the 11th century the "Officium Pastorum," "The Shepherds' Liturgy," included a crèche scene with singing angels and clerics acting as shepherds. When such drama outgrew the church building and moved into the open air, it was performed in the vernacular and began to include other characters, such as Herod and the devil, and local humour and dialect. The best-known English example is the 15th-century drama from Wakefield known as *The Second Shepherds' Play*, which has strong comic elements. In Spain such plays are called *autos de nacimiento*. In Germany they were called *Herbergsuchen* ("Search for an Inn").

Survivors of medieval European miracle plays abound: in the Philippines and Mexico they are called *pastorelas*, in France *pastorales*, in Brazil *pastorhinas*. They focus on the shepherds of Bethlehem who are told by an angel of the birth of Jesus. In Mexico the devil plays a part in the proceedings as he tries to prevent the shepherds from bringing their gifts to the Holy Family. Standard characters include Lucifer and his assistants, angels, shepherds, and the hermit, but many other parts vary locally. (See colour fig. 17.)

Los Pastores   A folk play of medieval origins that is performed in Mexico and the southwest United States at Christmas. It tells the story of shepherds on their way to worship the baby Jesus and the trials they encounter. The cast is large and full of colourful characters, such as the Devil and his little assistants, the *diabolitos*, who are furious at the news of a Saviour being born, a hermit, angels, a drunk named Bartolo, who will finally renounce his life of debauchery, and his wife. The plays may or may not be performed according to a script; in many instances it is oral tradition that passes along the dialogue and stage directions. The end of the play is often the singing of "Noche Buena, Noche Santa," the Spanish-language version of "Silent Night," in which the cast is joined by the audience.

"Pat-a-Pan"   A French carol from Burgundy written by the prolific Bernard de la Monnoye (1641-1728), probably around the year 1700. The Canadian composer Bruce Carlson has written a particularly beautiful arrangement of this tune.

> Willie, take your little drum,
> Robin, bring your fife, and come,
> And be merry while you play.
>
> *Turelurelu. Patapatapan.*
> *Come be merry while you play,*
> *On this joyous Christmas day.*
>
> God and man became today,
> More in tune than fife and drum,
> So be merry while you play.
>
> *Chorus*

Paul VI   Giovanni Battista Montini (1897-1978) was elected pope, taking the name of Paul VI, in 1963. In 1969 he demoted a number of saints, including St. Nicholas, from the calendar, making the traditional December 6 observations no longer mandatory.

The pope was a devotee of manger scenes, ordering a new one for the papal chapel and placing the image of the baby Jesus there himself. From 1968 he blessed the manger figures brought to St. Peter's Square by thousands of children on the Sunday before Christmas.

Peacock   An animal whose presence in Nativity art is a symbol of immortality, based on the belief that the bird's flesh never rotted and that its tail could renew itself. According to legend, anyone who ate a whole peacock would become immortal.

In Fra Angelico's 15th-century *Adoration of the Magi*, a peacock perches on the stable roof overseeing the startling events (see colour fig. 18). The bird was also a feature of medieval Christmas feasts and was often served with its cooked flesh presented inside its feathers.

Pease, R.H.   A printer and variety store owner of Albany, New York, who distributed the first American-made Christmas cards in the early 1850s. These were black-and-white cards depicting a family scene in the centre with pictures on the corners of Santa Claus, dancers at a ball, Christmas presents, and a building marked "The Temple of Fancy." The text read, "Pease's Great Varety [sic] Store in the Temple of Fancy."

Peerie Guizers   On the Shetland Islands it was the custom to go door-to-door in disguise to get a coin or treat in return for Christmas blessings. The peerie guizers also once ventured out on New Year's Day, but this has been replaced by the Scottish custom of FIRST-FOOTING.

Pelzmartin   "Furry Martin," a German helper who accompanies the gift-bringer if gifts are delivered on November 11, St. Martin's Day.

Pelznickel   "Furry Nicholas," a German helper who accompanies the gift-bringer. See BELSNICKEL.

Perchtenlaufen   In parts of Germany and Austria, wildly costumed *Perchten* figures go about before Christmas making noises and re-enacting the perpetual battle between good and evil, light and darkness, spring and winter. The two aspects of Perchta or BERCHTA, the kindly rewarder and vengeful punisher, are represented in the *Schönperchten* ("beautiful Perchten") figures and their ugly counterparts.

Père Noël   In most of France the gift-bringer is Père Noël, a tall old man with a white beard who is clothed – more like England's Father Christmas than the American Santa Claus – in a long hooded robe edged with white fur. Like Santa, he carries a sack (in some areas, a basket) filled with toys but, lacking a sleigh and reindeer, he travels about with a donkey. On Christmas Eve he enters the house down the chimney and leaves presents for children underneath the tree or in their shoes, which are placed by the crèche or the fireplace. It is customary for children to leave him a snack and some fodder for his donkey. An earlier French gift-bringer was the figure representing the Christ Child, known as Le Petit Jésus or Le Petit Noël, but he has largely been displaced by Père Noël.

Le Père Noël est une ordure (1982)   This French film by director Jean-Marie Poiré, also known as *Santa Claus Is a Louse*, has become a cult favourite. Set in an office of social workers on Christmas Eve, the black comedy deals with the adventures of a series of misfits who arrive for help. Nora Ephron attempted, with much less success, to remake this movie in English as *Mixed Nuts*.

"The Perils of Certain English Prisoners"   A story published for Christmas 1857 by Charles Dickens, though not written in its entirety by him. It concerns an English marine who battles pirates in Central America and who falls in love with a lady above his station in life.

"Personent hodie"   A hymn for CHILDERMAS found in the PIÆ CANTIONES of 1582. Musicologists have speculated that this song was written for the choirboys' feasts in cathedrals during the December 28 tenure of the BOY BISHOP. For an English version see "ON THIS DAY THE EARTH SHALL RING."

Peru   Christmas in Peru mixes the Spanish heritage of the country's colonial past with the native American experience to produce a noisy, pious, and colourful celebration. The season begins in late November, when Christmas markets open. Peruvians are devotees of the home Nativity scene and are always looking for new figures to add to the crèche or new backdrops and landscapes in which to display them; carvings by the native Quechuans, in wood or plaster, are becoming sought-after around the world. These crèches are set up in churches and homes and can become quite complex as pieces are added every year.

During December, fairs and festivals are common, with music in the streets played on native instruments such as the harp, Indian flute, and whistle. Peruvians have adopted the traditional *villancico*, or Christmas carol, and made it their own, singing them in Spanish or in native languages. Popular carols include "Allegria, allegria en Navidad" ("Joy, Joy at Christmas"), "Vamos pastores" ("Let's Go Shepherds"), "Chillín, chillín campanilla" ("Bells Are Ringing"), and "Rueda, rueda" ("Roll, Roll").

As in all of Latin America, Christmas Eve is the time for the family dinner and the midnight church service. Turkey is usually the main dish, with *papas a la Huancaína* (a potato salad) or *tamales*. *Paneton* fruit cake and chocolate is served for dessert, with champagne the beverage of choice. *Noche Buena* is the night when children open their presents and see what Santa Claus has put in the stockings placed by the crèche. At midnight the image of the baby Jesus is placed in the manger, and fireworks continue long into the night.

From Christmas to Epiphany, Peruvians continue to celebrate. There are bull fights in the cities, processions, more fireworks, dances, and parties. High in the Andes, in the Huancayo district, native miners hold the exotic Dance of the Beasts and Birds complete with masked dancers and animals they have snared to populate the manger scene in the churches. On January 6 Peruvians keep the old custom of the ROSCA DE REYES, the King's Ring, which contains a surprise hidden within.

Pesebre   A Spanish-language term for the crèche. See also BELEN and NACIMIENTO.

Pfeffernuss   A small, usually ball-shaped cookie flavoured with cinnamon, allspice, anise, and black pepper, made especially during the Christmas season in Germany.

Pheasant   This symbol, when found in Nativity art, means loyalty and faithfulness in marriage. (See colour fig. 18.)

Philipovka   In Eastern Christian churches, a period of fasting in preparation for Christmas. This penitential season is called *Philipovka*, the Fast of Philip, because it formerly began on November 15, the day after the feast of St. Philip and 40 days before Christmas, but it has now been reduced in some churches to the 15 days before Christmas. During this fast no particular penitential acts are required, but the faithful are encouraged to keep the season holy. Mondays, Wednesdays, and Fridays are traditionally observed by abstinence from certain foods.

Philippines   Christmas in the Philippines is a colourful and multicultural affair, with influences from Spain, Mexico, China, and the United States mingling with native customs.

The Philippine observance of Christmas is one of the most protracted in the world. Christmas carols are played on the radio as early as September, stores hold Christmas sales in October, while much of November is taken up in preparing foods and home decorations. Unlike North Americans, for whom the holiday is increasingly family-centred, Filipinos keep many customs that involve the whole community in the celebration.

The Christmas season officially begins on December 16 with the first of a novena of early morning masses. This is the pre-dawn *Misa de Aguinaldo* ("Gift Mass") when the faithful gather at 3 a.m.; it was once customary for bands to tour the streets to wake up the town for the church service. The novena culminates on Christmas Eve in the *Misa de Gallo* ("Rooster Mass") held at midnight, after which the family gathers for the *noche buena*, the midnight feast, that breaks the fast many have devoutly kept all day.

Foods vary regionally across the vast Philippine archipelago, and Christmas dining reflects the diverse cultural influences. Chinese ham is found on many tables, along with American roast turkey and the indigenous *puto bumbong* (sticky violet rice in bamboo tubes, served with grated coconut and sugar) or *pacpac* (fried pig's ears favoured on Luzon). The Spanish heritage of the Philippines can be seen in desserts such as almond *turonne* (nougat), *pastillas*, or meringue rolls.

Visitors to the Philippines cannot escape the sight of the *parol*, the ubiquitous five-pointed star lantern. The *parol*, representing the Star of Bethlehem, is found in every home, office,

school, and shopping mall. Originally made from bamboo sticks and rice paper and meant to contain a candle, *parols* are now often spectacular affairs, lit by electricity and made by community effort. In Pampagna, home of the San Fernando lantern festival, where each Christmas Eve prizes are awarded for the most stunning *parol*, the lanterns are fabulously large and have to be transported on the backs of trucks.

The *belen* ("Bethlehem"), the Filipino version of the crèche, is found in many homes. They range from simple homemade creations to more extensive commercially produced depictions of the Holy Family, shepherds, livestock, and the Magi gathered around the manger. Churches, too, display *belens* on the altar, every day adding a new piece and placing a figure of the baby Jesus in the crib on Christmas Eve. This is a custom brought to the Philippines from Mexico in the 18th century, when both countries were part of the Spanish Empire.

Another Mexican import is the *panuluyan*, a street drama and procession derived from the POSADAS. A couple depicting Mary and Joseph walk through the town on the evenings before Christmas requesting shelter. They are ritually turned down until they and their train of followers come to a shelter prepared for them. In some parts of the country, Mary rides a donkey and is padded to look very pregnant; in other areas she rides in a little cart.

The gift-bringers in the Philippines used to be the Three Kings, as was customary in areas colonized by Spain, and gifts were exchanged on Epiphany, which celebrated the arrival of the Magi. By the late 20th century, however, the pervasive influence of American culture created a generation gap – for younger people Santa Claus increasingly became the pre-eminent bringer of presents, and these were opened on Christmas Day. The Christmas tree found in many homes is another example of the spread of American customs.

December 28 is marked as Holy Innocents' Day (see CHILDERMAS) and, as in Spain, kept in much the same way North Americans keep April Fool's Day, a time to play pranks on friends and family.

The Christmas season ends on January 6 with Epiphany, or Three Kings' Day.

Philocalian Calendar   The earliest reliable documentation of a celebration of the birth of Christ on December 25. Known as the "Chronograph" or the Calendar of Furius Dionysius Philocalus, this is a set of chronologies from both secular and Christian sources. A list of Roman consuls contains the notation *I p Chr. Caesare et Paulo sat. XIII Hoc cons. Dns. ihs. xpc natus est VIII Kal. Ian de ven. luna XV* ("Christ is born during the consulate of C. Caesar Augustus and L. Aemilianus Paulus on 25 December, a Friday, the 15th day of the new moon").

Though the work seems to have been compiled in 354, it is believed that it refers to practices in place as early as 336.

Piæ Cantiones   A collection of 74 songs assembled in 1582 by Theodoric Petri and the source of much of the Christmas music sung today. Entitled *Piæ Cantiones ecclesiasticae et scholasticae veterum episcoporum* ("Devout ecclesiastical and scholastic songs of the old bishops"), this collection of medieval Latin songs was intended for the pupils of the cathedral school in Turku, Finland. Many of these songs seem to have been of Finnish origin and others from different European countries. The first English edition by G.R. Woodward was published in 1910, but before then musicologists had used the collection to create such English Christmas carols as "Good King Wenceslas" and "Of the Father's Love Begotten."

The Pickwick Papers *A Christmas party in an English country home, from* The Pickwick Papers *by Charles Dickens.*

Pickle, Christmas A glass pickle ornament is hidden on the Christmas tree on Christmas Eve and good luck (or an extra present) goes to the first one to find it. Originally a German custom from the ornament-making district of Lauscha, it has spread to the United States.

The Pickwick Papers A novel by Charles Dickens first published in serial form in 1836-37, with the December 1836 issue containing a description of a Christmas spent by Samuel Pickwick and his friends at the home of Mr. Wardle at Dingley Dell. The description of the dance, the parlour games, and the story-telling is reminiscent of a traditional rural holiday and lacks the notion of Christmas as a time for charity that dominates Dickens's 1843 *A Christmas Carol*.

> Now, the screaming had subsided, and faces were in a glow, and curls in a tangle, and Mr Pickwick, after kissing the old lady as before mentioned, was standing under the mistletoe, looking with a very pleased countenance on all that was passing around when the young lady with the black eyes, after a little whisper with the other young ladies, made a sudden dart forward, and putting her arm round Mr Pickwick's neck, saluted him affectionately on the left cheek; and before Mr Pickwick distinctly knew what was the matter, he was surrounded by the whole body, and kissed by every one of them.
>
> It was a pleasant thing to see Mr Pickwick in the centre of the group, now pulled this way, and then that, and first kissed on the chin, and then on the nose, and then on the spectacles: and to hear the peals of laughter which were raised on every side; but it was a still more pleasant thing to see Mr Pickwick, blinded shortly afterwards with a silk handkerchief; falling up against the wall, and scrambling into corners, and going through all the mysteries of blind-man's buff, with the utmost relish for the game, until at last he caught one of the poor relations, and then had to evade if blind-man himself; which he did with a nimbleness and agility that elicited the admiration and applause of all beholders. The poor relations caught the people who they thought would like it, and when the game flagged, got caught themselves. When they were all tired of blind-man's buff, there was a great game at snapdragon, and when fingers enough were burned with that, and all the raisins were gone, they sat down by the huge fire of blazing logs to a substantial supper, and a mighty bowl of wassail, something smaller than an ordinary wash-house copper, in which the hot apples were hissing and bubbling with a rich look, and a jolly sound, that were perfectly irresistible.
>
> 'This,' said Mr Pickwick, looking round him, 'this is, indeed, comfort.'
>
> 'Our invariable custom,' replied Mr Wardle. 'Everybody sits down with us on Christmas eve, as you see them now – servants and all; and here we wait, until the clock strikes twelve, to usher Christmas in, and beguile the time with forfeits and old stories. Trundle, my boy, rake up the fire.'

Pikkijoulu "Little Christmas" in Finnish, the custom of seasonal parties at office or home.

Piñata In Mexico a container, made of clay or papier-maché – decorated to look like any number of fantastic and colourful objects, such as birds, animals, stars, or clowns – containing the *colación*, candy, fruit, toys, or other treats, that spill out when the *piñata* is struck. Traditionally the *piñata* is suspended from a hook by a rope which can be moved up and down while blindfolded children try to strike it with a stick. It is a fixture at Mexican Christmas festivities. It derives from the Italian *pignatta* and was brought to Mexico by 16th-century missionaries.

Pintard, John (1759-1844) Merchant and civic leader in New York, founder of the New-York Historical Society and promoter of a new sort of Christmas. Dissatisfied with the rowdy and uncouth New Year's celebrations of early 19th-century America, he proposed a home-centred Christmas festival. He also introduced St. Nicholas to American literature, sponsoring an 1810 pamphlet showing the saint bringing Christmas gifts to children. Along with other KNICKERBOCKERS, he helped change the season from one of drunken, outdoor revelry to an indoor, domestic holiday centred on the family with the figure of Santa Claus playing an important role.

"A Pleasant Countrey New Ditty: Merrily Shewing How to Drive the Cold Winter Away" A 17th-century ballad drawn from the Roxburghe Collection. It was to be sung to the tune of "Drive the Cold Winter Away" or "When Phoebus Did Rest."

> All hayle to the days that merite more praise than all the rest of the year;
> And welcome the nights, that double delights as well for the poor as the peer:
> Good fortune attend each merry man's friend that doth but the best that he may,
> Forgetting old wrongs with Carrols and Songs to drive the cold winter away.
>
> The Court all in state now opens her gate an bids a free welcome to most;
> The City likewise tho' somewhat precise doth willingly part with her cost;

And yet, by report from City to Court the Countrey gets
the day:
More Liquor is spent, and better content, to drive the cold
winter away.

Thus none will allow of solitude now, but merrily greets
the time,
To make it appeare of all the whole yeare that this is
accounted the Prime,
December is seene apparel'd in greene and January, fresh
as May,
Comes dancing along with a cup or a Song to drive the
cold winter away.

This time of the yeare is spent in good cheare, kind
neighbours together to meet
To sit by the fire, with friendly desire each other in love
to greet:
Old grudges forgot are put in a pot, all sorrows aside
they lay;
The old and the young doth carrol this Song, to drive the
cold winter away.

To maske and to mum kind neighbours will come with
Wassels of nut-browne Ale,
To drinke and carouse to all in this house, as merry as
buck in the pale;
Where cake, bread and cheese, is brought for your fees to
make you the longer stay;
The fire to warme will do you no harme, to drive the cold
winter away.

When Christmas tide comes in like a Bride, with Holly and
Ivy clad, –
Twelve dayes in the yeare much mirth and good cheare in
every household is had:
The Countrey guise is then to devise some gambols of
Christmas play;
Whereas the yong men do best that they can to drive the
cold winter away.

When white-bearded Frost hath threatened his worst, and
fallen from Branch and Bryer,
And time away cals from husbandry hals, and from the
good countryman's fire,
Together to go to Plow and to sow, to get us both food
and array:
And thus with content the time we have spent to drive the
cold winter away.

Plough Monday *Merriment around a decorated plough is a feature
of Plough Monday, the end of the Christmas season.*

Plough Monday   In England, the first Monday after Twelfth
Day (January 6), when agricultural labourers returned to work
and, in many places, Christmas decorations were taken down.
It was also a time when decorated ploughs were paraded
through the villages to raise money for candles used in blessing the coming agricultural year – a ceremony in which a
plough was brought into the church – or just simply for a
party to mark the end of the holidays. The men who dragged
the plough were called Plough Stots, Bullocks, Jacks, or Jags,
and the implement itself was called the Fool. Should anyone
refuse to make a donation, the men ploughed up the yard in
front of the house in revenge.

The superstitious connection between the plough and fertility is seen in the folk belief that young women who draw the
plough, or even sit on it or touch it, will soon be married and
blessed with children. A related custom in Romania was called
plugusorul, in which boys took decorated ploughs from house
to house accompanied by bells and pipers.

Plough Monday in modern England is frequently the occasion for morris-dancing and St. George plays.

Plygain *The Welsh early-morning carol service, depicted on a
British Christmas stamp.*

Plygain   A pre-dawn church service on Christmas morning in
Wales, the last surviving remnant of the pre-Reformation
Sarum rite. It was customary for many to spend the long night
waiting for the service singing and celebrating in the company
of friends and family. The service was lit by special *plygain*
candles and consisted largely of singing carols. The service
was originally a Catholic ceremony, but it survived in the
Anglican tradition when Wales converted to Protestantism
and was kept alive in the 19th century by Methodist churches.
In Carmarthenshire, people paraded through the streets with
torches on Christmas Eve before the service. *Plygain* gradually
disappeared from most areas, because so many of the participants passed the time waiting for the service by getting drunk.

The name seems to derive from the Latin *pulli cantus*, or
"cock crow song," which suggests that carol singing was long a
part of the custom. A related observance that survives on the
Isle of Man is the *Oie'l Verrey*.

Podblyudnuiya   Russian songs formerly sung during Christmas
to accompany a fortune-telling ritual. Young people dropped
rings or other trinkets into a bowl (*bliudo*) of water which was
afterwards covered with a cloth and around which they sang
podblyudnuiya songs. At the end of each song, one of the trinkets would be drawn at random and an omen derived from
the nature of the words just sung.

Pohutukawa *Metrosideros excelsa*, called the Christmas tree of New Zealand, because it flowers in December with beautiful red blossoms amid dark green leaves. A pohutukawa tree grows on the cliffs at Cape Reinga at the northern end of New Zealand, the spot that the Maori believe is the departure point for the spirits of the dead. To say that someone "has slid down the pohutukawa root" is to say he has passed on.

The native Maori are wont to predict a long hot summer when pohutukawa trees bloom early. Unfortunately the pohutukawa have been endangered by the introduction from Australia of possums, who have made it their favourite food and eradicated it from some of the coastal areas. (See colour fig. 19.)

Poinsettia Also called Christmas Star, *Euphorbia pulcherima* is a shrub native to Mexico and known to the Aztecs (who called it *cuitlaxochitz*, or "false flower") for its use as a dye and medicine. Poinsettia is connected to Christmas through the Mexican legend of a child walking to church on Christmas Eve with only weeds to give the baby Jesus. Jesus miraculously turns them to beautiful red blooms, known ever after as *Flores de Noche Buena*, "Flowers of the Holy Night." They were used in Nativity processions by Franciscan friars as early as the 17th century. Brought back to the United States in the 19th century by ambassador Joel R. Poinsett, an amateur botanist, most are now grown in California.

The red part of the plant is composed of bracts, small inner leaves; the flowers are actually the bright yellow buds in the centre of the cluster. In the wild the plant can grow three or four metres high, but it seldom grows nearly so big in indoor pots. A milky latex in the stems and leaves can be irritating to the skin, but is not, despite common belief, fatal. Domesticated varieties are available in a variety of colours – white, pink, and even striped – but red is most popular at Christmas.

Poland Advent in Poland is full of saints' days that call for particular observances. On the eve of St. Andrew's Day, November 29, young people customarily play fortune-telling games to find out whom they will marry or when. On St. Barbara's Day, December 4, dances are held, and it is also traditional to place a cherry bough indoors in water in the hope that it will bloom before Christmas and bring good luck to the family. December 6 is St. Nicholas's Day, when children receive small gifts in the shoes they have left out for the saint. In some places the saint himself (known in Poland as Mikolaj) might appear in his bishop's robes and quiz the children on their catechism or ask them to recite a little prayer. Good children got treats and bad children received coal or twigs in token of the thrashing they deserved. The rest of Advent is spent preparing for Christmas, cleaning the house, baking, and obtaining the OPLATEK wafer for Christmas Eve dinner. Devout Catholics, intent on spiritual preparation, often attend the *Roraty*, the early morning mass where the Advent candle is lit.

Christmas Eve is the *Wigilia*, or Vigil, when Poles keep a 24-hour fast broken only when the first star is detected in the evening sky. The head of the house then breaks the *oplatek*, shares it with the family (and sometimes the family's livestock in the barn), and the feasting can begin. Because it is not yet midnight, the meal must contain no meat. The custom is to have an uneven number of meatless dishes (the quantity depending on the household's wealth) and an even number of diners, with one place left empty for a stranger, the spirits of dead family members, or the Holy Spirit. Straw is placed under the table or tablecloth in memory of the Christ Child's manger, and a sheaf of wheat, a fertility symbol, is placed in a corner.

Traditional Christmas Eve foods vary regionally, but most often include carp, which must be bought alive and kept swimming (often in the bathtub) until shortly before it is to be prepared. Mushroom and beet soups are favourites, as are dumplings with sauerkraut and other fillings, varieties of fish, potatoes, and noodles with poppy seeds. Desserts include strudel, fruit compotes, and *kutya*, a dish made with grain, nuts, or raisins and honey. *Krupnik*, a holiday brandy, is also served. After dinner the family goes to church for *Pasterka*, the Shepherds' Mass. Presents, brought by the Star Man, or the Little Star, or (increasingly of late) Santa Claus are opened after the *Wigilia*.

Christmas Day is spent relaxing with the immediate family and dining on food prepared beforehand. In honour of the Saviour's birth, no cooking, cleaning, or other work is done. December 26, Saint Stephen's Day, is a time for visiting, parties, and carolling.

Poles have a rich musical heritage, which is evident in the Christmas season. Carols, or *koledy*, are numerous and date back to the Middle Ages. Among the favourite Christmas hymns are "Weród nocnej ciszy" ("In Night's Deep Silence"), which begins the mass and "Bóg sí rodzi" ("God Is Born"), sung at the end of the mass. The 14th-century "W ZLOBIE LEZY" has become popular in translation as "Infant Holy, Infant Lowly." Carollers still go door-to-door in the rural areas of Poland, one carrying a star, one dressed as King Herod, and others as angels and shepherds.

Since the late 18th century, Poles have put up Christmas trees, but this custom is pre-dated by the *podlazniczka*, the top of a fir or spruce tree, which was hung from the rafters or on the barn door. These were decorated like the free-standing trees, with fruit, candles, and wafers. In the 19th century the importation of German ornaments triggered a nationalist reaction that led to the production of folk-art tree decorations. Present-day Polish trees are adorned with a combination of commercial ornaments and homemade decorations of straw, paper, and wafers, along with candies and fruit.

Crèches are important in the Polish celebration of Christmas, both in the form of "puppet cribs" and Nativity scenes. "Puppet cribs" are a type of puppet drama developed by the clergy during the 1700s, and involve not only references to the Nativity story but also secular satire. Crèches are found in many churches and homes, but the most spectacular ones can be seen in the annual contest held in Krakow. There, artists and amateurs compete to produce the most striking crèche, all of which must be modelled on the architecture of the city's St. Mary's church. Every year in early December, the entrants are put on display in the Old Market square.

The Polar Express A moody and atmospheric children's book about a magic train that takes a small boy to the North Pole on Christmas Eve. Although there is nothing much to the plot – the boy boards the train, visits the city of toy factories, is given a bell by Santa Claus, loses and then regains his gift – the real charm in this 1985 book by Chris Van Allsburg lies in the superb and evocative illustrations done by the author.

A 1988 animated short film was based on the book.

Polaznik In Slavic Eastern Europe, the *polaznik* is the first visitor of Christmas Day. His appearance is pre-arranged and ritualistic, and resembles the FIRST-FOOTER at the Scottish New Year, whose purpose is to bring good fortune on the house. On entering the home, he scatters grain and announces,

"Christ is born," whereupon a family member throws grain on the visitor and says, "He is born indeed." The *polaznik* strikes the Yule log so that sparks fly up, and recites a wish for good luck for the family and farm. Sometimes he places money on the log to symbolize the prosperity wished for in the coming year. He stays for the day, eats the Christmas meal with the family, and departs in the evening with a gift.

"The Poor Relation's Story"   A sentimental Christmas story by Charles Dickens from 1852, in which a family telling stories around the fire hears the poor relation tell of the rich life he leads in his imagination.

Pope's Christmas Message   A customary message to the world delivered by the Roman Catholic pontiff on or near Christmas Day, often on behalf of the cause of peace. One of the most famous of these speeches came in 1942, in the midst of the Second World War, when Pope Pius XII protested the fact that hundreds of thousands were being persecuted "solely because of their race or ancestry." The German ambassador to the Vatican complained that Pius was "clearly speaking on behalf of the Jews." In 1990 Pope John Paul II used the occasion to call for peace in the Persian Gulf as war with Iraq loomed; in 1998 he appealed for an end to the death penalty.

Portugal   The Portuguese prepare for Christmas in ways similar to their cousins in many other Latin countries: decorating the home, taking part in religious devotions, re-enacting the Nativity (the *Auto da Natividade*), and setting up the crèche. Known as the *présepio*, the manger scene appears all over, in schools, churches, and homes. The Portuguese have also adopted the Christmas tree, both natural and artificial, under which children expect to find presents on Christmas Eve. For centuries they have also cherished the Yule log, the *fogueira da consoada*, to whose ashes they have traditionally ascribed powers to protect against disease and thunderstorms.

As the big day gets closer, shoppers carefully select the main elements of the festive meals to come. The favourite dish of Christmas Eve, or *Vespera de Natal*, is the *bacalhau*, dried, salted cod from the North Atlantic. Bought in fish stores or supermarkets, these huge, flattened fish must be soaked for days before being boiled. Those shopping for turkey might seek out a dealer in live birds who will prepare the unlucky fowl in the old-fashioned way: the turkey has liquor poured down its throat and, after a short but intoxicating period of freedom, collapses. Its throat is cut, it is plucked on the spot, and then taken home to be bathed in lemon- and laurel-scented water before being roasted.

Christmas Eve means attendance at midnight mass, the big family dinner of cod and boiled potatoes, and the opening of the presents brought by Santa Claus or the Christ Child. The next day, *Dia da Familia*, or *Dia Natal*, the turkey is eaten, with cake, *rabanadas* (French toast), fruit, and wine for dessert.

In early January groups of children go about singing *janeiros*, songs about the baby Jesus or the coming of the Three Kings. As they go door-to-door they are rewarded with coins, cakes, or fruit. The season ends on January 6 with the eating of the *bola-rei*, or King Cake, which, like all Epiphany cakes, has a little surprise baked into it. Whoever finds a bean in his piece must pay for the cake at the next party.

Portugal has a number of remarkable customs associated with Christmas. Among them is the *Festa dos Rapages*, held in the northeast part of the country. It is part initiation and part rowdy Christmas festival. The *rapages* are teenage boys who are segregated for a short period between Christmas and Epiphany. They emerge in bright costumes, masks, and carrying sticks, and go door-to-door bearing gifts or performing a satirical play on the year's events in the community. At the end they doff their masks and attend mass. The *rapages* can only participate in the festival once. When it is over they are boys no longer and can now number themselves among the men of the village.

Las Posadas   "The Lodgings" or "The Inn," a nine-day Latin American celebration preceding Christmas which re-enacts the journey of Joseph and Mary to Bethlehem, where they are refused shelter at an inn.

Based on the suggestion by St. Ignatius of Loyola that a novena (a set of prayers on nine successive days) would remind the faithful of the journey to Bethlehem, the Spanish mystic St. John of the Cross put it into practice in 1580. Seven years later Friar Diego de Soria, hoping to replace native pagan midwinter celebrations, got permission to celebrate Christmas masses with a similar re-enactment in Mexico. Held initially inside the church, *las posadas* evolved into an outdoor fiesta. Shortly after dark a procession forms, often headed by a child dressed as an angel and followed by two more children carrying images of Mary and Joseph. Behind them comes a crowd carrying candles and accompanied by musicians, singing *posada* songs. When the procession reaches the house chosen for that evening's enactment, it divides itself into those playing the innkeepers and those playing the weary travellers. The travellers march to a closed door, knock on it, and beg entry in song. They are at first refused by the heartless innkeepers, who then relent and invite the pilgrims inside. After a prayer at a homemade altar, a party is held which usually includes the breaking of a *piñata*. A different house is chosen to host the festivities each night, and on Christmas Eve the procession includes a figure of the Christ Child carried by a couple chosen as godparents.

The *posada* custom is now found throughout much of Latin America, including the southwestern United States and California.

Posadero   The homeowner who is taking his turn playing the innkeeper in the *posadas* drama. It is his responsibility to prepare an altar where the image of the baby Jesus will be laid and to provide a place for the party that follows the entry of the procession. Neighbours drop by to help him prepare food and drink for the evening.

Powwow, Christmas   Many North American native communities, though largely converted to Christianity, still cling to the observance of older rites such as pipe ceremonies, medicine bundle rituals, and powwows, gatherings of dancers for competition, feasting, and celebration. Christmas has come to be one of the traditional times for these dances, such as those held by the Sarcees of the Tsu'tina Nation in Alberta, and Arizona's Hot Springs Christmas Powwow.

Prancer (1989)   Directed by John D. Hancock, this is the story of nine-year-old Jessica (Rebecca Harrell), who nurses an injured reindeer in the belief that it is one of Santa's team. Her attempts to restore the animal to its rightful place are thwarted by adults, including her father (Sam Elliott), but eventually all works out for the best.

Prang, Louis   (1824-1909) Christmas card entrepreneur. After emigrating from Germany to the United States in the 1850s, Prang worked as a printer. By 1870 he owned most of the steam presses in the country and had perfected chromo-lithographic printing. In 1875 he introduced coloured Christmas cards to the United States and could not keep up with the demand; 5,000,000 were sold annually. He viewed each card as an affordable work of art and wanted to educate the public taste, sponsoring annual design awards from 1880 and commissioning leading artists to contribute. Prang made Christmas cards so popular that competitors entered the market, and by 1890 cheap imitations from Germany had driven him out of the business. Thereafter he concentrated on the manufacture of art supplies and promoting the "Prang method" of developing artistic awareness in young people.

A Prayer for Owen Meany   Owen Meany is a stunted boy who senses that he was born to a Christlike destiny and who shapes his life to meet the self-sacrificial end he has foreseen for himself. In this 1990 novel by John Irving, Christmas – in the form of Nativity pageants, allusions to Charles Dickens's *A Christmas Carol*, and reflections on the Advent of Jesus – plays an important role.

The Preacher's Wife (1996)   A remake of the 1947 Christmas classic *The Bishop's Wife*, this film manages to succeed in its own right. Instead of a white Episcopalian bishop, the protagonist is a black Presbyterian preacher (Courtney B. Vance) in an inner-city neighbourhood. Tempted to transfer out of his struggling church to a massive new one (a move that would doom his neighbourhood), the preacher ignores his wife (Whitney Houston) and family. The angel Dudley (Denzel Washington) appears at Christmastime to reunite the couple and help the preacher re-establish his priorities. Directed by Penny Marshall, the film is full of glorious gospel music.

Presepio   The Italian manger scene and the centre of household Christmas observances. Italians became interested in the crèche starting in the Middle Ages; Rome's Church of Santa Maria Maggiore maintains one that dates from the late 13th century. From the mid-17th century, the nobility became fascinated with *presepi* and started to commission and collect them. The 18th-century King of Naples, Charles IV, had a very extensive collection, 1200 pieces of which are still on display. By 1800 these aristocratic *presepi* were vast, taking up whole rooms and coming complete with volcanoes, village scenes, and waterfalls. Common folk were encouraged to place a manger scene in their home by Catholic clergy such as the Dominican monk Gregorio Maria Rocca, who believed that a *presepio* in each house would improve the moral tone of Naples. Nowadays, communities stage living *presepi*, children make them in schools, and churches display them, but most important to the celebration of Christmas in Italy are those in the home. They are set up in December without the image of the Christ Child, which is put in place only on Christmas morning. Families collect the figures of the Holy Family, shepherds, animals, townspeople, and Magi and pass them on as heirlooms. American President Lyndon Johnson's wife, Lady Bird, began the White House crèche in 1967 by purchasing Neapolitan *presepio* figures.

Presidents, American, and Christmas   The evolution of Christmas in the United States is reflected in the way American presidents have marked the holiday, from the paternalism of slave-owning Thomas Jefferson to the political correctness of the Clintons. Here are some highlights of presidential Christmases:

1800 – John and Abigail Adams burn 20 cords of wood in an attempt to warm the presidential mansion to a liveable temperature.

1805 – Thomas Jefferson hosts a children's party and plays the violin.

1808 – Jefferson writes to his overseer approving a holiday trip to Washington for his slave Davy.

1811 – Dolly Madison serves eggnog at a White House party – guests include Henry Clay and James Monroe.

1815 – Dolly Madison's pet macaw attacks a little girl; following a Southern custom guns are fired all night to "shoot Christmas in."

1828 – Andrew Jackson buries his wife on Christmas Eve.

1829 – Andrew Jackson, recently a widower and orphaned as a child himself, gathers Washington orphans, his grandnieces and nephews, and stages a mock snowball fight in the East Room.

1835 – Jackson's chef makes him a sugar-frosted pine tree surrounded by ice toy animals; his nieces and her friends set out Christmas stockings; Jackson gets a pair of slippers, a cob pipe, and a bag of tobacco.

1837 – Future president Zachary Taylor defeats the Seminoles at the Battle of Okeechobee.

1845 – Workaholic James Polk ignores Christmas except for a Christmas Eve party for some Congressmen and their wives; the Polks shun liquor and dancing.

1856 – Franklin Pierce sets up the first Christmas tree in the White House.

1857 – Future president Ulysses S. Grant pawns his watch to buy Christmas presents for his family.

1860 – James Buchanan entertains a delegation of Pawnee natives.

1862 – Tad Lincoln intervenes with his father and wins a presidential pardon for "Jack," the turkey meant to be the main course for Christmas dinner; his father and mother visit Civil War wounded in local hospitals.

1863 – Tad Lincoln sends a Christmas parcel to Union troops.

1864 – Confederate President Davis plays Santa Claus to orphans in Richmond; Tad Lincoln invites a group of street children to dinner at the White House.

1868 – Andrew Johnson signs a pardon of southern rebels.

1874 – Ulysses S. Grant entertains the King of Hawaii.

1880 – Rutherford B. Hayes begins the custom of gift-giving to White House staff; each member gets a $5 gold piece.

1883 – Chester Arthur and his daughter's Christmas Club entertain 500 children.

1885 – Chester Arthur gives all federal workers a Christmas holiday.

1890 – The Harrison grandchildren celebrate Christmas at the White House.

1891 – Harrison assures reporters he will have an "old-fashioned Christmas tree" for his grandchildren and play Santa Claus himself.

1895 – Grover Cleveland is the first to use electric lights on a presidential Christmas tree.

1896 – The Clevelands hold a carnival for their three children and those of members of Cabinet.

1902 – Conservationist Teddy Roosevelt forbids his children a tree but is convinced by a Cabinet minister, a forestry expert, to relent.

1903 – All the Roosevelt children, plus Allan the dog, open their presents on the president's bed.

1905 – Roosevelt sends his old nurse $20 for Christmas and tells her he will play hide-and-go-seek with children in the White House.

1910 – William Taft's daughter Helen becomes a debutante in the Christmas season.

1914 – Woodrow Wilson pardons two prisoners.

1916 – Wilson is on honeymoon in Virginia with his second wife.

1917 – Wilson and his wife go to the theatre and a gala dinner, followed by charades.

1918 – Wilson commutes the death sentences of two soldiers sentenced for desertion; the presidential couple spends Christmas in France with U.S. troops.

1921 – After protests by their insurance company, the Hardings remove real candles from the Christmas tree.

1923 – At the behest of electrical companies anxious to promote Christmas lighting, Calvin Coolidge begins the tradition of lighting a tree on the White House lawn; Grace Coolidge begins the custom of singing carols on the North Portico.

1925 – NBC broadcasts the tree-lighting ceremony with the Marine band playing carols; Coolidge begins the tradition of a presidential Christmas address.

1926 – Grace Coolidge hosts a ball and dances with 60 boys.

1928 – Coolidge makes Christmas Eve a holiday for federal employees.

1929 – Fire breaks out in the west wing of the White House on Christmas Eve and destroys the executive offices.

1930 – Herbert Hoover holds a children's party to gather presents for the poor.

1932 – The Hoovers spend Christmas in Panama aboard the presidential yacht, *Sequoia*.

1941 – Winston Churchill spends Christmas at the White House; he and Roosevelt attend a Methodist service, because FDR believes no one sings hymns as "lustily" as Methodists.

1942 – The White House outdoor tree is not lit for security
-43   reasons.

1944 – Franklin Delano Roosevelt reads Dickens's *A Christmas Carol* aloud to his family for the last time.

1945 – Harry Truman gives copies of his V-E Day proclamation announcing the end of the Second World War as a Christmas gift to staff.

1948 – Truman begins his custom of anonymously sending Christmas dinner and presents to a poor white and a poor black family; he lights the National Community Christmas Tree by remote control from Missouri.

1953 – Dwight D. Eisenhower sends the first official presidential Christmas card and dispatches "bushels" of toys to 73 children at a Virginia orphanage.

1954 – A life-size Nativity scene is erected near the National Community Christmas Tree; it is an annual fixture until an American Civil Liberties Union lawsuit forces its removal in 1973 (the seasonal display in Washington is now called the Pageant of Peace).

1955 – Eisenhower pardons 42 prisoners (one of them in jail since 1898) and commutes a death sentence.

1957 – Mamie Eisenhower hosts a tea party for women reporters.

1958 – Eisenhower broadcasts a Christmas message from space via the first American satellite.

1959 – Premier Kruschev of the Soviet Union gives Eisenhower a collection of Russian toys and dolls.

1961 – Jackie Kennedy plays Santa Claus to 200 at a Washington children's hospital.

1965 – Lady Bird Johnson revives White House carol-singing for a state visit by German Chancellor Erhard.

1968 – The Johnsons hold several parties for poor children.

1969 – The Nixons mail out 39,000 Christmas cards.

1972 – Jesuit Philip Berrigan and anti-war protesters stage a morality play outside the White House with President Nixon cast as Herod.

1975 – Gerald Ford points to his Christmas tree and remarks that a couple of months ago neither he nor Betty expected to be in the White House.

1979 – Jimmy Carter orders the White House Christmas tree lights to remain unlit until the hostages in Iran are released.

1980 – The Carters mail out 100,000 Christmas cards; 1,000 volunteers are necessary for the effort.

1981 – Nancy Reagan gives a party for 178 deaf children with entertainment by two of the Osborne Brothers; the Reagans commission Jamie Wyeth to paint *Christmas Eve at the White House* for the presidential Christmas card.

1984 – The Nativity scene is restored to the National Community Christmas Tree display by Supreme Court order.

1989 – President Bush spends Christmas at Camp David, a custom he will keep for each of his four years in office.

1990 – The Bush presidential Christmas card is the first to depict the Oval Office.

1992 – Vice-President-elect Gore buys his wife, Tipper, a drum set.

1993 – President Bill Clinton begins a tradition of reading "A Visit From St. Nicholas" to school children.

1993 – None of the Clinton White House "holiday cards"
-99   mention the word "Christmas."

Prince, Christmas   One of a number of terms used for the figure presiding over social inversion festivities during the Twelve Nights of Christmas. See LORD OF MISRULE.

Prophecies   A number of passages in the Old Testament are read by Christians as prophecies of the Nativity of Jesus and its accompanying events.

The coming of a Messiah from the lineage of David is detected in Isaiah 11:1: "And there shall come forth a rod out of the stem of Jesse." The virgin birth is prophesied in Isaiah 7:14: "Therefore the Lord himself shall give you a sign; Behold, a virgin shall conceive, and bear a son, and shall call his name Immanuel." The presence of the ox and the ass at the manger is seen in Isaiah 1:3: "The ox knoweth its owner and the ass his master's crib." The arrival of the Magi is presaged by Psalm 72:10: "The kings of Tarshish and of the isles shall bring presents: the kings of Sheba and Seba shall offer gifts."

That the birth of the Messiah should be in Bethlehem is foretold in these verses from Micah 5:2-3, later quoted to King Herod quoted in Matthew 2: "But thou, Bethlehem Ephratah, though thou be little among the thousands of Judah, yet out of thee shall He come forth unto me that is to be Ruler in Israel; Whose goings forth are of old, from everlasting. Therefore will He give them up until the time that she who travaileth hath brought forth; then the remnant of His brethren shall return unto the children of Israel."

The Massacre of the Innocents by Herod is the subject of Jeremiah 31:15: "Thus saith the Lord; A voice was heard in Ramah, lamentation and bitter weeping; Rachel weeping for her children, refusing to be comforted for her children, because they were not."

An influential prophecy from ancient Rome found in Virgil's fourth *Eclogue*, written c. 30 B.C., suggested to the medieval Christian mind that even pagans had foretold of Christ's coming:

Prophecies *The prophet Micah predicts the birth of the Messiah in Bethlehem.*

The last great Age, foretold by sacred Rimes,
Renews its finish'd course: Saturnian times
Roll round again; and mighty years, begun
From their first Orb, in radiant circles run,
The base degenerate iron Offspring ends;
A golden Progeny from Heaven descends.
O chaste *Lucina!* speed the Mother's pains,
And hast the glorious Birth! thy own *Apollo* reigns!
The lovely Boy, with his auspicious face,
Shall *Pollio's* consulship and triumph grace.
Majestick months set out with him to their appointed Race,
The Father banish'd virtue shall restore,
And crimes shall threat the guilty World no more.
The Son shall lead the life of Gods, and be
By Gods and Heroes seen, and Gods and Heroes see.
The jarring Nations he in peace shall bind,
And with paternal Virtues rule Mankind.
Unbidden Earth shall wreathing Ivy bring
And fragrant Herbs (the promises of Spring)
As her first offerings to her infant King.

Protoevangelium of James A second-century pseudo-gospel that contains additional material on the Nativity and the life of the Virgin Mary not found in the canonical gospels of Matthew and Luke. From it we have the stories of the Virgin's parentage, Joseph's advanced age, the birth in a cave attended by a midwife and children from Joseph's first marriage, and the miracle of Salome the midwife.

In the Eastern churches, the *Protoevangelium* had some authority, but in the West it was rejected. Many of its contents were incorporated by Jacob of Voragine in his *Golden Legend* in the 13th century and thus became part of Catholic medieval traditions about the Holy Family.

Proverbs Folk tradition claims that the future can be more clearly seen at Christmas, and thus the season is a great occasion for fortune-telling. Proverbs from many countries make predictions for the coming year based on conditions during the Christmas season. See DIVINATION and SUPERSTITIONS AND CHRISTMAS.

Pseudo-Matthew, Gospel of An apocryphal account of the Nativity dating from the sixth century and related to the PROTOEVANGELIUM OF JAMES. In it is the story of the ox and ass adoring the baby Jesus, the midwives attending the birth, the bending down of the palm trees, the fall of the Egyptian idols, and other tales that became part of medieval legend.

The book is ascribed to the writer of the Gospel of Matthew but is clearly a later product.

Psychiatry and Christmas Sigmund Freud is known to have celebrated Christmas, and his followers in the psychiatric profession have not ignored the season in their quest for understanding the deepest secrets of the human mind.

Adrianus de Groot, for example, claims that the folk customs surrounding St. Nicholas represent all the stages of the human reproductive cycle, from courtship to the production of offspring. "The symbolism could hardly be more characteristic," states the good doctor, who helpfully emphasizes the clues we should all have noticed, "the *riding* on the rooftops of *houses*, the *pouring down of sweets* and other *presents* through the *chimney*, so that all these good things fall into the *shoe* or the *barrel* beside the *fire*." Treasure is of course semen, and the story of the three murdered students whom St. Nicholas revives is the story of the "male triumvirate"; their death is the "death of the phallus."

For Richard Sterba, female imagery is the key to unlocking the heart of Christmas. The chimney and the fireplace used by

Santa Claus to enter the house are the vagina and the vulva to the unconscious mind of the child, and presents therefore come out of the birth canal. Santa Claus, with his great belly, is a pregnant woman. In fact the whole process of shopping, wrapping, and keeping secrets is symbolic of pregnancy, just as the exhaustion that follows the opening of presents resembles that after giving birth.

A Christmas Carol's Ebenezer Scrooge, who hoarded money, is diagnosed as anal-retentive by Freudians. Michael Steig reminds us of the link between feces and money and speaks of the "excremental vision" of Charles Dickens. (Other psychiatrists have dissented, noting Dickens's love of food and feasting, and have pronounced him an "oral" personality.) Walter Bortz, on the other hand, points out that Scrooge was cured by Dickensian psychotherapy and urges sufferers of Christmas funk to follow Dickens's prescription of indulgence coupled with generosity.

In seeking to understand the foundations of the psychological disorders that appear in December, James Caltrell notes that the holiday season and the presence of one's father, God, Christ, Santa Claus, and Father Time produces a syndrome marked by "diffuse anxiety, numerous regressive phenomena including marked feelings of helplessness, possessiveness, and increased irritability, nostalgia or bitter rumination about holiday experiences of youth, depressive affect, and a wish for magical resolution of problems."

For psychoanalyst Bryce Boyer, the key to Christmas depression is found in unresolved sibling rivalries. He concludes that his patients sought to obtain penises, which they hoped would win their mother's love that had previously been given to other siblings. The worship of the Christ Child, adored by his mother Mary, awakens a frustration of never being as good as the favourite child. See BLUES, CHRISTMAS.

Pudding Clubs

In 19th-century England, one way for the working poor to save enough money to pay for the Christmas meal was to put some away each week into a "club." The most common form of these were held in public houses, and diligent savers could expect a goose and a raffle ticket for a bottle of spirits in the days before Christmas. A little-known variation of this was the "pudding club." In the months or weeks before Christmas, families could deposit a small amount of money with the local grocer; these funds would be safe from impulse spending and provide the necessities to make the Christmas pudding.

Pudding, Christmas

The traditional English seasonal dessert is the Christmas plum pudding, a round, solid object, boiled and often served in flaming brandy and crowned with a sprig of holly.

Plum pudding has its origins in the medieval Christmas pottage or porridge – thick boiled dinners which (if made for the rich) contained meat and fruit. Plums were so frequently used that all fruited foods came to be called plums; thus the stew became known as plum pottage.

By the 16th century it had established itself as such a symbol of the season that "Plum Pudding" was included in Ben Jonson's 1616 CHRISTMAS HIS MASQUE as one of the children of Father Christmas. During the time of the Puritan war on Christmas, the traditional pudding was banned along with mince pie.

By the 19th century, thickeners had been added, and the solid plum pudding became the featured dessert of English Christmas dinners as described by Dickens in *A Christmas Carol*. These were made with all due ceremony, and family members often took turns stirring the pudding before it was placed in a cloth bag to be boiled (see STIR UP SUNDAY). When Queen Victoria's family adopted the dessert it became an indispensable national holiday dish.

The charms that had once been put into the TWELFTH NIGHT CAKE were now added to the pudding. For example, a ring, button, thimble, and coin were dropped in, and the recipient could expect marriage, spinsterhood, bachelorhood, or wealth in the New Year. A number of superstitions are attached to the making and eating of Christmas pudding. Some claim that it must be made with 13 ingredients and that stirring ought to be done by all members of the family, from east to west. Those who do not eat any pudding are said to be sure to lose a friend in the coming year.

Christmas Pudding *The making of the traditional English Christmas dessert as depicted in* Punch.

Puddings are also popular in other countries at Christmas: in Scandinavia it is rice pudding, while in Ukraine and Russia it is *kutya*.

"Puer natus in Bethlehem"   An anonymous 13th-century Latin carol written in Central Europe, perhaps Germany or Bohemia, found in PIÆ CANTIONES. Its lyrics were translated into German, Danish, Dutch, and English, where it appears as "A BOY [or A Child] IS BORN IN BETHLEHEM." J.S. Bach used the tune for harmonization. By the 16th century the original melody had been supplanted by its descant, which is still used today.

"Puer nobis nascitur"   A 14th-century Christmas hymn preserved in PIÆ CANTIONES. One English translation is "UNTO US A BOY IS BORN."

Puerto Rico   In Puerto Rico Christmas has been shaped both by Latin American Catholicism and the country's almost century-long association with the United States.

The season begins with the *Misas de Aguinaldo* on the nine nights before Christmas Eve. These are the pre-dawn masses that originated in Mexico in the 16th century and that have spread to other lands colonized by the Spanish, including the Philippines. Musicians play local instruments, such as native guitars, *güiros* (percussion instruments made of gourds), and maracas, and accompany the singing. Afternoon carol masses are also a feature of the days before Christmas. On Christmas Eve the faithful attend the *Misa de Gallo* ("Rooster Mass") held at midnight, a more solemn affair than the *Misas de Aguinaldo*.

Christmas Eve is the *Noche Buena*, a time for celebrating at home with the family or with the community. The meal features a turkey or roast chicken or ham, with local vegetables such as plantains, yams, and Spanish rice. PASTELES are steamed in banana leaves, rather like *tamales*.

An exciting Puerto Rican custom on the days leading up to and following Christmas is the ASALTO, or friendly home invasion. Bands of musicians called *parrandistas* descend on the homes of friends or relatives and demand to be let in. These carollers have songs for every part of the event, from the ritual denial of entry to the tardy farewell. Once inside, they are given food and drink by their host before they leave for another invasion. A couple of verses from one of these *asalto navideno* songs conveys the spirit of the occasion and shows how similar the custom is to the English WASSAIL:

Have the doors open, because
we want to celebrate
with Christmas carols
on this happy holiday.

We want rice pudding
roast pork, pasteles, and rum
to flavour it all,
and delightful pork skin of Bayamon.

Christmas carols, *aguinaldos* or *villancicos*, are sung by *trullas*, bands of singers, sometimes clothed in bright costumes. The singers go door-to-door or farm-to-farm and serenade their listeners, who reward them with hospitality, food, and drink. As in the case of the *asaltos*, the hosts often join the singers and go along for their next visit.

Many Puerto Rican families now open their Santa-delivered presents on Christmas Day, reflecting the American influence, but the traditional day for gift-giving, as in most Latin countries, is January 6, Three Kings' Day, or Epiphany. Americans have also brought the Christmas tree and its ornaments to the island, but most Catholic homes also have a crèche, or *nacimiento*, with the figures of the Holy Family, shepherds, and Magi. Many of these figures are hand-carved by *santeros*, whose traditional art is still appreciated.

December 28 is Innocents' Day in Puerto Rico, when tricks and jokes are played as in the North American custom of April Fool's Day. There are, however, places on the island that still remember the original, grim reason for the Feast of the Holy Innocents: the murder of the children of Bethlehem by the soldiers of King Herod. These towns hold a pageant where folk dressed as Herod's men go house-to-house to kidnap the first-born boy from each family. Gifts are given to Herod's soldiers to redeem the children and a party is held to celebrate the rescue.

Vispera de Epifania, Epiphany Eve, used to be the night when children, expecting the Three Kings to bring gifts, would leave out a box of hay or grass under the bed for the camels and a little snack for the Magi. Though the tradition faded as Santa Claus became popular, it is now returning, along with parades of the kings and their brightly dressed followers on *Dia de Reyes*, January 6. The day is marked by festivals, parades, puppet shows, dancing, and parties. Those who receive visitors on Three Kings' Day were traditionally expected to return the visits eight days later, the so-called *octavas*.

Punch and Judy Show   The traditional English puppet play, popular with children and widely performed during the Christmas season. The figure of Punch, a cruel braggart with a hooked nose and chin, evolved out of the short, fat *commedia dell' arte* character Punchinello. Much of the action consists of his beating his loud, nagging wife, Judy. Children seem attracted to the slapstick humour of the glove puppets, to Punch's battles with authority and his caustic witticisms, but at least one English borough council has banned the puppets because they promote domestic violence. "Young children are very impressionable," said a Colchester council spokeswoman, "Seeds are sown at a very young age."

Punkinhead   Inspired by the success of Rudolph the Red-Nosed Reindeer as an advertising tool for the Montgomery Ward department stores, the Canadian retailer Eaton's was moved to develop its own Christmas creature, Punkinhead the Sad Little Bear, who became one of Santa's helpers. Punkinhead, with his distinctive orange hair, appeared first in Eaton's 1948 Christmas parade, and for the next decade could be found in a series of 13 promotional books and on many items such as pyjamas, records, children's furniture, and toys. He was also popular with Canadian children in the form of a teddy bear.

Punkinhead was the creation of animation legend Charlie Thorson (1890-1966), who had helped develop Snow White for Walt Disney, Bugs Bunny for Warner Brothers, and Elmer the Safety Elephant for the Toronto Police Department.

La Purísima   "The Most Pure," the name in Nicaragua for the Feast of the Immaculate Conception. See NICARAGUA and "NIGHT OF THE SCREAMS."

Puritans and Christmas   The Protestant Reformation created a number of new religious groups, each with its own ideas about Christmas. While Lutherans were concerned mainly with removing the cult of saints from Christmas celebrations, and Anglicans with cleansing the season of practices such as the BOY BISHOP, Calvinist Reformers insisted on a more thorough-going approach. Using what came to be known as

Punch and Judy Show *Puppet shows have long been a part of Christmas entertainment.*

the "regulative principle of worship" as their guide, they decided to do away with Christmas altogether. John Calvin's *Commentary of Jeremiah* makes clear that whatever the Bible has not expressly commanded in regard to rites and ceremonies must be disregarded by Christians:

> There is then no other argument needed to condemn superstitions, than that they are not commanded by God: for when men allow themselves to worship God according to their own fancies, and attend not to his commands, they pervert true religion. And if this principle was adopted by the Papists, all those fictitious modes of worship, in which they absurdly exercise themselves, would fall to the ground. It is indeed a horrible thing for the Papists to seek to discharge their duties towards God by performing their own superstitions. There is an immense number of them, as it is well known, and as it manifestly appears. Were they to admit this principle, that we cannot rightly worship God except by obeying his word, they would be delivered from their deep abyss of error.

Thus Christmas, along with a host of other practices of late medieval popular religion, was suppressed in those parts of Europe where Calvinists came to power. In 1561 Scottish churchmen attacked the holiday, and at the same time Calvinists in England, known to their enemies as Puritans, campaigned against it. Queen Elizabeth I ignored such complaints and celebrated the season of Christmas with gusto,

giving and receiving presents, seeing plays, dancing, and carousing. When she died in 1603 and was replaced on the English throne by James of Scotland, it was feared by many that the new ruler would set his face against Christmas. Instead, James I proved a strong supporter of popular amusements, commissioning plays for his Christmas enjoyment and ordering his nobility to spend their holidays on their estates, where they were to keep up the traditions of hospitality and neighbourliness that the season had come to represent.

During the reign of James's son, Charles I, Puritans renewed their call for the abolition of Christmas, which to them meant a whole heap of sins: drunkenness, social inversion, gluttony, and superstition. When they came to power in the Civil War of the 1640s, they set their sights on Christmas. On Christmas Day, 1643, Puritan-owned businesses that decided to remain open in London were attacked by apprentices. Some clergy closed their churches, and Parliament was able to find enough members to conduct business. In December 1644, Parliament commanded that the 25th be kept as a day of fasting, because the date coincided with the monthly mandatory fast. In January 1645, Parliament issued the Directory for the Public Worship of God: Sunday was to be the only holy day, and all old feasts were to be abolished. Later that year, old civic pageantry like the St. George's Day march, maypoles, and church ales were also discouraged.

John Taylor, the Water Poet, wrote regretfully of all these developments in his 1646 tract *The Complaint of Christmas*:

All the liberty and harmless sports, the merry gambols, dances and friscols, with which the toiling ploughman and labourer once a year were wont to be recreated, and their spirits and hopes revived for a whole twelvemonth, are now extinct and put out of use, in such a fashion as if they never had been. Thus are the merry lords of bad rule at Westminster; nay, more, their madness hath extended itself to the very vegetables; senseless trees, herbs, and weeds, are in a profane estimation amongst them – holly, ivy, mistletoe, rosemary, bays, are accounted ungodly branches of superstition for your entertainment. And to roast a sirloin of beef, to touch a collar of brawn, to take a pie, to put a plum in the pottage pot, to burn a great candle, or to lay one block the more in the fire for your sake, Master Christmas, is enough to make a man to be suspected and taken for a Christian, for which he shall be apprehended for committing high Parliament Treason.

Some showed their allegiance to the old ways by continuing to decorate the streets with traditional greenery. In the country, people kept churches open by force of arms, and the military had to suppress riots in many towns. In June 1647 Parliament made explicit the abolition of Christmas, Easter, and other Church of England feast days, substituting a monthly day of recreation in addition to the weekly Sabbath and monthly fast (on which days no recreation was permitted). The only other holiday was the anti-Catholic celebration of the failure of the Gunpowder Plot on November 5. On Christmas Eve, 1652, Parliament heard a Remonstrance Against Christmas and again reminded the public that "no observance shall be had on the five-and-twentieth of December, commonly called Christmas day; nor any solemnity used or exercised in churches in respect thereof."

But popular sentiment was not with the Puritans, who found that their substitution of fasts for feasts led only to grumbling and subversion. When the monarchy returned in 1660, Christmas came back with it.

It was a different matter in the New England colonies. Those Puritans who had emigrated to the New World took their anti-Christmas sentiments with them. Here is the account of the first Christmas spent in Massachusetts by the Pilgrims:

> Munday, the 25 day, we went on shore, some to fell tymber, some to saw, some to riue [split wood], and some to carry, so that no man rested all that day, but towards night, some, as they were at worke, heard a noyse of some Indians, which caused us all to goe to our Muskets, but we heard no further, so we came aboord againe, and left some twentie to keepe the court of gard; that night we had a sore storme of winde and raine. Munday the 25 being Christmas day, we began to drinke water aboord, but at night, the Master caused us to have some Beere, and so on board we had diverse times now and then some Beere, but on shore none at all.
>
> On the day called Christmas-day, the Gov'r called them out to worke (as was used), but the most of this new company excused themselves, and said it went against their conscience to worke on the day. So the Gov'r tould them that if they made it a mater of conscience, he would spare them till they were better informed. So he led away the rest, and left them: but when they came home at noone from their worke, he

found them in the streete at play, openly; some pitching the barr, and some at stoole ball, and such like sports. So he went to them and tooke away their implements, and told them it was against his conscience that they should play, and others worke. If they made the keeping of it matter of devotion, let them kepe their houses, but there should be no gameing or revelling in the streets. Since which time nothing hath been attempted that way, at least, openly.

In 1659, the General Court of Massachusetts enacted a law making any observance of December 25 subject to a five-shilling fine; the colony in Connecticut also banned Christmas and mince pies. Even when these laws were abolished, that corner of the United States continued to look askance at Christmas and was the last in the 19th century to be penetrated by its spirit. Christmas was an ordinary working day in Boston until 1856, and it was not until 1870 that schools in that city closed for a Christmas holiday.

Puss in the Corner An 18th-century Christmas game. "As for *Puss in the Corner*, that is a very harmless Sport, and one may romp at it as much as one will; for at this Game when a Man catches his Woman, he may kiss her 'till her Ears crack, or she will be disappointed if she is a Woman of any Spirit; but if it is one who offers at a Struggle and blushes, then be assured she is a Prude, and though she won't stand a Buss in publick, she'll receive it with open Arms behind the Door, and you may kiss her 'till she makes your Heart ake."

Putz From the German *putzen* ("to decorate"), it refers to the Moravian crèche scene, a central part of the Christmas season to those religious immigrants who were so influential in shaping the holiday in the United States. Like the Latin American and Italian Nativity scenes, they can be quite ornate, often occupying a whole room and taking weeks to build. Most, however, are small enough to place under a Christmas tree. They can portray not only the Holy Family in the stable at Bethlehem, but also a whole landscaped area with fences, buildings, foliage, and tiny characters.

Christmas Pyramid *A woman sells Christmas pyramids and crèche figures in a German market.*

A similar custom is found in northwestern Nova Scotia, Canada, where folk artists were famous for the miniature towns, farms, and churches that once were placed at the base of the Christmas tree.

Pyramid, Christmas A German decoration predating the Christmas tree. A wooden pyramid with shelves was decorated with greenery, cookies, candles, fruit, or figures representing the Holy Family. By the 19th century, pyramids coexisted in homes with Christmas trees and had become quite large, ornately carved, and often topped by vanes driven around by the warm air rising from candles. Some very large ones are now erected outside in town squares.

The German custom emigrated to North America, arriving first in Pennsylvania with the Moravians. In Canada it was transformed into the "cookie tree," where gingerbread and cookies were displayed on a tabletop tree. Similar structures in 18th- and 19th-century England were wrapped in gilded evergreens and held apples and nuts.

Quaaltagh The name of the "first-footer" on the Isle of Man (see FIRST-FOOTING). Unlike in many parts of Britain, the first visitor across the threshold on New Year's Day or Christmas could bring luck whether it was male or female (though men were preferred).

Questions and Commands An English Christmas game in which the commander bids his subjects to answer a question. If the subject fails to answer, he must pay a forfeit or suffer the consequences. "The Commander may oblige his Subject to answer any lawful Question, and make the same obey him instantly, under the Penalty of being smutted, or paying such Forfeit as may be laid on the Aggressor; but the Forfeits being generally fixed at some certain Price, as a Shilling, Half a Crown, etc., so every one knowing what to do if they should be too stubborn to submit, make themselves easy at discretion."

"Qui creavit coelum" A 15th-century Latin hymn written by English nuns, translated as "He by Whom the Heavens Were Made" or "Carol of the Nuns of St. Mary's Chester." It was one of the last Latin Christmas hymns written in England.

Quotes About Christmas Joseph Addison: "'I have often thought,' says Sir Roger, 'that it happens very well that Christmas should fall out in the Middle of Winter.'"

Louisa May Allcott: "Christmas won't be Christmas without any presents."

Dave Barry: "In the old days, it was not called the Holiday Season; the Christians called it 'Christmas' and went to church; the Jews called it 'Hanukka' and went to synagogue; the atheists went to parties and drank. People passing each other on the street would say 'Merry Christmas!' or 'Happy Hanukka!' or (to the atheists) 'Look out for the wall!'"

Ebenezer Blackadder in *Blackadder's Christmas Carol*: "I trust Christmas brings to you its traditional mix of good food and violent stomach cramp."

Erma Bombeck: "Adults can take a simple holiday for children and screw it up. What began as a presentation of simple gifts to delight and surprise children around the Christmas tree has culminated in a woman opening up six shrimp forks from her dog, who drew her name."

James Cameron: "Is not Christmas the only occasion when one gets drunk *for the sake of the children*?"

Santiago Carrillo, Spanish Communist leader: "For years Moscow was our Rome, the Great October Revolution was our Christmas. Today we have grown up."

G.K. Chesterton: "A turkey is more occult and awful than all the angels and archangels. In so far as God has partly revealed to us an angelic world, he has partly told us what an angel means. But God has never told us what a turkey means. And if you go and stare at a live turkey for an hour or two, you will find by the end of it that the enigma has rather increased than diminished."

Marcus Clarke: "Christmas in Australia is a gigantic mistake."

Marceline Cox: "Our children await Christmas presents like politicians getting election returns; there's the Uncle Fred precinct and the Aunt Ruth district still to come in."

James Gould Cozzens: "A cynic is a man who found out when he was about ten that there wasn't any Santa Claus, and he's still upset."

Danielle in *My So-Called Life*: "Do we have to keep talking about religion? It's Christmas."

Robertson Davies: "Early in life I developed a distaste for the Cratchits that time has not sweetened. I do not think I was an embittered child, but the Cratchits' aggressive worthiness, their bravely borne poverty, their exultation over that wretched goose, disgusted me. I particularly disliked Tiny Tim (a part always played by a girl because girls had superior powers of looking moribund and worthy at the same time) and when he chirped, 'God bless us everyone!' my mental response was akin to Sam Goldwyn's famous phrase, 'Include me out!'"

Les Dawson: "My mother-in-law has come around to our house at Christmas seven years running. This year we're having a change. We're going to let her in."

Charles Dickens: "'Not too much writing home allowed, I suppose?' said the father-in-law hesitating.

'None, except a circular at Christmas, to say they never were so happy, and hope they may never be sent for,' rejoined Squeers.

'Nothing could be better,' said the father-in-law, rubbing his hands."

Elvira, *Mistress of the Dark*: "Revenge is better than Christmas."

Ferdinand the Duck in *Babe*: "Christmas? Christmas means dinner, dinner means death! Death means carnage; Christmas means carnage!"

Art Fettig: "Some businessmen are saying that this could be the greatest Christmas ever. I always thought the first one was."

W.C. Fields (attrib.): "A Merry Christmas to all my friends except two."

Benjamin Franklin: "A good conscience is a continual Christmas." "How many observe Christ's birthday! How few, his precepts! O! 'tis easier to keep holidays than commandments." "O blessed Season! lov'd by Saints and Sinners, / For long Devotions, or for longer Dinners."

Kris Kringle in *Miracle on 34th Street*: "Christmas isn't just a day, it's a frame of mind."

Linus in *A Charlie Brown Christmas*: "Do they make wooden Christmas trees anymore?"

Robert Lynd: "Were I a philosopher, I should write a philosophy of toys, showing that nothing else in life need to be taken seriously, and that Christmas Day in the company of children is one of the few occasions on which men become entirely alive."

Don Marquis: "What I like about Christmas is that you can make people forget the past with the present."

Dr. Karl Menninger: "I could never see why people were so happy about Dickens's *A Christmas Carol* because I never had any confidence that Scrooge was going to be different the next day."

Michel de Montaigne: "For certainly it is a frenzy to go immediately and whip yourself, because it may so fall out that Fortune may one day make you undergo it; and to put on your furred gown at mid-summer, because you will stand in need of it at Christmas!"

Benito Mussolini: "This holiday which only reminds me of the birth of a Jew who gave the world debilitating and devitalizing theories."

P.J. O'Rourke: "There is a remarkable breakdown of taste and intelligence at Christmastime. Mature responsible men wear neckties made out of holly leaves and drink alcoholic beverages with raw eggs and cottage cheese in them."

Adam Clayton Powell: "Santa Claus is a white man's invention."

Harry Reasoner: "So if a Christian is touched only once a year, the touching is still worth it, and maybe on some given Christmas, some quiet morning, the touch will take."

Byrn Rogers: "Christmas, that time of year when people descend into the bunker of the family."

Mr. Rogers: "I think that if Jesus hadn't been born on Christmas, my mother would have invented the holiday."

Saki (Hector Hugh Munro): "Temptations came to him, in middle age, tentatively and without insistence, like a neglected butcher-boy who asks for a Christmas box in February for no more hopeful reason than that he didn't get one in December."

Eric Sevareid: "If Christmas didn't already exist, man would have had to invent it. There has to be at least one day in the year to remind us that we're here for something else besides our general cussedness."

William Shakespeare: "At Christmas I no more desire a rose Than wish a snow in May's new-fangled mirth; But like of each thing that in season grows."

The Sheriff in *Robin Hood*: "Cancel the kitchen scraps for lepers and orphans, no more merciful beheadings, and call off Christmas!"

Bart Simpson in *The Simpsons*: "Oh please, there's only one fat guy who brings us presents, and his name ain't Santa."

Upton Sinclair: "Or consider Christmas – could Satan in his most malignant mood have devised a worse combination of graft plus buncombe than the system whereby several hundred million people get a billion or so gifts for which they have no use, and some thousands of shop-clerks die of exhaustion while selling them and every other child in the western world is made ill from over-eating – all in the name of the lowly Jesus?"

Mother Teresa: "It is Christmas every time you let God love others through you . . . yes, it is Christmas every time you smile at your brother and offer him your hand."

Bill Vaughan: "The ideal Christmas present is money. The only trouble is, you can't charge it."

Evelyn Waugh: "The prospect of Christmas appalls me."

Geoffrey Williams and Ronald Searle: "Xmas is a good time with all those presents and good food and i hope it will never die out or at any rate not until i am grown up and have to pay for it."

P.G. Wodehouse: "Christmas will soon be at our throats."

Radishes See NIGHT OF THE RADISHES and MEXICO.

Railways, Influence of The development of Christmas as a time of togetherness and family reunion owes much to the spread of cheap rail travel in the 19th century. Before this the poor condition of the roads in winter meant that travel was infrequent, expensive, and too slow for a short Christmas holiday. After the advent of the railways, however, the poor in Britain were able to look forward to holiday travel, because the law mandated the provision of third-class carriages at a penny a mile. The railway network also brought thousands of boarding-school children home for Christmas. Railways meant the supply of fresh, inexpensive food for the city's festive dinners, and brought cheap, raw materials to the factories that turned out affordable consumer goods in mass quantities.

Rainbow In Christian art it is the symbol of God's peace. Some Renaissance paintings of the Annunciation depict Gabriel's wings shimmering like a rainbow as he converses with Mary. (See colour fig. 20.)

Rapee Pie In French *Pâté à la Râpure*, an Acadian meat pie served on Christmas and festive occasions in the French-speaking areas of Canada's Maritime provinces.

Rauhnächte In Austria and Germany, the Twelve Nights of Christmas are referred to as *Rauhnächte*, "Rough Nights" or "Smoke Nights," a time for ridding house and farm of witches and other evil spirits. Figures clad as devils and witches roam the streets and sweep the steps and stables with their brooms, driving out demons. Inside, families, often led by a priest, move through the house and use a censer to smoke out maleficent forces.

Reindeer Now an indispensable part of the imagery of Santa Claus, reindeer made their first appearance in 1821 in *The Children's Friend: A New Year's Present, to Little Ones From Five to Twelve*, an American book illustrated with colour prints of "Santeclaus" in a sleigh pulled by one reindeer. "Old Santeclaus with much delight / His reindeer drives this frosty night." Before too long the number of reindeer pulling Santa's sleigh was increased to eight by the poem "A Visit From St. Nicholas" by Clement Clarke Moore. Here we learn that the names of the deer are Dasher, Dancer, Prancer, Vixen, Comet, Cupid, Donder, and Blitzen. Students of Scandinavian mythology have pointed out the resemblance of the names of the first two reindeer to those of the goats pulling Thor's cart: Cracker and Gnasher.

In Lapland and Siberia, reindeer (*Rangifer tarandus*) have been domesticated and do pull sleighs, but only after they

Influence of Railways The Christmas train pulls into a London station in 1850.

have been gelded if male. Attempts by some ethnologists to link Siberian shamans to the figure of Santa Claus have proven unconvincing.

Reindeer Rule American concern over separation of church and state has resulted in a number of court challenges to Christmas observances by governmental bodies. In 1969, for example, the American Civil Liberties Union (ACLU) sued over the inclusion of a crèche at the site of the National Community Christmas Tree. In 1983 the ACLU sued over a municipal Nativity scene in Pawtucket, Rhode Island, but the Supreme Court decided that the presence of secular elements such as Santa Claus, elves, and reindeer had diluted the religious content sufficiently. This decision has been referred to since as the Reindeer Rule.

Reindeer Substitutes *Father Christmas rides an Australian kangaroo.*

Reindeer Substitutes Though Santa Claus travels by reindeer-drawn sleigh, other gift-bringers have found different ways to cover their territories. In Australia, for example, popular culture has given Father Christmas six white boomers (male kangaroos), while in the swamps of Louisiana, Père Noèl is pulled in a *pirogue* drawn by alligators and a red-nosed were-wolf. The Three Kings of Spain and Latin America travel by camel, and in the Netherlands St. Nicholas is mounted on a tall white horse. In parts of Switzerland he comes by donkey, and in the Czech lands he descends from heaven on a golden cord. In Germany the Weihnachtsmann is often seen walking with his pack on his back, but in Italy the Befana has been known to sail through the air on a broom. Hawaii witnesses Santa arriving through the surf in a dugout canoe wearing a toque and the native *lava-lava* (a kind of skirt), while Brazilian children are not surprised to see Papai Noel appear in a helicopter.

"Remember Adam's Fall" An English carol from the 16th century.

Remember Adam's fall,
O thou man;
Remember Adam's fall
From Heaven to Hell.
Remember Adam's fall;
How he hath condemn'd all
In Hell perpetual
Therefore to dwell,

Remember God's goodness,
O thou man:
Remember God's goodness,
His promise made.
Remember God's goodness;
He sent His Son sinless
Our ails for to redress,
Our hearts to aid.

In Bethlehem He was born,
O thou man:
In Bethlehem He was born,
For mankind's sake.
In Bethlehem He was born,
Christmas Day i' the morn:
Our Saviour did not scorn
Our faults to take.

Give thanks to God alway,
O thou man:
Give thanks to God alway
With heart-felt joy.
Give thanks to God alway
On this our joyful day:
Let all men sing and say,
Holy, Holy

Remember the Night (1940) Prosecutor John Sargent (Fred MacMurray) wants to put three-time shoplifter Lee Leander (Barbara Stanwyck) away for a long time but ends up taking her home to Mother (Beulah Bondi) during Christmas court recess. Director Mitchell Leisen and writer Preston Sturges created a lovely holiday movie with an ending that refuses to take the easy way out.

Réveillon From the French for "awakening," a late-night meal, served after the midnight mass in France, New Orleans, and French Canada, where it has come to be a central part of the Christmas season. In Brazil the *réveillon* refers to the celebration of the New Year.

Rhyming Slang In England nicknames are given to an object or activity based on a phrase that rhymes with the original name. Thus a railway guard is referred to as a "Christmas card." Those truly in the know often reduce the rhyming phrase to the initial (non-rhyming) word, so to inquire of a railway guard is to "ask the Christmas."

Other examples of Yule-related rhyming slang include "mince pies" for eyes; "Christmas Eve" for believe; "Yule logs" for dogs; "Christmas crackers" for testicles (knackers); and "Christmas crackered" for knackered or exhausted.

Riddle-Raddle Men In the Bavarian Alps, on St. Nicholas Day, the Riddle-Raddle Men, or the Buttenmandelhaut, come out to drive away demons. They put on fearful masks, cover themselves with sheaves of straw tied around the waist with rope, and burst from the barn shaking cowbells and rattles. Once they are blessed by St. Nicholas and a farmer's wife has

The Ring and the Rose *A comic army on the march in Thackeray's Christmas story* The Ring and the Rose.

sprinkled them with holy water, they go door-to-door with gifts for kids. Sometimes St. Nicholas reads from a book listing the children's good deeds and bad deeds and sermonizes on the importance of being good. The Riddle-Raddle Men then playfully carry the house's single women outdoors.

Riedesel, Baroness von   The lighted Christmas tree was introduced to Canada by Baroness Frederika von Riedesel, whose husband, Baron Friedrich, had brought 4,000 German Brunswicker soldiers in 1776 to reinforce Canada under General Carleton.

The Ring and the Rose   Inspired by the success of the Christmas works of Charles Dickens, English author William Makepeace Thackeray (1811-63) attempted his own series of seasonal stories. The most famous of these is *The Ring and the Rose; or the History of Prince Giglio and Prince Bulbo* of 1855, a mock pantomime complete with fairies, princes, princesses, and magic devices to render the owner attractive to the opposite sex. There was nothing particularly Christmasy about this or any of the other stories, and their popularity soon faded.

"Rise Up Shepherd and Follow"   This African-American carol was called "A Christmas Plantation Song" when first published in the 1867 collection *Slave Songs of the United States.*

> There's a star in the East on Christmas morn
> Rise up, shepherd, and follow!
> It'll lead to the place where the Saviour's born:
> Rise up shepherd and follow!
>
> *Leave your sheep and leave your lambs*
> *Rise up shepherd and follow!*
> *Leave your ewes and leave your rams*
> *Rise up shepherd and follow!*
>
> *Follow, follow, rise up shepherd and follow!*
> *Follow the Star of Bethlehem*
> *Rise up shepherd and follow!*
>
> If you take good heed to the angel's words
> Rise up shepherd and follow!
> You'll forget your flocks, you'll forget your herds:
> Rise up shepherd and follow!

Robin   A symbol of Christmas in England and the subject of numberless Christmas cards in the British Isles since 1862. Because the robin mates in December, its plumage is particularly bright during the Christmas season. Legends attribute the robin's red breast to its being burnt by flames while trying to warm the baby Jesus, or to its plucking out a thorn from Christ's brow at the crucifixion and being splashed by blood.

A curious feature of many Victorian Christmas cards was the image of a dead robin, presumably frozen to death. Freezing to death at Christmas was a common theme for 19th-century stories of poor children, and it may be that card-makers wished to provoke feelings of seasonal sympathy.

Rock and Roll and Christmas   Rock and roll, that blend of gospel, rhythm and blues, and country music that grew up in the mid-1950s and developed into the world's dominant musical form, has long included a number of Christmas themes.

Rock and roll is by nature an exuberant genre, based around dance rhythms and mating rituals, so it is unsurprising to see that worship is not a major topic in its embrace of Christmas music, aside from those renditions of sacred classics by popular artists. Generally speaking, "Santa Claus" is a name much more likely to be invoked by performers than "Jesus." Among the few exceptions are "Child of God" by Bobby Darin, "Gabriel's Message" by Sting, and "The Birth of Christ" by Boyz II Men. Elements of sincerity, if not piety, have also crept into songs such as "Thank God It's Christmas" by Queen and "Peace on Earth" by the unlikely duo of David Bowie and Bing Crosby.

Rock and roll is more likely to set toes tapping than souls soaring. Christmas hits from the 1950s include Brenda Lee's "Rockin' Around the Christmas Tree," "Jingle Bell Rock," by Bobby Helm, and "Run Rudolph Run" sung by Chuck Berry and written by JOHNNY MARKS. Since then this upbeat, celebratory tone has dominated Christmas music. Paul Young's "What Christmas Means to Me," Elton John's "Step Into Christmas," and "December Will Be Magic Again" by Kate Bush all found Christmas something joyful to sing about.

On the other hand, dashed Christmas hopes have led to thousands of rock and roll laments. "Christmas Eve Can Kill You" by the Everly Brothers sums up that sentiment, which is echoed by Roy Orbison's "Pretty Paper," "Please Come Home for Christmas" by the Eagles, and of course Elvis Presley's definitive "Blue Christmas." (See BLUES, CHRISTMAS.)

Social commentary has always been part of rock and roll, and that holds true when the music deals with Christmas. Simon and Garfunkel's "7 O'Clock News/Silent Night" mixes familiar carol music with the kind of grim news report the world is offered every night. "Christmas at Ground Zero" is a sardonic view of a nuclear winter by Weird Al Yankovic, while "Happy Xmas (War Is Over)," by John and Yoko and the Plastic Ono Band, offered a more hopeful perspective. Carlene Davis and Trinity ask about racial and social equality in "Santa Claus (Do You Ever Come to the Ghetto?)," and "Christmas in Vietnam" by Johnny and Jon laments the war that has separated lonesome soldiers from their accustomed Yule-time celebrations.

Ever since the 1950s, when Stan Freberg cornered the market in seasonal satires with such hits as "Green Chritma," "Christmas Dragnet" (alias "Yulenet"), and "The Meaning of Christmas," recording artists have tried to create Christmas novelty tunes. David Seville's "Chipmunk Song (Christmas Don't Be Late)" was a great success in 1958. Among the more bizarre performances have been Elmo and Patsy's "GRANDMA GOT RUN OVER BY A REINDEER," Yogi Yorgesson's "I Yust Go

Crazy Over Christmas," "Santa Claus and His Old Lady" by Cheech and Chong, and "Xmas at K-Mart" by Root Boy Slim and the Sex Change Band.

Rock and roll singers have contributed greatly to Christmas charities. Band Aid's 1984 "Do They Know It's Christmas?" led the way in collaborative efforts to raise money for world hunger relief.

"Rocking Around the Christmas Tree"   A hit for singer Brenda Lee, written by Johnny Marks, author of "Rudolph, the Red-Nosed Reindeer," in 1958.

Romania   Christmas in Romania is a colourful time of the year, full of old customs and community activities that honour the past. Though the country's main religion is Orthodox Christianity, Romanians keep their holidays according to the Gregorian calendar observed in Western Europe. The season begins on December 5, the eve of St. Nicholas Day, when children leave their freshly polished shoes out in the hope that the saint, whom they call Mos Nicolae (Old Nicholas), will pass by in the night and put candies and small gifts in them; bad kids may expect to find a switch in their footwear.

On December 20, when Romanians honour St. Ignatius, a curious custom takes place in rural areas. A pig is slaughtered and its bristles singed off with burning straw. It is then ritually censed and the sign of the cross is made over it by the head of the household. A banquet of roast pork follows, to which family and neighbours are invited.

Christmas Eve is the day for decorating the Christmas tree; in addition to the usual ornaments and garlands, there are (as in Hungary) candies wrapped in foil. That night children go door-to-door as *colindatori*, carollers, singing songs about the birth of Jesus. Sometimes they carry with them a *steaua*, a star on a pole; inside the star, a candle lights a picture of the Holy Family or another Bible scene. The houses they visit reward them with gifts of money, fruit, or sweets. The carol tradition is very strong in Romania; some of the favourite Christmas songs are "Astazi s-a nascut Cristos" ("Christ Is Born Today"), "Mos Craciun cu plete dalbe" ("Santa Claus's White Locks"), "Trei Pastori" ("Three Shepherds"), and "La Betleem colo-n jos" ("Down in Bethlehem").

The gift-bringer in Romania is Mos Craciun, a Santa Claus figure who comes on Christmas Eve and is said to enter the house through the chimney. (During the Communist era, the Soviet-sponsored Grandfather Frost was introduced, but he has now largely disappeared.) That evening's meal is likely to include a pork dish, soup, cabbage rolls, braided bread, walnut bread, and a pastry called *turta* whose thin layers of rolled dough represent the swaddling clothes of the baby Jesus. After church on Christmas Day, another large meal is consumed, along with heroic amounts of wine and plum brandy. Feasting at New Year's is also obligatory. Traditional dishes are turkey, sausage, head cheese, stuffed cabbage rolls, roast suckling pig, and, for dessert, squares of pastry with a fortune baked into each one.

The time from Christmas to New Year's is a period of traditional celebrations unique to Romania. In the *plugusorul*, or "little plough" ceremony, young men used to decorate a plough with ribbons and take it from farm to farm, reciting an old fertility poem that invokes the memory of the Roman emperor Trajan, who colonized the area in the first century A.D. Nowadays the plough has been replaced with costumed youth snapping whips, singing songs, ringing bells, and playing bagpipes. In the *capra*, or goat dance, which is performed until Epiphany and seems to have been a pre-Christian fertility rite, a man dressed as a goat or other animal performs a skit accompanied by singers and musicians. (A similar but less common ceremony is the *ursului*, or bear dance.) The *Viflaiem* is a kind of folk drama that has evolved since the 18th century and involves masked characters such as "Greybeards" and "Mistress Death." On New Year's Day itself, children go door-to-door with a branch decorated with artificial flowers called a SORCOVA and recite poems wishing people well in the coming year; as they speak they tap the listeners with the stick. Families often spread grain about the house as a symbol of wished-for prosperity.

Rosca de Reyes   The "King's Ring," the Mexican version of the Epiphany cake. A small figure representing the Christ Child is baked into the ring-shaped cake, and whoever finds it is expected to host a party on February 2, *El Dia de la Candelaria*, Candlemas.

Rosemary and Christmas   At one time a popular Christmas decoration, rosemary (*Rosmarinus officianalis*) has, since the 19th century, fallen into disfavour. The choirboys of Ripon Cathedral used to come into church on Christmas morning with baskets of apples stuck with sprigs of rosemary as a symbol of fallen man and redemption. St. Thomas More said of it, "'Tis the herb sacred to remembrance and therefore to friendship."

According to legend, rosemary got its aroma when the swaddling clothes of the baby Jesus were hung upon it to dry. Originally white in colour, its flower was changed to lavender when the Virgin Mary cast her purple cloak upon it during the flight to Egypt.

Round About Our Coal Fire   A small English book of 1734 filled with Christmas lore and ghost stories suitable for telling long into the night. This passage gives an idea of the spirit of an English Christmas of the early 18th century, with its focus on feasting, drinking, and community merriment; the notion of a child-centred, family-oriented Christmas was to appear much later.

> O you merry, merry souls, Christmas is a coming;
> We shall have flowing bowls, Dancing, piping, drumming.
>
> Delicate minced pies,
> To feast every virgin,
> Capon and goose likewise, Brawn, and dish of sturgeon.
>
> Then for your Christmas box Sweet plum-cakes and money,
> Delicate Holland smocks, Kisses sweet as honey.
>
> Hey for the Christmas ball, Where we shall be jolly;
> Coupling short and tall, Kate, Dick, Ralph, and Molly.
>
> Come bring with a noise,
> My merry, merry boys,
> The Christmas log to the firing;
> While my good dame, she
> Bids ye all be free,
> And drink to your heart's desiring.
> Then to the hop we'll go,
> Where we'll jig and caper;
> Dancers all a-row,
> Will shall pay the scraper.
>
> Hodge shall dance with Prue,
> Keeping time with kisses;
> We'll have a jovial crew

Round About Our Coal Fire *A Christmas feast portrayed in a wood-cut from the popular 18th-century book of seasonal entertainments.*

Of sweet smirking misses.
With the last year's brand
Light the new block, and
For good success in his spending,
On your psalteries play,
That sweet luck may
Come while the log is a tending.

Royal Christmas Message At 3 p.m. on every Christmas Day since 1932, the reigning British monarch has spoken to the people of the Empire and Commonwealth. The first to make a royal Christmas broadcast was George V, who had been requested to do so by BBC General Manager John Reith since 1923. Written by Rudyard Kipling, the speech was delivered from Sandringham Castle:

> Through one of the marvels of modern science I am enabled this Christmas Day to speak to all my peoples throughout the Empire. I take it as a good omen the wireless should have reached its present perfection at a time when the Empire has been linked in closer union, for it offers us immense possibilities to make that union closer still.
>
> It may be that our future will lay upon us more than one stern test. Our past will have taught us how to meet it unshaken. For the present the work to which we are all equally bound is to arrive at a reasoned tranquillity within our borders, to regain prosperity without self-seeking, and to carry with us those whom the burden of past years has disheartened or overborne.
>
> My life's aim has been to serve as I might towards those ends. Your loyalty, your confidence in me has been my abundant reward. I speak now from my home and from my heart to you all; to men and women so cut off by the snows, the desert, or the sea that only voices out of the air can reach them; to those cut off from fuller life by blindness, sickness, or infirmity, and to those who are celebrating this day with their children and their grandchildren – to all, to each, I wish a happy Christmas. God bless you.

Listening to the broadcast has since become a traditional Christmas afternoon event. Queen Elizabeth II made her first Christmas broadcast on radio in 1952, and on television in 1957. Like her father, George VI, and grandfather, George V, the queen used to broadcast her message live, but since 1960 the Christmas message has been pre-recorded, and sent in advance to Commonwealth countries for broadcast at a suitable local time. The television program incorporates material specially recorded for it during the preceding year. The speech is now also made available on the Internet.

"Rudolph, the Red-Nosed Reindeer" One of the great marketing coups of all time and one of the 20th century's most noticeable additions to the celebration of Christmas, "Rudolph, the Red-Nosed Reindeer" first appeared in 1939 in a promotional giveaway for Chicago's Montgomery Ward department store. His creator was advertising editor Robert Lewis May (1905-76), who conceived of an illustrated booklet with a Christmas poem that families could read every year. The story was to be about a rejected reindeer with few friends (like May in his own childhood) to whom Santa Claus would turn for assistance. Denver Gillen did the artwork for the booklet based on sketches made while visiting the city zoo, and May wrote the poem about the reindeer named Rollo. Or perhaps Reginald. Both these names, and others, were ultimately rejected in favour of Rudolph, the choice of May's four-year-old daughter. The company loved the result and gave away millions of the books throughout the 1940s.

In 1947 songwriter JOHNNY MARKS penned the famous lyrics that summarized the Rudolph story, but Marks couldn't interest any music publishers in his work and had to found his own St. Nicholas music company; nor could he find a singer willing to take a chance with a song about an advertising character. He was turned down by Bing Crosby, Dinah Shore, and Perry Como before Gene Autry, "The Singing Cowboy," recorded it in 1949, selling 2,000,000 copies in the first year alone and launching Rudolph to further success. The reindeer went on to appear in movies and books (in dozens of languages) and his image was used for a host of marketing devices and toys.

Rudolph, the Red-Nosed Reindeer (TV) (1964) This was the second animated version of Robert Mays's creation (the first was a 1944 cartoon) and seems to have become the audience favourite. Narrated by Sam the Snowman (the voice of Burl Ives), it is the story of a misfit reindeer who comes through for Christmas when he is needed. Directed by Kizo Nagashima and Larry Roemer.

Rudolph, the Red-Nosed Reindeer: The Movie (1998) A well-animated movie with an interesting cast makes this worth watching. John Goodman is the voice of Santa Claus, with help from Eric Idle, Bob Newhart, Debbie Reynolds, Richard Simmons, and Whoopi Goldberg. William R. Kowalchuk directed.

Rudolph's Second Christmas Written in 1947, this sequel by Robert May to his best-selling *Rudolph, the Red-Nosed Reindeer* lay in a drawer and unpublished until 1991, when it was discovered by the author's daughter. Like the original, it concerns animals that don't quite fit in: a dog that meows, a cat that barks, a canary that could talk but not sing, a parrot that could sing but not talk, a slow-moving rabbit, and a speedy turtle. Again Rudolph saves the day. Illustrated by Michael Emberley.

Ruins In many medieval representations of the Nativity and the Adoration of the Magi, the Holy Family is depicted sheltering in some ruins, often of classical architecture. These ruins represent the death of the old dispensation that Jesus came to change.

Russia *Carollers and a puppet theatre in rural 19th-century Russia.*

Russia Before the Communist Revolution of 1917, Christmas in Russia was celebrated with great solemnity as one of the high points of the religious calendar of the Orthodox Church and as a joyous midwinter festival by the population. Fasting began weeks ahead of Christmas, with all meat and dairy products shunned by the devout and no food eaten at all on Christmas Eve until the first star appeared in the sky. The traditional Christmas Eve meal consisted of 12 meatless dishes (in honour of the 12 apostles), and KUTYA, a sweet porridge eaten to ensure future prosperity and happiness. Priests might visit the home to sprinkle it with holy water, and the Christmas Day church service was massively attended. Folk celebrations involved the Christmas tree, carolling from house to house – singing *kolyadki*, songs of blessing and begging – mumming and masquerading (as described in Tolstoy's *War and Peace*), and visits from Saint Nicholas, the BABOUSHKA, and Kolyáda, a white-robed girl who travelled by sleigh and who personified the Christmas season. It was also the time of prognostication, ceremonies to predict the future, especially the identity of one's spouse. (See PODBLYUDNUIYA and DIVINATION.)

All this changed with Communism and the drive to suppress religion. Christmas celebrations were forbidden, and where they could not be utterly abolished they were channelled into secular New Year's rites. Thus the "New Year's tree," New Year's presents and feasting, and the replacement of Saint Nicholas and the Baboushka by Dyed Moroz (Grandfather Frost), his niece Snegurochka (the Snow Maiden), and the New Year's Boy. Calendar reform further confused the matter: while the government shifted from the Julian to the Gregorian calendar in keeping with the rest of the world, the Orthodox Church clung to the old ways of reckoning time. Therefore, in the Soviet Union, New Year's Day (January 1, Gregorian) occurred before Christmas Day (December 25, Julian), which served to weaken the impulse to celebrate Christmas.

The fall of Eastern European Communism and the death of the Soviet Union has brought a revival in religion in Russia, and the people are rediscovering traditional holidays and customs and trying to blend them with newer customs they have grown used to. Churches are filled with young people, and state officials now take part in the Christmas liturgies they once tried to repress. Television stations broadcast the Christmas Eve midnight mass from the Cathedral of the Epiphany in Moscow, and hundreds of thousands of Russians take part in the *Krestny Khod* ceremony of "walking the cross," in which a candle-lit procession of priests and congregants goes outside on Christmas Eve to circle the church before returning inside for a round of carol singing. Christmas observances have returned to millions of Russian homes, and many children wait until January 6, Christmas Eve in the Julian calendar, to open their presents. The singing of the *kolyadki* has been revived, mumming and fortune-telling continue to be popular, and the crèche, though not a traditional item of devotion in Orthodox countries, has been adopted by many Russian families.

New Year's celebrations continue to be popular nevertheless; the January 1 dinner will probably be a grander affair

Russia *A Soviet-era stamp depicting Grandfather Frost and the New Year's Tree.*

than that on January 7. Grandfather Frost and the Snow Maiden have now become commercial icons in the way Santa Claus is in the West; they are on display in shopping malls, public celebrations, and at private affairs. Children at year-end parties join hands around the Christmas tree and ritually call on the Snow Maiden three times before she appears and the festivities can begin. Though Santa Claus is making some inroads, Grandfather Frost remains the predominant gift-bringer both for those children who receive presents on New Year's Eve and those who get them at Christmas.

Sainfoin   The name of this leguminous perennial herb (*Onobrychis viciaefolia*) is from the French for "holy hay." The plant, sometimes called holy clover, is said to have lined the manger in Bethlehem.

Saining   Rituals to provide supernatural protection and good luck are often a part of the Christmas season. Saining customs include the English and Romanian wassailing of fruit trees (see WASSAIL), and the German SHOOTING-IN of Christmas. A remarkable example from Scotland involves the custom of drinking water from the "dead and living ford." Water from a ford over which the living carried the dead to burial was brought into the house on the last day of the old year, in silence, without the vessel it was borne in touching the ground. It was drunk by every family member in turn very early on New Year's Day and sprinkled over the beds. The house was then fumigated with juniper smoke. Thus by fire and water, evil and sickness were driven away from the house for the coming year.

Saint Nicholas   An American children's magazine, published from 1873 to 1943, named for the patron saint of children. It attracted the finest writers and illustrators of its time, including Alfred Lord Tennyson, Louisa May Alcott, L. Frank Baum, Rudyard Kipling, Jack London, Howard Pyle, Mark Twain, Arthur Rackham, Maxfield Parrish, Frederic Remington, and Norman Rockwell. Not surprisingly, it was a popular magazine for Christmas stories and poems. An 1876 tale by Edward Eggleton, "The House of Santa Claus, a Christmas Fairy Show for Sunday Schools," was among the first to surround Santa with a corps of helpful elves.

Saint Nicholas   A 1948 Christmas cantata, opus 42, by Benjamin Britten, text by Eric Crozier, about the life of the most famous Christmas saint, including the story of the boys pickled in brine.

Saki   The pen name of Hector Hugh Munro (1870-1916), journalist and short story writer who wittily chronicled the shallow lives of the upper classes of Edwardian England. Christmas, especially of the English country-house variety, was a favourite topic. "A Touch of Realism" illuminates the perils of Christmas parlour games, "Bertie's Christmas Eve" shows what happens when the gentry test the myth of animals kneeling in the stables at midnight, and "Reginald's Christmas Revel" exposes the dangers of house guests falling prey to boredom:

As a crowning dissipation, they all sat down to play progressive halma, with milk-chocolate for prizes. I've been carefully brought up, and I don't like to play games of skill for milk-chocolate, so I invented a headache and retired from the scene. I had been preceded a few minutes earlier by Miss Langshan-Smith, a rather formidable lady, who always got up at some uncomfortable hour in the morning, and gave you the impression that she had been in communication with most of the European Governments before breakfast. There was a paper pinned on her door with a signed request that she might be called particularly early on the morrow. Such an opportunity does not come twice in a lifetime. I covered up everything except the signature with another notice, to the effect that before these words should meet the eye she would have ended a misspent life, was sorry for the trouble she was giving, and would like a military funeral. A few minutes later I violently exploded an air-filled paper bag on the landing, and gave a stage moan that could have been heard in the cellars. Then I pursued my original intention and went to bed. The noise those people made in forcing open the good lady's door was positively indecorous; she resisted gallantly, but I believe they searched her for bullets for about a quarter of an hour, as if she had been a historic battlefield.

I hate travelling on Boxing Day, but one must occasionally do things that one dislikes.

Salome the Midwife   According to the apocryphal *Protoevangelium of James*, Joseph went in search of a midwife for Mary when it came time to give birth. He brought back to the cave two women, Zelomi and Salome, who were too late to assist in the delivery but who marvelled at the possibility of a virgin birth. Zelomi expressed her belief, but Salome, doubting, wished to make an examination herself. For her impudence Salome's hand was withered, but an angel urged her to place it on the baby who at once healed it – the first miracle of Jesus. The two midwives were often portrayed in Nativity art of the Middle Ages until the Council of Trent discouraged it as nonscriptural.

Salvation Army   The Salvation Army – part church organization, part worldwide social service agency – has become identified with Christmas charity since it was founded in London in 1865 by General William Booth. The sound of Salvation Army brass bands playing Christmas carols and the sight of street-corner kettles awaiting donations are a part of Christmas in many countries.

In 1891 Captain Joseph McFee of San Francisco set up the world's first Salvation Army kettle to collect money for Christmas charities. It was such a success that within a few years kettles were a common sight on the West Coast. In 1897 the idea spread to Boston; though some officers were reluctant to man the kettles lest they make a spectacle of themselves, enough money was collected to feed thousands. In 1901 the Salvation Army set up the first mammoth sit-down dinners for the poor in New York's Madison Square Garden, a custom that persisted for decades. This kind of communal Christmas dinner is still offered to the homeless, but around the world today the collections from street kettles also fund groceries, clothing, and toys for poor families, meals and visits for shut-ins, and services and supplies for prison inmates and their families.

At one time the Salvation Army employed the homeless to dress as Santa Claus while they manned the kettles, but the proliferation of street-corner and department store Santas confused children, so the practice was dropped. Nowadays many kettles are automated, with a self-ringing bell and a public address system broadcasting carols.

Samichlaus   Swiss-German name for St. Nicholas or Santa Claus.

Sandys, William   (1792-1874) English lawyer and carol collector whose publications helped save important Christmas music from extinction and did much to preserve the observance of the holiday itself. Sandys was an amateur musician and folklorist. In 1833 he published *Christmas Carols, Ancient and Modern*, which included 34 long-ignored songs, 40 contemporary carols from the west of England, and six French songs. Among the carols he helped popularize were "The First Nowell," "God Rest Ye Merry, Gentlemen," "Tomorrow Shall Be My Dancing Day," "I Saw Three Ships Come Sailing In," and "Joseph Was an Old Man."

"Sans Day Carol"   A Cornish carol named after the Breton Saint Day. Also known as "The Holly Bears a Berry."

> Now the Holly bears a berry as white as the milk
> And Mary bore Jesus, who was wrapped up in silk.
>
> *And Mary bore Jesus Christ our Saviour to be*
> *And the first tree in the greenwood, it was the holly.*
> *Holly, holly,*
> *And the first tree in the greenwood it was the holly.*
>
> Now the Holly bears a berry as green as the grass
> And Mary bore Jesus, who died on the cross.
>
> *Refrain*
>
> Now the Holly bears a berry as black as the coal
> And Mary bore Jesus, who died for us all.

> *Refrain*
>
> Now the Holly bears a berry as blood it is red
> Then trust we our Saviour who rose from the dead.

"Santa Baby"   In this holiday tribute in song to the give-and-take of personal relationships, Santa Claus is urged to provide a yacht, furs, jewellery, and other consumer durables to a young woman, who assures him she could be good if only her needs were met. Written by Joan Javits, Phil Springer, and Tony Springer, the song was a hit for Eartha Kitt in 1953 and was later recorded by Madonna, the self-anointed Material Girl.

Santa Claus   The most famous of the Christmas gift-bringers, Santa Claus is only about 200 years old, the descendant of older European figures and the product of a movement to produce a distinctively American Christmas.

The history of Santa Claus begins with SAINT NICHOLAS of Myra, an early Christian bishop of Asia Minor, whose cult grew throughout the Middle Ages and around whom numerous stories of kindness to children developed. By the 12th century he was the patron saint of children, and in his name gifts were given to little ones on his feast day of December 6 or on its eve. Children left out stockings or shoes for him by the window or door, as chimneys were rare in Europe until the 1500s. In the 16th century, religious reformers attacked the excessive devotion given to saints, and in Protestant areas Saint Nicholas lost his job as bringer of Christmas gifts. He was replaced either by the Christ Child or by secularized versions of himself, usually dressed in fur. Thus in 17th- and 18th-century Germany figures appeared such as Knecht Ruprecht, Pelznickel or Belsnickel (which meant "Furry Nicholas"), or Ru-Klaus ("Rough Nicholas"), who either accompanied the Christ Child (who came to be known as the Christkindl) or who appeared in his stead. In other Protestant countries such as England, the giving of gifts to children declined and there

Santa Claus *The 19th-century saw a number of versions of the American giftbringer. This one dates from 1845.*

was no particular gift-bringer. In Scotland, Christmas festivities of all kinds were forbidden by the Calvinist Church, and so gift-giving and merriment shifted to New Year's.

In much of the United States of the late 1700s, Christmas was a time of boisterous, outdoor fun; drinking was a major part of the season, as was feasting, noise-making, and wandering about at all hours of the night troubling one's wealthier neighbours for hospitality. During the first half of the 19th century, Christmas would be remade; collective rowdiness and social inversion were replaced by a child-centred, family-oriented holiday that rendered the streets safer and the merchants happier. Central to this important social change was the invention of Santa Claus by a small group of New York men of letters.

To some in the newly independent United States things Dutch were symbols of anti-British republicanism. St. Nicholas had been a rebel symbol in New York during the Revolutionary war, and with tensions still running high in the early years of the 19th century he would be useful again. In 1809 American writer WASHINGTON IRVING wrote a mock chronicle entitled *Diedrich Knickerbocker's History of New York* in which he claimed that the early Dutch settlers revered Sinterklaas, or Saint Nicholas, who visited every December. He was widely believed to ride a horse and wagon through the skies, slide down chimneys with presents, and smoke a pipe. Irving seems to have invented this Dutch-American attachment to Saint Nick; the first mention of him in the New York area dates to a dinner on December 23, 1773, in honour of the saint "otherwise called St. a Claus." The next year George Pintard, another member of the KNICKERBOCKER group, published a pamphlet in Dutch and English showing pictures of St. Nicholas dressed as a bishop, presents stuffed into stockings by a fireplace, a good child with treats, and a bad child with a switch. The verse read, in part:

Saint Nicholas, my dear good friend!
To serve you, ever was my end,
If you will, now, me something give,
I'll serve you ever while I live.

A couple of weeks later, another poem, this time anonymously written, appeared in a New York newspaper praising "Sancte Claus" for the gifts he brings, asking him to spare the rod, and promising, "From naughty behaviour we'll always refrain, / In hopes that you'll come and reward us again."

Within two years this newly minted legend of Santa Claus had spread far enough to provoke an attempt to disprove his existence. In 1812 Samuel Woods, in his *False Stories Corrected*, tried to debunk "Old Santa Claw, of whom so often little children hear such foolish stories." But already the myth was too powerful. By 1822 two more poems would be added to the Santa Claus canon that fleshed out his personality and helped ensure his survival in American Christmas celebrations. The first appeared in an 1821 book entitled THE CHILDREN'S FRIEND. In this poem we see very important elements in the development of Santa Claus: his connection with the northern winter; the reindeer and sleigh; his arrival, not on his saint's day, but on Christmas Eve; as well as the traditional carrot-and-stick approach to children's behaviour.

In 1822 a poem entitled "A VISIT FROM SAINT NICHOLAS," destined to be known popularly as "The Night Before Christmas," further elaborated on the nature of Santa Claus. The poem is usually attributed to Clement Clarke Moore, a prominent New Yorker, scholar, and theologian, who is said to have written it for his children. It appeared anonymously in the *Troy Sentinel* on December 23, 1823, and it was not until

1837 that Moore associated himself with the poem. In "A Visit From Saint Nicholas," we are given not one but eight reindeer and are informed of their names (see REINDEER); we see an elfin character, friendly and non-judgmental, clothed in fur; we note the descent down the chimney; and we see the Christmas Eve connection reinforced.

Moore's poem became widely known in the United States, and Santa Claus was soon adopted as the figurehead of a new sort of Christmas – more domestic and less boisterous, focused on December 24 and 25 instead of December 6 or 31, and capable of generating revenue for the merchants who began using Santa in their advertising. From the 1820s until the American Civil War of the 1860s, a number of images of Santa Claus appeared, each wildly different from the others. The first widely distributed picture of Santa Claus appeared in an 1841 newspaper and showed a smiling middle-aged Santa with a pointed beard in the act of entering a chimney. The cover of an 1846 piece of sheet music entitled "Santa Claus' Quadrilles" depicted a beardless young man with a cape and a sack of toys. Sometimes he was portrayed as a Dutchman with tricorn hat, red breeches, and yellow stockings; sometimes he wore a red fur-trimmed cap. Throughout the century he would be made to resemble a peddler, a buffalo hunter, and a prosperous merchant, but it was a German-born New York cartoonist who would help standardize the image of Santa Claus.

THOMAS NAST was a talented artist working for *Harper's Weekly* during the American Civil War. In his depiction of the Union war effort, he drew several pictures of Santa Claus: standing on a roof with his reindeer, while in the house below a wife prays for her soldier husband; watching over sleeping children; and bringing presents to Federalist troops in their camp. These pictures helped to associate Christmas with both patriotism and the hope of family reunion, important elements in the spread of Christmas observances throughout 19th-century America. Nast's Santa Claus was elfish, never quite full size, and clothed in fur suits – aspects that would, in time, change – but it was his kindly, bearded face under a fur cap that was to win the hearts of the American public. After the war Nast continued to draw Santa Claus and influence the way the world thought of him: in a North Pole workshop full of toys, keeping a list of good and bad children; a symbol, not just of the season, but of love for children.

As Santa Claus grew more widely known, as middle-class attitudes to child-rearing softened, and as Christmastime became less raucous and more domestic, many gift-bringers around the world came to resemble Santa. It was in the 19th century that Père Noël, Father Christmas, and the Weihnachtsmann came to be viewed in France, England, and Germany, respectively, as kindly, elderly conveyors of presents for children, and the wilder Christmas visitors such as Knecht Ruprecht, Ru-Klaus, and Belsnickel faded in importance or became subordinates. The Christmas ELVES of European folklore, often mischievous or deadly, mutated into milder creatures such as those who populated Santa's workshop or, like JULENISSEN, came to resemble Santa himself.

By the early 1900s Santa Claus was an omnipresent part of the North American Christmas scene: his image was on cards and in advertising; he appeared in stories, plays, and the new motion pictures; his surrogates could be seen in every department store, begging for charity on street corners, or leading Santa Claus parades. His image, once so various, had become more homogenized; he had the jolly, bearded countenance Nast gave him, boots, and a fur-trimmed jacket (usually red) bound with a broad belt. Sometimes he wore a cap and sometimes a longer robe, but he was distinguishable from his European counterparts, who generally wore a hooded garment and who tended to be more stately and less rotund. Magazine and commercial illustrators, such as Norman Rockwell and Joseph Leyendecker in the *Saturday Evening Post* (see colour figs. 10, 21), and Haddon Sundblom in his Coca-Cola ads, completed the process of presenting a standardized Santa Claus, recognizable around the world.

The first and second world wars sent millions of American military men overseas, and with them went their idea of Christmas and Santa Claus. Some countries, such as Japan, have adopted him into their own culture without too much dislocation of native seasonal figures, but in other countries, such as Latin America, his celebrity has driven out indigenous Christmas figures and changed gift-giving patterns. Consequently, nationalist opposition to Santa Claus appears around the world. He has been burnt in effigy in France, outlawed in towns in the Netherlands, beaten up in Bosnia, and criticized by Catholic bishops in Latin America ("fat drunk" was one of the kinder terms used). Even in the United States he has been the target of religious fundamentalists opposed to the celebration of Christmas; they claim that he is the reincarnation of pagan gods, and in several Southern towns his image has been lynched.

Despite these criticisms Santa Claus remains the embodiment of Christmas for hundreds of millions of people all around the planet and looks to be well-established for the future.

Santa Claus (1959)   Rene Cardona's Mexican film of 1959 was supposedly based on an e.e. cummings play; though that's not quite true, the film is certainly strange enough on its own merits. Santa Claus, played by José Elías Moreno, must battle demonic forces (clad in scary red tights and puffy shorts) and bad boys to continue his works of goodness. Luckily he is aided by Merlin and triumphs in the end.

Santa Claus: A Morality   A short play by the American poet e.e. cummings. Published in 1946, its two chief characters are Death and Santa Claus, who indulge in ponderous musings on the nature of belief and giving. It is alleged to be the basis of the 1959 Mexican movie *Santa Claus*, but there is little real connection.

The Santa Claus Bank Robbery   On December 23, 1927, Santa Claus robbed the First National Bank in Cisco, Texas. Dressed as St. Nick, Marshall Ratliff and three undisguised companions looted the bank and took hostages, but were greeted by police and heavily armed townspeople when they emerged from the building. In the shoot-out that followed, two officers and a bandit were mortally wounded. Though Ratliff and his two remaining partners temporarily escaped after a series of car-jackings and hostage-takings, they were forced to abandon the stolen money and were rounded up within a week.

The erstwhile Santa, who killed again in a failed escape attempt, was eventually taken from his jail cell by an angry mob and lynched. A piece of the rope used in the impromptu hanging is on display in the Callahan County Courthouse in Baird, Texas.

Santa Claus Bottles   In the late 19th century, the mineral water spa in Poland Springs, Maine, made bottles in the shape of Santa, which are now collectors' items of some value.

Santa Claus Conquers the Martians   Director Nicholas Webster has much to answer for with this cinematic turkey of 1964, also known as *Santa Claus Defeats the Aliens*. It seems that the children of Mars have become dull, passive, and materialistic from watching too much Earth television and its constant promotion of Christmas. Rather than simply turning off the TV set, the Martians decide to visit Earth and kidnap Santa. When they bring back the jolly old elf and two Earth children, reactionary elements on the red planet try to thwart all the Christmasy goodness that ensues. Look for Pia Zadora and Jamie Farr under their green makeup; close your ears during the introductory song, "Hooray for Santy Claus!"

Santa Claus Cup   An international polo tournament in Portugal that ends the country's annual polo season.

"Santa Claus Is Coming to Town"   Written on the back of an envelope in a bar in 1932 by Haven Gillespie (music by Fred Coots), "Santa Claus Is Coming to Town" could not find a singer until Eddie Cantor agreed to perform it on his 1934 radio show and in Macy's Thanksgiving Parade that year. The most popular recordings have been by Bing Crosby, the Andrews Sisters, and Perry Como, and in total 70,000,000 copies have been sold.

Santa Claus Is Coming to Town   (1970)   The team of Jules Bass and Arthur Rankin, Jr., is a veritable animated Christmas industry, having given the world, among other films, *Rudolph, the Red-Nosed Reindeer*, *The Little Drummer Boy* (I and II), and *Rudolph and Frosty's Christmas in July*. Here we have the story of a town in conflict. Young Kris Kringle wants to hand out presents to the children of Sombertown, but Burgermeister Meisterburger is opposed. Narrated by Fred Astaire, with other voices by Mickey Rooney, Keenan Wynn, and Joan Gardner. Critics have noted a decidedly hippie flavour to this effort.

Santa Claus Symphony   A symphony by William Henry Fry (1813-64) performed for the first time on Christmas Eve 1853. Fry was an American composer more famous for his 1858 opera *Leonora*. He studied in Europe and was a friend of Berlioz, but contemporary critics were unimpressed by his symphony.

Santa Claus: The Movie   (1985)   At the time, one of the most expensive films ever made, *Santa Claus: The Movie* leads the Christmas sweepstakes in special effects. Millions of dollars were spent making audiences believe that Santa (David Huddleston) and his reindeer really could fly and in constructing a vast North Pole workshop. After showing the origins of Santa and Mrs. Claus – a frozen medieval woodcutter and wife – the plot revolves around John Lithgow as an evil toy manufacturer (is there any other kind in Christmas movies?) and a gullible dwarf (Dudley Moore). Despite its enormous budget, director Jeannot Szwarc's movie never made an impact on critics or audiences.

Santa Claus World Congress   An international professional association linking Santa Claus, Father Christmas, Julemand, and other gift-bringing figures from around the world. It has met annually in Copenhagen since the 1960s with great fanfare, including parades, dances, and contests. Attendees discuss such issues as female Santa Clauses, uniform style, and efforts by the European Union to standardize the length of gift-bringers' beards – an issue over which they threatened to go on strike. Recent years have seen tension between members of the organization and the Finnish Joulupukki, who claims to be the most authentic Santa Claus, and who sees no reason to attend a meeting of mere imitations.

Santa Claus World Cup A competition held in Drammen, Norway, in 1994 between 30 Santa Claus figures from around the world. Events included fence and rooftop climbing, chimney sliding, and carolling. Judges were eight-year-old children in elf costumes.

The Santa Clause (1994) A very successful film for comic Tim Allen in which he plays Scott Calvin, an unhappy, divorced father who unwittingly becomes the successor to Santa Claus. When Scott causes Santa to fall from his roof and dons the old man's suit, he finds himself gaining weight, growing a beard, and attracting children who want to tell him their Christmas wishes. As he grows into his new role, adults worry about his mental health, but he finds he has repaired his relationship with his estranged son (a common theme in late-20th century Hollywood movies like *Hook, Liar, Liar*, and *Jingle All the Way*). Wonderful special effects and a good heart to this John Pasquin film make it a potential classic.

Santa Clawing Also known as "Santa Clausing" or "Sandying," this is a term used on Sable Island and parts of Nova Scotia for informal Christmastime visits of mummers, groups of folk of all ages and both sexes wearing disguises. On Sable Island groups of masked visitors would peer in at windows and announce their presence by beating on drums and playing homemade instruments. Once inside, they would play a song or act a skit and be given treats before going on to the next house. The practice seems to have died out after the Second World War.

Santa of the Year Award In 1995 the Santa Claus of Greenland Foundation instituted the Santa of the Year Award to be given each Christmas "to an individual person, who is internationally recognised for humanistic views and deeds and who . . . is committed to furthering awareness of the need for improvements in the welfare of children throughout the world." That year President Nelson Mandela of South Africa was given the award by the Premier of Greenland, along with $100,000 to be used for children's charities.

Santa With Muscles (1996) A universally despised film directed by John Murlowski and starring professional wrestler Hulk Hogan as a mean millionaire who becomes convinced that he is really Santa Claus.

Santicló Latin-American term for Santa Claus.

Santons **of Provence** Literally "little saints," *santons* are clay Nativity figures made in the south of France. They represent not just the usual figures about the manger – the Holy Family, shepherds, animals, and Magi – but also townspeople, pipers, travellers, merchants, and gypsies – in fact a microcosm of life in period costume. The custom of crafting *santons* came to Provence from Italy in the 18th century, and since the early 19th century there have been *santon* fairs – the one in Marseilles is held annually from St. Nicholas's Day (December 6) to Twelfth Night (January 6) – with prizes for the best figures and best crèche.

Saturnalia The ancient Roman festival honouring Saturn, god of the harvest, held from December 17 to 24. It was a time of obligatory merriment, suspension of quarrels, cross-dressing, social inversion, and masquerades. Only those essential to the merry-making, such as cooks and bakers, were allowed to work. Slaves and masters temporarily reversed roles, and a Lord of Misrule was elected to oversee the fun. Houses were decorated with candles and greenery and small presents were exchanged between friends; children were given little dolls (perhaps as a token of the time when human sacrifices were made to ensure fertility of the crop). Many of the customs proved hard to eradicate when Roman paganism was replaced by Christianity, and they seem to have clung to subsequent midwinter holidays such as Christmas, as opponents of Christmas have always pointed out. This 17th-century attack makes the basis for objection clear:

> The generality of Christmas-keepers observe that Festival after such a manner as is highly dishonourable to the name of Christ. How few are there comparatively that spend those Holidays (as they are called) after an Holy manner. But they are consumed in Compotations, in Interludes, in playing at Cards, in Revellings, in excess of Wine, in mad Mirth; Will Christ the holy Son of God be pleased with such Services? Just after this manner were the Saturnalia of the Heathen celebrated. Saturn was the Gaming God. And (as one saith) the Feast of Christ's Nativity is attended with such Profaneness, as that it deserves the name of Saturns Mass, or of Bacchus his Mass, or if you will, the Devils Mass, rather than to have the Holy name of Christ put upon it.

Schmutzli An intimidating companion to the Swiss Saint Nicholas. He carries a sack in which he threatens to stuff bad children. See HELPERS, SANTA'S.

Schwibbogen Arch-shaped candle-holders, a type of Christmas folk art from the Erzgebirge area of Germany. Based on the lamps worn by miners of the area, the first *Schwibbogen* appeared in the 18th century as a way to decorate the church during midnight mass. Later the candle-holders were placed in windows and used as home decorations. Nowadays they appear in many forms and have become a highly prized collectible. The name seems to have been derived from the German architectural term for arches on Gothic buildings.

Scotland Christmas in Scotland is the story of a holiday celebrated, banned, relocated, and now rediscovered. Until 1560 English and Scottish Christmas celebrations were similar. Merriment was widespread, carols were sung, Yule logs were burnt, Abbots of Misrule presided over parties and festivals of social inversion, and, according to Sir Walter Scott,

> 'Twas Christmas broach'd the mightiest ale;
> 'Twas Christmas told the merriest tale;
> A Christmas gambol oft could cheer
> The poor man's heart through half the year.

This began to change after 1561, when the Calvinist Church acquired power. In that year the Book of Discipline claimed that feast days like Christmas, Epiphany, and the Circumcision (January 1) were papist inventions and abolished them. This was reinforced in 1566 with the adoption of the Helvetic Confession, which explicitly omitted the clause recognizing the feasts of Christ. In the 1570s a drive against Christmas observances was undertaken: in 1573 the church session of St. Andrew's punished folk for observing superstitious days, including "Yuill-day." In 1574 it punished a baker who had held a New Year's party and shouted "Yuill! Yuill! Yuill!" That same year the session at Aberdeen tried 14 women for "playing, dancing, and singing filthy carols on Yule Day at even." The Glasgow kirk (the established Calvinist Church) in 1583 ordered excommunication for those who kept Christmas, and throughout Scotland bakers who made the Yule bread and those who sang carols were prosecuted. In 1593 the minister at Errol equated carol-singing with fornication.

Resistance to these bans was widespread, and they had to be continually repeated. In Aberdeen in 1606, the session condemned those who still kept Yule and New Year's, those who masked and disguised themselves, men and women who cross-dressed, and folk who danced with bells and celebrated in the streets or in houses. Prohibition met particularly strong resistance in the royal court, and there were appeals in 1598 and 1599 against Christmas celebrations at the court of James VI in Edinburgh. In 1618 King James (now James I of England) imposed the Five Articles on Scotland, which, among other things, mandated the observance of Christmas in the English style, but when religious hardliners assumed power in Scotland in the late 1630s they re-abolished the holy days and forced James's son, Charles I, to rescind the Articles. Repression seems to have worked in the 1640s; zealous clergymen searched homes at Christmas for signs of "the superstitious goose" or for weavers who had taken the day off work.

Parts of the Highlands and the Outer Hebrides never experienced the full impact of the Calvinist Reformation and so continued to celebrate Christmas in the old ways. Christmas Eve was known as *Oidhche Choinnle* ("Candle Night") from the practice of keeping lights in the windows. Yule bread and Yule cake, dancing, and feasting continued to be part of the Christmas season. Carolling died out in most of Scotland under the Church's prohibitions, but it survived in the Catholic Outer Hebrides. Groups called Christmas lads (*gillean nollaig*), song men (*fir duan*), guisers (*gaisearan*), or rejoicers (*nuallairean*) went about singing carols in Gaelic and wearing long shirts and tall white hats in imitation of a Catholic clergyman's surplice and mitre.

In the south the need for a midwinter festival was met by transferring the Yule celebrations to New Year's, when they were less religiously objectionable, though the kirk tried to control these festivities as well. So it was that in the more populous parts of Scotland, New Year's Eve, or Hogmanay, became the substitute for Christmas and the time when many of the old Yule-time customs were able to be observed.

The origin of Hogmanay is still debated, with some saying the word is derived from the French *aguillanneuf*, meaning either "New Year" or a New Year's gift, while others, probably on shakier ground, claim it comes from the French phrase *Homme est né* ("Man is born"), a reference to the birth of Jesus. Regardless of the origin of the word, it is a time of high celebration, with house parties, revellers in the streets, masked guisers, church bells ringing, and ancient customs (see GUISING). Among these traditions is opening the doors of the house at midnight to let the old year out and the new year in, and the choice of the first-footer (see FIRST-FOOTING). It is a matter of some importance who the first person across the threshold in the new year should be: dark-haired men are generally preferred, and there is a prejudice against fair-haired men or women of any description being first into the house. Some householders arrange for a family member to perform the first-footing, while others hire someone suitable. The first-footer should bring with him a suitable gift or *handsel*: a lump of coal or other symbol of fire and warmth, a cake to symbolize plenty, salt or a bottle of whisky

to symbolize the luxuries of life. Many homes still follow the Celtic custom of placing candles in the window on Christmas Eve and Hogmanay.

In the rural areas of Scotland, SAINING, or ritual cleansing, was required as the New Year approached. There were many approaches to this vital task; some involved censing the house and barn, people and animals with juniper smoke; in some cases holy water was sprinkled in every corner; in others an animal hide was loudly beaten and good-luck verses were recited.

Great good luck to the house,
Good luck to the family,
Good luck to every rafter in it,
And to every worldly thing in it.

Good luck to horses and cattle,
Good luck to the sheep,
Good luck to everything,
And good luck to all your means.

Luck to the good-wife,
Good luck to the children,
Good luck to every friend,
Great fortune and health to all.

Many seasonal customs have to do with fire. In Burghead, a tar-barrel, the *clavie*, is set on fire, and brave volunteers take turns carrying it on their head before it is smashed to bits. In the Shetland Islands, a 30-foot replica of a Viking boat is carried through the streets in the UP-HELLY AA before it is set on fire by torches. In Comrie huge torches, or *flambeaux*, are paraded through the streets before being thrown into the river.

Similar to the Haxey Hood Game in England is the Orkney Ba' Game, played annually on Christmas Day and New Year's Day between two sections of the town of Kirkwall. The inhabitants are divided between "Uppies" and "Doonies," who struggle for possession of a leather ball on the streets of the town. Heaving and grabbing, the players can tussle for hours as the "Uppies" try to propel the ball to the south end of Kirkwall while the "Doonies" hope to move it toward the harbour. Legend attributes the origin of this contest to the kicking of a hated enemy's severed head in medieval times.

Despite being the nation that invented haggis, Scotland has produced some delicious seasonal foods: shortbread, which is consumed in massive amounts in Scotland and exported around the world; the rich BLACK BUN; Athol Brose, a whisky-flavoured oatmeal concoction that can be drunk or served as a dessert; and the *clootie* dumpling, a boiled pudding containing good luck charms, served with a creamy topping for the children and an alcohol-flavoured custard sauce for the adults.

The Scottish resistance to Christmas continued until well into the 20th century, partly for patriotic reasons (Christmas was seen as an English custom), and partly for reasons of lingering Calvinism. Opposition broke down after the Second World War, when many Scottish troops had experienced Christmas customs and American Christmas culture was achieving worldwide penetration. Nowadays Scots tend to have the best of both worlds. They celebrate Christmas on December 25 with a tree, turkey dinner, and the visit of Father Christmas, but they cling to the old ways and honour Hogmanay as much as ever.

SCROOGE See SOCIETY TO CURTAIL RIDICULOUS, OUTRAGEOUS AND OSTENTATIOUS GIFT EXCHANGES.

Ebenezer Scrooge *Scrooge is forced to contemplate his own gravestone in* A Christmas Carol.

Scrooge, Ebenezer A rich miser whose redemption by the three Ghosts of Christmas is the centrepiece of Charles Dickens's 1843 *A Christmas Carol*. Dickens shows how Scrooge, though blessed at various points in his life with the love of his sister, a nephew, and a fiancée, turned his back on emotion to concentrate on the accumulation of wealth in the company of his business partner, Jacob Marley. When Marley's ghost appears one Christmas Eve to show how the afterlife punishes the greedy and uncharitable, Scrooge begins his journey to renewal.

By the time Dickens came to choose the name for his flint-hearted protagonist, the word "scrooge" already meant "to squeeze," and despite Ebenezer's change of heart, the name Scrooge has come to denote those who are tight-fisted and mean.

Scrooge (1935) Sir Seymour Hicks stars as Ebenezer Scrooge in this British adaptation of *A Christmas Carol*. Hicks spent much of his working life playing Scrooge, giving over 2,000 stage performances and appearing in a 1913 silent version. This was the first full-length sound motion picture of Dickens's classic. Director Henry Edwards chose not to show the audience Marley's ghost: it was visible only to Hicks, who played the entire scene by himself.

Scrooge (1970) A great cast is wasted in this musical version of *A Christmas Carol*. Albert Finney is Scrooge, Alec Guinness is the ghost of Jacob Marley, Dame Edith Evans is Christmas Past, and Kenneth More is Christmas Present, but collectively they can't do much with an uninspired Leslie Bricusse score.

Scrooged (1988) A rather nasty postmodern remake of *A Christmas Carol*, directed by Richard Donner and set in the high-pressure world of television production. Frank Cross (played by Bill Murray), who plans to air a live TV version of the Dickens classic, is a Scroogelike character himself, and in need of Christmas redemption. This is eventually provided by the Spirits, led by Carol Kane. As an attempt at comedy it is pure dross and its fumblings toward Dickensian pathos are equally ineffective.

It is a great pity the audience doesn't get to see the version of *A Christmas Carol* that Cross was preparing to broadcast that fateful night – starring Buddy Hackett as Scrooge and perky gymnast Mary Lou Retton as Tiny Tim, it would have been far more memorable than *Scrooged*.

"Season's Greetings" A popular, if somewhat meaningless, slogan (sometimes rendered as "Season Greetings") on late 20th-century North American Christmas cards. Its emptiness is a virtue of political correctness for those afraid to offend by mentioning a Christian holiday.

Secret Santa A popular custom of many countries where, in schools, offices, and other places of work, participants draw the name of someone to whom they will anonymously give a little gift before Christmas. In Brazil this is called *amigo secreto*; in Honduras, *cochombros*; in some parts of Canada it is "Kris Kringle."

"See Amid the Winter's Snow" A Christmas hymn written by English priest Edward Caswall (1814-78), with music by John Goss (1800-80).

> See, amid the winter's snow,
> Born for us on earth below,
> See, the tender Lamb appears,
> Promised from eternal years.
>
> *Hail, thou ever-blessed morn!*
> *Hail, Redemption's happy dawn!*
> *Sing through all Jerusalem:*
> *Christ is born in Bethlehem!*
>
> Lo, within a manger lies
> He who built the starry skies,
> He, who throned in height sublime,
> Sits amid the Cherubim.
>
> *Chorus*
>
> Say, ye holy shepherds, say:
> What your joyful news today;
> Wherefore have ye left your sheep
> On the lonely mountains steep?
>
> *Chorus*
>
> As we watched at dead of night,
> Lo, we saw a wondrous light:
> Angels, singing peace on earth,
> Told us of a Saviour's birth.
>
> *Chorus*
>
> Sacred Infant, all divine,
> What a tender love was Thine,
> Thus to come from highest bliss
> Down to such a world as this!
>
> *Chorus*
>
> Teach, O teach us, Holy Child,
> By Thy face so meek and mild,
> Teach us to resemble Thee
> In Thy sweet humility.

Serenading A term used in the Salvation Army for the custom of small brass ensembles going about playing Christmas music.

"The Seven Joys of Mary" The Seven Joys (and Sorrows) of Mary were a popular theme in medieval art and didactic literature. Though there are many songs and legends enumerating the various joys and sorrows of Mary, by the 15th century Franciscan monks had codified them and limited the number of each to seven. The official joys are:

1. The Annunciation;
2. The Visitation;
3. The Nativity;
4. The Epiphany;
5. The Presentation of Jesus;
6. Finding Jesus in the Temple;
7. Her Assumption into Heaven.

The Seven Sorrows of Mary are:
1. The Prophecy of Simeon;
2. The Flight into Egypt;
3. The Loss of Jesus in the Temple;
4. Meeting Jesus on the Way of the Cross;
5. The Crucifixion of Jesus;
6. Taking Jesus down from the Cross;
7. The Burial of Jesus.

The song below is based on a 15th-century English folk poem and was often sung by poor women who went door-to-door with a cup bearing images of the baby Jesus and Mary.

The first good joy that Mary had,
It was the joy of one;
To see the blessed Jesus Christ
When he was first her son:

When he was first her son, good man
And blessed may he be,
Praise Father, Son, and Holy Ghost,
To all eternity.

The next good joy that Mary had,
It was the joy of two;
To see her own son, Jesus Christ,
To make the lame to go:

Chorus

The next good joy that Mary had,
It was the joy of three;
To see her own son, Jesus Christ,
To make the blind to see:

Chorus

The next good joy that Mary had,
It was the joy of four;
To see her own son, Jesus Christ,
To read the Bible o'er:

Chorus

The next good joy that Mary had,
It was the joy of five;
To see her own son, Jesus Christ,
To bring the dead alive:

Chorus

The next good joy that Mary had,
It was the joy of six;

To see her own son Jesus Christ,
Upon the crucifix:

Chorus

The next good joy that Mary had,
It was the joy of seven;
To see her own son,
Jesus Christ, ascending into heaven.

Shepherds The Gospel of Luke (2:8-18) tells the story of the announcement of the birth of Jesus to local shepherds and their visit to the Holy Family.

And there were in the same country shepherds abiding in the fields keeping watch over their flocks by night. And, lo, the angel of the Lord came upon them, and the glory of the Lord shone round about them: and they were sore afraid. And the angel said unto them, Fear not; for behold I bring you tidings of great joy, which shall be to all people. For unto you is born this day in the city of David a Saviour which is Christ the Lord. And this shall be a sign unto you: Ye shall find the babe wrapped in swaddling clothes and lying in a manger. And suddenly there was with the angel a multitude of the heavenly host praising God, and saying, Glory to God in the highest, and on earth peace, good will toward men. And it came to pass, as the angels were gone away from them into heaven, the shepherds said one to another, Let us now go even unto Bethlehem, and see this thing which has come to pass, which the Lord hath made known unto us. And they came with haste, and found Mary, and Joseph, and the babe lying in a manger. And when they had seen it, they made known abroad the saying which was told to them concerning this child. And all they that heard it wondered at those things which were told them by the shepherds.

Theologians have often remarked on the importance of the choice of shepherds as the first to be told of the birth of the Saviour. Shepherds were notoriously dirty, infamous for their neglect of the Jewish rites of ritual cleanliness of body and utensils; their testimony, like that of thieves and extortionists, was not acceptable in court. The angels' visit to these debased characters seems to stress the universality of the Christmas message and the social inversion implicit in the Incarnation – the King of the Universe born in an animal shelter.

This exaltation of the humble has been the subject of drama and song ever since. Church liturgies have long honoured shepherds; the Office of the Shepherds at Rouen re-enacted the story before the midnight mass. In Poland the midnight mass is called the Shepherds' Mass, and shepherds' pipes are often played during the service. In special masses in the south of France, shepherds bring lambs into church and place them near the altar. PASTORAL DRAMA, stories of the shepherds' journey to see the Holy Family, is a big part of the Christmas season around the world. In Italy shepherds come down from the hills before Christmas to play their bagpipes before shrines, in churches, and in the streets. Carols that celebrate the role of shepherds include the English "While Shepherds Watched Their Flocks by Night," the French "Berger, secoue ton sommeil profond," and the German "Stille Nacht."

The 14th-century mystic St. Bridget of Sweden, whose spiritual revelations about the Nativity were important in shaping medieval depictions of the event, said that when the shepherds first encountered the Holy Family they wanted to know the sex of the child, "for angels had announced to them that

Shepherds' Field *The beautiful Shepherds' Field Chapel in Bethlehem is on the spot where the shepherds were greeted by angels on the night of the Nativity.*

the saviour of the world had been born, and they had not said it was a saviouress." When Mary showed them that the baby was a boy, they rejoiced and adored the child.

Today Christmas Eve celebrations in Bethlehem are held in SHEPHERDS' FIELD, where the angels made their announcement, but various denominations disagree over the exact site. (See colour fig. 22.)

Shepherds' Field   The field outside Bethlehem where the angelic host announced the birth of Christ to shepherds tending their flocks. The exact spot is a matter of some debate, but all agree it must be east of Bethlehem in what is now the village of Beit Sahour. Protestants favour the area presently owned by the YMCA; Catholics point to the site of the beautiful Sanctuary of the Shepherds church built to resemble a nomadic tent; Orthodox believers maintain the revelation occurred on the site of a Byzantine-era church. Services held in the area on Christmas Eve are very popular.

"Shepherds, Shake off Your Drowsy Sleep"   A 17th-century Besançon carol, "Berger secoue ton sommeil profond." The anonymous 19th-century English translation was arranged by John Stainer.

> Shepherds, shake off your drowsy sleep,
> Rise and leave your flocks of sheep;
> Angels from heaven around are singing,
> Tidings of great joy are bringing,
> Shepherds, the chorus come and swell!
> Sing noel, O sing noel, noel, noel, noel!
> Sing noel, noel, noel!
> Hark! Even now the bells ring round,

> Listen to the merry sound!
> Hark! How the birds new songs are making,
> As if winter's chains are breaking,
> Shepherds, the chorus come and swell!
> Sing noel, O sing noel, noel, noel!
> Now, comes at last the age of peace,
> Strife and sorrow now shall cease;
> (Prophets foretold this wondrous story)
> Of this heaven-born Prince of glory.
> Shepherds, the chorus come and swell!
> Sing noel, O sing noel!
> Sing noel, O sing noel!

Shoe the Wild Mare   A traditional Christmas game in 17th- and 18th-century England involving striking players on the foot.

Shoes and Christmas   Shoes have played a number of roles in Christmas observances around the world. The most common dates from the Middle Ages: on St. Nicholas Eve or Christmas Eve or Epiphany Eve, children set out their shoes so that the gift-bringer can fill them with treats or gifts. In many European countries, it is essential that the shoes be freshly polished. These same shoes often hold grass or grain for the gift-bringer's animals. A related use is to place one's letter to Santa or other gift-bringer in a shoe so that he will know what present to bring.

In Greece, some people burn their old shoes to prevent misfortunes in the coming year, while others burn them to prevent the monstrous *kallikantzaroi* from coming down the chimney to torment the family. In Scandinavian countries it is believed that shoes placed side-by-side on Christmas Eve will prevent a family from quarrelling in the year to come.

Throwing shoes is also a means of Christmas DIVINATION. A girl who successfully throws her slipper into a tree or who throws her shoe at a door at midnight and finds that it points toward the door will receive a marriage proposal within the year.

Shop Early Campaign Not a drive to begin the Christmas shopping season early, but a reform movement to prevent abuse of shop workers. Begun in 1906 by the American Consumers' League, the campaign hoped to eliminate the need for extended working hours (for which overtime was seldom paid) by persuading shoppers to finish their purchasing several weeks ahead of time. Its motto was "For the sake of humanity, shop early!" They pointed out that retail clerks, delivery boys, factory workers, and postal employees would all benefit from an end to the last-minute rush. The League praised those stores that stuck to their normal hours, and published a "White List" of those shops that required their workers to stay late. A similar drive for reforming Christmas was the SOCIETY FOR THE PREVENTION OF USELESS GIVING (SPUG). (See colour fig. 23.)

"Shop of Ghosts" A story by British writer G.K. Chesterton in which Charles Dickens, Richard Steele, Ben Jonson, and others who have written about Christmas discover a dying Father Christmas but in the end conclude that he is immortal.

Sibyls Ancient priestesses gifted with powers of seeing the future, sibyls were believed by medieval Christianity to have made prophecies concerning the birth and mission of Jesus. They were seen as proof that the pagan world knew of the coming of the Messiah and, as such, they feature in Christian art such as the Sistine Chapel. The Tiburtine Sibyl was said to have pronounced at the moment of Christ's Nativity the virgin birth of a king greater than the Roman emperor. (See colour fig. 24.)

"Silent Night" The most widely sung Christmas carol in the world began life as a poem, "STILLE NACHT" by Austrian priest Josef Mohr (1792-1848), in 1816. Two years later, preparing for the Christmas Eve service in Oberndorf's St. Nicholas Church, Mohr discovered that the organ was not functioning. Legend has attributed the failure to mice gnawing through the bellows, but it is more likely that the organ in the riverside church suffered from excessive moisture and rust in its works. Mohr asked the organist Franz Gruber (1787-1863) to compose a guitar setting for his poem, and the resulting composition was sung at the midnight service. (See colour fig. 25.)

The song would probably have been performed only on that single occasion and forgotten had a visiting musician not seen the music in the church in the early 1820s and taken it away with him. It was played throughout Austria and Germany for the next few years, growing in popularity. The authorship of the piece remained a mystery until 1854, by which time its lyricist was dead. The carol had been attributed to many different composers, including Haydn, Mozart, and Beethoven, but the director of the Royal Court Choir of Berlin, where "Silent Night" had become the favourite of King Friedrich Wilhelm IV of Prussia, researched the origins of the carol and succeeded in having its true creators credited for their work.

The song has been translated into over 300 languages. Its English version was written in 1863 by American Episcopal priest John Freeman Young (1820-85).

Silent night, holy night!
All is calm, all is bright.
Round yon Virgin, Mother and Child.
Holy infant so tender and mild,
Sleep in heavenly peace,
Sleep in heavenly peace.

Silent night, holy night!
Shepherds quake at the sight.
Glories stream from heaven afar
Heavenly hosts sing Alleluia,
Christ the Savior is born!
Christ the Savior is born.

Silent night, holy night!
Son of God love's pure light.
Radiant beams from Thy holy face
With the dawn of redeeming grace,
Jesus Lord, at Thy birth.
Jesus Lord, at Thy birth.

Silent Night, Bloody Night (1973) Typical Christmas horror fare: a small New England town, mysterious mansions, psychopathic killers, insane asylums, female impersonators. Directed by Theodore Gershuny.

Silent Night, Deadly Night (1984-92) Poor Billy has warped ideas about Christmas. Not only has his grandfather filled his head with tales of bad boys being punished by St. Nick, but his father was murdered by a thug in a Santa Claus suit. When Billy grows up and gets a job as a store Santa, it is only natural that he starts to punish and murder on his own. Jonathan Best played the young Billy, and Robert Brian Wilson played the adult axe murderer. Also known as *Slayride*, the film was directed by Charles E. Sellier Jr.

Protests about the movie's violence and its desecration of Christmas and Santa were so widespread that a series of profitable sequels were put into motion. The imaginatively titled 1987 follow-up was called *Silent Night, Deadly Night Part II* and featured Billy's younger brother, Ricky, up to much the same mayhem. *Silent Night, Deadly Night III – Better Watch Out!* (1989) kept the spotlight on Ricky, whose mental health had not improved, while *Silent Night, Deadly Night 4: Initiation* (1990) saw Ricky mixed up with pagan feminists and giant bugs. In *Silent Night, Deadly Night 5: The Toy Maker* (1992), the last of the sequels, the series ran out of gas and died a merciful death.

"Silver Bells" A song from the 1951 movie *Lemon Drop Kid*, sung by Bob Hope and Marilyn Maxwell. It was written by Jay Livingston and Ray Evans, who also wrote hits such as "Mona Lisa," "Buttons and Bows," and "Que Sera, Sera," all of which won Academy Awards. "Silver Bells" was later a hit record for Bing Crosby and was rated Number 8 in the American Society of Composers, Authors and Publishers' survey of the 20th century's best "holiday" songs.

Silvesterkläuse Every December 31 (St. Sylvester's Day) and January 13 (Old St. Sylvester's Eve), men of Urnäsch, in eastern Switzerland, don fantastic costumes and go in groups from door to door. Their outfits are intended to achieve three levels of grotesqueness: the Wüeschti, or "the ugly Chläuse," is covered in bark and branches and wears a frightful mask; the Schö-Wüeschti, or "less-ugly," is equally piney but less frightening; and the Schöne, or "pretty Chläuse," wears a huge bell or a massive headdress depicting a rural scene.

At each house they sing three *zäuerli*, or wordless yodels, and are rewarded with a drink, food, and money before going on to the next destination. Once part of the widespread phenomenon of Christmas BEGGING VISITS, the custom is now kept alive partly out of a love for local tradition and partly for the tourist trade it attracts.

Simon the Zealot   One of the original 12 disciples of Jesus, whose nickname has led some to link him with the violent anti-Roman resistance movement. Christian legend places him among the shepherds to whom the birth of Jesus was announced on Christmas Eve.

"The Simpsons' Christmas Special" (1989)   In the Christmas episode of the opening season of *The Simpsons*, Homer discovers he will not receive the holiday bonus the family has been counting on. He takes a job as a department store Santa but loses even that money at the dog track, where he wagers on a long shot named Santa's Little Helper. All ends happily when he brings home the losing dog as a present. Also known as "Simpsons Roasting on an Open Fire." Created by Matt Groening.

"Sleep My Little Jesus"   A 19th-century Christmas hymn by Adam Geibel, the blind Philadelphia composer who also wrote "Stand Up, Stand Up for Jesus"; words by Unitarian minister William Channing Gannett.

> Sleep, my little Jesus,
> On thy bed of hay,
> While the shepherds homeward
> Journey on their way.
> Mother is thy shepherd,
> And will vigil keep.
> O, did voices wake thee?
> Sleep, my Jesus, sleep!
>
> Sleep, my little Jesus,
> While thou art my own!
> Ox and ass thy neighbors,
> Shalt thou have a throne?
> Will they call me blessed?
> Shall I stand and weep?
> O, be it far, Jehovah!
> Sleep, my Jesus, sleep!
>
> Sleep, my little Jesus,
> Wonder, baby mine!
> Well the singing angels
> Greet thee as divine.
> Thro' my heart, as heaven,
> Low the echoes sweep
> Of glory to Jehovah!
> Sleep, my Jesus, sleep!

"Sleep Well, Little Children"   A 1956 song for Christmas by Alan Bergman and Leon Klatzkin, recorded by Rosemary Clooney, Vanessa Williams, and The Carpenters.

"Sleigh Bell Serenade"   A 1952 hit record for Bing Crosby, by Paul Francis Webster and Sonny Burke.

"Sleigh Ride"   Written as an instrumental piece, including hoofbeats and horse's whinny, in 1948 by Leroy Anderson (1908-75), who also wrote "The Syncopated Clock," "The Typewriter," and "Bugler's Holiday." Words were added in 1950 by Mitchell Parish (1900-93), who also wrote lyrics to "Stardust," "Deep Purple," and "Moonlight Serenade."

Slovakia   For the devout, Christmas in Slovakia begins on November 15 with the 40-day St. Philip's fast. A break in the solemn preparation comes on St. Nicholas Day, when the saint, known to Slovaks as Mikulas, visits children and deposits treats and small presents in their shoes or stockings, which are left by the windowsill. Advent is also the time for a thorough house-cleaning, buying baking supplies and festive foods, having the *oplatki* wafers blessed by the priest, and shopping for Christmas presents.

On Christmas Eve the tree is decorated, often with home-made ornaments, cookies, and candles; in many homes a crèche, or *Betlehem*, is placed at the foot of the tree. The sight of the first star in the evening sky is eagerly awaited; when it has risen, the meatless Christmas Eve meal can begin. On the menu are 12 dishes to honour the apostles, including mushroom or cabbage soup, fish, potato salad, *bobalky* (poppy seeds, milk, and honey poured over bread), vegetables, and Christmas cake. The dinner often begins with *oplatki* wafers, which are stamped with Nativity scenes. They are often smeared with honey and garlic and passed from hand to hand accompanied by a kiss. On farms, the father may give some of the wafers to the livestock along with an extra helping of fodder. Traditions associated with the Christmas Eve meal include a family blessing. A Slovak-American immigrant remembers a ritual performed by her parents:

> Father and we children were seated quietly around the table and put out the lamp. Mother came to the doorway and knocked three times on the door frame. With each knock Father would ask, "What do you bring?" Mother answered each time, "The Lord's gift." After the third knock Mother came into the room greeting us with, "Praise be to the Lord Jesus Christ" to which we answered, "Forever, Amen."
>
> Then Mother put some holy water into each of the four corners of the room and said the following prayer, "Good tidings be yours during these glorious holy days of the birth of Christ the Lord, may He bring you health, happiness and His abundant blessings, and after death that you will be taken up into His heavenly kingdom."

Sometimes the legs of the table are bound by a chain as a symbol of family unity. Candles are lit on the table and in the window, and a fish scale is placed under each plate for good luck. Hay or straw is placed in the room as a remembrance of the manger. Prayers are said, carols sung, and presents exchanged; the main gift-bringer in Slovakia is the Christ Child.

A well-loved old custom in Slovakia is the arrival of the *Jaslicakary* or Bethlehem carollers, men and boys dressed as angels and shepherds, who visit homes carrying a crèche, singing carols of the Nativity, and re-enacting the story of the birth of Jesus from the point of view of the shepherds. Like much pastoral drama around the world, there is attendant humour, often in the person of clownish figures, who bluster, threaten the children, and try to kiss the girls. The visitors are given refreshments, and when they leave they sing out their wishes for a happy and healthy long life for the residents. The family then heads off to church for the midnight service.

Christmas Day is also a time for church and family togetherness. On St. Stephen's Day people leave their homes and exchange visits. Partying continues until the end of the Christmas season, Theophany, the commemoration of Christ's baptism in the River Jordan and the revelation of his divinity.

Snacks for the Gift-bringer *Children lay out a treat for Santa Claus.*

"Slyseli jsme v Betleme"   A traditional Czech carol, translated as "We Have Heard in Bethlehem."

> We have heard in Bethlehem,
> Lies a Babe, a heav'nly gem.
> O'er the infant King, so lovely,
> Joseph and sweet Mary hov'ring,
> We have heard in Bethlehem,
> Lies a Babe, a heav'nly gem.

Snacks for the Gift-bringer   In North America it is customary to leave out a snack for Santa Claus to refresh him on his Christmas Eve labours. Children put out a plate of cookies and a glass of milk and perhaps a carrot for the reindeer. To their delighted satisfaction they find the next morning that the cookies have been devoured, the milk drunk, the carrot nibbled, and maybe even a polite note of thanks from the gift-bringer.

This custom has its historical antecedents as well as corresponding actions around the world. Its origins partly lie in the Eastern European and Scandinavian belief that the spirits of the family dead visit the home on Christmas Eve, when they find a place laid for them at the table and in some areas a bath or a bed waiting for them. Sometimes offerings are also left for the Holy Family. In the Austrian mountains it was the custom to leave milk for the baby Jesus and Mary during the time of the midnight mass, while in Brittany food was left out at night for the Virgin. A loaf of bread, a jug of milk, and a burning candle were placed on many Irish tables in case the Holy Family ventured by in the dark.

Today, children in Latin countries for whom the Three Kings are the gift-bringers leave an offering of hay for the camels on Epiphany Eve; in Puerto Rico children collect fresh grass, roll it in a ball, decorate it with lace, and leave it under the bed for the weary animals. In pre-Communist Cuba, children would leave tobacco, grass, and coffee beans for the Three Wise Men and their camels.

In England Father Christmas might find a mince pie and a shot of brandy. In at least one house in Cumberland in the 1950s, Father Christmas was left a glass of sherry, a cigarette, and half-a-crown. Children in Syria and Lebanon leave water and wheat for the Mule and Camel. In Denmark the house elf, or *nisse*, must have its saucer of rice porridge on Christmas Eve or things will go badly. The heat of the Australian Christmas means that Father Christmas often gets a cold beer, and a bucket of water for the white kangaroos that pull his sleigh. In the Tyrol, St. Nicholas's horse gets hay, while the saint is left a glass of schnapps. In Protestant areas of Germany the Weihnachtsmann looks forward to a snack of *Glühwein*, ginger bread, or *stollen*.

Snap Dragon   An English game played at Christmas since at least the 17th century. A bowl of raisins is soaked with brandy and set alight. Players reach for the fruit with their bare fingers while onlookers chant:

> Here he comes with flaming bowl,
> Don't he mean to take his toll,
> Snip! Snap! Dragon!
>
> Take care you don't take too much,
> Be not greedy in your clutch,
> Snip! Snap! Dragon!
>
> With his blue and lapping tongue
> Many of you will be stung,
> Snip! Snap! Dragon!
>
> For he snaps at all that comes
> Snatching at his feast of plums,
> Snip! Snap! Dragon!

A variation on this game was Flap Dragon, in which a lighted candle was placed in the centre of a mug of ale or cider. The challenge lay in getting a drink without extinguishing the candle.

Snegurochka   The Snow Maiden, Snegurochka, was a legendary figure in pre-revolutionary Russia, a snow-girl who appeared in winter and returned to the far north for the summer. She was used by Soviet authorities during the Communist regime as a secular personification of winter and to lead, with Grandfather Frost, New Year's celebrations. She is usually portrayed as a beautiful young woman with long blond braids and a blue, fur-trimmed costume. Snegurochka's popularity has continued since the demise of the Soviet Union and the return of older Christmas traditions to Russia.

Snap Dragon *The exciting Christmas game of Snap Dragon.*

Snow *Christmas and snow seem inextricably linked.*

Snow Snow has become so accepted a part of the Christmas landscape that even in tropical countries artificial snow is used as a seasonal decoration, and snowbound scenes illustrate Christmas cards around the world. Medieval and early-modern representations of the Nativity often stressed the cold and hardship suffered by the Holy Family, but snow was rarely included; Pieter Brueghel's setting of his Nativity cycle in a snowy Dutch village is an exception.

Snow became intertwined with Christmas only in the 19th century, when Santa Claus was portrayed by Americans as driving a sleigh pulled by reindeer and was identified with the North Pole. Victorian poets such as Christina Rossetti ("In the Bleak Mid-Winter") and Edward Caswall ("See Amid the Winter's Snow") then added snow to the vocabulary of Christmas hymns. Secular carols such as "Jingle Bells," "Sleigh Ride," "White Christmas," and "Frosty the Snowman" echo the theme.

Phoenix, Arizona, with an average December temperature of 23°C (73.4°F) dumps 10 tons of real snow around for its annual "Snow Daze" festival.

Sixteenth-century cooks also knew how to imitate snow, as this Christmas dessert recipe from *A Booke of Cookerie*, 1594, demonstrates:

> Take a pottle of sweet thick Cream, and the white of eyght Egs, and beate them altogether, with a spoone, then put them into your cream with a dishfull of Rosewater, and a dishfull of Sugar withall, then take a sticke and make it clene, and then cut it in the end foursquare, and therewith beat all the aforesaid things together, and ever as it ariseth take it off, and put it in to a Cullender, this doone, take a platter and sette an Apple in the midst of it, stick a thicke bush of Rosemary in the Apple. Then cast your Snow upon the Rosemary and fill your platter therewith, and if you have wafers cast some withall, and so serve them forthe.

"The Snow Lay on the Ground" A 19th-century West Country folk carol.

> The snow lay on the ground,
> The stars shone bright,
> When Christ our Lord was born
> On Christmas night.
>
> *Venite adoremus*
> *Dominum:*
> *Venite adoremus*
> *Dominum.*
> *Venite adoremus Dominum.*
>
> 'Twas Mary, daughter pure
> Of holy Anne,
> That brought into this world
> The God made man.
> She laid him in a stall
> At Bethlehem;
> The ass and oxen shared
> The roof with them.
>
> *Refrain*
>
> Saint Joseph, too, was by
> To tend the child;
> To guard him, and protect
> His mother mild;

The angels hovered round,
And sung this song,
Venite adoremus
Dominum

Refrain

And thus that manger poor
Became a throne;
For he whom Mary bore
Was God the Son.
O come, then, let us join
The heavenly host,
To praise the Father, Son,
And Holy Ghost.

Refrain

Snowdrops A white flower (*Galanthus nivalis*) used in Wales at the end of the Christmas season when decorations and greenery were taken down. A bowl of snowdrops was said to drive evil out of the house before the arrival of spring and to give the house a "white purification." They are also a flower associated with CANDLEMAS and are known around the British Isles by names such as Purification Flowers, Mary's Tapers, or Candlemas Bells.

Social Inversion Like the feast of Saturnalia that preceded it, Christmas has a long history of social inversion, of the world turned upside down, of the first being last and the last being first. It begins with the birth of Jesus in a lowly manger and the angelic announcement being made to a group of shepherds. It continued after Christmas had become a state holiday, with Byzantine court officials indulging in festive cross-dressing and parodying sacred rites. The FEAST OF THE ASS, the FEAST OF FOOLS, and the BOY BISHOP all had elements of social inversion, with the latter designed to reflect the Christian notion that one had to be like a little child to receive the kingdom of Heaven. Inevitably these reversals of the norm were abused, leading to irreverence and violence – clergy in Exeter in the 14th century, for example, took to throwing mud at each other during Christmas services – and they were suppressed by church and governments. Some echoes of these customs still exist: the Boy Bishop has been revived in some English churches; in Italy children are encouraged to preach at Christmas in front of the BAMBINO of Ara Coeli; and in many armies of the British Commonwealth, officers have traditionally served Christmas dinner to the troops. Some have detected social inversion in the Irish hunting of the wren on St. Stephen's Day, a bird protected all the other days of the year.

Society for the Prevention of Useless Giving (SPUG) The Progressive movement of early 20th-century America sought to reform a number of capitalist institutions, and SPUG's desire to modify aspects of Christmas giving grew out of this impulse. Formed in 1912, it aimed to eliminate the practice of supervisors receiving gifts from their underlings at Christmas. SPUG complained that this was a form of corruption and did not reflect any real affection on the part of the employees toward their bosses. Their publicity attempted to shame the supervisors and persuade the clerks not to buy these offerings; the campaign was ultimately a success.

Society to Curtail Ridiculous, Outrageous and Ostentatious Gift Exchanges (SCROOGE) An American group founded in 1979 that sought to reform Christmas by eliminating much

of its commercialism. Charles Langham of SCROOGE suggested spending a maximum of 1 percent of income on Christmas gifts. Its Four Principles are:

1. Try to avoid giving (and receiving) extremely expensive gifts, particularly the heavily advertised fad/status symbol items that are often not very useful or practical.
2. Make every effort to use cash rather than credit cards to pay for the items that you do purchase.
3. Emphasize gifts that involve thought and originality, such as handicraft items that you make yourself.
4. Celebrate and enjoy the holidays but remember that a Merry Christmas is not for sale in any store for any amount of money.

Sol Invictus The cult of the Unconquered Sun, celebrated in imperial Rome on December 25. The worship of the sun god was introduced under Emperor Elagabulus in the 220s, and under Aurelian in 274 it became officially linked with the empire's well-being. Constantine was a devotee of this sect, and despite the favour he bestowed on Christianity after the 313 Edict of Milan, he continued for a number of years to have images of the sun on Roman coins. Some historians speculate that the choice of December 25 as the date for the observation of Christmas was, at least in part, due to a desire to replace worship of the sun god with the Son of God.

Solstice Literally "sun standing still," when the sun reaches its highest or lowest point in the sky at noon. At the winter solstice, December 22, the sun is directly overhead at noon along the Tropic of Capricorn and the day is shortest in the northern hemisphere. This has traditionally been a time of celebrations involving light, greenery, fire, and the return of the sun. Such midwinter festivities have left their mark on the ways Christmas has been observed. See CANDLES, GREENERY, and PAGANISM.

"Sonatina in Diem Nativitatus Christi MCMXVII" Written by Italian composer Ferruccio Busoni and dedicated to his son Benvenuto, who had enlisted to fight in the First World War, this piano piece affirms the beauty and importance of Christmas in the midst of global violence.

Sorcova On New Year's Day in Romania, children practise a custom known as *sorcova*, derived from the word for "forty." They tap their elders lightly with a small branch or stick decorated with artificial flowers (also called a *sorcova*); the 40 light touches correspond to the 40 words of the poem they recite while doing so.

The Merry sorcova
Long may you live,
Long may you flourish,
Like apple trees,
Like pear trees,
In midsummer,
Like the rich autumn
Overflowing with abundance,
Hard as steel
Fast as an arrow,
For many years to come!
Happy New Year!

In Transylvania a similar custom is carried out by children who go door-to-door with a colourful handkerchief on a stick wishing householders well with the following verse:

As many lumps of coal in the hearth,
Just as many suitors to the lass;
As many stones in the river,
Just as many wheat stacks in the field;
As many chips from the cutter,
Just as many children around the hearth!

Sorrel Jamaican sorrel, *Hibiscus sabdariff*, is the basis of the island's favourite Christmas drink. The red petals are steeped in water for days with spices and orange peel, then strained and mixed with sugar and rum. Served cold, sorrel fuels the many parties held during Jamaica's holiday season.

South Africa Christmas in South Africa closely resembles an English Christmas, reflecting 19th-century British settlement and rule. The Dutch settlers of the country were largely Calvinist and had scant interest in Christmas; for them any merriment was reserved for New Year's Eve.

The gift-bringer in South Africa is Father Christmas, for whom children leave out their stockings on Christmas Eve (the more optimistic children leave out a pillowcase). Christmas dinner is sure to include the traditional Christmas pudding and Christmas crackers, which yield the obligatory paper hats. Boxing Day is the day to distribute gratuities to delivery people or the men who take the rubbish away. Children, as in England, demand to be taken to the pantomime to see "Babes in the Wood" or "Puss-in-Boots" over the Christmas vacation.

What distinguishes a South African Christmas from its European antecedents is that it takes place in midsummer.

The artificial snow used as decoration and the carols referring to a winter wonderland are in contrast to the sunny weather, which draws people to the beach or the mountains. Increasingly, makers of South African Christmas cards are adding local themes; in addition to the usual depictions of snowy sleigh rides and fur-clad Santa Clauses are pictures of native wildlife or Nativity scenes with a black Madonna and Child. The wonderful Australian custom of evening "Carols by Candlelight," so suited to a warm climate, has captured the South African imagination and is now a part of Christmas here, too. Barbecues and beach picnics for Christmas dinner are now much more common than in the past.

Native Africans, for whom Christmas was once primarily a family time of togetherness with little commercial pressure, are now being caught up in the round of present-buying and preparing for holiday feasts.

Spain Christmas in Spain begins with a dance. The Feast of the Immaculate Conception is celebrated in Seville Cathedral every December 8 with *Los Sieses*, the Dance of the Six; 10 boys in the costume of Renaissance pages whirl and step through a series of figures that symbolize the mysteries of the Incarnation and the Nativity. On the same day, in Torrejoncillo, the young men of the town don emerald-studded sheets and gallop through the streets, holding aloft the standard of the Immaculate Virgin. Townsfolk cheer them on, firing encouraging blasts from shotguns.

Outside, the signs of Christmas are everywhere. Christmas markets in Spain today haven't changed much from this lively

***Spain** A Christmas Eve market in the great square in Madrid, 1854.*

description, which appeared in the *London Illustrated News* of December 1854:

> The scene in the Great Square, in every corner of which are various packages – as sacks, boxes and baskets: and lambs, turkeys and other articles of good cheer – where the confusing and crowding are insupportable. The number of "Nacinnentos" (figures representing the birth of Christ) and images of every description is infinite, as well as rattles, back-scratchers, and other instruments of amusement. The place becomes a Babel, where a thousand different languages are spoken. On the one side are enormous pyramids of pomegranates of Andalusia, Valencia oranges, Arragonese apples; opposite are sellers of the walnuts and chestnuts of Gallicia, grapes and Malaga sweet potatoes. In another corner rabbits and hares are strewed upon the ground. Here also are castles of "pistache" and tables covered with almond cakes, songs of the sepulchre, and Castilian biscuits. Farther on are interminable columns of sweetmeat boxes, flanked with strong walls of tambourines, drums, pipes, etc. In the centre are the herds of turkeys of Castell, and capons of Biscay; and the "virtuous" pullets of Puercarral.
>
> The vast assemblage, seen beneath a bright sun, and clear blue sky, has a very animated appearance. The costumes are not the least attractive characteristics.

In Madrid the Plaza Mayor is taken over by the market stalls, and in Barcelona the Santa Lluíca fair is set up on December 13 outside the gothic cathedral. Among the Christmas goods on sale are materials to make or add to the family crèche, known variously as a *belén* ("Bethlehem"), *presipio*, or *nacimiento*. These Nativity scenes have been popular since the 18th century and are objects of pride, often handed down from generation to generation. Madrid hosts an annual *Exposición de Belenes* in the Museo Municipal.

An inescapable aspect of the Advent season in Spain is the *Loteria de Navidad*, the Christmas Lottery, the biggest in the world. Almost every Spaniard buys a ticket for this venerable lottery, which dates back to 1763, and everyone dreams of winning *El Gordo*, the "Fat One," the first prize. The draw for the hundreds of millions of pesetas in prizes takes place on December 22 and is covered live by Spanish media. It is traditional for the winning numbers to be sung by orphan schoolchildren. (Another lottery with a Christmas connection is *El Niño*, the Christ Child, which is held on January 7.)

December 24 is *Noche Buena*, the "Good Night" or "Night of Good Tidings," Christmas Eve. Highlights of the day are the midnight mass and the Christmas dinner. As church bells ring out, Spaniards make their way to the late-night *Misa de Gallo*, the "Rooster Mass." A number of remarkable church services are held around the country, such as the candle-lit mass in the mountain monastery at Montserrat, where the choir is renowned, and at Labastida, where shepherds enter bearing a lamb, and a shepherdess carries a representation of the baby Jesus. In Galisteo, a Nativity play is staged at dusk by the 30 members of the Brotherhood of God the Child, complete with shotgun-toting shepherds and slapstick antics.

After the mass families return home for dinner, which varies from region to region but is sure to be the most impressive feast of the year. *Pava*, or turkey, often stuffed with truffles, is the main course in some areas; along the coast it could be cod or *besugo* (red snapper). *Paella*, in one of its many ricey forms, is eaten across the country, as are the wonderful desserts for which Spanish Christmas is famous: marzipan, caramel custard flan, and *turrón*, an almond nougat, made both hard and soft. *Cava*, the Catalan version of champagne, is drunk in great quantities, as are liqueurs, wine, and coffee.

Some families have adopted the North American Santa Claus, or Papa Noel as he is known locally, as the gift-bringer on Christmas Eve (both Santa and the Christmas tree are recent imports), but most continue to wait until January 6 for a more traditional trio to arrive. Another Christmas Eve visitor found in the Basque country of northwest Spain is the Olentzero, who comes down from the mountains bearing gifts for children and telling the news of the birth of Jesus.

Christmas Day sees more festive eating, either of leftovers from the previous night's meal or another family feast, and perhaps another church service. It is also a time to sing many of Spain's famous carols, called *villancicos* or *goigs*: "Fum Fum Fum," the "Carol of the Birds," "The Son of Mary," "El Rei Herodes," and "En Belén Tocan a Fuego." For some it is time to participate in the "Urn of Fate," a kind of matchmaking game where names are drawn from an urn two at a time; the pairs are to be friends for the coming year. A little manipulation to secure the right coupling of partners has been known to happen.

December 28 marks the Feast of the Holy Innocents, a time for licensed foolishness. Friends and family members play pranks on one another, the media makes incredible announcements, and strange characters appear. In Alicante, *Els Enfarinats*, men with flour-caked faces, and *Els Tapats*, masked figures, roam about. Bystanders are levied fines and witty criticisms of local people and events are read out. Other towns have their own "Fools' Festivals." (See FOOLS, FEAST OF.)

In fact, the Christmas season in Spain is celebrated with all sorts of colourful festivals and ceremonies. In Fuentecarreteros, Cordoba, they celebrate *El Baile de los Locos*, "Dance of the Madmen," where, under the direction of a chief lunatic, seemingly deranged dancers parade through the streets and people's houses. At the *Fiesta de Verdiales* in Malaga, 20 bands of musicians gather at a country inn to decide who can play longest and loudest; the contest goes on for hours.

Spaniards see the New Year in with much partying and more festivals, many of them featuring a tree or a fire as a sign of renewal. In Centelles, the Pinewood Festival honours the martyred St. Coloma, who was burnt at the stake. A pine tree is brought down with great ceremony from the mountainside and erected first in the town square and then in the church. At Epiphany its branches are distributed to the inhabitants. The Cart Festival in Cogollos de Guadix sees the village youth collect firewood and cut down a pine tree. On December 31, "Cart Day" girls decorate the tree, which is carried into town, blessed, and its branches distributed. In the evening there is a children's procession for the baby Jesus, and at night a huge bonfire, which the whole town attends. In Spanish homes another festive meal is prepared, and the diners rush to eat 12 grapes between the first and last stroke of midnight. It is bad luck to leave a grape uneaten.

The Christmas season in Spain ends with a flourish. Everyone looks forward to the arrival of the Three Kings – known to Spaniards as Melchior, Gaspar, and Balthasar – on January 5. Their coming is heralded by the performance of solemn mystery plays about the Magi, and wonderful parades get underway as the kings arrive in each city on their way to Bethlehem and the Christ Child. In some towns they arrive by sea, in others they come by helicopter. In Seville the *Cabalgata de los Reyes Magos* features marchers, floats, masquers, dancers, and musicians as well as the kings and their attendants. During

Barcelona's parade, the kings collect the letters the children have written to them in their capacity as Spain's chief gift-bringers, and candies are thrown to the thousands of children lining the streets. At home the children leave out their shoes, filled with grass or grain for the kings' camels, hoping to find them covered with presents in the morning. They are seldom disappointed, though truly bad children are told they can expect only a lump of coal in their footwear.

On January 6 the custom is to eat a piece of the *rosca de reyes*, a kind of cake in the shape of a ring, which contains a bean and a little porcelain baby. The finder of the bean must buy the cake next year, while the person whose piece contains the baby must act out a dare.

Spiders and Christmas A number of European countries, particularly Germany and Ukraine, tell folktales about the role of the humble spider in Christmas. In one story with a number of variations, the Christ Child changes the spider webs on the Christmas tree into silver tinsel. In another, spiders delight the Christ Child in the manger by spinning a web above him in the night. Another story tells of a poor woman whose family is enchanted by the spider webs on the tree, which look silver in the morning sunlight. Because of these tales, it is said, an ornamental spider is often placed on the Ukrainian Christmas tree, and the tree is decorated with tinsel.

Spirit of Christmas (1995) This five-minute animated movie, which was intended by creators Trey Parker and Matt Stone to be a video Christmas card for a Fox television executive, spawned the foul-mouthed comedic phenomenon *South Park*, loathed by parents and educators around the world. Jesus appears to four boys and asks to be taken to the mall for a showdown with his arch-enemy, Santa Claus. The two fight until it is pointed out to Santa that there would be no Christmas were it not for the birth of Jesus, and that Jesus should realize Santa personifies the spirit of giving. Along the way vulgarity, violence, and indecent language abound.

SPUG See SOCIETY FOR THE PREVENTION OF USELESS GIVING.

Stable Though the gospels do not explicitly state that Jesus was born in a stable, the reference to his being laid in a manger has led to this conclusion. In Nativity art, the stable is often depicted in a ruinous condition, symbolic of the passing of the old world. The legend of the ox and ass and other animals attendant at the birth has been derived from the proposition that the event took place in a stable.

Non-canonical gospels and Christian historians as early as 150 A.D. have referred to Mary giving birth in a cave, and some have concluded that the stable was a grotto or cave used for sheltering animals, a not-uncommon feature of the Bethlehem area (see colour fig. 22). Nonetheless, the traditional depiction of the stable in art, in song, or in the custom of the crèche has been as a humble free-standing structure.

"Staffan var en Stalledräng" A Swedish Christmas song about ST. STEPHEN that conflates the legends of Stephen the protomartyr, and another Stephen, or Staffan, reputed to be a horse-loving missionary. This kind of hymn to Stephen would have been sung by "Staffan Riders" on December 26. It begins:

Staffan var en stalledräng
vi tackom nu så gärna
och han vattnade sina fålar fem

"Staffan Var En Stalledräng" *A Swedish postage stamp celebrating the legend of St. Stephen as a lover of horses.*

allt för den ljusa stjärnan
ingen dager synes än
stjärnorna på himmelen de blänka

Staffan was a stable lad,
Thanks now to the Lord.
He watered his five horses,
All for the bright star.
The dawn cannot yet be seen,
The stars twinkle in the sky.

Stainer, Sir John (1840-1901) English composer and carol collector. Working with Henry Ramsden Bramley, his editions in 1871 and 1878 of *Christmas Carols, New and Old* popularized 70 carols, including "The First Nowell" and "What Child Is This?"

Stamps The tradition of Christmas stamps was started in Canada in 1898 when post office officials decided to mark a reduction in the price of postage within the British empire by issuing a commemorative stamp bearing a map of the world with the empire in red and the inscription "XMAS 1898."

Canada did not follow this up, and there were no more stamps with Christmas themes until 1937, when Austria produced a stamp depicting Christmas roses. Two years later, Brazil issued one featuring the Three Wise Men and the Star. However, neither of these stamps was issued specifically for Christmas and so, to philatelic purists, the honour for the first Christmas stamps issued for the holiday season goes to Hungary, which in 1943 issued a set of three, depicting the Shepherds and Angels, the Nativity, and the Adoration of the Magi. It was not until the late 1950s that the use of special Christmas sets became widespread, with Spain, Australia, and the Vatican leading the way.

The first American Christmas stamp was issued in 1962, a four-cent stamp showing a Christmas wreath. Given the touchy question of the separation of church and state in American political life, it is not surprising that some criticized the post office for marking a religious observance, but postal authorities were undeterred and have continued to issue Christmas stamps with both secular and religious themes. (Since 1993 the U.S. Postal Service has referred to this distinction as "Holiday Contemporary" versus "Holiday Traditional," and the only text used is the inoffensive "Greetings.")

It was customary in many countries to issue stamps at Christmastime with a surcharge that would direct money toward various charities, and in some places it was compulsory

Star Boys *Groups of children follow a star on a pole in this venerable Christmas custom, illustrated here on a German postage stamp.*

to use these stamps when sending seasonal mail. Cuba financed an anti-tuberculosis campaign this way, and Costa Rica funded a children's home. See CHRISTMAS SEALS.

Star Boys One of the few remnants of the medieval plays about the journey of the Magi is the custom of the Star Boys. During the Christmas season in Sweden, Germany, Norway, Poland, Lithuania, Russia, and Alaska youth parade dressed as the Three Kings, following a star held aloft on a pole. Since the 16th century, Star Boys have gone from house to house to sing carols or present a pageant in return for hospitality and money, which nowadays goes toward charity.

Star Man In Poland, the Star Man, usually the village priest, quizzes kids on Christmas Eve about religious doctrine with rewards for correct answers.

Star of Bethlehem "Now when Jesus was born in Bethlehem of Judaea in the days of Herod the king, behold, there came wise men from the east to Jerusalem, saying 'Where is he that is born King of the Jews? for we have seen his star in the east, and are come to worship him'. . . . When they had heard the king, they departed; and, lo, the star which they saw in the east, went before them, till it came and stood over where the young child was. When they saw the star, they rejoiced with exceeding great joy." (Matthew 2:1-2, 9-10.)

One of the most fascinating aspects of the story of the first Christmas is that of the Star of Bethlehem, that mysterious celestial object that led the Magi to find the infant Jesus and the Holy Family. The earliest known reference to it in Nativity art is in a fresco from the first half of the third century in the catacombs of Priscilla in Rome; it features a man pointing to a star and a mother feeding a baby who clings to her breast. The star was featured in medieval mystery plays and is the topic of carols such as "Star of the East" and "We Three Kings"; it

appears on countless Christmas cards, on gift wrap, and millions of cookies are made in its shape. In its honour many countries believe that the Christmas Eve feast can begin only when the first star has appeared in the evening sky. The Star Man quizzes children on their behaviour in Poland, while Star Boys parade in many lands preceded by a star on a pole. A star is the top-most ornament on Christmas trees around the world. But what was the original star? Does modern science have an explanation for this ancient wonder?

Most early Christians were happy to explain the star in supernatural terms; non-canonical scripture and Church fathers often referred to the star as an angelic messenger. The modern mind, cool to the possibility of the miraculous, has preferred to seek naturalistic explanations. Four sorts of astral phenomena have been suggested as the Star of Bethlehem: a comet, a nova, a retrograde planetary motion, or a planetary conjunction.

In 5 B.C., Chinese astronomers reported the appearance in the skies of what has long been assumed to be a comet. The manifestation of a comet was always held to be of great political importance and to portend changes in kingdoms. This one was visible for 70 days, long enough to guide Eastern Magi toward Palestine, and had been preceded over the previous two years by astrological signs pointing to events in Israel. As to its appearing to hang over a particular spot in Bethlehem, defenders of the comet thesis say this might be possible if the comet were low in the sky and its tail was oriented vertically.

A nova or supernova is the thermo-nuclear flaring-up of a star so that it suddenly appears much brighter in the sky before gradually returning to its normal luminosity. Some have suggested that the object visible to Chinese astronomers in 5 B.C. was not a comet but a nova. The problem with this explanation is that novae do not give the appearance of moving.

Those who look to planetary phenomena have a number of options from which to choose. In 7 and 6 B.C. Jupiter went through a series of conjunctions (close alignments) with Venus, Saturn, and the star Regulus in Leo, thus astrologically linking kingship (Regulus) with Israel (the Lion). On the other hand, in March and April of 6 B.C., the moon occulted Jupiter – which represents kings – in Aries, the sign corresponding to Judaea. This first occultation could have sent the Magi hurrying west, and the second could have corresponded to the second sighting of the "star" after they left Jerusalem. A conjunction of Venus and Jupiter in August 3 B.C. and June 2 B.C. has been pointed to as a possible "star," as has a retrograde loop by Jupiter in 2 B.C. (here the planet would have appeared to be stationary on December 25).

So far no explanation has proven particularly compelling, and the solution to the mystery of the Star of Bethlehem continues.

Star of Bethlehem An ornamental plant, *Ornithogalum umbellatum*, with bursts of white flowers, which legend says first sprang up outside the stable when light from the Star hit the ground. The lilylike flowers are often used in Christmas bouquets, while herbalists have traditionally employed the plant as a cure for pulled muscles and scarring.

"The Star of the East" An American carol of the 1890s, words by George Cooper, music by Amanda Kennedy.

Star of the East, oh Bethlehem star,
Guiding us on to heaven afar
Sorrow and grief and lull'd by the light
Thou hope of each mortal, in death's lonely night

Fearless and tranquil, we look up to Thee
Knowing thou beam'st through eternity
Help us to follow where Thou still dost guide
Pilgrims of earth so wide

Star of the East, thou hope of the soul
While round us here the dark billows roll
Lead us from sin to glory afar
Thou star of the East, thou sweet Bethlehem's star

Star of the East, undimm'd by each cloud,
What though the storms of grief gather loud
Faithful and pure thy rays beam to save
Still bright o'er the cradle, and bright o'er the grave

Smile of a Saviour are mirror'd in Thee
Glimpses of Heav'n in thy light we see
Guide us still onward to that blessed shore
After earth's toil is o'er

Star of the East, thou hope of the soul
Oh star that leads to God above
Whose rays are peace and joy and love
Watch o'er us still till life hath ceased
Beam on, bright star, sweet Bethlehem star

"The Star Song"   A Robert Herrick (1591-1674) Epiphany poem, written to be sung at Whitehall Palace and a traditional part of many English Christmas festivals. The final verse refers to the practice on Twelfth Night of choosing a king and queen of the festivities.

(King 1) Tell us, thou clear and heavenly tongue,
Where is the Babe but lately sprung?
Lies He the lily-banks among?

(King 2) Or say, if this new birth of ours
Sleeps, laid within some ark of flowers,
Spangled with dew-light; thou canst clear
All doubts, and manifest the where.

(King 3) Declare to us, bright star, if we shall seek
Him in the morning's blushing cheek,
Or search the beds of spices through,
To find Him out?

(Star) No, this ye need not do;
But only come, and see Him rest
A princely Babe in's mother's breast.

(Chorus) He's seen, He's seen, why then a round,
Let's kiss the sweet and holy ground;
And all rejoice, that we have found
A King, before conception crowned.

(Three Kings) Come then, come then, and let us bring
Unto our pretty Twelfth-tide King,
Each one his several offering;

(Chorus) And when night comes, we'll give Him wassailing:
And that His treble honors may be seen,
We'll choose Him King, and make His mother Queen.

Steak   A Christmas game played in Finland. The player who is "It" sits blindfolded holding straws in one hand and a piece of rope or heavy yarn (the "steak") in the other. Players try to steal the straws without getting swiped with the steak; if one is hit, he becomes "It." In Sweden a variation of the game is called *Nappa Stek,* or "pinch the steak," and "It" has to guess who has pinched him.

"St. Stephen and Herod" This 19th-century picture portrays the myth of St. Stephen as a servant in the household of King Herod.

"Stephen, St., and Herod"   A medieval carol in which Stephen is portrayed as a stable lad in the employ of King Herod. When Stephen announces that a king has been born that night, Herod replies that if what he says is true, the roast cock on his plate will rise and speak. The dead bird immediately does so, crowing, "*Christus natus est.*" (See "THE CARNAL AND THE CRANE.") Herod then has Stephen executed: "Tokyn he Stevene, and stonyd hym in the way, And therfore is his evyn on Crystes owyn day."

Stephen's Day, St.   December 26 is the feast day of St. Stephen, the first martyr of the Christian church. What little we know about him can be found in the Book of Acts, where we learn that he had been chosen one of the seven deacons in Jerusalem and that his defence of Christianity resulted in his being stoned to death for blasphemy. Legend, however, has surrounded the proto-martyr with a host of stories linking him to Herod's household at the time of the birth of Jesus, to horses, and to the stoning of the tiny wren.

Ever since the 10th century, St. Stephen's Day has been associated with horses, probably because the season was a time of horse sacrifice in pagan Northern Europe, and a time of rest from agricultural work for both man and beast. In England it is a time to bleed horses to ensure their health for the coming year. In the 16th century, Tusser noted,

Yer Christmas be passed,
let Horsse be lett blood,
For many a purpose
it dooth him much good:
The day of St. Steeven,
old fathers did use.
If that do mislike thee,
some other day chuse.

Across Europe, December 26 is a time for horses to be fed extra food, raced, decorated, blessed by the priest, or ridden in ceremonies honouring their species. This is particularly true in Sweden, where "Staffan Riders" would race from village to village and sing songs in honour of the saint. Some have tried (not very successfully) to explain the connection between horses and St. Stephen by claiming it stemmed from confusion between the martyr in the Book of Acts and a later saint, Stephen of Corvey, martyred c. 1075, whose feast day is June 2. This Stephen was a lover of horses and was said to ride five of them in turn. (See "STAFFAN VAR EN STALLEDRÄNG.") When he was murdered, his unbroken colt took him home to Norrtalje, which became a shrine for horse-healing.

The water and salt blessed by the priest on St. Stephen's Day would be set aside to use as medicine for horses should they fall ill during the rest of the year, or to sprinkle liberally about the barn and yard to bring prosperity. The salt could also be thrown in the fire to avert danger from thunderstorms. In some places the blood drawn from horses on this day was thought to have healing powers. In Poland, the blessing of food for horses led to other peculiar rituals on St. Stephen's Day. In what has been interpreted either as a remnant of pagan fertility rites or a re-enactment of the stoning of Stephen, people would throw the consecrated oats at each other and their animals. It was also customary on December 26 for boys and girls to throw walnuts at one another.

St. Stephen's Day is also marked in Ireland and other parts of the British Isles by hunting the WREN, a bird considered protected every other day of the year, and parading about with its body. Wren Boys used to carry a dead wren on a branch from house to house, and sing an appropriate song to solicit money:

The wren, the wren, the king of all birds,
On St. Stephen's day was caught in the furze;
Though his body is small, his family is great,
So, if you please, your honour, give us a treat.
On Christmas Day I turned a spit;
I burned my finger; I feel it yet,
Up with the kettle, and down with the pan:
Give us some money to bury the wren.

Other customs associated with St. Stephen's Day include HOLMING. In Wales holming, or holly-beating, was the practice for young men to beat each other (or female servants) with holly branches. In Britain generally, December 26 is observed as BOXING DAY, a day for sporting events and hunting.

"Still, Still, Still" An Austrian carol of the 19th century.

Still, still, still,
The night is cold and chill!
The virgin's tender arms enfolding,
Warm and safe the Christ child holding.
Still, still, still,
The night is cold and chill.

Dream, dream, dream.
He sleeps, the Savior King.

While guardian angels watch beside Him,
Mary tenderly will guide Him.
Dream, dream, dream.
He sleeps, the Savior King.

"Stille Nacht" The original German version of "SILENT NIGHT" by Mohr and Gruber.

Stille Nacht! Heil'ge Nacht!
Alles schläft; einsam wacht
Nur das traute heilige Paar.
Holder Knab' im lockigten Haar,
Schlafe in himmlischer Ruh!
Schlafe in himmlischer Ruh!

Stille Nacht! Heil'ge Nacht!
Gottes Sohn, o wie lacht
Lieb' aus deinem göttlichen Mund,
Da uns schlägt die rettende Stund'.
Jesus in deiner Geburt!
Jesus in deiner Geburt!

Stille Nacht! Heil'ge Nacht!
Die der Welt Heil gebracht,
Aus des Himmels goldenen Höhn,
Uns der Gnaden Fülle läßt sehn,
Jesum in Menschengestalt!
Jesum in Menschengestalt!

Stille Nacht! Heil'ge Nacht!
Wo sich heut alle Macht
Väterlicher Liebe ergoß,
Und als Bruder huldvoll umschloß
Jesus die Völker der Welt!
Jesus die Völker der Welt!

Stir Up Sunday *Every member of the family must take a turn stirring the Christmas pudding.*

Stockings *In this illustration by Thomas Nast an ambitious tot tacks up a large stocking for Santa to fill.*

Stille Nacht! Heil'ge Nacht!
Lange schon uns bedacht,
Als der Herr vom Grimme befreit
In der Väter urgrauer Zeit
Aller Welt Schonung verhieß!
Aller Welt Schonung verhieß!

Stille Nacht! Heil'ge Nacht!
Hirten erst kundgemacht
Durch der Engel Alleluja,
Tönt es laut bei Ferne und Nah:
"Jesus der Retter ist da!"
"Jesus der Retter ist da!"

Stir Up Sunday   The last Sunday before Advent, deriving its name from the first two words of the Church of England reading for that day: "Stir up we beseech thee, O Lord, the wills of thy faithful people that they plenteously bring forth the fruit of good works." This has been parodied by generations of choirboys as "Stir up we beseech thee the pudding in the pot. And when we get home, we'll eat it up all hot." An English tradition requires that each family member takes a turn stirring up the Christmas pudding, and some insist the stirring must be performed east to west and with eyes closed. The day also announces to schoolchildren the approach of the Christmas holidays.

Stockings   Medieval legend says that St. Nicholas saved three daughters of a poor man from lives of shame by dropping bags of gold into their stockings (see ST. NICHOLAS). From

this came the tradition of setting out a stocking or shoe for the gift-bringer to fill with treats and presents. Given Santa Claus's usual means of entry, the fireplace was the logical location to hang up one's stocking, as can be seen in Clement Clarke Moore's 1821 "A Visit From Saint Nicholas":

> He spoke not a word, but went straight to his work,
> And filled all the stockings; then turned with a jerk,
> And laying his finger aside of his nose,
> And giving a nod, up the chimney he rose;

However, many people prefer to leave their stocking by the window, at the foot of their bed, or by the family crèche. For a time, after the middle of the 19th century, the stocking was eclipsed by the Christmas tree as the place to find one's presents, but in many families the two have long co-existed, with small presents and candies being put in the stocking and larger gifts ending up under the tree.

In England and British Commonwealth countries such as South Africa and Australia, it is customary for a pillowcase to serve as a stocking. In some areas the receptacle is called a "Santa Sack." (See colour fig. 26.)

Stork and Christmas   A medieval English ballad tells of how the stork, seeing the Christ Child cold in the manger, plucked out its own feathers to line his bed. Since then the bird has been the patron of babies and considered a protected species. In Christian art the stork is a symbol of chastity, vigilance, prudence, and piety; because it is the bringer of spring it is often depicted in the ANNUNCIATION TO MARY.

Strewing Eve   An old name in parts of the Netherlands for December 5, St. Nicholas's Eve. Just before St. Nicholas and Black Peter appear, Peter throws *peppernoten*, hard round spice cakes, and other treats down the chimney.

Sugarplums   Candies made of preserved fruit, often coated in chocolate. Clement Clarke Moore's influential poem "A Visit From St. Nicholas" speaks of children all tucked in their beds while "visions of sugarplums danced in their heads." In Tchaikovsky's *Nutcracker Suite*, the Sugarplum Fairy has a featured dance.

Sundblom, Haddon Hubbard   (1899-1976) A successful commercial illustrator in Chicago, Sundblom was asked in 1931 to produce advertising art for the Coca-Cola company. His depictions of a portly, red-coated Santa holding a bottle of Coke continued until 1964 and became popular Christmas icons in the United States. Though the image of Santa painted by Sundblom had already become standardized by the 1930s, it is fair to say that after these advertisements it was impossible for the gift-bringer to be portrayed in any other way.

Superstitions and Christmas   There are countless Christmastime superstitions. For those that deal with predicting the future – especially the identity of one's spouse or the weather in the coming year – see DIVINATION AT CHRISTMAS. For those that concern the fate of babies born on December 25, see BORN ON CHRISTMAS DAY. Those that deal with the dark side of the supernatural may be found in DEVILS AND EVIL SPIRITS AT CHRISTMAS, WEREWOLVES AND CHRISTMAS, and WITCHES AT CHRISTMAS. See also GREENERY and FIRST-FOOTING.

Social historians agree that one of the great uses of superstitions is to enforce widely accepted community standards. Thus togetherness and family solidarity are promoted by the

English superstition that everyone in the house must stir the Christmas pudding three times round – with enough vigour to see the bottom of the pot – and make wishes for the new year. So, too, with the Romanian practice of binding the legs of the Christmas table with a chain, or the Polish practice of family and guests staying at the table until, at a signal from the host, they all rise in unison and leave (should this not occur, the first to rise will die before the next Christmas Eve). British custom dictates that if you don't eat any plum pudding, you will lose a friend before the next Christmas, and that for every house in which you eat mince pies at Christmas you will enjoy a happy month in the coming year. In Scandinavia, some families place all their shoes together on Christmas Eve, so they may live in harmony throughout the year. It is easy to see why the peasantry, wanting to maintain the sanctity of the holiday, would tell tales of the bad luck befalling those who continued to work at Christmas – that the fairies or gnomes would attack those spinning maids who left wool on the distaff, or that he who laboured willingly during the Twelve Days would have to buy ale for the whole village. But what sort of collective wisdom can have produced the following superstitions?

– To keep in good health, do not wash yourself, take a bath, or change your clothing between Christmas and New Year.
– If you eat no beans on Christmas Eve, you will become an ass.
– If after a Christmas dinner you shake out the tablecloth over the bare ground under the open sky, crumbwort will grow on the spot. (Polish peasants, on the other hand, saved the crumbs from this meal so they could sow them in the spring and bring fertility to the land on which they fell.)
– If on Christmas Eve or Christmas Day you hang a washcloth on a hedge and then groom the horses with it, they will grow fat.
– If you have a fever on Christmas Eve, put three different kinds of food on the windowsill, and in the morning eat some of each, and you will be safe for the rest of the year, particularly from fevers.
– To protect cattle from sickness during the coming year, feed them hay put outside to freeze on Christmas Eve.
– For a year of prosperity, put a loaf of bread in the yard on Christmas Eve and leave it overnight. In the morning cut a piece of the bread, wet with Christmas morning dew, for each member of the family.
– To keep dogs from going rabid, feed them a piece of bread and butter on which silver filings have been sprinkled on Christmas Eve, New Year's Eve, or Epiphany Eve.
– If a dog howls the night before Christmas, it will go mad within the year.
– During the Gospel recitation of Christ's genealogy during the Christmas Eve mass, treasure reveals itself.
– A cricket chirping at Christmas brings good luck. (See "CRICKET ON THE HEARTH.")
– A meowing cat at Christmas is bad luck.

Perhaps the loveliest Christmas superstition is found in *The Golden Legend*, a medieval book of saints' stories: "What persone beynge in clene lyfe desyre on thys daye a boone of God: as ferre as it is ryghtfull and good for hym, our Lorde at reverence of thys blessid and hye feste of his nativite wol graunt it to hym."

"Sussex Carol"   A traditional carol from the west of England whose most usual setting is by Ralph Vaughan Williams (1872-1958). It is also known as "On Christmas Night" (though it refers to events on Christmas morning).

On Christmas night all Christians sing
To hear the news the angels bring.
News of great joy, news of great mirth
News of our merciful King's birth.

Then why should men on earth be so sad
Since our Redeemer made us glad?
When from our sin he set us free
All for to gain our liberty?

When sin departs before his grace
Then life and health come in its place;
Angels and men with joy may sing,
All for to see the new-born King.

All out of darkness we have light,
Which made the angels sing this night:
"Glory to God and peace to men
Now and forever more, Amen."

Swaddling Clothes   According to the Gospel of Luke, the baby Jesus was wrapped in swaddling clothes immediately after his birth. These were strips of cloth designed both to warm the infant and immobilize his limbs for health reasons. During the Middle Ages a number of places, Santa Maria Maggiore in Rome, Aix-la-Chappelle, and Wittenberg, claimed to possess relics of these clothes, but the Arabic Infancy Gospel, a non-canonical account from the fifth century, tells of a different fate for them:

And it came to pass, when the Lord Jesus was born at Bethlehem of Judaea, in the time of King Herod, behold, magi came from the east to Jerusalem, as Zeraduscht had predicted; and there were with them gifts, gold, and frankincense, and myrrh. And they adored Him, and presented to Him their gifts. Then the Lady Mary took one of the swaddling-bands, and, on account of the smallness of her means, gave it to them; and they received it from her with the greatest marks of honour. And in the same hour there appeared to them an angel in the form of that star which had before guided them on their journey; and they went away, following the guidance of its light, until they arrived in their own country.

And their kings and chief men came together to them, asking what they had seen or done, how they had gone and come back, what they had brought with them. And they showed them that swathing-cloth which the Lady Mary had given them. Wherefore they celebrated a feast, and, according to their custom, lighted a fire and worshipped it, and threw that swathing-cloth into it; and the fire laid hold of it, and enveloped it. And when the fire had gone out, they took out the swathing-cloth exactly as it had been before, just as if the fire had not touched it. Wherefore they began to kiss it, and to put it on their heads and their eyes, saying: This verily is the truth without doubt. Assuredly it is a great thing that the fire was not able to burn or destroy it. Then they took it, and with the greatest honour laid it up among their treasures.

Two Christmas sweets, the German *stollen* and the Romanian *turta*, are said to be made to resemble swaddling clothes.

Sweden It would be difficult to miss the arrival of Advent in Sweden: in the beginning of December, stores and buildings are draped in seasonal decorations and Advent calendars and their television tie-ins appear; Advent stars are placed in windows; and on every Sunday another Advent candle is lit in homes and churches. But the real beginning of Christmas is December 13, ST. LUCIA's Day, when by tradition the eldest daughter in each family rises early in the morning and dons a white dress, a red sash, and a lingon wreath with seven lit candles. She carries coffee and *Lussekatter*, special saffron-flavoured buns, to her parents; later in the day other "Lucy brides" lead processions of white-clad girls and STAR BOYS in schools, offices, and other public places.

Other Advent activities include shopping, baking, entertaining friends with a smorgasbord, writing Christmas cards, and decorating the home with greenery, candles, ornaments, and flowers. The Christmas tree is set up one or two days before Christmas; typical ornaments are those made of straw in many shapes, but they might also include a goat, angels, candles, red apples, glass balls, flags, and lots of candies and edible treats. The family crèche is a 20th-century addition to Swedish Christmas (it was long resisted as smacking too much of Catholicism in this Lutheran country) but one that has become very popular.

Christmas Eve is a day filled with well-loved traditions. It was once mandatory to begin the day with a bath, one person at a time in the family tub, to put on at least one article of new clothing, and to give the house a good scrubbing. Such acts would guard the home from spirits who gathered during the Christmas season. Many no longer observe these safeguards, but most continue to honour the custom of *doppa y grytan*, where the family gathers to take turns dipping a piece of dark rye bread into a pot of drippings. Later in the afternoon, after the family has watched the now-traditional Walt Disney programming on television, folk sit down for the big holiday meal. This begins with a smorgasbord of such things as pickled herring, meatballs, sausage, and jellied pig's feet, and includes *lutfisk*, *julskinka* (roast ham), cabbage, casseroles, and potato, with *risgrynsgröt*, the creamy rice pudding (with a hidden almond), spiced cakes, and cookies for dessert.

After dinner, many Swedes attend a Christmas Eve service. For others, it is time for the gifts to be opened. It was once customary for an anonymous giver to knock loudly at the door (thus the name *julklapp* for Christmas present) and throw in a wrapped gift. The present would contain a mischievous rhyme aimed at the recipient and might be deceptively wrapped. For a time the legendary gift-bringer was the *Julbock*, or Christmas Goat, but in the 19th century he was replaced in popularity by the figure of Santa Claus. The Swedes named the old gentleman Jultomten after the *tomte*, or household elf, who guarded the home and farm through the year and who had to be bribed with a bowl of pudding at Christmas. In homes with children, someone dressed as Jultomten comes to the house on Christmas Eve with a sack of presents, knocks on the door, and inquires, "Are there any good children here?" After opening the presents, families sing carols, read a chapter of the Nativity story, or dance holding hands around the Christmas tree.

Christmas Day is a time for an early-morning church service. Among the favourite Swedish Christmas hymns are "Var hälsad sköna morgonstund" ("All Hail Thou Radiant Morning-Tide"), "Nu så kommer Julen" ("Now Christmas Is Coming"), and "En jungfru födde ett barn idag" ("A Maid Hath Brought Forth a Child"). In snowy parts of Sweden, when it was customary to travel to church by sleigh, a race

home after the service was an exciting part of the day.

December 26, or Second Day of Christmas, is a time to pay special attention to livestock. Legend linked ST. STEPHEN (whose feast day it is) with horses, and this was once a time for the Staffan Riders, with their horse races and parades and

Sweden *A Swedish stamp celebrating the custom of racing sleighs home after church on Christmas Day.*

hymns to the saint. Nowadays it is another holiday, with plenty of time for visiting and parties.

New Year's Eve and Twelfth Night (January 5) offer more time for merriment. The traditional Epiphany custom in Sweden was for the Star Boys, dressed as the Three Kings, to walk about singing carols, following the Star of Bethlehem held high on a pole. Accompanied by figures dressed as Herod and Judas, who carried a bag, the boys collected money for their efforts. This tradition fell into disfavour as an occasion for disorder. A 1712 edict warned against "irresponsible boys and other loose persons who gather together to run about streets and alleys and prowl about the houses with the so-called Christmas goats, stars and other vanities." Today the Star Boys are mostly confined to a role in St. Lucia processions.

The final day of the Christmas season is January 13, known as ST. KNUT's DAY: "Twentieth-day Knut driveth Christmas out" is the folk saying. This is the day when children plunder the tree for any remaining candies or treats, final parties are held, and decorations are put away for another year.

Switzerland Switzerland is a country of different linguistic and cultural traditions, but each one makes much of the opportunity to celebrate Christmas in its own style.

As St. Nicholas's Day approaches, Christmas festivities begin. In the costume of a medieval bishop, Nicholas strides through towns scattering candies and fruit to children, checking on their record of behaviour, and listening to them recite a poem. He will visit schools, hospitals, and shopping areas and take part in a number of civic celebrations. On December 5 in Küssnacht, near Lake Lucerne, hundreds of marchers participate in the *Klausjagen*, the hunting of Nicholas. Men and women, carrying huge cardboard bishops' mitres decorated with lacy patterns and lit from within by candles, escort Saint Nicholas through the village. They are accompanied by whip-crackers, bell-ringers, and brass bands. On December 6 in Fribourg, Saint Nicholas rides through town on a donkey. He gives a speech about civic events over the past year and then joins the townsfolk for dinner. Other gift-bringers make appearances during the month as well. In the village of

Hallwil on Christmas Eve, a white-robed girl representing the Wienectchind (Christ Child) walks through the town carrying a lantern. She is accompanied by six other young women, and together they go about singing carols together and giving treats to children.

In Catholic areas of Switzerland the crèche is set out in homes and churches with figures of the animals, Mary and Joseph, and shepherds, but the baby Jesus is placed in the crib only at midnight on Christmas Eve.

Swiss Christmas trees are usually decorated on Christmas Eve away from the eyes of the children. The tree is lit by real candles and hung with garlands, glass balls, candies, and apples and topped by a star or an angel. When the children are admitted, the presents piled beneath the tree or hung from the branches are distributed. The family then sings carols and eats Christmas snacks before going off to a midnight church service. (In French-speaking parts of the country, some families delay opening presents until January 1 and some Swiss-Italian children wait until Epiphany for the arrival of the Befana.)

The gift-bringer varies from region to region. Depending on whether the local religion is Catholic or Protestant, and whether the population speaks French, German, Italian, or Romansh dialect, presents can be brought by the Christ Child, or Christkindli, usually represented as a white-clad young girl or angel; Saint Nicholas, called Samichlaus in German areas or San Nicolao in Italian; Père Noèl; the Befana; or the Gesú Bambino.

On December 25, Swiss of all denominations go to church and afterwards enjoy the main holiday meal. Fondues are a favourite in many parts of the country; using long forks, diners dip pieces of bread and meat into cheese mixtures or hot broth or oil. Switzerland is a land rich in desserts, from their fabled chocolate to many kinds of biscuits: *Mailänderli* (butter cookies), *Basler brunsli* (chocolate and hazelnut cookies), *Zimtsterne* (cinnamon stars), *Läbchueche* (spice-honey cookies), and *Chraebeli* (aniseed cookies). In Zürich, *Tirggel* cookies are made in wooden moulds that decorate the cookies in patterns and Christmas scenes.

A number of remarkable ceremonies and customs take place in Switzerland after Christmas Day. New Year's Eve is the feast of ST. SYLVESTER, and so the Swiss celebrate *Silvester* with gusto, dining out, feasting and making noise to bring in the new year. In the *Silvesterumzug* in Wil, hundreds of children march through the streets, carrying lanterns and singing carols. The tradition of the SILVESTERKLÄUSE in Urnäsch sees three types of grotesquely costumed figures go from farm to farm, yodelling and receiving hospitality. On Epiphany the holiday season ends with the traditional TWELFTH-NIGHT CAKE, inside of which are hidden tokens.

Sylvester's Day, St.   December 31 is the feast day of St. Sylvester, the fourth-century pope during whose reign (314-35) persecution of Christians ceased and Christianity received the favour of the emperor Constantine. In legend, Sylvester was supposed to have cured the emperor of leprosy and received Western Europe from him through the spurious Donation of Constantine.

In German-speaking countries, *Silvester* is the name given to New Year's Eve and its festivities.

Szopka   A remarkable Polish variation on the Christmas crèche. The city of Krakow holds an annual contest for the best decorated Nativity scene in the traditional *szopka* style, in which the crèche is always covered in foil and reproduces in miniature the city's cathedral. The entries are displayed in public and draw crowds of admirers.

Tante Aria An elderly female gift-bringer from the Franche-Comté area of France who descends from the mountains on Christmas Eve, bearing presents for good children and switches or dunce caps for the wicked ones.

Television and Christmas Though television was an invention of the 1920s, it was not until the 1950s that it began to have an effect on Christmas. In the early years of the medium, the first instinct of television producers was to duplicate programming that had proved successful on radio, and so television imported radio stars such as Jack Benny and Milton Berle and its short comedy, variety, and quiz show formats. As opera had long been a staple of radio broadcasting, it was not long before the first opera written for television was produced by NBC for the 1951 Christmas season, Gian Carlo Menotti's AMAHL AND THE NIGHT VISITORS. Though *Amahl* was well-received and is occasionally reproduced, the public did not warm to the genre, and there have been few Christmas television operas since. (Ballet, which was not a radio-friendly art form, has done much better than opera on Christmas-time television.)

A form that soon did succeed was the "Christmas special," an intensely promoted gathering of stars for an allegedly glittering one-off production. The first of these was "One Hour in Wonderland," broadcast on Christmas Day 1950 as the first of Walt Disney's television products. It featured the ventriloquist Edgar Bergen and his dummy, Charlie McCarthy, as well as previews of the new feature film *Alice in Wonderland*. Similar productions from the 1950s, such as "Holiday on Ice" with Sonja Henie and Julius LaRosa, and "All Star Jazz" with Louis Armstrong, Dave Brubeck, and Duke Ellington, have been followed by countless imitators.

In time, every television sitcom and drama was expected to have a Christmas episode. Few of these have lingered in the memory. Far more significant were the seasonal animated films, some of which became classics: *Rudolph, the Red-Nosed Reindeer* (1964), *A Charlie Brown Christmas* (1965), *How the Grinch Stole Christmas* (1966), and *The Little Drummer Boy* (1968). These are replayed every Christmas and seem to have a longer-lasting appeal than most of the live-action dramatic specials that come out yearly, each claiming to illustrate in some way "the real meaning of Christmas." Among the very few of these that have created a place for themselves are *The Homecoming – A Christmas Story* (1971), which turned into the long-running series *The Waltons*, *The Best Christmas Pageant Ever* (1983), and *A Child's Christmas in Wales* (1986).

Among the most-appreciated fare at Christmas are old movies. There seems to be an unending appetite for reruns of *It's a Wonderful Life*, Alastair Sim's *A Christmas Carol*, and *A Christmas Story*. In fact, watching television on Christmas has in many countries become a family tradition, worked into the day's schedule as securely as opening the presents or sitting down to dinner. While Britons and Commonwealth citizens watch the royal broadcast, Scandinavians are hooked on Walt Disney. All around the world, people turn on the television for the pope's midnight service from Rome.

Perhaps the most notable effect television has on Christmas is in its avalanche of seasonal advertising. Most retailers rely on Christmas sales to make their entire year profitable, and television is a prime means of influencing consumers. Though TV advertising has not produced Christmas icons the way printed media have – for example, the Coca-Cola Santa, Rudolph the Red-Nosed Reindeer, or Punkinhead – it is probably far more influential in determining what will be under the tree and how much money families will have to spend to keep children happy. See TOYS AND CHRISTMAS for the connection between television and popular playthings.

One country's attitude to television at Christmas stands out as unique. In Iceland television broadcasts are halted at 5 p.m. on Christmas Eve, so for a few hours families can enjoy dinner together, open their presents, and listen to a radio Evensong service without the lure of the tube.

Tertullian (160-220) Christian theologian of Carthage who wrote a treatise on idolatry that criticized the use of midwinter festive greenery and lights: "Let them kindle lamps, they who have no light; let them fix on doorposts laurels which shall afterwards be burnt, they for whom the fire is close at hand. . . . But thou art a light of the world and a tree that is ever green; if thou hast renounced the temple make not a temple of thy own house door."

He was also the first to call the MAGI "almost" or "as good as" kings and thought they were from different lands.

Theophany January 6 marks a number of traditions concerning the life of Jesus. In the West it is chiefly the time to celebrate the Epiphany, the manifestation of Jesus to the Gentiles in the form of the Magi, who had come to worship the newborn king. In the East it is the occasion of the Theophany, the descent of the Holy Spirit on Jesus at the River Jordan and the beginning of his ministry. It is the time for the final rite in the Ukrainian Christmas season, the celebration of the *Yordan*, or Feast of the Jordan. In other churches it is a time of the "Blessing of the Waters."

Theotokos "God-Bearer," the title given to the Virgin Mary by the Council of Ephesus (431). This led to certain types of artistic portrayal, as when Mary is depicted sitting on a throne with the infant Jesus on her knees.

"There Is No Rose of Such Vertue" An anonymous English carol from the 14th or 15th century and one of the first in English. Its most usual setting was written by Benjamin Britten.

There is no rose of swich vertu
As is the rose that bare Jhesu.
Alleluia.

For in this rose conteined was
Hevene and erthe in litel space,
Res miranda.

Be that rose we may weel see
That He is God in persones three,
Pares forma.

The aungeles sungen the schepherdes to
Gloria in excelsis Deo.
Gaudeamus.

Leve we all this werdly merthe,
And folwe we this joyful berthe.
Transeamus.

"There's a Song in the Air"   Josiah Holland (1819-81), physician and writer, wrote the words for this song, which appeared in his 1872 *The Marble Prophecy and Other Poems.* Musicologist Karl P. Harington (1861-1953) wrote the tune in 1904.

There's a song in the air!
There's a star in the sky!
There's a mother's deep prayer
And a baby's low cry!
And the star rains its fire
While the beautiful sing,
For the manger of Bethlehem
cradles a King!

There's a tumult of joy
O'er the wonderful birth,
For the virgin's sweet boy
Is the Lord of the earth.
Ay! the star rains its fire
While the beautiful sing,
For the manger of Bethlehem
cradles a King!

In the light of that star
Lie the ages impearled;
And that song from afar
Has swept over the world.
Every hearth is aflame,
And the beautiful sing
In the homes of the nations
That Jesus is King!

We rejoice in the light,
And we echo the song
That comes down through the night
From the heavenly throng.
Ay! we shout to the lovely
Evangel they bring,
And we greet in his cradle
Our Savior and King!

"The Third Day After Christmas"   An austere story by William Saroyan (1908-91) about a little boy who is abandoned to the cold by a neglectful father three days after Christmas and the people who try to help him. The sting in Saroyan's tale is that the third day after Christmas is CHILDERMAS, which commemorates the murder of the children of Bethlehem by King Herod. The author was himself raised in an orphanage.

The Thirteen Desserts   On Christmas Eve in Provence, it is traditional to serve 13 desserts at the post-mass dinner. The number 13 represents Christ and his 12 apostles. The desserts may vary to some extent, but must always include "the mendicants" (dried figs, raisins, hazelnuts, and almonds, which stand for the monastic orders of the Franciscans, the Dominicans,

the Augustinians, and the Carmelites) and *pompe à l'huile* (a brioche made with olive oil). Other options include nougat, oranges, apples, pears, fruit tarts, and *calissons* (marzipan). Breads are broken by hand, not cut, to ensure successful future harvests.

"This Endris Night"   An English carol from the 15th or 16th century. "This endris night" means "the other night."

This endris night I saw a sight,
A star as bright as day;
And e'er among a maiden sung,
"Lullay, bye bye, lullay"

This lovely lady sat and sang,
And to her Child did say:
"My son, my brother, father, dear,
Why liest thou thus in hay?"

The Child then spake in His talking,
And to His mother said:
"Yea, I am known as heaven King,
In crib though I be laid"

For angels bright down to me light:
Thou knowest 'tis no nay:
And for that sight thou may'st delight
To sing, "bye bye lullay."

Thomas's Day, Saint   Thomas was one of the original apostles of Jesus, known in the Gospel of John for doubting the resurrection and renowned in legend for also doubting the Assumption of the Virgin. He is said to have evangelized in India, where he met and converted the MAGI and was martyred. His feast day, December 21, is connected to a number of Christmas customs.

In England it was traditionally a day for poor women to be permitted to go door-to-door and beg for alms. This custom, called "Thomasing," "mumping," or "a-gooding," was considered an opportunity to do one's soul some good by showing charity. Thus this song sung by the indigent women:

Well a day, well a day,
St. Thomas goes too soon away,
Then your gooding we do pray
For a good time will not stay.
St. Thomas gray, St. Thomas gray,
The longest night and shortest day
Please to remember St. Thomas's Day.

The custom died out in the early 20th century as charity became more institutionalized and attitudes to begging hardened. Many registered charities in Britain, however, observe St. Thomas's Day by choosing to make their payments then.

In Central Europe, St. Thomas's Day was a time for driving out demons by making loud noises, cracking whips, letting off firearms, or ringing bells – all while wearing horrible masks – or by using incense and holy water and saying the rosary. In Bohemia, St. Thomas himself was said to ride at midnight in a chariot of fire to the graveyard, where he met the spirits of all the dead men named Thomas; there he blessed them, and as they returned to their graves he would disappear.

In other parts of Europe it was a time for schools to close for the Christmas vacation, an opportunity for social inversion, BARRING-OUT of teachers, or extorting treats from them. In some parts of Germany, the one who is last to wake up or comes late to work on St. Thomas's Day is the "Thomas Donkey." In Norway it was once the custom to have all preparatory work for the Christmas season done by St. Thomas's Day. A two-weeks' supply of wood for the stove had to be ready, else the saint would come and take away the axe; all baking and brewing had to be finished lest a string of kitchen mishaps take place.

Thorlak's Day, St.   St. Thorlak Thorhallsson (1133-93) was a medieval Icelandic monk and bishop of Skaholt famous for his attempts to reform his nation's churches and monasteries. His feast day is December 23, which is marked in Iceland by a meal of skate hash, similar to *lutefisk*, whose plain charms make the Christmas feast more appealing. It is also a day for decorating the Yule tree and shopping for last-minute gifts.

"Thou Didst Leave Thy Throne"   An English carol for children, words by Emily Elizabeth Steele Elliott (1836-97), music by clergyman Timothy Richard Matthews (1826-1910). Elliott, a clergyman's daughter, was deeply interested in philanthropy and in Evangelical Sunday school work, and published 141 hymns.

> Thou didst leave thy throne and thy kingly crown
> when thou camest to earth for me;
> but in Bethlehem's home there was found
> no room for thy holy nativity:
>
> *O come to my heart, Lord Jesus, there is room in my heart*
> *for thee.*
>
> Heaven's arches rang when the angels sang,
> proclaiming thy royal degree;
> but in lowly birth thou didst come to earth,
> and in great humility:
>
> *Refrain*
>
> The foxes found rest and the birds their nest
> in the shade of the forest tree;
> but thy couch was the sod, O thou Son of God,
> in the desert of Galilee:
>
> *Refrain*
>
> Thou camest, O Lord, with the living Word
> that should set thy people free;
> but with mocking scorn, and with crown of thorn,
> they bore thee to Calvary:
>
> *Refrain*
>
> When the heavens shall ring, and the angels sing,
> at thy coming to victory,
> let thy voice call me home, saying, "Yet there is room,
> there is room at my side for thee."
>
> *My heart shall rejoice, Lord Jesus, when thou comest and*
> *callest for me!*

Three Godfathers (1948)   See "BRONCHO BILLY AND THE BABY."

Three Kings (TV) (1987)   Three patients of a mental hospital escape from custody dressed as the Wise Men and riding a camel. Jack Warden, Lou Diamond Phillips, and Stan Shaw play the lunatic Magi who bring a new meaning to Christmas in Los Angeles. This made-for-television movie was directed by Mel Damski.

Three Kings' Day   A term for Epiphany, when the Magi are said to have arrived to pay homage and bring their gifts to the infant Jesus. In German it is the *Dreikönigfest*, and in Spanish it is *el Dio de Los Tres Reyes Magos*. In Belgium it is *Dreikonigendag*. In Germany and Austria the initials of the Magi are chalked on doors and barns, salt and chalk are brought to church to be consecrated, and kids wear paper crowns and carry large stars. In Portugal, where it is called *Dia de Reis*, mothers serve a ring cake called *Bolo-Rei* at children's parties, which contains fancy trinkets and a dried bean. The bean finder is crowned king and promises to make a cake for the party next year. Throughout the Spanish-speaking world, the eve of Three Kings' Day is when little ones put out their shoes for the Wise Men to fill with gifts on their way to Bethlehem and leave a treat for the camels of their caravan. See EPIPHANY.

"The Three Low Masses"   A renowned French short story of 1875, "Les trois basses messes," by Alphonse Daudet (1840-97), is supposedly based on a Provençal folk tale. The 16th-century priest Dom Balaguère is so greedy for his Christmas *réveillon* feast of truffled turkeys, pheasant, peacock, eel, trout, and wine that he falls prey to the tempting of the Devil and rushes through his performance of the required three masses. God decrees that the priest shall not enter heaven until he has celebrated 300 Christmas masses in his chapel. For centuries his ghost must haunt the altar until his sentence expires.

Tirggel   Elaborate moulds for making Christmas cookies in Switzerland, they are carved from wood and impress upon the biscuit elegant designs and Christmas scenes. Many have become collectible as examples of folk art.

"To Shepherds, As They Watched by Night"   "Vom Himmel kam der Engel Schar," a 1543 carol by the German reformer Martin Luther (1483-1546); translated in 1854 by Richard Massie.

> To shepherds as they watched by night
> Appeared a host of angels bright;
> Behold the tender Babe, they said,
> In yonder lowly manger laid.
>
> At Bethlehem, in David's town,
> As Micah did of old make known;
> 'Tis Jesus Christ, your Lord and King,
> Who doth to all salvation bring.
>
> Oh, then rejoice that through His Son
> God is with sinners now at one;
> Made like yourselves of flesh and blood,
> Your brother is the eternal God.
>
> What harm can sin and death then do?
> The true God now abides with you.
> Let hell and Satan rage and chafe,
> Christ is your Brother – ye are safe.
>
> Not one He will or can forsake
> Who Him his confidence doth make.
> Let all his wiles the Tempter try,
> You may his utmost powers defy.
>
> Ye shall and must at last prevail;
> God's own ye are, ye cannot fail.
> To God forever sing your praise
> With joy and patience all your days.

Todi, Jacopone da   (1228-1306) Franciscan monk and carol writer. Of noble birth and a lawyer by training, da Todi became a Franciscan after the death of his wife, and seemed "mad as a lark" to his contemporaries; indeed, he was imprisoned for a time by Pope Boniface VIII. On his tomb is inscribed *Stultus propter Christum, nova mundum arte delusi et coeli rapuit* ("A fool for Christ's sake, by a new artifice he cheated the world and took heaven by storm").

The common humanity with which the early Franciscans tried to depict the Incarnation and the Nativity is evident in this poem, translated by John Addington Symonds, one of a number da Todi wrote on this topic:

Come and look upon her Child
Nestling in the hay!
See his fair arms open wide,
On her lap to play!
And she tucks him by her side,
Cloaks him as she may
Gives her paps unto his mouth
Where his lips are laid.

She with left hand cradling
Rocked and hushed her Boy,
And with holy lullabies
Quieted her toy
Little angels all around
Danced, and carols flung;
Making verselets sweet and true,
Still of love they sung.

He died during the midnight mass on Christmas.

"Tomorrow Shall Be My Dancing Day"

A mystical carol from the west country of England which is sung by Christ on the eve of his marriage to the Church:

I would my true love did so chance
To see the legend of my play,
To call my true love to my dance.
Sing O my love, O my love, my love, my love;
This have I done for my true love.

Then was I born of a virgin pure,
Of her I took fleshly substance;
Thus was I knit to man's nature,
To call my true love to my dance.
Sing O my love, O my love, my love, my love;
This have I done for my true love.

In a manger laid and wrapped I was,
So very poor, this was my chance,
Betwixt an ox and silly poor ass,
To call my true love to my dance.
Sing O my love, O my love, my love, my love;
This have I done for my true love.

Then afterwards baptized I was;
The Holy Ghost on me did glance,
My Father's voice heard from above,
To call my true love to my dance.
Sing O my love, O my love, my love, my love;
This have I done for my true love.

Tourtière

The traditional French-Canadian meat pie served at Christmas Eve with ketchup or a chutney. Made of ground pork and veal with mashed potatoes, it is an irreplaceable comfort food in Quebec.

"Toyland"

Though having no direct connection to Christmas, the song "Toyland" is played frequently over the holiday season. It first appeared in the Victor Herbert operetta of 1903, *Babes in Toyland*, which was remade several times as a movie, most notably in 1934 with the comic duo Laurel and Hardy. Lyrics were by Glen McDonough (1870-1924).

When you've grown up, my dears,
And are as old as I,
You'll often ponder on the years
That roll so swiftly by, my dears,
That roll so swiftly by.
And all the many lands
You will have journeyed through
You'll oft recall,
The best of all,
The land your childhood knew.

When you've grown up, my dears,
There comes a dreary day
When 'mid the locks of black appears
The first pale gleam of gray.
Then of the past you'll dream
As gray-haired grownups do
And seek once more its phantom shore,
The land your childhood knew.

Toyland, toyland,
Little girl and boy land,
While you dwell within it,
You are ever happy then.

Childhood's joyland,
Mystic merry toyland,
Once you pass its borders,
You can ne'er return again.

Toys and Christmas

It is impossible in the modern world to think of Christmas without toys, but the mass manufacture of playthings for children is a comparatively recent phenomenon. Before the mid-19th century, most toys were handmade (there were guilds of toy-makers in Germany as early as the 15th century) and many were homemade. The spread of the industrial revolution in 1800s, however, meant that techniques of mass production coincided with a growing desire by the prosperous middle classes to provide toys for their children as Christmas gifts. Since then, commercially produced toys and Christmas have been inseparable.

The following is a list of toys given as Christmas presents in the last century or so. (The dates specified are either when the toys were introduced or achieved a particular prominence in the marketplace. All toys listed originated in the United States unless noted otherwise; where "U.S." appears, the entry refers to a toy introduced into that country from elsewhere.) It does not mention other gifts found under the tree, such as books, clothes, or sports equipment.

Those who decry the prevalence in recent years of toys associated with television shows or movies should note that this is a phenomenon common throughout the 20th century, as witnessed by the Betty Boop, Shirley Temple, Disney, and Tom Mix toys of earlier decades.

1867 – Parcheesi
1875 – Croquinole (Canada)
1878 – Martin mechanical mill (France)
1879 – Bateman model steam locomotive (U.K.)
1880 – Jumeau talking doll (France)
1884 – Magic Flute
1887 – Parker Bros.' The Grocery Store

Toys and Christmas *Families shop for toys at this 1877 exhibition.*

1888 – Reversi
1889 – Tiddley-Winks (U.K.); Flexible Flyer sled
1890 – Jumeau fashion doll (France)
1891 – Edison talking doll
1892 – Snakes and Ladders
1895 – Rossignol model train (France); Parker Bros.' The Game of Business
1896 – Ludo
1897 – Carlisle and French first electric train
1898 – Bagatelle; Nellie Bly board game
1900 – Ping Pong (U.K.); electric street car set (Germany)
1901 – Lionel electric trains; Mechanics Made Easy (U.K.)
1902 – Humpty Dumpty Circus
1903 – Teddy Bear; Crayola crayons; Plank Black Prince steam locomotive
1904 – The Landlord's Game (predecessor of Monopoly)
1905 – Eaton Beauty doll (Canada); Golliwog (U.K.)
1906 – Rook; Tootsietoys
1907 – Mechanics Made Easy becomes Meccano; Patty Comfort doll
1908 – Plasticine
1909 – Billiken Doll with Can't Break head; Star swing horse (U.K.)
1910 – Kathe Kruse unbreakable doll
1911 – Fairy auto-coaster; Hess clockwork Dreadnought (Germany); Little Daisy Pop-Gun
1912 – Kewpie Doll; Mohawk pedal car
1913 – Erector Set
1914 – Tinkertoys; Raggedy Ann
1915 – O gauge electric trains
1916 – Lincoln Logs
1919 – Tiss Me doll; Bing clockwork train (Germany)

1920 – Dolly Dingle paper dolls; Parker Brothers Lindy Hop Off; Milton Bradley Messenger Boy; Marx King Racer wind-up car; Hornby train (U.K.)
1921 – Parker Bros.' Wonderful Game of Oz; Buddy L Express dump truck
1922 – Tortoise & Hare game; Doctor Play Bag; Skaymo Bricks (U.K.)
1923 – Chinese Checkers; Andy Gump Roadster; York Western cap gun; Madame Alexander doll
1924 – Bye-Lo Baby; Barney Google scooter
1925 – Felix the Cat; Ives model train set; Arcade Mack dump truck
1926 – Bonnie Babe doll; Peter Pan board game; Parker Bros.' Touring Game
1927 – Spirit of St. Louis model airplane; Toonerville Trolley; Tootsietoy dollhouse
1928 – Yo-yo craze; Metalcraft Zeppelin construction kit; Sunbeam Race pedal car
1929 – Popeye Paddle and Ball; American Flyer model train
1930 – Little Orphan Annie paintbox; Rodeo Joe Krazy Kar; Mysto Magic Set
1931 – Betty Boop doll; Parker Bros.' Camelot; Keystone Ride-Em Steamroller
1932 – Lego founder Ole Kirk Christiansen builds first wooden toys (Denmark); Fisher-Price Granny Doodle; Flash Gordon Arresting Ray Gun; table hockey (Canada)
1933 – Tom Mix Straight Shooter pistols; Mickey Mouse radio
1934 – Shirley Temple doll; Lionel Union Pacific City of Portland electric train
1935 – Monopoly; Dionne Quintuplets dolls
1936 – Babe Ruth's Baseball Game; TiddlyTennis; Tom Mix Rocket Parachute
1937 – Snow White & Seven Dwarfs tea set
1938 – Fisher-Price Snoopy Sniffer; Gene Autry guitar; Ferdinand the Bull doll
1939 – Daisy Red Ryder air rifle; Princess Elizabeth doll; Charlie McCarthy & Mortimer Snerd car
1940 – View-Master; Hopalong Cassidy camera; Tootsietoy camouflage ambulance
1941 – Deluxe Kiddilac pedal car; Marx U.S. Army airplane
1942 – Donald Duck Choo Choo; Jack Armstrong Secret Bomb Sight
1943 – Jane Russell paper doll; Gilbert chemistry set; Buddy L fire truck
1944 – Dick Tracy Junior Detective Kit; Little Lulu doll
1945 – Slinky; Captain Midnight Magni-Matic Code-O-Graph
1946 – Tonka trucks; Donald Duck camera
1947 – Buck Rogers Atomic Pistol; Captain Marvel racing car
1948 – Scrabble; Cluedo (U.K.); Cootie
1949 – Marx "Mickey Mouse Meteor" electric train; Clue (U.S.); Candyland
1950 – Silly Putty; Cinderella toys; Hopalong Cassidy cap pistols
1951 – Alice in Wonderland phonograph
1952 – Mr. Potato Head; Howdy Doody marionette; Roy Rogers Quick Shooter Hat; Scalextric
1953 – Wiffle Ball; Flower Pot Men (U.K.); Superman playsuit
1954 – Paint-By-Numbers; Matchbox toys; Milles Bornes (France)
1955 – Davy Crockett craze; Lego (Denmark); Dragnet game
1956 – Play-Doh; Daisy Monte Carlo BB gun; Corgi cars (U.K.)
1957 – Pluto Platter (original plastic Frisbee); Tic-Tac Dough

1958 – Pluto Platter renamed Frisbee; Hula Hoop; Perry Mason game

1959 – Barbie; L'Ecran Magique ("The Magic Screen," French predecessor to Etch-A-Sketch); Careers; Troll Doll (Denmark)

1960 – Etch-A-Sketch (U.S.); Sea Monkeys; Chatty Cathy

1961 – Ken (Barbie's boyfriend); Frankenstein monster kit

1962 – Return of the Pogo stick; Yo-yo fad returns; Milles Bornes (U.S.)

1963 – Diplomacy; Midge (Barbie's best friend); Easy Bake Oven

1964 – G.I. Joe; Skateboards; Skipper (Barbie's little sister); Mary Poppins; Electric Football

1965 – James Bond Aston-Martin car; Super Ball; Marx Rock 'Em Sock 'Em Robots

1966 – Action Man (U.K. version of G.I. Joe); Twister; first Lego train; Tiny Tears

1967 – GI Joe Nurse; Talking GI Joe; Kerplunk; Duplo

1968 – Spirograph; Sindy doll (U.K.); Fisher-Price Little People

1969 – Hot Wheels; Talking Barbie; Booby Trap

1970 – Nerf Ball; Mod Squad; 3-D Chess

1971 – Ten-speed bikes; Katie Kopycat writing doll (U.K.); Clackers

1972 – Magnavox Odyssey video game system; Hacky Sack

1973 – Skateboards with polyurethane wheels; Mastermind; Dungeons and Dragons

1974 – Atomic Man; Mood Ring; Pong home video game system

1975 – Pet Rock; Wombles (U.K.); Rubik's Cube (Hungary)

1976 – Moon Base Alpha; Mork and Mindy; Happy Days play set

1977 – Atari 2600; Playmobil Playpeople; Slime; Othello

1978 – Star Wars toys; Battlestar Galactica

1979 – Mattel Intellivision; Legoland Space kits

1980 – The Empire Strikes Back; Rubik's Cube (U.K.)

1981 – My Pretty Pony (Hasbro's first attempt); Donkey Kong; Dukes of Hazzard car

1982 – Pac Man; Rubik's Cube (U.S.); My Little Pony; Colecovision; He-Man: Masters of the Universe; Indiana Jones; 3 3/4" GI Joe

1983 – Trivial Pursuit (Canada); Coleco ADAM; Cabbage Patch Dolls; Return of the Jedi; Rollerblades

1984 – Big video-game crash under impact of home computers; Care Bears; Lego Technic; Temple of Doom

1985 – Tetris (U.S.S.R.); Nintendo NES; Transformers; Pound Puppies; Ewoks

1986 – Sega Master System; Pictionary; Thundercats

1987 – Freddy Krueger slasher doll pulled from stores after protests; So Soft Ponies

1988 – Ghostbusters; Daisy Red Ryder Anniversary air rifle

1989 – Tetris (U.S.A.); Sega Genesis; Nintendo Gameboy

1990 – Teenage Mutant Ninja Turtles

1991 – Super Nintendo; Constructicons

1992 – WWF Wrestlers; Barney

1993 – Color Etch-A-Sketch; Star Trek: Deep Space Nine; Jurassic Park; Magic: The Gathering

1994 – Mighty Morphin' Power Rangers; Lion King; Pogs

1995 – Sony Playstation; Pocahontas

1996 – Nintendo N64; Buzz Lightyear; Tamagotchi; Tickle Me Elmo

1997 – Teletubbies; Share A Smile Becky (Barbie's friend in a wheelchair); Sing 'N Snore Ernie

1998 – Beanie Babies; LEGO Technic Robots' Revenge; Playmobil System X; Furby

1999 – Pokémon; Sega Dreamcast; Furby Babies; Bagpuss (U.K.)

2000 – Lego named Toy of the Century, Monopoly the Game of the Century, and the Yo-yo the Craze of the Century by the British Association of Toy Retailers

Trafalgar Square   A square in central London that honours British Admiral Horatio Nelson and his 1805 victory over a Franco-Spanish fleet. During the Christmas season it is customary for Londoners to gather there and sing carols under the great spruce tree which, since 1947, has been donated every year by the people of Oslo, Norway, as a symbol of their gratitude for British help during the Second World War.

A Trap for Santa Claus (1909)   An early Biograph silent film directed by D.W. Griffith. Included in the cast was Mack Sennett, who would win fame as a director of slapstick comedy.

Trapped in Paradise (1994)   A sentimental comedy that demonstrates the redemptive power Christmas is supposed to wield over even the most criminal heart. The Firpo brothers, Bill, Dave, and Alvin (Nicholas Cage, Jon Lovitz, and Dana Carvey), are considered by their flint-hearted mother to be collectively as intelligent as a bag of hair. They mean to rob the bank in Paradise, Pennsylvania, and make a clean getaway, but a series of disasters keeps them trapped in the small town over Christmas. Naturally, they fall prey to the warmth and folksiness of the inhabitants who take them in. Written and directed by George Gallo, this film has no surprises but a lot of charm.

Tree, Christmas   There have been numerous attempts to find an ancient pedigree for the Christmas tree, with various camps linking it to Babylonian, Egyptian, and Druidic precedents. The only real connection to these cultures is that greenery is, unsurprisingly, often a feature of midwinter festivals. Christian legend-makers have been active as well, attributing the origins of the tree to a dramatic encounter between the missionary St. Boniface and German pagans in the 720s. After chopping down the Oak of Thor at Geismar, Boniface is said to have pointed to a young fir tree as the new symbol to which the German people should look, ever green even in the midst of winter darkness.

A somewhat better-documented story for the origin of the Christmas tree lies in the history of the medieval "Paradise Tree." Among the many mystery plays of the Middle Ages, one of the favourites was the "Paradise Play," which recounted the story of Creation and the expulsion of Adam and Eve from the Garden of Eden. The stage prop that represented the lost Paradise was a tree (often a fir) hung with apples and round wafers in imitation of the consecrated Host. Even after mystery plays fell into disfavour, people kept alive their memory by erecting a "paradise tree" in their homes on December 24, the feast of saints Adam and Eve. Those who favour this account then blend it with the medieval German custom of setting up a pyramid of shelves at Christmas on which were placed candles and greenery. They claim that in the Rhineland area of Germany in the 16th century, the pyramid and the paradise tree were merged into a lighted fir tree hung with ornaments, the prototype of today's Christmas tree. A legend also says that about 1530 Martin Luther was struck by the beauty of the night sky and tried to recreate the appearance of the heavens over Bethlehem by placing candles on an evergreen tree. There is, however, no reliable record of a German tree bearing either decoration or candles in the 16th century and it is more likely that the trees were hung from the rafters upside-down or upright.

Estonians, for their part, claim to have used evergreen trees at Christmas as early as 1441; Latvians point to Riga in 1510, where an evergreen decorated with artificial roses was carried in procession to the town square and burnt; and Stow's *Survey of London* noted that in 1444 "a standard of tree [was] set up in midst of the pavement, fast in the ground, nailed full of holm [holly] and ivy, for disport of Christmas to the people." There is no doubt, however, that in 16th-century Germany accounts of Christmas trees in the home become more common. Evergreens were being sold in markets by 1531, and a 1561 decree from Alsace ordered that "no burgher shall have for Christmas more than one bush of more than eight shoes in length," presumably as a forest conservation measure.

It is not until 1605 that we have an account of a Christmas tree bearing paper roses (a symbol of the Virgin Mary), apples (reminiscent of the paradise tree), wafers (representing the Host), candies, and sugar lumps. Sixteen-sixty is the earliest account of candles being placed on a tree.

From Protestant areas of Germany, the tree spread slowly throughout Europe (largely by German royalty) and to North America. It came to England in the 18th century with the Hanoverian kings. Queen Charlotte, who married George III in 1761, had a yew tree hung with sweets and toys for local children at Windsor on Christmas Day 1800. Queen Adelaide, who married William IV in 1818, always had a tree, but the notion was slow to catch on among the English people, partly because the royal family was unpopular. The Christmas tree was introduced into France in 1837, when the German princess Helen of Mecklenburg brought it to Paris after her marriage to the Duke of Orléans. Empress Eugenie encouraged the tree during the Second Empire, and refugees from Alsace and Lorraine fleeing to France after the Franco-Prussian War helped to popularize it. It was not until PRINCE ALBERT of Saxe-Coburg-Gotha married Queen Victoria that the Christmas tree became part of the British domestic landscape. Albert had always had one as a child, and in the 1840s he erected them for his young family at Windsor Castle. When in 1848 the *Illustrated London News* printed an engraving of the royal family around a tabletop Christmas tree, the custom was quickly adopted by upper- and middle-class English homes. Albert helped spread the notion by sending trees to military barracks, schools, and hospitals.

Moravian settlers brought the tree to what is now the United States in the 1740s; it was imported to Canada in 1781 by Baroness Frederika von Riedesel, whose husband, Baron Friedrich Adolphus, had brought 4,000 German Brunswicker soldiers to reinforce Quebec from American attack. A second wave of German immigration in the 1800s helped the tree become more widely known. The first commercial tree lot in the United States was set up in New York City in 1851, when Mark Carr hauled two ox-sleds loaded with trees down from the Catskills. The first tree in the White House was erected by Franklin Pierce in 1856.

It was really not until the 19th century that the Christmas tree achieved widespread success, penetrating not only Northern and Western Europe and North America, but also Southern Europe, Scandinavia, Eastern Europe, and Russia.

The first trees, hung from rafters, seem to have been undecorated and small. When they became decorated, they remained small enough for a tabletop; some prosperous families had a separate tree and its own pile of presents for each person. In the 19th century the fashion was for bigger trees, but keeping them erect posed a problem. The trees were often

Christmas Tree *A Victorian family poses beside its Christmas tree.*

nailed onto a wooden stand or placed in a pail of rocks and sand; patented tree stands emerged in the 1870s but they were maddeningly inefficient for many years. Candles on trees were lovely to look at but very dangerous. Many families lit them only on Christmas Eve when the tree was revealed for the first time to the children; others had servants standing by with pails of water and wet swabs to extinguish any errant flames. Varieties of patented candle clips competed, but were eventually eclipsed by the electric bulb, which made its debut in 1882. It must be said, however, that though all of North America (under pressure from insurance companies) went electric, Europe continues its love affair with real candles.

In the late 19th century, Germans grew concerned over the effect the Christmas tree trade was having on their country's forests. Those seeking the perfectly shaped tree had taken to lopping the tops off larger trees, preventing them from growing any further. Laws were passed to prevent people from taking more than one specimen, and some called for the abolition of the Christmas tree altogether as an ecological safeguard. Among these was conservationist American President Teddy Roosevelt, who barred Christmas trees from the White House. In Canada, a woman's magazine suggested that a stepladder could be suitably disguised as a tree, or presents could simply be placed on a table. An American magazine suggested hiding wrapped gifts in a tub of bran or sawdust and letting children root around for them. Businesses began to sell artificial models; the goose-feather tree was quite popular, but the Addis Brush company produced a model based on their toilet brush that was capable of holding heavier loads of ornaments than the feather tree. Interest in artificial trees declined in the 20th century as real ones became easier to obtain, but the introduction of aluminum trees in the 1960s renewed the fascination momentarily. In North America, as the baby boom generation grew up and left home in the 1970s and 1980s, many parents replaced the real tree with a plastic one.

Ornamentation of Christmas trees has always been eclectic and extravagant (see ORNAMENTS). From the home-made decorations and edible treats of the earliest trees to the glass bulbs of Germany to the plastic innovations of Japan, each generation and nation has strived to combine meaningful tradition with dazzling effect. In the 19th century this meant huge trees with massive ornamentation, or trees with a theme – Egyptian, Oriental, or colour-coordinated models. National tastes also differ. Sweden favours straw goats and live candles; the Danes love their flag and heart-shaped ornaments; Polish trees have angels, birds, and stars; Ukrainian trees feature a spider among the tinsel and angel-hair; Hungarians prefer brightly wrapped sweets. Technology has played its part. The raw material for tinsel has evolved from silver to lead to plastic as manufacturing techniques have changed. Since the first patent for a tree stand was issued in 1876, they have been made to rotate while playing music, raise and lower the tree, or keep it supplied with water; almost anything is possible in a tree stand except an easy set-up and take-down. Christmas tree lights have been made to resemble cartoon characters, fruit, or angels; they can bubble, flash, or twinkle in sequence. It is impossible, however, to keep the cords from becoming tangled from one Christmas to the next.

Styles of tree have changed over time and also reflect national preferences. Nineteenth-century Germans preferred *tanne* trees with even branches to support hoops with candles on them lowered over the top. The cedar tree was fragrant, but lost its foliage too quickly and was replaced after the 1860s by the hemlock, which could not support much ornamentation. By 1900 the balsam fir from Maine had established itself in the eastern United States, where it remains pre-eminent. In the western states it is the Douglas fir; in the South the white pine rules; elsewhere in the United States the Scotch pine has a large following. In Hawaii, the Norfolk Island pine is admired for its symmetry, but many make the mistake of planting them in the yard after Christmas; they tend to grow very large and be a menace to house and garden. In Canada the favourite tree is the balsam fir, followed by the Fraser fir, Scotch pine, and White spruce. Norwegians incline to the pine and the spruce; it is a spruce tree that the city of Oslo sends every year to London's Trafalgar Square. The Christmas tree found in English homes is likely to be a spruce as well.

Trees, Non-coniferous, and Christmas   A number of legends have linked non-coniferous trees with Christmas. The "Cherry Tree Carol" tells how the tree bent down to make it easy for the pregnant Mary to pick its fruit. This was based on an earlier legend from a non-canonical gospel which relates how palm trees bowed toward Bethlehem to show the Magi the way. From this came the notion that every Epiphany Eve (or, according to some, Christmas Eve) since then, palm trees have bowed down in reverence to the holy birth. On the other hand, the aspen refused to bow as Mary and the baby Jesus walked past, so now it is always trembling.

When shepherds of Bethlehem arrived at the stable, they found the Holy Family cold, so they gathered ash logs, which, despite being green, burnt well and provided immediate warmth. Since then, though other logs will not burn if newly cut, the ash has always burnt brightly even if green.

Visitors to Egypt are often shown an ancient sycamore that has been named the Virgin's Tree because, after the Holy Family had fled from Israel, the tree opened itself up to shelter Mary and Jesus while Joseph was building their first house.

Trial of Bitter Waters   According to the apocryphal *Protoevangelium of James*, Mary and Joseph were required to take the Trial of Bitter Waters, an ancient test of guilt or innocence in an accusation of adultery. They survived the ordeal, to the amazement of the High Priest. The Trial was depicted in early medieval art but was seldom of interest to later artists.

Trinidad and Tobago   Christmas in Trinidad and Tobago is a time to look back on the old year and prepare for the new. The house must be given a thorough cleaning before being decorated, and a portion of the Christmas budget always goes to buying something new for the house or making repairs. The famous Black Fruit Cake is prepared well in advance to let the flavours develop. The same is true for the homemade drinks: plantain wine, sorrel, ginger beer, and *Ponche à Crème*.

Christmas food is plentiful, with the main course usually a ham, or perhaps a turkey, accompanied by sweet potatoes, PASTELLES, *calaloo* (a spinach-like vegetable) and crab, pigeon peas, and rice. Extra must be prepared for the relatives returning for the holiday from North America, and visitors that are sure to drop in on Christmas and Boxing Day. Most island families go to church for the Christmas Eve midnight service or the morning service on Christmas Day.

The most distinctive aspect of a Trinidadian Christmas is the music of the season, *parang*. The term is derived from the Spanish *parranda*, or "spree"; Trinidad was a Spanish colony until 1797, when it fell to the British. The music is a lively combination of Spanish and Venezuelan influences that have melded over the centuries. It was customary for groups of *parranderos* to go from house to house, singing these Christmas songs (in Spanish for the most part) and receiving hospitality in return. Like the *parrandistas* in Puerto Rico, they have songs to gain admission to the house and songs for performing inside. Today the traditional acoustic instruments have given way to electrified ones, and traditionalists worry about the modernization of the art form, but the spirit of the music remains the same. A new variety, called *soca-parang*, has emerged, praising Christmas with different rhythms and English lyrics.

Once Christmas has passed, Trinidadians begin to prepare for the onset of Carnival.

The Troublemakers (1994)   A spaghetti Western with a Christmas twist. Travis, the fastest gun on the plains (played by Terence Hill, who also directed this lightweight oater), has been instructed by his aged Maw (Ruth Buzzi) to bring his estranged brother Moses the bounty hunter (Bud Spencer) home for the holidays. The climax is a touching scene on Christmas Eve: a host of bad guys approaches the homestead with guns drawn and murder in their hearts, but at the magical sound of children singing carols, they drop their weapons one by one. The resulting showdown must therefore be settled with fists and blunt instruments only. Also known as *The Fight Before Christmas* and *Botte di Natale*.

Truce, Christmas   One of the undoubted benefits of Christmas throughout history has been its ability to bring a little peace into the world, however temporary, in the midst of war. We can see this first in the 11th century, when the Church promoted an international movement to reduce social violence. The Peace of God and, slightly later, the Truce of God were attempts to dissuade knights from harming unarmed peasants, women, merchants, and clergy and to convince them to restrict warfare to certain times of the year. Advent and Christmas were among the seasons in which war was to be prohibited; the penalty for breaking the truce was excommunication.

The notion of a Christmas truce caught on in many parts of Europe. Every year since the Middle Ages, the Finns have proclaimed a truce from their old capital of Turku at midday on Christmas Eve; nowadays the ancient proclamation is read by the city's mayor and broadcast on radio and television. The Swedes, Norwegians, and Estonians have followed a similar custom since about 1650. In medieval York, a piece of mistletoe was laid on the high altar of the Minister on Christmas Eve and left there for the Twelve Days of Christmas. At the city gates, a decree of peace and pardon was proclaimed for as long as the mistletoe remained in place. In medieval Scotland, the Yule-firth was a kind of truce that forbade legal proceedings in the week before and after Christmas.

During the Franco-Prussian War of 1870, French and German soldiers faced each other in trenches around besieged Paris. It is said that on Christmas Eve a Frenchman jumped out of his trench and serenaded the Germans with the beautiful "Cantique de Noèl" ("O Holy Night"). When the French singer had finished the carol, a young German responded with Luther's Christmas hymn "Von Himmel Hoch" ("From Heaven Above to Earth I Come").

Christmas Truce *German and British soldiers fraternize during the 1914 Christmas truce which temporarily brought World War I to a halt.*

This was a prelude to the most famous Christmas truces of all, which occurred during the First World War. On December 14, 1914, the German 107th Regiment of Leipzig left its trenches following its band, which was playing Christmas carols. Their singing induced the French to leave their shelter and join them for a time in no-man's-land and exchange presents. Similar spontaneous outbreaks of peace took place all through that Christmas season. On Christmas Day, German and British troops played soccer between the lines, with the Germans winning 3-2. Officers on both sides deplored such goodwill and tried to suppress it. The Germans pulled the Christmas-loving Bavarians and Saxons out of the front lines and replaced them with Prussian regiments, who were made of sterner stuff. The next year there were similar demonstrations of the Christmas spirit, but by 1916 the war had hardened participants on both sides and no truces seem to have taken place.

During the Second World War, some of the most vicious fighting took place on December 25 – at Hong Kong in 1941, and Stalingrad in 1942 – and no record of truces on Christmas from that conflict has survived.

The Truth About Father Christmas The first play written for radio in Britain, broadcast on Christmas Eve, 1922, by the BBC. It was written by Phyllis M. Twigg.

"Tu scendi dalle stelle" A favourite Italian carol, written in 1853 by the Neapolitan bishop Alphonsus Liguori.

> You came down from the stars, O divine King,
> And appear in a cavern in cold and ice.
> O my divine Child, I see you trembling here!
> How much it cost you to have loved me!
>
> You, the Creator of the world,
> Are lacking clothing and fire,
> O my Lord, dear little one,
> How much more this poverty makes me love you,
> Since it is love that has made you poor.

Tussie Mussies Small posies of herbs and aromatic flowers bound together. In the Middle Ages it was customary to carry such bouquets close to the nose to mask the vile stench of life before indoor plumbing; it was also believed that this was a way to ward off airborne disease. Nowadays tussie mussies are most often used to keep closets and drawers smelling sweet, but recently American craftspeople have begun to decorate Christmas trees with them.

Turkey The most widely served Christmas entrée today is the turkey, *Meleagris gallopavo*, a bird first domesticated in Mexico by the Aztecs and exported to Europe in the 16th century by the Spanish. It derives its English name from confusion with the guinea fowl, which was imported about the same time by merchants trading with Turkey. William Strickland, a Yorkshireman, introduced the bird into England and, in recognition, was granted a turkey cock on his family coat of arms in 1550. Before long it was accepted as a seasonal dish: THOMAS TUSSER in 1573 speaks of it as "Christmas husbandlie fare," but for centuries the goose remained the primary Christmas bird. Turkeys were raised in great numbers on farms in Norfolk and East Anglia, with huge flocks driven to market in London every Christmas; walking on the roads was difficult for the birds and they were fitted with special shoes for the journey, which could last as long as three months. It was not until the advent of rail travel and refrigeration in the 19th century that these drives ceased and turkeys were slaughtered before their journey. In 1851 the British royal family ate their first Christmas turkey, which from then on replaced swan as their seasonal dish. (See colour fig. 27.)

Americans are the world's greatest consumers of turkeys, since the two great end-of-year festivals, Thanksgiving and Christmas, both feature the fowl. Benjamin Franklin wanted to make the turkey America's national bird; he deplored the bald eagle's "bad moral character" and claimed his candidate was a "much more respectable bird, and withal a true original native of America." Since 1947 the National Turkey Federation has presented the president of the United States with a live turkey and two dressed birds at Thanksgiving. The annual presentation signals the unofficial beginning of the "holiday season"; after the ceremony, the lucky National Thanksgiving Turkey retires to a traditional farm to spend its declining years in comfort.

The bird is eaten all around the world. In Portugal, poultry farmers walk the streets of Lisbon with their flocks. When a buyer has chosen the turkey he wants, the farmer catches it, forces alcohol down its throat, and briefly releases it. The inebriated turkey soon collapses. Its throat is then slit and it is plucked and eviscerated before being soaked in salt water, perfumed with lemon and bay leaves, for 12 hours. The bird is then hung for another 12 hours before being cooked. The Brazilians have a similar love of turkey tenderized from within: they feed the bird a kind of rum called *cachaça* on Christmas Eve before it is slaughtered. In the southern United States, the custom of deep-frying the bird is growing, while in Mexico they eat the bird with a *mole* sauce, made of chocolate and chili peppers. In Spain they stuff the bird with truffles; in Burgundy they stuff it with chestnuts. In 1969 the Apollo astronauts' first meal on the moon was roast turkey.

Around the world families "pull the wishbone" – two people grasp an end and pull in opposite directions. Good luck comes to the one who ends up with the bigger piece.

Turkey Narcosis A jocular expression for the drowsiness felt after ingesting a large Christmas dinner. Turkey, like other protein-rich foods, contains tryptophan, an amino acid that induces sleep.

Turrón A traditional Christmas dessert in Spain and Spanish America, made of almond nougat.

Turtledove In Christian art, a symbol of purity. Joseph of Nazareth gave to the Temple two doves in a basket at the purification of Mary.

Tusser, Thomas Tudor farmer, writer, and musician, Tusser (c. 1524-80) is best known for the proverb "Christmas comes but once a year." From his observations on 16th-century agriculture and household management, we learn of many traditional English Christmas customs. His emphasis is on Christmas as a time of feasting and charity, both of which he claims are a good investment.

> Get ivy and hull, woman, deck up thine house,
> And take this same brawn for to seethe and to souse;
> Provide us good cheer, for thou knowest the old guise,
> Old customs that good be, let no man despise.
> At Christmas be merry and thank God of all,
> And feast thy poor neighbours, the great and the small.
> Yea, all the year long have an eye to the poor,
> And God shall send luck to keep open thy door.
> Good fruit and good plenty do well in thy loft,
> Then lay for an orchard and cherish it oft.
> The profit is mickle, the pleasure is much;
> At pleasure with profit few wise men will grutch.
> For plants and for stocks lay aforehand to cast,
> But set or remove them, while Twelvetide do last.

In his "Christmas Husbandry Fare," Tusser says

> Good husband and housewife, now chiefly be glad
> Things handsome to have, as they ought to be had,
> They both do provide against Christmas to come,
> To welcome their neighbour, good cheer to have some
> Good bread and good drink, a good fire in the hall,
> Brawn pudding and souse, and good mustard withal.
>
> Beef, mutton, and pork, shred pies of the best,
> Pig, veal, goose, and capon, and turkey well dressed;

> Cheese, apples, and nuts, jolly carols to hear,
> As then in the country is counted good cheer.
>
> What cost to good husband is any of this?
> Good household provision only it is;
> Of other the like I do leave out a many,
> That costeth the husbandman never a penny.

"Twas in the Moon of Wintertime" See "THE HURON CAROL."

"Twas the Night Before Christmas" See "A VISIT FROM ST. NICHOLAS."

Twelfth Night The night of January 5, the vigil or eve of Epiphany, is the 12th night from Christmas (if Christmas is counted as the first). In England, Twelfth Night was long a time of merriment to mark the end of the Christmas season. Masquerading was a common activity on Twelfth Night, along with dancing, cross-dressing, and gambling. It was a time of social inversion, when a mock king was elected to supervise the misrule.

By the 19th century its reputation of riotousness was working against it, and Twelfth Night was losing out to Christmas as the date for festivities. Victorian values were making the season more respectable and domestic. The gender-swapping and role reversals were theatricalized and absorbed by the PANTOMIME, where they became harmless family fare.

Twelfth-Night Cake In many countries it was customary to celebrate Epiphany with a feast on its eve, or Twelfth Night. A central feature of these festivities was a cake in which a bean or token was hidden. He who found it in his piece of cake was named lord of the evening's entertainments and could command guests to do his bidding. In France the cake was known as *gateau des rois*, or kings' cake, in honour of the Wise Men, whose feast Epiphany is; in Louisiana it is "king cake"; in Germany it is *Dreikonigskuchen*; it is the Black Bun in Scotland; in Portugal it is *bola-rei*; and in Spain it is *rosca de reyes*. See BADDELEY BEQUEST and BEAN KING.

Twelve Days of Christmas In 567 the Council of Tours proclaimed the 12 days between Christmas and Epiphany to be a sacred and festive season. Since then it has been widely accepted as a time of holiday and merriment; in many places all non-essential work was forbidden. In German-speaking territories, the time is *Die Zwölf Raunächte*, the Twelve Rough Nights, when it was advisable to guard against evil spirits with noise, masks, and smoke.

The Twelve Days are not calculated in the same way everywhere. In some places Christmas is counted, making Epiphany the 13th day. In England it is particularly confusing, because January 6 is Twelfth Day, but January 5 is Twelfth Night.

"The Twelve Days of Christmas" A seasonal ditty whose origins may lie in pagan magic counting songs or something very much like the old Latin hymn, with leader and responses building on each verse: one God, two testaments, three patriarchs or persons in the Trinity, four gospels, five books of Moses, and so on, up to twelve apostles. An early French version has one good stuffing without bones, two breasts of veal, three joints of beef, four pigs' trotters, five legs of mutton, six partridges with cabbage, seven spitted rabbits, eight plates of salad, nine dishes from the chapterhouse, ten full casks, eleven beautiful maidens, and twelve musketeers with swords.

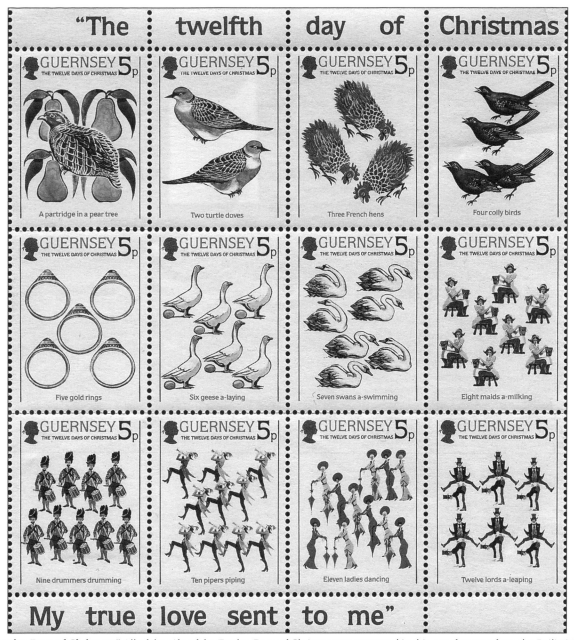

"The Twelve Days of Christmas" *All of the gifts of the Twelve Days of Christmas are portrayed in this set of stamps from the Bailiwick of Guernsey.*

Numerous versions abound, but the earliest in English is in the 1780 nursery book *Mirth Without Mischief*. A Christmas game called for a forfeit to be paid if someone missed or confused a line when it was sung in a group.

A myth circulating on the Internet in recent years has called the song a secret code by which English Catholics kept their faith alive during the years after the Reformation, when their religion was discouraged, but this appears to be just another cyber hoax. None of the so-called hidden meanings (the partridge representing Jesus, for instance) is particularly Catholic.

The present version, by J.O. Helliwell, is from 1842, but American regional variations have such things as "deer a-running" and "wolves a-howling," and New Zealand and Australian versions populate the song with indigenous wildlife, such as "a pukeko in a ponga tree."

The full complement of gifts is gathered together in the last verse:

On the twelfth day of Christmas
My true love sent to me:
Twelve drummers drumming,
Eleven pipers piping,
Ten lords a-leaping,
Nine ladies dancing,
Eight maids a-milking,
Seven swans a-swimming,
Six geese a-laying,
Five golden rings,
Four calling birds,
Three French hens,
Two turtle doves,
And a partridge in a pear tree

Ukraine Christmas in Ukraine begins with a 39-day season of spiritual preparation. It is a period of meatless fasting, reconciliation with family members and neighbours, and readying the house and farm for the festivities in honour of the birth of Jesus. This Advent period covers a number of saints' days that have had special traditions attached to them over the centuries, many of which involve divining the future or obtaining a spouse. The eve of St. Catherine's Day, for example, was a time for young men to fast and pray that they would be sent a good wife. On St. Andrew's Day young women would listen for the sound of dogs barking – that part of the village the noise came from would produce their future husband – or would hope to see their mate in a dream. On St. Nicholas's Day the gift-bringer visits children in the form of a stately bishop, perhaps accompanied by angels; he quizzes them on their behaviour and religious knowledge before distributing presents. Those who do not get to see the saint personally still set their shoes or a plate on the windowsill so that he can fill them with gifts in the night.

Meanwhile, everything is being made ready for *Sviata Vechera*, the Christmas Eve supper. The animals are given extra feed, and straw is placed under the table and the tablecloth in token of the birth that took place in a humble animal's stall. A candle is set in the window to guide the homeless, and an extra place at the table set for the stranger or the spirits of the family dead. The centrepiece is round, braided bread with a candle in the middle. The head of the family brings in the *didukh* ("grandfather spirit"), a sheaf of wheat that represents the trans-generational unity of the family, and places it by the icons on the east wall of the house. (It, and the Christmas tree, remain in the home until the eve of Epiphany, when they are removed and the *didukh* burnt.)

When the first star appears in the evening sky the dinner of 12 meatless courses can begin. The father reads a prayer and greets those at the table with the traditional "*Khrystos Narodywsia!*" ("Christ is born!") and is answered, "*Slawimo Yoho!*" ("Glory to Him!"). All may then begin to eat the traditional first dish of *kutya*, a grain porridge sweetened with honey that symbolizes life and prosperity. The remaining dishes consist of various types of fish, dumplings, cabbage rolls, beans, beets, assorted vegetables, mushrooms, soup, and fruit compote. After supper children hunt about in the straw for candies and perhaps take food to their grandparents or godparents. Carols are sung and the night ends with attendance at the midnight mass. (See colour fig. 28.)

(In the pre-Communist era, Christmas Eve was not a time of gift-giving; that was reserved for St. Nicholas's Day. Under the Soviet regime, St. Nicholas and Christmas were repressed and replaced with New Year's festivities and Grandfather Frost. In the diaspora, primarily in the United States and Canada, where hundreds of thousands of Ukrainians fled, many people adopted Christmas as the time of gift-giving and placed presents under the Christmas tree. But to assert their distinct cultural identity, they clung to the ancient Julian calendar, and so celebrate their rituals 13 days after the rest of the world and its Gregorian calendar – thus Christmas is January 7, and so on.)

With the preparatory fast ended, meat and foods prepared with dairy products can once more be eaten, so more feasting is sure to take place on Christmas Day. Families exchange visits and receive groups of carollers, who are rewarded with food and money for their efforts. Ukrainians take their carolling seriously and sing two types of Christmas songs: the *koliadky*, which are sung on Christmas Eve and Christmas Day, and the *shchedrivky*, sung during New Year's and the Feast of the Epiphany. Among the latter is the most famous Ukrainian seasonal song, "Shchedryk," by Leontovych, which is known in English as "THE CAROL OF THE BELLS." The traditional carolling group included someone dressed as a goat, someone to carry a pole with a lighted star, a bag-carrier, and, occasionally, musicians with folk instruments. The carollers first had to ask for permission to sing and, when admitted, sang a song for each member of the family, down to the smallest child. Sometimes they danced and presented a humorous skit involving the death and resurrection of the goat – clearly a hold-over from pagan fertility drama. The carolling always ended with the recitation of poems wishing prosperity on the house. Like the carollers, members of a puppet theatre troupe might visit Ukrainian homes during the Christmas season. Using a two-stage portable theatre the puppeteers would present a Nativity story and patriotic folk tales. (See VERTEP.)

New Year's Eve, or *Malanka*, is also a time of feasting and merriment, with rich foods, toasts, and carols. It is a night for spirited Ukrainian dancing and music. When Ukraine was part of the Soviet Union, Communist authorities encouraged citizens to treat New Year's Day as a substitute for Christmas, with GRANDFATHER FROST standing in for St. Nicholas as the gift-bringer.

The last day in the Ukrainian Christmas season is *Yordan*, or Epiphany, which celebrates the baptism of Jesus in the River Jordan. It is a time for priests to bless the waters in a ceremony to which people solemnly march with banners. Often this occurs outdoors on a frozen lake where a huge cross of ice has been erected. The priest will cense the waters, and three candles will be dipped into the water as a token of the necessity of baptism. After the ceremony the people return home with some of the blessed water to keep during the coming year.

Uncle Mistletoe A commercially inspired analogue of Santa Claus invented in the late 1940s by Marshall Fields department store in Chicago. Described as a "black-browed, winged sprite, wearing a cape and top hat," he lived with his wife, Aunt Holly, in Cozy Cloud Cottage (the creation of store designer Homer Sharp) on the eighth floor. Uncle Mistletoe attracted a loyal following of children, who joined his "Happiness Clubs," and he even made television appearances in cartoon form during the holiday season. In 1951 the Three Suns issued a 45 rpm recording entitled "Uncle Mistletoe," and he was the subject of a children's book. Collectibles of Uncle Mistletoe and Aunt Holly are still made for Marshall Fields.

Uncle Mistletoe was only one of a number of additions to the mythology of Christmas made by North American department stores. For others see PUNKINHEAD and RUDOLPH, THE RED-NOSED REINDEER.

United Kingdom See ENGLAND, SCOTLAND, and WALES.

United States In 1607 at Jamestown, in the Virginia colony, John Smith boasted, "Wherever an Englishman may be, and in whatever part of the world, he must keep Christmas with feasting and merriment! And indeed, we were never more merry, nor fed on more plenty of good oysters, fish, flesh, wild fowl and good bread; nor never had better fires in England." And so it developed in the southern colonies: feasting, gift-exchanging, lengthy visits, hospitality, dancing, fireworks, and SHOOTING-IN of Christmas were all aspects of the holiday season. The French influence in Louisiana, the English heritage in New York, and the Moravian and German settlements in Pennsylvania ensured that in most of the British North American colonies, Christmas was a special time of year.

In much of New England, however, with its PURITAN founders, Christmas was a time of sobriety and honest labour. In 1620 the Pilgrims, fresh from the *Mayflower*, worked on Christmas Day and built the Common House in Plymouth; the next year a quarrel broke out between those who wished to take time off to celebrate Christmas and those who believed they should not mark Christmas in any way. The opponents of Christmas won that struggle, as they did in 1659, when the General Court of Mass forbade the observation of Christmas on pain of a five-shilling fine. Connecticut banned Christmas and saints' days, mince pies, card playing, and musical instruments. Though many of these laws were eventually abolished, prejudice against the holiday lingered. In 1686 angry Puritans barred the new governor from holding a Christmas service in their meeting house and forced him to move to the Boston town hall. It would be a long time before Christmas became a popular holiday in New England.

The Puritans and other opponents of the holiday objected to the drunkenness associated with Christmas, as well as the noise, crowds of men out late at night, violence in the streets, and "CALLITHUMPIAN" music, all of which threatened the repose of decent men and their families. By 1800 a middle-class dislike of Christmas was growing in cities of the young American republic; the holiday, it was felt, had fallen into the hands of the lower orders, as in the case of the Boston "ANTICKS." Attempts were made to wrest Christmas from the dangerous sections of society and give it a more religious and domestic face.

This was accomplished in the early 19th century by a number of contemporary drives. Police cracked down all over North America on behaviour that had long been tolerated; the alcoholic excesses, the late-night wandering, and the extortionate MUMMING during the Christmas season were now banned and subject to prosecution. In this they were supported by editorialists. "Let all avoid taverns and grog shops for a few days at least, and spend their money at home," was the advice of the *New York Herald* in 1839. "Make glad upon one day the domestic hearth, the virtuous wife, the smiling, merry-hearted children, and the blessed mother." Churches began to urge that Christmas be a legal holiday so that families and their servants could spend time in worship and decent recreation. Most importantly, a group of New York antiquarians and writers invented a new kind of Christmas that was suitable to the prosperous classes.

John Pintard, WASHINGTON IRVING, and CLEMENT CLARKE MOORE were all conservative New Yorkers whose writings led to a revolution in keeping Christmas that was eventually to spread all over the world. Through his work in the New-York Historical Society, Pintard promoted the cult of St. Nicholas and introduced a Dutch version of the gift-bringer to American families. In this he was aided by Irving's *Knickerbocker's History of New York*, in which St. Nicholas, or Santa Claus as he was coming to be known, was portrayed as a flying sprite who brought presents, a picture that was completed by Moore's poem "A Visit From St. Nicholas," which blended the flying from rooftop to rooftop, the reindeer-drawn sleigh, the jolly corpulence of the gift-bringer, and the descent down the chimney in a way that had never existed before but that would prove irresistible to the public.

While this was happening other important forces were at work. The Industrial Revolution was making it possible to mass-produce goods for a newly prosperous country and make Christmas a gift-buying holiday. New attitudes to the family and the place of children were emerging, and these meshed well with the notion of Christmas as a family-centred activity. The Christmas writings of Charles Dickens were quickly adopted in the 1840s, and the holiday became identified with charity, reunion, and reconciliation. New waves of German immigrants were coming to America with their love of Christmas trees, carols, cookies, and gifts. By the 1850s the modern notions of Christmas were taking shape. Gone, or at least discouraged, were the forces of misrule and outdoor merriment; in the ascendant were Santa Claus, Christmas Eve gift-bringing, and children at the heart of the festivities. Those years also saw the first American Christmas cards and the first decorated tree in the White House.

Ironically, the horror of the American Civil War (1861-65) was to accelerate this process. It created massive family dislocation, homesickness, and a yearning for normality, a situation in which Christmas served as a metaphor for peace and restoration. Thomas Nast's drawings of Santa Claus visiting Union troops and of husbands, wives, and children yearning for each other on Christmas Eve served to present Christmas to the public mind as something deeply patriotic and traditional. When the war ended, the new domestic Christmas was inextricably woven into the American consciousness. It was no coincidence that President Andrew Johnson chose Christmas Day to sign a pardon for all those who had taken part in the rebellion.

The near-universal popularity of Christmas meant that commercial forces would soon get involved. It is important to note, however, that the overwhelming acceptance of gift-giving was not a result of merchandising pressure but rather a slowly growing demand from the populace that merchants strove to meet. Department stores hired Santa Claus stand-ins, store windows were decorated for the season, and opening hours were lengthened. The volume of Christmas advertising grew as the century progressed, and the time allotted for a national shopping season was extended until it preceded Thanksgiving in November.

Christians were aware of the contradictions involved in celebrating the birth of the Saviour with a festival of consumption. As Christmas became a feast of family prosperity so did American families strive to include charity among the meanings of the season. Children were taught to think of the poor when disposing of their Christmas allowance or their old toys. A number of important charitable institutions sprang up in the United States whose purpose was to provide to the poor the essentials of a middle-class Christmas: gifts for children and a sumptuous meal. These "Christmas Clubs" raised money among the well-to-do and distributed their charity to hospitals, orphanages, and Children's Aid societies, as well as holding mass banquets to which thousands of poor children were invited. (In 1902 a Christmas meal for 20,000 in New York's Grand Central Palace went awry when a free-spirited segment of the poverty-stricken youth indulged in an orgy of pie and cutlery throwing.)

By the dawning of the 20th century, Americans of all Christian denominations and ethnic backgrounds adopted Christmas and added their particular flavours to what was becoming a favoured national holiday. New American carols were written by Unitarians, Catholics, Lutherans, Episcopalians, and even Mormons. The French of Louisiana added the King Cake and *feux de joie*; the Moravians added the *putz*, cookies, and candle-lit services; Catholics added the Nativity scene, processions, and drama; and German Protestants, the Christmas tree. The Puritan rejection of Christmas had finally been overcome, and the vast majority of American Christians had made Christmas a central part of their church and social calendar. Americans were well on their way to producing a new kind of Christmas, one that could be exported to the rest of the world.

The key element in this was the development in the United States of Santa Claus. His emergence in the 19th century as a kindly, non-judgmental gift-bringer influenced native Christmas figures all around the world – what had in many cases been frightening, half-demonic spirits now became much more like Santa. We can see this particularly in the domestication of the *Jólasveinar* in Iceland and the gnomes and Christmas goats of Scandinavia. Francis Church's eloquent 1897 editorial "YES, VIRGINIA, THERE IS A SANTA CLAUS" made Santa much more than a convenient way of explaining the arrival of presents or an allegory of parental love; he was now the embodiment of faith, generosity, and idealism in a skeptical age, and Christmas was a time for believing in the possibility of goodness. These were notions that American cinema continued to support with films such as *Miracle on 34th Street* and *It's a Wonderful Life*. During the 1900s, Hollywood and the wars that sent American troops around the world diffused aspects of the North American Christmas into other cultures. Santa Claus, his arrival on December 24, the Christmas tree, snowy backdrops, and turkey found their way into the most remote celebrations of Christmas.

But this influence worked both ways. Massive immigration to the United States meant that a cross-fertilization took place, and the American Christmas was shaped by all the cultures that flocked to the continent. The following list of Christmas attractions in the United States will give an idea of the wonderful diversity of the holiday in that country.

Macy's Parade
As early as 1889 a New York newspaper claimed that "as soon as the Thanksgiving turkey is eaten the great question of buying Christmas presents begins to take the terrifying shape it has come to assume." Thanksgiving parades, especially Macy's in New York, usher in the American Christmas shopping season late in November. The Macy's parade is famous for its huge helium-filled balloons representing cartoon characters; the bow tie on "The Cat in the Hat" for example was 16 feet wide and his hat was two storeys high. Two million spectators crowd the 2.5-mile parade route, while another 50,000,000 watch at home. Presiding over the affair, of course, is Santa Claus, whose presence reminds children of the approach of Christmas and parents of the film *Miracle on 34th Street*.

Christmas Pageant of Peace
Early in December the president of the United States officially illuminates the National Community Christmas Tree on the Ellipse just across from the White House, and a month-long Pageant of Peace begins. Visitors can view the huge living Colorado Blue Spruce that is the National Tree and stroll along a boardwalk that connects it to 56 other living trees representing the 50 states, five territories, and the District of Columbia. Along this Pathway of Peace are model railroad displays, a burning Yule log, a Nativity scene (subject of years of legal wrangling about its constitutional appropriateness), and concert band performances.

Colonial Williamsburg
Williamsburg, Virginia, is the site of a remarkable village where life in colonial America is re-enacted. Electric candles replace real ones for the annual Grand Illumination, but all other decorations are made of natural materials such as greenery and berries. Visitors can see preparations for an 18th-century Christmas, take carriage rides, enjoy colonial-era Christmas meals, and learn how to make antique crafts.

Rockefeller Centre
The civic heart of the Christmas season in New York is Rockefeller Centre. In early December a massive tree is erected and illuminated with 29,000 lights, and the square is magnificently decorated. Up to 400,000 visitors a day enjoy the ice rink, admire the Art Deco architecture and murals, attend the nearby Radio City Christmas show with the fabled Rockettes, and admire the shop windows on Fifth Avenue.

Posadas, Farolitas, and Luminaria
In the southwestern United States, devout believers stage the POSADAS, or the search for lodgings of the Holy Family in Bethlehem. A couple representing Mary and Joseph, accompanied by followers, knocks at the door of a pre-selected house and begs a place to stay for the night. They exchange a ritual petition and responses until the couple is at last admitted, whereupon all pay their devotions to a little shrine and enjoy the hospitality of the house. This is often repeated nine times, culminating in a large celebration on Christmas Eve. Houses and yards are often lit at Christmas by *farolitas*, home-made lanterns in paper bags, or *luminaria*, bonfires.

Star Boys of Alaska
In Alaska, which was once owned by Russia and was evangelized by the Orthodox Church, a common sight at Christmas is a procession of STAR BOYS going about dressed as Wise Men. Following a lad with a star on a pole, they go from house to house singing carols to raise money for charity. On some nights they might re-enact the rage of King Herod and the search for the baby Jesus.

New Orleans Bonfires
Along the levees of the Mississippi during the Christmas season, people light bonfires in strange and wonderful shapes. According to locals, this is to help guide Papa Noel on his journey. On Christmas Eve paddle-wheelers cruise up the river carrying passengers to view these *feux de joie*, listen to a jazz band, and eat Cajun and Creole Christmas fare.

Sheepherders Ball, Boise
Many of the Basque settlers of the American west became shepherds, and this ball, inaugurated in 1929, is a celebration of both Basque culture and the approach of Christmas. The original dress code of blue jeans for the men and cotton dresses for the women is no longer enforced, and the traditional

United States *A matachine dancer of New Mexico.*

midnight auction of a live lamb and turkey for charity has faded away, but the original exuberance and Christmas spirit of the dancers remain.

Taos Deer Dance and Los Matachines
In Taos Pueblo, native Americans stage two distinct dances during the Christmas season: the deer dance, in which participants wear the horns and hide of the animals they have killed earlier in the year; and a medieval Spanish dance called *los matachines*, in which the battles between the Christian Spanish and the Islamic Moors are re-enacted.

Philadelphia Mummers' Parade
The rowdy mumming and riotous public behaviour that marked Christmas in the early 19th century was first suppressed and then channelled into expressions such as the Philadelphia Mummers' parade. Every January 1 for 12 hours, over 10,000 enthusiastic participants march and strut in a parade. Club members in elaborate costumes replete with jewels, sequins, and feathers compete in four divisions – comics, fancies, fancy brigades, and string bands – for prizes and bragging rights.

Though late in warming to the celebration of Christmas, the United States has been more influential than any other country in the past 150 years in shaping the holiday. Its version of Santa Claus has influenced the personality of gift-bringers around the world; its menu and holiday calendar have been adopted widely; and where it has not driven out indigenous ideas it, at least, co-exists with them. It is the only country to

have produced new characters in the Christmas myth in the last century: for example The Grinch, Rudolph the Red-Nosed Reindeer, and Frosty the Snowman. Its role in the 21st century Christmas will doubtless be as interesting.

"Unto Us a Boy Is Born" A translation by Percy Dearmer (1867-1936), one of the editors of the 1928 *Oxford Book of Carols*, of the Christmas hymn "PUER NOBIS NASCITUR."

Unto us a Boy is born!
King of all creation,
Came He to a world forlorn,
The Lord of every nation.
The Lord of every nation.

Cradled in a stall was He
With sleepy cows and asses:
But the very beasts could see
That He all men surpasses.
That He all men surpasses.

Herod then with fear was filled:
"A prince," he said, "in Jewry!"
All the little boys he killed
At Bethlehem in his fury.
At Bethlehem in his fury.

Now may Mary's Son, Who came
So long ago to love us,
Lead us all with hearts aflame
Unto the joys above us.
Unto the joys above us.

He the Source and He the End!
Let the organ thunder
While our happy voices rend
The jocund air asunder!
The jocund air asunder!

Up-Helly-Aa A remarkable procession held at Lerwick in the Shetland Islands, the term being derived from the Scottish "Upholiday" or Twelfth Day (though the ceremony always takes place on January 29). In this ceremony hundreds of men in Viking costumes parade through the town carrying torches and a large-scale model of a longship. The participants are called Guizers, and their chief is the Guizer Jarl. They are accompanied on their march by bands, and as they process they sing the "Up-Helly Aa Song." At the end of the march, the ship (a commemoration of the centuries of Viking rule on the islands) is set on fire while the Guizers sing "The Norseman's Home," ships in the harbour sound their sirens, and crowds cheer. Finally, after a long night of drinking, the Christmas season officially comes to an end for another year.

This is one of a number of Scottish ceremonies built around the notion of the cleansing power of fire. Though it looks pagan and antique, it really dates back no further than the 1870s, when the local Total Abstinence Society wanted an activity to replace the customary Christmas Eve and New Year's Eve drunkenness.

"Up on the Housetop" In "Up on the Housetop," Benjamin R. Hanby (1833-67) created one of the first American songs dealing with Santa Claus as well as one of the first secular American Christmas songs. Both Gene Autry and Hopalong Cassidy recorded this song.

Up on the housetop reindeer pause,
Out jumps good old Santa Claus;

Down thru the chimney with lots of toys,
All for the little ones'
Christmas joys

Ho, ho, ho!
Who wouldn't go!
Ho, ho, ho!
Who wouldn't go!
Up on the housetop
Click, click, click
Down thru the chimney with
Good Saint Nick.

First comes the stocking
Of little Nell
Oh, dear Santa
Fill it well.
Give her a dolly
That laughs and cries
One that will open
And shut her eyes

Chorus

Next comes the stocking
Of little Will
Oh, just see what
A glorious fill
Here is a hammer
And lots of tacks
Also a ball
And a whip that cracks

Chorus

Upholiday Literally "end of holiday," the term for Twelfth Night in Scotland, when festivities come to an end.

"Upon Christ's Nativity, or Christmas" A poem by Englishman Rowland Watkyns (fl. 1662).

> From three dark places Christ came forth this day;
> From first His Father's bosom, where He lay,
> Concealed till now; then from the typic law,
> Where we His manhood but by figures saw;
> And lastly from His mother's womb He came
> To us, a perfect God and perfect Man.
> Now in a manger lies the eternal Word:
> The Word He is, yet can no speech afford;
> He is the Bread of Life, yet hungry lies;
> The Living Fountain, yet for drink He cries;
> He cannot help or clothe Himself at need
> Who did the lilies clothe and ravens feed;
> He is the Light of Lights, yet now doth shroud
> His glory with our nature as a cloud.
> He came to us a Little One, that we
> Like little children might in malice be;
> Little He is, and wrapped in clouts, lest He
> Might strike us dead if clothed with majesty.
> Christ had four beds and those not soft nor brave:
> The Virgin's womb, the manger, cross, and grave.
> The angels sing this day, and so will I
> That have more reason to be glad than they.

Urn of Fate A sort of Christmas lottery in Spain and Italy. In Spain pairs of names are drawn from an urn and those who are matched are to be friends for the coming year. In Italy the urn holds small presents and people dip in to draw one out.

Van Dyke, Henry (1852-1933) American Presbyterian minister and short-story writer, many of whose works deal with Christmas themes. Some, such as "THE OTHER WISE MAN" (1896) and "THE FIRST CHRISTMAS TREE" (1897), were first read aloud to his congregation in New York as sermons.

"Venez divin Messie" A French-Canadian carol by the Abbé Pellegrin (1663-1745).

Venez, divin Messie,
Sauvez nos jours infortunés;
Vous êtes notre vie,
Venez, venez, venez!

Ah! descendez, hâtez vous pas,
Sauvez les hommes du trépas,
Secourez nous, ne tardez pas.

Voyez couler nos larmes.
Grand Dieu! Si vous nous pardonnez,

Henry Van Dyke *The popular American preacher and short story writer.*

Nous n'aurons plus d'alarmes:
Venez, venez, venez!

Refrain

Ah! désarmez votre courroux,
Nous soupirons à vos genoux,
Seigneur, nous n'espérons qu'en vous.

Pour nous livrer la guerre,
Tous les enfers sont déchaînés,
Descendez sur la terre,
Venez, venez, venez!

Refrain

Que nos soupirs soient entendus!
Les biens que nous avons perdu
Ne nous seront-ils pas rendus?

Seigneur, Vos saints oracles
A tous les siècles étonnes
Promirent ces miracles,
Venez, venez, venez!

Refrain

Si vous venez en ces bas lieux,
Nous vous verrons victorieux,
Fermer l'enfer, ouvrir les cieux.

Nous l'espérons sans cesse;
Les cieux nous furent destinés:
Tenez Votre promesse;
Venez, venez, venez!

Refrain

Ah! puissions-nous chanter un jour,
Dans Votre bienheureuse cour,
Et Votre glorie et votre amour!

C'est là l'heureux partage
De ceux que vous prédestinez:
Donnez-nous-en la gage:
Venez, venez, venez!

Venezuela Religion, music, and food are three essential components of Christmas in Venezuela. During Advent virtually every family erects a crèche in the home; it is a point of pride that every year the Nativity scene becomes more elaborate. In some homes the Nativity scene encompasses all of Bethlehem and the surrounding landscape, with dozens of figures moving toward the crib, where the figure of the baby Jesus will be placed on Christmas Eve. Though many Venezuelan families have adopted the North American Christmas tree, presents are often placed beside the crèche.

Starting on December 16, Venezuelans attend an early-morning mass called the *Misa de Aguinaldo*, where Christmas songs are sung. Traditional Christmas carols in Venezuela are called *aguinaldos*, and in times past the *aguinalderos* would go door-to-door, singing and playing folk instruments such as the *cuatro* (a small, four-string guitar), the maracas, and the *furruco* (a small friction drum). Then there are the *gaitas*, infectious Christmas songs that combine African and Latin rhythms.

The focus of the holiday season is *Noche Bueno*, Christmas Eve. The traditional meal consists of *hallacas* and *pan de jamon*. The *hallaca* is a cornmeal pie stuffed with pork or chicken, olives, peppers, vegetables, and raisins and wrapped in plantain leaves and boiled; making it is a family effort. The *pan de jamon* is bread stuffed with ham and raisins. Dessert may be *dulce de lechoza*, made of green papaya and brown sugar, slowly cooked for hours and served cold. Dinner is followed by attendance at the midnight mass. In the morning children wake up to find that El Niño, the Christ Child, has left them presents beside the crèche or under the tree.

New Year's Eve is celebrated with music, feasting, and fireworks. To welcome in the new year, there are also bonfires to burn effigies of Judas, who represents the old year. It is customary to eat a grape with every stroke of the clock at midnight, to be followed by a glass of champagne.

In the city of Mérida, a fascinating local custom is the *La Paradura del Niño*, or The Standing Up of the Christ Child. Here, the Nativity scenes in homes are particularly cherished; some are tabletop size, and some are room size, with all of Bethlehem portrayed in a Venezuelan-style landscape of mountains and rivers populated by figures that often look like the local people. On Christmas Eve the Holy Family is placed in the scene and every day the Wise Men are moved a little closer. On New Year's Day tradition dictates that the baby Jesus must be moved to an upright position and stay there until Candelaria (February 2).

If a friend or neighbour sees this is not done, the baby may be kidnapped, and the family who neglected their duty must hold a *paradura* party for the kidnappers and friends. They choose godparents for the Niño and arrange for musicians, candles, fireworks, and refreshments. A procession then sets out to retrieve the baby from the kidnappers' home. It is led by boys setting off fireworks, followed by the musicians, who will be mute until the baby is found, a pair of teens as Mary and Joseph, children as shepherds singing a carol about searching for the baby, and, lastly, the godparents. When the candle-lit procession gets to the house where the baby is stored, the Niño is handed over to its godparents wrapped in a handkerchief and joyous music breaks out. All then march joyfully to the home of the negligent family, where after the baby is replaced standing up, the party gets underway. Little kids may offer a poem of welcome, women will say the rosary, and all eat, dance, and drink until dawn.

The Christmas festivities come to an official end on January 6, the Day of the Reyes Magos (the Three Wise Men who visit Mary and the infant Jesus), when children again receive toys and candies.

"Veni redemptor gentium" One of the earliest of all Nativity hymns, written by Bishop Ambrose of Milan (339-397), translated by David Thomas Morgan (1809-86), and musical setting by Arthur Henry Brown (1830-1926). The song is a defence of Christian orthodoxy against heretical Arian views on the nature of Christ. Martin Luther made a German translation of the song in 1524.

> O come, Redeemer of mankind, appear,
> Thee with full hearts the virgin born we greet;
> Let every age with rapt amazement hear
> That wondrous birth which for our God is meet.
>
> Not by the will of man, or mortal seed,
> But by the Spirit's breathed mysterious grace
> The Word of God became our flesh indeed,
> And grew a tender plant of human race.
>
> Lo! Mary's virgin womb its burden bears;
> Nor less abides her virgin purity;
> In the King's glory see our nature shares;
> Here in His temple God vouchsafes to be.

> From His bright chamber, virtue's holy shrine
> The royal Bridegroom cometh to the day;
> Of twofold substance, human and divine,
> As giant swift, rejoicing on His way.
>
> Forth from His Father to the world He goes,
> Back to the Father's face His way regains,
> Far down to souls beneath His glory shows,
> Again at God's right hand victorious reigns.
>
> With the eternal Father equal, Thou,
> Girt with our flesh dost triumph evermore,
> Strengthening our feeble bodies here below
> With endless grace from Thine own living store.
>
> How doth Thy lowly manger radiant shine!
> On the sweet breath of night new splendor grows;
> So may our spirits glow with faith divine,
> Where no dark cloud of sin shall interpose.
>
> All praise and glory to the Father be,
> All praise and glory to His only Son,
> All praise and glory, Holy Ghost, to Thee,
> Both now, and while eternal ages run.

Vertep Ukrainian puppet theatre staged at Christmas. It originated in 17th-century Kiev, where students wrote and performed plays for this remarkable art form based on a two-storey stage that could be carried about by minstrels, teachers, or groups of actors. Wooden puppets, guided by wires, moved through grooves in the floors of the two levels. During the Christmas season students would take the *vertep* through the countryside, performing and receiving money and hospitality in return.

The play was divided into two separate, unconnected acts. The first, which took place in the upper floor of the miniature theatre, had a Nativity theme. Shepherds and the Magi come to visit the new-born Jesus and rejoice at his birth. Rachel, representing the mothers of Bethlehem whose children are murdered by King Herod, curses the king, who dies and whose soul is taken to Hell. The second act, which is in a lighter, more secular vein, is about the hero Kozak, who plays the bandura, smokes a pipe, and praises Ukrainian virtues while overcoming all who will deceive him. Both acts are accompanied by musicians.

A Very Brady Christmas (TV) (1988) The Brady kids, now grown-up, return home for Christmas with families of their own. Directed by Peter Baldwin and starring Florence Henderson and Robert Reed as Ma and Pa Brady, with Ann B. Davis as the housekeeper, Alice.

Vessel Maids In Yorkshire young women called Vessel Maids would carry about a box or a hoop twined with greenery containing a figure of the Holy Family. Singing as they carried it house-to-house during Advent, they could command a tip to see the box and give their blessing. It has been suggested, not convincingly, that this custom was a remnant of the worship of Dionysus, the Greek god of fertility. See WASSAIL WENCHES.

Villancico Originally a type of Spanish folk song, by the 17th century it had been linked with sacred texts, often on a Christmas theme. By the 10th century the term came to refer to Spanish or Latin American Christmas carols.

Virgin Birth In the New Testament gospels of Matthew and Luke are the accounts of Mary, a virgin, conceiving a child through the Holy Spirit and eventually bearing Jesus. The virgin birth has been an article of faith since the early Church, as can be seen in the Apostles' Creed.

The doctrine may have struck people of 2,000 years ago as much less startling or remarkable than it seems now; this was, after all, a common way for a god to appear in the ancient world. Aphrodite, the Greek goddess of love, was born in a seashell; Athena, the goddess of wisdom, popped fully grown from the forehead of Zeus; Mithra, the Iranian god of light, was born from a rock; Alexander the Great, who proclaimed his divinity and sought to be worshipped by his conquered peoples, claimed his mother, Olympias, was a virgin when she gave birth to him.

The non-canonical second-century PROTOEVANGELIUM OF JAMES states that Mary gave birth in a cave attended by a midwife and the sons of Joseph by his first marriage, while the eighth-century GOSPEL OF PSEUDO-MATTHEW harmonizes the two, saying that the birth took place in a cave and then, after three days, the family moved to a stable. There are three versions of the manner of Christ's birth. The earliest depictions, in the belief that Mary delivered in the usual fashion, had her resting on a bed, but late-medieval legend based on the revelations of St. Bridget of Sweden saw the Virgin kneeling to pray and the baby suddenly appearing in a blaze of light at her feet. Another medieval variation has Mary leaning against a pillar with Joseph spreading hay at her feet and the baby appearing on it bathed in light.

Vergil's *Fourth Eclogue*, 40 B.C., seems to prophesy a virgin-born baby bringing a new golden age. See PROPHECIES.

"The Virgin Mary Had a Baby Boy"   A traditional Trinidadian carol.

> The Virgin Mary had a baby boy,
> The Virgin Mary had a baby boy,
> The Virgin Mary had a baby boy,
> And they said that his name was Jesus.
>
> *He come from the glory,*
> *He come from the glorious kingdom.*
> *He come from the glory,*
> *He come from the glorious kingdom.*
> *Oh yes, believer!*
> *Oh yes, believer!*
> *He come from the glory,*
> *He come from the glorious kingdom.*
>
> The angels sang when the baby born,
> The angels sang when the baby born,
> The angels sang when the baby born,
> And proclaimed him the Saviour Jesus.
>
> *Refrain*
>
> The wise men saw where the baby born,
> The wise men saw where the baby born,
> The wise men saw where the baby born,
> And they said that his name was Jesus.

"A Virgin Most Pure"   In this version of the Gloucestershire carol, 16th-century words were set to an 18th-century folk tune. A number of variants exist, some called "A Virgin Unspotted."

> A virgin most pure, as the prophets do tell,
> Hath brought forth a baby, as it hath befell,
> To be our Redeemer from death, hell and sin,
> Which Adam's transgression hath wrapped up in.

> *Aye, and therefore be you merry,*
> *Rejoice and be you merry,*
> *Set sorrows aside!*
> *Christ Jesus, our Saviour, was born on this tide.*

> In Bethlehem Jewry a city there was,
> Where Joseph and Mary together did pass,
> And there to be taxed with many one more,
> For Caesar commanded the same should be so.

> But when they had entered the city so fair,
> The number of people so mighty was there
> That Joseph and Mary, whose substance was small,
> Could find in the inn there no lodging at all.

> Then were they constrained in the stable to lie,
> Where horses and asses they used for to tie;
> Their lodging so simple they took it no scorn,
> But against the next morning our Saviour was born.

> The King of all kings to this world being brought,
> Small store of fine linen to wrap him was sought;
> When Mary had swaddled her young son so sweet,
> Within an ox manger she laid him to sleep.

> Then God sent an angel from heaven so high
> To certain poor shepherds in fields where they lie,
> And bade them no longer in sorrow to stay,
> Because that our Saviour was born on this day.

> Then presently after, the shepherds did spy
> A number of angels that stood in the sky;
> Then joyfully talked and sweetly did sing;
> "To god be all glory, our heavenly King!"

"A Visit From Saint Nicholas"   One of the most important documents in the creation of contemporary ideas of Santa Claus, this poem was first published in the Troy *Sentinel* on December 23, 1823, with the introduction "We know not to whom we are indebted for the following description of that . . . homely and delightful personage of parental kindness, Santa Claus." Though most now attribute the work to CLEMENT CLARKE MOORE, some suggest the author was HENRY LIVINGSTON JR. Regardless of authorship, the poem was instrumental in popularizing in America the notion of a kindly, non-judgmental Christmas gift-bringer, his elfish appearance, the descent down the chimney, and travel by reindeer and sleigh.

> 'Twas the night before Christmas, when all through
>   the house
> Not a creature was stirring, not even a mouse;
> The stockings were hung by the chimney with care,
> In hopes that ST. NICHOLAS soon would be there;
> The children were nestled all snug in their beds,
> While visions of sugar-plums danced in their heads;
> And mamma in her 'kerchief, and I in my cap,
> Had just settled down for a long winter's nap,
> When out on the lawn there arose such a clatter,
> I sprang from the bed to see what was the matter.
> Away to the window I flew like a flash,
> Tore open the shutters and threw up the sash.
> The moon on the breast of the new-fallen snow
> Gave the lustre of mid-day to objects below,
> When, what to my wondering eyes should appear,
> But a miniature sleigh, and eight tiny reindeer,
> With a little old driver, so lively and quick,
> I knew in a moment it must be St. Nick.

"A Visit from Saint Nicholas" *"Merry Christmas to all, and to all a good night."*

More rapid than eagles his coursers they came,
And he whistled, and shouted, and called them by name;
"Now, DASHER! now, DANCER! now, PRANCER and VIXEN!
On, COMET! on CUPID! on, DONDER and BLITZEN!
To the top of the porch! to the top of the wall!
Now dash away! dash away! dash away all!"
As dry leaves that before the wild hurricane fly,
When they meet with an obstacle, mount to the sky,
So up to the house-top the coursers they flew,
With the sleigh full of toys, and St. Nicholas too.
And then, in a twinkling, I heard on the roof
The prancing and pawing of each little hoof.
As I drew in my hand, and was turning around,
Down the chimney St. Nicholas came with a bound.

He was dressed all in fur, from his head to his foot,
And his clothes were all tarnished with ashes and soot;
A bundle of toys he had flung on his back,
And he looked like a peddler just opening his pack.
His eyes – how they twinkled! his dimples how merry!
His cheeks were like roses, his nose like a cherry!
His droll little mouth was drawn up like a bow,
And the beard of his chin was as white as the snow;
The stump of a pipe he held tight in his teeth,
And the smoke it encircled his head like a wreath;
He had a broad face and a little round belly,
That shook when he laughed like a bowlful of jelly.
He was chubby and plump, a right jolly old elf,
And I laughed when I saw him, in spite of myself;
A wink of his eye and a twist of his head,
Soon gave me to know I had nothing to dread;
He spoke not a word, but went straight to his work,
And filled all the stockings; then turned with a jerk,
And laying his finger aside of his nose,
And giving a nod, up the chimney he rose;
He sprang to his sleigh, to his team gave a whistle,
And away they all flew like the down of a thistle.
But I heard him exclaim, ere he drove out of sight,
"HAPPY CHRISTMAS TO ALL, AND TO ALL A
    GOOD-NIGHT."

Visitation   The first chapter of Luke describes the visit of Mary, pregnant by the Holy Spirit, to her elderly cousin Elizabeth. The story of the Visitation was the basis of the "Ave Maria," the "Magnificat," and the notion of the unborn John the Baptist leaping with joy in the womb of Elizabeth. In early Christian and Eastern art, it was part of the Nativity cycle, but by the late Middle Ages in the West, the Visitation began to be portrayed with the focus on Mary.

"Voici le Père Noèl qui nous arrive"   A French-Canadian Christmas song made popular in 1931 by the legendary Mary Travers (1894-1941), "La Bolduc." Travers was a Quebec housewife turned singer-composer, whose songs celebrated the daily life of French Canada.

"Von Himmel Hoch, da komm ich her"   One of the few Christmas songs reliably attributed to Martin Luther, who wrote it in 1534 for a Christmas Eve service. It was published in 1535 accompanied by a German folk tune, but in 1538 Luther composed a new melody for it, the one still in use today. J.S. Bach used the tune in three harmonizations in the 1734 *Christmas Oratorio*. The best-known English translation is "FROM HEAVEN ABOVE TO EARTH I COME" (1855) by Catherine Winkworth (1827-78).

"W zlobie lezy" A medieval Polish carol, probably from the 14th century, translated as "Jesus Holy, Born So Lowly" or "Infant Holy, Infant Lowly."

> Infant holy, Infant lowly,
> For his bed a cattle stall;
> Oxen lowing, little knowing
> Christ the Babe is Lord of all.
> Swiftly winging angels singing,
> Nowells ringing, tidings bringing:
> Christ the Babe is Lord of all.
>
> Flocks were sleeping, shepherds keeping
> Vigil till the morning new;
> Saw the glory, heard the story,
> Tidings of a gospel true.
> Thus rejoicing, free from sorrow,
> Praises voicing, greet the morrow:
> Christ the Babe was born for you.

"Wachet auf! Ruft uns die Stimme" "Wake, Awake for Night Is Flying" (1599) by Philipp Nicolai (1556-1608). Nicolai also wrote "Wie Schön Leuchtet der Morgenstern," translated as "HOW BRIGHTLY SHINES THE MORNING STAR."

Waits In medieval England, waits were town watchmen whose job was to patrol the dark streets and sound the hours. Through the early modern period, however, the post evolved into a kind of licensed musician. The Shakespearean clown Will Kemp, who morris-danced to Norwich from London in nine days (the original "nine-day wonder"), speaks of being greeted by civic officials as he entered Norwich:

> Passing the gate, Wifflers (such Officers as were appointed by the Mayor) to make me way through the throng of the people, which prest so mightily upon me: with great labour I got thorow that narrow preaze into the open market place. Where on the crosse, ready prepared, stood the Citty Waytes, which not a little refreshed my weariness with towling thorow so narrow a lane, as the people left me: such Waytes (under Benedicite be it spoken) fewe Cities in our Realme have the like, none better. Who besides their excellency in wind instruments, their rare cunning on the Vyoll, and Violin: theyr voices be admirable, everie one of them able to serve in any Cathedrall Church in Christendome for Quiristers.

During the Christmas period they were allowed to go door-to-door and serenade householders in return for a gratuity. Their visits were not always welcome to those who were trying to sleep, and when their position was replaced by the regular police force in the 19th century, waits gradually disappeared as well from the Christmas landscape.

Wales Today the Welsh celebrate Christmas in much the same way as their English neighbours do, but there are lingering traces of an older Wales in some very distinctive seasonal customs.

A remarkable sight is the MARI LWYD, a horse's skull which is set on a pole and manipulated by an operator under a white sheet so that its jaws clash. It is accompanied by a group of men, who lead it from door to door and beg admittance with a ritual rhyme. A contest of wits between the householder and the visitors ensues, and eventually the group is let in, whereupon they perform various antics in return for hospitality. When it is time to go, the group sings a song of blessing and is off to the next house. This custom virtually disappeared in the 20th century, but has been revived in some areas.

The PLYGAIN was a Christmas-morning service held as early as 3 a.m. in which carols were sung by the congregation, who all held candles. Carols were sung by individuals, trios, quartets, and choirs until after the sun rose and breakfast beckoned. There were those who waited for the service innocently meeting with friends or making taffy, and those who spent the time getting drunk. It was the rowdiness of the latter that led to the custom being discontinued in the 19th century. The service was revived by Methodist chapels and can still be found in some churches.

On *Gwyl San Steffan*, St. Stephen's Day, it was time for HOLMING, a mutual thrashing of boys carrying holly branches; it was good luck to break the skin and see the blood flow. Blood flowed as well in the traditional bleeding of horses and other livestock that was carried out on December 26 and in the Hunting of the Wren. Groups of boys would capture the tiny bird and carry it from door to door in a little house expecting a gratuity. Sensitivity to animal rights has lately meant that the wren paraded about is artificial.

New Year's customs observed in Wales include FIRST-FOOTING, wherein the first visitor across the threshold on New Year's Day should ideally be a dark-haired male; women and red- or fair-haired men had to wait until someone more appropriate entered first. All debts should be paid by January 1 or indebtedness would grow during the year; nothing should be lent that day or the "luck" of the house would be gone. It was also a time for boys to go about with water drawn from a local well or stream. They would sprinkle it on doorways with an evergreen branch and sing a (now-enigmatic) song, hoping to be rewarded with a small tip. Sometimes they carried about a CALENNIG, an apple stuck with fruit, grain, and herbs.

On Twelfth Night (January 5) the Christmas greenery was to be taken down and the Yule log's remnants removed from the fireplace; its ashes would be planted with the spring crop to ensure fertility. On Twelfth Day the traditional Epiphany cake was shared and guests would look for the token baked inside. The lucky finders would be the king and queen and would preside over the day's festivities.

War and Christmas Christmas is usually an opportunity for wars to cease for a time in an official or unofficial TRUCE, but at least once the Nativity has helped cause a war. This sad occasion occurred when, ostensibly because of the theft, in

Wassail *A steaming bowl of punch for the chilly Christmas season.*

Wassail the trees, that they may bear
You many a plum, and many a pear:
For more or less fruits they will bring,
As you do give them wassailing.

To ensure fertility for the coming year, English farmers developed a number of variations on the wassail. On Twelfth Night, Devonshire men got out their weapons and went to the orchard. Selecting the oldest tree, they would form a circle and chant:

Here's to thee, old apple tree
Whence thou mayst bud and whence thou mayst blow
And whence thou mayst bear apples enow:
Hats full, caps full,
Bushels, bushels, sacks full,
And my pockets full too!
Huzza! Huzza!

After drinking some cider the men would discharge their (unloaded) weapons at the tree and head home. Traditionally, the women of the house were to deny the men entrance until they had guessed what sort of roast was being prepared for them. The man with the correct guess presided over the evening's entertainment. In other parts of England, fruit trees were wassailed by being sprinkled with cider, beaten with sticks, and bidden in rhyme to bear well. In Cornwall the song was sung with a cider jug in one hand and a branch in the other:

Huzza, huzza, in our good town
The Bread shall be white, and the liquor be brown
So here my old fellow I drink to thee
And the very health of each other tree.
Well may ye blow, well may ye bear
Blossom and fruit, both apple and pear.
So that every bough and every twig
May bend with a burden both fair and big
May ye ever bear us and yield us fruit such a store
That the bags and chambers and house run o'er.

In south Hampshire they threatened the fruit tree:

Apple tree, apple tree
Bear good fruit,
or down with your top
And up with your root.

This threatening of the orchard is reminiscent of a custom in Romania. The farm husband and wife go through the orchard at Christmas, she with her hands covered in dough and he with an axe. The man goes from one barren tree to another, each time threatening to cut it down. And each time, the wife pleads for the tree by saying, "Oh no, I am sure that this tree will be as heavy with fruit next spring as my fingers are with dough this day."

In the West Country it was also customary to wassail the oxen. On Twelfth Night men and women went into the stalls, drank from the wassail bowl, and took a cake from a basket decorated with greenery and placed it on the ox's horns. If the ox remained quiet it was considered good luck. In Hereford, a cake was stuck on the horns of the ox while the oldest person present chanted:

Here's to thy pretty face, and to thy white horn,
God send thy master a good crop of corn,
Both wheat, rye and barley, of grains of all sort,
And next year if we live we'll drink to thee again.

1847, of the silver star marking the place of Jesus' birth, a long-standing dispute over the control of the Church of the Nativity boiled over. The claims of the Catholic Church were backed by the French government, and those of the Orthodox Church were supported by the Russian government; the Turkish Empire, which controlled Palestine, was caught in the middle. Though this dispute was not sufficient in itself to cause an outbreak of fighting, it combined with other issues which together sparked the Crimean War (1854-56).

The causes of the Second World War were not remotely Christmasy, but the conflict did help spread the North American notion of Christmas. Santa Claus, turkey, and presents on Christmas Eve were all ideas carried by American troops wherever they were stationed and adopted by cultures around the world.

Wassail   The term "wassail" is derived from the Anglo-Saxon toast "*waes hael*," or "good health" (the expected reply is "*drinc-heil*," or "drink well"). To wassail is to drink to someone's health at Christmas, especially from a decorated bowl filled with a seasonal drink. The wassail bowl was traditionally filled with mulled ale or "LAMBSWOOL" and was adorned with ribbons.

"Wassailers" often referred to those who went door-to-door at Christmas with a wassail bowl expecting a gratuity for a drink, or to those who expected the householder to fill the bowl at each stop. See WASSAIL WENCHES.

The tradition of wassailing the apple trees or livestock is a venerable one. In the 17th century the poet Robert Herrick noted:

The rhyme was repeated in chorus, then the oldest threw a pint of cider in the beast's face. If he tossed the cake forward it was a good sign.

In Sussex and Hertfordshire we also have mention of wassailing the beehives.

Wassail Wenches Or "wassail virgins," English women who went door-to-door at Christmas, carolling and calling blessings on the homes they visited. George Wither's 17th-century poem "A Christmas Carol" says,

> The wenches with their wassail-bowls
> About the streets are singing.

On Twelfth Night in 1555 at Henley, in came "twelve wessells with maidens singing, with their wessells; and after came the chief wives singing with their wessells; and the gentlewoman had ordained a great table of banquet, desserts of spices and fruits." It is unclear whether these women were going house-to-house or were a spectacle arranged by the host, but this is the earliest reference to a custom that became widespread within a couple of generations.

By the 17th century it was a way for women to gather alms. The lawyer John Selden complained about "wenches with wassells" who came at New Year to present you with a cup "and you must drink of the slabby stuff, but the meaning is, you must give them monies, ten times more than it is worth." Despite Selden's misgivings, many rural areas considered a visit from the wenches essential for the family's luck for the coming year.

The cup was always decorated with greenery, such as holly or mistletoe, ribbons, or flowers and contained spiced ale, with apples, toast, nutmeg, and sugar. A 12-verse carol was often sung, or sometimes just the second verse:

> Good Dame, here at your door
> Our Wassail we begin
> We are all maidens poor,
> We pray now let us in,
> With our Wassail.

Sometimes the "GLOUCESTER WASSAIL" or the "SEVEN JOYS OF MARY" carol was sung.

Door-to-door wassailing eventually died out (except in some parts of England, where it was revived in the 20th century with money going to charity), but wassailing was retained inside the home. A bowl of hot spiced ale, with toast, apples, or Christmas cake floating in it, was served to guests. In Sussex the guests stirred it with silver spoons and walked "sunwise" around the bowl.

In time the wassail bowl gave way to a box, decorated with greenery and containing fruit and sugar or a decorated doll to represent the infant Jesus. Sometimes a second doll to represent the Virgin Mary was added. It was covered with a cloth or a glass front which was raised to allow viewing, in return for food or money. The carriers sang carols or wassail songs, and the object was known as a wassail box, vessel box, bezzle cup, milly (for Milady) box, or even Wesley-box. (See VESSEL MAIDS and MILLY BOX MAIDS.) In Leicestershire, children used to carry about a "Christmas vase" containing three dolls, representing Mary, Jesus, and Joseph.

Watch Night A custom developed c. 1740 in England by early Methodists, who kept a vigil of prayer and hymn-singing on certain nights. When held on Christmas Eve or New Year's Eve, it was usually as an expression of opposition to seasonal rowdiness and misbehaviour; in the 18th century, Christmas was not yet the domestic, child-centred holiday it was to become later. The custom was to pray until about five minutes to midnight and then observe silence until the clock struck 12, "when they exultantly burst forth with a hymn of praise and joy."

When used by American Episcopalians, it refers to a midnight communion service on Christmas Eve, accompanied by great music such as Gounod's "St. Cecilia's Mass" or Handel's *Messiah*.

"Watchman, Tell Us of the Night" *A 17th-century watchman patrols the streets with his lantern and weapon.*

"Watchman, Tell Us of the Night" An 1825 Advent hymn by Englishman Sir John Bowring (1792-1872), MP, governor of Hong Kong, and linguist; music by German Jakob Hintze (1622-1702), published in 1678, or by Welshman Joseph Parry (1841-1903) in 1879, or George J. Elvey (1816-93) in 1858.

> Watchman, tell us of the night,
> What its signs of promise are.
> Traveler, o'er yon mountain's height,
> See that glory-beaming star.
> Watchman, doth its beauteous ray
> Aught of joy or hope foretell?
> Traveler, yes; it brings the day,
> Promised day of Israel.
>
> Watchman, tell us of the night;
> Higher yet that star ascends.
> Traveler, blessedness and light,
> Peace and truth, its course portends.
> Watchman, will its beams alone
> Gild the spot that gave them birth?
> Traveler, ages are its own;
> See, it bursts o'er all the earth.
>
> Watchman, tell us of the night,
> For the morning seems to dawn.
> Traveler, darkness takes its flight;
> Doubt and terror are withdrawn.
> Watchman, let thy wanderings cease;
> Hie thee to thy quiet home.
> Traveler, lo, the Prince of Peace,
> Lo, the Son of God, is come!

Water There are a number of Christmas customs around the world in which water plays an important part. On New Year's

Day in England and Scotland, it was a custom to seek out the "FLOWER OF THE WELL," the first water drawn that year from a well. In Wales in the 19th century, boys rose early on January 1 and went about with freshly drawn water and a twig with which to sprinkle it on houses and people for good luck. They chanted the following puzzling verse and were rewarded with money:

Here we bring new water from the well so clear,
For to worship God with, this Happy New Year,
Sing levy dew, sing levy dew, the water and the wine,
With seven bright golden wires, the bugles that do shine;
Sing reign of fair maid, with gold upon her toe,
Open you the west door and turn the old year go;
Sing reign of fair maid, with gold upon her chin,
Open you the east door, and let the new year in.

In Brazil the mixing of African folk religion and Catholic beliefs has resulted in the festival of the goddess Iemanjá. On New Year's Eve hundreds of thousands of believers head to Copacabana Beach in Rio de Janeiro and send gifts to the goddess out on the water. If they float out to sea it is good luck; if they are washed ashore, the new year will be an unhappy one.

The Eastern churches celebrate two solemn water-related events. The first is the "Renewal of the Waters" on New Year's Eve, when new "St. Basil's Water" replaces the old year's water in jugs. The other occurs on Epiphany, which, among other things, commemorates the turning of the water into wine at the marriage in Cana and the baptism of Jesus in the Jordan River. Ukrainians celebrate this as *Iordan* and hold a ceremony where the priest dips a cross into the water and blesses it; believers then take the holy water home. In some churches the cross is thrown into the water and divers compete to retrieve it.

"The Ways of White Folks"   A poignant story from 1934 by African-American writer Langston Hughes (1902-67). A black domestic worker, overworked and underpaid, is searching with her young son Joe for inexpensive gifts on Christmas Eve when the boy is frightened by a man dressed as Santa Claus in a whites-only theatre.

"We Three Kings" John Henry Hopkins Jr. wrote the popular American carol.

"We Need a Little Christmas"   A spirited seasonal ditty that first appeared in the Broadway musical *Mame*, written by Jerry Herman in 1966.

"We Three Kings" There is no scriptural evidence of the Magi who came to present gifts to the baby Jesus being "three kings," but their number and occupation has become fixed in the popular imagination. This British stamp shows the now typical portrayal of the Magi.

"We Three Kings"   The words and music for this popular Epiphany carol were written by American clergyman John Henry Hopkins Jr. (1820-91) in 1857. It expresses the non-scriptural beliefs, held in Christian folklore since the days of TERTULLIAN, that the Magi who visited the baby Jesus were kings and that they were three in number. See MAGI.

We three kings of Orient are
Bearing gifts we traverse afar.
Field and fountain, moor and mountain,
Following yonder star.

O star of wonder, star of night,
Star with royal beauty bright,
Westward leading, still proceeding,
Guide us to thy perfect Light.

Born a king on Bethlehem's plain,
Gold I bring to crown Him again,
King forever, ceasing never
Over us all to reign.

Chorus

Frankincense to offer have I.
Incense owns a Deity nigh.
Prayer and praising all men raising,
Worship Him, God on high.

Chorus

Myrrh is mine: Its bitter perfume
breathes a life of gathering gloom.
Sorrowing, sighing, bleeding dying,
sealed in the stone-cold tomb.

Chorus

Glorious now behold Him arise,
King and God and Sacrifice.
Alleluia, alleluia!
Sounds through the earth and skies.

Chorus

"We Wish You a Merry Christmas" An English West Country folk carol, probably from the 16th century.

> We wish you a Merry Christmas,
> We wish you a Merry Christmas,
> We wish you a Merry Christmas,
> And a Happy New Year.
>
> *Good tidings to you,*
> *And all of your kin,*
> *Good tidings for Christmas,*
> *And a Happy New Year.*
>
> O bring us figgy pudding
> O bring us figgy pudding
> O bring us figgy pudding
> And a cup of good cheer
>
> *Refrain*
>
> We won't go until we get some
> We won't go until we get some
> We won't go until we get some
> So bring it out here.
>
> *Refrain*

Weather, Predicting the See DIVINATION.

Weihnachtsmann *An early 20th-century Weihnachtsmann steps off an elevator.*

Wenceslas *A Victorian Christmas carol turned the ancient duke into a charitable king.*

Weihnachtsmann When Protestantism ended the cult of saints in much of Germany, Saint Nicholas had to be replaced as the seasonal gift-giver and two figures emerged to take his place: the Christ Child and, in the 19th century, the Weihnachtsmann, or "Christmas Man." This secularized version of Saint Nicholas is depicted as an old man walking in a long robe with a peaked hood or winter cap; he carries a bag or basket of presents for the good children and switches for the bad. Weihnachtsmann-shaped ornaments and chocolates helped to popularize the image.

Well of the Magi The Well of the Magi has been associated in tradition with the place where the Wise Men, after leaving Jerusalem, caught sight again of the star that would lead them to the infant Jesus. The sixth-century Gallo-Roman historian Gregory of Tours asserts in his *Book of Miracles* that it was the custom of the people of Bethlehem to go there during Christmas, and cover the opening with blankets to shut out all light. In the darkness, with their heads under the blankets, the pure of heart (and only they) could see the Star of Bethlehem moving slowly across the water.

For centuries local guides used to point out to pilgrims a cistern midway between Bethlehem and Jerusalem as the miraculous well. Recent archaeological research has also linked the site to an early Christian sanctuary dedicated to the Virgin Mary, who, legend says, stopped there to rest.

Wenceslas, St. Václav the Good (903-29), duke of Bohemia. A pious Christian and advocate of closer ties with Germany, he was assassinated by his brother Boleslav I, who succeeded him as duke. Though it was once thought that Boleslav acted out of anti-German and pagan sentiments, it now appears he shared his dead brother's ideas and religion, and the murder was most likely the result of a family feud. Nonetheless, Wenceslas was regarded as a martyr to his faith; his tomb in St. Vitus's Cathedral became the site of pilgrimages and he was canonized, becoming in time the patron saint of Bohemia and, more recently, the Czech Republic. In Czech mythology he is a "sleeping king" (like King Arthur to the English or Friederich Barbarossa to the Germans) who will one day rise again when his nation needs him most. There appears to be no connection between the actions of the real-life duke and the hero of J.M. Neale's Christmas hymn "Good King Wenceslas."

We're No Angels (1955)   Three convicts escape from the French prison on Devil's Island at Christmas and plan to rob a family to finance their getaway. However, the three crooks (Humphrey Bogart, Aldo Ray, and Peter Ustinov) fall prey to the charms of family and the holiday season and stay to help their new friends thwart a villainous nephew, played by Basil Rathbone. Directed by Michael Curtiz, who had worked with Bogart on *Casablanca*, this film is not to be confused with the oafish remake that appeared in 1989.

Werewolves and Christmas   Christmas in some parts of the world is a time of increased activity by evil spirits, witches, and monsters of all sorts, including humans who can transform themselves into wolves.

In the Middle Ages, Olaus Magnus said that in Prussia, Livonia, and Lithuania, werewolves gathered on Christmas night and then spread out to "rage with wondrous ferocity against human beings . . . for when a human habitation has been detected by them isolated in the woods, they besiege it with atrocity, striving to break in the doors and in the event of doing so, they devour all the human beings, and every animal which is found within." At a certain castle the monsters held werewolf games, and those too fat to leap over a wall were eaten by their fitter comrades.

It was also a medieval belief in Latvia and Estonia that "at Christmas a boy lame of leg goes round the country summoning the devil's followers, who are countless, to a general conclave. Whoever remains behind, or goes reluctantly, is scourged by another with an iron whip. . . . The human form vanishes and the whole multitude becomes wolves." This transformation lasted for 12 days.

In Poland and northeastern Europe, it was believed that a child born on Christmas had a greater chance of becoming a werewolf, and ritual steps were taken to protect Christmas babies from this state.

Louis Frechette's *Christmas in French Canada* claims it was the belief in Quebec that "a man who has been seven years without partaking of the Easter Sacrament falls a prey to the infernal power, and may be condemned to rove about every night in the shape and skin of a wolf or any other kind of an animal, according to the nature of his sin. A bloody wound only can release him."

In Louisiana it is said that Père Noël travels through the swamps and bayous in a flat-bottomed *pirogue* pulled by alligators and accompanied by a red-nosed werewolf.

"The Wexford Carol"   A traditional Irish Christmas carol, one of the few attributed to that island of poets and musicians. Some claim that though the carol was popular in the Wexford area, it was really of English origin, derived from the ballad "All You That Are to Mirth Inclin'd."

> Good people all, this Christmas-time,
> Consider well and bear in mind
> What our good God for us has done,
> In sending His beloved Son.
> With Mary holy we should pray
> To God with love this Christmas Day:
> In Bethlehem upon that morn
> There was a blessed Messiah born.

Werewolves and Christmas *Legend has long said that men can become wolves during the Christmas season.*

The night before that happy tide,
The noble Virgin and her guide
Were long time seeking up and down
To find a lodging in the town.
But mark how all things came to pass:
From ev'ry door repell'd, alas!
As long foretold, their refuge all
Was but an humble ox's stall.

Near Bethlehem did shepherds keep
Their flocks of lambs and feeding sheep;
To whom God's angels did appear,
Which put the shepherds in great fear.
"Prepare and go," the angels said,
"To Bethlehem, be not afraid;
For there you'll find, this happy morn,
A princely Babe, sweet Jesus born."

With thankful heart and joyful mind,
The shepherds went the Babe to find,
And as God's angel had foretold,
They did our Saviour Christ behold.
Within a manger He was laid,
And by his side the Virgin Maid,
Attending on the Lord of Life,
Who came on earth to end all strife.

There were three wise men from afar
Directed by a glorious star,
And on they wandered night and day
Until they came where Jesus lay.
And when they came unto that place
Where our beloved Messiah was,
They humbly cast them at His feet,
With gifts of gold and incense sweet.

"What Child Is This?" The tune to this carol is the familiar "Greensleeves," which dates back at least to the 16th century and which was once ascribed to England's much-married monarch Henry VIII. The song is mentioned in Shakespeare's *The Merry Wives of Windsor*.

The words are by the Victorian English hymnist (and insurance executive and poet) William Chatterton Dix (1837-98), who also wrote "As With Gladness Men of Old" and "Like Silver Lamps in a Distant Shrine." The harmonization is by John Stainer, who may have been responsible for bringing words and music together.

What child is this, who, laid to rest
On Mary's lap, is sleeping?
Whom angels greet with anthems sweet,
While shepherds watch are keeping?

This, this is Christ the King,
Whom shepherds guard and angels sing:
Haste, haste to bring him laud,
The Babe, the Son of Mary!

So bring Him incense, gold, and myrrh,
Come peasant king to own Him,
The King of kings, salvation brings,
Let loving hearts enthrone Him.

Raise, raise the song on high,
The Virgin sings her lullaby:
Joy, joy, for Christ is born,
The Babe, the Son of Mary!

"Which of the Nine" A Christmas story from Hungary by Marus Jókai. A poor shoemaker with nine children is made an offer by his wealthy landlord: if the cobbler will give up one of his children, the rich man will adopt the boy and make him a gentleman. Naturally, the poor man refuses to part with a single child, even if it means a life of leisure for the lucky one. The rich man, who has been annoyed by the family's carol singing, then makes another offer: 1,000 florins if only they will not sing any more. They try, but find they cannot, and the father quickly returns the money.

> With that he put the bill down upon the table and rushed breathlessly back to his waiting family. He kissed them one after another; and lining them up in a row like pipe organs, he sat himself down on his low stool, and together they began to sing again, heart and soul: "On the blessed birth of Our Lord Jesus Christ . . ." They couldn't have been happier if they owned the whole of the great big house.
>
> But the one who owned the house was pacing through his nine rooms, asking himself how it was that those people down below could be so happy and full of joy in such a tiresome, boring world as this.

"While Shepherds Watched Their Flocks by Night" Nahum Tate, later Poet Laureate of England, wrote the words to this carol c. 1696. In his lifetime, Tate was perhaps best-known for being the author of a version of Shakespeare's *King Lear* that comes to a happy ending.

The song has been graced by many tunes, but the most popular is from G.F. Handel's 1728 *Siroè, King of Persia*.

While Shepherds watch their flocks by night
All seated on the ground
The angel of the Lord came down
And glory shone around.
"Fear not," said he, for mighty dread
Had seized their troubled minds,
"Glad tidings of great joy I bring
To you and all man-kind."

"To you in David's town this day
Is born of David's line
The Savior who is Christ the Lord
And this shall be the sign:
The heav'n'ly babe you there shall find
To human view displayed
All meanly wrapped in swathing bands
And in a manger laid."

Thus spoke the seraph and forthwith
Appeared a heavenly throng
Of angels praising God who thus
Addressed their joyful song:
"All glory be to God on high
And on the earth be peace
Goodwill hence-forth from heav'n to men
Begin and never cease."

White Christmas In 1914 a new type of service was introduced into some North American Protestant Sunday schools for Advent: the "White Christmas" service in which children were encouraged to bring gifts to be distributed to the needy. This became a popular tradition in many churches, and it continues to this day, collecting canned food, toys, and money to make Christmas for the poor a little easier. In some churches it is called "White Gift Sunday" from the custom of wrapping the offerings in white paper.

"White Christmas"   A 1940 Irving Berlin tune, still the biggest-selling Christmas song of all time, having sold over 100,000,000 copies. Bing Crosby's version alone sold 31,000,000. Little wonder that Berlin called it "the best song anybody ever wrote."

On screen it was sung in the Bing Crosby/Fred Astaire classic *Holiday Inn* and appeared again in the remake titled *White Christmas* with Crosby and Danny Kaye. "White Christmas" won the Oscar for best song of 1942.

White Christmas (1954)   Bing Crosby sings Irving Berlin's "White Christmas" for a third time on the big screen (first in *Holiday Inn* and then *Blue Skies*) in this lamely plotted story of two song-and-dance men in love with two song-and-dance women. Crosby and Danny Kaye team up with Rosemary Clooney and Vera-Ellen to save the country inn of retired General Waverly (Dean Jagger). Directed by Michael Curtiz, who at least had *Casablanca* to look back on proudly.

Wichern, Johann Hinrich   (1808-c. 1888) German Protestant pastor who began an influential movement inside the Lutheran church for social action. In 1833 in Hamburg, he opened the Rauhe Haus for orphaned or neglected children. His lighting of a nightly candle during Advent helped inspire the custom of the Advent wreath, which spread throughout Germany.

Wigilia   The fast on Polish Christmas Eve that ends when the first evening star appears.

Window   In Christian art this opening in a wall implies penetration without a violation of the interior. Especially popular in northern medieval artists' depictions of the Annunciation, a window's clear glass signified the virginity of Mary.

In many countries it is customary to decorate windows at Christmastime and particularly to place candles in them. This serves to welcome the stranger or, legendarily, to light the way for the Holy Family on Christmas Eve.

Winkworth, Catherine   (1827-78) English translator of foreign carols who specialized in songs originally written in German. Among the Christmas songs she introduced into English were "All This Night My Heart Rejoices," "From Heaven Above to Earth I Come," "Wake, Awake, for Night Is Flying," and "O Morning Star, How Fair and Bright." She is credited with helping the German choral tradition spread to the English-speaking world.

Wise Men   See MAGI.

Witches at Christmas   In parts of Europe, Christmas is the time of increased demonic activity on Earth. All sorts of evil powers, furious at the celebration of the birth of the Saviour, roam the dark roads and the skies of late December, looking for a chance to do evil. Consequently, Europeans developed ways of keeping witches and other maleficent forces at bay during the holy days.

In the Middle Ages there was often confusion between good female spirits and bad, and a saint in one area might be regarded as a witch in another. Lucia, for example, is celebrated as a saint in Sicily and Sweden, but in Central Europe she is the frightening Lutzelfrau, who disembowels bad children and punishes lazy girls. Frau Berchta or Perchta can be a stealer of children in one part of Germany or the bringer of Christmas presents in another. In some places she leads the Wild Host, a gang of cursed souls, in others she leaves

Witches at Christmas *Witches prowl the night in this old woodcut.*

surprising gifts for those who help her. On Twelfth Night in some areas, fish and rolls have to be eaten. If someone chooses to ignore this menu, Perchta will come and cut open his body, fill him with chaff, and sew him up again with a ploughshare and an iron chain.

It was best to stay out of the way of such figures and keep them from gaining admission to the house. In Norway, it was considered a wise precaution to put away brooms lest witches find them and ride about on them. To keep witches from coming down the chimney, fires were kept burning all night. Salt sprinkled on the fire also helped, as did choosing dry spruce, which always provided an abundance of sparks. Making the sign of the cross with a brush dipped in tar would protect doors to the house and barn.

In Austria, the Twelve Nights are known as the *Raunächte*, or "rough nights"; this is a time for driving evil spirits away with incense, loud noises, or a broom. Figures clad as witches and devils walk the streets with brooms, literally sweeping away unwanted spirits. In England it was a time to polish the silverware so that spirits could see their faces and thus be deterred from stealing.

It should be said that there are good witches at Christmas as well. In Italy the Befana, who is depicted as an old crone flying about on her broom, brings presents to children on Epiphany Eve. Her equivalent in Russia is the Baboushka. In the Franche-Comté, the gift-bringer is also depicted as a witch, Tante Arie, who comes down from the hills with her presents on Christmas Eve.

Women Will Have Their Will, or, Give Christmas His Due   A 1642 tract in which Londoners argue over the celebration of Christmas. Mrs. Custome represents the traditional keepers of the feast, while Mrs. New-come stands for the Puritan opposition to celebrating Christmas. Despite allowing full expression to the Puritan argument, the epilogue concludes:

> *Christmas* is the welcommest Time,
> That does come through the Yeare;
> For't maketh many joyfull hearts
> And fills the World with Cheare.
>
> Now Tom and Tib, and lustie Jack
> The time in Mirth doe passe;
> And each in kitchen or the Hall
> Is towsing of his Lasse.
>
> As long as there the fragrant Fire
> Doth spit out its fierce Flames

There is no ceasing of their Mirth
Nor period to their Games.

But now the Log of Logs is burnt,
The Hall-chimney leaves smoaking;
Good folkes farewell, for I will stay
No longer in it poaking.

Women's Christmas   *Nollaig na mBan*, the Irish term for January 6, Epiphany, to contrast with *Nollaig na bhFear*, Men's Christmas, on December 25. In some places the day was marked by the serving of food enjoyed by women: a high tea with cakes and sandwiches. In other areas it was the time for women to relax and watch other family members do the cooking and housework for a day.

Wrap, Christmas   Though most Christmas presents today are wrapped, this was not always the case. In the 19th century, gifts were placed under the tree, hung on its branches, or placed in piles on the table. The children of the house would be kept out of the room in which the tree was being decorated on Christmas Eve, and when allowed to enter they would see the tree and unadorned presents for the first time. In Scandinavia, gifts were thrown into the house after an anonymous person knocked at the door (thus the name for presents, *Julklapp*). It was not until late in the century that wrapping became common.

Why then wrap the gift? A very simple explanation is that some cultures set the tree up earlier than Christmas Eve and placed presents under the tree that had been sent from other family members. An unwrapped gift on Christmas morning meant that it had been dropped off in the night by Santa Claus.

Christmas Wrap *Hiding presents in a tub of bran was an early form of Christmas wrap.*

Hiding the gift also heightens the pleasure by prolonging the moment of revelation and perhaps disguising the contents. In many places, such as the Netherlands and Sweden, it is considered good fun to disguise a gift with deceptive wrapping or by placing it in an unlikely spot. In Victorian England, this trick was called a Yule Trap. Another reason for wrapping a gift in colourful paper is that it transforms a commercial, mass-market product into a personal treat.

Christmas Wrap *A novelty photo from the 1920s shows the importance of wrapping Christmas presents carefully.*

Stores discovered that wrapping was also good advertising. By 1900 retailers of luxury goods were wrapping their merchandise in paper that identified the source of the gift and thus announced that the package contained a costly item. (By 1910 stores were discovering that pre-wrapping an item as a Christmas gift increased sales of goods that were otherwise unlikely to be considered as presents. Putting a bow on a set of wrenches, for example, increased the likelihood of it being bought at Christmas.)

Gift paper in the 19th century was usually coloured tissue paper; ornately designed wrapping paper came to the fore in the first years of the 20th century. But early wrapping was not always a question of parcelling a gift in paper. Much ingenuity was expended on devising ways to present gifts. There was the Fairy Snowball, in which gifts were first wrapped in paper and then rolled in cotton batting. More gifts were added and the cotton kept being rolled around them, keeping the form as round as possible. When everything was rolled up in the cotton, the package, now resembling a huge snowball, was tied up with twine. Then there was the Magic Well: a box large enough to accommodate a child was painted to look like a well. The child filled buckets dipped into the well with presents. One of the oldest tricks, practised in many countries, is the presentation of an enormous box, which when opened yields a smaller package, which when opened contains something still smaller, and so on until a tiny present is revealed – very tedious to the recipient but guaranteed to provide endless mirth to the giver.

Wreath   A circular garland usually woven of flowers or greenery, traditionally denoting victory or honour. Olympic victors were crowned with laurel; Roman military heroes with oak. A wreath of ivy at a drinking party was said to combat drunkenness. In Christian art a wreath is often held by angels over a saint. At Christmas it is made of holly and other greenery

Wren *A procession brings the wren to an Irish village on St. Stephen's Day.*

symbolizing eternal life and the Nativity of Jesus in the midst of winter; it also presages the Crown of Thorns worn by the crucified Jesus. Advent wreaths are often used as centrepieces and are placed around the Advent candles. Hanging a wreath outdoors at Christmas is a recent phenomenon that may have derived from the custom of a funeral wreath on the door to indicate mourning.

Wren, Hunting the

"The wren, the wren, the king of birds,
St. Stephen's Day, was killed in the furze.
Although he is little, his honour is great,
And so good people, give us a treat."

"We hunted the wren for Robin the Bobbin,
We hunted the wren for Jack of the Can,
We hunted the wren for Robin the Bobbin,
We hunted the wren for everyone."

On St. Stephen's Day the wren, a protected animal all the rest of the year, may be hunted and its tiny body paraded about by boys, hoping for a gratuity. This was the custom in parts of France, England, Wales, Ireland, and the Isle of Man, and perhaps represented a hold-over from the days of animal sacrifice at midwinter.

In Ireland the Wren Boys wore a traditional costume and went door-to-door, trading feathers of the bird for money with which to hold a party. Today the bird is artificial and the money raised by the visitors goes to charity.

On the Isle of Man, the wren was killed at daybreak on Christmas, paraded about, and buried with a circle dance performed in the churchyard – only then could Christmas begin. The killer had good luck through the rest of the year and the highly prized feathers were brought aboard boats to protect against wreck and drowning.

At Carcassonne, France, the Wren Boys went out in late December; the first one to kill a wren was named king and ruled in state on Epiphany, when he received a gift of money from the bishop and town officials with which to have a party. This custom seems to have faded away by 1830.

Why the wren? This may be an example of SOCIAL INVERSION, that turning of normal rules upside down during the Twelve Days of Christmas. A tiny, inoffensive bird that it is shameful to harm the rest of the year now becomes the target of hunters. Numerous stories are told to justify the choice. One says that St. Stephen was hiding in the furze from his enemies when he was betrayed by the wren; another says that Jesus was betrayed to soldiers in the Garden of Gethsemane by the wren. A variation says that the Irish were sneaking up on Danish invaders when the latter were woken by a wren; another claims the Irish were about to surprise Oliver Cromwell's men. Whatever the reason, the bird is now protected by animal-rights legislation and has no reason any longer to fear St. Stephen's Day.

X-mas An abbreviation for Christmas derived from "X" (*chi*), the first letter of the Greek word for Christ. Though the term has a long and honourable history, some modern Christians have misunderstood it as a disrespectful kind of shorthand unsuitable for the solemn origin of the name.

Xerotighna Dark pastry balls thrown onto roofs to appease evil spirits during the Christmas season in Cyprus.

Ximbomba Also known as a *zambomba*, a friction drum featured in Spanish Christmas music. Coming in several sizes, the *ximbomba* consists of a round pot with a membrane of skin or cloth over the top opening. A rod is tied into the skin and makes a strange drone or rumble when rubbed. It is used to accompany Spanish *aguinaldos*.

A similar drum can be found in Hungary (where it is made from an iron pot with a pig's-bladder covering), in the Netherlands, where it is called a *rommelpot*, in Venezuela, where it is the *furruco*, and in Brazil, where it is the *zabumba*.

Y aura-t-il de la neige à Noël? (1996) *Will There Be Snow for Christmas?* is the English title of this enormously depressing drama about an exploited French country woman (Dominique Reymond) and her seven children. The father of her children (Daniel Duval) exploits his farm family as cheap labour while he keeps another family in town. The sense of their harsh daily life through the changing seasons as Christmas approaches is explored, but it's tough going for the audience, too.

"Ya viene la vieja" A traditional Spanish carol whose English translation is "Come, My Dear Old Lady."

> Come, my dear old lady,
> With a little present
> That you love so dearly.
>
> *Offer it to Jesus.*
> *We're weaving a garland of green lemon leaves,*
> *For sweet Virgin Mary, the Mother of God.*
>
> Kings of Orient riding,
> Cross the sandy desert,
> Bringing for the Baby
> Wine and cookies sweet.
>
> *Chorus*
>
> Kings of Orient riding,
> Guided by the starlight,
> Bringing to the Baby
> Gifts of love, this night.
>
> *Chorus*

Yawning for a Cheshire Cheese An 18th-century English Christmas game wherein, as midnight approaches, the guest with the most impressive yawn wins a cheese.

The Year Without a Santa Claus (1974) Christmas animation specialists Jules Bass and Arthur Rankin Jr. tell the story of the time Santa Claus (Mickey Rooney) almost cancelled Christmas, of the brave elves who contend with Heat Miser and Snow Miser, and the role of Mrs. Claus (Shirley Booth).

"Yes, Virginia, There Is a Santa Claus" On September 21, 1897, the *New York Sun* printed the following:

> We take pleasure in answering thus prominently the communication below, expressing at the same time our great gratification that its faithful author is numbered among the friends of *The Sun*:

> Dear Editor:
> I am 8 years old. Some of my little friends say there is no Santa Claus. Papa says, "If you see it in *The Sun*, it's so." Please tell me the truth, is there a Santa Claus?
> Virginia O'Hanlon

> Virginia, your little friends are wrong. They have been affected by the scepticism of a sceptical age. They do not believe except they see. They think that nothing can be which is not comprehensible by their little minds. All minds, Virginia, whether they be men's or children's, are little. In this great universe of ours, man is a mere insect, an ant, in his intellect as compared with the boundless world about him, as measured by the intelligence capable of grasping the whole of truth and knowledge.

> Yes, Virginia, there is a Santa Claus. He exists as certainly as love and generosity and devotion exist, and you know that they abound and give to your life its highest beauty and joy. Alas! how dreary would be the world if there were no Santa Claus! It would be as dreary as if there were no Virginias. There would be no childlike faith then, no poetry, no romance to make tolerable this existence. We should have no enjoyment, except in sense and sight. The external light with which childhood fills the world would be extinguished.

> Not believe in Santa Claus! You might as well not believe in fairies. You might get your papa to have men to watch in all the chimneys on Christmas eve to catch Santa Claus, but even if you did not see Santa Claus coming down, what would that prove? Nobody sees Santa Claus, but that is no sign that there is no Santa Claus. The most real things in the world are those that neither children nor men can see. Did you ever see fairies dancing on the lawn? Of course not, but that's no proof that they are not there. Nobody can conceive or imagine all the wonders there are unseen and unseeable in the world.

> You tear apart the baby's rattle and see what makes the noise inside, but there is a veil covering the unseen world which not the strongest men, nor even the united strength of all the strongest men that ever lived could tear apart. Only faith, poetry, love, romance, can push aside that curtain and view and picture the supernal beauty and glory beyond. Is it all real? Ah, Virginia, in all this world there is nothing else real and abiding.

> No Santa Claus! Thank God! he lives and lives forever. A thousand years from now, Virginia, nay 10 times 10,000 years from now, he will continue to make glad the heart of childhood.

The unsigned editorial, later revealed to be the work of FRANCIS PHARCELLUS CHURCH, was not given any prominence that day – it was the seventh article on the page and ran below commentaries on New York and Connecticut politics, the strength of the British navy, chainless bicycles, and a Canadian railroad to the Yukon – but it soon became famous around the world. The exchange between Church and Virginia O'Hanlon was reprinted every year until the newspaper ceased publication in 1950. Movies were made about the story (see below), in 1932 NBC produced a cantata (probably the only editorial set to classical music), and in 1996 a musical by David Kirchenbaum and Myles McDonnel appeared.

Yordan *An Orthodox bishop lowers his cross in the water during the* Yordan *ceremony.*

Yes, Virginia, There Is a Santa Claus (1974)   An animated version of the story of the little girl who questions the existence of Santa Claus. Jim Backus narrates.

Yes Virginia, There Is a Santa Claus (TV) (1991)   Charles Bronson plays the *New York Sun* editorial writer Francis P. Church, who must answer little Virginia O'Hanlon's question about the reality of Santa Claus. Directed by Charles Jarrott, with Ed Asner as Bronson's boss and Richard Thomas as Virginia's father, this movie ignores almost every historical fact. Church is portrayed as a tough guy and a hard drinker, shattered by the death of his wife in childbirth. In reality, Church was a Baptist and total abstainer from liquor whose childless wife outlived him. Virginia was portrayed as the daughter of poor Irish immigrants; in fact her father was a doctor.

Yodelling   Yodelling is the practice of wordlessly singing by frequent shifts between chest tones and head tones. In the Tyrolean Alps, masters of this art form have yodelled their praises of the Christ Child for centuries, in churches and across mountain valleys, improvising or basing their songs on traditional carols. The ZÄUERLI yodels are also a part of the Swiss custom of SILVESTERKLÄUSE. During the famous 1914 Christmas truce of the First World War, some German troops entertained the Allies across no-man's-land with a demonstration of yodelling.

Yordan   The celebration of the EPIPHANY or THEOPHANY, the final day of the Ukrainian Christmas season, whose name is derived from the River Jordan, where Christ was baptized. On this day Ukrainians celebrate a blessing of the waters, either a river, lake, or sea, or a container of water indoors. After the ceremony people take away some holy water for the home.

In the Gregorian calendar, this takes place on January 19, which is January 6 in the Julian calendar.

Yorkshire Christmas Pie   An 18th-century English example of the cook's art, in which a boned turkey was stuffed with a goose, which was stuffed with a fowl, which was stuffed with a partridge, which was stuffed with a pigeon. This was put inside a pie crust and surrounded with rabbit and other game and four pounds of butter. The enclosing crust was shaped to resemble a turkey, and the massive pie was then put into the oven to bake. These pies were often sent from Yorkshire to London as gifts and were made sturdy enough to survive the travel.

You Better Watch Out (1980)   Directed by Lewis Jackson, with Brandon Maggart starring as a psychopathic Santa, this low-budget thriller achieves some real Yule-tide menace. Santa vows, "But if you're bad, then your name goes in the Bad Boys and Girls Book, and then I'll bring you something . . . horrible." Also known as *Christmas Evil* and *Terror in Toyland.*

Yule   There is still no scholarly agreement on the derivation of the term "Yule," with rival camps pressing the claims of early Germanic words meaning either "wheel" (as in the cycle of the year) or "feast." Most are agreed, however, that it was brought to England and Scotland by Danish invaders in the ninth and tenth centuries and that it came to be another word for Christmastide in England by the 11th century. In Scandinavia it probably first referred to a winter feast (even this is debated, for there is no mention of such a festival before the 13th century) and then, as in England, came to be attached to the Christmas season.

The commonly held notion that Yule was celebrated by pagans on the winter solstice has now been discounted – the astronomical knowledge of the early Germans was sketchy at best – and Yule seems to have been a two-month period from mid-November to mid-January. This was a time for slaughtering livestock that could not be kept over the winter, feasting on the meat – particularly pork – and drinking.

Yule Bread   A large round cake made in Scotland, also known as Yule Cake or Yule Bannock. Scottish churches prohibited it as part of the 16th- and 17th-century drive against the celebration of Christmas.

Yule Cake   A cake in the shape of a YULE LOG, popular as a Christmas dessert in France and French Canada (see BÛCHE DE NOËL).

In Durham, England, this was a term for YULE DOUGH.

Yule Candle   In England this is a large candle that must last all Christmas Day or bad luck will result. In the 18th and 19th centuries, chandlers gave candles to customers at Christmas and they were also considered a suitable gift for the poor to give to the rich.

In Scandinavia, the Yule candle burnt over the night of Christmas Eve. The remains of the candles were a blessing when smeared on ploughs or in the form of a cross on animals. The remnants were thought to provide protection against thunder.

Yule Dough   In England in the 18th century, Yule dough, or "dow," was a small pastry baked in the shape of a baby and presented by bakers to their customers, just as chandlers passed out Christmas candles to their clients. It was probably once intended to represent the Christ Child.

Yule Lads   Icelandic Christmas elves. See JÓLASVEINAR.

Yule Log   The custom of placing a large block of wood on the fire at Christmas. The selection and laying of the log are often attended with ceremony and celebration, and its remnants are believed to possess miraculous powers.

The Yule log is a widespread tradition. The first mention of the custom, in Germany, dates from 1184, and it was eventually found in the Italian Alps, the Balkans, Scandinavia, France, and the Iberian peninsula. The first mention of it in England comes from the 17th-century poet Robert Herrick, who learned of it in Devon, where it seems to have been well-established by the 1630s. Most parts of England and Scotland adopted the custom, except in Lowland Scotland, where forests are scarce and where many Christmas practices were suppressed by the Calvinist government. Eventually the Yule log would cross the Atlantic and become part of Christmas in the United States and Canada.

In France it was customary for the family to go out together to find the best log for the BÛCHE DE NOËL, while in Norway the father went out alone. In England the log had already been selected at the previous Candlemas (February 2) and set out to dry. It was bad luck in the United States to buy the log, while good luck fell on those who selected it themselves from wood on their own property. In Serbia the log was cut before sunrise on Christmas Eve and brought into the house at dusk by candlelight.

Ceremonies · for · Christmas

Yule Log The Yule Log is kindled with the remains of the previous year's firewood.

Dragging the log home was a time for high spirits. Logs were often decorated with ribbons, and people encountering the procession would raise their hats in salute. The youngest member of the party could claim a ride on the log as it was pulled through the snow.

Once home, proper ceremony was required for the laying of the log. In 19th-century Newfoundland, when the Back-Junk, as the Yule log was called, was set in the fireplace and lit, the father of the house went to the porch and discharged a firearm to announce the deed to his neighbours. The oldest male in Serbian households was responsible for placing the log on the fire and saying a prayer for the family and crops. In Dalmatia the log was decorated with leaves and flowers before being brought in. As it entered the house the log, or *badnjak*, was sprinkled with wine or grain.

In Montenegro a piece of bread was placed on the log and wine was splashed on the wood, a custom similar to that observed in 16th-century Lombardy. There, the family gathered while the father, uttering a blessing in the name of the Trinity, placed the log, or *zocco*, on the fire. Juniper was placed under it and money on top (these coins were later distributed to the servants). The father then took a drink of wine, shared it with his family, and then poured three libations on the log. In other parts of Italy, the Yule log is the *ceppo*; in Tuscany, Christmas is called the *Festa di Ceppo*. In the Catalonian area of Spain, children were blindfolded and led forward to strike the *tio*, a hollow burlap-covered log, and to their delight candies and treats would emerge.

The French Nobel Prize-winning poet Frédéric Mistral had vivid memories of the Yule log ceremony in his native Provence:

> For my father, who was so faithful to ancient custom, the feast of the year was Christmas Eve. That day the farm-labourers left off work early, and my mother gave each of them, in a napkin, a splendid *galette à l'huile*, a roll of nougat, a bunch of dried figs, a cheese from our own flocks, a celery salad, and a bottle of old wine. And then the servants went off in every direction to "place the Log" in their own country and their own homes. Those who stayed behind at the farm were the unfortunates who had no family; and sometimes relatives, an old bachelor, perhaps, would arrive at nightfall, saying: "Merry Christmas! I've come to place the Log with all of you." Then all together we went in a joyous crowd to find the Christmas Log, which – the tradition was strict – had to be a fruit-tree. We lugged it back to the farm, in line, the eldest at one end and I, the youngest, at the other; thrice we paraded it round the kitchen; and then, as we arrived again in front of the hearthstone, my father solemnly poured over the log a glass of old wine, saying:
>
>> "*Allégresse! Allégresse!*
>> *Mes beaux enfants, que Dieu nous comble d'allégresse!*
>> *Avec Noël tout bien vient!*
>> *Dieu nous fasse la grace de voir l'année prochaine,*
>> *Et, sinon plus nombreux, puissions-nous n'y pas être moins!*"
>
> And crying all together "*Allégresse! Allégresse! Allégresse!*" – "Happiness! Happiness! Happiness!" – we placed the Log in position on the fire-dogs; and as the first tiny flame darted from it, my father recited, "*A la bûche, boute feu!*" and crossed himself.

In most areas it was necessary to light the Yule log with the remnants of the previous year's wood. Robert Herrick's poem points this out and stresses the necessity of clean hands while doing so:

> Come, bring with a noise,
> My merry, merry boys,
> The Christmas Log to the firing;
> While my good Dame, she
> Bids ye all be free;
> And drink to your heart's desiring.
>
> With the last year's brand
> Light the new block, and
> For good success in his spending,
> On your Psaltries play,
> That sweet luck may
> Come while the log is a-tinding.
>
> Another to the Maids
>
> Wash your hands, or else the fire
> Will not tind to your desire;
> Unwashed hands, ye maidens, know,
> Dead the fire, though ye blow.

The remainders of the previous year's log (or its ashes) had other, more wonderful, uses. In Germany a log was placed on the fire on Christmas Eve or Christmas Day, charred a little, and then taken off. When a storm threatened, this wood, called the *Christbrand*, was put on the fire again as a guard against lightning. The French have been known to use remnants to cure cattle of diseases or prevent mildew in wheat. In Portugal the remains of the *Sepo de Natal* are kept and burned again to prevent harm from storms. Other ailments that are kept at bay with pieces of the Yule log are toothaches, hail, house fires, and chilblains. Mixed with fodder its ashes help cows calve; in the soil it keeps crops healthy; in the well it keeps water sweet. A curious inversion of this custom used to be practised in the Scottish Highlands. There, early on Christmas Eve, the head of the house would go out and seek a twisted root or stump; bringing it home he would carve it into the shape of an old woman. This piece of wood was called the *Cailleach Nollaich*, or Christmas Old Wife, and represented all the evil that needed to be destroyed if the family were to prosper. It was placed on the evening fire and reduced utterly to ashes so as to keep misfortune from the door for the next year.

Different cultures prefer different woods for the Yule log: the English will look for ash, pine, or oak; the French for fruit wood; the Scots, birch; and the Serbs, oak.

In the United States before the Civil War, it was customary on many plantations for slaves to be given a holiday for as long as the log burned. The wood was therefore sprinkled with water to prolong the vacation, and it became a proverb in the South that any wet wood "has as much water as a Christmas log."

In Devon, the ASHEN FAGGOT substitutes for the Yule log. A chunk of ash is cut and bound with nine bands of wood, preferably from the same tree. It is then burned on an open fire, which itself is lit by a piece of last year's faggot.

Even in the United States the Yule log custom lingers in surprising ways. Since 1933 a Yule Log Hunt has taken place annually at Palmer Lake, Colorado. A tree chosen for the Yule log is cut down and then carefully hidden. Those who join in the hunt must all wear capes and hoods of red or green in imitation of the days of old England, when choosing a Yule log was an important part of the Christmas celebration. Once found, the log is dragged into town with great ceremony, with the person who has found it riding upon it.

On Christmas Eve and early Christmas morning in 1966 WPIX, a New York television station, broadcast an uninterrupted three hours of a Yule log burning in the fireplace, accompanied by carol singing. It was in black and white, based on a 17-second loop of the fireplace in the residence of the mayor of New York. This innovative piece of programming (sometimes called the world's first music video) attracted a large and grateful audience over the years – some of the million or so viewers would even move televisions into their empty fireplaces to heighten the effect. The tradition was carried on until 1990 (the fire scene was eventually reshot in colour and with a longer seven- to eight-minute loop) and has been revived for the age of cyberspace – the station now features the burning log on its Christmas Eve Web site.

Yule Swain Yule Swains, Yule Goblins, and Yule Lads are all terms for the tricksome Icelandic Christmas elves. See JÓLASVEINAR.

Yule Trap A 19th-century English custom of disguising one present by hiding it in another or in deceptive wrapping.

Zacharias An elderly priest in the Temple at Jerusalem. The Book of Luke (1:5-25, 57-66) recounts how Zacharias and his wife, Elizabeth, are visited by the angel Gabriel, who announces they will have a son who will be named JOHN (later to be known as the Baptist). In the apocryphal *Protoevangelium of James*, it was Zacharias who assisted in selecting a spouse for Mary and who was murdered at the altar during the Massacre of the INNOCENTS.

Zakk A type of bagpipe made of dogskin and played by Maltese pipers during Christmas celebrations.

Zambomba See XIMBOMBA.

Zampognari Italian shepherd bagpipers who are famous for playing hymns at Christmas to the Christ Child. In the 19th century it was their custom to descend from the hills in December and come into the cities, where they would serenade images of the Virgin and Child – they claimed it was the sound of shepherds' pipes that lulled the baby Jesus to sleep – and drop in at carpenter's shops to pay their respects to Joseph. In return for an offering they would also play outside homes.

They still appear in traditional costume in Rome, southern Italy, and Sicily, where their arrival is a sign of Christmas. See "CAROL OF THE BAGPIPERS."

Zäuerli A wordless yodel emitted by the men of Urnäsch as they go in disguise from door to door in their customary SIL-VESTERKLÄUSE procession on December 31 or January 13.

Zelomi A midwife of Israel, one of two attendant at the birth of Jesus, whose story is told in the *Gospel of Pseudo-Matthew*. Zelomi and Salome were brought by Joseph to the cave where Mary had just given birth. Zelomi proclaimed in amazement that Mary remained a virgin despite the obvious signs: "Lord, Lord Almighty, mercy on us! It has never been heard or thought of, that any one should have her breasts full of milk, and that the birth of a son should show his mother to be a virgin. But there has been no spilling of blood in his birth, no pain in bringing him forth. A virgin has conceived, a virgin has brought forth, and a virgin she remains." Salome, however, had doubts, and examined Mary, whereupon her hand was withered, only to be cured moments later by touching the baby.

Zelten In Tyrol peasants on St. Thomas Eve once baked the *zelten*, a pie filled with dried fruit, which was blessed with the sign of the cross and sprinkled with holy water before being placed in the oven. It was not eaten until St. Stephen's Day or Epiphany, when it was cut with great ceremony. Smaller pies were made for the maidservants, who observed the custom of carrying the food home to their relations at the Christmas holidays. When a young man wished to marry a maid, he asked, as an expression of his love, to carry her pie; if she agreed the engagement was on.

Ziemassvetki The Latvian term for a midwinter festival, but which has now come to be synonymous with Christmas.

Zinzendorf, Count Nicholas von (1700-60) German church reformer and, as founder of Moravian settlements, importer of Central European Christmas customs to North America.

A Saxon aristocrat, he offered refuge on his estates to remnants of the persecuted Protestant sect known as the Moravian Brethren in 1722. Becoming the leader of this little church, he incurred the wrath of German religious authorities and was banished. During his exile he established new Moravian congregations in Europe and England. From 1741 to 1743 he travelled to America, where he oversaw new settlements, particularly one at Bethlehem, Pennsylvania, which saw its first church service on Christmas Eve, 1741, when von Zinzendorf lit a candle and led his followers into the stable singing a hymn. From these settlers came a number of Christmas traditions that have proved popular in America, such as the Christmas tree, the PUTZ, seasonal recipes, and carols.

Zocco In Lombardy, the Yule log is called the *Zocco di Natale*. In a 16th-century ritual, the family gathered while the father, in

Zampognari *Italian pipers play before a shrine at Christmas.*

Zwarte Piet *Black Peter brandishes his switches and accompanies St. Nicholas through a Dutch street.*

the name of the Trinity, placed the log on the fire. Juniper was placed under it and money on top; these coins were later given to the servants. The father would then drink wine, share it with his family, and pour three splashes on the log. Ashes of the *zocco* guarded against hail.

Zwarte Piet   The gift-bringer's HELPER in the Netherlands. Zwarte Piet, a black-faced figure in the medieval dress of a Moorish servant, accompanies St. Nicholas on his visits to Dutch children in late November and early December, culminating in the gift-giving on the eve of the saint's birthday on December 5. He tosses candy to children but also threatens to stuff bad kids in his sack and take them back with him to Spain for the next year. Recently he has been criticized for racial stereotyping by advocates of multiculturalism.

Zwetchegenmännchen   "Prune people," a German Christmas custom, especially popular in the Nuremberg area. Colourfully decorated figures are made of prunes, nuts, raisins, and figs and serve as seasonal decorations.

Copyright Holders' Acknowledgements

The following people and institutions graciously gave permission to use their material in this encyclopedia:

Amador Publishers (www.amadorbooks.com) for the excerpt "Credo" from their 1995 book *Christmas Blues: Behind the Holiday Mask*, eds. Gatuskin, Miller, and Wilson, which accompanies the article "Grinch."

The Australian Tourist Commission for the photo accompanying the article "Australia."

The Canada Post Corporation for permission to reproduce the images of the following postage stamps, copyright © Canada Post Corporation: Huron Carol set, 1977 ("The Huron Carol"); Christmas Parade set, 1985 ("Parades"); and Santa Claus set, 1991, Foreign Santa Claus set, 1992, and Foreign Santa Claus set, 1993 ("La Befana," "Grandfather Frost," "Reindeer Substitutes"). Reproduced with permission.

Andrew Galloway for the photograph that accompanies the article "Pohutukawa."

The Frederick Harris Music Co., Limited, Mississauga, Ontario, Canada, for permission to reprint the English text of "Twas in the Moon of Wintertime" ("The Huron Carol") by J. E. Middleton. All rights reserved.

The images of the following postage stamps are reproduced by kind permission of the Lord Chamberlain and the British Post Office, copyright © The Post Office. All rights reserved. United Kingdom: "Good King Wencelas," 1973; "Hark! The Herald Angels Sing," 1982; "The Holly and the Ivy," 1982; "I Saw Three Ships," 1982; "We Three Kings," 1982; "The Devil's Knell," 1986; "Glastonbury Thorn," 1986; "Boy Bishop," 1986; "Plygain," 1986; "St Augustine" ("December 25 Events"), 1997. Guernsey: The Twelve Days of Christmas set, 1984; Christmas miniatures set, 1988 ("Baboushka," "Balthazar," "France," "Gaspar," "Julenisse," "St. Lucia," "Melchior," "Wenceslas").

Thora Gunnasdottir of Iceland's House of Christmas (www.jolahusid.com) and artist Brynja Eldon for the illustrations accompanying the articles "Jólasveinar" and "Laufabraud."

Oxford University Press for permission to reprint the lyrics of the following carols from the *Shorter Oxford Book of Carols*, eds. Parrott and Kyte: "Blest Mary Wanders Through the Thorn" ("Maria durch ein Dornwald ging"); "Infant Holy, Infant Lowly" ("W zlobie lezy"); "Joseph, Dearest Joseph Mine"; "Unto Us a Boy Is Born." Copyright © Oxford University Press, 1993. Words reproduced by permission. Licence no. 05224.

Manfred Fischer and the Stille Nacht Gesellschaft for the illustration accompanying the article "Oberndorf."

The Luxembourg City Tourist Office for the photo accompanying "Luxembourg," copyright © Luxembourg City Tourist Office.

Corbis Graphics for permission to reprint the illustrations accompanying the articles "Bethlehem," "It's a Wonderful Life," "John Canoe," "Krampus," "Massacre of the Innocents," "Miracle on 34th Street," "Pantomime," "Pastoral Drama," "Prophecies," "Shepherds' Field," "Sybils," "Ukraine," "United States," "Werewolves and Christmas," and "Zwarte Piet."

Mick Tems for the photo accompanying the article "Mari Lwyd."

The National Gallery of Art, Washington, D.C., for permission to reprint the following images: Juan de Flandes, *The Adoration of the Magi*, Samuel H. Kress Collection, © 2000 Board of Trustees, National Gallery of Art, Washington, c. 1508/1519, oil on panel ("Melchior"); Fra Carnevale, *The Annunciation*, Samuel H. Kress Collection, © 2000 Board of Trustees, National Gallery of Art, Washington, c. 1448, tempera (and possibly oil) on panel ("Annunciation to Mary"); Jan van Eyck, *The Annunciation*, Andrew W. Mellon Collection, © 2000 Board of Trustees, National Gallery of Art, Washington, c. 1434/1436, on canvas transferred from panel ("Rainbow"); Fra Angelico and Filippo Lippi, *The Adoration of the Magi*, Samuel H. Kress Collection, © 2000 Board of Trustees, National Gallery of Art, Washington, c. 1445, tempera on panel ("Peacock"); Giorgione, *The Adoration of the Shepherds*, Samuel H. Kress Collection, © 2000 Board of Trustees, National Gallery of Art, Washington, 1505/1510, oil on panel ("Shepherds"); Giovanni Bellini, *Madonna and Child with Saints*, Samuel H. Kress Collection, © 2000 Board of Trustees, National Gallery of Art, Washington, c. 1490, oil on panel ("Madonna and Child"); Filippino Lippi, *The Adoration of the Child*, Andrew W. Mellon Collection, © 2000 Board of Trustees, National Gallery of Art, Washington, c. 1480, tempera on panel ("Adoration of the Child"); Vittore Carpaccio, *The Flight into Egypt*, Andrew W. Mellon Collection, © 2000 Board of Trustees, National Gallery of Art, Washington, c. 1500, oil on panel ("Flight into Egypt"); Gerard David, *The Rest on the Flight into Egypt*, Andrew W. Mellon Collection, © 2000 Board of Trustees, National Gallery of Art, Washington, c. 1510, oil on panel ("Joseph").

The Norman Rockwell Family Trust for permission to reprint the works of Norman Rockwell accompanying the articles "Homecoming," "Letters to Santa Claus," "Mistletoe," "Santa Claus," and "Shop Early Campaign." Copyright © 2000 the Norman Rockwell Family Trust.

Anthony Olszewski for permission to reprint the photograph accompanying the article "Opposition to Christmas."

The Silent Night Museum, Oberdorf, Austria, for permission to reproduce the painting accompanying the article "Silent Night."

The United States Postal Service for permission to reproduce the image of the postage stamp "Emily Bissell" ("Christmas Seals"), copyright 1980. All rights reserved.